C000025492

James Mitchell

Beyond The Islands

An Autobiography

**MACMILLAN
CARIBBEAN**

Macmillan Education
Between Towns Road, Oxford, OX4 3PP
A division of Macmillan Publishers Limited
Companies and representatives throughout the world

www.macmillan-caribbean.com

PB ISBN: 978-1-4050-1417-5
HB ISBN: 978-0-230-02220-1

Text © Sir James Mitchell 2006
Design and illustration © Macmillan Publishers Limited 2006
First published 2006

Designed by Carol Hulme
Typeset by EXPO Holdings, Malaysia
Plate section photographs courtesy of
Sir James Mitchell Collection
Cover design and plate section by Andrew Magee
Cover photographs by Marcus Lyon

Printed and bound in Thailand

2010 2009 2008 2007
10 9 8 7 6 5 4 3 2

"Perhaps it is the struggle that gives value to life, and not so much the ultimate result."

Jawaharlal Nehru: *Toward Freedom* (1936)

"The history of society shows that no body of men ever obtained a widespread ascendancy, never secured general respect, unless they deserved it."

John Lord: *Beacon Lights of History* (1883)

Also by Sir James Mitchell
Caribbean Crusade
Guiding Change in the Islands
A Season of Light

*To my loving daughter Gabija
and my editor Jehan Senaratna,
who did not write his novel*

Contents

Acknowledgements

In a strange way, this book wrote itself. The story kept flowing from my pens, propelling itself forward despite the intrusions of surgery. Like my islands in the Grenadines yearning for development in the 1960s when the bankers from England and Canada thought I was crazy to begin the task, we all kept going.

When I started to represent these islands, there was not much beyond what was Bequia seen by the Arawaks – no jetties, no roads suitable for cars and trucks, no electricity, no telephones, no airports – the legacy of colonialism. Who then would have imagined I would have steered islands like Mustique, Bequia, Canouan, from thatched huts to glossy pages in architecture magazines.

That it was possible I have to thank the fishermen, soaking in the sea spray from dawn to dusk; the farmers and their sweat; the loyal old market ladies I brought into the shade in the capital; and countless others from every walk of life in my beloved St. Vincent and the Grenadines, and in many other countries along the way, who have lived out my vision for this land. I thank too, the countless persons whose faith in me never wavered and who are not mentioned.

Despair I know descended on my daughters Louise, busy with her battle with the Financial Action Task Force, and Sabrina, busy with our family hotel, her children Ondine and Ella and basketball administration, as they witnessed the mountain of written pages I kept producing, and which they suspected would end up in their laps.

Rescue came with a heroine to whom I am profoundly grateful. My former secretary in the Prime Minister's Office, Angela Mercury, seasoned in my hieroglyphics, for whom we had secured training in Jamaica, was only too ready to transcribe everything at home onto her computer, ready to email back to Bequia or Caracas. I don't know what I would have done without her.

Then Jehan Senaratna arrived. In him I found a kindred spirit. He had grown up like me in the Third World, Sri Lanka, secured degrees in America, lived there and in Europe, working in the stock market, ending up in Caracas representing Dow Jones, the *Wall Street Journal* and the *Economist*. I had known him in an earlier spell as a journalist in Bequia. He was friends with Sabrina and her husband Junior, and had co-authored with Sabrina a coffee table book on St. Vincent & the Grenadines (SVG) for a French publisher. A worldly editor who had grown up in the tropics was just the person I needed to assist me. I owe Jehan a great deal more than I can say. As he read my story he was ready to postpone writing his novel and abandon both Caracas and his incisive reportage on turbulent Venezuela.

Fortunately, each day he checked his editing with Sabrina and worked through the manuscript with her. She, like me, had to face the shock of his heart attack. She carried on. Thanks to her, picking up the thread from Jehan, the book took its final shape. Thanks too to Louise, the book got finished: she demanded that I stop writing.

I also wish to thank all those friends who were constantly ready to refresh my memory including SVG Ambassadors Edwin Laurent in Brussels and Kingsley Layne in Washington D.C.

Indeed, let me thank all the partners in our beloved New Democratic Party who helped to build this country, and whose support encouraged my success and inspired me to tell our incredible story for posterity. Thanks also to fellow Prime Ministers in the Caribbean and the wider Commonwealth who shared these exciting times with me.

I am also indebted to Marcus Lyon and the staff of his Glassworks Studio near Westminster for all their meticulous restoration work on my photographs, especially those barely surviving the ageing process in the humid tropics. I am fortunate to have kept my diaries in the safe deposit of my bank, and so they became available to reveal those historic moments in Nicaragua, Hungary and along the Cambodian border.

It would be remiss of me not to express profound gratitude to those erstwhile strangers worldwide who ensured that my thirsting soul savoured other civilizations.

Helianthus, Bequia, 2005

List of illustrations

Glossary of abbreviations

Lomé Agreement	The European Convention for Aid to ACP Countries (named after the capital of Togo)
MIGA	Multilateral Investment Guarantee Agency
NDP	New Democratic Party
OECD	Organization for Economic Cooperation and Development
OECS	Organization of Eastern Caribbean States
ONR	Organization for National Reconstruction
OPEC	Oil Producing and Exporting Countries
PNM	People's National Movement
UNC	United National Congress
PC	Privy Councillor
SCMFA	Standing Committee of Ministers Responsible for Foreign Affairs
SDF	Special Development Fund
SNOWI	Senior Naval Commander at the West Indies Squadron
SSU	Special Service Unit
SVG	St. Vincent and the Grenadines
UNCTAD	United Nations Conference on Trade and Development
WAND	Women and Development
WIBDECO	Windward Islands Banana Development and Exporting Company
WISA	West Indies Associated States
WTO	World Trade Organization
UBC	University of British Columbia
UWI	University of the West Indies
UNESCO	United Nations Educational, Social and Cultural Organization

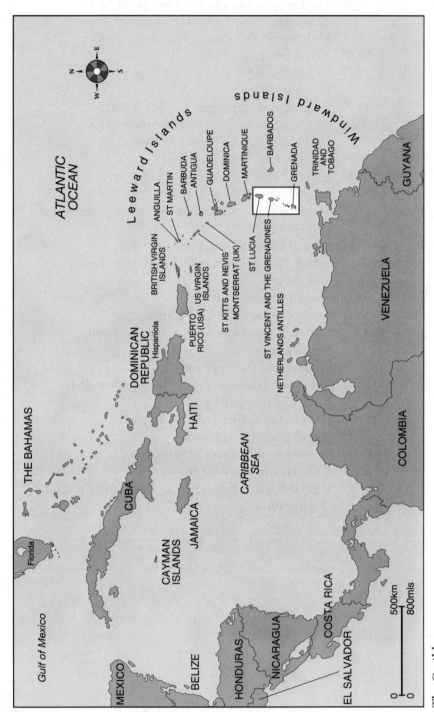

The Caribbean

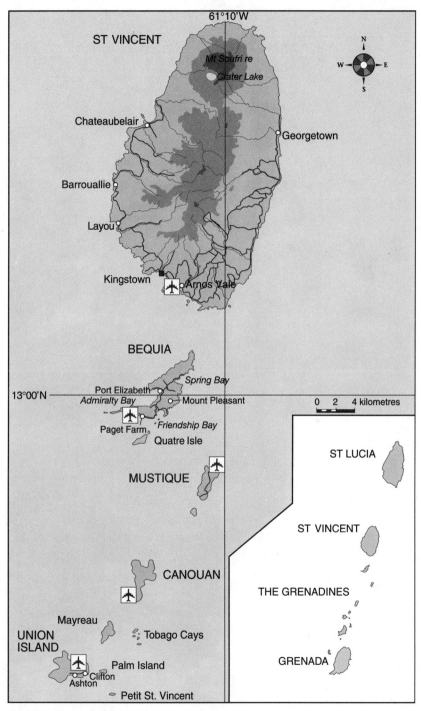

St. Vincent and the Grenadines

1

Memories of a Commonwealth Meeting

Every time I see a gruesome picture of the amputees in Sierra Leone, I wonder if I made a mistake. Could I have done more during my involvement with West Africa? Could we have stopped the carnage? Who could have imagined that, in our time, a human being would have to choose how much of his limb should be chopped off? What scars must remain on the very souls of those tortured and maimed for life!

It doesn't seem that more than ten years have passed since November 1995 when I met up with two Prime Ministerial colleagues, Goh Chok Chung of Singapore, and Jean Chrétien of Canada, bright and early one Sunday morning as I took my morning exercise around Millbrook golf course in New Zealand. We were at the Commonwealth Heads of Government retreat. They were playing golf and strolling around while I ran. I had not played golf for years, although in my youth I won the college championship in Trinidad.

We were all quite relieved to have just settled our position ejecting Nigeria, but were only too aware of other challenges facing us in West Africa. After I left the Prime Ministers of Canada and Singapore, on the way to my room I saw two rather desolate Africans engrossed in conversation on their porch. They were the President of Sierra Leone and the Foreign Minister of The Gambia, V. E. H. Strasser and B. I. Jagne. Both had recently come to power through military coups.

The day before, the Conference had thrown President Sani Abacha's Nigeria out of the Commonwealth and they were worried as to whether or not we would be doing the same to their countries. For if the powerful and oil-rich Nigeria was dismissed so harshly, smaller states like theirs could easily suffer the same fate. They had been in the Conference for two days and had seen how the ground for the ostracism of Nigeria had been laid. They must have been worried too, in retrospect, about their prospects of survival on the way home, because other leaders had been

1

overthrown while away at a Commonwealth Heads of Government Meeting (CHOGM).

They invited me to join them. They were young men. Men under thirty had led the coups in both Sierra Leone and The Gambia. They had not been born when I went into politics. Seizing power, they discovered, was a lot easier than holding it. The President of Sierra Leone did not look like someone who could even swat a fly. (The extraordinary circumstances that permitted him to succeed will have to be a subject for competent army historians of West Africa, not me.)

But the two leaders conveyed to me that they hoped the Commonwealth Heads of Government Meeting (CHOGM) would not treat Sierra Leone and The Gambia the way it had dealt with Nigeria. "We want help," one said and explained that their countries were very different from Nigeria, and didn't want to defy the Commonwealth.

I sensed they might not have been able to go home if, on their watch at the CHOGM, their countries were ejected like Nigeria.

"Could you get the message across for us?" they asked in unison. I agreed to try.

At the CHOGM retreat, over two days and nights, Kings, Presidents, Prime Ministers, and their wives or partners, mingle freely in the world's most informal international gathering of leaders. There are no fixed seating arrangements. You sit at random, join a table. You wear no label except the gold pin that marks you as a Head of Government.

So at a coffee break, I singled out John Major. I told him that I had met the leaders of the delegations from Sierra Leone and The Gambia earlier in the morning, and they indicated to me that they need our help.

"We shouldn't give them the Nigeria treatment," I said, and added, "Perhaps we can steer them another way."

I knew John Major. In the Malaysia CHOGM I had chided him about the poll tax. At that time he was Foreign Secretary. That tumultuous day when he leapt into prominence as Chancellor of the Exchequer, I was his first guest at No. 11 Downing Street.

"James, if they want help they must say so," he said.

So I went back to Foreign Minister Jagne of The Gambia and Captain Strasser of Sierra Leone, and delivered the message. When the caucus of leaders resumed they both made the statements of request. I supported the idea that we should recognize that these young leaders needed our help, and that our generosity of spirit must be demonstrated.

Chief Anyouku, the Secretary General, thanked me later for my intervention.

I didn't think that, as a Nigerian, he would relish the prospect of *three* West African states being suspended. The Conference established how the Foreign Ministers would place The Gambia and Sierra Leone within their purview. My country with its limited resources could not stretch itself to the frequent travel required of the Foreign Ministers, so the matter passed out of my hands.

Later that day, Foreign Minister Jagne invited me to visit The Gambia. He said that when he got home he would have his President confirm the invitation. The young President of Sierra Leone thanked me and he too said he would like me to see his country. I told him I had a dear friend from University days who was once his High Commissioner at the Court of St. James, and that I would love to go there one day.

I told Chief Anyouku that I would be willing to go to West Africa to follow up if ever it became necessary. I had developed great confidence in him for his handling of the debate on Nigeria's fate. As the barbs against his country flew, he kept cool and retained his charm. All those of us who had been nervous about electing such a man for the post of Secretary General instead of a retired Australian Prime Minister could only be pleased with his performance on that occasion.

Some months later, when the Commonwealth Foreign Ministers were having difficulty leading The Gambia back to a new constitution and elections, Chief Anyouku called to ask if I could travel there and prod things along. By this time the British were already bogged down in Sierra Leone. The next I heard of President Strasser of Sierra Leone was that he was studying in England. Every vampire in the region was sucking the blood of that country, its diamonds the motive for the violence, the amputations.

The Foreign Ministers of the Commonwealth were still making no progress, so I went to The Gambia to see what I could do to induce the military to return the country to democracy. I think I succeeded. Indeed, even before I influenced their return to democracy, they named a market and a street after me. I was the first head of government to make an official visit and confront the Provisional Ruling Military Council.

If I had gone to Sierra Leone too, could I have made the difference? Could I – or the other Prime Ministers in the Commonwealth collectively for that matter – have saved Sierra Leone from 20,000 limb amputations of men, women and children? Some 50,000 women and girls were raped in the quick civil war fuelled by diamonds. Did we in the Commonwealth fail them?

My Gambian experiences, and the fraternal relations we developed, including the state visit of President Yahya Jammeh to my home town, and the return visit of our Governor General, have their own chapter later in this book.

PART I

Formative Years

2

Growing up in Bequia

I was born in Bequia, one of the smallest inhabited islands in the Caribbean. In 1931, its population was less than a thousand. At the beginning of this new millennium, we are up to 5,500, with many of us Bequians spread out across the United States, Canada and the United Kingdom. I recently discovered an enclave of Bequians living near the marinas of Florida's Fort Lauderdale – not a surprising place for a people whose culture is steeped in sailing, from schooners in the old days to yachts today.

There was only one midwife on the island, Nurse Hazell, who lived into her nineties. She delivered every baby in Bequia, walking miles to perform her duties, even at night, though there were no streetlights then. There was not much money in circulation in those days. The colonial government must have paid her a few shillings, but I am sure her grateful patients supplemented that with generous supplies of corn, peas, the odd rooster, and sun-dried fish.

My mother's first child had been a miscarriage. She told me she rested for two months to make sure I made it into this world. (As one of the select few who actually retired as Prime Minister in the Caribbean I am sure many of my political enemies must have wished that I had been another miscarriage.)

Our home was on the beach, surrounded in season by fields of corn and pigeon peas. There were ladies from the village of Hamilton who tended these fields with their hoes, and I remember them sitting in the shade and cleaning cotton, clearing out the parts stained by insects, and removing dried twigs blown by the wind into the open pods.

My grandmother Sarah was a classic West Indian matriarch. She was known to everyone else as Nen Sarah. Nen was short for Nennen (perhaps an African tribal term akin to Auntie). To me, though, she was Granny. My grandfather, a Canouan sea captain and shipwright, bought the land on which we lived, and where our family business is today, in 1897 for 12 guineas, as a wedding present for my grandmother.

"Sail oh! Sail oh!" That was the cry I heard in my youth. A ship was coming home.

In the 1930s there were no yachts in Admiralty Bay. Today there are billions of dollars' worth, from modest single-handers that have crossed the Atlantic to manicured mega-yachts of old-money families and the *nouveau riche*.

"Sail oh" was the exciting sound echoing across Admiralty Bay when a sailing schooner returned. The residents in Sugar Hill – a high point on Bequia – could see the ship first, and as she tacked into the bay, Hamilton village on the other side would respond. Our sailing ships and their crews would be gone for months, sailing on to the Guianas for rice and sugar, and salt from Anguilla, to be transported to the other islands of the West Indies. Bequia built its own boats. Our shipwrights in the Grenadines settled in other islands and taught them too how to build boats.

"Sail Oh" was our contact with the outside world. Its sound brought great happiness to the island, for crews came from every village, Hamilton, the Harbour, Mt. Pleasant, La Pompe, Lower Bay and Paget Farm. And every sailor, not just the Captain, brought home his bounty for his family: condensed milk, Argentinean corned beef, Portuguese sardines and codfish from Canada. Alas, no prime frozen and sealed tenderloin from the United States then – there simply was not any refrigeration for it.

I remember well a schoolboy joke about a sailor on my father's ship who told his wife Lestelle: "The girls in Puerto Rico sweet like stars, they passing you with perfume, dollar a drop." She told the story to her co-workers in my grandfather's home, and complained that her man never actually brought her any of that perfume! For years I wondered if that hearty Bequia sailor had only *passed by* the perfumed Puerto Ricans.

The Bequia of my youth was free from noise. The sounds you heard were that of a human voice, a bird singing, the waves breaking on the shore, the infrequent sails of a schooner flapping in the wind, or an anchor chain rattling to the bottom in Admiralty Bay – sounds now gone through the progress of development I helped to engineer. The only metallic clanging came from the church bells saluting the dawn and blessing the sunset with the holy rhythm of the angelus. And a bell too summoned us to school. There were no mechanical sounds: no cars, no motor-cycles, no power or electrical tools, no chainsaws. Not a single boat had an engine. My family who had been in the shipbuilding business and owned ships in the eighteenth century and into the twentieth century, up to the beginning of the Second World War, did not sail in powered ships.

A shipwright, Benjamin George Compton from Hampshire, England, came to start the shipbuilding business in the Caribbean. He took on a local apprentice named William Alexander Mitchell who married the daughter born to Compton with a native woman. The Compton--Mitchell dynasty built, up to 1950, some 68 ships, from Anguilla in the north, to Grenada in the south.

So more and more ships were built in Bequia. Every carpenter was a shipwright, for it was the earnings from being a shipwright that led to the building of wooden homes and the beautiful gingerbread lattice-work bordering the roofs.

Shipbuilding and sailing ships were our lifelines. The young men who sail on yachts yearly to and from Newport carry on our wonderful tradition. All over the world, our men toil on bulk carriers, still bringing home their savings to enhance the quality of our homes; and also bringing that experience of life in other lands, making tourists feel welcome here.

My immediate family built a succession of schooners. As they sank, more were built. *Alternara, Fauna, Water Pearl, Gloria Colita.* The *Juliana*, which my father sailed from Bequia to the United States, passed through Cuban waters. On my state visit to Cuba, as Prime Minister, I was able to tell President Fidel Castro that my family contact with Cuba had been established in the 1930s. My mother, now in her nineties, had sailed on that voyage. Fidel invited me to come back with her to revisit Cuba.

Single families built most of the sailing ships – they had names like Ollivierre, Stowe, Adams, Wallace, Tannis, Jarvis, Gooding, and Davis. Each family in Bequia produced its own ships. "A partnership is a leaky ship" was the slogan of the private sector in those days, before the term Company Law entered our vocabulary.

The sailors were away from Bequia for months at a time, sometimes years. My recollection of my father is faint. He was only home for long periods when our ship had sunk and he was building another. The *Water Pearl* went ashore in Park, in north-east Bequia, on her way back to Guyana from St. Vincent. Apparently a porpoise had been harpooned on a previous trip and the line got caught between the keel and the "false keel" (an addition to the keel to help the ship sail into the wind) which hung loose, making it impossible to steer the ship.

And thus we started building the *Gloria Colita*, the largest wooden schooner built in the Caribbean, all of 165 feet long, with three masts.

(The earlier ship *Juliana* also had had three masts. She dwarfed all ships built before her in Bequia.) How my father undertook such a task in the Great Depression of the 1930s, I cannot imagine.

The ships were built with local cedar frames tooled into shape by the curved adze. No tool has damaged more feet than the adze, because it required the shipwright to bend over with the wood on the ground between his legs. Our family had tree-filled estates in Hope and Isle à Quatre, so we had no difficulty finding wood for most of the timber frames. But frames for certain parts of the ship were carefully sought by shipwrights who could tell by looking at the tree if the curve of the wood was right, and so we also bought some frames from the McIntosh family in Spring.

My father and grandfather built the *Gloria Colita* beside our home. The bow leaned over the shore and the stern was well into the hill. The three masts were great trunks of Douglas fir from Canada, towed into Bequia harbour. Each in turn was measured for length and the thinner ends put aside for smaller craft. Meticulously, each trunk was turned into a square with a long chalk line marking the two sides, then rolled to be marked again to complete the square. The shipwrights used axes to demarcate sections to be peeled away by the adze. From the square, the whole process was repeated to shape the trunk into an eight-sided cylinder, then to 16, to 32, and finally as close to a perfect circle as possible. By the time the process was reduced to the final strips to be shaved away, the planes were ready to produce the beautiful smooth surface, showing the long veins of the wood to be greased from one end to the other. It would take eight men some three weeks to process and produce a single spar. I was proud the shipwrights still used this method when they created the teak flagpole that stands on my Bequia residence.

Meanwhile, I remember going with my father on the ferry *Corona* to the capital, Kingstown, on Saturdays to buy supplies for the construction and to pay off the market lady and butcher who had been sending supplies to our home when he was at sea. My father was a towering figure. As we walked through the town, with me holding the edge of his pants, he'd stop and listen to all manner of people pleading with him to take them to faraway places. I loved visiting Gibson the blacksmith and seeing him pound the red-hot iron into a shape my father wanted for the ship. I remember romping on my father's big belly when he was lying on the floor. But he was not home often.

He had lost many ships and had told many friends, "When this one I'm building goes down, I go with it." She took 21 days to launch. She was stuck in the sand and the *Corona* was sent to Carriacou to borrow a screw jack – an iron device to move the ship closer to the water.

Enormous quantities of food had to be cooked each day for all the men and women from all over the island who came to help. The cattle to be slaughtered came from our estate at Hope. The goats and sheep came from Isle à Quatre. They were cooked in enormous old sugar cauldrons. There was great feasting because everyone came to give a free hand to launch the ship, and they had to be well fed. We had to hire the cooks and the maids. Cooking and more cooking, pulling on the ropes around the ship – and singing sea shanties. There was great ceremony with people seated everywhere eating, telling tales and singing.

I still can hear the melodious sea shanties:

Oh tell me what the white man had for dinner
Mosquito leg and sand fly liver
Blow my bullyboy, blow.

Oh Rosie was a windj'er
Walk along, Rosie, walk along.

And the frustration, day after day, waiting on the tides to give some help.

When she was finally launched, the *Gloria Colita* was a magnificent spectacle with her sails up. She was a clipper on the water. Legend has it that even before her mainsail was up, she had reached Kingstown. All of Kingstown came to the waterfront to see her tack and sail to anchor.

Drums of corn, dried peas, and farine had been stowed beneath the decks for the long voyages my father planned. They would take stones from the rocky beaches off Isle à Quatre and transport them to Guyana and to Curaçao or other islands in the Netherland Antilles to sell. Later on, in many of my early campaigns in the countryside, many an old man would tell me that it was my father who took him to some Dutch island to help him start making a living. The very successful farmer Basil Bascombe, a millionaire in his own right although he was barely literate, who worked with me when I was Minister of Agriculture trying to market a stock pile of arrowroot, once related a story to me about how his barrow – a large pig – was sacrificed on my father's ship. They were becalmed for days, and my father told him no wind would blow unless some blood was shed. After the pig was slaughtered, and the pork was eaten, the breeze returned. (My father being a skilled navigator probably understood the changing features in the sky, and could anticipate the breeze was coming – by which time the pork was safely in the pot.)

My uncle Newton Ollivierre, my grandmother's brother, sailed as mate with my father. "Baby Lou" Lewis and Uncle Jim Gooding were also crew on the *Gloria Colita*. When the three learnt that my father was sailing from Curaçao to Alabama they literally got cold feet. They did not want to go in the cold winter, so they returned home. My father made the voyage safely with his new Venezuelan crew. Trade had begun between the United States and Cuba. His last load was lumber.

And then the cable reached Bequia in January 1940: "*Gloria Colita* found abandoned. No souls on board." I remember the exact spot on the beach outside the schoolroom where I was told. I got home to find a weeping village. Bequia's foremost navigator had perished. The largest ship ever built in the Caribbean was picked up by the US Coast Guard in the infamous Bermuda Triangle. Her sails were still up, but torn. With a cargo of lumber, she was still afloat, her decks awash. She was sold later, and repaired. We got a few dollars but not enough to pay off the debts.

In the family archives, in an old album, I found my father's last picture, and the tattered receipt for $32.50 dated January 30, 1940 from the Mobile Bar Pilots Association; his final communication to the family. On the back of the photograph was an inscription. "Fighting with the cold. Just came from the Custom House. Met the Manager taking pictures for advertisement of the oil." With it was a money order of $5.00 to the family and the servants. I got a dollar.

With the *Gloria Colita* gone, we were left only with the *Corona*, our small packet boat – ferrying messages, mail, goods and passengers to St. Vincent and back – earning no more than a pound a week. Beyond the tears, I learned lessons that served me well as a Minister of Finance. Indeed, I never had a problem with the International Monetary Fund. "Much to praise, little to fault" is what the IMF said of my management of the economy. You learn from life.

The return fare on our ferry was one shilling per person. I remember my grandmother settling up on a Friday afternoon with the Captain and crew. We had done exceedingly well if we collected 20 shillings, or £1, for the week. The bounty was shared, one third for the crew, one third for the maintenance and operation of the ship, one third for the owner.

The packets were sailing sloops. They had great long oars to assist when becalmed close to land. Out came the oars near Devil's Table at the entrance to Bequia, and when going into Kingstown harbour. But the wind and currents would be too strong sometimes and carried the ship low down the leeward coast and the ship would return to Bequia without making Kingstown.

The packets had an open bilge over which the passengers sat on two planks. Decaying vegetable matter washed down between the round stones used as ballast produced an awful smell, guaranteed to produce instant seasickness.

I remember my grandmother sending me to Spring with three shillings out of the six she earned to pay off debts on timber used in our sunken ship. But there was some compensation. The plantation owner, Mr. McIntosh, would have his stable boy drive me on the horse and buggy back to town. Seventh Day Adventist that he was, the horse and buggy had to be home before sundown on the Friday evening. Later, his son Cecil, who considered himself a literary and political pundit, was one of my harshest critics. For a long time, his weekly column's subject was me. So I told my Cabinet colleagues who became worried from time to time, that Cecil's problem was that he could not come to terms with the idea that the little boy who used to walk to his father's house with three shillings had become his Prime Minister.

But the disappearance of my father still churns my inside when at the funeral of any seaman, even today, the hymn is intoned:

Eternal Father, strong to save,
Whose arm hath bound the restless wave,
Who bidd'st the mighty ocean deep,
Its own appointed limits keep.
O hear us when we cry to Thee,
For those in peril on the sea.

Early in the life of my Frangipani Hotel (of which more later), I met one Christmas day an American family seated in the bar waiting for our special Christmas lunch, and the father suddenly announced that the family was sailing out. The Christmas winds were howling. It was raining furiously.

"Where could you be going in this weather?" I asked.

"We are sailing north. We have changed our mind. We don't feel like celebrating," he declared.

I got to the bottom of the story. The family had lost a son who had fallen overboard in the Bermuda race that year, and suddenly they felt it would be sacrilegious to celebrate. I sat and told them my story. I told them how the blow of my father's disappearance in the Bermuda

Triangle wrought havoc in my family, but with the years I have put it behind me as my mother had done. She had lost not only her husband, but also her father, in a storm.

"So please stay," I said. "You don't have to pay for the Christmas lunch. You need company today. Your family must not be alone. Take some comfort out of my family's triumph over the sadness we too have known in this house."

He looked at me, and then at each member of his family in turn, and agreed to take up my offer.

I grew up with strong religious training. Each day I went to church – three times on Sundays. I had a beautiful white cassock and a silken rope around the waist. I served at the altar. The priest, Fr. Owen Mallet, gave me a souvenir bible from his ordination by the Archbishop of York in England. That bible, decades later when I was Premier, was inscribed by the Archbishop of Canterbury when he visited our country, and it kept me company around the world.

There were also the visits on certain weekends to the Holy Cross Anglican Church in Paget Farm. We would walk more than three miles on a Saturday afternoon. I would spend the night either at the home of Uncle Newton, who had sailed with my father, and his wonderful wife, Aunt Jane, or in Gellizeau with Aunt Ethel, my grandfather's sister. I used to think how terribly far it was to go and serve in Church in Paget Farm. I suppose it would be a hard grind even today for a seven-year-old boy. The waves on the reefs in Paget Farm were a strange sound with which to go to bed, as there were no waves crashing on the shores of Admiralty Bay on the other side of the island where we lived. Today the young people can't hear those sounds in Paget Farm. We have built a $75-million airport that extends even beyond the reefs. Progress?

And so I learned my way through the Christian liturgy and the Bible, and the knowledge has served me well in both my personal and political life. The experiences of my youth, however, were sufficient to permit me to be cynical about the mischief and abuse I suffered later in my political life, at the hands of various religious bodies. I have ended up disillusioned about the Church.

3

Youth and the Sea

In 1921, a violent hurricane in the West Indies devastated the island of Canouan. The hurricane also took the life of my mother's father. He had rowed a boat out from the beach in Bequia to rescue a passing Union Island schooner and never returned. So like me, my mother lost her father at the age of nine. She was an attractive teenager skipping rope among her girl friends on Porter's Wharf in Kingstown when a swaggering hulk of a sea captain from the *Alternara* first saw her. He proposed later while she was still in High School.

Bequia had no secondary school then and indeed had none even after I had left home for University. But my grandparents were always hospitable to teachers. A headmaster named Cato, whose son was to precede me as Prime Minister, and whose grandson became one of my Health Ministers, occupied a room on the lower floor of our home, and a Barbadian tutor lived on our estate at Camel. The fees at his school were a penny a week, or an egg on Monday mornings. My father and aunts were sent to school in Barbados, living in a home we rented there. It was after his time on Barbados that my father took up an American correspondence course in navigation and became Bequia's first navigator, taking Vincentians seeking employment to other lands, and Cubans into the United States. My mother was sent to the coastal town Barrouallie in St. Vincent to go to school and learn the piano. That was early in the twentieth century. Sadly today, a hundred years later no one gives piano lessons in rural St. Vincent.

My father's sisters were sent to the United States to study medicine and nursing. It was quite revolutionary in the West Indies, early in the twentieth century, to invest in the education of women. My aunt Eulalie Lee was probably the first woman to be sent from the Caribbean to study medicine abroad. She came to prominence during the Second World War when she had accompanied her husband, also a doctor, when he returned to army duty in the United States. On the train on the way back she was forced out of the whites-only section, and rather than

15

accept the indignity of the colour bar, took to the railway tracks. She damaged her ankle, initiated a class action and won a settlement that enabled her to purchase a home in the all-white enclave of Martha's Vineyard in Massachusetts.

My aunt's uncompromising response to racial discrimination must be trait I've inherited. For my grandmother's mother, Caroline Wilkinson, was the fruit of a liaison between landed gentry from Bequia and a house slave, descended from the Fulani tribe in West Africa. A marriage was proposed by the plantation owner to the mother of the child, but the Anglican Church decreed that it should take place at the back of the church and not the altar. The house slave declined.

So the teenager (my mother) married the sea captain and the family moved to Curaçao. My genealogy is a true Caribbean cocktail. By the time I had to deal with apartheid in South Africa in the 1980s at the United Nations, and at the Commonwealth Conferences, I could speak with the authority of my inheritance – that those of us who are a blend of Africa, Europe and India are at a loss to understand the lack of faith in racial harmony. My white mother with her blue-grey eyes descended from the Wallaces of Scotland. My father's line, apart from the Fulani slave, emerged from French-Jewish pirates named d'Ollivierre who had children with a respected English plantocrat named Warner. So I suppose it was my destiny to deal with the resolution of some serious twentieth-century racist problems, in my own way.

I once had to address a gathering in celebration of William Wilberforce and the abolition of slavery. I told them the identification of hard work in the Caribbean with slavery was indeed for me a more worrisome burden than the history of slavery itself. Equating hard work with slavery is a bane of Caribbean society. All those who only want to work 30 hours a week, all those who want to work only four hours a day, are now democratically free to do so. For me, however, the working day is 15 hours.

As I said earlier, I was born beside a shipyard. There were boats being built, repaired and renovated on both sides of our home and on the beach in front of the house. My father was building again and my mother wanted to give him a son. I was almost another miscarriage. When I arrived, the midwife shouted from the window to the shipwrights, "It's a son." And "Son" became my nickname all through life, and in conferences around the world.

My grandfather was not the explorer that my father was. He sailed throughout the Caribbean and to the United States, and brought home treasures not available in the islands; red wine for himself, and white for my mother. And in her nineties now, Mama still insists each day on her quota of white wine.

There is a tale about how my wandering father bet his boyhood friend Spence, the Customs Chief in St. Vincent, that he could smuggle in rum on his ship at any time. Six months later, they were waiting for him with hammers to lift the floorboards of his ship – and found nothing. My father said he had forgotten about the bet, but that night he raised the anchor to which the cask of rum was tied, and invited the customs staff back aboard the ship the next morning.

"I now declare my cask of rum from Guyana!" he exclaimed. Everyone had a stiff drink and enough to take home.

I didn't hear all those stories about my legendary father until he was gone, and I was a schoolboy in Kingstown.

One vacation, I was hiking on the eastern side of the island with an older member of the family. Looking toward Mustique, we saw the periscope of a submarine and its wake on the surface of the water. We did not discuss it. But the silence did nothing to dull the pain deep down in me.

Survivors of schooners torpedoed between the islands had been saying that they saw a big bearded captain on the deck of the German U-boats, and that that person was my father. A legend had developed that the enemy needed a skilled navigator who knew the islands, to lead them to places where they appeared, to places only my father could have known. The Germans had taken him off the *Gloria Colita* in the Bermuda Triangle in 1940, according to the legend.

Of course I would have loved to believe that my father was alive. But proof of that never came. The U-boats once went right into Castries harbour in St. Lucia and blasted a ship while my stepfather was in charge of the port. He, of course, took my mother and drove the other way in their little Morris.

My grandfather, after whom I was named, always hoped that, at worst, I would keep the family tradition alive and become a sea captain. I once wrote about that in a school essay.

We returned to the island and found that some visitors were cutting his timber without permission. My grandfather pointed out to me which part I could chop off and bring home for him to sell subsequently to a shipwright. I cut the frame in two even pieces so that I could lift them. He shook his head at me. I had made both pieces of wood useless for shipbuilding. The curve was needed for the belly of a ship. It was my first serious lesson in the family legacy of shipbuilding.

My grandfather had his own way of looking at the world. Whenever someone died, a bell would toll in town. He would say to me: "Boy, go into town and find out if one of my enemies is dead." When I reported him the name of the deceased, he would often say: "Oh, he was a good man. He was not a thief." Later, when I was looking for development finance in the Arab countries, I was reminded of my grandfather when I heard one of their proverbs: "If you sit on your steps long enough, and you are patient, you will see the body of your enemy pass." Alas, the bells no longer toll for anyone in Bequia.

My paternal grandfather, nicknamed Old Harry, was a self-made man. He had captained sloops that plied the islands and saved his money. He bought our four acres in Belmont, suitable for boat-building, and near enough to the Harbour.

His success with purchasing property engendered jealousy, and he was always in court with thieves and trespassers. Only property owners voted in those colonial days. There were less than 50 votes in the Grenadines. I knew my grandmother voted, but my paternal grandfather could not be bothered. My grandmother was the caring soul, ready to share meals with all visitors.

Years later he was still ready to build me a ship and launch my career as a sea captain. That cut no ice with my mother and stepfather. One had lost both a husband and father at sea and the other had lost his best friend. So I found myself on course to be an agronomist. It was to be on the land, and not the sea that I found a career, although I later did study navigation when working in London.

I grew up learning about boats. I learnt how to roll the oakum on my legs. I learnt how to caulk a seam. I knew how to boil the pitch and seal the seam. I knew how to trim the sails and how to move the ballast and how to steer and to tack with the wind; how to dismast the sails, empty the ballast, bail out a swamped boat and sail again to meet 40-foot waves at sea. If I did not know all this, I might have perished at sea on many an occasion and (I like to think, immodestly) St. Vincent would never have had a liberal to lead them away from communism.

When I became Agricultural Research Officer in St. Vincent, my cousin Cyrus Mitchell and I would sail to Bequia for weekends. The boat we used belonged to my uncle, and was not by any means a yacht. She was a glorified fishing boat with a deck and engine, and a tiller and rudder, hinged behind. On one occasion Cyrus and I sailed my uncle's boat to Bequia and on the return nearly lost our lives in the 40-foot waves we encountered.

On the Sunday afternoon we sailed from Bequia back to Kingstown. Our main sail needed mending. An old sailmaker in Hamilton fixed it for us. The boat also had a leak. A friend tacked on copper sheeting with some grease beneath. As we rounded the point from Bequia we met the schooner *Gardenia* coming down the Bequia coast from Barbados. They shouted for us to turn back. We did not give it the slightest thought. Cyrus was a teacher and had to get to work on Monday morning. My job at the research station needed me to start the week.

Hardly were we at sea when confronted by massive waves, wind and a strong current, and then I understood the warning from the *Gardenia*. In the midst of this roaring sea the rudder floated up, knocking the tiller out of my hand. The little sloop was totally uncontrollable. Without a word, Cyrus stripped and swam to the rudder, using it to help him get the tiller. I rushed to stop the engine and lower the sails. It was close to sundown. I could only see my cousin intermittently between the waves. I unloosed the main sheet and timed when I could throw it to him. Thank God I got it to him. I pulled him, the tiller and the rudder back aboard. I then had to bend over the stern and mount the rudder, tying it to the gudgeon while Cyrus held my feet so I would not fall over. We raised the sails again, started the engine and brought the boat under control.

But then she started to leak. Cyrus had to go below and bail. I was steering and dumping the water overboard. We bailed all the way to Kingstown, getting in after nightfall, and tied up alongside the jetty. We found the leak again: the patch had come off. So we plugged it from the inside this time.

Cyrus later migrated to Montreal. He was rushing one night with his wife to see her father who had had a heart attack, and drove under a truck. All three were buried together. Had Cyrus not made it back to the boat with rudder and tiller all those years ago, I too, like my father and grandfather, would have been one of Shakespeare's mariners of whom he wrote: "of his bones are coral made."

I have survived other frightening experiences, and sensitivity to mortality has always inspired in me a diligent use of time.

Of course, I was not the only leader in the Caribbean to have experience of the sea. There was also John Osborne, a dear friend in Montserrat, whose toughness in dealing with rough weather equipped him well as he tried to keep his country going after much of it was blown apart by the volcano. And there was the redoubtable Captain George "Fergi" Fergusson from Barbados and the aimiable Sir Emile Gumbs Chief Minister of Anguilla. Captain Fergi, Errol and I once sailed together in the *Ecstasy*, borrowed from the prominent Barbadian family, the Goddards. We caught over 20 dorados and kingfish sailing the Bequia channel, and later dined on selected portions of them at the Frangipani Hotel.

Long before going into politics, Sir Emile captained one of the most elegant schooners in the West Indies, his beloved *Warspite*, and brought me a shipment of pineapple suckers from Antigua. He once sailed to Kingstown needing urgent help. He was broke at the time but Allan Gunn, a yachtsman and partner in the old firm John H. Hazell's Sons & Company Ltd., could not let such a beautiful ship go without help and generously assisted him. Emile never forgot the kindness. Later, Emile and I teamed up in a collaborative effort to redesign our EC currency notes, an option granted us by the Monetary Council of the East Caribbean. We took control of the back of the $10 note. He sent in an old picture of *Warspite* and I provided Admiralty Bay. I think we worked out better compromises than the European Finance Ministers, who, years later, designed their faceless euros. (And our model of a single currency for separate nations was functioning successfully decades before the euro came into being.)

Sir Emile always laughs whenever we meet, and he recounts what he thought was a practical joke I played on him. The Bequia Airport, funded by the European Union and supported by all Caribbean governments, deserved to be properly opened. So I invited all heads of government, and a host of bureaucrats from our region and Brussels.

Accommodation had to be found all over Bequia. Sir Emile was sent to Moonhole, a somewhat incongruous resort built in the rocks at the end of Bequia. Tom Johnston, the retired American marketing genius who designed the place for his friends, allowed no glass windows or any precise measurements. I had allowed him to proceed without planning approval, which would have required specifics. Johnston was into ecotourism before a Costa Rican architect invented the term.

Sir Emile had entertained me lavishly and had escorted me through the fine wine cellar at the Malliouhana, his premier resort in Anguilla. Quite reasonably, he had assumed I would be keen to return the royal treatment, and show off a facility as sumptuous as the result of investments he had brought to Anguilla. He could not believe he would be treated to an *al fresco* toilet, without a roof or doors, but looking out on a magnificent seascape.

He made a great show of his feigned chagrin. "Son, do you know that the shit house has no doors in the place you sent me?" he asked.

"Come on, Emile," I said. "You're no stranger to fresh air – the *Warspite* didn't even have a *washroom*."

I think he forgave me when I sent him 2000 coconut plants after Hurricane Luis devastated his country in 1995.

After my father vanished with his Spanish crew in the Bermuda Triangle, my mother moved to St. Vincent and married Alf Baynes, the Comptroller of Customs, who was a family friend. He had stayed with us in Bequia before. He was very ambitious for his new family, and a wonderful protector. He was promoted to St. Lucia and shortly thereafter my brothers and sister were taken to St. Lucia. I was left with my grandmother, Sarah.

Granny took me one Friday on our ferryboat *Corona* to sit the Grammar School entrance exam before the headmaster, the revered Don Lopey. Within an hour, I was pronounced suitable. With two pounds paid into the treasury, my first term began. I took up residence with a friend of my grandmother's, who put me up while I went to school in return for Nen Sarah's modest contribution to the household.

Mother Cropper, who presided over the household, was a comely white old lady with her retired civil servant husband, who all day sat looking out through the window and tending his bandaged sore leg. They lived in Middle Street at the lower end of the town. The house was comfortable and adequate but lacked the more sumptuous fare awaiting me from our estates in Hope, Isle à Quatre, and our corn and peas from Belmont.

Food supplies were limited in Kingstown. Flour was a rarity. The Second World War and the German U-boat menace were very much alive in the West Indies. Indeed, quite a few ships were torpedoed in our waters during the conflict. I can recall seeing the burnt faces of English sailors as they came ashore in their lifeboats. Some of them had been scalded swimming in flaming oily water away from their sinking ships. I can also remember how I was sailing home one Saturday on our ferryboat. An English Harrison cargo ship had taken on board the entire year's production of Sea Island cotton. She passed us in the channel, and was torpedoed just west of Bequia right before our eyes. Bequia fishing boats went out to rescue the crew. Many a mattress and pillow were made out of the cotton that washed up on the beaches.

I remember that Mother Cropper would bake a cake on Saturdays, and the whole house was filled with its wondrous smell. On Sundays we would get the first slice after lunch, which was quite enjoyable, an enriching feeling to be diminished by the admonition that the rest of the cake had to last all week for the six of us in the household, four adults and two children. I once opined to Mother Cropper that her slices of cake during the remainder of the week were so thin that one of these days I expected the knife to shave itself. I would be happy to have my week's allocation in one gulp. "Then you'd have nothing to look forward to each day after school," she kindly reminded me.

Mother Cropper boiled guava jams and jellies to supplement the family income, and even taught me how to stir the jam speedily in her beautiful copper skillet over the hot coals, to ensure it came in at the right texture for setting, without being burnt. I learnt too how to make guava cheese, after the pulp had been squeezed through a muslin gauze, sugar added and the mixture stirred constantly in the copper skillet until, sputtering like porridge, it came in and was poured on to wide tins to be cooled and dusted with fine sugar. I used to get the trimmings and was entitled to lick the pot. The rest was sold to a neighbour's shop.

Such were my early lessons in allocation of resources. Early days too and long before the calories of banquets around the world extended my waistline.

Dinner sessions also thanked the Lord for making us truly grateful. A very mean Lord, I often thought. I listened in wonder to the intricacies of the elite in our society as revealed by Aunt Vida, one on Mother Cropper's spinster daughters who worked the island's telephone exchange of a few hundred lines. Aunt Vida (she was not an aunt, but the mores of the time dictated such respect) while plugging in her connections could save the time of various ladies by bringing them up to date on the whereabouts of other callers whose conversations she had gleaned earlier that day. She knew who was sick and the remedies prescribed.

They were a holy household, with loyalties split between the Methodist and Gospel Hall churches. I'd go with them to either on various special sessions when a preacher with new enlightenment descended from Barbados or Trinidad, but they allowed me following the stern injunctions of my grandmother to stick to the Anglican faith and the liturgy I knew by heart. But I was ready to go to any church, a practice useful for later political niceties. As a matter of fact, on Sunday nights I would visit all the churches, beginning with the Roman Catholics, as they finished earliest, when I could see my girlfriends out of their protective school uniforms.

I looked forward to vacations in Bequia. It was only for Easter, Christmas and August vacations that I could get home. There was no way one could sail every day between the islands and get back to school on time. It's a very different story now, since I privatized the ferry service. Many parents in Bequia, including teachers in the Bequia secondary schools, now send their children to school daily in Kingstown.

My childhood visits home increased after the businessman, Grafton Hazell, built a yacht to visit his lady in Bequia. I would get a ride with them after taking the bus from Kingstown to Villa where his yacht was moored. His was the first yacht owned by a Vincentian.

Then tragedy struck one Tuesday morning, and transformed my life. The Headmaster summoned me to his office, and asked me to sit down. "Mitchell, your grandmother Sarah is dead," he said. My grandmother had died on a Friday, and was buried on the Sunday. No boats had sailed from Bequia in the rough September weather, so I was told only on the following Tuesday. I thought very much about this, when decades later, I negotiated telephone services for the island with Cable and Wireless.

My mother and stepfather came down from St. Lucia and collected my brothers and sister. I was left to go to school in St. Vincent. That single decision, to leave me to grow up a Vincentian, rather than a St. Lucian, led to my political career in St. Vincent.

The first election I ever won was at school, when it was thought that the school needed to move from three to four competitive houses. The school competitions were in both scholastics and sports. A group of students met in a classroom to select a new leader and I was chosen to mould a random selection of boys into a spirited team. We called it "School House." Some great friendships were forged then, and have withstood the test of time and migration to distant lands.

Every generation has difficulty communicating with its successors about the hardships it encountered. The youth today, who drive to school or are dropped off by parents, cannot imagine how my friend George Richardson, founder of our Vincentian group in Montreal, walked three miles from Questelles to school every day, or how Vincent Cabral rode his bicycle 15 miles over rugged roads to Park Hill at weekends. The kind of route marches we did, walking miles from school at 3 p.m. and into villages on dusty roads towards Layou, only to return at 3 a.m., would be torture for our youth. Our entire cadet corps and scout troops did this regularly. For fun! My stepfather had great pride in the day he walked all the way from Georgetown to Kingstown, and then became Victor Ludorum at an athletic event in the afternoon, while my friends and I used to swim across the bay, from Kingstown to Edinboro, to meet up with girls. My exploration of the coast line, outside the harbour into which I plunged from surrounding cliffs, instructed me in the feasibility of the US$18 million cruise ship berth I later negotiated with the Kuwait Fund and the European Investment Bank.

I used to love spending vacations in Isle à Quatre with my grandfather and got along well with his new lady. He was a cheerful philanderer who sired 22 children by five women. The island was busy with workers from Paget Farm, in the south of Bequia, tending the fields of corn and peas, reaping the oranges and sapodillas. From the numerous sheep and goats, there was plenty of mutton for all. The fishermen who tended seines on his shores had to give him some of the catch. What was not cooked right away was salted and sun-dried, there being no refrigeration in the Grenadines at the time.

I have a wonderful memory of my Grandpa, sitting outside at Corkscrew Hill, looking at the sunset while eating his dish of pickled roasted sprats and farine rolled in his hands. He would belch and say, "King George did not enjoy his supper tonight better than me!" And his boast went further as he relished his island:

I am monarch of all I survey
My right there is none to dispute
From the centre right round to the sea
I am Lord of the fowl and the brute.

He taught me his skill in management too. Once, we were taken from Friendship to the island in a fishing boat. The fishermen were pleased to do him favours because he provided them with timber to build their boats. I was so glad to reach land; I jumped off the boat and scampered up the hill. That evening at supper Grandpa summoned me to Corkscrew Hill. "You jumped out of the boat. You did not say thanks, you did not help to haul up the boat," he scolded.

"Grandpa," I remember saying, "I am small and not strong like the fishermen."

"No, boy. That's not the point," he said. "I, too, am not as strong as the fishermen. I did not help to pull either. But I put my hand on the boat."

So I learned that a leader leads by being part of the team. You have to be seen to be a team player. It was a principle with which I endowed my Cabinet colleagues in the management of a country.

In the summers off from school, I joined farm labourers pounding sacks of dried peas, and shelling and grinding corn. The memory of those long, dry afternoons later sparked my later concerns about global warming today and its possible effect on changing seasons. May, June and July were rainy months. August was dry. Today there is no produce to process in August. The rains come later.

Holidays in St. Lucia in the forties were also wonderful. My first trip was on a Compton-owned schooner, carrying fuel in drums to the American base at Vieux Fort. The Americans were very much in evidence with their powerful transport vehicles. A police officer, Sergeant Biddy, a friend of my stepfather, treated me to my first Pepsi Cola from the American canteen. Like my first romance, I still remember the taste of my first Pepsi. The other thousands of gallons I have imbibed never tasted the same.

I remember what a glorious sight it was, looking down upon Castries and the northern end of St. Lucia and Martinique from the Morne. And I was back in the bosom of my mother. No hugs from all the aunts and caring friends of my mother could ever equal it. I did not know then how lonely my life was destined to be, spending years away from my family in the Grenadines, living in the Prime Minister's residence with security police and government staff, dedicated to service, missing my children.

Castries was welcoming, and I made a lot of friends. They gave me a new nickname because my feet intertwined like an X when I walk. To this day even eminent QCs in St. Lucia, like my friend Kenneth Montplaisir from those days, call me – the longest serving Prime Minister of St. Vincent and the Grenadines- "X."

I joined them in schoolboy pranks. Castries was then a beautiful city of three-storey wooden houses. But they had no sewage system. All buckets in the basement were carried nightly to a place called Shit Alley on the edge of town. A ship docked there collected waste daily and dumped it beyond the entrance to the harbour. A horn sounded every night, the signal for the scavengers to collect their buckets of human waste. These ladies had an awful job, and some worked for more than one home, and carried a second bucket that was often perched precariously on their heads.

Some youngsters were not beyond the prank of tying a string under a walkway that could sweep the precious cargo off the ladies' head: – an event that brought out the fire brigade hose the next day, to peals of laughter. The Captain of the ship, from the island of Canouan, who daily sailed the precious cargo out of the bay, was frequently taunted by the youth who got him to chase them in all directions.

Question: "Captain Eli, what is your cargo?"
Answer: "Dry shit and paper."

Later in life, I remembered these scenes when I saw the squalor and garbage of poverty in developing countries in Africa, Latin America, and even in Haiti. I marvel at the progress we have made in most of the Caribbean in becoming middle-income countries.

Back then in St. Lucia, it was a rough ride on the dirt roads along the coast and through valleys of sugar cane, although it was quite pleasant through the orderly villages. I still recall how the buses had to make three-and four-point turns to round some corners, and the precarious rides, often skirting the edge of precipices protected only by clumps of bamboo.

I also made good friends among other schoolboys in Castries. Their school was Catholic whereas mine at home was a government grammar school. To get to the beaches we would walk a couple of miles over the hill to Vigie. Castries had a wharf in town whereas Kingstown had only a pier. Big ships came alongside in Castries, built as a transfer coaling station, whereas at home, the cargo came ashore in lighters with massive oars. Alongside the wharf, we played water polo. Being a good swimmer I took to the sport readily.

Adult suffrage had not yet come to the islands. My stepfather, as Colonial Treasurer, possessed some of the appropriate regalia: corked hat, tunic, sword and emblem; but they were not as resplendent, with the ostrich feathers reserved for the Governor.

A great fire once swept through Castries. I was back home in school and got on the relief boat that was dispatched from St. Vincent. We stopped along the leeward coast and scores of farmers brought yams and tannias to the beach for us to take on board. I reached Castries in time to see the roof of our magnificent three-storey wooden house collapse. My parents were camping out in disused army barracks that had been built in the old days when regiments were stationed in St. Lucia. We shared the building with the Judge's family.

As I was about to graduate from the fourth form in our grammar school, I had to choose between the Classics and Science. I abandoned Latin and was going for Chemistry and Botany. The Headmaster Lopey was the Latin teacher, and wanted the best students in his classes. So he was quite upset when I chose Science under the Barbadian, Woody Blackman. But I was quite happy to stay in English, absorbing some ten Shakespeare plays, Bernard Shaw, and poetry from Chaucer to the romantics, Keats and Wordsworth. Thus began my odyssey into Science, from which I never returned.

While I was very busy in the Cadets and Scouts, becoming head of both and devoting after-school hours to those activities, I was not very good at either cricket or football. I would occasionally hit a six, and score a goal from time to time, but did not excel. My main contribution to the game of cricket will be remembered more for the pavilions I built in my country as Minister of Finance.

Having passed the Cambridge School Certificate in all the subjects I undertook, including Chemistry, I was ready to migrate, along with my schoolmates, to work in the Dutch Antilles oil refineries. But my stepfather would have none of it. My grandfather reiterated he was ready to build me a ship. To that too, my parents vehemently objected.

"You will stay in school and win a scholarship to university," was my stepfather's final say.

There was, however, an upside. It meant more holiday trips to St. Lucia on sailing sloops. One trip took three days. The majesty of the Pitons on all the St. Lucia brochures was totally lost on a hungry schoolboy with nothing to eat but dry rations on a becalmed sailing sloop.

Once in a while it was more luxurious, going deck class on a French cruise ship, the *Duc D'Amale*, via Barbados; one night to Barbados, a day ashore, and the next night to St. Lucia. To get into cabin class, I remember befriending some French priests. That was when I was first introduced to Benedictine liquor. I would sleep in the cabins, refuse to awake when called by the crew – I had a good excuse as I knew no French then.

The great excitement for me besides holidays, however, was the Inter Schools Tournament in another island. We were off to Dominica to engage that island, along with the boys from Grenada and St. Lucia. The sailing ship (which had an engine) came up from Grenada, picked us up, and we made it in a couple of days to Dominica.

We slept on school benches for two weeks. We competed in cricket, soccer and athletics. I was Prefect, Sergeant, Troop Leader, head of School House and chosen as extra for all teams, but good at none. But the Vincentian group never wanted to leave me behind.

We swore that in Dominica we would not be eating their mountain chicken which we thought, having not seen it, to be no more than a glorified frog. Lo and behold, we were entertained one Sunday by a farmer. The first course was chicken soup. We had all relished the mountain chicken before we knew it. We were ignorant of the fact that we had eaten one of the world's great delicacies: frog's legs.

But the serious business was to win this scholarship and get to University for a profession. In those colonial days, the country awarded only two scholarships every three years. It meant I had to sit the finals twice – once at the end of my studies, and again the next year, when the scholarship was offered. Nothing was going to stop me.

In the final year, we had no Chemistry teacher, but I had learnt the syllabus the year before, had good textbooks, and even taught my colleagues. Two of them, Richard John and Cecil Cyrus, became eminent physicians.

My grandfather would never give me more than a shilling as pocket money, but he would pay for the books I ordered COD from England. He was always proud to go into Barclays Bank in the city when he came to town. He prided himself on having Barclays' shares in England.

One of my old aunties with whom I was staying once complained to him that I was studying girls. She had seen my letters from some girls in Dominica and St. Lucia. I shed tears for my shilling that day. But the old philanderer, my grandfather, didn't care about the complaints as long as my school reports were satisfactory.

"Never mind her," he said to me, referring to the old auntie as he took out the money. "When she got pregnant and she wasn't married, and the priest asked her to explain, she said it was for the Holy Ghost."

Sensitive to her probable reaction if I told her that Grandpa was still giving me money, I dared not reveal what he really thought about her, until much later when I was already Prime Minister.

My dear Aunt Cleve transferred to St. Lucia and worked with Cable and Wireless. Every time government business took me to St. Lucia, I made it my duty to visit her and see that she was comfortable. She left me her modest two-bedroom house and it turned out to be more valuable than the gratuity I received from Parliament for over 35 years of service. But back then, I was bending my mattress so that my feet would press against the bed boards, ensuring I was too uncomfortable to oversleep. I'd awake early every morning to study, determined to secure that scholarship. Early rising, an early swim, a cold shower and a breakfast with a spoonful of whale oil paid off. I remember, too, those War years when there was no flour. We got by with fried breadfruit and cassava farine. I received the coveted Lady Musgrave prize in 1949, a copy of Trevelyan's *English Social History*, a fine exposition of influences on our heritage, needing a lifetime of experiences to really relish.

I came first in Science.

When those exams were over, I did not know what to do with myself. I had studied so hard that, with suddenly nothing to do, I felt a great emptiness. The Science class celebrated. We mixed up rum punches, went along the coast in a boat, plunged off the rocks and got drunk.

Most of us had been accepted into a University and were headed overseas to study, or make a life elsewhere.

It was the first time I got drunk. The second and last was at a wine-and-fondue party in London's Kensington. With all that I later had to consume as a parliamentarian of the liquor-smuggling Grenadines, I had to know how to hold my drink.

With nine months on my hands before I could enrol at the Imperial College of Tropical Agriculture in Trinidad, I temporarily became a Science teacher at St Mary's College in St. Lucia directly under the Science Headmaster, Brother Canis of the Presentation Brothers, allowing him to concentrate on administration. With my first salary of $90 for the month, I gave my mother $30, opened a bank account with another $30, deposited $20 on my first wristwatch and kept $10 to buy cakes and fizzy drinks.

I teamed up with other young teachers, Derek Walcott, Garth St. Omer, and Perry Husbands, none of us dreaming where fate would take us. Derek certainly had no clue he was to win the Nobel Prize in Literature. Many of our students too climbed the ladder to success. Michael Chastanet, on whose report I declared he was "resting on his oars," became a shipping magnate. Edsel Edmunds as Ambassador joined me in the Banana Wars against the United States, Barry Auguste as Head of Protocol in Eric Williams' government received me at Piarco on several occasions. George Odlum became the respected Foreign Minister of St. Lucia, his oratorial skills honed in the halls of Oxford, and often displayed with great passion on our political landscape. He was to be among the few from the Caribbean to earn an obituary in the *Times*.

But it was now time to move on!

4

Imperial College of Tropical Agriculture in Trinidad (ICTA)

I really would have liked to study medicine, but there was not enough money to do so. I was enrolled to study Agriculture, but with no role models to emulate, I had no idea what I would do in the field.

The ICTA campus was large and gracious. Lovely green lawns, meticulously landscaped with elegant Saman and yellow Poui trees. It was an almost male enclave – only four women; two in my class and two postgraduates.

I remember ending up in the Dean's home on my first Sunday. His wife was the College doctor, and I had twisted my ankle going across a gutter. It had already been damaged shortly before in St. Lucia, playing soccer. It turned out that the Dean's and Doctor's daughter – the first of two female students in the history of the college – was to be in my class.

All the professors and lecturers were English, except for one or two assistants in Engineering who had done well in previous years. Most of the students were English too, and the rest in the graduate class came from the Colonies, including Rhodesia, Malaya and South Africa. The place was set up mainly to teach the English how to manage the resources of the tropics. These students were already graduates from Cambridge, Oxford and Reading. The minority were the West Indian scholars from the region, most of whom were undergraduates.

My first Economics class served me throughout life, in business and in politics. The English lecturer laid out before us the factors of production: land, labour, capital and management. At question time, I asked why management should be put alongside the other three, and was told that that was the reason why I was at the University.

ICTA's main rule was simple: You failed a subject and you were out. At the end of the first term, a Grenadian student fell by the wayside.

We were down from 24 to 23. Years later, at a Conference of the Heads of Government of the Caribbean under the Chairmanship of Prime Minister Eric Williams, chaos in the same campus where I had studied arose on our agenda. I suggested that the University, now controlled by West Indians, should return to the English standards of my day: "Fail a subject and you're out." It sounds harsh, but that *was* my recipe for student agitation. Students today are allowed too many repeats.

Evenings at ICTA were elegant occasions. We dressed in ties and white shirts for dinner in the hall beginning at seven. From five-thirty onwards, all students were invited to drinks with a professor or lecturer of their choice. Each of them would put up their names on the notice board and you wrote your name down under the name of the person you planned to visit. The professor or lecturer would pick up the list later, and expect you for drinks – usually rum, whisky, vodka or gin. They were also teaching us the social graces. Certain students looked forward to socializing with certain lecturers, but social contact did not save you if you failed the exams.

I remember one Sunday going to Blanchisseuse Beach in the school wagon with some English students, including the female postgraduate. We were swimming offshore and the current swept in. I was first back ashore. From the beach I could see how the current was moving. I went back in to help her. She was panicking, and I told her I was back to keep her company. I did not rush to her, as I knew what *not* to do. She was not drowning but could have done. I told her to swim with me and the current and that we would come ashore lower down. We made it in fine style.

Another memory that stayed with me was my foray into golf. All the West Indians had signed up for soccer, cricket and hockey. The English and South Africans predominated in rugby and golf. I was the only West Indian signing up for golf. It so happened that the college had enlisted the help of an American professional to teach golf. On the first day, the golf students all gathered on the first tee. The pro turned out to be a black man. All the white students walked away, leaving me alone with the gentleman.

"I'll teach you to flog their arses," he told me.

The college could not break their contract with the black golf pro, so I was the sole beneficiary of his instruction. I became an object of ridicule, because for three weeks, he taught me the swing only. My West Indian friends thought it a big joke, me swinging the clubs for weeks without a ball. By the second year I became champion and was the only West Indian on the college team that included professors and lecturers. By the time other West Indians wanted to learn, there was no coach again!

There was to be another lesson for me in racism. Among the two Africans in the graduate class was a student from Sierra Leone. He had already graduated from Reading University in England, and was brilliant at rugby. When the College rugby team went to play against the management of the Oil Fields in San Fernando, the African was not allowed in the Club House.

Quite incensed by this, I organized all the first years to vote him as Captain of the football team. He was elected. But when the time came to pick the College team (although by this time we were close friends) he left me out and chose several white players. I demanded an explanation.

"I am choosing my team on the basis of ability not race," he explained. "You go and rest your twisted ankle."

Bad manners also got me into trouble. I was a top student in Geology. Professor Hardy invited a group every Wednesday night to his office for a tutorial. The tutorials were casual and friendly, and concentrated on how to communicate using refined English.

On one such evening, I was celebrating my birthday and did not turn up. "Mitchell! You have no manners," greeted me the following Wednesday. "Why did you not call and say you would not be coming?"

Very self-assured, I said that I was celebrating a birthday.

"Never let me hear you are doing that again at this college. I'll be having a birthday party and I will invite you," he said. "It's only when you are old that you should celebrate, for then each year is a challenge."

He visited St. Vincent in his retirement as a guest of the planters, the Hadleys, whose son Victor maintained the family tradition, becoming one of the island's top flower exporters. I had the professor over for dinner and reminded him of his advice.

The early 1950s were wonderful years to be at college in Trinidad. The school was a prestigious institution, respected for research in cocoa, sugar-cane, and sugar technology. Our lecturers had experience from all over Africa, India, Malaya, on top of their academic achievements. They understood their mission. Their lectures were replete with experiences of life. One veterinarian had been in the trenches with the horses in the First World War. The Second World War had ended little more than five years ago and Churchill had lost the election.

I enjoyed all the subjects. I excelled in Geology, loved dealing with the animals, and was fascinated with the history of agriculture, from the spice trade that led to the discovery of the West Indies, through the export of logwood to dye fabrics in Europe, right up to the role of sugar in the development of the City of London. Sadly, nobody, including our intellectuals, cares a hoot today about the logwood trees.

The lectures from Professor C.Y. Shephard on the history of tropical agriculture served me well in guiding my nation through changes. In seminars organized by the Eastern Caribbean Central Bank on policy guidelines, I had the confidence of history in my veins, knowing that our monocrop culture in sugar cane and cotton and cocoa would all pass. The old religions that inspired generations would fade, and a new ethos would come. It was hard going, but the agriculture of slavery gave way to other eras of survival. The lands which produced logwood for dyes gave way to beach resorts, and I knew that the cane fields would someday become golf courses.

Adult suffrage came to St. Vincent during my first year at University. My stepfather's brothers were elected. I promptly wrote requesting my government-granted allowance be increased. It went from $25 dollars to $50 a month, my first benefit from adult suffrage.

It wasn't a lot of money by any means. By the time I finished paying my laundry bills – for my white shirts for dinner – not much was left. With the increase, however, I was able to take a weekend off once a month and take the train to Port of Spain. It was during those journeys that it struck me how serious the English were about Train Spotting as a hobby. One of my graduate friends, an Englishman who spent his hours off studying trains while I was out on the golf links, would, for instance, forever complain about train number 33: "She hasn't got a whistle."

Back at college, it was serious business twice a week to get to the farm, milk the cows, and clean the cowsheds, all before breakfast and lectures. My first outing in the rice swamps to plant seedlings was a novel experience for someone from parched Bequia. My water boots flooded, and I joined the Indian ladies barefoot and did my job.

But I was to run into trouble with Animal Husbandry. All my dreams of doing veterinary medicine collapsed. We were given an assignment to write a paper on caring for a donkey for a day. All I could think of was the way we loaded up the ass for a good day's work on our estates. I duly prepared the donkey's work schedule and determined the size of stick needed to prod the beast along. No grooming for me. But it wasn't what my teacher was looking for.

The next disaster was with guano fertilizer. In that assignment, I went beyond the chemical analysis and nutrient value for plants, and did some research in nature magazines on the birds in the Galapagos and the quantity of their excreta. I calculated the output of a bird per day throughout its lifetime, to the absolute consternation of the professor and chaos in the classroom. I did not intend to be funny. I was environmentally sensitive long before it became fashionable. I did not want the resource exhausted.

If I had thought I was a brilliant scholar leaving St. Vincent, I was quickly disillusioned, faced with the competition from British Guyana and Jamaica. But today, those wonderful schools of the 1940s are hardly even a shadow of their former glory. The prestigious school in Georgetown, Guyana, is creaking from the disrepair it has fallen into under communism.

The Americans were still at the bases in Trinidad, and the Gaza Strip, the street where the girls flourished, was very much in business. The houses where they worked operated as registered clubs. You had to sign in. As students we were not going to put our own names down. But we did duly register as our various English lecturers, and had great fun among ourselves the next day as they pontificated before us. "I wonder if he knows he was in a brothel last night," the students would whisper as the teacher gave his lesson. Having only to pay the shilling for taxi fare, I became a habitué in Laventille.

I think my initiative in early research was rewarded when I wrote to the King's Ranch in Texas for information on their famous breeding of Texas cattle. Redemption from my earlier misdeeds was complete. My pass in Animal Husbandry was secured. The volume of information I presented was overwhelming.

Succeeding in exams meant I was able to be in Trinidad for three carnivals. Every island in the Caribbean has some kind of carnival, but that was not so in the early 1950s. As a matter of fact, some Trinidadians and I organized the first carnival in St. Lucia. But the real Carnivals are in Rio, Trinidad and New Orleans. The others are still trying to catch up.

Trinidad is not rich in beaches. The bikini seldom has opportunity to reveal the glory of flesh in that country, a real shame because nowhere in the world has India, Africa, China and Europe blended so thoroughly as in the texture of the Trinidadian woman. But Carnival atones for the shortage of bikinis on the beaches.

My first Trinidad carnival began on a Saturday with a ride into town on the train. I settled down with a hamburger and banana split. My $20 had to see me through until Wednesday morning. I shouted at the Queen shows (beauty contests) as though I was the sole arbiter of quality. A lass whose attention I sought (but never got) was placed sixth in one show.

When vacation came, eight of my friends had failed their exams. I was lucky. I got a job in cocoa research under the Economics lecturer. A Jamaican, a Guyanese, a Montserratian and I found lodgings in Curepe. The Jamaican and Guyanese worked in a sugar factory. The routine always began at 3 a.m. when we were picked up, then headed for the cocoa fields all over Trinidad. We had to be on location to meet the labourers at 7.00, worked until 2.00, and made it home. We carried our lunch with us and the East Indian labourers later introduced me to roti.

Once we returned to pick up our lunch from where we had left it, covered by an oilskin, and there was a massive snake coiled over it. I preferred to go hungry. We would run into snakes about every other week. An East Indian labourer chopped one in two from a branch over my head, and a section of the snake fell on either side of me. That graphic picture is still with me half a century later.

The second year at the Imperial College was a monumental test of memory. Entomology, botanical classification, and Pathology had to be digested and regurgitated. My room was full of lists and charts, and I learnt to identify every plant and insect disease in the tropical kingdom, complete with Latin names that I absorbed easily, given my earlier forays into Caesar's *Gallic Wars*.

My photographic memory developed at ICTA was to serve me well at my next university in Canada. I could go to their plant museum and recognize the species of the plants in the Canadian wilderness as well as any Canadian.

I was before the microscope one afternoon examining the mandible of the sand fly when the lecturer interrupted. "The King is dead. Long live the Queen," he declared. Elizabeth II had just ascended to the English throne, from a tree house in Kenya where she was on honeymoon with her new husband, Prince Phillip. But not for a second did I then imagine Her Majesty would one day visit me, alighting from the Royal Yacht *Britannia* moored right in our very own Bequia harbour. I went back to my study of the mandible and wings of the sand fly.

With a developing interest in the history of Tropical Agriculture inspired by Professor Sheppard, I spent hours roaming the library and digesting ancient texts. I once came upon the history of nutmeg. It was advocated as an eminently suitable plant to be cultivated after the abolition of slavery because the trees produced a wonderful shade under which white planters could comfortably collect the nuts themselves. Decades later, after American intervention helped depose the Communists in the isle of spice, Grenada, I told the Director of USAID (who was seeking my guidance on helping our neighbour) about the cultivation of the nutmeg, and warned him that Grenadians would be expecting a lot of shade from the US.

I got quite fed up of lectures on the control of insects and diseases. One day, trying to move on to something I thought more interesting, I challenged the lecturer.

"You keep teaching us how to control pests and diseases," I said. "Why don't you teach us how to eliminate them?"

"Young man," he replied, "the insects will inherit the earth, not humans."

I learned many other lessons in those days that stayed with me throughout my life. One afternoon at the horse races, for instance, ensured I'd never be much of a gambler. A brief encounter with nicotine similarly convinced me that smoking was not my thing. I might never have tried it at all if a fellow student had not told that smoking improved concentration. Dutifully, wanting to maximize my results at study, I bought a tin of du Maurier cigarettes. Later, engrossed in Chemistry formulae that night, I lit it up. Having no ashtray I was resting the cigarette in the fold of my beautiful and expensive textbook. The next thing I knew, the book was on fire. That was the end of my indulgence in nicotine. I reckoned I didn't need that kind of help to concentrate.

Other lessons I learned were sometimes hilarious. Our Jamaican friend, "Wacky" Kennedy, complained one night that he could not sleep because of a pain in his scrotum. We discussed the issue at length and it was agreed that he had caught a cold in that area of his anatomy. I prescribed Sloan's Liniment.

It wasn't long after his careful application of my gooey medication that he nearly fainted with pain. We had to use up all the ice in our refrigerator to give him some relief. We had him squat in a basin of ice. The next year, in our class on horses (namely draught horses, of course!), the veterinary surgeon was lecturing on swollen testicles and I sought guidance on the use of Sloan's.

"You'd kill the horse," the Vet shouted,

Needless to say, I had to hide when I next saw my Jamaican friend. But I'm happy to say he survived his condition – and my prescription – to become a successful manager of sugar factories in Jamaica, and fathered many children.

My Soils lecturer, Professor Hardy, loved the earth. He patented tests on soils, including the widely used Hardy's Sticky Point Test. He loved the feel of the earth and designed and quantified a simple test to determine the ratio of clay and sand in a soil. Originally a botanist, he taught himself the structure of soils. He was one of the earliest environmentalists. When he spoke on the evolution of the earth's surface, it was as though he was imparting a religious truth, and indeed he was in a way. The line from the hymn – "A thousand ages in thy sight are like an evening gone" – was the embodiment of the evolution of a soil, from rock, humus, sediment, wind, rain, through the centuries, a living experience in infinite time.

In Vancouver some years later, I was to meet Professsor Hardy's soul brother in Soil Microbiology, Professor Laird, whose theme was "earth to earth, dust to dust," and who specialized in the role of soil organisms and bacteria in the evolution of our landscape.

In my final year one morning when we were on the farm chatting away about our futures, I told my colleagues that if I passed the exams I would be looking for a salary in four figures, far beyond 1000 BWI dollars. The lecturer overheard and looked at me as though I was a real fool.

"You will not be worth that on graduation," he said.

"Why not?" I demanded.

"Because you have no experience," he said.

"I thought you taught us everything," I challenged.

"We did not," he said. "There are certain things in life you have to learn for yourself. You will be worth a thousand dollars when a disease wipes out your farm and you are still farming. You will be worth three thousand when you have survived pests, diseases, flood, drought, hurricane, volcanic eruption – in fact, if you can survive all disasters you can call your price," he went.

I didn't realize at the time that I was not only getting a lesson in management, but also a pointer about life's ultimate tutor – experience.

A fire started by an unknown once destroyed my Mt. Pleasant farm. My daughters were delighted. Little girls under ten do not relish being awakened at first light to water plants in a mountain far away from their beds. When I turned up the next week with three times as many orange, lime, grapefruit, mango and mahogany plants for the driveway, they were horrified. But years later, when Hurricane Lenny deposited four feet of sand in our hotel dining-room, my daughter Sabrina was ready for business in three days.

Instant readiness to recover from disaster became a hallmark of my political life, for tribulations were not only the result of hurricanes destroying our livelihood, the banana industry, but also from the havoc caused by political jealousy.

Agricultural Engineering was my nemesis, however, during my final year at ICTA. Each Friday afternoon, we would go to the farm shed to take apart implements and machines. The work began with the process of greasing our hands down. In desperation, I said to my buddies, but within hearing of the English lecturer, that the only thing I would really remember was how the soap grease worked to clean my hands. When the three-hour final exams came, he gave me a brush cutter with a universal joint that was hell to put together. I failed the practical.

But my theory was excellent and had put me over the 50 per cent mark; and fortunately for me, the Soil Science professor who had cautioned me about my bad birthday manners was powerful on the examination board. The Principal told me later, when I went to collect my diploma, that Soil Science won me the day. The Professor of Soils had insisted that he who excelled in his subject deserved to graduate.

I had succeeded in all but one of my Trinidad endeavours – the golden necklace and heartfelt attention that I had bestowed on a certain young lady, sadly, yielded me nothing. On my last night in Trinidad I visited her and said my tearful farewell. The next time I heard of her was when her husband, a military man, was my protocol officer on a visit to Eric Williams.

I was all set to go on to another University. But first I went home to my grandfather in Isle à Quatre who came up with me to the Bank in St. Vincent and gave me the exact 2200 BWI dollars I calculated would get me to Canada and the University of British Columbia for a year.

5

Canada/University of British Columbia (UBC)

I left Trinidad from the Chaguaramas Bauxite terminal where my uncles were working. I had secured a cheap passage on a bauxite boat all the way along the 60° line of longitude toward Nova Scotia and into the St. Lawrence River. The fare for the trip was $180. I was the lone passenger among the Norwegians operating the ship. The Captain knew only a few words of English.

The ship – which I had picked because I judged that it would fit my time schedule to register at University – was the slowest of the fleet. The first day at sea was spent washing the ship free of the reddish brown bauxite dust and cleaning the cabins where it seemed to have seeped through every crack in the doorway.

My sole reading matter was a two-volume copy of Boccaccio's *Decameron*. I had pretty well gone through the first volume in three days, but soon I realized how slow our ship was. At dawn, we would see another ship on the horizon, and by 2 o'clock, she had passed us. They were all on the 60° line, going the same way to Canada. I frequented the bridge and checked the charts. After seven days I realized we were only half-way. I began to ration my pages of the *Decameron* so that I would have some reading matter all the way.

The weather was fine. No hurricanes were coming our way. The first land in sight at the end of the journey was the bleak coastline of Nova Scotia. I spent time on the bridge checking out the lighthouses and isolated houses scattered along the coastline. I could see no people or signs of activity.

"What do these people do?" I asked my Norwegian host and Captain.

"In summer, they fish, they f***. In winter they don't fish."

I went ashore in Montreal, having got past the medical checks at the port, and made my way to a youth hostel that Friday night. The

39

next morning, I went to a travel agent and requested a Greyhound bus ticket to Vancouver. It was only then that I realized how much that slow Norwegian ship was really going to cost me. The travel agent pointed out that I would reach Vancouver on Tuesday night at the earliest, one day too late for registration at the University, which was on the Monday.

If I took the Greyhound, it would have meant that I would not make the academic year, and that without a student visa, I would have no legal status in Canada, so I had no alternative but to spend $300 on an airplane ticket. The travel agent took pity on me, took me to a restaurant after I had bought the ticket, and said he would take me to the airport later.

I went into Eaton's Department Store to buy myself a felt hat to prepare for winter. At the top of the escalator, I approached an attendant, turned on my charm, and asked for help, only to be briefly taken aback when she just stared back at me.

The object of my attention turned out to be a mannequin.

The journey to British Columbia wasn't uneventful either. The airplane was a four-engined propeller design. As we lumbered across Canada, I awoke in the night to see one of the engines on fire, as the plane landed at an airport somewhere in the prairies. No big fuss. We changed planes and went on. I got into Vancouver on Sunday afternoon and made my way to Fort Camp at the University of British Columbia.

British Columbia lived up to all my dreams. In geographical magazines, I had seen wonderful pictures of winding roads beside the edges of the lakes in mountain valleys with conifers everywhere. The homes were so beautifully landscaped, spotted with pine trees and apples! To this day, I have not seen a campus as beautiful as that of the University of British Columbia. So much space! Wonderful mountain scenery, a whole peninsula to yourself, beaches strewn with driftwood for wiener roast parties, wrapped in blankets. I could still enjoy the luxury of the scenery, and the company of beautiful students, even as I slaved away 17 hours a day for seven months.

The campus had two camps, Fort Camp for single students and Acadia Camp for married ones; both began life as wooden structures with varnished plywood floors for soldiers training in the Second World War. The girls' dormitories, though, were made of different stuff. They had beautiful clay brick structures with glass and curtains. In the two camps some 700 girls and 1,000 boys shared a common dining-room. We had breakfast, lunch and dinner, cafeteria style, with random seating and unlimited food. The lines moved quickly, and in the evenings, we hung around no more than 15 minutes. The girls' dormitories were forbidden territory, but boys and girls could share the glorious landscape.

I registered for the two-year honours course in Agronomy and Soil Science. After I had paid the fees for tuition and residence and meals for the academic year at Fort Camp I was left with $55. There were no telephones in the Grenadines, and therefore no way to get in touch with my beloved Grandpa.

I wrote home but it was going to be six weeks before I could expect a reply. Impending penury dictated a change of coursework. As things stood, not only would I have to go a full two years for the honours programme, I would have to go back and upgrade my calculus. I quickly looked for an alternative, and found one that solved my problem, although it left me with more on my plate than anyone in the Faculty of Agriculture. The Dean's office checked my credits and suggested that if I increased my workload from the 18 units a year I had signed up for on the honours course, to 22 units, I could get the basic degree in one year, and enter the Master's programme.

But I was still close to broke. The student job advice bureau beckoned. I went to a bowling alley for a two-hour stint for 65¢ an hour. But the bus ride was 30¢ return. So I perched myself between the bowling alleys on a narrow ridge, jumping from one side to side and keeping out of the way of the flying pins for my two hours. Dripping with perspiration, thirsty and hungry, I bought a hot dog and Pepsi. That was another 60¢. I wasn't going to save a fortune this way.

When I got back to the dormitory I realized I had left my precious 12-dollar hat behind. I called the bowling alley but it was not to be found. I was already $11.60 in the red in my first venture into the Canadian economy – rather dubious credentials for someone who was to attend his first Commonwealth Finance Ministers' meeting in Toronto years later.

The next weekend I vowed to do better. As an agricultural student, I could earn some money gardening. I set out on Saturday afternoon with the address of a lady who had advertised for someone to prune her apple tree. An hour later, hopelessly lost, I rang the lady, who gave me directions. Half an hour later, lost again, I rang again and she discovered I didn't know the difference between East and West Vancouver. She told me to stay put and came to collect me.

I had never seen an apple tree before I came to Vancouver, let alone pruned one. She provided a saw, shears and clippers, and, looking like a true professional, I walked around my quarry, sizing up the situation.

The branches were laden and low down near the ground, choked by grass around the trunk which would be difficult to mow.

As I began working, I engaged the lady in a discussion about the age of the tree, its yield of apples and their quality and ended up convincing her that the low branches had yielded too much, and would probably not continue to do so. Moreover, I said, she should be able to walk around the trunk of the tree without having to fight the underbrush that had developed. I chopped and packed the branches. She was pleased and later let me use the phone to call a friend with a car to take away all the apples she did not need. I had enough under my bed to trade for a couple of weeks.

To further supplement my income, I took a job delivering telephone directories, when a friend asked me to join him in the venture. The deal was one penny per book for me, one for the car, and one for him. We went to the warehouse and drew lots – and wound up with deliveries to homes in North Vancouver. It would have been far more lucrative if we had drawn apartment blocks in the southern part of the city.

We paid a toll to cross the bridge to North Vancouver, and set about delivering in the snow. The driveways of the rich were long and dog-infested, and the books were very heavy. By the end of the day, we had not even made enough to cover lunch and the toll back across the bridge. That was the end of my career in the telephone-directory delivery business.

Luckily, I got a job instead delivering the campus mail from 5 to 7 o'clock three mornings a week for $28 a month. The job turned out to be quite a catch after I had earned my stripes during the Christmas vacation delivering mail. Later, whenever November came around and I was signing my 3000 Christmas cards as Prime Minister, I always remembered my early delivery days.

Except for the few texts I owned on Organic Chemistry and Plant Physiology, I had to rely on the library for books. My routine was to get to the library by 8 o'clock and study until 10. Three nights a week, and at weekends, I had to walk through the snow for half an hour to the greenhouse for my research on the effect of growth-inhibiting hormones on the post-generation growth of rape seeds in various nutrient media and soils. I would get home about midnight. Despite my full schedule and workload, I enjoyed the lectures. My fellow students, unlike those with me in Trinidad who were expecting to work in the offices of their Civil Services, were basically from farms. Their enthusiasm was infectious. Back home in the West Indies, the children of the wealthy did not have the ambition: they were already comfortable with the family fortune. In Canada, the richest girl in our Biochemistry class was also the most diligent. I saw then a great difference between the children of the rich in developed countries, and the careless rebelliousness of their counterparts in poor countries.

The lecturers were also superb. They were scholars in their fields. The professor of Soil Classification, to cite but one, was a very dedicated scientist from Alberta who once revealed in class, in his constant monotone, that his lifestyle was about to change.

"All my life I have devoted to the top six inches of earth," he said. "This morning, I have been told they have found oil beneath my farm!" And then he just went on with his lecture on permafrost.

My Soil Bacteriology teacher was the philosopher, Professor Laird. Soil Bacteriology teaches the role of organisms and how they painstakingly play their part in the evolution of soil, death, decomposition and decay, returning the essential elements to the earth. Thus I learnt the meaning of the funeral ceremony: earth to earth, ashes to ashes; and how transitory our own flesh is, in the cycle of the universe.

At the Range and Pasture Management exams, I was more than the Canadians' equal in identifying species. I remember delivering my thesis only a few minutes before the closing hour and my tutor kindly telling me delivery was only a formality. He had read all the drafts, he said, and was pleased with my research, which was part of work he would later publish.

I had chosen to go to UBC because it had diverse programmes of study – not just Agriculture – and because I loved West Coast scenery. I did not want to go to another agricultural college with student conversation limited to one field of study. The decision proved to be the right one. Among others, I attended lectures on the role of the Catholic Church in Polish history, and was well prepared to see at first hand how the Church and Pope John Paul II took on communism at the political level.

I concluded my first year and had a chat with my tutor. I remember his advice to me that I should always respect other academic disciplines if I wished to gain respect for mine, and never to be lavish with my opinions unless asked because everyone thinks they know about plants, trees and flowers.

Funds remained a problem. On the bus, going to the railway station for training as a sleeping-car porter, a friend joined me with the newspaper, which published the exam results. Mitchell, James F., was listed with distinction. No work that day; I threw a great party the night the exam results were published.

After graduating, we all set about looking for summer jobs. I was offered an attachment in the Provincial Agriculture department at a rather low wage, which was not enough to pay for another year's tuition and meals. The best money for students was to be made in the mines or on the railroad. I knew that my mother was claustrophobic and would die if she heard I was 1,000 feet below ground. So the trains it was, working as a porter between Vancouver and Winnipeg, with an occasional diversion to St. Paul, Minnesota.

What a wonderful lesson in scheduling it was, getting into Moose Jaw for a two-minute pause at 2:30 a.m. to let off passengers from the sleeping car. Like everyone else, I became proficient in making 28 beds in an hour, and taking them down in 20 minutes. I learnt a lot about the service industry on those trains.

Tips were our lifeblood, as we had to buy meals in the dining-rooms. Poached salmon followed by the blueberry à la Mode was the ultimate indulgence for a starved West Indian student, particularly on a Sunday afternoon beholding the mountain passes between Banff and Lake Louise.

We devised other ways of saving. For instance, you could swap a meal for a bunk, if you had a bed to spare. One night I was in charge of empty cars inside British Columbia, and struck a deal in the dining car and kitchen. They requested one car for all but the chef whom they insisted must sleep in a separate car. I had my sumptuous salmon and put them all in one car. They rebelled. I could not understand the need for the separate car.

The chef was quickly asleep but what a thunderous snore he had! I swear the company could have replaced the train whistle or the fire alarm with his snore. It was unevenly explosive; there were long periods of silence, and small snores, which accumulated for a big bang. The uncertainty would drive you crazy. He was one of those Eastern Europeans who had fled from communism. They used to be described as DPs, or "displaced persons." Today, they are classified as "refugees."

My bank balance improved. I got to know by heart the times of arrivals and departures along the route. I kept the spittoons shining. Polishing shoes became routine. And we slept when we could. One Sunday afternoon, a train inspector presented his identification when he found me sleeping in a corner. He upbraided me with the obvious charge – sleeping on the job. Mercifully, Pepsi Cola had a great billboard in those days that came to mind in my time of need.

"The pause that refreshes," I said to the inspector.

"I like your humour," he said, "but don't try it twice."

On one occasion, quick thinking came to my aid during a stop in Winnipeg. I was walking down a street in that city when I saw some Indians drop to the ground on their stomachs. Instinctively, I did the same. Some fellow students from Trinidad thought I was crazy. But "when in Rome, do as the Romans do," was my first instinct, which turned out to be the right one. The black tornado cloud was ripping down the street and my friends were lucky to be pinned against a doorway.

By the end of the summer I had enough money to register in graduate school. Before I did however, a black Southerner who claimed to be the president of the Student Union somewhere in Tennessee offered to get me a scholarship at his university. He said that his campus needed someone like me. I was vaguely interested and bounced the idea off an elderly American railway porter who had made Canada his home. "Jim, boy," he said, "you stay right here in Canada. Down there they'll call you a liberal. Both the blacks and the whites will crucify you. You don't care a damn about colour. You are going to have a problem!"

I took his advice and stayed in Canada.

After I had paid all my fees for the coming year, and paid the necessary deposits on my rent for digs outside campus, I still felt rich enough to buy a car with a friend, with the idea of travelling to Mexico for Christmas. My friend, Bill Donawa, spent days in the second-hand car lots and finally turned up with a Ford convertible, the model seen in the film *From Here to Eternity* about GIs in the Pacific. But the car never made it through its inspection. Each light pointed in a different direction no matter what was done to it. We never got to Mexico and the car was an almost total loss for me.

Years later when I was Prime Minister and waiting in the first-class lounge of an airport, I ran into my partner again. He promptly returned the $300 badly invested two decades earlier. He had more honour than many of my political friends. He had become a successful veterinarian, and still had a summer home in Vancouver, together with a clinic and a restaurant business in Barbados.

But back in Vancouver all those years ago, the loss forced me to return to my weekend gardening to keep body and soul together. But my coursework was fascinating. In one Soil Classification class, we embarked on a forensic project, analysing samples of soil from the boot of a dead criminal to determine the area he came from. Others were doing entomological research, confirming our conclusions by analysing maggots in decaying tissue to determine how long ago the person had died. I didn't know it then, but I was getting valuable exposure to forensic techniques that served me well as Minister of Security later on.

I delved into other disciplines too. My friends in Philosophy invited me to their private sessions at home on Friday evenings, to luxuriate in the history of civilization with diversions into home-cooked Chinese food. I was so taken with the subject, I took a graduate course in the Philosophy of Science, and another in Symbolic Logic.

In other ways my life changed. I suddenly wanted to explore Europe, and go beyond the colonialism into which I had been born. I was fascinated with European history and thought I should take a year off as many other students were doing. I had read all of Hemingway, and then graduated to Steinbeck and Kerouac. Now I wanted to visit the land of Wordsworth, Keats and Shelley that had absorbed me in scholarship for years in Kingstown.

With two degrees I felt I was a professional, and had enough to fall back on. So, after a year of graduate studies, and a basic course in Spanish, more savings from working on the trains, I terminated my service in Winnipeg, and took a train to Montreal for the ship to England. It was time for a break from academia.

Before leaving, I rolled up my diplomas from ICTA and UBC in a poster of a buxom (and quite naked) Marilyn Monroe advertising Bearing Engineering and Supply Co., and shipped them home to my mother in St. Lucia. I never knew where those diplomas were, until many years later my mother, now in her nineties, outlived all her friends in St. Lucia and came back to Bequia to join me. She had them still, carefully rolled up in my poster stamped "posed by Marilyn Monroe." My mother had never unrolled the folder marked "Certificates." So much for vanity.

The Canadian Pacific trains had become part of my being for two summers, working over 20 hours a day, often on a nine-day shift with one night off. It was good money. But as I became a passenger on that last ride from Winnipeg to Toronto, and Montreal, enjoying the gorgeous colours of the autumn leaves falling from the trees, spreading their golden hue on the Laurentians, I knew I was saying goodbye to one chapter of my life and the discipline that began with bending my mattress to win a scholarship. Now I was ready to explore the world. Hemingway would carry me to Spain and the bullfights.

When I became Prime Minister, and was negotiating further investment by Canadian Pacific and their subsidiary Maple Leaf Mills, in our joint flour business, I returned the inscribed clothes brush, my souvenir tool as a porter, to the President to decorate his office.

I took a cheap passage on a liner to Le Havre and Southampton. A former German soldier shared my cabin, and regaled me with stories of girls in Lille during the Occupation. He was going home, fed up with Canada, but still dreaming of finding a French wife.

6

Spain

I entered Europe a citizen of the United Kingdom colonies, on a passport – complete with the raging lion in the corner to prove it. Nobody eyed me suspiciously or asked how long I wanted to stay, or whether or not I was looking for work. None of the "uniformitis" from which our immigration and customs officials suffer as they seek to protect our sovereign identity in the Caribbean today. In the 1950s, I was welcome, or ignored, as a wanderer in Europe.

In Trinidad as a student I had been bombarded with BBC world news about the frequent demise of short-lived French governments, but a colonial stepping onto the pavements of Europe in the 1950s could not fail to be impressed by the grandeur of the architecture in London and Paris.

Colonialism at home made one feel caged with the way life was ordered by alien authorities. For instance, a Governor in St. Lucia once decided that the Judge better deserved the home assigned to the Colonial Treasurer, my stepfather, and much to my mother's anguish moved them to a lesser house. But walking through London and Paris for the first time as a colonial student, was simply overwhelming, and shattered all my preconceptions about our colonizers. I did not feel jealous of them. I simply knew we had a long way to go. In the meantime, let me enjoy myself, I thought. Let me get down to Spain where I could be anonymous and discover my soul.

The Canadian dollar bought a lot of pesetas in those days, so I left enough in a Canadian bank in London to pay my passage back to the West Indies, and set out for Barcelona, wine, paella and castanet dancers. I had enough money for three months in a *pension*, so I settled down and began to discover Spain. The *pension* harboured a group of young dancers. They rose late for breakfast and were never allowed out of sight of their black-jacketed chaperon.

My knowledge of wine was limited. I had read that the Spaniards went to the bullfights with leather pouches from which they squeezed their *manna*, the local wine that kept them going through the day. By my second bullfight I was similarly equipped. I relished the spectacle of the bullfight. Sunday after Sunday in Barcelona I would make my way along Las Ramblas to the Correa, almost out of town, and shout and scream like the Spaniards, and afterwards join the throngs walking homeward.

Franco then was all-powerful. My cadet training ensured my deference and I saluted the Guarda Civil whenever I passed. They must all have thought I was one of them on my day off. I became a fan of El Greco, viewing his paintings in the museum nearby quite frequently. When you visit a museum regularly and find yourself constantly ending up before a particular blue painting, it is as though you have discovered a friend.

I managed a couple of days in the delightful fishing village San Feliu de Guixols indulging in their fabulous paella with a sample of all that abounded in the Mediterranean Sea. How boring was our chicken peleau! How elegant were the fish markets with hand-painted tiles of squid and mollusks and various species of fish. Why were our fish markets so filthy? I was influenced by all those impressions on my first state visit to Japan where I secured the first $12 million investment in the Caribbean for the grand fish market that I named "Little Tokyo."

In Barcelona, I enjoyed the Mediterranean climate and the spectacle of families – usually three generations in each group – strolling the Ramblas in the evenings. Was the congestion of a city bringing them together? We had no such daily fraternity in our part of the world.

My Spanish experience was cut short suddenly by a letter from home. It was time to say goodbye to the castanet dancers and the wines of Catalonia. My favourite was Extressima Bach. But my obstinate refusal even to sprinkle olive oil on my salad earned from the waitress in the *pension* my new nickname "Sin aciete."

My grandfather had died. I was quite shocked. In the letter I learnt that his promise to me that I should have a share in the family island of Isle à Quatre was no longer in force. So it looked as though I would not have free access to the cedar wood to build the schooner as he had suggested. No more the entitlement of the ragged rascal scampering around the rocks on the coastline of his island inheritance. My degrees in Agriculture seemed to be my only property. I felt it best to return.

I found an Italian liner carrying West Indians to England, and others going all the way home, took the cheapest fare, and mingled with the middle-aged carpenters who didn't want to work in the rain and the cold. They did not even like the wine, and sweetened it. One of them was quite a rogue, I remember. He told the story of his hunting dog in the islands, which found its way home after he sold it, prompting him to sell it over and over again. He was also constantly trying to seduce a pregnant passenger, suggesting she needed continuous sex to "keep the baby's passage free."

On that same ship, however, I did meet a first-class passenger, who later turned out to be the politician I was so proud of when he won the election in Guyana, challenging the colonial *status quo*. He was Cheddi Jagan. I never imagined then that the day would come when, in Mustique after I had become Prime Minister, I would be chairman of a meeting of colleagues that would decide to establish observers in an election that would return him to power before he died.

7

An Agronomist

I disembarked from the Italian liner in Martinique and, with my slender belongings, made my way to the wharf where the schooners from St. Lucia were unloading provisions and taking up cases of margarine and French delicacies. They were leaving that night. The next morning I was in Castries.

My parents had built a new home in Vigie, my stepfather having been promoted to the top of the Civil Service bureaucracy, and their split-level house had beautiful views of the island and looked out across the ocean to Martinique.

I did not rush to find a job. Many friends I had made during school vacations had migrated and some were still in university. I became a beachcomber. Every morning, apart from a few retirees, I would have Vigie beach to myself, and roamed from one end to the other. Walking barefoot on the sand, being occasionally splashed by the waves, is wonderful therapy. I would rise early and write, then take to the beach, and write again. The impressions of all the Canadian cities, imperial London, and delightful Barcelona, filtered through my consciousness. That was all in the past, and I was home now.

And one day, in the midst of this relaxed existence, my first job fell into my lap. The Chief of Agriculture, an Anguillan graduate of Cornell University named Swithin Schouten, drove his jeep into our yard. "Son, I need you in my department," he called out to me. "I don't have anything good enough to match your qualifications, but it will be a start."

By then, I was ready for the open fields and the countryside. Salary was not a priority. So, nominally, I became Cocoa Agronomist in charge of propagation and distribution of cocoa plants all over St. Lucia. My immediate boss was Charles Cadet who was later to serve me as High Commissioner in London in our joint St. Lucia/St. Vincent Mission.

Charles immediately directed my attention to the inspection of a virus in the cane fields, and a yellowing of the banana leaves. There was no laboratory to test anything. There was no research library in the offices either. But answers had to be found. Fortunately I had shipped home some of my textbooks from Trinidad.

We set upon a plan that I should tour the whole island and familiarize myself with conditions, the good, the bad and the indifferent. Some banana fields were in excellent condition especially when young. Not all the sugar fields were infected, so there were varietal differences. The bananas, as the bunches were demanding extra nutrients, were yellowing and short of potassium. Other banana trees were falling over. We made the early discovery of nematodes, a parasitic worm.

I got along very well with my boss Swithin Schouten and we became friends. He had bought a plantation with a beach near Castries and we would often go there after work. The place was virtually abandoned. He set about building a beach house. His supervisors who were in charge of the project would meet with us and report to him on the progress. One evening I ventured a suggestion, but Schouten was silent until the supervisor left. Then he said, "Your suggestion was excellent, but your timing is wrong," adding: "At the end of the day, a worker is tired and glad his day is finished. That is no time to give him new ideas. I will call him to my office in the morning and tell him I thought overnight about your suggestion."

It was a valuable lesson which stayed with me through life. You do not give new instructions at the end of the day! A good motto for most situations, although somewhat irrelevant to a Minister of National Security dealing with a crisis.

I also worked during that time with Dr. Graham Louisy, who later became one of St. Lucia's most prominent veterinarians. Indeed, I still tell a funny story involving Dr. Louisy, who was later honoured for his years as a distinguished civil servant with a Castries administrative building named after him. A country farmer was trying to justify the quality of a young calf, a product of Dr. Louisy's bovine artificial insemination programme. "Which bull is the father?" the farmer was asked, to which he proudly replied: "Dr. Louisy."

Humour in this vein reached an even lower level in one of our practicals on insemination at the stud farm in St. Joseph, in Trinidad, when a prisoner who was doing time on the farm indicated that he thought the tube-like receptacle used for collecting the bull's semen – designed to approximate a cow's warm vagina – would be a welcome innovation among his colleagues.

St. Lucia was poised in those days for the conflict of interest between the cultivation of sugar-cane and bananas. I attended political meetings in Castries where the drama was unfolding. Bananas were beginning to provide continuous weekly employment in place of the long gaps between the planting and reaping of canes. The social dominance of the banana farmer was distinct from the hired cane-field worker, and was inspiring new hope. It was a theme that fascinated me and one that would be a recurring issue in my political life. I could sense that a continuation of the history of agriculture learned at the Imperial College was unfolding before my eyes.

But I was to leave in the midst of those weighty decisions. The St. Vincent government, responding to my enquiries, offered me the post of Research Officer, and I moved back home to begin work, with a three-bedroom house provided on a farm three miles from town. I was delighted to be home with three farms under my command.

My boss Hugh McConnie and the second-in-command, the enthusiastic Con De Freitas welcomed me enthusiastically. Hugh had moved beyond the technical work to administration, with a desk full of files and endless correspondence, including writing briefs that went all the way to the Colonial Office. Con, unlike present-day agriculturists, hated the office, and was happy only in the fields, with his clothes stained and boots muddied. Together, they set out my agenda.

My post was designated Agricultural Research Officer, but my responsibilities were spread far and wide. Research and demonstration of good practice in a whole range of crops all over the island had to be combined. I was put in charge of propagating stations, including our famous Botanic Gardens, which came into being with the breadfruit brought in 1793 by Captain Bligh on his second voyage after the mutiny on the *Bounty*. The job included growing ornamentals, and the distribution of economic plants, cocoa, various varieties of citrus, mango and avocado. On top of all that, I had to supervise the upgrading of all livestock, bulls and cows, sheep, goats and donkeys in the countryside.

One of the farms, Ottley Hall, was allocated to the prison. It was my job to guide the prison warders on the crops to be planted, tended and fertilized. There was also a separate home for the aged poor. They too had land under cultivation, and I had to inspire them.

On the main farm at Campden Park, we set out additional new clones of cocoa and established a system of recording yield and growth. Bananas were coming into their own, and I was determined to prove to the farmers that I could get better yields than they could. And I did just that, netting a record income.

I had some poultry farms built, imported high-yielding leghorns for egg production, and others for chicken production. The records we assembled demonstrated to the farmers how to distinguish between egg and poultry-meat production, and how to combine both. I got the merchant Gerry Palmer to import specified feeds. I encouraged visits from farmers and explained things to them.

It was during that period that I discovered an allergy to feathers. One night I got very ill. I could hardly breathe – my first-ever bout of asthma. Why did my genetic inheritance from my grandmother descend on me so suddenly? The vet next door, the late Dr. Earle Kirby, came to my rescue, prescribing anti-histamine pills, and told me to limit my visits to the poultry farm. Later, I had similar problems on my travels around the world, and my advance teams had to ensure that my hotel rooms were free of down pillows.

In St. Vincent, meanwhile, our farm produced handsomely. Yams, tannias and lots of milk from our demonstration herd. Dr. Kirby was a lover of calf liver, and so the young culls from the herds were usually destined for our table.

Following up on my thesis at University in Canada, I set about researching herbicides. The herbicide being used at the time was sodium arsenite, which produced instant results and was popular with the farmers who used it between crops. The merchants had brought in great quantities of the stuff. But sodium arsenite was terribly dangerous and was killing the earthworms and organic life.

I had to get good results from alternatives fast. I imported organic herbicides from Dow that I knew would degenerate and not linger and poison the soil, but they were more expensive. I pleaded with the bureaucracy. I pleaded with my superiors. I demonstrated to the farmers. I published my results and advice but only met with modest success. But the fact that I was producing other results in the fields and on the farms tempered the personal criticism. My publication on weedicides became a guidebook to farmers and extension officers in the department.

We were doing other research in cotton, arrowroot and sugar-cane. The wealth of knowledge in dealing with all those crops later sustained me in the formidable battles I had to fight restructuring the economy when I took over as Prime Minister. Indeed, I had to be very firm in contributing to our first manifesto in the Labour Party and eventually had to mobilize the full authority of the Food and Agriculture Organization to close down the sugar industry.

But my job in the 1950s was to make the industry more profitable. I tried out random applications of fertilizer to establish the ratio of nitrogen, phosphate and potassium required. I also kept track of the varietal responses to certain viruses. Cotton was a real problem. Our wonderful long staple Sea Island cotton provided great nutrient for the insects. All malvaceous plants in the island – like okra, so beloved in local dishes – had to be exterminated, as they were alternate hosts even when the cotton was not growing. It was hard work for the women in the sun, picking cotton. It was hard work again in the shade cleaning out the boll weevil damage. Under the circumstances, there was little profitability in growing cotton.

An Indian geneticist named Dr. Chaudhuri was busy at the time with arrowroot research. We wanted a variety that would be easy to harvest, rather than the long tapering roots, but didn't find it. So we brought in new varieties from Brazil, but again with no improvement. Our great St. Vincent arrowroot was destined to be a crop grown in sandy soils, relatively easy to reap, and destined to survive only with farmers working for themselves.

I did additional things free of charge. When the school was short of a Chemistry teacher, I would volunteer to help students prepare for exams. Later, as Prime Minister, remembering all the free help I gave, I could not come to terms with the inflexibility of teachers' unions.

My working day usually began very early, and in the evening I would go for a swim off Lowman's Bay, the coconut estate. I remember a narrow escape during one such evening. On the hill overlooking the bay was the watchman's residence. That evening he seemed to be going crazy. I was too far away to hear what he was saying, but swam quickly back to the shore to see if he needed help. But it wasn't him that needed help, but me. From his vantage point, he had seen an enormous shark in the bay and had been trying to get me to come ashore! From then on my swim has always been parallel to the beach.

I had another escape of a different kind on the leeward coast. A truck named "Justice" belonging to the former politician Edmund Joachim, laden with arrowroot, was in the centre of the narrow road, leaving me very little room to pass. My little Morris happened to stall right on the edge of the precipice, beginning to roll toward a drop to the sea a couple of hundred feet below. Fortunately for me, the truck reversed a little, and the workers sprang out and steadied my car, letting me get out safely. They then lifted the car back on to *terra firma*.

Indeed, when I look back on my life and all my escapes on land, sea and air, I can only surmise that guardian angels really do exist.

My pineapple trials, meanwhile, were successful. I had imported suckers from Martinique and Antigua, red Spanish and black Antiguan varieties, and they were thriving. I demonstrated to the farmers how they should be spaced and thinly fertilized. But, in the end, the fruit took too long to bear and they could not wait. In retirement, my friend Chief Minister Gumbs, visiting me at my home, Helianthus, recalled that he captained his *Warspite* delivering my pineapple suckers. Years later, when I was Minister of Agriculture, we had to start pineapple production all over again.

I got along well with the workers. I was lucky to have Mr. Rupert Lockhart, an old gentleman, as my farm manager. He was not an academic, but a great disciplinarian and a firm manager. His walking stick was part of his style. We would meet on Saturday mornings, assess the work of the previous week, and plan for the next week. I left more and more of the management to him while I moved around the countryside for research purposes, and to instruct the assistants in the fields.

At weekends, I would sail to Bequia. It was usually two or three of us in my Uncle Cyril Mitchell's 28-foot boat, *The Grenadines*. It was the boat he used to campaign from island to island and to bring his copra to Kingstown.

The first federal election in the West Indies took place when I was a practising Agronomist. Looking back, I have to say honestly that despite all the passion in my later political life that I directed to Caribbean union and other important issues, I was not focused on politics at all in those days. My energies were directed toward establishing my reputation as an agronomist and farm manager. I enjoyed seeing the result of my efforts in cultivation. Those who have planted a garden know how one's mind relates day by day to the growth one has induced, and how it becomes an absorbing passion.

However, I listened to the federal campaign. Leaders from other islands were passing through, talking in a few villages and the city, and moving on. I cannot remember anything about them other than the way they marketed themselves, and how they were most successful in their home base.

My uncle Cyril, who had done his stint in the Dutch oil refineries in Aruba, taken there by my father, was campaigning in the Grenadines for Sir Alexander Bustamante. He had been trying his luck at politics in the Grenadines himself, and came within a hair's breadth of winning on more than one occasion.

My single political contact in those colonial days was with our Chief Minister, Mr. Joshua, at that time a firebrand trade unionist. The workers on the plantation and at the research station wanted an increase in salary and I conveyed that to him. The owners, in this case the government, had to sanction the increase. I sent forward their request, but there was no response for several weeks. The workers decided to strike. The response was quick: the Chief Minister arrived, asking to negotiate with me as manager.

I simply and respectfully indicated that the government owned the plantation which was doing well, as the figures of income available to him showed, and I indicated what we could pay. But the poor fellow was not yet in control of the Treasury, and had to direct his frustration at the Colonial Administrator. The workers got their increase and continued to support their Chief Minister.

The work was interesting, but my mind was still set on exploring the world. The more I felt I had established my reputation in agronomy, the more I wanted to move on, sample the world, continue from where I left off in Barcelona, and discover more of Europe.

So one day, after considerable thought and in accordance with my contract, I gave notice to leave. A friend indicated that I could get better wages in British Guyana, but I did not accept. I had saved enough money to put up a deposit on land beside our home in St. Lucia, which I quickly inspected. Then I bought a ticket on a Geest banana boat, and headed for England.

The banana boats had six cabins for passengers. The food was good and the passage to Wales took nine days. My fellow travellers were a doctor from Grenada named Stan Friday who was returning to pursue a fellowship in surgery, and a couple of girls from St. Lucia who were going to study nursing. I arrived in London in the fall of 1961, thirsty for knowledge of life and the world.

A Guyanese friend from my ICTA days, Eamon Nicholson, whom I had inducted into the ways of golf, had left the Bookers sugar refineries to study law, and he offered me lodgings in North London, around Stamford Hill.

A Trinidadian introduced me to Gallop Poll Officers in Piccadilly, and I joined him, randomly selecting names from the archives of the British Museum to make up lists of people to survey. He had been involved in the Trinidad Labour movement, and his Communist sympathies swelled with the launch of Sputnik and the defeat of the American-inspired invasion against Castro in the Bay of Pigs.

The British Museum became my intellectual home, as I wandered through the history of civilization, brooding over Egyptian monuments amid recollections of Mark Anthony from the school play, Shakespeare's *Anthony and Cleopatra*. A citizen of the colonies discovering the British Museum cannot be less than awestruck and amazed.

My communist friend was of the opinion that all foreign exhibits should be repatriated to the corners of the earth whence they were stolen, a thesis to which I was not particularly sympathetic for the simple personal view that with such repatriation poor wanderers like me would remain bereft for life of their acquaintance.

My Gallop salary wouldn't stretch to many indulgences, and London expenses were soon eroding my agronomy savings, so I took a job as a "supply," or temporary, teacher. One had to be capable of giving a class in Chemistry, Physics or Biology at any grade in a secondary school for a few days when the regular teacher was ill or absent.

It was an obvious choice for me. The city was short of Science lecturers, I had nine months' experience at the Catholic St. Mary's school in St. Lucia, and my two degrees put me in a relatively high-earning capacity. The extra job suited me all the way. In two days, I made more than a week's pay at Gallop.

I was posted in the divisions between Kensington and the East End, the latter a decidedly hostile environment where free textbooks supplied by the London County Council were used more as missiles than reading material, and the condition of the texts told of previous wars. I was shocked to discover that all the regular teachers were accustomed to this level of chaos in the secondary moderns, knowing how much my friends and I at home treasured the books my grandfather imported for me from the famous bookshop Foyle's in London.

Occasionally an assignment would last a few weeks. Various techniques had to be deployed to divert the students from their pranks and get them to settle down and listen. A psychology of negative inspiration sometimes worked. "Do you want to make more money than your father or less?" Or, "Do you want me to lock away the books and talk to you or be silent, for if the Headmaster comes I will tell him the books are no use to you anyway ..." And so on.

So I became Mr. Silent and the students learnt a few things. I was invited to stay at the school and became permanent.

I enjoyed the weeks off and began writing again, and spending a lot of time in the bookshops seeing what was being published. When I resumed work, having been reassigned from the Notting Hill office, I'd go to the Tube (the Underground subway) and plot my journey to arrive after the morning break, but after a cup of tea at the train station along the way.

One night a friend and I went to a show in Kensington and missed the last underground train back to North London. There we were, two unkempt West Indians, wandering through salubrious South

Kensington after midnight when a policeman drove up to check us out. It was obvious we did not belong in that area. He picked us up, and drove us to the boundary of his beat. "Keep going north," he said. "Don't you turn back into my district!" It was a wonderful conversation piece for many years in my lunches at the House of Commons.

Certainly I learnt to be strict with time. No train, bus or plane ever left me again. It was as though those old timepieces at the British Museum and their successors had been designed for my benefit. I learnt, too, the distinction of classes of neighbourhoods. I have witnessed, in my political life, and at a distance, the argument in Britain about its types of schools, the grammar school, the comprehensive, and the secondary modern. I taught in all of them for two years. My experience would never let me look kindly on the abolition of the Chelsea Grammar, to be replaced by something like the Holland Park Comprehensive. My Physics classes in Chelsea were a joy. Well-dressed boys and girls all wanted to understand everything thoroughly. Lowering the good to a common denominator can never attain standards of excellence.

Female science teachers seemed to be a rarity and one day I found myself as the only male teacher at a Convent in Ladbroke Grove. The Mother Superior, the Headmistress, was also head of the Science department and wanted to concentrate on administration while someone took on her teaching responsibilities. The fact that I was the alternate of the Reverend Mother Superior gave me status. But my real challenge was not in the disciplined classroom but during a rainy lunchtime when the girls could not get out in the open. There was a large indoor sports centre with an second-storey balcony overlooking it.

What was I to do with seven hundred girls on a rainy day?

"Sir, could we have some music in the hall?" one of the girls asked.

I soon found myself dancing the lunch hour away with all of them, having such a time of it that we did not even hear the bell. When I looked up to see the Mother Superior in the balcony laughing away, I thought my easy income as a supply teacher had just ended.

But I was wrong.

"What a glorious idea," said the Mother Superior. "From now on, anytime it rains, I know what to do with them."

And then came the winter of 1962 with fog and smog to end all London winters.

I had moved to East Acton by then, as I wanted my own space. The afternoon of the great fog, I was on the bus from Ladbroke Grove to Shepherd's Bush and East Acton. The driver who had been on the route for 15 years got lost. We all got out and it took me until 8 p.m. to feel my way home. You could not see beyond an arm's length. When I got home my white shirt was black, my handkerchief ruined.

I put on my gas fire, filled the slot with copper pennies, and felt awful. The next three days were hardly any better. I could not venture out. My chest was exploding. A friend of mine, an English nurse at the Hammersmith hospital, made me a cup of tea and consoled me. I was not as badly off as the three who had died in her ward in the hospital that day, she said. Indeed, the evening papers she brought me had the headline "Fifty-six dead of bronchitis today."

Sadly, our affair did not survive my recovery. But I learnt from various articles in the media that the gas heater in my room was leaving unburned sulphur dioxide in my immediate atmosphere. After negotiations with my landlady on my rental charges, I invested in a small electrically heated fan. The romance of the coal fire in London ended with the legislation passed in the wake of the 1962 fog.

Bronchitis apart, life never got better than lighting the fire in Egerton Gardens on a Saturday evening before going to the theatre, returning with the warm beautiful creature from Wales – who shall remain unnamed but for the nickname "China Flood" – whom I would awake in the mornings with my Canadian-style pancakes, coffee and the Sunday papers.

It is so good that we only have one life. Heaven is wonderful to contemplate, but it becomes more real in the imagination with a delectable foretaste.

8

Hitch-hiking and Living in Europe

Philip Greaves, a great Barbadian friend, was in London at that time studying law. Our friendship began in St. Vincent where he was teaching Latin, and I was a Research Officer. We did not dream then that we would later be Ministers of Government at the same time in our respective countries. We decided to team up hitch-hiking, being of the generation inspired by Jack Kerouac's *On the Road*.

One Whitsun weekend, we met in Acton with new rucksacks on our backs, and rode the bus to the end of the line, and hiked to the highway.

I must say we started out in style. The first car to pull up was a vintage Rolls-Royce. I thought the old lady had broken down. But it wasn't so. A distinguished gentleman summoned us to join him. Our destination was Cardiff, for a weekend in Wales to enjoy the countryside. We learnt quickly how to engage a generous host by honestly talking about ourselves, but without asking too many questions. He did say, however, that he had never been to the West Indies but had been "almost everywhere else."

A quick succession of rides, and we were in Cardiff, and with the youth hostel identity cards we had earlier collected in the Strand, secured lodgings for a few shillings. The next day we set out for the beach and it seemed as if all of England wanted to get to the coast for the Whitsun weekend. Needless to say, the rocky "beaches" were not our cup of tea. Coming from Barbados and the Grenadines, we could not imagine a beach to be so full of rocks. That was the end of our pursuit of beaches in Britain. We charted our course from maps and changed our plans to explore the Wye Valley along the river.

Back on the road again, a small car pulled up, absolutely filled with children. We excused ourselves and said that we'd wait for another ride but the driver would have none of it. He put our rucksacks in the boot, and had the children ride in our laps.

"Take the ride as far as you can go," he advised. "Further north they are prejudiced."

Our West Indian complexions were evidently not going unnoticed. But that particular gentleman was pleased that we wanted to explore Wales. Newtown was our first stop, and in the hostel we were taken to the kitchen to peel the "spuds." The fraternity was wonderful. We were the only West Indian hitch-hikers and were destined to have that distinction all summer long wherever we went.

Back in England, we went on to the wonderful old town of Shrewsbury, the name of the home in St. Vincent that would house me later as Prime Minister. In Coventry, we saw the bombed-out cathedral; half-restored alongside its controversial sculpture. We went to Stratford-on-Avon to see a play and all the Shakespeare we had studied came alive right before our eyes.

We returned to supply teaching and summer vacation came quickly. Having earned our spurs hitch-hiking in Britain, we decided to tackle the continent. Philip and I mapped our route through Belgium, Germany, Austria, Yugoslavia, Italy, Switzerland and France, and back to England, but we set out separately.

I had my first taste of Belgian beer during a pleasant night in Brussels — no one would have won any money then betting on my later life in politics waging the Banana War (of which more later) in Brussels. Continuing my trek, the regular routine was to take public transport to the farthest end out of the city, and then, "thumbs up" on the side of the highway.

After leaving Brussels, securing a succession of lifts, I suddenly found myself in dire straits, penniless in a foreign country. Out on the highway, waiting for a ride, it was a little chilly so I had on my light coat. I got a lift. Inside the car, it was warm. The kind driver, after I had expressed my thanks, put me down on the highway further on because he was travelling in a different direction.

But, lo and behold, I was chilly again. I had forgotten my coat in the car. And that coat had my meagre savings and, even more importantly, my passport. I was suddenly stranded in the Belgian countryside (*sans identification et sans un sou!*). I hitched another ride to the nearest town and made my way to a police station. Fortunately, my French was good enough to explain my predicament.

Although I was deep in despair, within an hour there was comfort. The driver had discovered my belongings and deposited them at another police station, and the news was circulated to the one I was in. I waited. A police car turned up and delivered my passport and money, and left me with an eternal respect for the Belgians.

Had the kind driver not returned my possessions, I would have had to hitch my way back to England, sleeping on park benches until I knocked on my benevolent landlady's door. I would then have had to wait for a tax refund to pay her back. In all the nightmares I have had over the years, I never dreamt of losing my identity.

Much later, I was able to tell this wonderful story to King Baudouin at a garden party in Tokyo at the Emperor's enthronement. A whole world was opening up for me and my wandering spirit.

I got into Aachen in time to see an elegant wedding with the bride and groom descending the steps of a beautiful old church to mount a white horse-drawn carriage. The closest we in the islands came to this was a couple riding off in a donkey carriage after the first wedding at our elegant Canouan resort as a Grenadian lady, Shadel Compton, returned to her roots.

There must have been something burning within my soul that drove me from the settled routine of a country agronomist to the spontaneous existence of a hitch-hiker, moving from country to country, city to city, lonely roads to highways, resting on park benches and cooling down at the foot of fountains, for indeed I was seeking nothing.

Perhaps it was my father's spirit; sailing from one end of the Caribbean to another, from Venezuela to Alabama, and as far as his sailing ship and dried provisions would let him. Or perhaps it went deeper down, in my New England ancestry, whaling from Bedford to Bequia, or the French privateer that cavorted with the English ancestry!

Whatever it was, I wanted to keep moving.

The autobahns were exhilarating. In Germany, some English hitch-hikers told me the great highways were invented by Hitler to invade other countries. Now it was my turn for a singular odyssey, and I loved it. I remember enjoying the music playing in the German youth hostels.

Having established some competence in French and Spanish, I thought I knew enough languages for life. And surely, I thought, with English, I should have enough to tackle Europe! It worked, for the cities. But the villages in Germany were a different story, so I bought my first and only German grammar book. What really motivated me, I remember, was that I felt I was paying more for my beer in the parlours than the Germans were.

That night in the hostel in Frankfurt, I approached a young brother and sister after dinner and asked them to teach me the basics. I wanted to be able to count, to understand how to measure time (how long to get to so and so), how to buy the essentials, like bread, milk and sausage, and how to thank a driver properly for a ride.

It was not long before the brother got disgusted with me. "You want to speak like a woman!" He said, obviously recognizing that my intonation was more like that of his sister. The fraulein however did not abandon me. She took me to the shop next morning to buy my sausage, bread and milk, while she waited outside. After I thanked her, we said goodbye and I put away my rations for the day. But the milk was too thick – I had bought cream.

In my enthusiasm to get to Heidelberg, the famous university town that to me was synonymous with great German literature, I made a mistake that I regretted throughout my political life. Mannheim was flooded with posters announcing a meeting at which the Chancellor Adenauer was to speak. Much later, my NDP party, battling communism in the islands in the 1980s, was the beneficiary of funds from the Adenauer Foundation, used for youth seminars across the region, teaching about fiscal prudence and international finance.

I should have stayed that night and heard him speak, but I was anxious to get to Heidelberg. Other hitch-hikers who joined me the following days talked about Adenauer's speech and were thrilled to have heard him.

One Saturday afternoon, soon after that, I helped someone save the life of a young girl. I was in Ulm, the beautiful Cathedral town beside the Danube, lying on the grassy bank of the river and looking towards a bridge, when I heard screams.

Another young man and I ran down to where the river curved. He plunged in and swam toward the screaming girl. I ran to a jetty that was jutting into the stream in time to see him grab the girl, and shouted to him to swim toward me. I stretched out and pulled both of them up to safety. She had apparently jumped off the bridge some hundred feet up, hoping to commit suicide. I remember the folk who came to take her away asked if I wanted anything for my help and I told them I had already been amply paid by the courtesies I was receiving in Europe.

This was my second rescue, since the English student in Trinidad.

The sound of the church bells the next Sunday morning in Ulm was a glorious spiritual gift as I knelt in the empty church alone, thinking about the drowning girl and praying for the soul of my drowned father. I drew a sketch of the river and the steeple behind it on the back cover of the German theological text I was reading, wishing I were a better artist. I simply could not put down on paper what was going to be forever etched in my memory, a portrait of the agony in that young girl's soul as she took the plunge.

What strange destiny brought me thousands of miles to be on the banks of the Danube that day!

My first lessons in German white wine came from the free samples at Heidelberg Castle, the Rhine wine experience certainly better than my earlier forays into the nameless reds of Barcelona.

On to Salzburg after Munchen and, lo and behold, from the middle of nowhere on the ramp of the autobahn coming out of a restaurant, was my friend Philip Greaves. His ride had taken him in for a meal. I felt like Stanley and Dr. Livingstone.

"Philip Greaves, I presume!" I said.

"Indeed," he replied, with a great laugh.

We decided to carry on to Salzburg, and beyond, together.

On the morning before we got into Salzburg, we were invited into a farmer's home for breakfast. He was pleased to have West Indians as he had sampled Barbados rum and wanted us to imbibe his Austrian fare, Slivovitz. I don't know about the animal kingdom, but for human beings certain first impressions remain for life. Later, when an Austrian of noble birth invested in Union Island at home, I was ready to give him my oldest bottle of rum, from a cask that had been found hidden in the back of a storeroom in one of our bonded warehouses.

Philip regaled me with his experiences, including going to Berlin to see The Wall and the tanks. We decided to take in some churches and museums. In the youth hostels, discussions with other hitch-hikers centered on places of interest as well as the hospitality of car owners who gave us rides. Most of the youth in the hostels were hitch-hikers in the days before hitch-hiking became a menace to society and a new generation clawed their way to success (for a few days, I should add). I am glad mine was the civilized period.

The most disgusting encounter I had in a hostel was with a totally dishevelled and dirty English youth. He must only have been successful with the truck drivers – most of the rest of us obviously realized that, above all, we had to be clean to attract a ride. On the night we met him, before going to bed, he took off his filthy shoes, slowly peeled off his socks and threw them against the wall. "They don't stick," he said. "Not ready to be washed."

In Salzburg, I met a Swedish student, and we romantically climbed mountains together, and fell in love. She became a good friend, destined to hitch-hike with me again the next year when she came to London for Christmas. We spent a Sunday walking in the Vienna Woods, and after the museums, music in the streets, the churches and the old architecture of Vienna, Philip and I decided we had to check out communist Yugoslavia. I had read Marshal Tito's biography, *Tito Speaks*, and was fascinated by the distance he was keeping from the Russians.

As we left Vienna on the way to Graz, we saw a series of poles with bouquets outside small vineyards and discovered that local white wine was on free offer to sample. Apparently, the custom was to advertise in this fashion and have the city dwellers stock up. We were again the only West Indians around and they were ready to give us a few bottles but we had to decline, as they would have been heavier than all our possessions. A bottle of water or a box of milk was all a hitch-hiker wanted.

The farms all over Europe too were eye-openers. It was an education, to say the least, to see the beautifully tended fields; to see, for instance, more cabbages in a single field than the entire Caribbean's cabbage crop. There is no doubt in my mind that the worst thing slavery did to the Caribbean's people was to leave behind the lingering notion that hard work is to be despised.

Back to my travels. Klagenfurt was a celebration. We found a pleasant and affordable family-run *pension* where we were the only guests. The three beautiful daughters attended us in the dining-room and were fascinated with us, a compliment we lavishly reciprocated. In tune with the times, they called us Lumumba and Castro, Philip the clean-shaven of darker complexion and yours truly with his mop of wild hair and black beard. We told the mother we would like to marry them, two of us to marry three, as we could not choose honestly between them. They wanted us to stay longer and make up our minds. After two nights of banter, it was again time to move on.

I am still in love with mountains and lakes around small towns. Perhaps it was the Caribbean Sea around small hilly islands like my own Bequia that gave me a feeling of belonging. Klagenfurt's scenery was much like the interior of British Columbia, but British Columbia towns can't match European elegance – and their rich history.

And so to Tito's Yugoslavia. We assumed all Europe had the same quality of transport and were spoiled by the ease of getting a ride in a car. A Dutch vehicle would give us a ride in Germany; an English car would pick you up in Germany, and a Belgian in Austria. There were no Yugoslavs offering rides.

But we did manage to enter Yugoslavia in a beautiful Mercedes with an extraordinarily beautiful lady (accompanied). There were a lot more guns at the border here than elsewhere, and we were warned there would not be many cars and rides in Yugoslavia. Such was my first taste of communism. (Philip had already gone to the border of East Berlin.)

We made it to Rijeka, a coastal town. There were no hostels, so we secured accommodation advertised at a tourist information centre. We climbed about 120 steps in a building without lifts, noting the furtive peepholes at the doors. A claustrophobic country, I thought. In the town square, old men were drinking white wine. Poverty was everywhere. I regret to say one's memory lingers on the smells of human body odour.

On the coast, we visited a beautiful resort at Opatia, with a restaurant beside the sea. We did not dine there but sought our goulash at a cheaper establishment. We knew nothing about the language, but I decided to unload all my small change to see if I could get a bigger note. The waitress smiled and pocketed it all.

Philip with his knowledge of Latin and Greek had done well in the rest of Europe. (In fact he had even bought a German dictionary and was making quite an effort solving German crossword puzzles.) But trying not to end up in the women's toilet proved quite a challenge. We took a bet, as to which was which, and each of us went into one of the two possibilities, only to rush out in consternation. There were women in both. We were relieved, soon afterwards, to discover that the women were cleaners.

The rural coastline of Yugoslavia was simply superb, but was largely undeveloped. We took a train to Trieste. There were no cars on the highway. When we reached Trieste and saw the amazing development of villas on the Italian side of the border, a stark contrast to barren Yugoslavia, any lingering enthusiasm I might have had for socialism as a response to imperialism perished. How could two countries with the same climate, the same scenery beside the sea, the same resources, be so different? Trieste in the 1960s was alive. The opposite side of the Adriatic seemed asleep. Lessons on political leadership were sinking in.

I was to discover a similarly tragic difference in our part of the world where the boundary between an absolutely bare Haiti adjoins the forest of the Dominican Republic, a boundary visible from the air, an environmental disaster created during a century of misrule.

We went on to Venice; centuries of civilization awaiting us. No comparison to anywhere else on earth! Italian genius at its best! We made it to the hostel and then to San Marco plaza by gondola. We had arrived.

I met up with three Canadian girls who were also hitch-hiking, lingered a while with them as Philip went on, to return to his law classes in England. I stjll had a few pounds and could afford to drift.

I travelled across industrial Italy, down to a fishing village in Alassio where I met another charming girl, a German, whose father had survived the Eastern Front. She, like me, had read a lot of Hemingway and was ready, after dinner, to consume a bottle of grappa with me on the beach, until we lost her earrings. I remember wishing I had the resources to manage a replacement. We searched again fruitlessly the next morning for the earrings. Later, we settled for a coffee and I picked up an English newspaper and learnt that Jamaica had voted to leave the West Indies Federation.

As I made my way through France and up to Switzerland, my diet changed from bread, wine and sausage to chocolates. And in the middle of the day, luxuriating in all kinds of wonderful, Swiss filled chocolates, dropping the wrappers on the ground as I walked around, I learned an environmental lesson I later often imparted as Prime Minister. The image of an old lady bending to pick up my chocolate wrappers in that Swiss mountain village has remained indelibly carved in my consciousness.

"English?" she asked me.

"Yes" I replied.

"In Switzerland, we have a place for these," she said, and pointed to the basket on the lamp pole.

I thank Switzerland for making me into garbage cleaner. In the back of my jeep, there is often an empty box to collect the wrappers of corn curls and plastic cups to be deposited in the skips, to keep the scenery of my corner of the Caribbean the way that old lady would have wanted. I am pleased to say I have never littered the world since. Indeed, I proclaimed the 1980s the Decade of the Environment. That old Swiss lady prepared me to take on the Global Environment Facility, signed up to by my Minister in Brazil.

At the end of it all, I could say no more than I loved the countryside of every country in Europe. I had lived for six weeks on £65, less than the tips and service charges I would have to leave for a night at a five-star hotel, later, as I travelled on behalf of our taxpayers.

I had encountered wonderful generosity and kindness; bread, wine, cheese, milk, sausage and fruit had sustained me. Exposure on the roads, discovering life among other wandering youthful souls in Europe, sleeping in strange places, in bunks among strangers with strange languages, prepared me to understand the European Community, to copy its agricultural policy with my own introduction of an agricultural marketing protocol for our free trade area early in my political career, just six years later.

Back in London, my landlady Viola Dummett had not rented my room in East Acton and was glad to see me. She loved to meet my friends when I introduced them to her on Sunday mornings, especially since she could only barely keep up with the nationalities of all the *au pairs* and students who went through her house. "Jim! Where is that one from this time?" she would often ask me.

I used to invite her across for a cup of tea after my room was thoroughly made up, we had finished breakfast, and my guest for the night was ready to go. "All these European girls," she would say. "Jim, when are you going to settle with one of these lovely English girls? I liked the Welsh one, you know."

She was a middle-class Guyanese Creole woman whose husband, a company director, had shipped her to England after her sons and daughter had emigrated. She, I think, fancied the city lights, while her husband probably found the young Indian flames at home reinvigorating. Her son Jack, whom I knew from my Vancouver days, introduced me to her, suggesting I take over his room as he was taking his Canadian bride to Guyana, leaving the city lights to be a pioneer in the jungle. Apart from someone to keep her paraffin stove working, my landlady loved the idea of having a man in the house, particularly one who knew her son.

Later, I found out that she had deliberately not rented the flat when I wandered off for the summer in Europe. She would put it up for rent but turned down the applicants as too scruffy – as if my wardrobe went beyond my teaching suit and the ochre and black turtle-neck sweater my Swedish lass whom I had met in Austria lovingly knitted for me.

By the end of that summer, having paid no rent during my travels, and anticipating the tax refund I would collect for not working, I had plenty of money to live on until the next cheque from my supply teaching job. The Notting Hill teacher recruitment centre was ready to receive me again, so after a shilling at the Laundromat to clean my white shirts, I was ready again for the battle zones in the East End secondary moderns.

My education in Science had left a great void. Every city in Europe, every old building, is a lecture on history. I had studied Sir Francis Drake and his voyages; I knew about Columbus, but no history lesson taught in a classroom can match travelling to a country, and getting a feel of the place over the ages.

In London, I set about to educate myself further. I bought Trevelyan's series of books on Garibaldi. I started too on Gibbon's *Decline and Fall of the Roman Empire*. Steadfastly, I read all I could about Italy, from the Roman Empire up to the modern Treaty of Rome. Later, a friend suggested old bookshops in Hampstead, and I picked up my 1848 edition of Gibbon.

I would work for a few weeks, read and write for a few weeks. My Swedish friend came to London for Christmas, and we decided to hitch-hike together to Spain and back to Scandinavia.

Those became my Castro years. It seemed that everywhere I went, I was mistaken for Castro. We were alongside the road in the Costa Blanca one day, and a truck laden with bricks gave us a ride to a construction site. (The coast of Spain was in a building boom. The fishing villages were being transformed.)

"Aqui tengo Castro," the truck driver called out to the workers, who dropped their tools and flocked around me:

"Donde estan los canones?" they wanted to know. (Where are the guns.)?

I did not want to fall into the clutches of Franco's guards, nor did I want to offend them, but I was loath to give up the charade. So I said I was on an exploratory mission, and that I would return another day with the "canones."

At a train station another day, a porter said to me under his breath, as I passed: "Fidel Castro, bienvenido a la España."

It was all good stuff to amuse my host, the real Fidel Castro, on my official visit to Cuba 37 years later. When we met again in New York for the United Nations Millennium Summit at a reception hosted by Japan's Yoshiro Mori, his *abrazo* was very enthusiastic.

"Thanks to you, I am still alive," he joked. "They don't know which one of us to shoot."

My Swedish friend and I did not make it to the running of the bulls in Pamplona, but got there a couple of days later when prices were lower. We got a cheap, but modern, apartment and enjoyed life. Later, in the mountains of France, we visited the cave where blue Roquefort was produced. And on a cold night in the forest, I discovered how right Omar Khayyam was, as we shared a jug of wine, a loaf of bread and the warmth of a sleeping bag.

Why would I ever want a second life!

We went from France to Germany, before heading for Denmark and Sweden. In Hamburg one evening we went to a restaurant to have some goulash, and a drunken German came up and wanted to fight me.

"He thinks you are Jewish," my friend told me.

Some of the patrons, quite embarrassed, pulled him away from me and offered to pay for our meal, but he returned. But now that I knew that the majority was on my side, I was ready to fight.

"What annoys me, coming from the Caribbean," I said, with my friend translating, "is the situation in Palestine."

From the Caribbean! Suddenly, the Caribbean became the problem. "Fidel Castro, we don't want you here," one of them shouted. Most West Germans hated Castro. It was time to quit the scene.

That night in the male section of the hostel, the lights were out, and I was relaying the events to my fellow hitch-hikers, expounding on the anti-Jewish feeling still lingering in Germany. An English hiker, in the darkness responded: "We don't have any anti-Jewish sentiment anymore in Britain. Our feeling is against West Indians."

"Thank you very much," I said in the darkness. "I am one."

My mixed ancestry has seen me mistaken as a member of just about every ethnic group. In London, I was caught up in an Arab demonstration outside the American Embassy when a fellow rushed up to me and asked, "Where are we meeting?"

So I suppose it was quite appropriate for me to attend a Bar Mitzvah in Vermont with my friend Jill Bobrow and, on another occasion, secure an Arab outfit in Kuwait to wear at home to a banquet I hosted for the Muslim President of The Gambia.

It is a good thing my wandering days are over. These days, I would be deemed a terrorist, given that my bionic knees, implanted in the Hamlet Hospital in Copenhagen, simply couldn't seem to get past metal detectors.

Back in London again, wanting to live by myself now, I found a one-bedroom flat beyond Shepherd's Bush, on the way to East Acton, on a direct bus route from the West End, past the paintings on the wrought iron railings enclosing the Park. My flat was two avenues from the corner where the bus stopped near the pub and the fish and chip shop. Although trained in Chemistry, I was, like the rest of England at the time, unaware of the carcinogenic properties of newsprint, and quite regularly had my fish and chips with a small tin of Heinz mixed vegetables I warmed by immersing the tin in boiling water. It was a very satisfying meal for fewer than three shillings.

It was during that time that I went to the Old Bailey to watch the controversial trial of *Lady Chatterley's Lover*, a book accused of depravity, of corrupting not only merry olde England, but millions reading English across the globe. I remember getting in line early, and going back in the entrance queue to join a girlfriend only to be told hours later that the court was full.

And I continued writing, and finished my first novel about life in Trinidad, much influenced by James Jones' *From Here to Eternity*. In the end, I decided my attempt was too personal and no good. I threw it out and started again.

I decided to take on the theatre. I would go to Shaftsbury Avenue and walk around the West End looking for last-minute ticket deals for the "Gods" – the highest gallery where the cheapest seats were available. I remember constantly having to hold back sneezes for fear that I would grind the play to a halt. London fog in the 1960s was not kind to me.

My unrestrained laughter was however relished by the actors, as I was capable of infecting the audience appropriately. I was uproarious in my laughter but totally ashamed if the actors moved me to tears, which I would quickly dab away with toilet paper. I doubt if there were very many theatre-goers at the time who saw more plays than I did.

If I wasn't enjoying the play, I would always leave during an intermission, a habit that may have offended one British Under Secretary, much later when I was Prime Minister, when he had been detailed to entertain me on my official visit to Mrs. Thatcher. I suggested to him during the play *Goa* that we go to dinner after the intermission. (When I met him subsequently at another Banana War Meeting, I asked if he had recovered from *Goa*. He was too polite to say he had not recovered from me.)

When I went to the theatre in modern-day London as Prime Minister, I paid more for a single ticket than I paid for forty shows in my wandering youth.

The assassination of President Kennedy propelled me on to the front page for the first and last time in the British press. I jumped on a bus from Shepherds Bush toward Bond Street and ran to the American Embassy. The photographers were there to catch me as the second person signing the condolence book.

I never told this to the American Presidents I met, nor did I mention it to his daughter Caroline, when with her family she sought privacy and anonymity one Christmas in my Villa Helianthus, my 20-year building project, vacant when Mustique was full. The letter, responding to our condolences on the tragic death of her brother, spoke of the happier times peacefully on holiday in Bequia, which our note evoked.

Nightclubbing was another great hobby during my time in London. The Marquee, I remember, was a wonderful place that really got going after about ten on Saturday nights once the band had been recharged at the Coach and Horses, a nearby pub. To get to the Marquee, you got off between Oxford Circus and Bond Street, took a side street to the smoke-filled basement, which was usually full of *au pair* girls from the continent.

My friend from home, Shake Keane, was the flugelhorn player, along with two Jamaicans and two Scots. The bandleader, Joe Harriott, played saxophone, Coleridge Goode was on bass, Bobby Orr on drums and Pat Smythe on piano. After an hour or so, the cigarette smoke would usually prevail over my eagerness to discuss world events with the *au pairs*, and my runny nose would drive me to the surface for fresh air. I always had to plan on ten shillings for a night out, including my round at the Coach and Horses.

I remember another club called the Downbeat, in Soho, down a dark corridor and a seemingly never-ending flight of steps, with as good an entrance to Dante's Inferno as you may ever encounter. It was a hole in the wall for musicians and their ilk, from the dance studios, the theatre pits, and the symphonies. They came with their instruments, and the spirit of the night flowed spontaneously into morning.

Shake had migrated to England with a trumpet and volumes of unwritten poetry in his head. He was the first in our school to excel in Chaucer and Milton and Keats, and several generations of English classics, an endeavour, alas, totally abandoned in our independent nation today. Shake graduated from the trumpet to the flugelhorn, lovingly crafted by a German instrument-maker, and played it with deep emotion. He played too in theatres, at poetry and jazz sessions, sometimes at the readings of some of his own creations. His last performance was in Norway, after which he succumbed to cancer in November 1997. So highly regarded was he, *The Times* published his obituary. His poem, written as a birthday gift to a child in the Lake District, "Once the Wind," survives still in the *Oxford Book of Children's Verse*.

Then there were the naughty lines at one poetry and jazz session about the birth of Princess Margaret's son:

Little Lord Lindley, Little Lord Lindley
Ten little fingers, ten little toes
A cool ten thousand a year I suppose.

I never imagined this would be the beginning of close contact with that line of the Royal Family, whom I would come to know when Princess Margaret built a house in my constituency. And who would have imagined that the bum at the back of the audience in an ochre and black sweater would later deliver an eulogy among Mustique millionaires for Princess Margaret!

Back to work as a supply teacher, Chelsea and Holland Park represented my graduation from the battle zones in the secondary moderns of the East End. I often wonder what became of the lad who threatened to bring his father, a dockland tough, to deal with me.

"I'll bring my dad from the docks to deal with you," he screamed as I pinned him against the wall to the cheers of the girls who thought my handling of him was long overdue.

"You tell your dad I'm the son of a sea captain and that I too worked as a stevedore unloading 100 pound sacks of peanuts for eight hours, but I am now trying to get some Science into your nut," I told him.

The next day we had his reply. "Dad says he likes ships and their captains," he said.

About that time, my hitch-hiking friend from Barbados, Philip Greaves, was living on Fitzjohn's Avenue off Finchley Road, and told me of a flat near him. I moved in, but the landlord did not approve of the Swedish lady who passed through daily, and informed me that he had rented me only a single room for three pounds, and his five-pound doubles were not available.

Shortly after I moved into the Finchley Road area, the Queen opened the modern Hampstead Library. ("Modern", that is, in the 1960s. A modern library today does not smell of books. That romance of feeling a text and holding the inspired author in your hands has long ago vanished.) But the Hampstead Library was to be my home. The librarians got to know me and left me undisturbed as I delved into the history of the Hapsburgs and the unification of Italy.

Reflecting that one day I should return to the Caribbean, I also registered in an evening class on navigation. An old navy Salt, aspiring to but not quite making it into upper-class status, couldn't understand why a West Indian would want to be competent in yachting. His first lecture was his best, on safety at sea: (1) no short cuts; (2) never set out to sea without water. "And I don't mean the ocean," he added.

So I learnt, unbeknownst to my mother who had had me swear to have nothing to do with the sea, how to calculate the depths of waters around England using the tide tables, and how to use the Northern Star as a guide. In my part of the world, it would be the Southern Cross.

My writing was again in full swing. I taught for a few weeks, calculated my expenditure and savings, and went back to trying my hand at a novel again. Then I met two English people who changed my life: George Ordish, an entomologist with an appetite for good wines and the history of civilization, and Melba Kershaw, a staid and meticulous editor. George was an Englishman, cultivated in intellect, taste and grace. He entered my life quite fortuitously. My Trinidadian communist friend with whom I worked at Gallop put me on to him and Melba when the vacancy for a scientific writer in their establishment arose. They needed someone trained in tropical agriculture with knowledge of plant pathology to edit one of their texts. I signed up. I was on probation for three months after which I produced my first edition of Pest Articles and News Summaries. The hierarchy was pleased with my work.

My sojourn in Spain had trained my taste in cheap "plonk", and I was ready for a course in French sophistication. George was a founding member of the English "Wine Writer's Circle." I couldn't imagine how such a group could be created, but in due course I was to discover more of George's idiosyncrasies. He took me to tastings with him after a snap course in civility. "No matter how much you need it, spit it out until I give you the signal to swallow before we leave." I graduated.

But even after several decades of postgraduate indulgence, I am still not bold enough to refer to a wine as peachy, black currant or damask. I go no further when I discover a great wine, whether it is on the yacht of my friend Simon Murray in Hong Kong harbour, or while bringing in the Millennium at the Great House in Mustique than simply to enjoy the golden moment.

I have become an unabashed wine enthusiast. For instance, during World Bank and IMF meetings, touring the Hong Kong harbour on a luxurious cabin cruiser to have a look at the enormous airport under construction, the sophisticated selection of red wines was the most memorable part of the journey, compared with the shameless jostling of the world's leading bankers and financiers to get in the dining-room with the Chinese Prime Minister. On that tour, my Director of Planning, Laura Anthony-Browne, the only female National Authorizing Officer in the Third World dealing with the European Union, accompanied me. Laura, a dainty lone parent and Methodist preacher, abhorred alcohol. But she respected my leadership just as I respected her competence.

"Neither you nor I may ever have a chance to drink such a great wine again," I told her. "Remember that our host Simon, beyond being our Honorary Consul in Singapore, is Chairman of Deutsche Bank (Pacific), an old Foreign Legionnaire who must know his wine. His reputation is at stake with this wine. Remember Christ changed water into wine when there was none available!"

It was a good enough pitch to convince her at least to taste the wine, after which she acknowledged its excellence. My Finance Director, Maurice Edwards, who was also with us, needed no such persuasion.

Back in London, I had to leave my temporary office while I was cleared by the Secret Service for a possible permanent job in the British Scientific Civil Service. It took a full six weeks, and I remember taking it so seriously I did not even laugh at the graffiti in the London toilets for fear of running into a trap. I was thinking of moving out of Hampstead to cheaper lodgings after a month, but was carefully instructed by Melba that for a job in Chancery Lane in the City I also had to have a "proper" address. (I was not one for being pretentious – the worker's cap I once wore so embarrassed an English girl that she never answered my phone calls again. If I were a good cartoonist, I could have made a fortune on a series named "Bringing Up The Native." I have since become allergic to caps of all kinds and stick to hats even full of holes and not completely protecting me from the skin cancer that has afflicted some of my friends.)

The security clearance came through. I asked to see the report, but there was nothing to see. Security clearances were simply, I learned, "Yes" or "No." I wished of course that I could have applied that rule as Minister of National Security dealing with applications for residence in my country, but lobbyists, in and out of Cabinet, rendered such clarity impossible.

So I became signatory to the British Official Secrets Act and swore that I would reveal no critical information for 22 years thereafter. My work became Crown Copyright reserved. I became ensconced in the fourth floor of the Tropical Products Institute on Gray's Inn Road, not far from the underground vaults of ancient London silver. We produced three journals on insect control, plant disease control, and weed control. I was put in charge of plant disease control under George Ordish. Our boss Dr. Hopf was a stocky German scientist, a man of few words, whose specialty was bilharzia control. Our mission was to inform the plant chemicals trade and to keep workers in the tropics informed of the latest advances in pest control.

I enjoyed the job and the people with whom I worked. In due course I was launched into the scientific conference circuit, meeting eminent biologists and reporting on their findings. I did however refrain from publishing the results one scientist revealed on the various parts per million of various pesticides in his body, when in the aftermath of an operation on his intestines he had analysed the tissue secured from his surgeon.

Once, to attend a conference at the Long Ashton Research Station, I stayed overnight at a hotel in Bristol, found a pub nearby with whole casks of various sherries and ports, and concluded that the two villages in Union Island in the Grenadines named Clifton and Ashton must have been imaginatively named by a Bristol sailor.

Once every three months, the editorial staff journeyed to Oxford to meet with our Board and report on our work. It was a morning affair, leaving us time to wander through the civilized bookshops and indulge in an appropriate pub lunch.

I was well settled into my nine-to-five routine, living in Hampstead and working in Chancery Lane, joining my boss George and his friend Melba Kershaw who edited our sister journal, *Tropical Science*, twice a week for some good-value wine, pork sausage or cheese in the pub for lunch. On my own I discovered a Hungarian goulash joint where a feast cost three shillings.

I had not settled long into the job when my predecessor, a pathologist named Leach, called to say that he could get me a job in his office at the FAO in Rome. Rachel Carson's *Silent Spring* hung like an ominous cloud over all our work in pesticides, and I was toying with the idea of returning to university and writing in this field. I thanked him, saying I was not ready for Rome, that I had not finished with London.

A river of scientific publications flowed across my desk and faithfully I collected the latest revelations that would enlighten researchers in developing countries. One day, when a paper turned up on the soil microbes useful for biological warfare, I realized why I had signed the Official Secrets Act. This was the time when I was still turning up at the "Ban the Bomb" demos at Trafalgar Square, one at which I heard Kenneth Kaunda and other leaders of Africa's struggle for independence.

I did not photocopy the article. It was not necessary. Soil microbiology was one of my fascinations, and I felt I thoroughly understood the role of microbes in enhancing the quality of the soil and life in general. But this paper was on soil organisms in human biological warfare. (I didn't know then that biological warfare was one day to be a burning political issue on which I should have to make a statement.)

"What did you think of the article?" George asked, over the bottle of Chablis in our cubicle in the pub. He had seen me poring over it earlier.

"I'd rather be reading about wine and Omar Khayyam and the love of life," I responded.

George made me comfortable. With a few publications to my credit, he nominated me as a Member of the Institute of Biologists, a title that to this day proudly accompanies my political honours. He was interested in old books and told me how, on occasion, we could find a good text in wheelbarrows carted around by the so-called Barrow Boys for next to nothing. One day, we found the *Life and Love of an Insect* by J.H. Fabre, and, on another, pages of an old atlas that threw some light on the Venezuela-Guyana border dispute, a real historic piece. He was interested in the history of the Incas, dealt in Colombian figurines, grapes and wine making, and lectured on all sorts of subjects while his wife translated Dutch works into English. He and I published a chapter on world fungicide usage for Academic Press, London and New York.

When I left London, he returned to Devon, but not before he published a tome on London pigeons called *Pigeons and People*, co-authored by the wife of the Attorney General Elwyn Jones. This contact was to influence the resolution of a later battle on our constitution.

Melba, too, retired. I visited her later, when I was Prime Minister, at her lovely flat in Notting Hill where cancer was taking its toll on her delicate frame. She offered me any book in her library. I looked for the nineteenth-century cartoons, but she had sold them in an auction, so I settled for the *Decameron* in memory of her love of life.

The black doorman at the London Marriott, where I was staying, noticed my tears as I alighted from the diplomatic limousine. "Sir James, are you all right?" he asked.

"Thanks for your concern," I said. "I have just visited a dying friend whom I shall not see again."

Melba read the two novels I had written and thought them eminently publishable. I continued to rework them, especially the second, on weekends, while I slaved away as a scientific editor during the week. I got into a circle of budding writers and there were perhaps hundreds milling around. In one of those amorphous parties serving wine and cheese among the blooming literary set, I met a Canadian girl who was art editor for the publisher Longman. She was also a part-time model. Her name was Patricia Parker, from Toronto, Canada. She seemed pleased that I had scoured all the museums in London, Paris and Barcelona, in addition to my fascination with the architecture of Europe's old churches.

Every group of wanderers in London had its own cluster of compatriot friends, even though they had all individually drifted into London for a new experience. It was like that for the Australians, the Rhodesians, the Swedes, the natives from the West Indies as we proudly called ourselves, and also the Canadians.

Pat invited me to meet some Canadian friends, Marion and Dennis Hebb, both literary scholars, at Belsize Park for dinner. Dennis was so taken with the history of furniture that he became apprenticed to learn the craft. He apparently had a reliable source of funds from home to allow him his furniture studies. Marion, slim, elegant, and bespectacled in thick frames, seemed to be tolerating his idiosyncrasies. We became great friends and would tour Hampstead Heath together with their daughter Sarah in the pram.

Later, after Pat had returned to Canada for a year and came back to London, I suppose to see more of me, she and I celebrated our wedding at their house, following a ceremony one Saturday morning at the Hampstead registry.

One of the friends I met was a rather dishevelled young writer with a strange deep monotone voice who told me she was working on her first novel. We went out together afterwards to a show. Pat confided to me that this girl persistently got better marks than she did in English at Victoria College, and for that reason, she decided to major in History. In 1964 Peggy Atwood was determined to be a writer.

Later, when my political career had advanced to premiership, she had published, as Margaret Atwood, *The Edible Woman* and *Surfacing*, both of which she sent to us. Her devoted husband, the very sturdy Graeme, was a fervent bird-watcher whose passion was behind their first Caribbean trip. They visited Tobago where he could see his birds, and she brought him to Bequia along with their daughter Jess, to stay with us. She took over one of the all-wood rooms at our Frangipani Hotel and wrote solidly for three hours every morning.

Peggy's fertile mind could plunge into the life around a well in an abandoned plantation, and with the same fascination, observe tombstones in the yards behind the homes in Petit Martinique. We sailed the Grenadines and behind the cold defence of a rather stern personality, she occasionally revealed a dry humour.

I ended up helping Peggy edit *Bodily Harm* – the book she was writing in Bequia – during a two-week visit to Toronto around the time I had lost my Alliance government and nearly been killed in an ambush in the banana fields. She wanted me to check the tropical ambience. Through Peggy, I met Charlie Pacter, the artist, famous for his variations on the new Canadian flag. He was doing building renovations at the time. Peggy dedicated the book to Graeme, James and John.

Back in London in 1963, Pat suggested we move in together into Ed Victor's flat higher up the hill in Hampstead. He was starting his business as a literary agent for writers, but had taken some months off in New York. Almost 40 years on, Ed's most recent success was getting some of Iraq's deposed leadership as clients. The *Weekly Telegraph* revealed how he had signed up *Comical Ali* with a contract in excess of the £500,000 on offer.

My cousin John Compton visited us immediately after he had captured the government in St. Lucia. He had got from my mother the address to our studio flat off Finchley Road – which we found after Ed returned from New York – and came to see me. I threw a party for him, and invited my Trotskyite friend, the cricket writer, C.L.R. James, and the two of them – the fervent nationalist and the idealistic communist – had a most memorable (and loud) argument on the destiny of the Caribbean. Later that was a battle I repeated often at home too, given my liberal inclinations after that visit to Yugoslavia as a hitch-hiker drove all thoughts of socialism out of my consciousness.

I remember having to intervene and steer the conversation to cricket where most West Indians find more common ground than in politics. My contribution was that the trampled cricket pitches needed to be ploughed up and aerated every few years. Aerobic rather than anaerobic conditions would put more life into the pitch.

The Windward Islands transformation into bananas and away from plantation sugar-cane was just beginning then, and John, who had led the rebellions in the cane fields after his pursuit of development economics at Cardiff, was ready to receive the paper I had done on the need for a Caribbean presence in London to maintain contact with the market. The fact that I had earlier put forward the idea to Swithin Schouten, my old boss in St. Lucia, had not endeared me to the powers-that-be in the industry at home. Quite correctly they had deemed me "a rolling stone."

Schouten, who enjoyed my company, also visited me in England. I took him to the Isle of Wight to see the prototype plane an Australian was designing, called the Islander, which became and still is the work-horse plane of the Grenadines. I introduced him also to the London silver vaults. He bought a dozen beautiful Russian samovars, and left them in the stored luggage at the Cumberland Hotel. I often wondered what became of them.

It was time again to contemplate my own destiny.

The fragmentation of the West Indies seemed ridiculous in my mind as I read deeply into the history of Europe, from the Roman Empire to the Hapsburgs, and the unification of Italy. The Treaty of Rome had been signed, old enemies were unifying, while we in the Caribbean,

1. Capt. Reginald Mitchell, my father, aboard the *Gloria Colita* in Mobile, Alabama, 1940

2. Joseph Ollivierre, my maternal great grandfather

3. Sarah Mitchell (neé Ollivierre), my paternal grandmother

4. Original home with *Gloria Colita* being built, circa 1937

5. Lois Gooding, my mother as a young girl dressed for a wedding, circa 1920

6. James (Harry) Mitchell, my grandfather

7. James Mitchell as a schoolboy, age 6, with father seated behind

8. Armistice Day, Sergeant of Cadet Corps, 1949

9. Launching of *Gloria Colita*, 1938

10. Found abandoned in Bermuda Triangle, February 1940

11. As a schoolboy at the St. Vincent Grammar school (2nd from right)

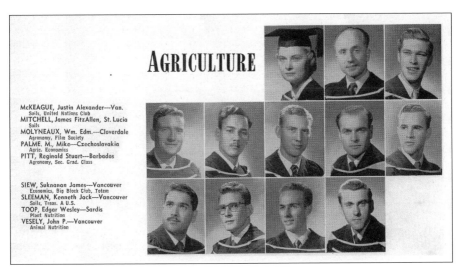

AGRICULTURE

McKEAGUE, Justin Alexander—Van.
  Soils, United Nations Club
MITCHELL, James FitzAllen, St. Lucia
  Soils
MOLYNEAUX, Wm. Edm.—Cloverdale
  Agronomy, Film Society
PALME. M., Mike—Czechoslavakia
  Agric. Economics
PITT, Reginald Stuart—Barbados
  Agronomy, Sec. Grad. Class

SIEW, Suknanan James—Vancouver
  Economics, Big Block Club, Totem
SLEEMAN, Kenneth Jack—Vancouver
  Soils, Treas. A U.S.
TOOP, Edgar Wesley—Sardis
  Plant Nutrition
VESELY, John P.—Vancouver
  Animal Nutrition

12. Student at University of British Columbia, 1955

13. With colleagues in the Cadet Corps

14. With a friend, Harvey
Demorest, downtown
Vancouver on a Saturday
night, 1954

15. Student at Imperial College of Tropical Agriculture, Trinidad
(2nd row from back, 4th from right)

16. Golf Champion at Imperial College – students and professors team, 1954
(2nd from right)

17. Signing the condolences book at the US Embassy in London, on the assassination of JFK, Photo courtesy of the *Daily Telegraph*

18. Marriage photo; Hampstead Registry, 1965

19. With daughters Sabrina and Louise, 1972

who had no wars between us, were drifting apart. I dreamt that I could make a difference. Life was slowly pointing me home again.

Shake, who used to take me to various theatres for poetry and jazz sessions with his artsy colleagues, was leaving for a contract to play in Cologne. Both Pat's and my living arrangements were also about to be affected by a policy perspective that was floating in the press about the need for both government and the private sector to decentralize away from London. Pat's firm Longmans was contemplating moving out, and my publication's offices were destined for Oxford. Success in my work had brought the offer to become an established Civil Servant and that meant living in or near Oxford – and settling into a mortgage. It also meant that Pat and I would very likely be living in different cities in England.

The savings I had sent home had completed payment on my acre in residential Vigie in St. Lucia with a superb view of Castries harbour and the West Coast. The savings too had secured land in Bequia. My friend Philip had returned to Barbados and was writing me about his glorious love affair, marriage, legal practice and plunge into politics.

I also had knowledge that the foreign investors were pouncing on the Grenadines, Mustique, Canouan, Prune Island (that became Palm) and Petit St. Vincent.

Pat and I decided to move to my home in Bequia and open a hotel. Preparing to leave London, we bought Norwegian hotel crockery from the Scandinavian design centre and Austrian cutlery, packed up 30 boxes of books, including all of Pat's manuscripts on art, and my one suitcase of clothes, and left to start a new life in an island without running water, electricity, telephones, and, as she was to discover, with ants ready to consume every morsel left behind. (Four decades later and into the Millennium, the Frangipani Hotel uses the same Norwegian crockery, with the manufacturer Porsgrund replenishing our stock after digging into its archives some years ago for the original design. Repeat guests identify affectionately with this institutional preservation.)

At midnight on the last day of 1965, we took to a cabin on a banana boat, with me vomiting for three days and quickly losing my reputation as the son worthy of his intrepid sea captain father. On a bright clear morning with an almost cloudless blue sky, the banana boat docked alongside at Bridgetown harbour at the end of its Atlantic crossing. It was a much-improved Barbados; different from the days of my youth, when ships moored out in the bay and the beseeching crews of small rowboats offered to take you ashore for a shilling.

Philip Greaves came to our cabin and invited us ashore with him for lunch and to call on the Premier of Barbados, Errol Barrow. It was my first visit to a Premier's office. Up the steps and past the secretaries, we went into the simple office where Errol left his desk immediately, welcomed us and reflected on the good times he had had with Canadian colleagues in the Battle of Britain. There I was, hardly an hour back in the Caribbean, in the presence of an affable easy-going leader, smiling beyond his open-necked shirt, his strange and unique voice exuding confidence and what I discovered the people called charisma.

This was the beginning of one of my greatest friendships among the leadership of the Caribbean, sadly ending with the eulogy I was invited by Cameron Tudor to give the thousands of grieving Barbadians in the Savannah. Errol loved Europe. He seemed pleased that the new postwar generation of West Indians, who like him had imbibed European culture, were ready to deploy their experience in moulding their countries in the Caribbean.

He had moved Barbados away from association with the East Caribbean, launched his own currency, and was preparing for Independence. And he was no stranger to my home, Bequia, I discovered.

"Bequia is another home to me," he said. "My father preached there."

A Barbados reporter interviewed the young man coming out of Errol's office. It was a simple story about a university graduate going home to launch a new political party and start up a hotel in the Grenadines. Its release was to be the beginning of my troubles. No one in St. Vincent liked either idea.

After we got to St. Vincent, a small ferryboat operated by old men who had worked with my grandfather on our boat landed our boxes on the beach of our new home in Bequia. We called on Estella Frederick, a neighbour and old servant of our family, who had become a popular baker of bread in a fired-up oil drum with coals above and below.

She welcomed us home, and gave us some warm bread, and the keys to our family house.

PART II

*Launching a Political Career
(1966 to 1974)*

9

Starting a Political Party and the Frangipani Hotel

My political career was launched in a hail of stones in the city centre. The Eighth Army of Liberation that had ushered in adult suffrage some 15 years before had crumbled in dissent and in the wake of its more aggressive counterpart, the People's Political Party. A middle-class legal element, the St. Vincent Labour Party, propped up by the remnants of the plantocracy, was leading the challenge. I descended into this maelstrom like an unwelcome bolt of lightning.

Both parties, never agreeing, nevertheless spotted an intruder to be crushed instantly. Enemies got together to screech obscenities in both my ears and this process took even more tangible form when a woman, offering to shake my hand, presented some faeces which simply ensured that the right hand I proffered for her handshake would not hold the microphone that evening.

So much for my grand idea on political union in the Caribbean!

Tip O'Neal had not yet discovered the legacy he was to leave the American people: "All politics is local." No decades of apprenticeship for me. The baptism of fire was a final exam. My idea of starting a political meeting with a calypso recording was a total disaster. (I cannot blame my friend, the optician Edgar Adams, for loaning me the music. I thought it was a good cultural idea.)

The bankers were just as cruel. Well dressed and, I thought, eminently presentable, I called on every bank manager in Kingstown seeking a loan for our proposed hotel, there being no bank in Bequia. They had read the press statement from Barbados. One manager summed up the mood accurately: "You wish to build a hotel in the Grenadines where there is no electricity, no telephones, no water, no jetties, and no transportation; and you want to go into politics? Politicians are a bad risk!"

I went to St. Lucia where my stepfather, a retired colonial treasurer, still had some clout. I mortgaged the land I owned in St. Lucia, purchased with my savings as an agronomist, and transferred the money to St. Vincent.

A young German Architect, Klaus Alverman, was living aboard the only little yacht in the bay of Bequia, anchored off the Frangipani's shore. The 28-foot boat, destined for a solo sail around the world, was christened *Plumbelly* during its construction on the beach beside our home, after the astute eyes of a ship builder noted that the ship's belly was a reflection of the Bequia plum.

Klaus had just completed the design of a holiday home for the American investor, Gustav Koven, who had bought a substantial part of my grandfather's Hope Estate from the daughters who inherited it. He learned shipbuilding from Bequia boat-builders and in the process became familiar with Guyana timbers in the production of the Koven home, which I admired a great deal.

Meanwhile, my political life began to take shape. The pillars of Bequia society gravitated towards me, and embraced me as the brightest son of an extensive and well-beloved family who had come home after his travels around the world. They saw Kingstown's ugly reaction to my entry into politics as abuse by the infidels on "the mainland."

In Bequia, the village of Hamilton led the charge of my supporters, including Edrich Harris, nephew of my old nanny Amelia, who had been a life-long supporter of Clive Tannis, sitting Member of Parliament for the Grenadines. Edrich had become disillusioned with Tannis after the latter failed to help in the rescue of his schooner, the *Edward H*, which sank off a reef on the west end of Mustique, taking with it Edrich's life savings.

Tannis, who had been in school with me, had survived many political challenges from my Uncle Cyril, and his family controlled the shipping in and out of the Grenadines, the ferryboats, and the cargo ship transporting all the rice and sugar, and the movements of workers to the Barbados cane fields. (Uncle Cyril wanted me to join his campaign for one last try against Tannis, but his supporters did not like the idea.)

As my first political rally approached, Casembe Bonadie (who had abandoned my Uncle Cyril's political campaigns that he had chaired several times), Claude Gurley and Victor Frederick, came to visit me in our little porch in front of the cottage.

"We brought you a hymn book and some good music," Casembe said with his raspy voice. "You have to choose some hymns and print them up for the congregation. You got to play this record of sacred music before the meeting starts. None of this calypso foolishness you started with in St. Vincent."

And so it was that, "O God our help in ages past," the enchanting hymn that so graciously reveals the essence of the Christian dream, became the signature tune in all my political overtures, summoning the faithful, and the disbelievers too, to bear witness to my unwavering cause, seeking comfort for my people, over three decades of political life.

Cousins from my grandmother's side, the intrepid whalers Joey and Athneal Ollivierre, also welcomed my return. Uncle Louis and Griffith, who had sailed with my father, also came on board. So too another sailor on my father's ships, retired and running the New York City Bar, Baby Lou Lewis.

The villages of Hamilton, Port Elizabeth and Paget Farm lined up. Mt. Pleasant, did not like my Uncle Cyril, partly, I suppose, because of proprietorship of the valley of neighbouring Hope Estate, in which they always trespassed. In any case, they saw more kinship in me because of the close family linkages through my mother. I discovered that I was related to more people in Bequia than anyone else; the families Ollivierre, Wallace, King, Davis, Adams, were all in some way connected to me, and when I attracted the Fredericks, Lewises, Bonadies and Stowes, Bequia was covered.

I walked and walked and walked, through the ditches, and climbing over the rocks, through the bushes to renew acquaintances and cultivate new friends. Bequia had no infrastructure; just a couple of wheel strips here and there, including of course, the road to the MP's home. With billions in property values in today's Grenadines, it is hard to imagine the cynicism in those days on the one hand, and the desperate hope on the other, that greeted my plans to secure a sound infrastructure and a good quality of life for all time.

The Grenadines, the land of my birth to which I returned in the mid-1960s from a gracious Hampstead in London, had hardly moved beyond the pastoral idyll of my youth, with the women still hacking away the soil, backs bent with their hoes sowing the crops of corn and peas, and the fishermen sailing their double-enders all day long to serve a fickle market in Kingstown, only to sail homeward at night, ready to start the day's toil again before dawn. The wonderful old buildings in Europe, the churches that took decades and hundreds of years to build, had taught me the patience it takes to create a civilization. Eric Williams' *Capitalism and Slavery* had instructed me on how some of those civilizations were the fruits of our labour in these islands, and somewhere in between, I knew I had to fashion a perspective to guide my sleepy heritage.

Edrich Harris was the son of Daniel Harris, a retired boatswain of the Harrison liners, whose living room in Hamilton was adorned with posters of the funnelled ships and the picture of a coloured lady sitting upright in a tall chair that he declared was the Empress Josephine. The senior Harris had a grand His Master's Voice gramophone brought from England, and, as a child, I would go to listen as he cranked it up with the bent handle on a spring, and play music on Sunday afternoons after Sunday School catechism. The colonial administration had made him a Justice of the Peace, and he comported himself in the village with the authority of a king. Edrich, like his father, had saved his money from the Harrison liners and had come home and invested his life's savings in the *Edward H*, the loss of which left him with nothing to do but eke out a living in a rum shop – and some bitterness.

Tannis had also lost the support of the seafaring community, the owners of the ships, the sailors and the fishermen, because members of his family who had saved their hard-earned money made in perilous shipping in their schooners, carrying drums of oil in the U-boat-infested Caribbean seas of the Second World War, were now in a position to commandeer the transport of goods from neighbouring islands, and also among the smaller islands of the Grenadines. Those who were their partners, like the shipbuilding Coziers, resented the way revenue was shared.

With my support in Bequia reasonably assured, I had to make my political way into the southern Grenadines. I sailed across, with my supporters in tow, to meet the villagers of Mustique, which Colin Tennant had bought for £45,000 from the Hazell family in 1959. No sooner had I set foot on the island, than the new manager (who had got the job through the MP I would be opposing) drove right at me in Mustique's solitary jeep, and I had to jump out of the way to keep my legs from being broken.

"A private island," he said. "No politics here."

"No polling station here then," I replied. "I'll have to discuss this with the Attorney General."

It was raining; the ground was soggy, slippery with mud glued to our bare feet. Mosquitoes descended on us, assailing the eyes, nostrils, ears and necks. As you responded they descended to the knees and ankles, then back to the ears. They were penetrating my mop of hair and biting my skull. The French explorers, who had named the island *Moustique*, had needed no great imagination.

The weather cleared. The labourers on the cotton plantation gathered under a tamarind tree, collected dried cattle dung, scattered it in a circle and lit it for the smoke to drive away the mosquitoes. I stood in the centre with the smoking cattle dung like a halo around me and began my speech. Such were the challenges greeting me in what was for decades to become my beloved constituency after my farewell to the comforts of England.

Some of the workers had Bequia connections to the Ollivierres. Others were related to Victor Frederick, who accompanied me. They all knew my father or the legends about him. The scene of my first political meeting in Mustique was what is now the homes of the Channons, *Clonsilla* and *Phibblestown*. (Paul Channon later became the scapegoat for the Lockerbie disaster for the simple reason that he was Minister of Transport at the time and wasn't in England because he was holidaying in Mustique.)

I kept on down the Grenadines, armed also with an open letter given to me by Mailings Compton, a distant cousin, sea captain and patriarch in Canouan who had settled in St. Lucia, calling on his widespread family to embrace me as one of the clan. In Union Island, I discovered that there were old folk who remembered that my maternal grandfather had lost his life in the 1921 hurricane when he left shore in a small boat in an attempt to rescue a Union Island crew. Many of the folk from Union Island were working at the waterfront in Trinidad and were listening to Eric Williams at Woodford Square. They were quite ready for an intellectual explaining the language of infrastructure development. It was time for the simple amenities of life: electricity, telephones, secondary education and a jetty.

But it was not only academia that helped me jump over the hurdles. Early one Saturday morning, after a reasonable and somewhat skeptical audience the night before, I was rowed out in the rain among the other passengers to the anchored ferryboat. The engine wouldn't start. All kinds of theories were being discussed on the engine's problems. A succession of tools, parts, batteries, and experimenting mechanics, came on board to lend a hand. In the meantime the agent of the governing party, a young fellow of Portuguese descent, was giving a running harangue steeped in old West Indian folklore that there was a traitor on board, and that evil spirit was me. He spoke with the authority of the Government.

After the problem was solved, we motored out, but my presence continued to attract comment and much laughter. I said nothing and waited. Out at sea in the tall swells of the Canouan channel, the ship, without sails to steady its motion, was tossing to and fro like a cork. I timed the rolling of the ship and as she leaned to leeward, I charged across the saloon with the ferocity of the ocean itself, gripped my accuser by the throat and pinned him against the pane. He was limp in my hands as he tried to reach for the gun in his pocket, but his breath, and the colour in his face, was gone.

"Another word from you and I'll pitch you overboard," I yelled at him and called for someone to take the gun from his pocket.

The captain, "Shorty," arrived amidst the commotion, and I requested he keep the gun until I left the ship. The passengers cheered. And suddenly, I was something of a hero. I remember some passengers' remarks: "I thought he was a softie, but he's not only got a brain but a strong hand." And "The boy is a man."

The story of the incident took wings in the islands. The humiliation I had endured in the market square meeting in the city was suddenly part of the past. (Much later, and after many fluctuations in our political fortunes, my victim on the mail boat came to me for some assistance and I was glad to be able to help him. We exchanged some assets to our mutual advantage; a car for an acre of land. I apologized for my behaviour. We became friends.)

The fledgling political meetings we held in Bequia – in Port Elizabeth under the Almond Tree, and in Paget Farm at the crossroads – went well under the experienced chairmanship of my veteran ally Casembe Bonadie. Casembe and Claude Gurley would turn up after lunch and sit for a couple of hours in our porch planning the meetings.

I was busy gathering support, and obviously succeeding because one day, my old French and Mathematics teacher from Grammar School, J. L. Eustace, came to Bequia to see me. He had just joined the Labour Party, he said, and wanted me to align myself with him. We gave him a room at the hotel and I set up a meeting with the group of elders that were now my advisers. They agreed that I could join the Party but on one condition: that I be the candidate for the Grenadines. He took the message back but the party leadership decided that I should join first, and only then would they decide.

That left the situation too vague for my supporters and me. Joining the Party, however, seemed a good idea, but I needed to talk to the top man about it. So another friend, Philip Veira, a merchant whose moral support I remembered when competing for the scholarship to university, and who also operated a shop in Bequia, and another in Kingstown first rented from my grandfather's sister, offered to accompany me to the legal office of the leader of the party, Milton Cato.

Phillip was brief and to the point. "I bring Son Mitchell to be the candidate for the Party in the Grenadines. OK," he said.

The office was upstairs at the Reliance Printery, two rooms – a waiting room with a couple of benches, and the inner room with a desk littered with papers and a dusty cupboard with books on some shelves. Cato was pleased to see me. He remembered that I had supported him in the federal election, even though I had not succeeded in influencing the workers at the Campden Park estate to vote for him.

I took the opportunity to enquire what progress he had made as my attorney on securing title to the land I had inherited in Bequia, a brief I had given him years ago and which my sister Gloria had followed up several times. He was vague about it and said he didn't quite remember the details. So I made two decisions that day: to accept him as my political leader, and to fire him as my family lawyer.

I went right away to see Alex Hughes who was a Cato supporter and he was pleased I was joining the Party. He said he would take over my legal matters – I wanted a company formed, and I needed to have the court relieve my aunt of a trust so that my brothers, sister and I could register our title. The trust was complicated. One of the trustees, Aunt Adeline, had died the year before from an allergic reaction to a bee sting. That left the other aunt, Dr. Eulalie Lee, a Brooklyn pediatrician, as the sole surviving trustee. Adeline's only child was a Professor Vance Christian at the Cornell University Hotel School in up-state New York. He visited and gave me authority for us to approach Dr. Lee, and have the land divided into three parts. No matter how chaotic the boundary, we all wanted beach frontage.

I wanted all this settled quickly and Dr. Lee (who did too), with adequate resources at her command, hired the powerhouses in Barbados – Henry Forde, now Sir Henry, and Harold "Bri" St. John, now Sir Harold, the future leaders of that island. We all met in Alec Hughes' office and, in short order, the problem was settled to everyone's satisfaction. In the end, it turned out to be a surveying matter to unravel rather than a legal problem, and an agreement was signed.

The people involved in that transaction, as I hinted, later played important roles in this region's development. Henry Forde was married to a Vincentian whose aunt, Clarie Paynter, was my landlady in my scholarship year. His wife was also a friend, whose wife was cousin to the Surveyor we appointed, Inky Williams, an old schoolmate of mine, who in due course became the Chief Surveyor in my Government, settling land disputes all the way to the Privy Council and MIGA (the Multilateral Investment Guarantee Agency). Henry defended me later in a Commission of Enquiry that came to naught and "Bri" St. John became Prime Minister of Barbados and signed his support for the Bequia Airport funded by the European Union.

But I am getting ahead of myself.

With the boundary around the Frangipani Hotel settled and the company incorporated, I was ready to settle down with my family in Bequia. My brothers in St. Lucia were St. Lucians really, and preferred to keep their assets there. My brother Reginald wanted to build a home on my piece of St. Lucian land and the other brother, George, married to a Norwegian, preferred the cold climate of Canada where they had met, and was aspiring to the security of the Ottawa Civil Service.

I wanted to keep the family structure in the business however and allocated them, after the exchanges in St. Lucia, 35 per cent of the shares in the business. With 65 per cent controlling interest and secure title, I was ready to develop.

I had to pay early attention, too, to fundamental landscaping. The hill behind our proposed hotel was barren and the highway narrow. I gave land for the expansion of the public highway, and cut down an old mango tree that had sustained the neighbourhoods in my youth. The established Sunny Caribbee Hotel had undergone a change of ownership, bought by Colin Tennant, descendent of an English industrialist who had made his fortune in bleach, and was now building a tennis court. Tons of beautiful soil was an encumbrance and we paid Henry Nicholls, the sole truck driver on the island, $7 a load to deposit it all on the rocky perimeter of our hotel. Everyone was shocked that I was actually buying dirt. The beautiful poui trees blazing their yellow glory at Easter, as a backdrop to our establishment, are now a seasonal glory commemorating this extravagance. I introduced the poui trees to Bequia. When they bloom, you can sit under them and relish the joys of creation.

The family home, which we were converting into the hotel, had been built in 1927. The 1921 hurricane had flattened everything in the Grenadines that didn't have a steep peaked roof, so the family home had been built with experiences of how to withstand any future hurricane. The home had changed little, maintaining its original design.

From the vantage point of his boat looking to the shore, Klaus conceptualized the old house as a hen that needed two chicks on either side to balance its perspective, and a porch for privacy in the morning and evening to look out on Admiralty Bay. The two chicks became the bar and the dining room. Beneath the concrete porch were suspended four steel bolts to hold the Tilley lamps to illuminate our evenings. With five rooms sharing a bath, and three members of staff, after a year of construction interspersed with the campaigns, the Frangipani opened in January 1967, at US$11 per night, including meals.

With these modest beginnings, the Frangipani became the gateway to the development of the Grenadines, welcoming the yachts and investors from abroad, and cultivating in my own mind the advantage of risk and private sector-led growth. The choice of a name for the hotel required some strategic thinking. My early immersion in botany had left me with an enduring affection for the Latin taxonomy of the plant kingdom. I wanted a tropical plant name for the hotel, a plant that would flower in the dry season and yield its aroma at the peak of the winter tourist season. I loved too the euphony in the name *frangipani* and remained fascinated by the history of its fragrance. In the twelfth century, an Italian nobleman took time off from his official duties as baker of the Holy Sacrament to indulge his hobby, blending volatile oils that produced this tantalizing perfume, which later became the favourite fragrance of Catherine de Medici. French explorers, centuries later, identified the scent of the tropical flower and gave the tropical plant its name, listing it as *Plumeria rubra* and *alba*, in honour of the French botanist Charles Plumier. So Frangipani became the name of our hotel with a rich botanical history, touched by Italian and French imagination, fondly called "the Frangi" by *afficionados*.

But there were other family intrigues to resolve. My grandfather, nicknamed "Old Harry," in spite of providing funding for my continuing university studies in soil science, sustained his abiding faith in shipbuilding and exploration of the oceans as pillars of the family fortune, and to preserve that destiny ordained that his first male grandchild should inherit Isle à Quatre, his island with the curved cedar timbers. My aunts Eulalie and Adeline, normally hostile to each other, connived instead to get him to sign a deed, during his declining health, transferring the island to them. He recovered enough to moan to his field workers: "What shall I tell the boy when he returns from university?"

Then, with Adeline's sudden death from an allergic reaction to bee sting, Eulalie chose to deprive Adeline's only son, Professor Vance Christian of the Cornell Hotel School, of his inherited share of the island. Vance was in the forefront of organizing university wine courses in the United States and was in demand as adviser on the establishment of hotel schools around the world. Lonely, without children of his own, he sought my advice. I retained Tajmool Hosein, a leading legal luminary in Trinidad, alongside my Saturday-night cognac friend Othneil Sylvester.

Aunt Eulalie even ventured a belated appeal to the Privy Council in England, which went before Chief Justice Allen Lewis. Justice Lewis asked her lawyer: "Under what authority may I extend the time for appeal to the Privy Council?"

"My Lord," the lawyer replied, "the rules are silent on the point."

"So should you be," ordered the Chief Justice.

The title was eventually entrusted to me, thus sustaining the only legacy in the Grenadines through four generations over a century. In the family tradition, a sunken ship was but a cause for reflection and a time to contemplate a new design. In Old Harry's view, the island should always be there with its profusion of white cedar trees, their branches agelessly bent in the wind, available to become the timbers of ships. He was proud too that he was the only man in the country with shares in a bank in England. Early in the last century he knew how to convert his diligence as a shipwright and sea captain into capital, and how to let his capital work for him. Thus came the legacy, Quatre Isle Resort.

10

First Election and the Labour Party

Meanwhile, the political climate was heating up. Elections were not far off and the governing People's Political Party turned up in Bequia to launch their campaign. For the first time since my fiasco in the city, they met fierce resistance.

I was in the southern Grenadines. I instructed my supporters not to lob conch shells at opponents during rallies on Union Island, as was their practice. I didn't mind them blowing the shell, which effectively drowned out speeches, and was a more than adequate expression of distaste. I also joined the campaigns on the mainland. My previous years as an agronomist in the countryside provided me with fertile subjects for my speeches. I was comfortable with topics in agriculture and trade, blending it with my experiences in other Caribbean islands, Canada and Europe.

But differences in approach surfaced quickly. Our party leader, Milton Cato, had grown up in the sugar-cane farming village of Georgetown, and never forgave the sitting government for trade union practices that led to the closure of the sugar industry. Our party's draft manifesto included therefore restoring sugar. Having done research in sugar, in the field and in the libraries at the Tropical Products Institute where I worked in England, all the technical and marketing information at my command instructed me to abandon this crop. Moreover, it created employment only for a few months. Bananas were showing enough results to produce a better quality of life in the countryside. At a meeting to draft the manifesto, I demanded that if I were to be spokesman on agriculture, references to revival of sugar be deleted. The battle of the generations began.

On my first tour with the Party in the Grenadines, the Party continued its line of attack on the then Prime Minister, Ebenezer Joshua, and bemoaned the collapse of the sugar industry. But the people of the Grenadines wanted to hear about roads, jetties, electricity, telephones, education and medical services. Above all they wanted an attack on their parliamentary representative, Clive Tannis – not Joshua and sugar.

But Clive was the cousin of Hudson Tannis, the party candidate in Kingstown, who wasn't about to attack his cousin. That was fair enough, I agreed. So it was settled that I would help on the mainland, but they would leave me to deal with the islands of the Grenadines, each with their own peculiarities and needs.

My final days of campaign were a naval strategy. I had learnt that my opponent, while losing in Bequia to my Uncle Cyril, always partially compensated for it with a majority in Canouan, Mayreau and Union Island. His method was simple. After voting in Bequia, he sailed south on his ship, *The Whistler,* which was contracted to collect the ballot boxes. There were no telephones in the islands to report the count before he collected the boxes.

To beat him, I supplied the police with contradictory information on my planned political meetings, all of which were approved. Consequently, no one could anticipate my movements.

I spread the word that I was not bothering to hold the Saturday night meeting in Port Elizabeth, and would concentrate on Paget Farm on Sunday. The rum shops that supported me were well supplied to entertain while my opponent conducted his rally. When the noise died down, my campaign boat, the *Eood,* slipped away from its mooring and drifted out of the bay. I did not allow the engine to be started until I was sure the sound would not reach any of the villages.

We arrived in Mayreau, an island of thatched houses and very sad homes, at dawn. I visited every home and we all went to pray in the Catholic Church. Then I went on to Union Island for a series of whistle stops all day. In the late afternoon, as we were leaving for Canouan, *The Whistler* arrived with my opponent. It had been late morning by the time he heard that my campaign ship was not in the bay. He had set sail for Mustique, but when he got close and did not see us anchored there, he continued on his way south.

He lost the votes in Mustique. He made the same error in Canouan, sailing into the bay without stopping. By the time he reached Canouan at night, after a useless detour in Union Island, the police informed him that he had no permission for a meeting, but he could begin when I concluded. But I kept on until midnight. His crew was told that I would be leaving Canouan when the moon rose, but I knew I had to win in the Southern Grenadines so I stayed till noon the next day.

As we sailed toward Bequia, we flashed a mirror – and soon, every mirror in every bedroom in Paget Farm came to life. The whole village was glistening with mirrors signalling triumphant enthusiasm. The people of Paget Farm, calling themselves the Rock of Gibraltar, had stood firm.

The women in Paget Farm had marched with fervent determination, chanting, "We shall fix the roads, we shall fix the roads," all the way from Paget Farm to Port Elizabeth. The dirt roads incensed them. They were fed up of going to Church with bare feet and a bottle of water to wash between their toes, and putting on clean shoes before entering the Church.

By the time the elections came, we were very sure we would win two more seats to capture the government. But, in the end, the only new seat captured by the Labour Party was my own in the Grenadines. The governing party, the PPP, held five seats to our four. One government seat was won by only five votes. My Grenadines were rejoicing in the hope and glory of a new dawn after 15 years of neglect in Opposition, ever since adult suffrage.

I knew I was home and dry. My political career had begun. My first daughter Sabrina was born three weeks later. The conversion of the family home into a hotel was almost complete. With a three-month-old baby, and my new career, the hotel opened for business in January 1967. It was hardly smooth going.

Our very first lunch order, which was to be carried into town on a tray for the staff of Barclays Bank, nearly led to the dismissal of our first waitress. Barclays would set up in Bequia twice a week for three hours and it was most convenient for them to have lunch brought to their office. But the waitress was too proud to be seen going into town with an apron and a tray.

My wife Pat had worked her way through the University of Toronto as a summer waitress at Banff Springs Hotel and had no trouble serving the bank staff who became permanent customers. We already had an account with them holding my St. Lucia funds.

We decided to keep the waitress on, and she soon learned to smile all the way to the bank, as we did.

We ordered supplies each day from St. Vincent, nine miles away, with a note to the ferry captain, and when they arrived, I would row out to the jetty in a boat I bought for that purpose. For the bar, we needed two blocks of ice a day, and three on Saturdays to keep us going at weekends. The blocks usually arrived rather melted down and missing a few chips broken away by the crew for their rum mix on the voyage.

Our first barman, a white retired seaman who claimed he knew the bars of the world, did not last long. He would hold up a glass to eye level to measure portions, and should anyone dare ask, "How are you today," he would take it quite seriously, proceeding with lengthy discourse into his diabetes, explaining with glass in hand, his method of daily urine tests akin to measuring drinks being poured for the customer. My kinship with the sea, alas, had misled me into thinking that a sailor, familiar with watering holes around the world, would qualify as a barman.

Some beautiful old classic wooden yachts occasionally graced the bay, as did the destroyers in the West Indies squadron, and we learnt how to cope with sudden demand for great volume, investing in a kerosene refrigerator which required one to get on one's knees to keep the flame nice and blue, something that always reminded me of those childhood church outings, kneeling in response to quiet signals from my grandmother.

Amelia Duncan, the trusted and faithful servant adopted at the age of four by my grandmother, and who had become my second mother in residence in Belmont, came to work for us. As her family slowly disintegrated around her with death and emigration, she had drifted into catering for a succession of Anglican priests, and had even done a spell in Aruba. With no children of her own, Amelia's three loves were our family, the Royal Family and the Anglican Church. When I returned, she abandoned the Sunny Caribbee Hotel where she was employed as a cook, simply giving notice: "My Son is back."

She had pictures of various members of the Royal Family across her bedroom walls, and her excursion into Aruba had expanded her interest into the Dutch Royals as well. Whenever I travelled out of the Caribbean to Europe, she would ask if I was going home, which meant to her was I going to see the Queen.

The only access to our six-room hotel was a walk from the wooden pier in town, down a path along the beach, making the transportation of our supplies and guests' luggage quite a challenge. To solve the problem, I negotiated with a shipwright to buy his second-hand, ten-foot, double-ender that he used to get along the shoreline and harvest for his fish pot. A gallant and strong soul rowed it all the way from Friendship, around West Cay, to our hotel in Belmont, a six-mile trip. The boat had two wooden oars, the cinnamon handle of each spliced and braced to a white cedar blade with a copper strap to reduce friction between the wood and the two fixed oar pins.

This delivery system turned into our first advertisement. My wife Pat painted the whole thing yellow with shades of Frangipani flowers, complete with the logo clearly visible. (It also served to make our guests feel that their luggage was safely in the hotel's hands and not disappearing with a strange bearded man in a rowboat.)

We would buy vegetables and fruit from Kingstown every day, sending a shopping list at 6 a.m. through a member of the ferryboat crew from whom our market lady Enid faithfully collected it. The market was a minute's walk from the jetty, and from her market stall she could see the ferry arrive. Dutifully, the same crew member delivered her payment in cash each week in an envelope. No questions ever arose; none of price, stolen goods or rotting fruit.

Although I began the system, rowing the boat myself to the jetty except when I had to be in Parliament, as our fortunes improved, we later employed the man who was living with our laundress to be in charge of the boat. She had already proved her reliability, coming to work at dawn, scrubbing all the laundry on a grooved board, in a two-compartment concrete sink (one for soapy water, the other for fresh). She would hang the laundry out to dry on lines in the sunshine, and had to be keeping a constant eye out for sudden rain and retrieve it all in time. Our ironing was done with the original pot, complete with a chamber of hot coals, constantly replenished from the adjacent coal pot. Fortunately, glamorous silk had not yet graced the Grenadines.

A retired Canadian doctor, Dr. Corbett, was the island's sole medical practitioner. He had served the Eskimos and was therefore comfortable in remote places. By 10 a.m. he was already ensconced in a rum shop with his unusual toast, "First for the day and God knows I need it." A visitor's bruised foot had got infected with the diatoms from the sea. "Would he come and look at it?" I asked. "Tell him to throw some strong rum over it. I have no antibiotics – these tourists, when they go to heaven, they'll get septic wings!"

One night, Pat and I were expecting a friend for dinner. We waited and waited. He did not turn up. There was no way to contact him until the next day. His explanation was simple. He was not hungry.

The hotel got busy very quickly, and Pat was usually worn out by the end of the day. Her friend from University of Toronto, Marie Kingston, who came on a holiday never to return, ended up helping her. Marie later became involved in the management and remained the Frangi's company secretary almost 40 years later. I took over the job of baby-sitter at nights. Our baby Sabrina seemed allergic to the night. For her, that was screaming time, leaving Pat with no chance to rest. So I used to walk her every night on the sandy beach in Belmont. She loved the warmth of my chest and the cool night air. I would sit with her on the trunk of an almond tree, with the waves lapping at my feet, until she fell asleep.

Meanwhile, after the drunken celebrations of my victory, and thank-you meetings, in all the islands of the Grenadines, I visited our party leader, Milton Cato, at his home in Calliaqua. He had done nowhere near as well as he had hoped and was dejected. Late into the day, he was still in pyjamas, and wearing dark shades: no semblance of dignity, only dejection, none of the Churchillian-in-defeat defiance. He was surrounded by his cats. I was ready to resume political meetings, he was not. And the old guard of the party had no stomach for it; they retreated.

The best I could get out of Milton Cato was that we should seek refuge in a legal challenge. He gave me some election results to take to Alec Hughes who was holidaying beside Princess Margaret Beach in Bequia. I rowed down and delivered the messages one evening. Alec was at the time working with me setting up my company and was pleased to discuss the political scene with me.

But before returning to Bequia, with the help of young activists – De Souza and Commissong – we launched an attack on the government in the market square. "Fair play or fight" was the theme I heralded for the anxious masses, and the town reverberated to my call.

At the very first session in Parliament, I approached the Hon. Sam Slater, who had won by five votes and whose seat we were challenging in the court, and asked him to cross the floor. "Quite improper," I was told that day by my colleagues at lunch.

The country was shortly to move one step from colonial status into statehood and, in the process, our Parliament was to be expanded from nine seats to eleven with the Government having the right to determine the additional two seats. Although it was a clear case of gerrymandering, the court was moving slowly and it seemed that time would run out on us. More and more people were taking to the streets, and some riots broke out resulting in the Government lumber warehouse being set on fire in the night.

I drafted a letter to the Colonial Secretary in London calling for a constitutional conference to review the situation. My old teacher Eustace had won his seat from Herman Young, who had defected from the Labour Party, and he signed above me. We took the letter to the office of Milton Cato, and invited him to sign above us as leader. He was not happy to do so, but capitulated after we threatened that if he tore it up, we would write another and dispatch it to London without him.

I was satisfied we had a case. How could a government unilaterally expand a parliament when it had won a majority by one seat with five votes, and had lost the popular vote? To the surprise of the party, London acceded to our request.

Before leaving for London, we had a party meeting in the home of Levi Latham in Mesopotamia, who had retained his seat in Parliament, to prepare for the conference. I was aghast. All the talk was about women and food. It seemed they were leaving London up to what they deemed "the brains" in the party. On the way to London, I stopped in Barbados and met with Errol Barrow. I had been his guest at Barbados' Independence celebrations, and his High Commissioner in London, Sir Lionel Luckoo, who also represented Guyana, was instructed to help get my message across to Her Majesty's Government. Milton Cato, meanwhile, was talking to the Opposition, Barbados Labour Party.

In London, my old boss, George Ordish, was still at the Tropical Products Institute. He and the Attorney General's wife had jointly published their work on the pigeons of London, she under the pseudonym Pearl Binder. She also had a nickname, Polly. George arranged for me to have tea in the residence at the Inns of Court the Sunday before our Monday Conference. Polly arranged my meeting with her husband at nine o'clock the following morning.

Triumphantly, I took the tube from the Cumberland Hotel at Marble Arch where we were staying, but holy hell broke loose when I told Milton Cato, leader of our delegation, that I had secured a call on the Attorney General after having tea with his wife a while ago. "Leave the legal matters to the lawyers," he bellowed at me.

I went to my room and cried. Here was I, having abandoned a comfortable life in England and uprooted myself for a life in politics at home, headed in a direction to what looked like total disaster. But Eustace consoled me. "This conference was your idea," he said. "You must see it through. Go and see the Attorney General. To hell with Milton's pettiness."

Timidly I climbed the stairs of the elegantly polished interior of the Attorney General's Office. The centuries assailed me from the paintings of all the formidable previous occupants of the lofty post. I was promptly ushered into the presence of Sir Elwyn Jones, whose wife had told him that I had left London after five years in the city, that I had served well in the Institute, that I was intelligent and should not be a waste of his time.

I knew I had to come to the point quickly. The West Indies Act; a government with a challengeable mandate was about to use the constitution to consolidate itself; I sought no more than British fairness; thanks for listening! Sir Elwyn Jones indeed listened attentively and his Secretary took copious notes. He thanked me for my visit and said no more than that my information was instructive and that he would see that Judith (Hart, Secretary in charge of the Constitutional Conference) understood.

That was as great a half an hour as I ever had in politics. The meeting resulted in a new order, with the boundaries to be redrawn into 13 constituencies but with the British to appoint a Boundaries Commission. A new Administrator, Hywel George, would be appointed. That night at the Cumberland I did not even feel like eating. I wanted to be alone. Eustace knocked on the door. "Son," he said, "your tears were not in vain."

At the Hyde Park luncheon hosted by Judith Hart, our conference chairperson, I was seated beside Tom Sewell, a top civil servant in the diplomatic corps. We discussed one common interest, farming. He and his wife extended a personal invitation to me to visit their home the next day. At Guildford station, he turned up in his Rolls. It was a 20-minute drive to his Surrey farm. Family dispatches from the King and decorations from the last war decorated the powder room. I commended his lavatory literature. "One has to find a place," he said.

His wife was from good Scandinavian stock. The sherry and port were excellent. Their children's portraits were done by a Russian artist, the lady explained. She had boundless energy. She took us on a tour of the farm, explaining her specialty in intensive beef-rearing. They introduced me to neighbours who worshipped Ian Smith. I showed them pictures of my wife and daughter and extended invitations to my home in the Caribbean.

Tom came to St. Vincent later on a mission to oversee our implementation of conference decisions. We were delighted to host him, at the Frangi, and reveal some of our family history. Tom and I became friends. When I returned for the full statehood constitutional conference in London, he was ready to host me at lunch at the Travellers Club, much to the annoyance of my wife Pat, then passing through from a holiday in Sweden, and totally contemptuous of my going to the all-male elitist enclave.

The results of the conference seemed to have impacted on Sam Slater. He was ready to cross the floor, but was nervous about the rumour circulating that I was a candidate for floor-crossing too. Indeed the Joshua camp made overtures to my friend Philip Greaves, and

Joshua himself made a play to John Compton, declaring that he could handle Cato, "The Magoffy," as he described him, a soubriquet earned by pomposity, but he wanted "the cousin of yours on his side, he's a terror on the rostrum."

But the Kingstown Club was the nemesis for Joshua's PPP. Hilary Da Silva, a Portuguese merchant, was the go-between in the negotiations. Slater resigned, creating another constitutional crisis. The Government was dissolved. We were involved in my second general election within a year.

Before leaving London, I called my old buddies in the Tropical Products Institute. From the receptionist to the directors, mine was more than a prodigal's welcome, to be once more honoured in our favourite pub off Holborn, with good old Stilton, crackers and Chablis, more sentimental in value than any banquet: savouring the company of old friends sharing the transition of my life from science into constitutional wrangles. When we got home, it was as though the whole of St. Vincent had come to the airport to meet us. The chant "fair play or fight," rang through the town.

I had won the battle for fair play.

11

Trade Minister and Statehood

The Colonial office sent out their new Administrator Hywel George. He came accompanied by his wife Edith and three young daughters. The British supervised the election. With the Grenadines safely under my control, I spent more time in St. Vincent plodding the length and breadth of the countryside. I spent a lot of time too in the city, helping our candidate Hudson Tannis.

And so we won the next election.

I became Minister of Trade, Agriculture, Labour and Tourism and found that my first challenge was to market a surplus arrowroot crop. Arrowroot had replaced sugar by then, but we had overshot our production goals that year. There was arrowroot in storage in the country, arrowroot at the port, and more arrowroot at a rented old stone building amidst the cobblestones in the centre of the city.

My natural instincts – to go out and sell the product – proved revolutionary. Never before had a Minister made it his business to secure a market for the farmers. In the past, it had been left to the old plantocracy that controlled the lands. The purchasers would come to St. Vincent and dictate the price.

After making some initial enquiries and extracting some commitments, I led a delegation to New York to meet with our purchasers, Staley, accompanied by the Manager of the Arrowroot Association, Vin Sprott, and Martin Barnard, a young university graduate representing the plantations. The New York buyers outlined the slenderness of the market, but assured us they would, "as usual," pay a high price for the Grade 1 and less for lower grades. We adjourned for lunch. In the washroom Martin noted that my silence was markedly different from all the noise I had made at home. But I kept my strategy to myself.

The hospitality of the buyers could not be faulted; ample cocktails and pleasant conversation without any rush to the negotiating table. I did not hesitate to drink. The wines were very good. It was obvious to me that they were trying to improve my mood, so to speak, before I signed away our farmers' arrowroot. But the rum sessions with fishermen had bolstered my tolerance, and I must still have been too sober for their liking because, when we returned to the office, they brought out reinforcements to negotiate with me.

At the last moment, I told them our second-grade arrowroot would be sold in the Caribbean, and that left them with Grade 1 at the higher price only. The New York office finally conceded that they had no authority to negotiate on that, and that a plane would take us to the head office. And so the next day we were flown to Decatur, Illinois. We had an even better dinner at their golf club, and closed the deal on prices for Grade 1 and lesser-grade arrowroot. My reputation as a trade negotiator was established, and I became the darling of the farmers.

But the starving fishermen in my constituency were still waiting. Before dawn each day, they sailed to St. Vincent to dispose of their catch and sailed home at night. It was a tedious life. Eventually, the foreign private sector came to my rescue.

A Frenchman from Martinique, Andre Beaufrand, bought beach property in Union Island, and built a hotel and fine restaurant, and then turned his attention to purchasing fish, lobster and conch for export back to Martinique. He then also built a slipway to service small yachts.

Another investor, a husky American named Crosby, brought in a trawler, designed lobster traps and engaged some Paget Farm fishermen to build them. Baited with the never-before-used cattle skin, the traps worked wonderfully. But the lobster divers panicked, fearing the American's traps would eliminate supply.

I remember drawing from the memory of rat traps on my grandmother's farm in Bequia, as I tried to pacify the divers at a public meeting. Granny had bought some powerful traps and I thought the end of the rats was nigh, but, decades on, rats still thrived. No trap at sea would permanently deplete the lobster stock, I assured them. Traps were universal, I said, adding that, moreover, they would serve in old age when they could not dive any more.

But my message failed. The traps were burnt. Crosby married a beautiful girl from Dorsetshire Hill and returned to the US. At the end of my political career, the traps did come into their own, but long after many divers had perished with the macho scuba diver's nightmare, the bends.

Another pressing problem in Bequia was the infamous over-the-sea toilet. Under the Almond Trees, the grand diversion from the usual gossip, scandal and political diatribe was watching the action from the toilet at the end of the jetty, a small house with male and female quarters for personal relief through a hole in the floor and to the sea. I decided to abolish the sea toilet and build facilities on land.

The Antique ninepenny chart of Admiralty Bay in 1811 drawn by Captain Dovers, RN, identified the ruins of the old wharf built by the crew of the *Ringdove*, deeming the Bay very secure for careening ships and coppering their bottoms. In 1966, when I returned from England, sailing schooners were still being careened there (but without copper), and the sea latrine was poised at the end of the jetty (to rescue America, we now have a razor wire fence on the beach!)

But the toilet met an early demise. We staged a grand opening. My chairman Casembe Bonadie announced, at the toilet's grand opening, that an old lady would have the job of dispensing sheets of toilet paper, "depending on your movements." But, alas, supply could not keep up with demand, which skyrocketed as the good citizens of Port Elizabeth claimed enough "movement" to secure extra paper to stock up their bathrooms at home. The toilets were blocked with stones, and with that, our first institution of public health collapsed.

One day I got home to find a telephone installed, the crank-handle version. The British Administrator had issued a challenge: "How dare you be a Minister of Trade, Agriculture, Labour and Tourism without a telephone!"

On the regional Caribbean scene, however, things were looking up. A fledging free trade area promoted by Errol Barrow of Barbados, Forbes Burnham of Guyana and V.C. Bird of Antigua had risen out of the ashes of the collapsed Federation. The constant news of new links in Europe, where former enemies like France and Germany were forging a union, reverberated in the Caribbean. Barrow invited the regional leaders to join him in Barbados.

Many who survived the Federation, playing advocate or spoiler, were very much around. Eric Williams, the scholar of Trinidad, Robert Bradshaw of St. Kitts – a black aristocrat if there ever was one – the flamboyant Eric Gairy of Grenada and most of the others were there. I was Trade Minister on our delegation.

The meeting took place in the Garrison Savannah, an old brick military building. The atmosphere was cordial. Jamaica's Hugh Shearer, with his sparkling humour, accompanied by his articulate Trade Minister Bob Lightbourne, seemed keen to atone for Jamaica's sins, as that country's withdrawal from the Federation had led to its total collapse. Trinidad's Williams led us in economics, which was his forte, but later, however, his expertise was not so evident in the manner he handled the resources of his country when the oil boom created soaring inflation.

In just a couple of days, we created some viable institutions. First-class lobbying and trading-off were in full swing. We in St. Vincent made a pitch for the seat of the Caribbean Development Bank but were a non-starter without an international airport. Barbados secured the Bank, and Guyana became the regional headquarters of the Secretariat in spite of the later furious objections of Edward Seaga, the Finance Minister of Jamaica. Jamaica and Trinidad settled for further university development. The small islands would seek compensation in trade for lack of economies of scale. I put forward the concept of a Caribbean agricultural marketing protocol based on the Treaty of Rome.

A whole series of meetings with the Regional Secretariat in Guyana began. The Trade Ministers were charged with following through on all the Barbados decisions, and what a responsibility it was! We started a search for a common external tariff. It meant going through the tariffs in every island and country on long spreadsheets typed on wide typewriters, working long hours into the night and sometimes through until morning. How simple life would have been if the word processor, computer and photocopier had been invented!

We struggled to get a harmonization, or rather an unbalanced harmonization, of fiscal incentives in place that would give advantages to smaller countries. The larger territories advanced their industrialization. I concentrated on my pet project, the trade in agricultural produce. At one meeting I had an altercation with the Barbados delegation on the trade in cooking oil. The Barbados Trade Minister, the redoubtable Captain George Fergusson, twisted his face in contempt for my arguments. His officials were squirming and shuffling papers before him, which he continued to ignore.

"You are finished?" he asked when I was done.

"Yes," I replied.

"Mr. Chairman," he said, "I want to tell that distinguished Trade Minister from St. Vincent that he is not my equal. His father, Captain Reg and I controlled the movement of goods in these islands and when I went to Bequia, he was a naked little boy on the beach and I would put him over my lap and spank his behind. His father was my equal, not him. We were explorers. Let the officials work on this during the coffee break."

There was no way I could respond.

Captain Fergusson was a very interesting character. He was not terribly good-looking, but had a great smile, and was a charmer. He had recently shot an intruder at his gate for interfering with his dog, and when asked at one meeting to explain how he could walk in Georgetown alone at night when everyone was fearful of the "choke and rob" gangs, the Captain pulled his pistol from his pocket there in the meeting and repeated the defence he had proffered at the courts in Barbados: "I have a reasonable apprehension of dread."

Fergusson had the distinction of being the only government minister in our part of the world for whom an extradition order was made. The Brazilians wanted him for smuggling. He was also indicted in Guyana for piracy, after he boarded a ship that had rammed his own ship and jolted some of his men into the sea. He held up the captain and commanded him to pick up his crew. Errol had to negotiate his release.

Fergusson taught me one ministerial trick – how to abolish price controls on fish, a condition imposed by the Japanese for their funding of our fish market. "Wait until the high season when the dorado and kingfish are in abundance and abolish the controls then," he said. "When fish become scarce later on, the public will have adjusted to market conditions."

When he retired, Fergusson was still sailing. He took a yacht out one evening to entertain a young lady, and was found drifting weeks after he had been assumed dead. He was picked up by a freighter in the Atlantic and carried all the way to Spain. When he got off the ship on his return, Al Gilkes, a Barbadian reporter, met him and asked how a navigator of his calibre had gotten lost.

"If you had a lady like this alone on a ship, you too would get lost," was Fergusson's reply.

At one level I was securing markets, but quietly also I was bringing in shipping business for my constituents and improving services such as mail delivery by establishing a mail contract with the ship, *Friendship Rose*. All three owners and partners in the Adams and Lewis family had arrived together in my office. Sailing with a few shipments of rice from Guyana they had saved enough to put down a deposit on a Kelvin diesel engine, and I had secured them a two-year contract on delivery of mail in the Grenadines. To my absolute astonishment they informed me that they were about to register the shareholding in the ship, and wanted to know how many shares I required for my help. "The days of this kind of representation in the Grenadines are over," I told them.

Back home, I took to the schools at night in the countryside expounding how to grow carrots. They were not rhizomes like arrowroot, but grew from seeds. Trinidad, which had been a traditional market for our yams, tannias and sweet potatoes, provided a more structured market now, including one for carrots. We did well.

Trinidadian Trade Minister Kamaluddin Mohammed, always seated next to me in the Guyana trade meetings, became a good friend, and the bond between our countries deepened. However, our friendship and mutual respect did cause me some grief later.

At the next Heads of Government meeting in Trinidad, Kamal was presenting the visiting delegates to his Prime Minister, Dr. Eric Williams. Dr. Williams said to Cato, "I understand you have a brilliant Trade Minister!" and held my hand warmly, saying that he would chat with me later. My boss did not like that at all. Eric Williams was a legend in the region, known for his formidable intellect.

Back home in Bequia, meanwhile, the battle was for infrastructure. The Commonwealth Development Corporation, or CDC, owned our electricity plant, and with the help of the administrator Hywell George, the Executive prevailed on them to introduce electricity into Bequia. Accordingly, two second-hand 50-kilowatt generators – Dormans that had been standby outfits at an airfield in England – were duly installed.

After a public meeting in Paget Farm, we proceeded to Port Elizabeth. Ceremoniously we left the Almond Tree public meeting in the candlelight procession to the generating plant, blew out our candles, and I switched on electricity on October 9, 1968 for the first time in the Grenadines.

The load on the generators was heavy; they nearly caught fire the first night. We solved that problem but sadly, when I visited the station on Christmas night just little more than a month afterwards, demand had already exceeded supply from one generator and I was told that one engine was under maintenance and we would have to turn off some lights in town because the other simply couldn't cope. Underestimating demand in developing countries was a battle to overcome.

The proposal on updating our old cranky telephone system on St. Vincent had come before the Executive Council and our Minister of Communications, Sam Slater, was put in charge of the negotiations with Cable and Wireless. The Executive Council thought I should assist him. Slater sat at the meeting with the British team in his office after lunch, not the greatest time for the senior man who had crossed the floor before the election to join us. Lunchtime to him was whisky time at the Kingstown Club. He fell asleep, and I extended the agreement to include all the Grenadines, with a special private-sector component for Mustique.

When questioned by the Executive Council the following week about the inclusion of the Grenadines, Slater quite graciously asked them what did they expect after putting me on the negotiating team.

The Grenadines were forging ahead.

The Petit St. Vincent Resort was taking shape. An American paper-maker magnate named Nicholls had seen the island from the deck of a yacht, bought it from the owners in Grenada's Petit Martinique, and put Captain Hazen Richardson in charge of construction. A Swedish architect, Arne Hasselquist, who had visited me with a rucksack on his back and sought my blessing as the Member of Parliament, took on the designs.

Palm Island, originally a sandfly-and-mosquito sanctuary where the mosquitoes and sandflies were fabled to force cattle to swim the channel for refuge in Union Island, had been leased for one dollar a year for 99 years. Before my time, an intrepid mariner, the Texan John Caldwell, who had written the book *Desperate Voyage* about his sail from the Pacific to the West Indies, built a resort, leaving the Government with $12\frac{1}{2}$ per cent ownership, a minority interest that yielded nothing.

I had to go along with the agreements we inherited on Palm Island and other islands, and eagerly waited for one of them to expire. While I did so, the question of Mustique arose. We had before us a proposal from Colin Tennant on concessions for Mustique, modelled to a large extent on agreements made by the Bay Street leadership of The Bahamas: it comprised 33 years' duty free concessions and a 99-year tax holiday to be legislated in Parliament. I did not like it. The English administrator, Hywel George, sent it to the Colonial Office for review. Confidential cables from London were then coded, and only one civil servant had access to the code. When deciphered it read: "Proposal will blast hole in the Bank of England."

My hand was strengthened. I demanded too that as Representative of the Grenadines the negotiation be my responsibility. In the Executive Council, our new Member of Parliament, Hudson Tannis, had been Tennant's lawyer, Tennant having also bought the 22-acre prime site in Bequia, the Sunny Caribbee Hotel, from Tannis's family. I settled for a 20-year concession for both duty and income tax, with payment to be made for the public services, like customs and police, and the establishment of a primary school. To cap it, the Government would receive $50,000 a year. The agreed goal was to create a unique resort with villas to promote tourism. To the surprise of the Council, I accepted the role of Director to look after Government (and my constituents') interests on the Board of Directors of the Mustique Company.

A few events and the decisions I took during my tenure as Trade Minister stand out in my memory. The demands of the farmers for instant payment for their carrots being exported by the newly organized Marketing Corporation meant that I needed a cash flow in advance of the funds coming in from Trinidad, the buyer. Our import of sugar and rice, serviced by the Royal Bank and Barclays, meant that I should join the accounts. The Royal Bank lost the million-dollar transactions. The Manager, who had refused my hotel loan when I was starting up the Frangipani, reached my office, pleading for a piece of the action. "Politicians," I reminded him, "are a bad risk."

My determination to get rid of the surplus stock of arrowroot had carried me around the Caribbean. My stepfather's brother, Rudolf Baynes, a member of the Executive of the ruling Labour Party and a former government minister who had improved my stipend at college up to $50, was Chairman of our newly formed Marketing Corporation. We travelled to Trinidad, Aruba and Curaçao. On another mission we did the northern islands, St. Thomas, St. Maarten and Anguilla. I was pleased to see the Aruba refineries, even though the operation was being scaled back and one town that was the centre of activity in the old days had become rather derelict. Aruba had been an early career option had I left school without staying on to win the scholarship. Some folk in St. Maarten, operating the guest house where we stayed, knew my stepfather and were pleased to meet me. The merchants were amazed that we were still producing arrowroot, but they had none on their shelves.

Anguilla had achieved their secession and Ronald Webster, their Chief Minister, was in a simple wooden building over which his flag with three dolphins flew. He proudly gave me a flag. There was only a three-room guest house on the island, named Hodge's. The land was spartan, still shipping out salt that dried on the edge of a pond. Like us in the Grenadines, they had wonderful and empty beaches. Their robust seafaring determination had earned them their identity. We in the Grenadines had much in common with them – the shipbuilding and seafaring personality, with sailors working on ships around the world and bringing the savings home. When I was a little boy, salt from Anguilla was stored in what is now the reception area of my Frangipani hotel. Before electricity and refrigeration, salt was the prized commodity for survival in the islands, used for curing fish and pork.

After my arrowroot mission, Anguilla came on the agenda of the Carifta Council. Guyana's Sonny Ramphal and St. Kitt's Paul Southwell were putting forward a resolution based on the Wooding Commission inquiry into the St. Kitts/Nevis and Anguilla disturbances after British intervention, calling for the restoration of the integrity of the state. I had seen the secret report in St. Vincent and did not like it. My instinctive rebellion against the neglect of the Grenadines aligned me with the Anguilla cause.

The resolution was about to be passed, so I demanded a discussion of the report, and quickly discovered that few had seen it. I threatened that if the resolution were passed, I would call a press conference and report that most were ignorant of the report. By the time the next Council meeting was called, Anguilla had settled back into its British status. My intervention, seeking to sustain respect for Anguillans admired in the Grenadines for their response to the contempt they suffered, I gathered later, bought time for the Labour Government in Westminster to extricate them from the acute embarrassment of so-called re-colonization.

Years later, reminiscing over a drink, our legal adviser to the Organization of East Caribbean States, the retired Judge Barry Renwick, told us how he was sent to hold court in Anguilla from St. Kitts when the rebellion was in full swing. He was met on the wharf by the defenders of Anguilla freedom who promptly informed him that no court based in St. Kitts would be allowed to sit again in Anguilla. Barry bargained. He understood their concerns. He simply wanted to go to court. They should accompany him. At the courthouse, Barry put on his robes, and rose with all the dignity his English training had bestowed to say, "The Supreme Court is now in session. The Supreme Court is adjourned."

With all the wonderful history behind us of the fierce battles throughout the perilous times among the armadas of the French and English, and Dutch and Spanish, beyond the images of conquest and cunning of the pirates and buccaneers, never in the history of political warfare in the West Indies has there been a more elegant experience of instant assault and spontaneous retreat than Barry's assault on Anguilla, sustaining legal propriety and sovereignty, alas, for a single moment.

Neither has there been in the history of the Caribbean a funnier manifestation of those ancient words of wisdom: "He who fights and runs away, will live to fight another day." This is part of our folklore, and this was probably the spirit inspiring our clever Grenadian jurist.

Anguilla manages her own affairs now and is a proud member of the Caribbean Community, offering some of the finest resorts in our region, complete with membership of the East Caribbean Supreme Court. A single statement to the Anguillans by Premier Bradshaw had sparked their revolt. "Statehood will come and you will not stop it. There will be no more England to complain to. If you do, I will make Anguilla a desert."

Despite my sympathy for Anguilla, I pursued my goal of political union at every turn. It was easy with the frequency of regional meetings to do so. And many ideas floated around, links between Grenada and Trinidad, St. Vincent and Guyana, but I felt the first goal should be unity among the small islands of the East Caribbean. Eric Gairy of Grenada once thought we should bring in the Turks and Caicos and the Cayman Islands. Le Blanc of Dominica felt the only way we could avoid the pitfall of the first federation would be to choose a capital by putting the names of the countries in a hat. I proposed that St. Vincent unite with any. John Compton indicated that he liked the "call for any." Nothing happened. Political union continues to elude the islands up to today.

There was also the memorable issue of "banana boxes." At the Tropical Products Institute, I once read an article on restructuring the banana industry in Ecuador using boxes, packaging individual bananas instead of exporting entire bunches as we were still doing. As Minister of Trade, Agriculture and Tourism, I wrote a memorandum outlining the advantages of this boxing technology which implied that the organic matter of the stems would return to the fields, rather than be a nuisance to be disposed of in England. I canvassed the idea with John Compton and Eric Gairy, and we commissioned a study on the establishment of a boxing plant using internationally competent auditors.

The report suggested that St. Lucia, which produced the most bananas, would get the plant and Geest Industries, our purchasing agents, were deemed suitable investors. An alternate choice, Papelera Industrial of Venezuela, was an unknown quantity. I had visited the Geest farms in England, and had seen their extensive production of potatoes and tulips linked to Dutch operations. Geest was diversifying and it made sense for us to do the same.

But the auditors were also Geest auditors. At a meeting in St. Lucia, I hammered away at the conflict of interest and we all decided to go to Venezuela and visit the Papelera plant. Grenada, with Gairy's interest in Venezuela stimulated by years close to that country while he worked in the refineries in Aruba, was promoting Papelera. We struck a deal with St. Lucia that they would have the plant, but we would decide on investment after checking with Venezuela following our visit. Nan Ducray, the Dominican Minister, a fat and jovial soul, went along with this. After the sumptuous exposure in Caracas visiting factories and lunching in luxury in the Jockey Club, before we left Venezuela Ducray came to my room to seek help writing his report.

Geest had influence in our council through Minister Sam Slater and his friend Hilary Da Silva, our Banana Association Chairman. But Sam was no match for me in public meetings at the market square when I pointed out that, with Geest, there would be no profit for us in boxing bananas, as the boxing operation would swim deep in their West Indian expenses before our price was determined.

In the end, we gave the deal to Papelera.

St. Lucia agreed that the next industry would go to one of us in the Windwards. Polar beer seemed interested, but declined. Heineken then made a successful pitch in St. Lucia and that did not go down well with us.

Being involved with commerce and agriculture was not the only responsibility I assumed as Trade Minister. There was also the problem of the "working week." It came about this way. As a Member of Parliament in a plural country of islands, with only sailing ferries for transportation, and with home, family and business in Bequia rather than the capital, Kingstown, a weekend comprising Sunday only was totally inadequate. In London I had become a Friday lover. Friday ended the week. Not so in St. Vincent. Saturday was the busiest business day and the Civil Service worked also on Saturday mornings.

I decided to have a go at the Chamber of Commerce. Let us forget about the Wednesday half-day/Saturday full-day and exchange it for Wednesday full-day and Saturday half-day. Simple. The Chamber agreed to it as an experiment for three months. It was not so simple for cricket. It was wonderful to split the week with a midweek break for cricket on Wednesday. I was to learn throughout my political life that sports and culture are enshrined with their own aura of irrational mystique. It was as though cricketing in flannels on Wednesdays was enshrined in the Treaty of Utrecht when England secured pre-eminence in the islands.

After much hullabaloo, the sporting fraternity agreed to try it with the business folk. The shift to Wednesday full-day and Saturday half-day worked well. Toward the end of the three-month trial period I enquired of the Chamber whether we should continue. They who had insisted that the change should only be experimental accused me of experimenting with them. No thanks, they were not returning to half-day Wednesday. Among other things sales in construction materials all day Wednesday had soared.

Next I put to our Executive Council that we should abolish the Saturday half-day in the Government service by putting in more hours

Monday to Friday. Four hours on Saturday could be deployed by starting at 8.00 rather than 8.30 and some minutes added after 4.00. Civil Servants then wanted to know how their children would get to school on time! Surely they could sort this out individually. In any event, they did not come to work on time. The legal profession wanted the Registry opened on Saturdays. We agreed. That could be done with rotation of working time. In every case, members of society had to be coaxed into making the slightest change which improved their lives. So thanks to having a businessman Minister from the Grenadines, the working week in the country was restructured for all time.

But I was still left with the physical problem of getting through the traffic in town on a busy Friday. The traffic then was routed down the commercial sector of Back Street, and circled the market toward the jetty in front of the police station.

The Administrator had secured for me a United Nations town planner from Sweden as a technical assistant in my agricultural department. I asked him to design a road at the back of the town, between Kingstown Park and McKie's Hill, to take some traffic out of the centre of the city. He pointed out that this could only be a narrow one-way street and that a traffic study of the entire town was needed. Schoolboys were deployed. The Swedish planner then made two recommendations. The first was that the traffic be completely turned around in a different direction. I liked this as it meant I could get to the ferry jetty without going through the market. Secondly he proposed a reclamation of lands, widening Bay Street, and putting other roads on the reclaimed area.

At our first meeting at Shrewsbury House, the entire Executive Council and a host of Civil Servants, I put forward the Swedish plan. It was not only accepted but was deemed to be too modest. We would also reclaim the entire front of the city, not simply between the jetties. And so I secured the relocation of a new Grenadines jetty away from the commercial sector.

My final stroke on getting to Bequia from Kingstown was worked out with the owners of *Friendship Rose*. With businesses closing for lunch between 12.00 and 1pm each day, the ferry should not leave at 1.30. Leave at 12.30 certainly. So a longer weekend was introduced, and holidaying between the islands remains a pleasure for all Vincentians.

I will end this chapter by relating some incidents involving four men; Forbes Burnham of Guyana, Milton Cato of St. Vincent, Bob Lightbourne of Jamaica and Sir Ellis Clarke of Trinidad and Tobago, who all affected my ministerial career and events.

The first two were law students in London together. They sat finals in the same year, Burnham with modest grades and Cato with a conditional pass. When they met again in Caribbean political circles, and Burnham did not recognize Cato, the latter felt terribly insulted, only to be flattered by an invitation to a red-carpet State visit to Guyana when Burnham sensed that a linkage with St. Vincent could provide black votes to overwhelm the Guyanese voters of Indian extraction. Cato returned with an album of photographs, which he showed us with enthusiasm. A sweetener was in the mix: he showed us his draft memorandum for St. Vincent to become an associate state with Guyana rather than England. We would break the colonial yoke in a single stroke. The West Indies Act provided for it.

My visit to Guyana had exposed the evidence of the creeping communism that I did not relish. My hitch-hiking days in Yugoslavia had instilled enough repulsion. Burnham wanted black votes to shore up his thin black majority over the Indians. Cato relished an umbrella to fend off the rain from Joshua's PPP. We were in a little room away from the Administrator's office that Saturday morning. My view was that we should take our chances with the British rather than embrace socialism. The pretty pictures from Guyana fell flat on our audience.

It was while we were in Anguilla that I lobbied Rudolf Baynes or "Sir Rudy" as he was nicknamed. Businessman that he was, he found the idea of linking with socialist Guyana quite abhorrent. The message went through our Executive.

At my subsequent cocktail party the evening before another Carifta Council was convened in Guyana, Burnham's voice boomed through the room when he saw me: "I've got to be careful with these young intellectuals." In my long association with Guyana and Burnham, I never assumed he had forgotten his frustration at my thwarting his plans. As he moved to command the heights of the Guyana economy, seizing control of the sugar plantations, the bauxite mines and renaming the bauxite town Lynden after himself, I kept a respectful distance. He had the intellectuals in the region on his side. Anti-colonialism and socialism were identical.

The Carifta Council was my training ground. Understanding the Caribbean economy. Understanding the leadership. Sorting our principles, theory and practice. I noticed that Jamaica, Barbados, Trinidad and Tobago were superbly prepared for every item on the agenda, completely ready with a brief from a specialist civil servant.

Jamaica's Bob Lightbourne consistently impressed me. His laurels from the longest session in Geneva of the International Sugar Conference and the millions in entertainment lavished by his Jamaica delegation, created a formidable aura around the man. He never carried a briefcase. His baggage handlers rose through the ranks and headed ministries. Pleas, entreaties (almost tears) and cogent arguments were his stock in trade. Listening to him was a daunting experience, as you never knew where next he would strike. At our first meeting in London together on bananas with Lord Chalfont, then Minister of State for the Foreign and Commonwealth Office, however, his persuasiveness got him nowhere. He congratulated me on my support, even saying I would develop into a great trade minister. When we adjourned to the pissoir in the elegant washrooms of the Foreign Office, where on the way a portrait of a notable presence in St. Vincent hung, I told him that the British saw our argument but they were constrained by their terms of reference.

"You will have to go to Singapore," I said to Bob. "You'll have to help the British sell arms in South Africa."

Back home, I was listening as usual to the BBC World Service reporting on the Commonwealth Heads of Government Conference in Singapore. When I heard that a committee was set up, including Jamaica, to deal with the thorny issue of sale of arms to South Africa, I knew that our banana market was secure.

Once, at a meeting in Guyana, a message came from President Burnham that I needed to return to St. Vincent immediately. At the airport I was greeted by my stalwart albino friend, Walter Bynoe, along with Ormond Hazell, brother-in-law of my ministerial colleague Hudson Tannis, part-owner of the ship *Rosarine*. The Commissioner of Police, Colonel Anderson, a serious Jamaican who had settled in St. Vincent, was also there. There were disturbances in Bequia, they said. The police station in my stronghold at Paget Farm had been sacked. The Police Commissioner wanted to know how many men I needed to go with me to restore order.

My answer was: "None." I collected my public address system at home in Bequia and went to Paget Farm in the only available taxi, getting into the village at dusk. Swarms of people were awaiting my return. They complained that they had told the engineer Arthur Dalrymple, a Dominican professional, that they were tired of his visits to measure the roads, that it was time for action on road construction to begin, as they already were in St. Vincent. The engineer had sought police protection and eventually left the village with the police. The villagers had then pelted the police station with rocks.

My meeting began with what, by this time, had become my theme hymn "O God our help in ages past." Silence followed the hymn.

I thanked the crowd for sending their message of frustration, which I shared with them. That said and settled, I told them they needed to continue to trust me to deliver, and some more patience was required of them.

When all was at peace, police reinforcements arrived in a truck, again arousing the crowd's anger in the dark streets lit only by the lamp on my rostrum. I told the police to return to Port Elizabeth, that I would call on them after the meeting and arrange for them to resume control of the station. I continued the meeting, and instructed the crowd to disperse. The fundamentals of democracy had been expressed. Law and order were an important part of the process and the police were there to sustain the democratic process. They understood what I was saying and capitulated.

My explanations were not welcome in the Executive Council. The Chief Minister, Cato, who was proud of his past as an administrative sergeant in the Canadian Army, fancied the notion of an armed intimidation of protestors. My dissertation that the will of the people was paramount did not cut much ice. My argument that while I was working to build up markets for agricultural products from the main island, these results did not matter in my constituency where the fishermen and the sailors simply wanted their roads fixed, fell on deaf ears.

As it turned out, this was just one more conflict of principle between us among a series that surfaced later, and it should have warned me of future anguish. I sensed the climax being forced upon me, but I remained a team player, working to ensure that our individual effort and collective results enhanced the party and the country.

In opposing unity with Guyana, I was not prepared to jump from colonialism to communism. Nor did I see how we in St. Vincent would fit into the racial conflict of separate parties for Indians and blacks. In the Paget Farm Rebellion, I sought the triumph of argument over arms. Anguilla was a case of people accusing the government of benign neglect. Fortunately, my stock at home was rising among the farmers with success in marketing their produce alone.

Meanwhile we were moving out of our colonial status. The Administrator Hywel George guided us along the way. I had fended off association with Guyana: we would become an associated state with Britain. The English experts drafted our Constitution. I was absolutely disgusted when my constituency, the Grenadines, were called "the dependencies of St. Vincent". I sponsored tourism promotion, naming us St. Vincent *and* the Grenadines. Such was the genesis of the name of our country. The constitutional conference was plain sailing.

Sir Ellis Clarke, a refined London University-educated advocate, diplomat and eventual President of Trinidad and Tobago, was relegated to the second tier of celebrities for our statehood celebrations. Premier Milton Cato had made his personal selection of dignitaries and friends for the official banquet at Young Island. More invitees were turning up than the hotel could host, so it was with a sense of great relief that the Cabinet accepted my offer to entertain the Second 11 on my verandah at Casson Hill at my own expense. All other Ministers were going to the big show.

Sir Ellis, accompanied by Lady Clarke, was representing Trinidad and Tobago. He was then no more than Chairman of BWIA, but he was the personal representative of Dr. Eric Williams, the Prime Minister. My wife Pat and I ensured that we had a better wine selection than the other banquet with our spill-over from the Frangi stocks. Our French wine came down from Martinique in the holds of the sloops chilled to carry red snappers from the Grenadines, a trade of fish one way and wine in return, in which the French were certainly not disadvantaged.

Sir Ellis remembered that party. When I became Premier and was in Trinidad for the Caricom Heads of Government in the sessions where we recognized Cuba, Sir Ellis had become President and was hosting the leaders for a dinner at the official residence. I had gone off to meet my constituents from Union Island who were working in Trinidad – the Selbys, the Hutchinsons, the Wilsons and the Johns. They were prominent stevedores on the Port of Spain waterfront.

To my utter embarrassment, the dinner was held up until I arrived, but the guests were not unduly upset, as it turned out, because Trinidad and Tobago never served more champagne than during the tenure of Sir Ellis. His Muslim successors kept a dry palace. I apologized to Dr. Williams, the Prime Minister, explaining that in fact I was cultivating his PNM supporters from my constituency.

"Ellis insisted," he said. "I don't know what you did to him."

Sir Ellis's (or was it Lady Clarke's) unnecessary return of my hospitality, keeping the entire lot of Caribbean Prime Ministers waiting to dine, was rather touching. My friendship with Sir Ellis and his wife continued to blossom after that first lunch I hosted for our statehood celebrations. He always remembered it.

But there was also another party for statehood. Colin Tennant, pleased with his concessions in Mustique, threw a grand party. The Vincentian workers gobbled up the food, but not so a man nicknamed "Old Trimmingham" in the village. I asked him the next day why he did not come to the party.

"If the English have anything for me," he said, "they should bring it to my home."

He gave me a lesson for life. All that I would negotiate for the poor should be delivered to their door!

12

Running as an Independent
(1972 to 1974)

One universal truth about politics, in the islands and beyond, is enshrined in the politician's prayer: "My enemies I can take care of, but God protect me from my friends." All this I was to experience in association with other political parties and in the creation of my own.

Success in government breeds jealousy, and failure, sometimes, delivers its just reward. Breaking into new markets for arrowroot, shipping the bananas in boxes so that they could reach European supermarket shelves in excellent condition, creating a new environment for practical cooperation in our region, all for the benefit of the government to which I belonged, yielded praise in some circles, and suspicion in others.

As Minister of Lands, I had produced a plan for the expansion of the overcrowded town of Barroualie into the neighbouring estate at Keartons, only to be deemed interfering by another Minister. And, voting with the Opposition, to ensure the lowering of the voting age to 18 from 21 before, and not after, the elections, made me a marked man. My objection to the sacking of a ministerial friend did not help.

I also realized that tardiness in developing a program for electricity in Union Island, with Bequia and Mustique's supply already in full swing, exposed my electoral flanks in the south.

I was alone. I had to decide my political future. I decided to resign from the Government. The Labour Party called a meeting and expelled me. Only one voice was raised for me, that of the insurance broker Cyprian Hypolyte who loved to campaign with me. The parliament was quickly dissolved, assuming that I did not have enough time to campaign for re-election outside the Party.

As noted in the previous chapter, throughout my boyhood and up to the beginning of my political career my beloved Grenadines were known as "dependencies" of St. Vincent, and in the very first publication my

Ministry of Tourism sponsored, I launched the name St. Vincent *and* the Grenadines, which, at independence, became our official title. The citizens of the Grenadines had tired of their "dependency" appellation, for, indeed, we took care of ourselves. We were certainly not dependent for our livelihood: the sailors worked the world's seas and oceans, and we fed ourselves through seasonal toil in corn, peas and cassava for our farine, sumptuously enhanced with an abundant supply of fish, lobster and conch.

The peasants in St. Vincent looked to the mountains, and our maritime culture focused on the horizon and distant lands. Indeed, my father, the first navigator in the islands, knew the route to Curaçao and Aruba where he took many Vincentians away from the cotton fields to construct the refineries in the 1930s.

From the inception of adult suffrage, eliminating the right to vote based solely on property ownership, our first mass-based party, the Eighth Army of Liberation, practised musical chairs in parliament, and along the way, floor-crossing continued to be a surprise. Clive Tannis, Herman Young, and Samuel Slater all crossed the floor.

Such were the early experiments in democracy in the colonial era. The two political parties, the Labour Party and the Peoples Political Party (which had stoned and desecrated my first political meeting in the city) now had the field to themselves. This time, though, I had a seat in parliament. As in the marriage ceremony, the intention was: to have and to hold.

The London tears that accompanied my secret meeting with the Attorney General in England had not been in vain. Colonialism had given way to statehood. The Parliament was expanded to 13 seats. Tears and other loneliness had also preceded my present predicament. Early in my time in the Executive Council; for example, a row with the doctor in my constituency, an American for whom we had to legislate away the restrictive provisions that allowed only UK training to be recognized, was undermining my status over the shortage of drugs, for which we were all responsible, and the Council was not taking my predicament seriously. I took the day off, drove to the foothills of the Soufrière Mountain and walked alone beyond the coconut plantation, beyond the lush bamboos and into the tropical forest until I reached the clearing of wide slabs of stones with a stream trickling through. I lay on my back, looked through the clearing to the sky, rolled over and drank the pure water in the stream. My scientific training had eroded much of the naivety out of my Christian faith, but faith I knew, and especially at that moment, faith was needed, and deep down I had come to my own deep spiritual understanding: the kingdom of Heaven is within you.

Now jealousy surrounded me in Cabinet, though I was popular with the business community and the farmers. The Chief Minister had objected to my leading another arrowroot mission to the United States, but the self-made planter Basil Balcombe prevailed. Our arrowroot I discovered was needed for carbonless paper in the early computer industry. I guaranteed production. I settled a dispute too in New York between the dock unions, the ship and the arrowroot purchaser relating to our exports being frozen in a snow-storm. The disputes between my colleagues the Minister of Health and Education J.L. Eustace and Chief Minister Cato led to the former's dismissal. I sensed that colleagues were disappointed that I did not perish when I climbed the volcano to inspect an incipient eruption. And I was making no headway with electrification in the southern Grenadines. So I resigned from the Government.

I set out on a comprehensive tour of all the islands of the Grenadines, visiting every home. In the village of Ashton, beneath the majestic peaks of Olympus and Parnassus, on the steps of the Harvey family a child brought the news: "Parliament is dissolved."

"God has delivered them into our hands," I offered to the gathered friends.

"You will have to be an Independent," they advised, "but talk to them."

A group of young intellectuals, calling themselves the Education Forum of the People, which had emerged out of the group that regularly met on a bridge to discuss the social agenda, visited me for a talk. They liked my style, and I would like to think, my substance. Before becoming a Minister I had slept in the home of Dr. Kenneth John; Arnhim Eustace, the young economist, had helped me with the statistics in the publication on agricultural exports I had sent on to my old Institute in London; Parnel Campbell, not yet a lawyer, but destined to become my longest-serving Attorney General, was also among them; so was Kerwyn Morris, a biologist. They were all graduates from Canadian universities. The "Black Power" images coming out of Trinidad were filtering through the Caribbean and some of this settled on the group. My attention to the Education Forum had earned me ridicule in Cabinet as the "Archbishop of Black Power".

They arranged a meeting with the hierarchy of the PPP to meet with me at Luther Robertson's Lyric. Luther was the agent of National Bulk Carriers for the recruitment of seamen and was therefore popular in my constituency. Our Labour Government had nationalized his contract for private-sector management of the port, without compensation, and the legislation was an outstanding encumbrance disallowed by the Colonial Secretary and therefore not *kosher*. The language was something like "Her Majesty's Government will not exercise the power of approval."

We went into Othneil Sylvester's legal chambers for the meeting. I had written to Joshua seeking membership in his PPP. Under the lingering influence of my former opponent in the Grenadines, Clive Tannis, who had planned to run for a seat in the mainland, the PPP came to no agreement with me. In retrospect their rejection of my overture was to change the political landscape of our country and region for all time.

The Labour Party selected one of my distant relations working in the fishing department under me, Errol Ollivierre, to run against me in the Grenadines. They figured that the large Ollivierre family, the largest in the constituency, would abandon me. I told my relation and opponent Errol that he should collect the $15,000 offered by the Labour Party before nomination day, since after that day he would be abandoned. (He lost and never got the money as I had predicted.) His father, the very distinguished gentlemen, Louis Ollivierre, sailed with us on *Friendship Rose* to sign my nomination paper in Union.

My Permanent Secretary in the Ministry, George Leigertwood, revealed to me how the Premier, having appointed himself to replace me as Minister of Trade, Agriculture and Tourism, turned up in full glory to assume control. He visited every department, and ingratiated himself with the staff before closing the door on himself in my former office.

I had once played on the Leader of the Opposition, borrowing a pair of dentures from a dentist, and holding them up to taunt him during a debate in parliament. I pointed out that with the extraction of all his teeth, the honourable member's argument was toothless. These dentures were left in my drawer. They were instantly construed by the visiting Premier as a curse I had left behind.

I thoroughly enjoyed myself campaigning as an Independent. Canouan had secured cheap lands for homes, Union's secondary school was under construction and a jetty had been built, there were telephones in three islands, and the seamen of Mayreau were getting jobs. Mustique was moving ahead. Colin Tennant had invited me to London to meet with Viyella, the fabric people. They wanted all the Sea Island cotton we could produce, but I could not see how at the price being offered we could overcome the pests and diseases, and replace bananas. Princess Margaret had accepted the offer of a plot of land in

Mustique. So Colin held a party at his home in Chelsea redecorated with myriad glass in shades of blue and turquoise, reflecting the colours of the sea and beaches around Mustique, and Princess Margaret graced the occasion. I was delighted to have her presence in my constituency.

One moonlit night in Union, at the green corner crossroads in Ashton, I spoke solidly for three hours. Teaching had taught me that a sip of water sustained the timbre of the voice. The old ladies had brought their chairs, the children were in their laps or on the ground at their feet, the men peeped out from the rum shops, the porches and verandahs were full. Eric Williams, their idol from their contact with Trinidad, had made his name in Woodford Square. This green corner was to be my square. I took the crowd through the failures of the Federation, the institutions being created around the Treaty of Rome and our feeble copy in Carifta. I explained how I had extricated the Labour Party from the statehood trap set for us in the earlier constitution. I told them what I had seen in the south of France where tourism was only money vested in buildings and there was certainly nothing to touch the God-given beauty of our Grenadines. It was vision that created inventions, it was vision that created opportunity, it was vision that created wealth.

I still remember the spirit of that meeting. It was one of the greatest of my political life and certainly the most seminal.

I recall a signal event the next day. I was resting and lying on the grass in the shade behind a rum shop, having bought an ample supply of six-dollars-a-bottle smuggled whisky. An old lady, Tanty Ma, well into her seventies, passed the rum shop. The men inside accosted her.

"Tanty Ma, you like the meeting last night. We want to hear you!"

Tanty Ma could not see me, but I could hear her.

"The meeting was all right, but I did not like how it finished."

"How you mean?"

"The girls in Ashton," she continued, "they are not bright. I see fellows come with a jeep and take away Son Mitchell after the meeting. If I was a young girl he would have to sleep with me. I was not going to allow a young man with all that brains slip away. He would have had to sleep with me and when I was done with him for the night he would have to come back. Tanty Ma would have had had a bright son to look after me today."

"It's not too late, Tanty Ma," the men in the rum shop told her. "He is lying on the ground behind the shop."

I rose to greet the old lady. She greeted me in a firm embrace. I told her that I was sorry I wasn't around when she was young. Politicians around the world face many temptations, but seldom an opportunity so unfortunately lost through a disparity in age. When I visited to celebrate Tanty Ma's 100th birthday, bringing her greetings from the Queen, she was still telling how she loved me, and repeating how many amorous encounters we had missed.

John Compton, Premier of St. Lucia, was in Bequia on holiday and joined me for a rousing rally in Paget Farm. He loved to have me negotiate on bananas with him in London and the crowd relished his presence.

And so I won the election as an Independent member for the Grenadines. I suppose I am the last of the lone rangers. My opponents won six seats each, and I had held the Grenadines against all comers, winning 57 per cent of the vote. Immediately petitions on irregularities in other polls were lodged in the courts, but panic seized their ranks. It was far easier to capture me and gain an instant majority.

Errol Barrow, Prime Minister of Barbados, was on the line. "Son, you have what it takes to be a Premier. Hold firm!"

The new telephone service inaugurated in Bequia was thoroughly tested. My line was hot. I listened to callers until my elbow became sore, resting on the edge of the book shelf with the telephone. Kingmakers in abundance, but none with Errol's message from St. Vincent. They never declared their individual mission, but it was clear that they sought to influence me for personal gain. A politician who is not cautious with hypocrites is doomed to oblivion sooner than necessary.

The Frangipani Hotel bar, the night the vote was announced, over-flowed. All Bequia seemed to be there as though I had already captured the government. My supporters knew the drifters from the other parties and were chanting them down. I pleaded their forgiveness, handed them drinks, and began my campaign for the next election.

Days passed and no government was formed. Then the pilgrimages began to arrive from St. Vincent. Quite unnecessarily, I think in retrospect, I told the press that I had gone fishing. For the remainder of my political life, I became "the Bequia Fisherman," a derogatory term that slipped into memory when I attracted millions from the Japanese for our fishing industry, long before fellow governments discerned my strategy.

The Labour emissaries came first, led by Levi Latham, an affable peasant, controlling the Marriaqua constituency while he farmed his wife's estate. He was a friend to whom I did not want to say goodbye, as he had sided with me on the dismissal of our Education Minister. I did not think he spoke with the authority of the Party. The boss was needed himself, was our message. By this time I had gathered my kitchen

Cabinet around me, sailmakers, shipwrights, whalers, sea captains. Not a group to be fooled or trifled with.

The PPP team arrived on two separate boats with the leader Joshua and his Secretary General Owen Walker on the second ship. Joshua was picked up by the Police Inspector, St. Clair Robinson, a jovial character but a firm disciplinarian, who during the Second World War had defended Kingstown against German submarines in a rowing boat with a .303 rifle. He had no use for the Labour Party as they had connived with the police chief to ship him into the Grenadines where the Chevrolet, a gift from his brother in Brooklyn, could not be driven.

"Son Mitchell never attacked you, Josh, during the whole campaign," he told the leader.

I invited the intellectual trio from the Educational Forum to be my guests and advisers during the impasse. We held the meeting in my unfinished home. I was offered retention of the Ministry of Trade, Agriculture and Tourism where it was thought I had done a great job. I suggested that I wanted all election petitions withdrawn, and that we should form a national government in coalition with the other side.

All this was to lead nowhere. Two decades of hostility, one side posturing as the right kind of people to lead the country forward, and the other side responding with contempt while they cultivated the hearts of the poor, did not produce the ingredients for any cocktail the people would relish. Self-serving selfishness had yet to be exposed.

No agreement. "Fine," said Errol, "go into Parliament, sit in Opposition and choose your issues."

The Governor General, Sir Rupert John, my old teacher of the romantic poets and British conquest of empire, quite rightly reappointed the existing government. Errol Barrow was on the line again. "I called Joshua and told him that I trust you to work with him, but that he must get his men to join him in signing an affidavit expressing confidence in you, and have it signed by a Justice of the Peace." So Joshua and his PPP team agreed to form the Alliance Government with me, and I was the agreed Premier.

Amidst sentiments ranging from caution to relish among my new colleagues, I was sworn in as Premier, but not without a Shakespearean analysis by Joshua, something to the effect that insecurity is man's mortal enemy.

I became Premier also with responsibility for Trade, Agriculture and Tourism. Joshua took the Ministry of Finance. Othneil Sylvester, the lawyer in whose chambers we held the first abortive meeting, became Minister of Communications and Works. With him I developed a close working relationship. And so we settled down. I offered Joshua the Premier's residence to live in, but he would not abandon his modest home. His wife, however, "Mammy," as she was widely known, was delighted to commandeer the grounds with all its fruit trees, breadfruit, mangoes, grapefruit and avocadoes, and she was not beyond keeping a few pigs on the compound. I moved into Shrewsbury House.

The Carifta Council in Guyana continued to demand my attention and I enjoyed going to Guyana. My Chivas Regal, illegal in that country, had smoothed my relations with Forbes, the Prime Minister. Importing hard woods from Guyana to expand the hotel and build our first home brought me in touch with the Indian industrialists. Dinners in their homes, with curried goat, shrimp and roti, were as good as any West Hampstead restaurant.

At the home of Sam Ghany and his wife, I cultivated the friendship of Cheddi Jagan. His wife Janet had visited Bequia and stayed one night at our hotel, an expenditure that led my critics to ascribe communist leanings to me. I learnt about Guyana first hand. Burnham while meticulously sticking to his "socialist" image by nationalizing the means of production, had undermined Jagan's communism, leaving him with only his rhetoric and the undying loyalty of the poor Indian minority he represented.

Guyana in those days had, apart from its ancient Stabroek market – the only public market I knew selling gold – a great selection of shops. The nascent garment industry was yielding good cotton shirts at wonderful prices. I found a great shop for lights and lampshades run by an old Portuguese man. He got to know my face as I visited at each council meeting and bought a shade or two. It so happened that I did not have enough money to buy one shade I fancied, so I requested that it be listed among his future orders.

"Take it, Mr. Mitchell," he said in a quiet voice. "You can pay me when you come again. I shall not be ordering again. The people who used to buy beautiful lights are leaving this country. Business is dying. One day the lights will go out in Guyana. I too am leaving."

What prophecy! That sentence, "the lights will one day go out in Guyana," haunted me and still haunts me as I think of Guyana three decades later. As I travel through Africa, Latin America, when I see the devastation that comes in the wake of stupid left-wing policies, I became fearful for our own Caribbean.

I was appointed to settle disputes in Guyana, but even as I listened to the current arguments, I remembered the wise Portuguese and the lampshade that he credited me.

Antigua experienced a change of government. The new leader, Walters, was savage in his criticism of the old order. He thought that in the same way he had "disposed" of V.C. Bird, it was time for the likes of Bradshaw, Eric Gairy and Eric Williams to go! I asked Eric Gairy what he thought of the remarks.

"A bird of passage, Brother Mitch," he said, prophetically.

Eric had attended our opening of Parliament, where unfortunately the Governor was booed. He decided to make a response in the throne speech. "Fire him," Eric advised me with the words hardly out of the Governor's mouth.

After such grandstanding, Walters deigned to send his brother to make requests of Williams. Seething with quiet and dignified rage, Williams had him ushered into his office to present his letter. Williams listened. When the White Hall silence descended on the hapless messenger, Williams simply pointed to the wastepaper basket. "Put it there."

I understand that the same destiny, much later, awaited the correspondence from Grenada's leftist revolutionary Maurice Bishop.

At home my first challenge as Premier was a prison riot. Self-righteousness all too readily relieves the boredom of confinement, and with the slightest encouragement the status quo will be challenged. The leader of the majority in our coalition, Mr. Joshua, was to remain eternally in mental opposition, willing to side with any cause challenging authority. Living in a house overlooking the prison, it came to my knowledge that his finger was in the pie. At the Cabinet meeting it was decided that we would both visit the prison after lunch. Before the appointed time I had armed police outside the prison gates.

Joshua and I went in and confronted the warders. They had little to say, except, "Things got out of control." I ordered a prison search by the warders with the police at their backs. So the warders had to do the job between the hostile prisoners and the police. All kinds of knives, cutlasses and tools of various description and length, along with cigarettes and US cash were found. Items missing from Haddon Hotel over the hill were retrieved.

So it seemed the prisoners were in and out at nights with the connivance of the warders. The weapons, on display at the police headquarters, sent a message of quick confidence in our alliance.

My second challenge was over a land reform lecture I had given in Trinidad about the dangers of nationalization and collectivism. The author, I presume, had to be exposed by the PPP. A delegation from the heartland of Joshua's constituency in Greggs, Lauders and Lowmans turned up in the compound beneath the Cabinet room with placards calling for the acquisition of the Lauders Estate. I sought an excuse, ignored the smirk in the Cabinet room and met with the demonstrators, thanking them for their suggestions with an assurance of action. In the continuing Cabinet I sought authority to meet with the planter, Fred Hadley.

Fred was a merchant in town at Hadley Brothers, doing well in the sale of agricultural chemicals. He quoted his price and I called on the Minister of Finance, Joshua, to pay up. With some show of arrogance, Joshua declared that that was a problem for his colleague in Government, the Financial Secretary, whom he insisted to be his sworn enemy. (Joshua still used the term "they." I could not get him to accept the principle of "we.") It really was an unbridgeable divide between trade union rabble-rouser and Minister of Finance, one that, I am afraid, old Joshua never really crossed.

At the Lauders banana-boxing plant, there was a single ice-box, with a slab of ice transported from the city, to cool the beers and stout needed by the sweating farmers and truckers after they had delivered their fruit. With the credit available from the Banana Association, production boomed. A prosperous community began to grow. Hundreds of refrigerators were shipped in to the new homes. I once asked a farmer from the area how well he was doing with the land I had secured for them. "I received none," he said, "as I had land before. But what I am glad about is that now everybody has bananas, thieving done!"

In Haiti, it was my turn to give the feature lecture at a Caribbean Tourism Conference. Rex Nettleford from Jamaica was also speaking, but I recall best his abhorrence of the tours laid on. "I am a bad tourist. I don't want to see sights."

I chose the theme "To Hell with Paradise." My wife Pat accompanied me to Haiti. After her studies in the history of art, she wanted to witness the Haitian painters at work, and with our new experience of tourism at our hotel in Bequia, getting the feel of how a tourism policy should be directed, she agreed to collaborate on my presentation.

My basic idea was a rejection of the high-rise Miami model as the vision of paradise. Our islands were all marketing paradises, and to my mind even then, the model had nothing to do with the unique Caribbean style we should be creating. Hell broke loose in the press conference. "In one stroke you have destroyed all the marketing we have been writing about!" "You can't be an hotelier!" "Do the other tourism ministers agree with you!" "Where do you go from here to get investors!" And so on.

I explained that I did not want to replace the Miami image with a single alternate architecture. I wanted diversity, but diversity adjusted to the Caribbean scenery. Bring in all the luxury you want to attract tourists, but I don't want a bunch of identical units lacking individuality at our beachfronts.

With some timidity Pat and I, after this blistering attack, went to the reception being hosted by Baby Doc Duvalier. One journalist approached me. In writing his copy it had struck him that my thoughts were amongst the most original he had heard for a long time. "Your stuff makes good copy. You are really smart." I don't think I ever made the front page of the *New York Times* again.

We were in a grand hall in the Palace standing in a horse-shoe arrangement, with Baby Doc at the heart of it all. Beside him was Robert Bradshaw, steeped in the love of the black Haitian revolution that my friend C.L.R. James had so gloriously described in his book *The Black Jacobins*, and a purchaser and collector of Haitian art, standing between me and the young President, his wife and his mother.

The champagne toast was sounded by the protocol officer. "The President for Life, President Duvalier." All, bar none, including me and my wife, responded to the chorus.

But the President for Life did not drink his champagne. He raised it only to his lips and then handed it behind his head to the military officer behind him.

"If he can't drink his own champagne," I intoned to Bob Bradshaw, "I shall not be drinking this either. I have champagne in Bequia."

Bob grabbed Pat by the arm and led her away, saying something to the effect that her husband was insulting the greatest man in our region. They apparently had more useful discussions about Haitian art. We bought two pieces of banana art, made out of the dried sheath of the banana leaf, which portrayed lively dancing, and this became the genesis of the banana art in St. Vincent. Pat also bought, directly from an undiscovered artist in the hills, two pieces with leaves of plants transfigured into birds. The artist, Sepierre, later made his name in *Time* magazine and his prices jumped beyond our means.

Carifta, the Caribbean Free Trade Area, was beginning to put a smile on the Caribbean Conference. Jamaica was on board, while Eric Williams and Willie Demas of Trinidad were urging faster movement towards deepening Caribbean integration. I got along well with Eric Williams. I escaped his disdain for fools. From time to time he arranged a lunch or dinner in the far corner of the Le Boucan dining room at the Hilton Hotel, a meal that always concluded with a $20-dollar tip for our waitress (a good tip in those days). We dined alone. He sought my assessment of the East Caribbean States. He liked my idea that we should seek collective independence. I worked out with him how we should do an economic analysis and then take the constitutional challenge at the second stage. He agreed to provide $20,000 for stage one.

Early in the life of my Alliance I had hosted a weekend meeting in Petit St. Vincent with Compton and Gairy on freedom of movement. We named it the Petit St. Vincent Initiative. My confidence in the success of this venture was encouraged by an editorial at home the week before urging that I demonstrate my desire for political union. Gairy promptly and quite correctly disabused me of any optimism, saying that we should plan to deal with opposition including the media. He was right. Why did we leave out Dominica? Why did we not include this or that, and so on? By the time we met in Grenada to resume plans, Gairy had lost interest and announced that Grenada would pursue independence.

Within three months of being sworn in as Premier, I accepted an invitation to lecture to CADEC (Christian Action for Development in the East Caribbean) at the St. Augustine Campus of the UWI (University of the West Indies), in a building constructed on an old student football field. In my introduction, I told the students the lesson in racial equality I had learnt on the soccer field from a Sierra Leonean, and hoped they were learning more to equip them for life than I had learnt outside the classroom. I didn't think they appreciated the message. My talk on land reform though was hot stuff. It set out my policy position on land reform, pontificating on how our economics needed to be restructured to expand purchasing power and create a property-owning democracy. At the height of the Cold War, I was staking my position on the centre ground, engendering animosity both from the communists who wanted this target of deprivation sustained and the plantocracy who were nervous about my liberal beliefs.

Already fascinated by my capture of the premiership, the Trinidad media readily reflected my message. Here was someone whose appointment as a Head of Government was no more than a shaky constitutional manoeuvre. Yet a challenging policy was already issuing forth. Moreover, alarm bells sounded as I was enlisting the support of the church in my cause. By the time the energy crisis, with its frustration with OPEC, descended a year later I was going further, calling for diversification in agriculture, more intensive use of the land and import substitution. I devised slogans like "No culture without agriculture," and "Dig a better life." My coalition partners instinctively recoiled.

"That Mitchell, if we let him put down roots, we will not uproot him easily."

A new era of relations with our southern neighbour Venezuela took shape with the joint venture between the Windwards Governments and Papelera Industrial. The banana-boxing plant was opened with flourish in St. Lucia, the same weekend as the Halcyon Days Hotel and the Hewanorra International Airport.

Shortly after becoming Premier the Venezuelan Government invited me for an official visit to cement and expand relations. Dr. Aristides Calvani, the Foreign Minister, had spent some of his youth in Trinidad and was anxious, as we were, to deepen our relations. They wanted to award me the Order of Simon Bolivar. The British representative in Kingstown summoned me to a meeting, and reminded me that as we were not Independent, I fell under the rubric of British diplomatic protocol. Expressed in simple language, this meant that there was a convention dating back to Queen Anne which ruled that British Ministers did not accept foreign dog-collars, so I should be guided accordingly.

Off I went with my wife Pat to Caracas on a Venezuelan plane. I was surprised to see how little time it took. There was my first red carpet, and a guard of honour, awaiting me. I laid my wreath at the foot of the monument for Simon Bolivar, and had pleasant discussions with President Caldera on the way forward. Then it was brought to my attention how disappointed Venezuela was that I had refused their highest honour. Such was the message, apparently, in the communiqué from London. No such thing, I assured them. Accordingly, a meeting was arranged at the British Embassy that evening in the garden after dinner: a Venezuelan protocol officer, the British Ambassador and myself attended. I said, "I will take the award, thank you."

So the next night I was decorated with the Order of Simon Bolivar, Gran Cordon, in the presence of Cabinet, Generals and Admirals, and the top echelon of the land.

My tour took me into the interior to see the newly constructed dams, the new cities, and the new farms in Valencia flourishing with citrus. It looked as though the oil wealth was pouring into the countryside. There seemed to be waves of prosperity everywhere.

Politics is like sailing. You have a course before you sail.

Canada has always enjoyed a bond with the West Indies. Early in the last century Canada's tourism in the Caribbean rested on the famed "lady boats," *Lady Nelson*, *Lady Hawkins*, *Lady Rodney* and *Lady Drake*. My mother's uncle, Timmy Gooding, was one of their captains and

I remember pictures of him in his golden epaulettes. The Second World War put an end to this luxurious cruise among the islands when a German U-boat that had escaped into the Atlantic, reported to be fuelled by Vichy supporters in Martinique, shelled *Lady Nelson* inside Castries harbour.

My stepfather, Alf Baynes, the Harbour Master at the time, scrambled my mother and brothers and sister into his Morris Minor and took off into the hills. The ship was looted. Wonderful Canadian ice cream was not allowed to melt. A St. Lucian peasant, jealous of the furniture in city houses, secured a refrigerator to take home to his village, to hold his clothes.

The West Indian Federation received more Canadian largesse. Hankering after the sentimental journey on the "lady boats," we were delighted to receive two new ships, symbolically named in the culture of the two lands, *Federal Palm* and *Federal Maple*. By the time I became Premier in the 1970s, the boats were in massive debt. One of them ran aground in Jamaica, damaging the rudder. A ministerial meeting was called to solve the problem; ample proof to me with my family background in shipping that governments could not run a ship. I proposed that our governments get out of shipping. Subsidies had reached unimaginable heights. These federal ships were the only ones losing money in the Caribbean. Every seaman knows where to find a bargain in every port, but our captains were purchasing all stores in Trinidad. The philosophy of subsidies for sea transport found ready adherents in later advocates for state-managed airlines.

But not all Canadian aid produced laudatory results. Canada gave us our first coastguard, a second-hand wooden fishing boat. On a visit to Mayreau, I discovered a very sombre constituency, as there were no drinks to share from smuggled bounty. My constituents felt threatened by the presence of a coastguard limiting their smuggling. I had to allay their fears. "Come on, the boat's engine is noisy. Can't you hear it coming?" Out came the drinks. At Independence we were embraced both by the Canadian officials in the World Bank, and by the Irish in the IMF – a dispensation guaranteed to produce a lunch in Washington once a year.

More fruitful were the Canada–Caribbean conferences with every new Canadian Prime Minister. I tried to get Brian Mulroney interested in helping me build a centre for the performing arts, only to be strongly advised by my close friend in Canadian diplomatic circles, De Montigny Marchand, that one does not make those kinds of requests as a developing country. Canada would help in productive enterprises or institutional strengthening, but not in promoting our aspirations in the field of culture.

Canadian Finance Ministers made every effort to cultivate us. They carried our message into circles where we had no standing. Paul Martin, Jr., in my last World Bank/IMF Meetings in Prague, listened sympathetically to our country's banana and sugar travails. He trusted that we would be honest in offshore financial dealings. The Barbados experience with its double taxation agreement with Canada had been mutually satisfactory. We had to find a way to keep democracy alive and beyond the drug culture encouraged by the offshore banking practises of some of our fellow Caribbeans.

No shame had been worse for our leadership than after the Canadian-Caribbean Summit in Jamaica. Then, the Chief Minister of the Turks and Caicos had been videoed in a Miami hotel with a lady in a negligee and afterwards receiving a bribe. We all as leaders made noises on his behalf. But in London the British invited me to a room upstairs in a building not far from the House of Commons to see my colleague on the video greedily wolfing sandwiches, the glimpse of the negligee, and the drug money stuffed in pockets. What a disgrace! When my turn came for accusations, and the American Embassy published that unsubstantiated rumours had indicated that all political parties in St. Vincent received drug money, I invited the Ambassador and the DEA point man to my home in Bequia. I hosted a reception for all the Americans in Bequia, dozens of them. My hotel was full, so the DEA friend stayed with me.

"Let these gossiping Americans tell you all about me. If one of them can tell you I am in drugs, I shall resign. My family has little cash, but we are propertied. We are what you call in America, old money. You can bug my house. You can tap my phone. Please let me know when you substantiate that I am trafficking drugs! I am a descendant of captains, not passengers!"

The Colonial Office in London, not unnaturally disappointed at the failure of the West Indies Federation, the loss of valuable colonies in Africa, the Middle East and the Far East, and the territories of Trinidad, Jamaica and Guyana opting out of British control, had to devise a strategy to lessen the drain of the remaining Caribbean states under their control on the UK Treasury. With statehood came the loss of "grant-in-aid" of administration. And so one day the letter came from the Bank of England informing us on a single sheet of paper that the revered institution would no longer guarantee our currency. We had to balance our books.

The Council of Premiers of the West Indies Associated States met and appointed Bradshaw and myself to meet with the Governor of the Bank of England. Our meeting was scheduled for late morning. We were ushered into the prestigious surroundings and graciously received. We stated our concern. They listened and took us to lunch. Bradshaw was left to do the talking. My brain was racing through all kinds of doomsday scenarios. Bradshaw produced an old glass bead which he claimed was one of those used in Africa for the exchange of slaves. The bead was passed around. Its significance was lost on me on this occasion. Bradshaw pocketed his bead. We returned home and developed our currency authority, determined to ensure that henceforth we would hold the equivalent of the value of our reserves in US currency.

October 1973 and the energy crisis descended on us in the small islands without notice like yearly hurricanes, the only difference being that this hurricane was not a Caribbean hit-and-miss affair. All islands were struck. I knew from my background in soil chemistry that the price of nitrogen in fertilizer would go through the roof, and fertilizer prices would rocket. The cost of food would escalate, and the cost of living was going to soar.

I issued a policy statement. In the crisis we would have to reassess our essentials – food, clothes and shelter. The only area where we could escape the looming disaster was the production of our own food. Back to the land!

We assembled a task force, economists like Arnhim Eustace, Kingsley Layne, Basil Williams and people from Customs like Sammy Joshua and Jeoffrey English, along with a Home Economics teacher, Adeline John. We went through the Customs tariff and drew up a formidable list of fresh and tinned imported foods to be banned. We could grow what potatoes we needed with seed imported from Holland, and export the surplus. We could make more furniture. We could produce all our own meat, vegetables, jams and chutneys.

So I thought. Hardly had our beautiful new potatoes come out of the ground than Geest, with their extensive potato fields in England and empty ships coming for bananas, slashed the price and dumped potatoes on our markets.

I met often with Eric Williams. He sought my views on agriculture and where I thought fertilizer prices would go. He was supremely confident. He was beginning to see the endless opportunities for Trinidad's oil wealth under the OPEC umbrella. We discussed how the Caribbean should respond to the energy crisis, Trinidad being a beneficiary. I pressed for food security. The Caribbean Food Corporation was born.

One of our lunch meetings was aborted by the tropical storm Alma. My plane had to be diverted en route to Tobago and arrived at night in Trinidad when Williams was entertaining a West African President. He adjourned a Cabinet meeting the next day to be with me, saying that he would have the coastguard plane take me home.

We again discussed the commission which I was setting up to study the economic and constitutional future of the associated states. At home, the attention Williams paid me exacerbated the jealousy seething in my coalition. How could Williams be sending me home on a plane? Word reached me that Joshua was saying, "He's behaving like a Head of Government without a party behind him!"

In our region, apart from the Food Corporation, the Carifta Council was trying to come up with strategies to offset the perils of OPEC. Lightborne of Jamaica was dreaming up a bauxite cartel. A weekend meeting was called in Barbados with Jamaica, Trinidad and Guyana to deal with sugar. I recall that Errol Barrow, Errol Mahabir and Burnham were there. They were also wondering how to deal with the associated states against the independent Caribbean countries as we moved from Carifta to the Caribbean Community. I told Errol to find Joshua, as he was in Barbados, a suggestion to which he responded that Joshua would be welcomed at lunch the next day, but I was needed for "serious" discussion. I should have known that all these manoeuvres were weakening my hold on the Premiership.

I went by special charter to the meeting being held at Sam Lord's Castle. The independent Caribbean countries were ready to establish diplomatic relations with Cuba. They were worried about some of us having to seek British approval for the creation of the Caribbean Community, Britain being responsible for the foreign affairs of the associated states. We had to secure British approval, which they considered an insult to the region. They were worried too about our sensitivities about being left out. I suggested that all governments at the Carifta Council level should participate in the creation of the instruments of the Community, and then the independent territories should sign the treaty. With the Community Treaty in place, we the associated states would seek approval of the British and we would sign subsequently.

I remember too we were watching the TV news during our meeting, observing Gairy in his white suit glaring at the trade unionists that had imposed an embargo on Grenada for its quest of independence. Forbes thought Gairy looked like Hitler.

Then the issue of creating the sugar cartel was raised. It did not take me long to advise against this one. "You'll succeed in discomforting Europeans with high prices for two summers only. When you do, they will produce beet sugar and your sugar prices will never rise again," was the essence of my advice, based not on politics but on my knowledge of agronomy.

We had also some important sessions in England. I attended the first meeting of Commonwealth Trade Ministers in London, when Britain announced her entry into Europe, and invited us to plan how we could benefit by her decision.

Then came our first meeting in Brussels with the Africans and the Pacific countries. We had prepared meticulously at the Carifta Council and our team in Brussels included Bradshaw from St. Kitts, Cameron Tudor and Barndford Taitt from Barbados, Sonny Ramphal from Guyana, and P.J. Patterson from Jamaica.

On the way to London, Bradshaw had brought along cases of whisky, brandy, vodka and gin. We were staying overnight in London at the Cumberland, the liquor stored in the baggage room. I tried to leave some behind, but Bradshaw would have none of it. He had correctly recognized that having the liquor supply meant that his suite in Brussels would be our conclave.

Our approach to Brussels won the Africans and Pacific to our side of the argument, and so Sonny Ramphal presented our united case to Europe, a procedure that in turn created the concept of the ACP, or African Caribbean and Pacific group of countries. The Europeans were paying attention to our development in trade, with aid geared to self-sustaining growth.

Sonny Ramphal, Cammie Tudor, Branford Tait, Willie Demas, P. J. Patterson and myself had brought about the ACP.

And so in due course was created the first Lomé Convention that was to prove one of our era's greatest efforts at co-operation between the rich and the needy. At the end of the meeting we were all going our own ways. In the hotel in Brussels, I chatted with some African politicians. They were off to Liège to look for guns. Or so they told me.

Sonny Ramphal really launched his international career with that ACP presentation to Europe. Guyana was driving onwards to becoming the Co-operative Republic with Forbes as President while Sonny secured the last knighthood from the Queen bestowed on a Guyanese citizen.

My cousin Vance (of whom I have spoken earlier with regard to his assistance in straightening out the family inheritance situation) invited me to Cornell University from time to time. I enjoyed Ithaca and rural America. He was getting well established in the wine industry in the United States, and had set up the university's first wine course. In recognition, he had received a set of gold wine glasses with the crest of the White House as a present in honour of his advice to the Nixon banquets. I once challenged his boast of the quality of California wine, but was surely disgraced in the tasting he set up in his Ithaca home with French and American wine. He had me lecture his graduates in Cornell on my philosophy of tourism in the Caribbean.

"Whatever happened to the chaos on the campus?" I asked him when on an earlier visit I predicted the total confusion of the Vietnam protests would ruin the place.

"It's all over: it brought down Johnson," he said.

I couldn't believe it. In our Caribbean when students and professors hold on to a rag, they didn't let go.

The American administration thought I needed some exposure. They awarded me three weeks in their Young Leaders Programme. I could choose where I wanted to go, what I wanted to see.

I chose:

1. A bit of US history: Boston and Philadelphia;
2. To understand the political system: Washington, the White House, and the Congress;
3. Out of curiosity: Cape Canaveral;
4. To refine my interest in animal husbandry: the King Ranch in Texas;
5. To understand tourism even more deeply: Las Vegas;
6. For sentimental reasons and my interest in wine: California to see if the American West Coast was as beautiful as Vancouver, and a trip to the state's Napa Valley to confirm or refute the truth put forth by my cousin in Cornell about the superior viticulture in the production of the new wines.

The large American seed-merchant firm, Burpee's in Philadelphia, was one of our suppliers, so I scheduled a visit to their operation to see if we could in some way turn business around and be a seed supplier instead of a user, cultivating something different at home. Another good idea still unfulfilled.

Washington meanwhile was in the thick of the Watergate scandal. My tour of the White House culminated in the evening, through an invitation from friends in Ottawa, with the Canadian Embassy reception where all eyes were glued on President Nixon on television.

My ascendancy to the Premiership had been somewhat anticipated by the Canadian High Commission in Barbados which had been following political fortunes in St. Vincent and reporting to Ottawa that the two main political parties were well balanced and with a little shift, Mitchell would be Premier. I learned subsequently in diplomatic circles that the typist had left out the 'f' in 'shift', only to get a reply from Ottawa asking about the constipation.

I thought it obvious that I should enlighten the Americans at the party pondering the results of the Nixon impasse. What a pity they did not have a provision in their constitution for a "no confidence" motion. Lo and behold, the next day word came from home that the exact motion was lodged at home against me. The Opposition thought it arrogant that I should leave the country for three weeks when a no-confidence motion had to be treated within two weeks.

So I lost my visit to Cape Canaveral and the King Ranch, went home to dispose of the motion at my government's expense, and resumed my American journey to Las Vegas.

Neon signs advertising weddings, divorces and breakfast anytime along the streets, and fortunes made and being lost, ushered me into the city of quickest gratification on earth. On the lavish bed in Caesar's Palace, I felt like a Roman Emperor, and Las Vegas was certainly a great place to fiddle. The young lady I ran into told me she was on probation from a court in California! Las Vegas certainly influenced me to keep casinos out of the Grenadines for a long time, and when we recanted, I put a threshold of a hundred-room hotel for the casino before a license was entertained. Our style of tourism without gambling survived.

On my return from the American experiences, I issued a letter of thanks, but commented that I thought that with the quality of California's wine it was time Pan American served the local vintage on international flights. More importantly, I came to the conclusion that our slender coalition, with only a single-seat majority in parliament (created essentially out of distaste with others) would become in time a breeding ground for mischief. Blend a tenuous alliance with internal jealousy, resentment and bribery becomes quite a reliable stalwart – in such a situation, tranquility readily gives way to turbulence.

I had always seized the opportunity to be out of the island if only to let the boss of the other side of the coalition assert his dominance. That apparently was not enough. He complained that the image accruing from my land reform program would mean that I could never be removed in the future. The prestige learned by performance in regional negotiations should have rested elsewhere. "If you leave Mitchell here too long, you will never get rid of him," Joshua kept saying.

I enjoyed working with the somewhat cantankerous old man. I respected the struggles that had moulded him. A schoolteacher of the old school, brought up on the "Royal readers," he loved his pithy and often gnomic quotations: "If I knew, is God's secret!" And when the bureaucrats proposed that guards at the port be made pensionable, he railed, "That port and customs is a bastion of fraud. They collect a pension every day." He had been charged for sedition in the period of his agitation for the sugar workers. He blasted the Attorney General, Keith Alleyne, with: "He charged me with sedition in a time of peace." To give him his due, a life of struggle against the plantocracy and colonialism had left an indelible mark of opposition in his veins. He loved jousting with the enemy: the Colonial Office; the Commissioner of Police; the Government. But he was the government, I was wont to tell him, and the Colonial Office had gone home. His confidant, Othneil Sylvester, Minister of Communications and Works, who had seen him through the constitutional conference in London, could only sigh: "Son, man, he has the devil in him."

The parlour games were harmless, but the policy decisions in our response to the energy crisis, the proliferation of food imports that our farmers could produce, linked to our back-to-the-land appeal, and the clarion call for our land reform program, alarmed the greedy merchants who anticipated a fall in their ill-gotten gains.

One Monday morning, my Cabinet Secretary George Leigertwood informed me on return from a Bequia weekend that the rumour was abroad that the leader of the other side of the coalition, Mr. Ebenezer Joshua and his wife Ivy, had both crossed the floor. A foreman of a road construction crew, nicknamed Red John, came to my office and said he had seen the gentleman counting wads of money in his McKies Hill home. I thought this strange, when another colleague, my Minister of Education Alphonso Dennie, the week before had announced that he had rejected a bribe to cross the floor, for which he had been congratulated by the soon-to-be-discovered defectors.

13

Collapse of a Coalition

A slender coalition with a one-seat majority became an obvious target. Alphonso Dennie had given up his tenure as a popular headmaster in a primary school for a political gamble. He became our Minister of Education and secured the establishment of the Petit Bordel School, the largest on the leeward coast. One of the opposing parliamentarians was entrusted with $75,000 in cash and made Dennie the offer to cross the floor. Dennie declined, even though the cash would have made him a home-owner. He reported the incident to me and to Joshua, the leader of his party.

At this time, tensions were surfacing in our Cabinet. Joshua, who had instigated the demonstration that had demanded I put my rhetoric of land reform into action, calling for the acquisition of the Lauders Estate in his constituency, continued to misplace Cabinet papers requiring his signature as Minister of Finance to pay Fred Hadley the sum of EC$165,000 I had negotiated toward purchase of the estate. We had other papers prepared for his signature, but he refused to permit the Treasury to pay up.

I shipped out Joshua to a university grants committee meeting in Jamaica and, acting as Finance Minister in his absence, authorized the payment, much to the jubilation of the peasants in his constituency. Joshua was furious when he returned, claiming that the Cabinet had thrust a long knife in his back. He also had an altercation with Housing Minister Victor Cuffy about the allocation of funds for a housing project. Cuffy pulled a gun on Joshua, and was restrained by Clive Tannis, while Joshua seized a heavy glass ashtray to throw at Cuffy, and was restrained by Othneil Sylvester. In typical metaphoric style, Joshua threatened Cuffy: "When I cut you away from my political umbilical cord, you're finished." Cuffy did contest subsequent elections in our group and failed. But he came into his own later as President of our Human Rights Association.

In the end, Joshua accepted money to cross the floor, unlike Dennie, who had honourably rejected it. As political fortunes fluctuated over the years, with the merchants disillusioned with the taxation imposed on their gross earnings and supporting my alternate policies, I got confirmation from the magnanimous contributor himself.

With the collapse of our government and loss of office in the subsequent election, Dennie resumed teaching, finding a job in Barbados, and later rejoined our administration as Chairman of the Electricity Company. His eyesight failing with the passing years, he became an impoverished victim of democratic change, without a pension. I called on him from time to time, responding to his requests. "It is great," he said to me once, "to see the general looking after a fallen soldier." I wonder what his legacy of integrity teaches his successors, short on morality, and our society in general, now that Dennie has fallen on hard times, when once, he could have changed his fortunes by accepting a bribe.

Dennie, Sylvester and Cuffy refused to attend Joshua's funeral. I read a lesson, both for Joshua, and later his wife, meeting their expenses with state funerals. I could not bear to see his living conditions in his last days. I changed his furniture. I gave him a police driver. I tried to build an institution of respect and later, a climate of modest comfort for those who served the people.

Our countries, like St. Vincent and the Grenadines, are small, but this should not mean that we who serve them should not subscribe to international standards of decency. How else will we build our nations and at the same time persuade citizens of other lands developed through the sweat and sacrifice of their forebears, to share their bounty with us, when we seem incapable of looking after ourselves?

I named our main airport in honour of Joshua before he passed on.

PART III

Sole Opposition
(1975 to 1984)

14

Formation of the NDP

Eight years on, as Member of Parliament for the Grenadines, I was facing my fourth election. Joshua and his wife's defection had triggered the poll. They abandoned their party and I had announced the dissolution of Parliament for a general election within 90 days. Othneil Sylvester, a key player in the constitutional negotiations with Joshua in their party, gave me his support, along with the Party's Executive General Secretary, the charismatic Owen Walker.

Of the fragile Alliance I was the sole survivor. Milton Cato promptly announced that with all but one seat at his command, he led "the strongest government in the world." He appointed Joshua as Minister of Trade, Agriculture and Tourism, and Joshua's wife sat also on the government benches.

The Governor, Sir Rupert John, apparently wished to appoint me to lead the Opposition, much to the annoyance of the government. The Constitution was clear. The reality was obvious. There was no one else who opposed the government. I sat alone in the Opposition while a motion to amend the Constitution was presented to prevent the Governor from appointing a Leader of the Opposition on the basis of seniority in Parliament, or who secured the most votes in the previous election, in the event that there were two or more in Opposition.

Mine was the sole vote against this constitutional manipulation. A division of the house yielded the result I anticipated, and Mrs. Joshua, who voted for the change, became Leader of the Opposition with the legal right to appoint as Senators two cronies. So our country made history!

The rape of our constitution was digested with hardly a murmur in St. Vincent. Civil society, including the churches, maintained an elegant silence. My colleagues in the region were equally silent. I wonder if this same butchery of our constitution were attempted in today's political arena whether it would be so gracefully accepted. Not with the freedom of the airwaves I introduced!

The disgust expressed by the Governor, a former United Nations staff member in the Bureau of Human Rights and himself a lawyer, ensured his removal. In his place came Dr. Sydney Gun-Munro, a retired surgeon who had served well in the city and for whom I had secured the job he requested as an ordinary medical officer in Bequia. With his prestigious career behind him, the doctor had tried to unseat me in the Grenadines. But he had refused to do any medical work in Mustique or the Southern Grenadines, and this forced me to split the constituency into two medical districts. So when he became a candidate for the constituency, it was easy to explain that he did not care to give service even in the area of his competence. (Sir Sydney was still in office when I became Prime Minister in 1984, and offered to resign, but I invited him to stay while my government put its house in order. His successful reputation as a surgeon only served to enhance my political ascendancy, ensuring feebler opponents in the future. He was a doctor and I was a pragmatist! As a Grenadian scholar in England during the Battle of Britain he was found in a morgue and presumed dead.)

I settled down in my role as the sole de facto opposition. The people of the Grenadines constituency never wavered. The seamen were making money working away from home, all over the world, on the New York-based National Bulk Carriers, owned by D.K. Ludwig, and transporting ore and oil. I had called on the New York office myself. The company's agent Luther Robertson was a reliable friend. My constituents were dependable sailors and willing to be away from home for long periods, and their savings were going into splendid new houses.

The people of Mayreau were happy. For generations they had squatted on the island owned by the Eustace family and when after a full day of negotiation the trustee of the island, Dr. Parmenas Eustace, refused to agree to sell the government land to house the people. I had the acquisition published in the *Gazette* and acquired 22 acres for them. Dr. Eustace even suggested that I should accept a piece of the land for myself instead of working on the people's behalf.

My children were going to the Kingstown Preparatory School. They were singled out for harassment even by the tuck vendors with trays of snacks outside the school. This was an early family price paid by my young children for my being in politics. We brought them to Bequia. We supplemented school by teaching them at home, along with some of their friends. Distant education with the American home study Calvert School was another alternative. The secondary education I helped to create in Bequia was becoming dominated by an Anglican priest. Teachers were marking right answers wrong and vice versa. It was time to lean on relatives in Canada, and one by one, while I was in opposition, Pat and I parted with our girls, putting up with their tears at the airport, and sent them to a private girls' school, Branksome Hall in Toronto, safe from abuse.

One evening, two fervent Joshua worshippers, Conrad Forbes, a vegetable trafficker, and Simeon Cumberbatch, a shopkeeper, walked the miles uphill to Cane Hall where we were staying in my father-in-law's home in St. Vincent, and called on me to form a new party. They were determined to see the end of Joshua for his sell-out (their term) of their beloved People's Political Party (PPP) which had done so much for the poor ordinary man.

Alphonso Dennie, my defeated Minister of Education, called from Barbados to say that I must enlist Owen Walker as my secretary as he would know the grass roots and the abandoned rural leaders. And so the campaign in the countryside began with Forbes and Walker. We travelled from one end of the country to another in my little yellow Volkswagen Beetle. I would take the map of the island, and plan random trips to various villages. It was as though I were once again an agricultural extension officer carrying a message of technology to the farmers, but this time it was a political message of hope. I had kindled the flame of land reform and import substitution that could revolutionize life in the hapless rural districts. Poverty could be set aside if you farmed for yourself and were not just a wage-earner.

As the message went home to Joshua's supporters that his coalition with the Labour party did not serve their interests, I welcomed them into my ranks. Walker and Forbes, known in the villages as former Joshua advocates, helped me sell the message of abandonment of old and now useless allegiances. Joshua's voice in the meantime was muted in Parliament.

As our relentless struggle continued, my yellow Volkswagen became more than a symbol of opposition; it became an enduring gesture of protest. No other vehicle in the history of St. Vincent survived more ruts, loose gravel, unpaved village roads, floods, hurricanes and volcanic eruption than my dear Beetle. All day long I would travel with a couple of friends, fortified with dried biscuits and a slice of yellow cheese. We were called "The New Party."

There were no ferry boats on Sundays plying between Bequia and the mainland. Sundays were well suited to campaigning as more people were lazing around in the afternoons in their villages. To meet with them meant chartering a speedboat from a cousin, William Gooding, at US$75 dollars per trip. Four trips in a month consumed my salary in Parliament.

In the midst of all of this, my father-in-law, Clayton Parker, went to the immigration office to renew his residence permit, a permission to reside in the home he had built. After three hours of humiliation, he received a temporary permit, but vowed to sell the house and return to Canada. I lost my place to stay during my constant travel to the mainland when hitting the campaign trail and attending Parliament.

Fortunately, my poet and musician friend Shake Keane and his wife, whom I had brought back from Germany, where he was on contract playing his flügelhorn in Cologne, to head up the Department of Culture, had built a home not far from the Parker residence in Cane Hall. They offered me a room. Times were rough; I sold a piece of beautiful mountain land where I had hoped to produce vegetables for the hotel and sent the funds to supplement school fees in Toronto.

The strategy of the governing Labour Party to eliminate all residual influence of the Joshuas began to unfold, even as they were demolishing any institutions I had established. The Department of Culture headed by Shake Keane was disbanded. ("We can't eat culture," was their slogan.) His wife Lou, an English teacher at the government-owned grammar school, was becoming uncomfortable. Shake took up teaching 20 miles away in Georgetown and was away five days a week. Lou moved into the management of the Mariner's Inn Hotel.

By December 1975, within a year of the ignominious defeat of our group in the general election, Walker and I were ready to launch our new political party. By this time, we had a name. A group of us had got together to put some kind of party structure in place, at the home of J.L. Eustace in Montrose. He still harboured his resentment at being sacked as Health Minister. In the Alliance government, he was elected our Speaker, much to the annoyance of Cato who then had to treat him with respect, until the no-confidence motion was before us. I had a merry old time debating the motion, waiting for the hour when I could announce the dissolution of the House before the motion was able to pass.

In this formative group were Forbes, Walker, a merchant George Reddock, John (Cherry) Smith, a bus driver and shopkeeper, George Stevens, retired from the Aruba oil refinery, Neville Richards, a carpenter, Milton Mayers, a contractor, and Tseldon Morris, a budding draughtsman. We had before us the names of the existing parties in St. Vincent – Labour, People's Political – and words such as Congress, Convention and Movement. Then there were the adjectives liberal, socialist, conservative, democratic. I liked the word democratic and its connotations. I had a reservation about using the label "new". It was fine while the party was a novelty, but what of its future! Cherry Smith had a prophetic answer, "The party must always be new. It must always find new people. New ideas. The older the party, the newer it must be." The name "New Democratic Party" was proposed by Cherry Smith, and his name survived in our party's folklore as the one who named the NDP.

On December 5, 1975, the New Democratic Party was launched in the Market Square and the event was reminiscent of my return from London: a hail of stones and a rostrum showered with human excrement. The election rules had been amended during our Alliance administration, providing additional symbols for political parties. Our NDP chose the key as its symbol. It was easily marketable. That first meeting promulgated my leadership as party President with Owen Walker as Secretary-General. We were in business. Our baptism in stench did not deter us! We set out our principles, including the pursuit of political union among the islands. Unilateral and unco-ordinated independence would leave us small islanders vulnerable, we argued. Divide and conquer!

Our formative group held a second house meeting. Two new faces joined us: Eldon Smith, a vendor who collected turtle shells from the fishermen to export to Japan, and Jerome Burke, both former PPP stalwarts.

We were delighted with the launching of the Party. I congratulated George Reddock on his brave stand upholding the Party banner throughout the meeting. It was time to get down to business. I presented a cheque for one hundred EC dollars, the first written in the name of the Party. We opened an account in Barclays Bank. We secured a two-room office in the city above a supermarket at a rental of $75 a month. A hairdressing salon, "Ella's," moved in beside us. We arranged to have a telephone and a post-box. George Stevens manned the office. George Reddock became our Treasurer.

In Opposition we had already humiliated the Government with one defeat. They had mounted a Commission of Enquiry into the Kingstown Board, essentially to discover corruption in spending 65,000 East Caribbean dollars on the retaining walls in Cane Garden, on the highway beside the family of a Minister. We had appointed a Guyanese architect named Mitchell to design a government building, and our opponents assumed that he was a relative of mine.

I had been on my farm in the hills of Bequia on the weekend, with a single helper, rolling away the stones to make a conservation terrace.

My superstitious helper did not like the mocking bird squawking at us. "He has a message," he said. Shortly afterwards, a policeman, Wendell Wright, who later became a member of our Central Committee in his retirement, presented me with a summons to appear before the Tribunal on Monday.

The Tribunal was meeting at 4.30, a time designed to have a full audience after business closing hours. I challenged the Commission. The filled hall groaned. They felt they had caught all the other Ministers, and here was the final fish. My grounds were simple. The law permitted me to be represented by counsel and the notice did not provide me with ample time to secure the presence of counsel. The announcement of my counsel as the distinguished Henry Forde of Barbados and the forced adjournment of the hearing raised doubts in the hearts of the believers. So the hearing was deferred.

Sylvester, who had earlier represented the Ministers, was waiting to challenge the validity of the Commission in Court at the end of the proceedings, making a mockery of it all. Henry differed on timing, while agreeing with the substance of Sylvester's argument, that the Board being investigated had been abolished by law.

I requested that I be allowed one hour to testify before the Tribunal. I did not want to allow the public to construe that I was hiding corruption under a legal argument. And so I hammered away. The new Chairman, Bert Commissiong, had been a friend in London days. He was anxious to establish his name, following the resignation of Alex Hughes, my business lawyer, on grounds of ill health. I had cautioned him some days before, outside Parliament, that Hughes had not been in hospital, that I could, as he knew, look after myself, and that he should be cautious.

Our petition was filed in the Supreme Court. The Court ruled in our favour. No Commission of Enquiry into political conduct in our Caribbean has ever done more than enhance the honeymoon of new governments, and in the subsequent verdict of the voters, it had never warranted the extraordinary expenditure. The Court was impartial at that time.

After launching our Party, we planned our first convention at Petit Bordel. The constitution I had drafted on the basis of Errol Barrow's Democratic Labour Party and John Compton's United Workers Party, refined here and there by my friend Emery Robertson, was adopted by those attending. Petit Bordel nestled as a narrow bank beside the ridges of the leeward coast. The acoustics of the narrow valley were wonderful. Shake Keane played his flugelhorn. The music, singing and chanting, and the flow of drinks kept the atmosphere buoyant. The sounds sailed up the valley. An old lady came up to Shake and declared: "Your music sounds like the trumpet of an angel in heaven." Thus was inaugurated the New Democratic Party.

In the meantime, in Opposition I had more time to help with the hotel. Our clientele was expanding among the more adventurous Americans and Canadians. More yachts were anchoring in the Bay, and occasionally I would clear them to make way for a sea plane that pulled up on the beach. An irate guest demanded I do something about the cacophony of the crowing roosters. The Winchester rifle I had bought in Ithaca remedied that. Shake was happy to spend the weekend with me at the Frangi, playing his flügelhorn with the local string bands.

Shake Keane's life was poetry and music. Poetry was scattered about his house. I collected some of the poems and dispatched them to a competition in Cuba. He won the Casa Las Americas Prize. His wife Lou found more lucrative employment in Union at Anchorage, where her French and German could be deployed.

France was discovering the Grenadines. The Union Airport I had authorized Andre Beaufrand to build over the swamp, perilous as was its approach to the sea, became the gateway. Shake soon took off for America. He teamed up with one of his students, Margaret, who had earlier taken up residence with us. We ate frequently at Edgar Adams' Fishnet restaurant where local fare was good enough for an NDP dinner with me selling 75 per cent of the tickets. Our dinners were a financial success, as I could sell twice the number of tickets, knowing that the middle class would support my cause clandestinely, but not show their faces.

With Shake and Lou leaving the mainland, I had to find new lodgings. A retired policeman, St. Clair Robinson, gave me shelter in Arnos Vale. He became my trusted companion on the campaign trail and sailing between the islands on the yacht *Sapphire* that I shared with John Compton and my brother Reginald.

All year long I recorded the grievances of the people in my cheap school exercise books, slipping in too the jokes on the pathetic misdemeanours of our government. It was all saved for the budget debates, the only time I was allowed on radio. In one session in Parliament I had left my rules at home and had picked up the airport regulations instead. This did not stop me from waving the book at the Speaker on a point of order.

My budgetary presentations lasted for up to three days. The purchase of batteries for transistor radios went up. Way up in the mountains the farmers were listening. Fishermen camping on the beaches in remote islands were listening. An audience developed in St. Lucia and Barbados, and of course the people in Grenada's Carriacou and Petit Martinique, longing for representation, were seeing me as the voice of all the Grenadines. My humour delighted my audience: serious stuff hammering at the consumption taxes was blended with the outrageous cost of a lady's panties. I have never subscribed to the politics of anger, as I always felt that a good-natured attack was more lethal..

One year I returned to my island home to collect some documents needed for the debate, intending to return the next day. Weeks before, an old lady had visited me with her worrying dream, that I had missed the ship that was to take me northwards. Listening to the debate I realized the Government was getting ready to wind up the debate that night without me. Remembering the lady's dream I chartered a speedboat to rush me across the channel to Parliament. I had forgotten my jacket. My friend St. Clair Robinson came to meet me and loaned me his. The late-night Parliament nearly fainted on my arrival. I began speaking and we adjourned. They had to listen to me for several days. When I stopped speaking, the public turned off their radios.

One night, in the debate, all the tyres of my Beetle were slashed. I had to beg a ride home from a stranger. The Parliament refused the compensation I sought. The denial reminded me of their refusal, even when I was in government, to pay for the tuxedo I had to rent when I was instructed to go directly from Venezuela to London without the right clothes. Such was the evolution of our fiscal discipline. Thanks to family inheritance, and our own diligence, my economic independence was able to buttress my intellectual competence. New tyres for my beloved Volks consumed half of my salary as an MP. Step by step, in the darkness alone that night, my resolve hardened to remove this government from office!

Fearlessly alone in Opposition, as the days, weeks and years went by, I programmed myself, choosing silence, whisper or explosion. The time came when I decided it was ripe to enlighten Ministers on the other side of Parliament about the opportunity I had left behind for help from the European Union to improve our hospital, only to be greeted by an incredulous, "What's the European Union?"

We drove my little Beetle to death going from village to village. Beneath the floorboards, we could see the roads, and shifting pieces of cardboard kept out the dust. I did not mind that I had no audience at some meetings. One or two was good enough. We would leave Arnos Vale before dawn and reach Fancy at the northernmost end of

St. Vincent, where there was a beautiful view of St. Lucia, and join the folk in the church. The village of Fancy had no electricity. Each night they could see the lights of St. Lucia. I promised them that one day the St. Lucians would see *them* at night. I remember sailing one night with John Compton from St. Lucia toward St. Vincent.

"Surely," he said after we had been at sea for three hours, "we should be seeing St. Vincent!"

"We will not," I replied. "The northern end of St. Vincent is represented by Joshua's party. They are in darkness."

It was painful to see some of the things we had secured in the Alliance government fall away. My navigation school in Bequia slipped away to Jamaica, much to the grief of our sailors for years to come. The deal I had worked out with Sir Linden Pindling in regional lobbying to cede him the hotel training school in the Bahamas, while he supported my navigation school, fell by the wayside as I demitted office.

Our opposition gained momentum because of our arguments, and thrived on the Government's heavy-handedness. Quite early on they had tear-gassed the teachers marching to demand the minimum additional wage of $75 that I had instituted for all public servants. In their support I had stood alone outside the central police station where the two union leaders were arrested without bail. I quietly told the young policeman sent to arrest me that he should tell the officer-in-charge I had informed him that a Member of Parliament cannot be charged for loitering anywhere in the country. An MP's job included loitering. Both jailed union leaders, Yvonne Francis Gibson and Mike Browne, later became Ministers of Education, Yvonne with me, and Mike on the other side.

Being alone in Opposition did not upset me. Being alone is not loneliness. Nor did the straggling attendance at my village meetings daunt my spirits. My confidence in my view of the world deepened as I saw what was going on in the islands. That youthful experience, against which I rebelled, having to rise early and be in empty St. George's Cathedral at six every Saturday morning saying mass with Canon Frederick was to serve me well.

"Young man," the old priest had pontificated. "It does not matter if there is no congregation. What matters is that we serve our God."

15

International Visitors and Residents in Bequia

Sir Anthony Eden, later Lord Avon, was the first celebrity to take up residence in Bequia. He came here after Suez. He was here before royalty in other Grenadine islands. He bought a home from my mother's aunt Betty and her husband Owen Wallace. I remember the home with proud pictures of her son in the US Marines. I used to visit them on vacation; most of the time was spent shooting dozens of pigeons on Pigeon Island, with me, the smallest of the raiders, assigned to clambering through the bush to retrieve the scattered prey. This youthful misadventure guided my later legislative project to protect the threatened species.

The beaches of Friendship and La Pompe were a beachcomber's paradise for Sir Anthony. The fishermen's discourse with him did not go beyond their catch of the day. Ill health took him onwards to Barbados, and then back home. He left behind a modest trust that we used to give a garden prize.

By the time I returned from England in the mid-1960s, Americans had purchased the east and west of Bequia. The Wagners had taken over Industry Estate. A group from Ohio led by Karl Fisher had purchased Spring Estate, and Tom Johnston, an early retired public relations executive, had commenced his pristine architecture on Moon Hole.

Johnson had secured a waiver from the planning authorities for his free-form iconoclasm, prohibiting workmen from using levels and squares. His investing friends trusted his judgment in building their homes with access either over the cliffs or by boat. The Moonholers overnighted at the Frangi to catch the early ferry or to avoid bruising their shins in the night. I had to draw the line on a physical planning waiver for Moon Hole when Tom Johnston died desiring to be encased on the crumbling rock which had inspired his dreams. A burial site had to be proclaimed by Cabinet and gazetted, a three-day rush, commandeering health officials, soil experts, civil servants, printers, but in the end, approved for eternity. Jim Wholey and Ray Du Bois became good customers and friends, and were delighted to welcome me in the Washington circuit on one of my World Bank/IMF jaunts. Ray, who volunteered to help me wash glasses in the busy Frangipani kitchen, became an Under Secretary of Defense in the G.W. Bush Administration, continuing afterwards to refresh his soul sailing in the Grenadines on our yacht *Pelangi*. Ezra Stoller, the Washington photographer, also became a Moon Hole and Frangi habitué.

The arrival of the airport was an unwelcome intrusion on Moon Hole's isolation, but it meant access by road and a means of exit by plane for medical attention for ageing settlers. Direct foreign investment stimulated our construction industry and this was matched by the savings by sailors transforming their homes.

Sandy Meisner, in the prime of his success directing the Playhouse School of Theater in New York, descended on quaint Bequia along with his friend Jimmy Carville to build a home overlooking Friendship Bay and the fields of corn, cassava, and peas. When I got to know them and asked why they chose this inaccessible site with this steep entrance, Sandy simply philosophized that, "How green was my valley," the name of the wonderful novel about Wales, reflected Bequia in time and place. Before you could realize it was happening, Sandy and Jimmy had trained the children of sailors, fishermen, and peasants to produce *Jesus Christ Superstar* in 1975, both in a school auditorium and the St. George's Cathedral, to the stunned amazement of Vincentians wondering what had come out of Bequia. Not satisfied with this, they persuaded the captain and owner of the freighter *Arlingham*, neighbour Cosmos Sylvester, to take the group to Grenada, two years later, to present Handel's *Messiah*.

Our blaring rap music today at two in the morning is therefore a descent into Hades. And a German diner at the Frangi, deafened by a religious crusade, intoned to me, "In Germany we worship silently."

For several summers, a troupe of young actors from New York followed Sandy to Bequia for further instruction on a rudimentary stage in a Friendship dining room. Sandy and Jimmy had adopted an almost homeless hearing-impaired youngster whom everyone called Boulou. As a young Trade and Tourism Minister, I was delegated to find two ancient cannon to present to Penetanguishene Fort in Ontario which was being restored, a gesture I co-ordinated with Bill Davis, then Minister of Education in the Ontario Government. (Ontario schools were raising funds to build us a secondary school.) Following up on these contacts, Ontario authorities at a lunch offered to get me a collection of hearing aids and some technical assistance to go with it. Boulou was one of the first recipients and he knew how to show gratitude. He acted out the behaviour of a cock crowing, letting me know in no uncertain terms that for the first time with my Ontario-procured hearing aid, he realized that certain antics of the cock meant it was crowing.

Boulou made a success in Manhattan with his office-cleaning business, but the trio was always in Bequia for Christmas, when Jimmy, his natural white beard flowing in the wind as Boulou rang the bell in the dinghy for the Santa Claus ritual in the bay, slid through the numerous yachts toward the children on the waterfront. An early guest was Wallace Shawn, who had our staff try out a one-act play.

The *Arlingham,* used for the Grenada Handel trip, was falling apart. Ever willing to help, Captain Sylvester volunteered to replace the ferry in order to get folks home to Union for Christmas. I sailed with them. The *Arlingham* barely made it into Union before sunset. We had enough daylight to get out and beyond the reef of Clifton Harbour when a dark north-easterly squall plunged us into night. The lights of the ship went out. Captain Sylvester took the sole flashlight into the engine room to see what was happening. I took up position outside the bridge in the driving rain, held out a handkerchief to get a bearing and instructed the helmsman how to steer between Mayreau and Union. I calculated the time and estimated our distance before giving the direction to change from west to north. When the squall lifted we were due west of Canouan. My constituents were home for Christmas. The *Arlingham* had avoided the reefs.

Not long after this the captain felt it was time to scuttle his ship. He let me have the massive wheel which we disconnected in the ocean, shortly before she went on her final journey to the depths! I plunged from the deck and swam to our waiting water taxi. The wheel now presides over the Frangi dining room, a fond memento of Sandy, Jimmy, Captain Sylvester and Handel's *Messiah* in Grenada.

The Frangipani prospered but the neglect of the expanding Grenadines took tangible form in the collapse of our electricity services and every business reliant on power had to purchase their own generator. I decided the time had come to purchase a reliable engine after the arrival of young economists from the CDB to analyze demand in response to my entreaties in and out of Parliament. I knew it would be years before a CDB project materialized. I became my own generation engineer, learning to read the dials.

As I was monitoring my generator one night at dinner I noticed in the shadows a tall, thin, lanky fellow folding up a frame in a white sheet. It turned out that he was a wandering American soul hoping I would help him sell his painting. He was broke and needed some money desperately. We took his painting to the light: a wonderful seascape, revealing the marvellous tones of the reef and the grasses beneath all the variations of blue and aquamarine of the waters beside a Grenadines beach. He wanted $600 for the painting and an advance from the hotel.

"It's a deal," I told him. "I'll mark it up to $750, and you have an immediate credit of $300 at the hotel. So go ahead and have a meal."

Within a week the painting was sold at my quoted price, and Brian Keeling was in business. He produced others on demand and we put them on show in the Frangi foyer. He was also commissioned to paint a special scene from the balcony of an American home-owner. Then it was time to go. He had made enough to travel home, but not before giving me a surrealistic seascape, which was a bit too way-out for my taste. I sold the painting to a German guest and I wrote Brian telling him that he had another advance of $750 dollars, as I would really like him to return one day and do me a traditional seascape of the Southern Grenadines. He returned with a wife. I got my painting showing a parched landscape in the dry season, beautiful reefs, and storm clouds about to descend on the parched earth. Brian has his own gallery now in the States. I was pleased that the Frangi launched his career.

We helped, too, an American girl, who painted ships and sunsets on driftwood. Forever empathetic to wanderers – a sentimental hangover from my drifting hitch-hiking days in Europe – I was enchanted with the wanderlust of two young American male college graduates. Inspired by Fenger's canoe voyage in the 1920s, they bought a native fishing boat to sail to the Panama Canal and thence up the coast back home to California. "It is the bliss of ignorance that tempts the fool," Fenger had advised, "but it is he who sees the world." As they outfitted their craft on the beach beside Frangi, everyone questioned their departure date. Quietly, they took off. They made it out of the bay but only to Paget Farm for repairs. Relieving themselves under manchineel trees and cleaning up with the dried leaves blistered the cherished organs. Fishermen provided cure and solace. The seafarers made it to Canouan, but while they were asleep ashore the boat was wrecked in the surf. I found them days later forlorn at the waterfront in the city and took them to the home I had as Trade Minister, leaving them to spend the weekend in my housekeeper's care.

On Monday morning the housekeeper was in rebellion about the pair's filthiness. I had hoped they would wash their clothes and clean up for the interview I had arranged for teaching jobs. In their condition I could not present them to a personnel officer, no matter what their university grades were, and I told them so. "I thought you were a kindred spirit," one of the two declared.

"I admire your spirit of adventure, but I think you need to return to your American mainstream."

Two winters later, a mother turned up at the Frangipani, thanking me for saving her son, who was settled in a bank. "Thank the fishermen who tended the manchineel blisters on their balls," I told her.

Smoothing the way for youth wandering far from home brought me, years later, cherished comfort in moments of solitude. Strangers had been kind to me in my own wandering days with few funds in Canada and Europe. I owed a particular debt of gratitude to those who piloted me as a hitch-hiker in the back alleys and highways in Europe, ushering in my age of enlightenment about the European mind and the ways of the world. This immersion in the natural beauty, centuries of culture and refinement of Europe saved me from chauvinism and the inanity of island politics, and in trying times in reflective moods, steered me to the distant shore.

16

Bequia Regatta

Five yachts do not a yacht club make. Yet such was the St. Vincent Yacht Club, augmented by the rental of boats from the Caribbean Sailing Yachts enterprise, for which I as Minister of Lands negotiated a lease of the sea-bed at Villa. The Whitsun Regatta to Bequia attracted also other charter yachts and cruisers from Barbados and Trinidad: three wonderful days of sailing to and around Bequia and on the final day around St. Vincent. The off-day was for the sailing fishing boats.

One day on the beach I met the Englishman Hodge Taylor and suggested we form a *sailing* club in Bequia, definitely not a *yacht* club. The sailing club would be for yachts folk, fishermen, home-owners, and anyone who loved sailing. Hodge agreed. We fixed a date to meet one night at the Frangi with Pat and my fishermen organizing team, Ermina Antrobus and Kenneth Allick.

We settled the principles for our club and regatta. All sponsors must be thanked, all expenses of the regatta published. And it would be a fun regatta. We would not want to compete with the prestigious races such as the Rolex. The gathering proposed that I become Commodore, but I declined, stating that I was already President of my newly founded political party, and I did not want the sailing club to be politically tainted. But our Whitsun Regatta suffered competition none the less from the Antigua Sailing week. When the boats went north, after the charter season, there was no reason to sail south back to Bequia.

The Grenada Revolution of Maurice Bishop gave me the chance I wanted. All the yachts suspected of being a source of guns to overthrow the revolution were thrown out. The Grenada Easter Regatta vanished from the calendar, so I decided we should move ours in Bequia into the Easter slot, fully confident that by the time the revolution collapsed our Bequia Regatta would have staked its claim permanently on the Caribbean year.

The excitement with capturing the Easter slot from communist Grenada for our yachting festival soon brought forth the wrath of our diminutive Anglican Rector, with appropriate fulminations against my cardinal sins in leading the people astray. How dare we have fun sailing on Good Friday when all good Christians should be in church for three hours?

My response that ships sailing the world did not cut their engines in remembrance of the crucifixion cut no ice. My wife Pat had other ideas. We placed the hours of the Easter church services in the Regatta Programme, sponsoring the generous presence at those services of the rich spouses of visiting yachting folk, whereupon after all criticism vanished. Publication of these church services, for all churches, became a permanent feature of the Regatta Programme.

The Easter Regatta and the Bequia Sailing Club became great successes, attracting the fishing boats and sloops from Carriacou, Petit Martinique and Tobago. The ancient fraternity of the offshore islands (neglected by governments) found new areas of bonding, as Bequia sailors looked forward to taking part in the races in Carriacou and Tobago. The Trinidad posse led by Rawle Barrow became an annual feature. The Barbadians also flocked in, their wives filling the hotels. And whoever was cruising the Grenadines, from Germany, France, Italy, Britain, or New Zealand, was ready for our fun regatta.

Our bar at the Frangi became a central reference point for the yachtsmen. Raul Barrow always tells the tale of how I was helping to serve in the besieged bar when a visitor asked, "So you are also the Prime Minister?"

"Yes, I am."

"If you are the Prime Minister, I am the King of England."

The Easter Regatta became a national festival, second only to the mainland St. Vincent carnival, generating wide enthusiasms in shore activities, alas with volumes of noise pollution obliterating the serenity of Admiralty Bay.

The club thrived. My original injunction that it be non-political worked. Enemies who claimed I did nothing in Parliament became Commodores. But I also pulled in political celebrities. John Compton sailed with us and distributed prizes. Ray Robinson, too, languishing in Tobago before regaining his country's premiership once more, and his wife were my guests handing out prizes at the regatta.

John Compton, my brother Reginald and I had bought a 26-foot Westerly *Colibri* which we sailed in our regatta. I used it to bring Prince Charles to Bequia when his naval assignment brought him to St. Vincent in July 1973 while I was Premier. I think the Palace authorized his sailing with me because the Senior Naval Commander of the West Indies Squadron "Snowi" had previously tested my seamanship. Snowi sailed with us in a regatta, when I almost crashed Colibri on the rocks off an islet and tacked dramatically at the absolute last moment. "Sorry gentlemen", I said, "my nerve gave". "Brilliant", declared Snowi. My other companions thought I had intended to harvest whelks.

Then we bought *Sapphire*, a 36-foot ketch in St. Thomas. With the help of a South African, we sailed the yacht three nights and two days out of sight of land to Martinique. In the loneliness of the ocean, my friend Patrick Cullen told the story of how he and others had plotted in the yacht club at home to raid Robben Island and release Nelson Mandela. They did not execute the plot for fear of failure and the loss of Mandela's life. I told President Mandela the story when I met him at the New Zealand CHOGM, and that Patrick was outside the prison holding a flag when he was released. Mandela offered generously to meet him, but Patrick died in a car accident before I could make the arrangements.

17

Independence and the 1979 Election

Cato had described his government as the strongest in the world, but it soon began to flounder. Brushed aside in Cabinet as an irrelevance and ignored by his once worshipful supporters, Joshua and his wife abandoned the Government they had help to build and joined the Opposition. I urged him to return to the market-place and tell the people his side of the story. He had a wonderful reception to his speech, and he decided to repeat it the next week, only to find that the crowds the week before were satisfied with the upset and now were nowhere to be seen. He had fired his last cannon. The leader that had aroused the masses, challenged colonialism and fought the plantocracy, had abandoned his friends and in the process outsmarted himself.

The thoughts of Independence were pervasive among the Associated States, Grenada's Gairy having led the way and survived all the mischief and tumult. I urged Joshua that we should separately go through the countryside and mobilize opinion on the framework of the new constitution. Some civic groups formed their own organization around the subject. Hardly had dialogue began than a motion was placed in Parliament purporting to be a mandate for Independence. It was challenged in court and brushed aside. The Colonial Office was concerned about getting the results they wanted quickly. The Caribbean did not have to fight for Independence. The constitutions were already being written in London. But only the experience of Independence would really point to the kind of constitution required.

Our volcano erupted on Good Friday 1979. It started the night before while the steel band was playing at the Frangipani and we could see the incandescence in the sky. The red flames of the eruption could be seen in the islands 50 miles away. Barbados, 100 miles away, received ashes. The ash would eventually get into the upper currents beyond the immediate atmosphere and circulate around the world.

Twenty thousand people were evacuated south from the volcano. Some families were moved to Bequia and never returned to the foothills of the volcano. Refugee camps in schools were set up for months. The government became a dispenser of largesse with the aid that flooded in from all quarters. Constitutional discussions on Independence became a non-subject. We sent food from our hotel to the refugees in the Bequia School.

As I witnessed the unkempt, ragged refugees in their camps, the mothers with their brood separated from home and husbands without their basic amenities, I remembered an acquaintance who had quenched my thirst in the Carib country on the campaign trail. I was moved to instruct the Treasury to commit my entire salary to the Soufrière Emergency Fund. Folly. I did so while still sensitive to the memory of the tyres of my Volks slashed in the grounds of the Parliament while I debated the budget late at night only to have to beg a ride home. Certain Labour ministers and their acolytes boasted of the maplewood-smoked hams cluttering their kitchens from the Canadian relief supplies. A single policeman was charged, and forced to resign. (He emigrated to Canada!) They called the loot "Bowdow," a marksman's term for the bull's eye in target practice. Such were the easy pickings. Meantime in Bequia, out of our own resources we fed the refugee Caribs.

With the newly-acquired popularity of the Government, it was an opportune moment for the British to announce Independence. Never mind the refugee camps. I wrote to the Premier indicating that I would require proper notice of a Conference in London, and that I would want to arrive in London at least three days before the Conference. I do not know if the Premier was frightened about the kind of mischief and lobbying I had carried out in pursuit of statehood, but I got my invitation on a Friday when the banks were closed and I could get no money – and we should be leaving on Sunday for a meeting in London on Monday. Joshua, too, refused the late invitation saying in the common parlance: "Late invitation is for dog."

And so the Independence was granted with no opposition present.

I was invited by John Compton to the St. Lucia Independence celebrations. There was to be a procession of yachts in Castries harbour, and our jointly-owned boat, *Sapphire*, he requested, should be present. So I sailed there with a friend and an American poet, Richard Dey. The British delegation arranged with John that I have a meeting with them in St. Lucia.

The hotel suite at La Toc was well prepared for the meeting. The British Minister, Ted Rowlands, was flanked by a retinue of officials, all with pens bristling to record my surrender to their too hastily imposed Independence without concessions to our economic needs. They needed our independence far more than we did to take the strain off their Treasury.

They welcomed me, regretted this and that, expected me and my party to do this and that – and so on. I decided at the celebrations for St. Lucia's independence that I was not going to be flattered: I did not turn up to the meeting to be silent. I spoke up. I told Ted Rowlands that, being Welsh, I expected him to ditch us without notice, the same way a Welsh girl had treated me in England. They were ditching us when 20 per cent of our population was in refugee camps. We did not know when the volcano would erupt again. On that day in St. Lucia, the Opposition was venting public ridicule. George Odlum and his brother Jon (later a Parliamentary Secretary) were hanging an effigy of Rowlands in Columbus Square.

Thus was ended 300 years of colonialism. I would have preferred it if St. Lucia, Grenada and ourselves had done it together in a joint effort. Another chance at Caribbean unity ignored. In my case, from being sole Opposition I became the longest-serving Prime Minister in the Caribbean.

I did not attend our Independence celebration. I went to Canada to be with my children and stayed with the Parkers, my in-laws, who lived in a simple, comfortable home on the Niagara escarpment with a marvellous view all the way to Toronto, beside a protected forest with trails that seemed perfectly designed to calm a turbulent mind.

The *coup d'état* on my doorstep in Grenada sent shock waves throughout the Caribbean. That sort of thing was for Haiti, the Dominican Republic and, of course, Cuba, but not my English-speaking Caribbean and its Westminster-style democracy.

The birth of Grenada's independence had caused much pain. Incensed that the British had allowed Eric Gairy to lead the country into Independence, conservative elements in association with the waterfront workers brought the island to a halt. Regional trade unions were ready to lend moral support and boycott movement of supplies into the island. Without replenishment of fuel stocks, internal transportation would cease. Gairy sternly resisted the pressures and was sworn in as Prime Minister. The strike crumbled. The battle was not with the imperial power but at home. Gairy who had been virtually exiled by the imperial powers to neighbouring Carriacou had been triumphant in previous elections. He triumphed again! He paved the way for other small islands to receive independence.

My own quest for independence as a group with influence drifted into history.

Maurice Bishop's revolution now hung like an ominous cloud over the Caribbean. The myth that "this couldn't happen here" was destroyed in a single day. Left-wing intellectuals championed Bishop's socialism even in the halls of our University of the West Indies. Some saw it as justice for the slaying of Bishop's father. Others claimed tyranny was at an end. The Mongoose Gang, akin to Haiti's Ton Ton Macoute, which roamed the villages beyond the control of the police had been destroyed, it was claimed. The truth to the contrary was not to be revealed until the confessions made in prison were exposed by inmates. Gairy's pontificating about UFOs and divine inspiration at the UN undermined his credibility. Grenada had fallen between Scylla and Charybdis, or as we say in the islands, between the devil and the deep blue sea.

I heard about Gairy's overthrow from a yachtsman who came ashore at the Frangi bar. I tuned in my radio: Grenada's single radio station was recording the surrender of police stations one by one to Bishop's rebels. The guns smuggled in barrels from the United States had done the job. Cuba was ready to consolidate the "revolution" – their AK 47s added might. A communist takeover in the Caribbean was complete. Bishop hosted the radicals of the region and they issued their "St. George's Declaration" of common principles, followed by a demonstration with placards, "St. Vincent next!"

I got a call from Conrad Adams, a storekeeper in Union, early the next morning asking if he should give refuge to a fellow who had escaped Grenada on a fishing boat and had reached Union, absolutely soaked, without a change of clothing. It turned out to be Derek Knight, Gairy's chief adviser and one of his Ministers whom I had met at many meetings. I remember we had discussed oil and gas exploration off Grenada, shared the theory that the offshore reserves beside Trinidad and Venezuela may also be within our waters all the way to Barbados. Derek had taken me to Point Salines to show me the area in Grenada where they contemplated building an international airport, slicing a couple of hills and filling a few bays. I told Conrad to take care of Derek and give him every courtesy.

When next I heard about Derek, he was a refugee in Canada, much to my amusement, because he had once strenuously objected to the idea of an Air Canada bail-out of our struggling airline LIAT on the grounds that he would have nothing to do with the new imperialism and Canadian multinationals.

I had sensed that my absence from St. Vincent at Independence would trigger the dissolution of Parliament and a call for elections. That was exactly what I wanted. All our candidates were ready for the first challenge to our New Democratic Party, except for Joshua's constituency in South Central Windward. We had two candidates interested, but neither wished to give way, not trusting each other. But the constituency was the bedrock of our land reform programme, and if I were to lead the country, I thought it would be best if I did so from the mainland. Moreover, if Joshua were defeated, we would become the traditional party for the disadvantaged poor.

But it was a tricky time for us. We had negotiated the purchase of a second estate, Diamond, as part of the program, but Bishop was confiscating estates and property in Grenada and my opponents were equating our orderly purchases to a "communist" bid to dispossess property owners, with slogans like: "If you have two cattle the Communists will take both."

And so "better the devil you know" provided the sanctuary for the governing party. The voters had no time to make a distinction between a left-wing radical and a centrist liberal. One night close to the election date, my candidate for East Kingstown was ambushed; his car was shot up, and two people were wounded. I inspected the car at the police station. The police had no evidence of the attackers. I called on the Commissioner and requested protection for me that night as I understood that I was the next target. He was anything but protective. "I do not take sides," he said.

At sundown, I was with my faithful friend St. Clair Robinson in the village of Hadleys. There was a great commotion in the street. A car with gunmen had arrived looking for Son Mitchell. A shop-keeper named Pompey hid me under his counter. Robbie, a former policeman, met the assailants and told them I had gone further up the village. As they continued on, we escaped. We drove a long circuitous route to the village of Greggs where there was great jubilation when we arrived alive. They had heard that I was dead. They had seen assailants hiding in the banana fields that afternoon on the Mesopotamia Road and since then, the village had sent men out with cutlasses to defend me.

The people put me up in the family home of Alston Lewis, who had stepped aside to allow me to be the candidate for the upcoming election. The women formed a cordon around the house and chanted hymns through the night while the men patrolled with cutlasses until daybreak.

After midnight, a man came to the village to take me to "a safe place." Robbie told him to keep going, that he would bring me to the foot of the hill shortly. As the man left the village, he was greeted with a hail of bullets and was ordered to stop. "I did not get him," he shouted over and over again. "I'm alone, I'm alone!"

I lost that constituency, but not my life. Joshua, too, was defeated. The third candidate, Offord Morris, won for the Government.

I had turned over my seat in the Grenadines to Cosmos Cozier, whom my Party had recalled from New Jersey where he had migrated with his family. He had been a popular Revenue Officer in Bequia, but unknown in the Southern Grenadines. He still won handsomely.

Our party also won the North Leeward constituency though not without some drama. On the Sunday morning when we arrived in Chateaubelair and Fitz Hughes to launch my friend Robbie as candidate, throngs of people mobbed our entourage with the chant, "No Calder, No Key." I sensed their affection for me, but they were unhappy with my choice of candidate. "Bring Calder and a Bible!" I demanded. The youthful Calder Williams arrived. I demanded he swear allegiance to me and the Party. He won the election.

North Leeward relished their symbolic presence in our party. Their John Smith had named the NDP. The first convention launching our Constitution had been hosted by them. My surrender of my parliamentary salary to their volcano fund had registered among them. Over the years the affection from that end of the island continued to flow towards me. I was glad that Robbie was no longer the candidate so that he could be with me that night in Greggs when my life was on the line.

18

Union Island Uprising

As soon as the results were announced, the island of Union exploded. The people there could not bear the thought of another five years of Labour neglect, with their island being the punishment posting for out-of-favour teachers and policemen. The young people, led by the radical "Bumba" Charles, stormed the police station, blasting a hole in the building, and chased out the five policemen.

Recalling the Paget Farm experience, the new Prime Minister, Milton Cato, declared a State of Emergency and invaded Union. I announced that I would be prepared to use my influence to restore order without resort to violence. No one listened. Barbados sent in a regiment to Union Island to restore order, even though the youngsters had long vacated the police station. Twenty-two boys and girls, aged between 16 and 22, were chained together and flown to St. Vincent to be greeted by jeering mobs. All the seats but those for the pilot and the armed policemen were taken out of the aircraft to make room for the chained youngsters on the floor.

Union's leading business people, Conrad and Amutel Adams and Wycliffe Hutchinson, who by no means sanctioned the breakdown of law and order but were deemed Opposition supporters, were taken from their plush homes and incarcerated in the dungeon prison of Fort Charlotte, with a bucket (which was seldom emptied) for sanitary use.

Cosmos Cozier, frightened by the draconian turn of events, slipped out of the country, handing me his letter of resignation from Parliament, leaving the Grenadines seat empty.

The Barbadian troops, assisted by their Vincentian counterparts, searched every island in the Grenadines for weapons, fearing a proliferation of Cuban arms from Grenada. But not even a bullet was found. In the end, the only casualty from the operation was the shooting of a Vincentian policeman, Superintendent Cox, by one of his own men.

I went to Union a few weeks after the fiasco to give cheer to the families whose sons and daughters were in prison, still uncharged. The Barbadians were still there, enjoying themselves. And while they slept, in the dead of night, I toured the village of Ashton accompanied by my friend Sydney Alexander, who had in many campaigns walked miles between the villages carrying the battery for my public address system.

Meanwhile, Calypsonians throughout the Caribbean were inspired by the Barbadian occupation. One of the songs, "Boots, Boots, Government Boots," became very popular with Barbados' Tom Adams, the central satirical target for his "swift attack on Communism" 100 miles away!

Our party had only one other seat in Parliament – the North Leeward seat held by Calder Williams. But, manipulated by others on the mainland, he distanced himself from me and appointed his own senators.

I have always believed that a people get the government it deserves. I was also resigned to the fact that, after the election, the Government was going to enjoy a honeymoon. So I threw myself into work at our hotel. The Ministry of Works found it appropriate to harass me further by removing sand from the beach beside my hotel. I knew the State of Emergency declared after the Union problem could not go on forever, but we just worked even harder servicing our guests.

Eventually, the by-election was called and when polling day arrived, the political climate was still fraught with danger. Indeed, at one point outside a polling station, my supporters had to seize a weapon drawn on me by a Government Minister.

Wanting to anger the Government further, and to let both St. Vincent and Barbados know that the spirit of the Grenadines would not be broken, I had decided to go beyond the uprising, and framed a resolution, "The Grenadines Declaration," calling for a referendum on self-determination. Grenada's revolution, I was satisfied, was the cause of our electoral defeat, but I was determined that it would not cost me a second election. However, it was all very tense and even good friends were nervous.

Campaigning to recapture my seat, in the aftermath of the Grenada Revolution and the Union Uprising, I sailed from Mayreau with my friend Dick Richards in his small open boat, which had hardly enough room for both of us and the cow on its side in the bottom of the boat, its feet strapped together. The gunwale of the boat barely rose above the level of the sea and it was my job to free the cow should we all be swamped. We made it to Union. The old ladies who witnessed our arrival swore my angels protected me. Dick, though, on a later voyage on a bigger ship he captained, sadly vanished without a trace. I moved back to Parliament. I was determined to restore the dignity of my islands trampled on by the boots of the Barbadian army.

I won my seat handsomely. Back in Parliament, I went on an extended holiday from its proceedings, and concentrated my energies on consolidating my constituency and the family business.

The Government, meanwhile, trying to consolidate its power, brought a Bill to Parliament stating that a citizen may be arrested for intent to commit a crime. There were no clauses relating to the evidence that would be required to establish "intent." It would be pure mind-reading or, in reality, an effective tool to persecute opponents. Amid civil society protests and demonstrations, the Bill was withdrawn even before the second reading and formal debate.

Nora Peacock devoted her editorial in the *Vincentian* to my silence on the issue. An odd criticism: my silence had spoken volumes.

As these events unfolded, I set about planning for the next elections which were still years away. I kept up the pace on all fronts. Up and down the country I toiled, holding meetings at night in the capital with a lantern loaned by a one-legged shopkeeper, Elias Roach, whose humour was legendary among his customers. Roach also had some valuable words for me: "If it were not for the kicks, the football would not score a goal." And more intuitively, about the regional scene, he ventured: "One of these days, these islands will fight one another."

Back in Bequia, as I have already noted, electricity demand was exceeding plant capacity. (Many years later, after we formed the Government, I summoned the manager of Shell and demanded that his company install a bulk storage plant within three months. They agreed to do so. When my Government installed new generating equipment and our standby generator was no longer necessary, I was happy to give it to investors starting up the resort in Canouan.)

Meanwhile, the Cubans continued building an air base in Grenada, an intermediate point between Cuba and Africa to facilitate Cuban subversion in Angola. (I really didn't imagine the Cubans could build the Grenada airport, and in an interview with Don Rojas, whose father Frank had been Joshua's public relations man, I said so, much to the annoyance of Grenadians.) The airport was a matter of grave concern to the Americans whose ambassador Milan Bish was based in Barbados. He invited me to a breakfast at Young Island to discuss the issue. Construction was now almost complete. The ambassador, a heavy-set

Midwesterner of ruddy complexion, expressed American concern that Grenada's airstrip would become a staging point between Cuba and Angola where the Cubans were fighting the South Africans.

I told him the Americans should recognize the point of view of the Grenada Chamber of Commerce which supported the airport project. The US could not attract support in Grenada against the wishes of the private sector and the people, including Grenadians in the United States. I did my best to explain to Ambassador Bish that airport construction was vital to Grenada's development and that I wished we could do the same. I would not condemn the airport. Moreover, I said to him, "You will need that airport when the time comes to invade." Following the meeting, I issued a statement on Grenada: "He who rides a tiger will end up inside."

In St. Vincent, several opposition parties of varying complexion had come into existence. The death of Taffie Woods occasioned a by-election in Central Leeward. The left-wing United People's Movement agreed to join with us in the campaign, supporting our candidate Herbert Young, a civil servant and son of a former Member of Parliament. We didn't win that seat but came within a hair's breath with a 14 per cent swing. Our candidate and his wife were in tears, but I was jubilant, as the swing foretold a general election victory for my party.

At the home of the formerly jailed Teachers Union leader Yvonne Francis-Gibson, I met with the leftists to plan strategies for the next election. They were anxious to secure the majority of seats even though they had not yet made it to Parliament. At the close of the meeting I called for a discussion on communism and Grenada. My line was simple: Grenada had cost me an election and I would not let it happen again. My party opposed military rule and seizure of property. We would not let the image of Grenada affect our chances in St. Vincent. They bizzarely insisted the early Caribs were communists and St. Vincent should "return to the fold."

The implosion occurred. Bishop and his Minister Jacqueline Croft, who was pregnant with his child, were mercilessly killed; dozens leapt to their deaths from the fortress prison. Today, the bullet holes in the prison's metal basketball stand are a testimony to the multiple executions there. I called the left-wing group, the United People's Movement, and they agreed to co-operate with me, supporting our candidate Herbert Young, a civil servant and son of a former MP, as their own candidate. But the group would not agree to a joint statement on Grenada. I issued my statement to the media. "The people of Grenada cannot speak for themselves," I said in my broadcast. "We, their neighbours, have to speak for them. We have to act. If we do not have the means, we must on behalf of the people of Grenada seek help for them." It was broadcast over the region. CNN called. I declared boldly that the people of Grenada were in no position to respond and we neighbours owed it to them to call for external assistance on their behalf. I heard later from leaders like Winston Whyte who were then imprisoned in Grenada that my call was heard by them on transistor radio. For many, it was the first ray of hope in the most dismal episode in Caribbean history.

I caught our Government flat-footed. They were preparing to send a Minister to speak with the murderers. That, in my view, would be the act of recognition that the illegal regime of Bernard Coard needed. This gave me my cue to attack the Government for attempting to recognize an illegal regime.

Three months after my meeting with Ambassador Bish, the Americans invaded Grenada. They did not have proper maps when they needed them. They bombed the hospital. At the time of the landings, a yachtsman sailed into Carriacou, and, as he anchored, fired his ceremonial bow cannon. A white flag went up on the police station. So Carriacou surrendered to a yachtsman. I sailed my yacht *Sapphire* to the southern end of my constituency, beside Grenada. I was in our territorial waters when an American battleship approached. "Cut your engines," they said. I put up my British Virgin Islands flag and sailed into Clifton Bay in my own constituency in Union.

Having distanced myself from the leftist league both in Grenada and St. Vincent, I positioned our party in the liberal centre-ground. Taxation on gross income fuelled opposition to the Government and the experience of my premiership combined with the memory of our bold politics to overcome the energy crisis were now creating some enthusiasm for us. Our team was spread across the disciplines in society – business, teaching, youth leadership, and the professions. We were, in effect, both a working and a middle-class party. As Parliament dissolved to prepare for elections, I announced a threshold below which there would be no income tax, effectively relieving masons, carpenters, and certain hotel workers of their burden.

To the surprise of the diplomatic community, right beside Grenada there was a new Government. Barbados was caught out again. Assuming another uprising, Union style, their coastguard was heard by our taxi drivers on VHF radios in our waters. The Barbadians planned to arrest me this time. They did not deny it when I raised the issue at a meeting of the Regional Security System where I now I held the position as Minister of Defence.

PART IV

Prime Minister Mitchell:
The First 10 Years (1984 to 1994)

20. Weekend in Wiltshire, 1964

21. Opening of Frangipani Hotel, January 1967

22. Political event Paget Farm, Bequia, circa 1967

23. A Labour Party march in Kingstown, 1966

24. Campaigning, 1966

25. Toasting "Baby Doc" Duvalier at the Palace in Haiti with Pat and Robert Bradshaw

26. Inaugurating a road project, Alliance Government, 1973

27. 1972–74 Alliance Government. Standing l to r: Alphonso Dennie, Carlyle Payne, Victor Cuffy, Clive Tannis, Ivy Joshua, Jerome Burke, Othneil Sylvester; Seated l to r: self, JL Eustace, ET Joshua

28. After Bequia Regatta with John Compton, 1973

29. Meeting West Indian cricketers at Arnos Vale, 1973. From left: Mike Findlay, Vibert Bute, Stanley Hinds and self

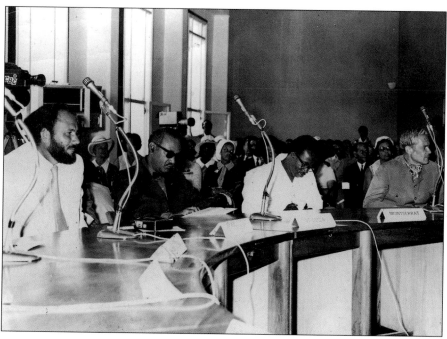

30. Early Carifta conference, Guyana. From left: self, George Mallet (St. Lucia), Austin Bramble (Montserrat), Michael Manley (Jamaica)

31. Switching on electricity in Bequia, 1968

32. With Premier Compton at a regional conference, circa 1973

33. Inspecting La Soufrière volcano eruption, 1972

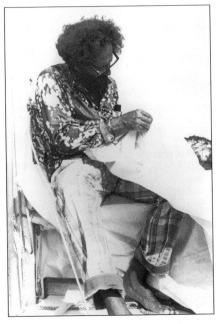

34. Mending a sail on yacht *Sapphire*, 1979

35. Campaigning in St. Vincent, 1984

36. Victory Parade, 1984 General Elections

37. Last photograph of the Executive
    Council, 1969. From left: Alcalde
    Warner (Attorney-General), Hywell
    George (last British Administrator),
    self, Milton Cato (Chief Minister),
    Levi Latham, JL Eustace, Hudson
    Tannis. Missing: Sam Slater

38. Carifta negotiations preparing for Lomé
    meeting with trade ministers;. From left:
    PJ Patterson, Brandford Taitt, self, Willie
    Demas, Sonny Ramphal

39. Crowning the Carival Queen, the late Donna Young in St. Vincent, 1985, among other
    Caribbean Queens

19

First Term: First Decisions

With eighteen years of parliamentary experience, in government and opposition, I was finally trusted to lead the country with a team without an hour's experience.

Our first Cabinet meeting within the first week, was very short. We took two decisions:

1. to appoint my life-saver, St. Clair Robinson, to be a Justice of the Peace, a title which as a retired policeman, he coveted;

2. to appoint a committee to examine the public finances and debt, with direction to give a preliminary report within a month and a final one within three months. Literally, I wanted a balance sheet so that I could begin to plan. I had drafted the terms of reference while I was in Opposition. I had discussed them with St. Aubyn Clarke, who was with ECLAC in Trinidad, while he had been moored on a yacht outside the Frangipani. Noel Venner, a retired colonial Vincentian economist who had lectured our party convention on the state of the economy, was made Chairman. I requested the Caribbean Development Bank (CDB) to relieve Arnhim Eustace as Secretary, and my own accountant, a school friend, Joe De Freitas, was installed to audit the books.

Our first budget was based on the preliminary report. Then I took off for the Commonwealth Finance Ministers meeting in Toronto and the World Bank/IMF meetings in Washington. The Canadians had invited me to go with them to the funeral of Indira Gandhi, but I declined as it was too early for such a distant exercise – a refusal that I still regret.

At the Toronto meeting I was a schoolboy taking notes. The jargon of international finance and structural adjustment were a foreign language I was determined to learn. My bright young advisers, Karl John and Gillian Nanton, took me aside during the luncheon adjournment and pleaded with me to shut up. They did not want to be embarrassed by the Bequia fisherman. I noted that each time Michael Wilson, the

Canadian Finance Minister, left the room to take a call, Tom Adams, the Barbadian Finance Minister and Prime Minister, continued smoothly. At the evening banquet Tom was at home toasting the Canadians with appropriate asides on the Canadian baseball team, the Blue Jays, of whom I had never heard.

To my surprise, Wilson invited me, as I had been paying such close attention, to be a concluding speaker. My officials did not squirm. By the time we reached Washington, I was ready to spread out my ideas on the management of our country's economy and its projections to the World Bank and IMF. Both bodies listened politely.

I bought every book with a title I thought I might need and collected every free publication available from the Bank and Fund. I was going to re-educate myself. Beholden to no one for my success, I was determined to carve our own path through the international financial jungle. Land reform creating a property-owning class, agricultural diversification away from the dominance of the sugar industry, tourism targeting the upper- and middle- classes in North America *and* Europe, would be my aims. Reducing taxes too would enhance confidence at home and encourage foreign investment.

The CDB released Arnhim Eustace, my economist from the Ministry of Trade era, now in the projects department, to be my Financial Secretary. I gave him one instruction. *No deficit.* No one was going to embarrass me with not being able to pay civil servants, or having to borrow from Jamaica to pay our university contribution as had happened before.

To restructure the sugar industry that had lost $45 million dollars in five years was not going to be easy. The FAO agreed to do an analysis. Arnhim Eustace, anxious to protect the CDB wicket, did not relish my insistence that the study should state categorically whether the industry was feasible or not. The FAO consultants arrived, and we could not agree on the terms of reference.

I met with the consultants at the official residence in Montrose one Friday afternoon, lectured to them on the rise and fall of crops in tropical agriculture, took them through the linkage between soil types and cane varieties, and finally the length of time the technology needed to develop profitability while the debt increased and world prices fell.

On the Monday morning a subdued Gillian Nanton, who had urged silence to me in Toronto, apologized, and informed me that the consultants had been suitably impressed. "We cannot fault this Prime Minister. He has a grasp of the subject that is frightening."

When the report was available, we closed the sugar industry. We increased the import of molasses from Guyana and continued to produce Sunset Rum. The differential in the price of imported sugar and local sales was used to reduce the sugar debt. Bananas took over the sugar fields. The farmers preferred year-round income and employment. In due course we captured the sugar-growing constituencies.

The figures in the Committee's report on public finances revealed an appalling drift toward bankruptcy. Even though we had begun to generate a surplus above the Government's expenditure, the Government-owned National Commercial Bank could not cash our cheques. We therefore had to borrow from the Central Bank. The Government-owned companies and statutory organizations were simply writing cheques with reckless abandon, and they were all losing money, be it in shipping, hotels, the dairy company, the water authority, and, of course, the sugar industry.

I was under no illusion that we were voted in with affection. The other side was voted out. The former Prime Minister gloried in his status of being Prime Minister, while his ministers gave priority to their law offices and businesses. One of them had been found guilty of contempt of court; another was abused by waterfront workers in Barbados. Their Minister of Agriculture deemed the worker's savings to be languishing in the Provident Fund, and turned over the money to the sugar industry to invest!

Inside the central committee of my own Party early dissension boiled over, with an incipient parochial flavour. Being from the Grenadines, where there was no public water supply, I was deemed insensitive to the cries of people of St. Vincent proper on the installation of water meters, and that alone would lose us the next election. My response was that those who did not want meters should do as the people in the Grenadines did and build expensive concrete cisterns and install gutters around the homes. They would then know the cost of water.

To the public cries that I was charging for God's water, I suggested they go in the river with a bucket, and that the bucket had to be bought, and that the workers in the water industry needed wages and not prayers. God may inspire workers, but he does not pay salaries. Before the television screen I sat one morning with a half glass of water. I compared the dollar a day to be charged per home through the metered system with the dollar for a shot of rum, and I gobbled the water down. "How much are you going to pay to have water to cook and keep the family clean?"

The women's vote lined up behind my argument. I accepted responsibility for the reckless statements made by some of my campaigners,
but we had to address the issue of solvency in our water authority,
access to investment, and distribution in every village in the remotest
part of the countryside. Our Chairman, an industrialist, Monty Maule,
his deputy Beverly Reddock, the Board and Engineer Managers, the
Grenadian Noel and later Daniel Cummings, stuck to our policies
without ministerial interference. With the legislation we copied from
St. Lucia, we became the envy of water authorities in the region,
including those of St. Lucia.

Contrary to my campaign rhetoric, the operator of the government-
owned ferry, *Grenadines Star*, informed me that the ship had $80,000
dollars in the bank. "In which case," I said, "please continue to manage
it." Two weeks later he requested funds to buy engine parts, boldly
asserting that the reserve was his own funds. "In which case," I added,
"please deliver the key." It turned out that the debts were almost the
value of the ship. We put it out to tender, for its original purpose, to
move equipment and materials, and privatized the ferry service.

At a school debate, a young lady won her prize asserting that I had
taken this ship out of service to ensure that Vincentians could not enjoy
the Grenadines! Today the private sector has produced the best ferry
service in the region with spare capacity for evening parties.

By June 1985 I was ready to confront the Caribbean Group for
Co-operation in Economic Development (CGCED), an amalgamation
chaired by the IMF, with the World Bank also participating, before
the international donor agencies which had already received guidance
from the Paris Club.

Jean Pierre Amsel, an IMF staff member, took me into his confidence
at lunch. "All governments," he said, "have grandiose plans when they
come to office and falter along the way. When you spoke in September,
we thought you were just another person who said one thing and did
another. Now we know you are serious with your strategy."

The donor response was favourable. The French, the British,
the European Investment Bank, USAID and the World Bank were
all ready to support design studies on infrastructure with a view to
implementation.

I attended the sessions for other regional governments established
before me, only to find they were in trouble with their deficits, while
they had long shopping lists without a strategy beyond dependence.

Foreign policy for a newly independent country, where there was no
experience among either political leaders or bureaucrats, was probably

the greatest task for such countries in the second half of the twentieth century. Metropolitan dominance was supposed to be terminated, only to be replaced by the yearning to belong somewhere. Out of this desire to be different emerged the non-aligned movement, with a greater feeling of involvement with the United Nations.

Being Premier, beyond my salutary excursion into Venezuela, did not equip me to be a Foreign Minister. But the long Friday afternoon walks as a little boy to pay off the family debts my father had incurred to build the ship in which he perished had helped to prepare me to be Minister of Finance.

John Compton came across from St. Lucia and spent a few days with me. His advice ranged through the whole gamut of government, how to handle security, funding for micro projects, the limitations in the Constitution on rearranging the public service, the United Nations and foreign policy choices.

Taiwan and China: two Chinas, or one China? My predecessor, at Independence, had opted for Taiwan. Technical assistance from Taiwan in agriculture was producing hill rice, and shrimps on sandy soils, neither of which I thought feasible. But in a housing project the Taiwanese technocrats had the wrong voltage. Matters of detail, not principle; I decided to do nothing rash, but to listen it through.

The United Nations protocol office met me at the airport in New York. Wonderful were all these trappings of Prime Minister, but I was soon deflated with the reception going on in our own offices where I was greeted with champagne in plastic glasses and a washroom "down the corridor."

An invitation came through to visit Japan. Why did other Prime Ministers elected before me not go to Japan? I enquired. They had been invited but turned down the offer. Would they repeat the offer to St. Lucia? I would be happy to go with Prime Minister Compton.

A charming petite girl, a graduate of not more than 20, turned up to show us Tokyo the first Sunday morning. She had volunteered to be with us, having already done her 75-hour week. The palace gates were our first stop. A Sunday market with all kinds of electronics was the second. The next day we went to *Asahi Shinbun* to see the greatest daily consumption of newsprint in the world. No interview was asked for. Then a scheduled meeting with the Finance Minister had to be postponed because of a Cabinet reshuffle. By the third day we were getting bored with tours. What was the reason for our invitation? My Government was generating a surplus. I did not come to Japan to see sights: I was here to do business.

So we went to a fishing village and witnessed the farming of all kinds of molluscs and fish to regenerate the coastline. The Minister of Forestry was available that night to receive us in a splendid restaurant served by geishas. The real thing! We had to deposit our shoes at the door. My beloved distant cousin, the distinguished Prime Minister of St. Lucia, alas in honouring this ritual at the same establishment, removed his brogues only to lay bare the holes in his socks. St. Peter's acolytes at the entrance to the pearly gates could not have been more polite. New socks appeared. Third World dignitaries had obviously been received at the restaurant before. I thanked Heaven that my Marks & Spencer's footwear had not let me down.

Then there was the question of whaling. My ancestors learnt to harpoon whales on New England fishing ships and the tradition survived in Bequia as the lone whaling outpost in the New World. Greenpeace-type activists appointed by St. Vincent had captured our seat in the International Whaling Commission. Their stand, I learnt, was in direct contrast to our allowed annual quota for hunting whales in our 28-foot whaling boats. My predecessor had agreed at Independence to have our seat on the Commission paid for by Greenpeace. The one paying the piper was calling our tune. I discovered to my amazement that one Dr. Christopher Davey, an Englishman in Florida, a man I had not met nor had he ever come to St. Vincent, was representing our interests. Did he really think that I, with my membership in the Institute of Biologists, was a species exterminator?

Our export of a few hundred pounds of arrowroot cut no ice with Japanese traders. The Japanese made it quite plain that no one needed to buy their products if the quality and price were wrong. Aid would come on the basis of other principles. They were interested in our votes to secure a seat on the Security Council. We should both adopt consistency on the Whaling Commission. Both Compton and I guaranteed performance.

I offered them a prime site for a fish market in our capital if they built one like theirs. Our dawn visit to the Tokyo fish market exposed a total new vision of the fishing industry. No protocol there. Keep out of the way of the auctions, the wholesalers, the retailers, the vendors. Real excitement!

Our negotiations started with a meeting in a Minister's office. It had all the precision of Japanese high-tech instruments. The officials with their notepads take their places on the high chairs, the Minister sits with you in the centre of the room around a low table. Our two officials, Geffrey Providence and Leslie Clarke, sat nervously but well-prepared.

An American, a world-wide lobbyist for Japanese whaling interests, Alan Macnow (married to a Japanese woman) ensured us that more than all our needs would be addressed if we supported the Japanese stand on whaling which corresponded to ours. The whaling people took us to a Karaoke club. Three Singapore girls, straight out of the glossy advertisements for the national airline, were part-time hostesses. They were in Japan to learn Japanese. We also met a school teacher doing part-time work. She agreed to show us Tokyo the next night. That was to be our last outing.

The entourage of the whaling dignitaries assembled in the foyer of the New Otani Hotel to take us to dinner. As we were about to leave, my school teacher arrived, bedecked in the finest livery and bowed past the group. I stayed behind. We had lost our hosts! She summoned a taxi. The driver was a part-time dealer in precious stones and quickly lost me in dialogue on the subject. We meandered through Tokyo and down a narrow lane to a small restaurant whose sole chef was the school teacher's friend. There was only one table. Behind the chef was an enormous menu written on the wall. Being an hotelier, I could not understand how such a hole in the wall could serve such an exhaustive menu. "Never mind" she said "order what you want. I am paying."

In the United States I would have been certain that I had run into a CIA trap. Warm *saki* to start. In a few minutes a van stopped at the entrance, and all kinds of crabs, molluscs, shrimps, eels and fish were disgorged. The night was getting serious. Could I cope?

"How are you feeling? the St. Lucian Prime Minister asked the next morning.

"Call me a Samurai," I suggested. "I now know why the Sun rises in the East."

Twelve and a half million dollars later I opened the best fish market in the Caribbean. I named it Little Tokyo.

For those readers unfamiliar with St. Vincent and the Grenadines, it is a plural country of two distinct geological ages. The people on the mainland, St. Vincent, have the culture of the land: the people of the Grenadines belong to the sea. One group looks to the mountains, the other to the horizon. I am in between – a sailor who studied agriculture. I had gone out on a political limb beyond the Union Uprising calling for a referendum to seek self-determination in the Grenadines, and now, the destiny of all the islands was in my hands.

It did not take me long to realize how leadership directly affects the lives of one's people, either by what you do, plan, or fail to do. I had seen poverty in rich countries, and at the conferences around the globe, saw the widest range of personalities influencing decisions. Leadership was why Singapore, Taiwan and South Korea moved ahead, while Africa retreated. The Americans may call it management, but I became satisfied that the quality of life in a country does not depend on resources, but on leadership.

In evaluating events around me, I kept returning to my nautical underpinnings, feeling that running a country is like steering a ship and that that ship cannot be allowed to drift. The captain must set a course before he leaves port. The course can undoubtedly change: external forces change; the weather changes. But the captain must still know where he wants to go.

As I became more and more involved in leading my country, I sensed that the plantation owners – who had dominated our land for more than a century – no longer wanted the responsibility for the thousands living on their estates. They would prefer to invest elsewhere, such as the tourist industry. I knew, too, that agriculture had to become more competitive for us to survive, and that meant responsibility for production in the hands of the farmer, caring for an area that he and his family owned and could manage, instead of being a wage-earner. I had declared that love of country begins with owning a piece of it.

We were bent on land reform bearing all those changes in mind. Time and again in politics, the unexpected has been the norm, and so it was again. Here we were, elected with land reform as the foremost element in our agenda, to find suddenly that a group of Danes from the TVIND organization settled on a small area on our leeward coast, had purchased Orange Hill, our largest plantation. Rehabilitation of wayward Danish youth was not a part of my mandate, sympathetic as I am to the basic principles – we could not afford the luxury of becoming a rehabilitation centre for aliens. But creating a viable peasantry out of menial plantation labourers was. And in the battle against communism and its all-pervasive intellectual rubbish, creating a property-owning democracy was a clear answer.

I summoned Martin Barnard, a scion of the Barnard family who had sold the 5000-acre to the Danish consortium and told him, "The Government will pay whatever anyone else will pay."

"You are too late, Sir," he replied.

"A government is never too late," I insisted.

Promptly, we in the Government agreed to an acquisition. But it was not at all simple. My friend and former Minister in the Alliance Government, Othneil Sylvester, was the lawyer for the Danes. He had set up a tangled web of local companies to control the assets, and his manoeuvres had imposed a severe strain on our earlier political alliance and friendship.

Big stakes were involved. I got in touch with Karl Hudson-Phillips of Trinidad and Tobago and asked him to guide us through the legal tangle. We offered the exact sum registered on the deed of conveyance, some $5 million, within a matter of days. It was refused.

Karl advised that we could seek a declaration of forfeiture. He presented all the cogent arguments against evasion of the alien land-holding licence, and how the Government could secure the estate without compensation. Instinctively, I rejected that suggestion. I did not want to have to explain to the Danes, the Europeans, or the world, that my government had secured property without compensation using a legal loophole.

Having established our legal position, we were ready to begin an orderly transition of ownership, but the move was further complicated when the outgoing landlord did not compensate his workers. We had to maintain production throughout an orderly transition.

Eustace Gulston of the Organization of American States (OAS) office came forward with a proposal on technical assistance. Surveys had to be undertaken; roads designed; areas allocated to housing, a playing field, and social infrastructure. The farmers would lease the land and the lease payments would go towards freehold ownership. Credit for fertilizer and other inputs would come from the Banana Association.

The legal battles went beyond the local court, the appeals court, and all the way to the Privy Council. The Privy Council upheld our rights, and approved our procedures except for our failure to pay interest from the date of acquisition.

Priority in allocation of farms was given to those who worked on the plantation, and then to those who came from the neighbouring villages. Poor people, who once faced the wrath of the magistrate's court for stealing a coconut, now owned the trees. Soon, their children would go to secondary schools.

One somewhat humorous incident highlighted the immense changes. At the land distribution ceremony as a triumphant people gathered to receive their letters, one worker declined. He preferred to work for people. He did not know how he would be paid if he worked for himself!

The banks that had historically ignored the people of the Carib Country, in and beyond Orange Hill, would in turn review policy. The area ceded to the Caribs by the British for 200 years was not deemed credit-worthy. I recalled how they had once considered me a bad risk.

It certainly was a continuing struggle to get the banks into financing development. At a meeting with managers of Barclays, Nova Scotia, CIBC and the Caribbean Banking Corporation (CBC), they declined. to participate. I tried to argue for a lower rate for mortgages for housing, but on this they refused to co-operate. I told them I was working on agriculture, and that this would stimulate the construction industry. We were still importing cement from Venezuela and Colombia, contrary to Caricom preferences. All to keep building costs down.

The CDB did organize a middle-income housing project for me at a 10.5 per cent annual interest rate, but I would have none of it. We had to break the image of the double digit. I wanted loans under 10 per cent.

We redid the numbers and the spreads from our pension funds and called in the banks, again warning them that housing loans would be available at 9 per cent, and that while I wanted commercial banks to survive, should they fail to match the rates at the government-owned bank, they would be out of business. The next week, breaking all the traditions of the past, an advertising sign on government-matching housing mortgages rates went up outside Barclays Bank.

Concessionary funds began to flow to our Orange Hill land reform project, converted to Rabacca Farms Ltd. We needed a single entity, outside of governmental control and bureaucracy, to distribute the land with some degree of equanimity. At the World Bank, the official designated for this kind of assignment was an Australian. We soon discovered how kindred were our spirits, for at two extreme corners of the world we had both studied Hardy's method of soil testing and Russell's *Soil Conditions for Plant Growth.*

The regional NGO, WAND, specializing in women and development, sought to be part of the process. I told them I had women in my Cabinet, that women ran my business, that apart from the messenger, I was the only male in the PM's office. I would be looking after the women in Orange Hill. We set a world record with one-third of the beneficiaries in our land reform being women. In time, they turned out to be more politically loyal than most of the men, who didn't even bother to feign gratitude.

Asia beckoned again. Seoul, South Korea, the poster proclaims, is where the East begins and never ends. The language was like that of our own people who declared that St. Vincent was "the natural place to be," as though Tierra Del Fuego, the ultimate home of all lost luggage from Caribbean destinations, did not possess its own singular charm.

Chen Doo Yuan received me in his palace. I thanked him for the gift of jeeps they sent us yearly, which helped the police and various ministries. That I should have come to the World Bank/IMF meetings along the same route where the Korean airline had been shot down by the Russians was to him a feat of bravery. I explained that it was a cold calculation that mistakes like that were not made twice, and that I expected that airline route to be the safest for a long time.

The South Koreans were anxious to demonstrate their wonderful economic recovery in a quarter of a century. At Lucky Gold Star's company headquarters, I went into the room of a think-tank where a dozen young graduates, all in white overalls like in any operating theatre were exchanging ideas on design. My team were impressed that a shop assistant in the small shop where she made her silken kimonos would kneel on the floor to wrap a housecoat for her customers. It was a natural gesture to her, something that would normally have been deemed a return to slavery by our folk.

My Minister of Trade, Marcus De Freitas, noted that the bowing in the East exceeded any courtesy in our entire history. (He appreciated my quip that the South Koreans were bowing all the way to the Bank.) They later put economic development before democracy and then shipped Chen Doo Yuan to a monastery after he was accused for misconduct. I always wondered how he fared.

Marcus was travelling a great deal at the time. The Dominican Republic destroyed his hopes that we could compete with them in fruit sales to the US – their costs were lower because they had 14-year-olds picking mangoes. When they joined us in the ACP, they had also promised not to compete with us in selling bananas to Europe, but their commitment was as serious as the cartoon referee in the soccer match between Iran and Iraq when he requested they did not shoot.

Stimulating our economy by exploring new avenues also took us to Colombia. Through our Development Corporation, we received an invitation to visit that country, and their embassy in Port of Spain made all the arrangements. The delegation was to be headed by me as Prime Minister. Our team consisted of the Attorney General, Emery Robertson, my Fiscal Adviser, Gillian Nanton, Fitz Richardson, Richard Joachim and Dick Gunn from the business community, and Jeffrey Providence from the Development Corporation.

It was a dire trip! The Twin Otter taking us to Martinique to catch the Air France connection to Colombia was caught up in some inter-tropical convergence zone which created the foulest weather imaginable as we were leaving St. Lucia for Martinique. The normally over-powered Twin Otter was rattling like an orchestra under an insane conductor while Martinique was totally obliterated. Going back to St. Lucia was out of the question, and Dominica was not night-landing country at the best of times. We circled around Martinique for some three-quarters of an hour, and finally the Martinique pilot plunged the aircraft through an opening in the black clouds and on to Lamentin Airport – already under a foot of water. Our shoes were wet but at least we were in the terminal building and not swimming, lost in the raging sea.

Some start for the Colombia saga!

Full protocol was arranged: guard of honour; red carpet lunch with President Velisario Betancur at a table full of the most beautiful yellow roses I had ever seen; a visit to the vaults of the Central Bank to see the incredible collection of exquisitely intricate gold ornaments made by the Indians long before the Spanish Conquest.

We went on to Medellin, landing between the mountains, weaving from buildings to the airstrip. A hair-raising experience. We were delighted to attend the opening of their new airport and, later, made our exit from there. That too was a scary exercise.

Medellin is a beautiful city, with ordinarily sensible people. We had a wonderful Sunday in the hills, at La Marguerita del Ocho restaurant where entire families seemed to be on an afternoon picnic. The restaurant was an enormous barn, with tables arranged around a dance floor where three generations of Colombians enjoyed the festive guitars and quatros. When the music stopped, the youngsters took over with soccer, and it was time to grab your glass of wine firmly. In one corner corn was roasted; in another, grilled steaks; in another, ribs. With quiet aplomb, right through the centre of the dining room, old men rode horses with their grandchildren, and the pooper-scoopers followed in train.

Up the hill, the young girls escorting us pointed with disdain to the homes of the Mafiosa. In the factories, we saw how hard the ordinary people worked for a pittance making garments, brass lamps, plastic toys.

Our security escorts were a strange collection. There was the standard uniformed group, but I was absolutely fascinated by two old fellows looking every inch typical peasants carrying innocuous straw baskets under their arm. Inside each basket was a short lethal automatic weapon. To this day, these fellows remain a mystery to me.

The black gentleman who seemed to be our contact and interpreter in Colombia was excited to take us to our final meeting with the Mayor of Medellin. Construction companies were ready to invest in houses, or anything funded through the CDB where Colombia was a contributor. I told him that I would rely on him as Mayor to ensure that no one with drug connections got in on the deal.

All this was supposed to be delivered through our interpreter. My Barcelona Spanish, while quite rusty, had been revived after a few days and I could understand more than I could speak. I knew the interpreter had not transmitted my views. I repeated my message about drug money. The interpreter still did not deliver my message.

So I spoke in Spanish.

The black contact man simply disappeared. Our bill, and my presidential suite, was no longer complementary. The construction companies came to St. Vincent later and put up two sample houses and some engineers produced a conceptual plan for our Union Island marina.

But our wandering in Colombia was over. Both the Mayor and the Attorney General that we met were shot later, at different times. Political killings? A falling-out with the drug barons? It is hard to say. Colombia is a beautiful country, as beautiful as any on God's earth. But the beauty of its roses and orchids is not enough.

I later returned to Colombia under totally different circumstances, having been invited to attend the inauguration of President Barco. Parnel Campbell came with me. Our route took us through Venezuela to meet up with Diego Arria (a Mustique home-owner), who had arranged a private plane to Bogota. We were at the home of Carlos Ardilla, the largest individual sugar producer in the world, with what appeared to be hundreds of armed bodyguards deployed in the gardens of the spacious villa. It was not until the evening that the foreign office people knew we had arrived. There were several ex-presidents and others at the private dinner, but my Spanish was not quite up to it participating in the heated and amiable discussion.

The inauguration of a Colombian President is an occasion like none other. The change over to Chen Shui-Bian in Taiwan was a school play compared to the Colombian war zone. Several Presidents, past Presidents, presidential hopefuls and Prime Ministers were in our hotel. The reception area became a military command centre with all kinds of transmitting equipment manned by hard-faced officers. Armed personnel were everywhere: inside the lifts; with guns trained on the lifts as they appeared; with weapons ready at each end of the corridors. Along the presidential route to the palace, tanks paraded in the street. People lined the route and were looking out of buildings, seemingly oblivious to the amount of weaponry deployed around them on the route, from roof tops, and at every manned intersection. Pillion riders on motorcycles faced backwards, their hands on their triggers. Campbell was a nervous wreck, fearing an accident could trigger confusion. "More serious stuff than *High Noon!*" he said.

After all the excitement, Diego took me to meet with Carlos Andres Perez in his suite. He was enthusiastic about helping us in the islands if he was returned to power.

My country seemed to be ducking the issues of international responsibility, gaining membership of institutions on the cheap. We were in the International Whaling Commission with an NGO paying our dues and representing us. As mentioned earlier, after my first speech at the United Nations, our New York office presumed to celebrate with champagne in plastic glasses, a gesture that I maintained was suitable only for a beach picnic. I had already declared the stationery in the PM's office to be no better than cheap toilet paper.

I discovered that we were in the Commonwealth on the cheap too, as an Associated Member, contributing reduced fees but extracting valuable technical co-operation. If I couldn't dine in the officers' mess, I wouldn't be relegated to "take away" – so I decided that either we, as a country, were to be seated at the Commonwealth Heads of Government meeting with some dignity or not at all. I paid up our full subscription and achieved a touch of class which I maintained thereafter. I always took along a Minister as part of his or her political education. Eddie Griffith accompanied me to my first CHOGM in The Bahamas.

Before going to Nassau, I had a visit from a British Conservative political whip, Bowen Wells, whom I had got to know when he worked for CDC in Guyana. Bowen had defeated Shirley Williams at a recent general election, one of the major upsets in the Thatcher victory. I had begged him to take up my cause on Independence, rushed on us while one-fifth of our people were in the refugee camps, evacuated from the villages under the volcano. But he wanted to make his maiden speech on the lofty subject of Zimbabwe's Independence instead.

Bowen's views on apartheid South Africa had been tempered by his Caribbean experience. He came to plead with me to help Margaret Thatcher through the war on apartheid looming over the impending Nassau Summit. He had no clear instructions beyond requesting me to ensure that the Commonwealth held together, and that Britain was not left in the cold.

And icy cold it was! At the first plenary on South Africa, it was pure drama. Kenneth Kaunda launched into his tearful entreaties with his white handkerchief wiping away the tears running down his cheeks. Those who had seen it before told me it was his routine piece of theatre, but it did not shake the Iron Lady. She had a wonderful record helping Zimbabwe and the Mozambiquans with funds and technical aid for railway repairs and was committed to help, but she was not going to destroy British industry. I hate to say it, but her speech came across as a tirade. The Conference Chairman, Sir Lynden Pindling, harassed at home with his own troubles, was the essence of poised dignity.

When we adjourned for coffee in the large hall splendidly set out with mid-morning snacks, Mrs. Thatcher sat alone. All the other Presidents and Prime Ministers were huddled together at the other end, the Africans chatting in their own tongues, the Pacific and Caribbean groups keeping to themselves..

I took my cup of black coffee over to Mrs. Thatcher and introduced myself. "I'm the new boy on the block, Madame Prime Minister, may I join you?"

"Certainly," she said.

She sat there as immobile as a statue, her features frozen in the chill she had imposed on us, the remnants of the Empire on which the sun once never set. Her invective on South Africa had poured outward like the smoke from a blast freezer. I began by telling her how I admired her policies and what a wonderful idea it was to get rid of those miserable council houses in England, and how I had fought the communists in the Caribbean. I was an hotelier and was set on a privatization course in shipping, airlines, farming and hotels, as well as getting rid of public-sector companies that were bleeding the taxpayers and the pension funds.

The British Prime Minister relaxed.

"Do you think, Prime Minister, that this conference should end with two conclusions?" I asked her eventually, getting to the reason I was talking to her.

"What do you mean?" she asked.

"One British, one others," I said.

"Certainly not."

"In which case, Madame, we have some work to do, don't we!"

"Indeed."

"Could I tell the others?" I asked.

"Why not?" she responded, nodding her approval.

I went to Rajiv Gandhi who had spotted me chatting with Mrs. Thatcher.

"The Lady wants a single conclusion," I told him.

The Conference then went on to other issues and South Africa and Mandela were temporarily abandoned for the Sunday Retreat.

At drinks before lunch, I chatted with Sir Geoffrey Howe who seemed to have gleaned the outcome of my chat with Mrs. Thatcher and its impact on the draft being contemplated by Sir Lynden. I took advantage of this opening with Sir Geoffrey to tell him about the impossible requirements his officials in the Caribbean were imposing on my road project in the Carib Country, an area neglected since Britain secured a settlement there hundreds of years before. A traffic study was needed where there was no traffic because the roads were impassable. So I had asked British officialdom to secure for me the services of the geniuses that had produced the feasibility on the Falklands Airport. Sir Geoffrey found the irony rather engaging and smiled as his officials took notes. He said he would see what could be done.

HMS *Britannia*, in all her gleaming glory, was anchored in Nassau. The Queen was hosting her African Kings, Presidents and Prime Ministers. Her presence was the key ingredient of the CHOGM. Each head of Government would disappear from the meeting, on cue, to have an audience with Her Majesty. I had my 15 minutes, and we talked mainly about preparations for her visit to St. Vincent.

The Queen's banquet was delayed, for the first and, I am sure, the only occasion during her reign. There were two methods one could get to the ship: one by a circuitous route along the highway and the other by launch across the bay. We who came by car ran into the demonstration with placards "The Chief's a thief," but we made it in on time. I thought the slogan had a touch of humour. The Bahamians, however, were not bellicose.

Tired of waiting for the boat passengers, Her Majesty joined us on the deck.

"Where are the boat people?" she asked. (This was the era of Cambodian boat refugees and the wrath of Pol Pot.) We roared with laughter. Her Majesty enjoyed bringing off a good joke.

The first of the "boat people" eventually to climb the gangway was the King of Lesotho. That day, Kings, Presidents and Prime Ministers were boat people and teased mercilessly for it.

The CHOGM Retreat is where the Commonwealth takes on meaning. The Retreat is the continuing bond between member countries, and heads of government get to know one another on a personal level, which results in all kinds of continuing co-operation on issues, international voting, appointing personnel, approving venues for sporting events, and so on. Discussions at the Retreat are the ultimate in informality, except for the Chairman and Secretary General who retain central responsibility.

The Bahamians had found for us each a luxury home in Lyford Cay. On the Sunday morning session, Rajiv Gandhi came to me and said he wanted Kenneth Kaunda (or KK as he was called) to sit between us, and that we would have to cheer him on to accepting the formula on apartheid. Mrs. Thatcher had agreed with the small group, Pindling, Bob Hawke and Brian Mulroney, to set up an eminent persons group to visit South Africa, see Mandela in prison, and report back to the Chairman who would transmit their findings back to us.

KK was leery of running into a trap. The group would be representative of the Commonwealth's shades of opinion, and capable of independent judgment. I tapped KK on the muscle of his leg. "Let's go with it," I pleaded.

He paused. The Africans seemed to be taking their cue from him. The Navy man from Nigeria, and Museveni from Uganda, were especially accommodating. I liked the matter-of-fact way Museveni stated his business.

The Africans agreed. And then the whole conference agreed. No voting; just the sentiments of common understanding.

The decision would buy time for Mrs. Thatcher. No agreement was reached on sanctions, but we were moving along. It was a compromise. We were all pleased with ourselves. But when we were all set to leave The Bahamas all hell broke loose with Mrs. Thatcher and the media. Had she compromised? she was asked.

"A teeny weeny bit," she replied, holding up a thumb and forefinger with the barest gap between them

Never would a tiny thumb and forefinger cast so immense a shadow over the painstaking conclusion of a serious conference. One by one, the leaders were forced to retreat into the familiar areas of boycott in sport, and the Commonwealth Games in Edinburgh became the next tragedy of the intransigence against apartheid sanctions. That singular gesture of meanness proved to be quite unnecessary.

We were back to square one with the British attitude. Fortunately the eminent persons were assembled, including Dame Nita Barrow from Barbados.

One great exchange in the plenary was between Mahathir Mohammed of Malaysia and Bob Hawke and Margaret Thatcher. It concerned an Australian of British descent who had been found in Malaysia with drugs on his possession, for which the penalty was death. Mahathir explained that all visitors signed the immigration form that stated the penalty on drugs quite plainly.

"The Prime Ministers of Australia and the UK need not be worried yet. The drug dealer will not be hung until after the appeal."

Bob Hawke pretended to be dismayed. The Nigerian naval officer loved it. At lunch he joked about it with me: "I shall not hang them until after they have appealed," he said, laughing. He liked that kind of justice.

I was back home in Bequia when the BBC reported another attempted coup in Nigeria, adding that the Government would allow the plotters to appeal their execution. There we go again, I thought. CHOGM revisited.

But it was time to get down to business. I had been introduced by John Compton to Moses Matalon, the Jewish Jamaican, who, with his construction company, was transforming the northern end of St. Lucia, linking Admiral Rodney's island to the mainland and dredging the swamps behind the hotels for a marina. Every evening, the fog blowers blasted the sites to drive out the sand flies and mosquitoes that had dominated the habitat for millions of years, and those little beasts had become the chief beneficiaries of the island's tourism, feasting on pale legs and converting them into reddened monstrosities.

Moses came down to St. Vincent on his yacht. He had sent his people to study our coastline. Moses was a philosopher engineer. He came to the point quickly. He could see what had to be done, and where it would get you. Extending our airport into the sea was our best option to enhance our tourism.

Cruising to Bequia on his yacht, we were looking at the flag for which I had set up a committee to re-examine the design and make recommendations. Our flag was one of the most expensive to construct, as it carried the coat of arms with our motto *Pax et Justitia* ("Peace and Justice") which therefore required it being legible on both sides in a double imprint. Then it was wrapped with a breadfruit leaf. It took a gale to get our flag flying. It sagged always limply from a mast.

"Whatever you do," Moses said, "do not change the colours blue, green and gold; they are the most beautiful colours in the rainbow. Forget about black and white!"

Public response to redesigning the flag was enthusiastic. Some 75 new designs were submitted. The Committee, chaired by Bassy Alexander, a surveyor and columnist, assisted by Joy Sprott, an old friend and business woman, Fr. Ulric Jones, selected three winning designs. We had a public launching in the centre of town, with Minister

John Horne, one of our cultural protectors, in charge. We flew the new designs in different locations alongside the old, and all were rejected.

My government had a problem on its hands.

Around that time, I had a meeting scheduled in Geneva with Bozo Dabinovic, our Maritime Commissioner, and Gloria Davy, an opera singer originally from St. Vincent. After we had dispensed with the ship registration business – which was in its infancy – and finished with a good meal at the Hotel des Bergues, I told them about the problems with redesigning the flag. I had actually intended to find a professional designer in London on the way back, but they said they knew someone who had just redesigned the Geneva coat of arms. They were enthusiastic about helping. So I took them to my room, showed them the new ideas from the competition, and a selection of the drawings, telling them I wanted to keep the blue, green and gold, and that I loved the gems theme that was recurring in some of the designs to replace the crest.

The next morning, they introduced me to Julien Van der Waal who had just returned from a vacation in France. I told him that he could try the breadfruit leaf – one that I actually carried in my briefcase – as a take-off on the Canadian maple leaf, but that I loved the theme of gems and the blue, green and gold.

He said he needed 48 hours. That was fine with me because it gave me time to study more thoughtfully the standards we needed to improve to establish a successful ship registry.

Julien reported on schedule. He demonstrated that there was no way that the breadfruit leaf would not be deemed a copy of the Canadian's leaf motif, and that it was "unimaginative, unimpressive and boring." I was very keen that our flag should be nothing like that. After all, the flag flutters in the breezes around the world, competing aesthetically with others from around the world. It was only natural to want one that succeeding generations could relate to with pride.

Julien did not disappoint. He revealed his various combinations of green gems in the golden centre. They were outstanding. The gems leapt out of the flag! When I saw the design in the shape of a V with the green taken out of the top of the V, I knew I had a symbol for St. Vincent, and that the diamonds would represent the plural nature of our islands.

He presented a design with lines defining the size and location of the diamonds in relation to the boundaries of the coloured stripes. The meticulous geometry could be expanded or reduced irrespective of size and even school children could easily reproduce it.

My prayers were answered. My instinct told me we now had an enduring symbol of our national pride that would compete with the designs of the world. I asked Julien how he managed to come up with such an amazing design in 48 hours, when all the talent in my country could not manage for so many months. In response, he related a story to me.

Picasso was once invited to draw a sketch for a waiter in a restaurant. He scratched a few swift lines and said, "That will be $5,000."
"You mean you charge me $5,000 for a few seconds' work?" the waiter asked.
"No," Picasso replied. "For 40 years' work'."

My design, Julien concluded, was not 48 hours', but 20 years' work. He was so pleased to be the designer of a flag, he charged nothing. I invited him to visit us when the Queen came, and we raised the flag.

On the way home I was scheduled to meet the Vincentian Community in Montreal, the group chaired by George Richardson, my school-mate who used to walk four miles to and from school. Vincentians beamed when they saw the new design and declared their support. Armed with the influence of that section of our Diaspora, I presented that final version that had incorporated the themes of our competition and the Cabinet agreed.

The Flag Committee, but for a few loyal souls, resigned. How dare we not accept their recommendations! I could understand their touchiness, but I had to find light at the end of the tunnel. Our young democracy had to learn the distinction between a committee's opinion and Cabinet's responsibility.

I dispatched the design for Royal assent and it was duly signed "Elizabeth R." We ordered the flags from Canada in time for the royal visit. Her Majesty was in St. Lucia and the text of her address to be delivered in St. Vincent had been forwarded to the *Britannia*. I received a call from the Private Secretary on the trip, saying that the Duke had suggested, and the Queen had approved, that she make a reference to the flag in her speech. Such crowning glory I could not have anticipated and we all began preparations for the visit.

Such an event demands meticulous presentation. Every minute of the Sovereign's time has to be planned with the approval of the Palace advance team. We were not in office long enough to have a project to be named in her honour, so it had to be a "people" occasion, having Her Majesty meet her subjects. The ancient wooden government house that had been home for the British Administrator from time immemorial was refurbished to minimal acceptable standards.

The best organizer in our administration was Parnel Campbell and I put him and Police Commissioner Toussaint in charge of all preparations. The prisoners were pleased to help, and I arranged for them to be present during the Sunday morning service in Victoria Park.

Our Archbishop, unfortunately, could not restrain his unrelenting enthusiasm. His sermon exceeded his allotted time, as he evidently thought he should send a message to the world's nuclear powers from the inspiration apparently received directly from the Supreme Authority. The Duke sitting beside me could not restrain his disgust. "Why do these people talk about matters on which they are ignorant?" he said to me.

The Archbishop's long peroration delayed our departure for Bequia, and at lunch on the *Britannia*, the ship's engines roared at full speed, making the table shake.

"Archbishop shudders," the Duke exclaimed. There was nothing I could add but, "Indeed."

Bequians relished the first-ever visit of their Queen. I wanted her to be among us in style, not only for the political enrichment her presence brought us, but for Her Majesty to identify with Port Elizabeth, the first town to be named after her when she was a princess. Her father had retroactively approved the naming after the burgesses of the town had been told that the Sovereign's name could not be used without royal consent. They then requested the Governor General to correct the misdemeanour. We can boast of the sole retroactive approval by the Sovereign. The Queen and the Duke planted flamboyant trees in stone circles where, to this day, plaques recall their presence.

My wife Pat hosted the garden party for 50 guests on our hotel grounds and the model boat-builder Lawson Sergeant presented a model of the Royal Yacht based on drawings confidentially loaned to him. The children lining the streets in Kingstown and Bequia kept their flag, the gems, as their personal souvenir.

Julien was delighted to be presented to the Queen. This signal honour was enough compensation for his work. He found a common interest with the Duke, in suggesting marketing strategies for the World Wildlife Fund.

After the celebrations, *Britannia* moved on to the privacy of Chatham Bay, and I returned to the duties I had been elected to perform. With their own man as Prime Minster, the constituents of the Grenadines enjoyed their newfound status, rejecting the colonial designation as a dependency of St. Vincent. They would show the mainland they were equals; they would carry their share. And I, as Prime Minister, did not even need my police escort after I boarded the ferry for Bequia.

The security detail simply picked me up at the Kingstown pier when I returned to the city to go to the office. I was public property then. The ferry boat became an office in which my constituents could express their needs: jobs, school books, health subsidies, references. And from the time the *Friendship Rose* docked in Bequia, the whole island knew I was home and the phones at home and the hotel started ringing.

With all passengers crowded in the *Friendship Rose*, there was great intimacy in conversation. When Neil Armstrong landed on the moon, an elderly shipwright was skeptical: "What worries me is if she doesn't shine any more."

Meanwhile, I worked on improving basic facilities throughout the villages of St. Vincent. Every path to the denigrated Baptist churches was paved. The old ladies could now wear their shoes to church without having to wash off the mud at the entrance. Splendidly, for our political image, my opponents picked on this meticulous attention to the village roads and tried to ridicule it saying we were building "gouti tracks," referring to the wild agouti which crashes through the bush making its own path. But the poor country folk were grateful for the roads and "building gouti tracks" became part of our political folklore. My strategy was to improve the lives of the rural poor even as I negotiated preferences in Europe so that the banana industry could flourish.

My burden of looking after the Southern Grenadines was lifted when I appointed Mary Hutchinson as a Senator. She had cried on my shoulder after visiting her husband Wycliff, a businessman who had been incarcerated at the Fort Charlotte prison after the Union Uprising. A devout Christian and school teacher, she was well respected and made my life easier, shouldering the burden of the southern islands while I struggled to master the intricacies of the Treasury, the jealousies arising within the police force over promotion and the random impositions in foreign affairs.

The need for improvement was evident everywhere. For instance, I visited police stations soon after being sworn in as Prime Minister, and was shocked at the state they were in. The men at the headquarters in the city were sleeping on pieces of foam that seemed to have been cut out with a dull cutlass. There were no sheets at all; the showers were green with mould; the toilets leaked; and they went to work in the mornings without even a cup of coffee or tea. I ordered instant repairs and bought two electrical kettles for the police headquarters out of my own pocket.

Rebuilding police stations was put into our fiscal plans and were in time executed. But wherever the police failed to respond promptly to citizens' requests for help, I got the unexpected criticism: "Son, you made them too comfortable. They don't want to patrol the streets."

The vacuum I created by withdrawing from service the government-operated landing barge, improperly used to transport passengers, was promptly filled by Captain Jeffrey King, an intrepid mariner, who bought the 94-foot *Vicky* in Norway, purchased lots of fuel and a powerful radio transmitter and asked his way across the Atlantic from other sea captains until he made landfall in the Grenadines. In turn, my cousins in the Gooding and Ollivierre families organized various joint ventures, purchasing other second-hand ferries in Europe, providing a far more frequent and reliable service than the government, including air-conditioned lounges with restaurant and televisions where fanatics could follow a Test cricket match in South Africa. Privatization said goodbye to the days of crowded passengers and discomfort on benches in the cabin of the last faithful ferry schooner, *Friendship Rose.*

20

First Term: On the International Stage

The Reagan presidency would have been totally vacuous without his triumphant visit to Grenada celebrating the monumental pin prick of the communist balloon. It was as incontrovertible a victory as Mrs. Thatcher's in the Falklands and Tony Blair's quick step in Afghanistan. Liberators deserve their moment of glory.

All of us in the East Caribbean that had moved in under the American umbrella, giving international respectability to the intervention, were invited to receive the President on our turf.

I told the US Embassy in Barbados that it would be an honour to meet the President, but I would not "be part of the decoration." A little shocked by my daring, they actually responded, enquiring what I wanted. "Scholarships for the young people to study in the United States," was my straightforward request. Lo and behold, the highlight for us in the President's address to the vast crowd in St. George's was the announcement of Presidential awards for student study in the United States.

My view was that this kind of thing would encourage young people who were critical of the invasion to reap some permanent reward from it. A few students secured places at Cornell in Hotel Management and Engineering. Some teachers, too, even though ungrateful to us, took some short courses. Later, the US administration changed tack, offering what they thought Caribbeans deserved, namely places in historical Black colleges. And eventually, the grand pronouncements forgotten, the programmes soon vanished from the American agenda.

Our private meeting with the President at Government House, in the company of Casper Weinberger, was an amicable affair with Reagan reading from his five bullet points. For our pains in Grenada, our spokespersons Eugenia Charles and John Compton, who had been hawks on the Grenada invasion, wanted to know if the US had any special consideration for us.

The President announced a grant of US$5 million dollars. The funds came through the East Caribbean Central Bank under a project named "Trade Support Grant." We had to file documents on trade statistics to justify the draw-down and each Prime Minister had to sign up for his share. It was a bit of a sham and I asked the USAID Director to accept the signature of the Cabinet Secretary instead. He would have none of it, so I signed on in the porch of my Bequia home. With our share, I built the banana roads between Mesopotamia and Lauders, in the area above the place where once my opponents tried to assassinate me. Grenada, alas, did not get their bombed-out hospital rebuilt! They got a lot of planning advice from some Harvard and Yale geniuses, and many tours of American businessmen. I think Blaize, the new Prime Minister, got free prostrate treatment at Walter Reid, but he still perished, while in his own constituency of Carriacou the roads were flaring up with dust.

American medical students, never threatened, returned to the US, kissed the ground and commemorated the Grenada victory – and helped to launch the second Reagan presidency. It was, for the American people, another war they had won, even if most had no idea where it was or that there was hardly any danger to their troops or citizens. That fact was brought home to me by an incident on my way back from the Commonwealth Conference in Vancouver.

I entered the US through Seattle rather than the usual Toronto/New York route, and, at the immigration desk, I had the usual incredulous greeting.

"St. Vincent and the Grenadines. Where is that?"

"Near to Grenada. Surely you heard of Grenada."

"I've heard of it. We invaded it, but where is it?"

Grenada once more invaded my political consciousness. The American Embassy, worried that my unexpected victory in St. Vincent might presage an unlikely outcome in Grenada, fretted also that the excesses of the former regime might remake Eric Gairy as an anti-colonial hero, where he had previously been regarded as a conspirator in the murder of Bishop's father.

Taking the coastguard boat from St. Vincent, John and I met with Herbert Blaize, the lonely leader of the old opposition to Gairy, at his home in Carriacou, along with representatives of other parties in Grenada. The erudite Winston Whyte thanked me for the ray of hope with which I had inspired them in prison before the troops landed. He like the others was anxious to see Grenada really reborn like a phoenix out of the ashes.

The parties had enough to digest and we agreed on another meeting to be held in my territory, this time in Union. Tom Adams, the Barbados Prime Minister, wanted some of the action. The aggression of his troops in my constituency did not endear him to me. He had however written a somewhat apologetic letter, following it up with a call, and I forgave him. So he asked to be invited to Union for my next meeting with the Grenadians.

Conrad Adams and his wife Amutel, arrested during the Barbados "Boots" operation to quell the Union Uprising, were our hosts. Looking out across the turquoise waters and the reefs offshore from the Adams' verandah, with a table set with a typical Grenadines array of drinks and seafood, we were all set to reposition Grenada on the world stage. The Adams family, no relation to the Barbados Prime Minister, were thrilled to demonstrate their humanity and triumph beyond the injustice meted out to them in the St. Vincent prison, where I had not been allowed to bring them any comfort.

Tom Adams was totally subdued in the home of those he had helped to torture. I chaired the meeting. Herbert Blaize, the Anglican lay reader, led the prayers with what was to be noted later as his substitute for careful analysis: "Bind us together, Lord, bind us together." Essentially we had to resolve three issues: an anti-Gairy alliance, its leadership, and the name of the party. Blaize's physical frailty, his former experience as a Chief Minister, and his age allowed the younger men to concede him leadership. Creation of a single party proved more bothersome. The word Labour, evocative of Gairy, was easily ruled out. National, Democratic, Congress, Movement, Party were all bandied about. My own party had a label, New, and we settled for New National Party and agreed the metaphoric symbol of a "house" as a hopeful image for Grenada's reconstruction.

Tom Adams flew back to Barbados and announced *his* success even before the Grenadians could get back home and discuss events among their people. My witnessing of the agreement, however, sustained the momentum. Federal agents of the US consulted with me, and with the funds provided, I designed and had all the posters and publicity material printed at Braithwaite's printery in St. Lucia.

The night of the election I slept in Union, listened to the results that went as we had planned, and at dawn took the coastguard boat to Carriacou to wake up Blaize, get him dressed, and prepare him to meet the international press that was streaming to Carriacou. A few pictures of the palm trees, the beaches in Carriacou, and a few sentences from the slow-speaking Blaize, were enough to tell the world that the

Grenada infringement of New World democracy was over. Grenada, Carriacou and Petit Martinique could now slip out of the news.

After Blaize had dispensed some US cash to his party supporters, we settled down to some fried eggs and discussion of formation of the post-revolutionary Grenada government. I could not believe my eyes when Blaize began to write out the portfolios he was keeping for himself, Finance, Foreign Affairs, Security, Trade and Leadership of Parliament. I told him he was crazy. I was the boss of my party. I created my party out of the wilderness. He was Chairman of a hurried coalition. He was old. He had to give the young people elected around him some work to do or there would be trouble. He refused to change. The effort I had put in to create his success was totally ignored. He was a Prime Minister now. In Blaize's mind there was not the slightest scintilla of respect for the source of his authority. Right away, and even before he took the boat to Grenada, I knew his Government would fall apart.

In despair I rang John Compton who was attending the Miami Conference on the Caribbean. "All is lost," I told him. He called Grenada, to no avail. We went to the opening of their Parliament for a few hours. I could not face with any ease the honourable men whom I had persuaded to join this unworkable alliance.

At home, the former Prime Minister, having barely made the deadline to qualify for the kind of pension he had legislated, resigned and we captured his seat with a customs broker, Louis Jones, in the wake of the court insistence that a former Minister repay the monies he had twice collected for freight for goods, consigned to his Ministry on his ship. There were other issues of corruption brought to my attention, but I was not interested in securing for myself the title of witch-hunter.

And while the Commonwealth Heads of Government were prepared to help us pursue political union, what was happening at home? My first effort was with the Petit St. Vincent Initiative on freedom of movement in 1972. The players were Eric Gairy, John Compton and I. The second was my address written in the Lawrence's home in Mustique and delivered in Sir Rupert Briercliff Hall in Tortola in 1987, to all the Prime Ministers, Chief Ministers, Ministers and diplomats. Whenever I was invited to address any group I developed the theme of unity. In St. Kitts, addressing the Chamber of Commerce I phrased it in terms of economic necessity.

Perhaps the most seminal was the paper presented to the Heads of Government at the Organization of East Caribbean States (OECS) in St. Lucia, in October 1986. The paper was in response to the suggestion made by Herbert Blaize at a breakfast meeting while we were all attending, as Finance Ministers, the annual meetings of the World Bank and the International Monetary Fund in Washington. Eugenia Charles of Dominica, Kennedy Simmonds of St. Kitts/Nevis, John Compton of St. Lucia, and Herbert Blaize of Grenada were all enthusiastic. Lester Bird, who had far more clout in Antigua and Barbuda than his father, the Prime Minister, was subsequently briefed by us.

The OECS set up a high-powered technical committee to carry the proposals further. The committee comprised some of the most formidable and prestigious brains in the region, Willie Demas, President of the Caribbean Development Bank, Alister (later Sir Alister) McIntyre, Vice Chancellor of the UWI and former Secretary General of UNCTAD, the Untied Nations Conference on Trade and Development, Vaughan Lewis, Director General of the OECS, and Crispin Sorhaindo of the Dominica Treasury and the CDB, later President of Dominica.

Billy Herbert of St. Kitts was designated to monitor progress on behalf of his country. Billy had been much involved as lawyer in the Anguilla separation and was deep in the offshore business in Anguilla while being chief adviser to Kennedy Simmonds. It did not take Billy long to inform me that the men in the islands north of us would be keeping their flag and identity in the United Nations. As Ambassador Plenipotentiary he was not contemplating any diminution of his status. As we began consultation in the various territories, Billy was still expected to lead discussions in the Leeward Islands. He led the cheering against unity. Years later, Billy vanished without a trace. It was suspected that his pleasure craft had exploded one weekend at sea, and there was speculation that his guardianship of offshore-held IRA funds might have been responsible for his death. Aerial searches in the Caribbean revealed nothing. His true tale has not yet been told.

Antigua declined to have any truck with our unification exercise. Functional co-operation was their agenda, albeit with the regional institutions in serious debt. So we set up the Constitutional Assembly of the Windward Islands – Dominica, St. Lucia, St. Vincent and Grenada. The Opposition and civil society were represented. A momentum developed. Various consultative sessions were held in each island. A Secretariat was appointed. The Churches claimed to be interested, but it was rather telling that in Catholic St. Lucia a Methodist represented the so-called religious support. The youth organizations were quite negative. My analysis that public opinion on unity would always reflect the "not yetters and yes butters" annoyed certain intellectuals, one whom in due course became one of our guardians in the judiciary.

Political union in the Caribbean is like a football, kicked about by all the players – and spectators – without ever going into goal. It reminds me of soccer in the war years of my youth, when we had one leather ball that had to be sown and patched every Saturday during intermission, and was stuffed with grass because rubber tubes weren't available. When the grass in the ball was soaking wet, kicking the ball was akin to kicking a dead animal. No joy at all.

Some objected that the quest for union by parties to the right was inspired by Washington, as though Washington had a new view on the Monroe Doctrine, or even cared. The truth is that succeeding generations of leaders want their individual taste of power, and cannot imagine power on a regional scale. Insularity is the easiest cause to espouse. The notion of a regional assembly petered out.

Vancouver! What a delight to return as Prime Minister to a CHOGM in a beautiful city that had nurtured me in my salad days. The Canadians have a wonderful country and a great quality of life, even though some, including my children, find Europe more exciting. But the Canadians have moved forward, decade after decade, eclipsing countries like Argentina that had greater wealth earlier in the twentieth century.

Knowing that I was a graduate of the University of British Columbia, the Secretary General, Sonny Ramphal, chose me to be one of the lead speakers at the Vancouver CHOGM. In accordance with the practice I had developed to extend the experience of people inside my Cabinet, I took along Parnel Campbell this time. We had our own office. I had arrived with a draft speech, and we worked and worked on my speech late into the night before the opening session. About 2 a.m. we were going down the corridor to leave and discovered the RCMP and protocol officers rehearsing the opening ceremony. Lo and behold, we saw two agents propping up a limping third person, and all of a sudden, the limping person walked normally. On enquiry, the explanation turned out to be a practice session to carry in Herbert Blaize, the Grenadian Prime Minister, without a wheelchair! How embarrassing for my neighbour, Grenada.

My speech was a success. Knowing the Canadian psyche and its inherent conflict between Quebec and the West, I turned Prime Minister Mulroney's welcome to us on its head by welcoming him to Vancouver as I knew the city before he did. Mrs. Thatcher was pleased that I thanked the taxpayers of the rich countries for their aid. Kenneth Kaunda was also a lead speaker, and somewhat stunned by my oration.

"James, you come from such a small place, and you make such a great speech."

"Mr. President," I replied. "When you don't have size on your side to command attention, you have to rely on quality."

"Have you been to Africa?"

"No."

"In which case I want you to be my guest in Zambia and address my party convention."

I was only too pleased to accept.

My daughter Sabrina had accompanied me to British Columbia, and took a few days off from studies at the University of Toronto where she was in her first year. At the retreat, she made good friends with Rajiv and Sonia Gandhi. They too invited us to visit them. My presentation on political union in the East Caribbean brought offers of help from Brian Mulroney; Rajiv left his seat, sat behind me and offered India's expertise in drafting a new constitution.

Mine was the only intervention at CHOGM that sought assistance in enlarging our states through surrender of sovereignty. Thereafter (and I attended five more CHOGMs) Caribbean leadership sang the constantly recurring litany of the plight of small states, entreating attention to our suffocation in the whirlwind of globalization, praying that the mills of God would no longer grind that exceedingly fine—but doing nothing! Finally President Museveni of Uganda could stand it no more. In Durban in his blunt fashion he asked, "Why are you people always complaining about your size? Why don't you do something about it!"

Sabrina and I never made it to India. Rajiv was assassinated before we could travel. Many a day I reflected on our discussions and wondered what life would have been like if we had co-operated on drafting a new constitution.

The sudden deaths of two Prime Ministers, Forbes Burnham and Tom Adams, shocked me profoundly. Tom had chatted amiably with me in the VIP lounge in Barbados a few weeks before the news of his death. He respected me after the Union Island meeting that steered the Grenada parties to victory. The British Government sent Baroness Young to represent them at the funeral.

Forbes Burnham never reminded me of my thwarting of his ambition to bring St. Vincent under his wing, but I suspected when I looked at him across the table at meetings he did not forget it. He had found other means to satisfy his lust for power. At a secret caucus in Barbados among the leaders, he sought our support for cancelling the visas of professionals who had migrated from Guyana, making them stateless. We needed a strategy to deal with the brain drain, he argued.

"Imagine," he said. "I found a Guyanese engineer selling aloe vera cream on the streets in Toronto."

"Forbes," I replied, "if an engineer is reduced to being a street vendor, it is more a reflection on you than him."

Edward Seaga, the Jamaican Prime Minister, poked me. "Touché," he said.

At a Caricom meeting, I asked Willie Demas to explain how in the town of Lynden, Burnham had secured over 100 per cent of the votes. Demas, a meticulous economist, excused it as an exaggeration.

I took Milton Cato and his wife Lucy, his nephew Burns Bonadie, former Secretary-General of the Caribbean Congress of Labour, to attend Tom's funeral as part of my official delegation. They were buddies of Tom. Indeed Milton was presumed to be very much under Tom's influence. Milton had refused to have me accompany him to the St. Kitts funeral of Bradshaw, but I did not remind him of this. Far better to usher in a touch of enlightenment in the evolution of political grace in our part of the world. I paid my own way to St. Kitts. Bradshaw's heavyweight successor, Paul Southwell, showered me with courtesies. An eminent Shakespearean at conferences, he prided himself in possessing a good turn of phrase. He had sought my support when we were finalizing the procedures for the Chairmanship of the Common Market (ECM) and that it should begin at the bottom of the alphabet, with St. Kitts/Nevis first, and St. Vincent and the Grenadines second. Nice idea, but I didn't see our neighbours buying it.

The Federal Flag of the West Indies that I had seized from the mast of my agricultural station in Campden Park on my departure was unfurled over the grave of Bradshaw and tossed in his coffin. Thus was interred the last remnants of our doomed West Indies Federation.

With the death of Forbes Burnham, Guyana was thrown into another election. The PNC election machinery remained intact, and Jagan's PPP with the Indian majority support relegated to Opposition. Once more the cries of foul play reverberated through the region, but the armed forces, loyal to the PNC, kept the lid on the boiling pot.

Dominica's Eugenia Charles, rocketed to prominence by her television appearances in Washington, beside President Reagan, anxious again to be the bastion of democracy in our region, demanded that Guyana be thrown out of the Caribbean Community and that the Secretariat be moved from Georgetown.

One of the great failures of our collapsed Federation was ascribed to the exclusion of Guyana. The thought played a part in the creation of Carifta when Guyana was awarded the Secretariat. Being part of the delegation that had agreed to a belated redress of previous shortcomings of this historic oversight, and while I had no sympathy for the election rigging in Guyana, throwing them out did not seem to me to be a sensible option.

The Trinidadian publisher of the tabloid *Bomb*, Satnarine Maharaj, came to Bequia with his editor Ian Gooding, my cousin, to do an article on me as the wind-surfing Prime Minister. I was photographed, athletically sailing among the yachts in Bequia's Admiralty Bay. Maharaj contended that the leadership of his Hindu temple in Guyana had supported Hoyte, the PNC President. Desmond Hoyte was his friend and he suggested I do something to help him. That weekend also in Bequia for a lunch at Mac's Pizzeria was a new acquaintance, a Mustique home-owner, Diego Arria, and his beautiful wife Tiqui, along with Peppone Della Schiava, President of Italian Fashion Designers. I asked them if they would help me host a private meeting of Prime Ministers in Mustique. They readily agreed. So did Harding and Mary Lawrence whom Diego had introduced me to a few weeks earlier, and whose beach house was vacant.

While I had been in the wilderness of Opposition, the only people who had time for me were the villagers, the same folk who had attended my cattle-dung meeting. So I was exceedingly cautious about friendship with the Mustique crowd, sensitive as I am to the political truism: the friends you meet on the way up are the ones you meet on the way down. Diego had attended the opening of our new Parliament and had brought along the Prime Minister of Portugal, Francisco Balsemao Pinto, who was his house-guest in Mustique. Colin Tennant realized that his concessions on the island were coming to an end, and he did not relish the prospect of having to negotiate with me again, 20 years on. I learnt that Diego, fresh from his governorship of Caracas, knew his politics and commented that "the place was littered with political corpses of those who had underestimated Son Mitchell."

Desmond Hoyte was ready for a meeting. So was Eugenia Charles. I sounded out other colleagues, and they were all ready – Bri St. John of Barbados, John Compton of St. Lucia, Kennedy Simmonds of St. Kitts/Nevis, and Herbert Blaize of Grenada. I chartered the planes to take us to Mustique, and engaged a friend, Flora Gunn, to be hostess, and Mustique settled down to coastguard surveillance and the invasion of Prime Ministers. The villagers loved it. Their man, ignored for years, was on centre stage.

The expansive verandah looking across the sea to Canouan and Isle à Quatre in Plantation House was the setting for the confrontation on the withdrawal of the Secretariat from Guyana, and the attack on the rigged elections in Guyana. Desmond led off with a long description of the elections, the votes in the various regimes, and how he had got beyond the black vote to encompass the Indians. Eugenia did not believe him and said so. We talked around the socialist policies, seeking to ascertain whether or not with the demise of Burnham, Guyana would be going in any new direction.

I put it to Desmond that if the Indians voted for him then he should lift the ban on importation of flour so that they could have *roti* without smuggling. I explained further, pointing to the wide expanse of Caribbean Sea beneath us, how the shrimp boats from Guyana brought us the beautiful large shrimps for our tourist industry and how I had personally arranged to supply them with flour from St. Vincent. He replied that Guyana had no foreign exchange to buy flour. So I proposed that we barter the flour for Guyana timbers. The same merchant in St. Vincent who had shares in the flour mill, Philip Veira, also had a lumber warehouse.

I wanted us to keep talking. The service at the villa was wonderful, excellent pastry with the coffee and fresh juices. By the time we were getting ready for lunch, I outlined a compromise. We would not challenge the legitimacy of the Guyana election in exchange for a change in Burnham's leftist policies. We would accept the results, but it would be the last time. Any future election must have observers. We undertook also not to say this in any press release. Our release would say only that we had come to an understanding in the best interests of the region.

Harding Lawrence himself was at hand in his beach house as our host for lunch. He was delighted to hear that we had settled our differences in Mustique. Desmond, I gathered, did not have an easy time back home lifting the ban on flour, but he eventually had his way. Our friendship matured. St. Vincent wanted rice for our mills and we got involved in resuscitating a country mill and exporting rice. Our manager, Ken Boyea, who had steered me into having executive medical examinations in Toronto after the sudden death of Tom Adams, was instrumental in the development.

All the Prime Ministers were pleased with the Mustique results. The Caribbean could forge ahead, but we would keep our eyes on Guyana's electoral processes. In the confidences we exchanged, Desmond reflected on the final hurdle to Guyana's Independence in 1964. Duncan Sandys, the British Tory Colonial Secretary, convinced Jagan of British impartiality, hinting how Britain never accepted anything but the Westminster first-past-the-post system, and Jagan expounded on television how he trusted the British. When Sandys came down on the side of proportional representation, it was too late for Jagan to retrieve the situation.

21

Second Term: No Opposition

In 1989, it was time to call elections. We had fulfilled most of our promises. The economy was buoyant. The sugar industry, close to penury, had been superseded by banana production at favourable prices and offering greater employment. The village roads had been paved and paths surfaced in impossible terrain. My constituency in the Grenadines had been split into two and Mary Hutchinson was ready to represent my former supporters. The city of Kingstown received an additional seat, taking the total to 15 seats in Parliament. Our team had lost a few Ministers. David Jack, too old to take on the strenuous weekly visits to the distant Carib country, had agreed to stand down and offered up support to the head teacher at Fancy, Monty Roberts. We had held a retreat in Canouan where we agreed on two important matters that, amazingly, were never leaked. One was that David would go "upstairs" to be Governor General, and the other on what date we would hold the election.

The Trade Minister, Marcus De Freitas, did the honourable thing in standing down while his family name was cleared in an unfortunate financial problem in Toronto. His place was taken by the veteran female Trade Unionist and teacher Yvonne Francis-Gibson, who also had been jailed by the Labour party for protest during the November teachers' demonstration.

A slightly modified testament to our IMF success was emblazoned on campaign T-shirts: "Much to please, little to fault." (The IMF's original line: "Much to praise" was considered too lavish, and with not enough emotion to attract the voters.)

Our final rally in Victoria Park attracted probably half the voters, about 24,000. The local artist Dinks Johnson had done a large satirical picture of the Opposition leader, Vincent Beache, standing amidst garbage on the beach. It amused the crowd endlessly. But when the banner carriers were taking away the ugly portrait, I called on them to bring it on stage so that I could have a good look.

211

"Do you want any Opposition?"

"No," they screamed.

"Let me have a good look at this picture," I said. "Because one day you will be doing the same thing to me."

No one of course was in a mood to accept my prophecy, but in that moment of glory, I wanted to let them know I knew too much of history and the fickle nature of the public not to realize how short their memory usually is, and how insatiable the public appetite to destroy their former heroes.

My speeches on political union had once been interpreted as an escape route for failing popularity at home and the critics could not believe our total victory. I was thankful that I had invited observers from the Trinidad Human Rights Association, led by Ramesh Maharaj, who pronounced the election free and fair. (Ramesh in time became a stern Attorney General in Panday's UNC government, surviving its demise with dignity. And the battles he won graced him with the experience to uphold my integrity, threatened as it was in retirement, keeping at bay the vultures of the second Labour inquisition, while in solitude, unperturbed, these memoirs blossomed like the rain tree I planted outside my window, even as the profanity of the slanderers, hypocrites and usurpers was laid bare.)

With no Opposition, our Constitution did not provide for a Leader of the Opposition, and in turn, no senatorial appointments by him. Our Acting Governor General, Henry Williams summoned me to instruct me to the contrary, and how in his own deliberate judgment, he could appoint an Opposition. I disagreed. My Attorney General, Parnel Campbell, sided with Williams, and secured letters from the law faculty of the UWI, and others, to justify the position. He had in mind certain persons whom he thought would be eminently suitable to lead the Opposition.

I had armed myself with the phone number of Buckingham Palace and knew my way to Her Majesty from previous experience. When Governor General Lambert Eustace, whom I had resurrected from anonymity, addressed a convention of youth attacking my government, I refused to put up with it. Earlier on, he had infuriated me by refusing to forward my recommendation for a knighthood for our most successful businessman, Philip Veira, the only one who had moved from merchandizing to manufacture and marketing products in the region. I recalled a relevant quote from Kipling: "If you can keep your head when all around you/ Are losing theirs and blaming it on you..." But I wasn't about to "make allowances for the Governor General doubting too" – I reported him to his boss, the Queen, calling the Palace at 9 a.m. London time. He was after all no more than a post-box between me as Prime Minister and the Queen, as Sir William Heseltine had put it to me at the Vancouver Summit.

The Private Secretary wanted to know what my wishes were.

"None," I said. "I am simply serving notice that he be invited to retire."

Sir Lambert was shocked when I kindly agreed to the date he chose to retire.

"I can wait, Your Excellency," he said.

"What do you mean, you can wait?" I replied. "Your dismissal has been agreed."

With that experience in mind, I made my way to London for consultations. Karl Hudson-Phillips had set up an appointment for me with an eminent barrister and Queen's Counsel, Mr. David Turner-Samuels, at Cloisters Chambers, in the Inner Temple. Turner-Samuels had been briefed by Hudson-Phillips on the fairness of our election, that the independent observers were satisfied and that there should be no impediment to a faithful interpretation of the Constitution.

The eloquent analysis of the consultation delivered as I looked out on the courtyard in the Inner Temple totally overwhelmed me. It was not that I was pleased to hear what I had hoped. The opinion given seemed absolutely incontrovertible. However, a verbal opinion was inadequate. I requested a written opinion and a statement of costs. The latter amounted to 1000 guineas.

At the Foreign Office, the message was identical. At any time that a Governor General finds himself in a position to exercise solely his deliberate judgment, he should be mindful that he is the Queen's representative, and, if in doubt, should consult Her Majesty.

I faxed back to the Cabinet Secretary Irma Young. I told her to inform the Acting Governor General, Henry Williams, that I had received appropriate professional and diplomatic advice at the highest level, and that nothing should be done until my return.

I returned with the appointment of David Jack assented by Her Majesty, awaiting only my signature and date, and presented the written opinion to the Acting Governor General, Cabinet and the Press. I then went to Government House at 2 p.m. on the Monday afternoon, thanked Mr. Henry Williams for his service to the nation, and informed him that he had two days to demit office as the new Governor General would be sworn in at 5 p.m. on Wednesday. I also told Mr. Williams that the view expressed in London was that, when in doubt in the exercise of deliberate judgment, a Governor General should consult the Palace. He sealed his fate by saying that if he did so, the palace would tell him to accept the view of Cabinet, something he was not about to do.

"Should you think of doing anything rash," I told him, "please understand you are already dismissed. Her Majesty has already signed the instrument for your successor."

I did not enjoy being ruthless, as it might have appeared, but there are times when one needs to act in accordance with the 11th Commandment: "Save thyself." And I knew that there was no shortage of legal talent in the region to raise the alarm were I to infringe the Constitution. In any case, it is totally unnecessary to create opposition. Opposition will arise on its own from treachery, ambition, self-righteousness, greed and impatience. When opposition is genuine, the Peter Principle governs politics as much as it does the rest of human affairs: when incompetence embraces arrogance to the delight of new opportunists, "the old order changeth."

I gave the Cabinet early guidance: remember those who sang hosannas for Christ in the morning, cried, "Crucify him" in the evening. With our absolute power, I said, we should do nothing that we could not face as ordinary citizens without that power.

Early into my second term, I visited Malaysia. Our first stop was Bangkok. It was the closest I would get to Mandalay, where I had longed to go ever since my headmaster objected to the "lascivious" way I presented the Kipling poem the night before our Speech Night. "Mitchell, you will learn 'If', instead," he said, banishing forever my schoolboy plan to titillate the audience with overt innuendo.

Bangkok was the most fascinating place I'd come to in the Far East. I was at the Oriental Hotel, again looking upon a scene reminiscent of the Grand Canal view in Venice, with all the barges and exotically designed boats plying their trade. The city had its own smell. Its craftsmanship was exquisite. I particularly liked what they did with teak. I thought I would like to import all my doors, frames and borders from here. Really I didn't think there was a wood finer than that teak for a house.

The next day, we got a female tour guide to take us to the golden temples, the Emerald Buddha, and for a ride on one of the small precarious junks that plied the filthy river. For years, she exchanged Christmas cards with my office. These were the days before e-mail and I never knew what became of that hospitable lass.

We decided to see the interior, and a visit was arranged for us by Janice Compton, the St. Lucian PM's wife, and daughter of St. Lucia's Governor General, Sir Frederick Clarke. Janice knew a diplomat at the

US Embassy who invited us all to inspect the refugee sanctuaries on the Cambodian border.

The landscape was flat on the way to Aranya. Rice fields abounded. I loved the bus stops with their temple-shaped roofs. The vegetation could have been Trinidad or Guyana, but the architecture of the bus stops, the temples along the way, and the little edifices built for spirits were what you would say defined Thailand. These ornate spirit roofs were gaily painted. You passed them in various sizes; some you could lift by yourself, while others would have needed a truck.

By the afternoon, we were going through a series of checkpoints ahead of the refugee camps. A diversion here and there to a military outpost, and a 20-minute wait for clearance in each. The fields were now in a deplorable and abandoned state. Not Guyana now, but Trinidad where fields became dilapidated in pursuit of oil money.

We finally reached our destination, the last camp before the Cambodian border, where some 48, 000 people were surrounded by a series of barbed-wire fences and ditches with soldiers pointing guns in both directions. No one was to escape into Thailand. We gathered that there were some other camps scattered along the Thai-Cambodian border, filled with refugees of all ages, strong men, old men, boys, mothers, children, old folk, all living in a bamboo world. Bamboo houses. Bamboo furniture. Bamboo beds for babies and old folks. No sheets, no blankets.

We split up. My Foreign Minister, Alpian Allen, went off to visit the buildings housing the handicapped who had lost limbs as a result of the fighting, the landmines and the war in the Cambodian forests. We visited the school, the classrooms, and the bamboo prison. Interestingly, inside this camp of no escape to Thailand or return to Cambodia, there was a system of justice with penalties, imposed by others similarly trapped.

What could we do? At the time I was preparing a speech for the United Nations on refugees. Had my American sponsor brought me here to taste powerlessness? The numbers in all the refugee camps exceeded our populations in St. Vincent, Grenada, St. Lucia and Dominica. Would our people ever know how lucky they are? For those in camps, one meal a day – United Nations gruel for babies, warriors and old ladies. For the children, water came from a truck. No sowing, no reaping.

Janice spotted a little girl in a T-shirt that said: "Nobody knows his destiny." The ultimate in irony, a discarded piece of clothing from a distant land, to a child unlettered in English.

The men in the camps looked strangely fit. Upon questioning, I learned that they slipped back into the Cambodian War and were reunited with their women, ensuring that there was another generation to be conceived and delivered on bamboo cots. A mature refugee who spoke with easy authority wanted to know if we wanted to adopt children. As a Prime Minister, he could let me have a dozen. To confirm his offer, mothers came with beautiful children in their arms and deposited them in our arms. I wanted to cry.

Our American sponsor did not improve the situation. "The United States will get them home for you. We can make the arrangements," she said.

How was I going to explain back home, with all our own poverty and unemployment, that I was bringing 12 orphans from Cambodia? I just didn't have the guts to do it. I considered selling it as a fine St. Vincent gesture to move up in the world's league of burden-sharing, but I couldn't do it. With all the interviews I have faced with the media and all those who ask me to encapsulate my life, I have never been able to tell the truth about Cambodia, how my heart was torn – and how my political instincts betrayed a piece of my soul I left in that wilderness.

At 11.30 p.m. we were back in the hotel beside the river, not too late for a beer and some shrimps. The High Commissioner, Dick Gunn, and his wife nearly fell over themselves when we turned up. They were sure we were dead because there had been shelling that day in one of the refugee camps. What would have been the press release to send home? "Prime Minister captured by Pol Pot." Or perhaps, "Prime Minister blown apart stepping on a land mine. Nothing to send home for a state funeral."

It was all too much for one day. I asked at the desk if the watermelon-carving course was on the next day and went to bed thinking about the child I had not adopted.

The next stop was Malaysia. Immigration forms tell a lot about a country. Usually the longer the form, the more backward the country. Zero drug tolerance assailed you from the Malaysian immigration form. I recalled the Nassau CHOGM where Bob Hawke and Mrs. Thatcher had laboured to save the life of the Aussie/Brit who had been apprehended for drugs in Malaysia.

Kuala Lumpur, the year's host to the CHOGM, looked marvellous with its well-tended gardens full of ornamental plants, but if you lay on the ground too long the speed of vegetation growth was such that you would be covered easily.

I ran into John Major, seated alone in the hotel lounge. I told him my party supported the Conservative Party, and how I admired

Mrs. Thatcher's pursuit of privatization, but I thought their poll tax contravened all principles of fair taxation. I did not expect an argument; I wanted to see my friends succeed. No one, let alone me, dreamt that the man declining to respond to the obvious, would soon be the beneficiary of the poll-tax fiasco.

The ease of meeting and talking with other Commonwealth heads is what is so good about CHOGMs. However there are some surprises. For example, you would think that West Indians found affinity with the Africans, but not all did. I could talk any time to Kaunda, Rawlings and Museveni, but there was no way you'd get much out of Moi or Banda. My friend from the Maldives, Gayoon, was always going on about sea-level rise and climate change. The ungracious among us would joke that his diminutive stature meant that he too was endangered. I did not make it when he hosted the Finance Ministers, but heard from Seaga how when travelling by boat between the hotel and the conference islands, he vomited every time.

On the first night of the retreat at Langkawi's Pelangi hotel, a fine village of teak luxury, I sat with Prime Minister Bob Hawke and his wife Hazel, and the Sultan of Brunei and his wife, who had on a pink diamond ring recently discovered in Australia. Bob and Hazel examined the stone which they had only heard about and expressed the view that it was beyond their reach. I liked the Malay name Pelangi. I decided to use it to name the second-hand yacht my hotel was buying. The word seemed harmonious with frangipani.

Good governance and the environment were the agenda of the next day. It was time, we thought, that Commonwealth countries should observe one another's elections. I advanced the view that it was most important when you did well that your elections be certified, especially if you won all seats. Benazir Bhutto quickly asked Secretary General Ramphal if I were crazy.

"He did win all seats!' Ramphal assured her.

Thank God, I thought again, that I had invited the international media and the Human Rights Association to certify our election results!

My final contribution to the meeting was to put forward a motion that we should establish an international commission on the tangle nets that were indiscriminately scraping the oceans.

My NDP had won all 15 seats in the second election. We had gone all the way to the Privy Council in London to confirm our land acquisition of the largest estate in the country. The pittance-per-day workers became farmers, their children moved to secondary school. The roads built with Mrs. Thatcher's aid money produced dozens of

Japanese vans in the Carib Country, replacing the two buses built on the backs of trucks. No longer did the country folk have to rise at 3 a.m. to spend all day in town. They could get to the city day and night. The fishermen were proud of their Japanese market which they called Chinatown as they could not tell a Japanese from a Chinese.

My Grenadines had, I admit, suffered some neglect, but I was preparing them for round two. I was not going to let the Vincentian jealousy of the Grenadines vent itself again as had happened when I was Premier. Every road opening was televised and the villagers put on a show in their own style, letting the nation know about the ease with which they could now get a box of Ju-c and a cylinder of cooking gas to their doors.

And the Commonwealth Conferences were coming up every two years. Our country was getting real value for money in this club, getting real exposure in the councils of the world, not like the UN where you glimpse the leaders in the corridors and chat with the ones next to you in the preordained positions where you stand to be photographed.

Kenneth Kaunda invited me to visit Zambia to address his Quinquennial Conference of the United National Independence Party. My trips to Venezuela had prepared me for red carpets, timed landing at airports, and 19-gun salutes. I did not miss the other two salvoes reserved for the Queen or my Governor General. The ambassadors that lined the tarmac seemed pleased to meet me as it took them from their desks sending newspaper clippings back home and I was creating another cocktail opportunity for them to bemoan the life of small states that could disappear in their lakes.

Kaunda was not available to dine with me the first night, so I was entertained by the Chief Justice, some parliamentarians and military protocol. Mandela was at the time suffering from pneumonia, and they were worried that the total liberation of Africa would halt. I urged them to take comfort from the news that meticulous South African expertise was attendant on him, that the people who initiated heart transplants would know how to look after a lung and it meant that South Africa was desperate to keep him alive. Two Vincentians called on me and joined the dinner. Dr. Regisford had worked with the troops in the Zimbabwe struggle (he came home and later died of AIDS, probably being infected by wounded guerrillas, but not before he had advised me to delay an operation on my knees), and an educationalist named Macauley Peters. (I brought him home to lead our Ministry of Education.)

Mulungushi was a rock in the bush in Zambia. It was around that rock that KK had launched his party and that was where he returned every year for his party's convention. There was no town or village in sight. It was a forest. A convention stage was built and in the vicinity a line of little huts for the visiting dignitaries. The huts were two single beds in a room and beside them a metal stand with a white enamel basin and an ewer with water, two towels and soap. Between the huts, at the back, was a latrine or two to be shared with other dignitaries.

KK attracted a lot of friends. All Africa seemed to be there in the huts – Mengistu of Ethiopia, Museveni of Uganda, Dos Santos of Angola, Sam Nujoma of Namibia, Oliver Tambo of South Africa, Joachim Chissano of Mozambique, Mobutu Seso Seko of Zaire and Yasser Arafat of Palestine.

We dined together for two nights and two days. Arafat dined alone. He invited me for breakfast as I was his neighbour with Tambo on the other side. I apologized to the Palestinian leader for the Caribbean's lukewarm support for his cause, but there were many Jewish-American tourists visiting our islands. Gairy's support of Palestine had cost his country dearly. Arafat quietly told me he was ready to recognize Israel. This was 1988 and my Jewish friend Trafford in Mustique couldn't understand why I didn't inform the world. I replied that I was not going to betray confidences of a relaxed moment, of either my girlfriends or my political friends.

Sam Nujoma of Namibia was all smiles. He knew about the African manoeuvres to ensure his country was next in line for liberation. Oliver Tambo was more reserved and KK kept him company eating with his fingers, delving into the stewed game and yams and tannias with quiet aplomb. The best joke was offered up by Chissano on Emperor Bokassa whom I then understood to have exceeded all expectations of Norman Vincent Peale's *The Power of Positive Thinking*. The Emperor abhorred the word "No." *No* did not exist in his vocabulary. A lieutenant was once accompanying him on a state visit outside his country. The lieutenant did his duty beside the Emperor night and day. On the last day Bokassa asked his man: "Officer, have you eaten?"

"Yes, Your Majesty, yesterday."

I did not dare trespass on the geniality of my African hosts to ask if on the state visits away from home host governments indulged the Emperor with his internationally famous cuisine (even though historically our Caribbean ancestors were reported to have also enjoyed their enemies).

Mengistu was the most easily distinguishable among the leaders. He would march with us through the lines of chanting African women, singing about how the Africans had crossed the Zambezi and planned to cross the Limpopo one day. But Mengistu would be no easy target for any assassin attending the festivities. He had six flanking bodyguards with the same pale brown complexion, almost identical features and blue casual uniforms.

I ventured to get an opinion on how he was coping with famine. A shrug. I had once long ago categorized politicians into: those who want to be, those who want to have, those who want to do. The basic French verbs: *être*, *avoir*, and *faire*. He belonged to the "be" category, the cock-of-the-roost type, which I think are the worst. There's nothing as dangerous as one desperate to be Number One. I had had my sample of that at home with my predecessor. I prefer to deal with those on the take, the "have." At least they do not stand in the way of your own performance.

I was later to meet Prince Ermias of Ethiopia through one of his sponsors, Baron Carlo Amato. He has a beautiful wife and two charming sons. I brought him to St. Vincent knowing how well his visit would be appreciated among the Rastas. They flooded the streets in front of my offices and I arranged for a delegation from them to meet with him in the Cabinet. They were finally touching the flesh of the direct descendant of their God Haile Selassie. "My grandfather was never interested in drugs. He guided African unity!" he told them, but it was not what the Rastas wanted to hear. They weren't looking for policy guidance.

Prince Ermias invested me with the insignia of the Order of Emperor Haile Selassie the First, a title that my Trinidadian adviser on protocol, Reggie Dumas, suggested be held in abeyance while I sought to be of service to Africa.

My fondest recollection of the expression of African power was the mellifluous chanting of the women preparing breakfast in this forest for thousands of delegates. And the chanting accompanied us as we walked together each morning to the dais where we sat for two days of speeches and always the energizing responses after each speech:

"One Nation?"

"One Nation!"

"One Party?"

"One Party!"

"One Leader?"

"One Leader!"

"And that leader is?"

"Kenneth Kaunda."

I was the sole representative on the rostrum from the West. And I was the last to speak. Gorbachev was blasting away about *glasnost* and *perestroika*, and I was sure it was relevant to African liberation. I was expecting the peace dividend from the end of the Cold War to provide funds for peaceful development such as fighting desertification in Africa. I did not dream that Africa itself was to provide the greatest market for the arms trade. In my speech I pleaded with the Africans on their bush fires. "If you love your country, why burn her?"

KK accepted my invitation and came to see me after we had won all the seats. We named the stand, where he addressed our people in Victoria Park one bright and sunny day, after him. It was the first time Africa reached St. Vincent. We were all proud. The folks even went along with Kaunda's chant: One Nation, one party, one leader and that leader? "Son Mitchell!"

I took him to Bequia. We visited the banana fields. He was impressed with our houses, the way our people dressed. He stayed with our Governor General at Government House. The morning he was leaving he had a serious question.

"James, how do you achieve such quality of life in a small place?"

All I could venture was: "Mr. President, when you have little you have to use it wisely. I come from a family that knew how to save and build."

I was sorry for Africa. I would have loved all those who wanted to steer us back to an Africa they knew not, to see the poverty, disease, the lack of hope – the sign in the tall hotel warning you to put away everything and lock your suitcase, clearly suggesting that even a manicure set a lady had given me for Christmas was obviously a needed treasure. I wished I could do more for Africa than show them my complexion that had emerged through the centuries of liaison between Europe and Africa. But I couldn't.

However, I was glad that our Commonwealth solidarity ensured that Zambia paid KK his gratuity and pension after he had put aside one nation, one party, one leader and cried for Africa all over the world. I will be passing on the carved chest he gave me, now outside my room, to a museum, but I still wonder if I will ever return to Mulungushi. Will the new liberators of Zambia who changed their Constitution to remove Kenneth Kaunda's citizenship posthumously allow his ashes to return there?

My next voyage abroad was to the Caricom Heads of Government Conference in Barbados, where I did battle with President Forbes Burnham of Guyana. Burnham, a man full of himself, always moved with consummate style and would enter a conference room with a great deal of flourish, buttressed by nervous minions flitting about him. He had studied law in England after the Second World War and the tone of his speeches was imbued with a certain Churchillian flair. His hand-crafted leather shoes were a subject of much sniggering in the corridors, but one had to be well prepared to take him on.

The *casus belli* for the conflict was this. I had procured a tennis net in Miami for my Frangipani Hotel tennis court and it had been placed for safe keeping in the cabin of the captain of Bernuth Lines. The ship was diverted to Guyana before entry into St. Vincent. Captain Oren King, a distant cousin, quickly lost the argument on undisclosed personal effects in his cabin, and my tennis net was seized and taken away by Guyana Customs officials.

Thus I decided to assail Guyana at the Conference, not really expecting any retrieval of stolen goods as I would have been quite happy if my net were deployed to produce a South American champion. Amidst the free-flowing debate on the harmonization of our trading policy in the Caribbean and all the mechanisms needed to be put in place to stimulate economic development, I said that we need occasionally to pay attention to detail, and our bureaucracy ought to be restrained in over-zealous execution of duties, even to the point where the name of the country is besmirched and confidence eroded. As a founding father of the extended Carifta, I was alarmed at the extent to which both the letter and spirit of our Treaty were abused. Indeed these divisions, to my mind, gave a totally new dimension to the meaning of "free" in "free trade."

And so I revealed the disappearance of my tennis net from the Bernuth Line's Captain's cabin in Georgetown harbour and braced myself for a blast from Burnham. Because he was cornered, I expected a real oratorical flourish from him.

But silence was all that greeted me. And: "Son, how dare you!" was all that I got from some of his colleagues at lunch.

With the weight of the discussions and Seaga's postulations on halting the sale of armed helicopters to South Africa, the tale of my tennis net, I was certain, had, like other lost causes, slipped into oblivion. But, lo and behold, as I opened my door the next morning at Sam Lord's Castle, there was my tennis net outside the door. The ruler of Guyana had chartered a LIAT plane to deliver my humble piece of sport equipment.

One of the Guyana minions accosted me on the way to the conference: "Prime Minister, did you get the thing?"

"Thank you very much. I got the thing."

Politicians often confuse their speech with actions, as though the sound of their voice is so wonderful that it becomes the substance of reality. Forbes Burnham never said a word about my net to the Conference. He demonstrated in one gesture the magnificence of his personality, and in the process gave birth to a story that became a legend among our sea captains. Later, I learned that chartering a passenger plane to deliver my tennis net was small beer. Burnham once shipped a gold bar by the hand of a Chinese employee in the sugar industry to be cashed in London to pay his embassy staff. He did not trust an Afro-Guyanese or Indian to do the job.

I was pleased that I had urged the lifting of restrictions on the importation of flour into Guyana so its citizens of Indian ancestry could make their *rotis*, and was always conscious that we should do more to help that country if we could. British Guiana had become independent with the name Guyana – later a Republic, as the Cooperative Republic of Guyana. Sir Walter Raleigh's earlier quest for gold in this continental territory, a place larger than England, became celebrated in the name of El Dorado, a majestic fifteen-year-old rum, aged in oaken casks, and the myth of gold triumphant. With socialism inspiring the government and opposition, even as an all-pervasive racism also reduced choice, the threatened souls, like my tennis net, escaped from the commanding heights of the economy to islands less endowed.

Following flour, my second project for the English-speaking South American republic involved its sand. I had learnt from Professor Hardy's course in soil science at ICTA that much of the rain forest in South America was over quartz sand and the forest had come into being over the millions of years sustaining itself on self-generating organic matter. When the forest was cleared and not thinned carefully in timber removal, the inert sand was exposed. In the course of my frequent travel to Guyana, all the way from Timeri Airport, I saw the mounds of sand and always wished we had that kind of sand for building at home.

At one CGCED meeting in Washington held in the austere top floor of the IMF, the Caribbean delegation faced up to the international institutions and all the donors, the European Union, France, Great Britain, the United States and Japan. We were castigated for not having an environmental project of our own. The World Bank, under the auspices of the newly formed Global Environmental Facility, was preparing a project to deal with solid waste from ships under the Marpol Convention designed to stop pollution of the seas.

I prepared a project overnight, with the central idea that we would take sand from Guyana, where vast quantities existed, and use it in the islands for the construction industry, to save the beaches. Equipment to mine the sand and deliver it to barges would be required in Guyana, and offloading equipment, storage and distribution facilities would be required in the islands.

All the donors were excited when I presented my paper the next day. They all wanted to fund the project: USAID, the British, the Europeans. I chose the European Investment Bank, as I was partial to working with Luxembourg after the excellent relations developed over the Bequia Airport. I knew Jean-Louis Biancarelli, the Lending Operations Director, would deliver.

The EIB's risk capital was deployed and a brilliant feasibility study was produced. I hosted a meeting of the Caribbean Planning Experts. And, then, all kinds of mischief surfaced.

The objections began with warnings that the endeavour would bring South American snakes into the islands. We contended that workers would surely see the snakes in the sand poured on to the barges. No, they said. It would be snake's eggs. And if not snake's eggs, then diseases. I had to wield my background in microbiology, arguing that, with a few cultures in test-tubes, this could be debunked in days. Antigua had its sand in Barbuda. Dominica had crushed rock, and so on.

When I drew attention to the feasibility study in St. Vincent, no company or individual would take it on. One New Year's morning, about to take a swim at Lower Bay to wind down from another legendary party at the Frangipani Hotel, the Old Year's night, I was accosted by a group of friends about the sand project: Francis Bynoe, the sea captain, Nik Kuhne, a resident German adventurer who owned a tug and who had settled in Bequia after a stint of trading in West Africa, Nolly Simmons who led a small construction company, and the businessman Sylvester Simmons, owner of De Reef restaurant and beach bar who had run once as a candidate against me. They could do the sand project, they said.

Between them, they had all the expertise to make the project work. I set up a meeting for them with the lawyer, Hans Matadial, to form a company named Sandpiper. The EU representative was visiting me that week. He met with Sylvester and authorized the use of the feasibility study to secure a bank loan, which the National Commercial Bank approved. The next week, Nik and Francis were off to Morgan City, Louisiana, and commissioned the construction of a barge. In six months, the barge was built and ready to come home, but with a diversion to Venezuela to deliver equipment for oil rigs, earning a freight of some US$90,000.

Two types of sand were moved around: the white quartz sand from Guyana, and the grey coarse volcanic residues from Martinique. The company then commissioned a second barge. Bequia used up 20,000 tons in a year. Mustique, Tobago and, eventually, Grenada, became markets. The new luxury project in Canouan appreciated the salt-free sand.

We decreed that no sand from beaches would be used in government construction. The Opposition whispered that I had shares in the company and that, in prohibiting the removal of sand from our beaches, I wanted to stop the poor from owning a home.

In Parliament I told the honourable member for Central Leeward that he should not only destroy the beaches of Layou and Barrouallie, but also that he should use trucks to do so. He should not then complain that it would be an act of God when the sea swells attacked the villages. The sand was our best defence in the hurricanes. The unscrupulous unfortunately continue to mine our beaches with front-end loaders and steal sand at night. The next hurricane attacked and devastated Layou and Barroualie just as I had warned.

The trade in sand thrived, even attracting the pirates off the Guyana coast. One such pirate cut and stole the towline between the tug and the barge! The captain and crew of the tug could only gaze in absolute consternation at the flagrant piracy and reconcile themselves to shortening the line to the barge when the interlopers left. Captain Kuhn complained to the agent in Georgetown who declared that he could find the towline for $1,000!

It was all too much. Better to use the tugs and barges elsewhere: the company decided. Sandpiper had secured a new powerful tug in Italy. A Guyanese ship was commissioned to bring the sand from Guyana. Let the Guyanese deal with the Guyanese, we thought. Alas, the Guyanese ship never reported precisely its date of departure or expected time of arrival. Then one day, the ship, *Fiona R*, ran into Hurricane Lilly off Tobago. The ship, Captain Randeram and his crew, all disappeared.

I leased a corner of Admiralty Bay to Sandpiper for storage of sand. They purchased a small dredge and restored our beaches in time to confront our first hurricane out of the West, Lenny, with its monumental waves that pounded the shorelines while I was in Kuwait securing the loan for the extension of our airport in St. Vincent.

In retirement, with occasional time on my hands, I visit the great mounds of imported sand, have a beer with friends, and indulge myself with my memories of a night in Washington, DC, when I set out hopefully to save our beaches and the glorious views of the sunset in our islands.

In 1984, a Dutchman representing the European Economic Community in the Caribbean, Johannes Ter Haar, called on me to pay his respects shortly after I assumed office. He brought me up to date on the functioning of the Lomé Convention which I had in part negotiated in 1974, outlining the structures of the national programme of direct help to individual countries and the regional aid programme. Europe was disappointed that our region had not accepted its procedures on procurement of commercial aircraft, and the funding had been withdrawn. He also explained the regional programme and how it had developed in Africa, building roads and bridges between countries. Well, no roads or bridges could be built across the Caribbean Sea and the demise of the aircraft assistance was a *fait accompli*. My brain went into overdrive. Should I get my neighbouring governments to designate the Grenadines – which every tourist to the region loved – as a regional centre and thereby eligible for the receipt of funds? It seemed to me then that it might just be feasible. Daily excursions were coming to Union Island from Barbados, Tobago, St. Lucia and Martinique, so I thought, why not my beloved Bequia?

St. Lucia's John Compton agreed. Blaize owed me a few good turns. Bri St. John in Barbados, previous Minister of Tourism, had been championing the value of regional packages (Barbados hotel displays had brochures on them describing the value of a combined Barbados-Grenadines holiday). Day excursions to the Grenadines were being marketed from Martinique, St. Lucia and Tobago, much to the annoyance of mainland-based Vincentians, who saw this innovative marketing as threatening our sovereignty. But I was prepared to advance regional tourism. All my correspondence conferring support for the Bequia Airport as a regional project entitled to aid was forwarded to the regional European Office for onward transmission to Brussels.

Trinidadian business was aiming to spread its wings. Sydney Knox had successfully built up Neal and Massey as the formidable industrial giant in the region, and was urging their banker Royal Bank to incorporate the St. Vincent Royal Bank branch. The licence was approved at a meeting I chaired, and the Caribbean Banking Corporation (later to be renamed the Royal Bank of Trinidad and Tobago – RBTT) was thus created, spreading its wings throughout the Caribbean. Anthony Lucky, the bank's lawyer, later became a Court of Appeal judge in Trinidad and moved on to the court in Hamburg for the Law of the Sea convention.

I invited Ray Robinson of Trinidad and his wife Pat to join me at the Bequia Easter Regatta and help me distribute the prizes. Needless to say we discussed the Trinidad political situation, particularly the rumour of the eminent demise of the PNM (in the previous election, my friend Karl Hudson-Phillips had secured 90,000 votes for his ONR, and no seat).

Knox and Hudson-Phillips were buddies. I had held discussions with Karl about Opposition collaboration to overcome the Westminster difficulty of third parties. I arranged a meeting at my Montrose residence between Knox and Robinson, suggesting that if Karl co-operated with Ray, they would be in a strong position to liaise with Basdeo Panday's Indian team and dethrone the PNM. It turned out that Basdeo agreed to the joint attack on the PNM, with Ray as leader. But Karl decided he would not be a Minister under Robinson as Prime Minister, but would support a merger. The important thing, though, was that Ray Robinson too was supporting my campaign to gain regional aid for Bequia.

When we got to Guyana for the next Caricom Heads of Government meeting, Desmond Hoyte, our host, was in the chair. He understood that my agenda among the plethora of topics on trade, health, communication, and external affairs was the European regional programme. Ninety million ecus were available. But funding for agricultural projects was a complex and complicated matter.

It seemed as though my subject would not come up. All day long we debated apartheid in South Africa. Every Caribbean leader had to exceed each other's exuberance on the topic. Everyone agreed we abhorred apartheid and that Mandela should be freed. Every speaker repeated what others had said. I waited until the day was almost over, then said that I had nothing new to add to the clearly presented South African debate, and that I would host in St. Vincent at our expense a meeting to resolve the agricultural issues that were holding up the allocation of the European funds.

St. Vincent had been rather negligent in hosting regional meetings because we had no large hotels. But we managed. We settled the agricultural projects. I was thus able to get our proposals for regional assistance to Brussels before the end of July and before my Dutch friend, Johannes Ter Haar, was posted to Africa.

Suriname by this time had acceded to the Caricom Treaty and was therefore entitled to funds in the Lomé Convention for the Caribbean. Commander Desi Bouterse had taken control, and his ambassador J. Harold Kolader indicated to me that his approval should be sought on a regional programme. My Minister Burton Williams had visited

Suriname and paved the way for us to meet in New York when he was visiting the United Nations.

We met for lunch in Manhattan. I sensed that Bouterse was examining how best to take Suriname forward now that he had military control. Sensitive to the Bishop fiasco in Grenada, we discussed how he should return the country to democracy before it was too late. My suggestion was to get the people to approve a new constitution through a properly held referendum that included an amnesty clause. Suriname needed the aid for the road and ferry linked to Guyana, across the Essequibo River, a clearly much-needed project and highly desirable. Bequia was again blessed by the support it gained from a grateful Suriname.

And so as the region gained EEC funding, my hopes for a Bequia airport grew. I was marketing an idea. I suppressed my glowing enthusiasm with my progress, confiding in my Director of Planning, Karl John. Some colleagues bought into the project in response to my favours. Others simply acquiesced to what they thought was an unattainable fantasy of mine. But at least no Caribbean leader was as negative as my predecessor at home who declared an airport in Bequia would only happen over his dead body, even though the World Bank had pointed out that: "The Grenadines are the area of most potential for tourism, requiring pre-development of certain basic facilities, notably jetties and air strips."

The Third Lomé Convention became my bible, occupying pride of place on my bed table and travelling up and down to Europe with me. "Conditions Precedent to Disbursement," the most mystifying psalm in the development religion, was the altar at which I worshipped. I studied with a theologian's zeal the framework of European aid to its poorer regions, even though the formula for them was different from mine.

On Grand Anse beach I secured from John Compton early one morning approval for our joint appointment of Dick Gunn, President of our Chamber of Commerce, to be High Commissioner in London and Ambassador to Brussels. Our budget committed £20,000 to European representation, and keeping both our banana and airport lobbies active and visible. While the Europeans were graciously listening, bureaucracy in the Caribbean bombarded the EEC with interminable memoranda confusing our cause, and a request for a further meeting. Dominica's Eugenia Charles and I, along with Secretary General Rainford, were dispatched to meet with the European Directorate. The Barbados ambassador hosted us in his splendid retreat in the Brussels woods and again all the ambassadors elaborated on how things were to be done if we were to be successful in Europe.

The Secretary General presented his brief the next morning (as he had apparently done before in several exchanges with Europe). The German Director Erich Wirsing was quite blunt. With nothing new that he could see, there was no further point in the meeting. Eugenia was anxious to take up Dominica's chairmanship of the ACP Council and she left me to carry on.

I explained that I was not beholden to Trade Ministers at home, that I had a mandate from the Prime Ministers to resolve the issues, that I was determined to conclude the business, and I would report on the telephone to seek approval from my colleagues along the way.

Apparently the sticking-point was the distribution of the 90 million ecus among the portfolios, that is, how much should go to trade or tourism or communications or education and so on. I said I did not mind if communication was expanded. The Europeans were expecting this. We juggled the figures; we discussed policy, self-sustaining growth, and so on. The Secretary General was dismayed. I sought an overnight adjournment, got Eugenia's blessing and spent the night and a considerable fortune on the telephone. One by one the Prime Ministers gave their blessing, St. Lucia, Grenada, Trinidad. I covered the East Caribbean, but had difficulty finding my friend Errol Barrow, the newly elected Prime Minister of Barbados.

I finally got on to Errol at 2 a.m. Miami time in a Miami hotel. His Belgian girlfriend was there with him, and they were both worried about her father who had recently suffered from a heart attack. I listened to Errol discussing with her when they could both travel to Belgium to visit her father. Patiently, I returned to the subject of the Lomé Convention. Errol was short: "Son, I trust your judgment."

The next day I initialled the agreement and brought it home for ratification and public signature. My faith in Errol Barrow and his Democratic Labour Party proved well justified. Bequia Airport in his opinion, as a lover of flying and aircraft, was long overdue. He declared his intention to be the first to land there.

I loved Errol Barrow. He was warm, gracious and I remembered his splendid paunch flowing beyond his morning coat at Independence. When his party won, I left a meeting in St. Kitts for the cookout he put on at his beach house, and that's where I first met his delightful Belgian companion. Not long afterwards, after a meeting of the Central Committee of my party, I called Errol to invite him to be the feature speaker at our convention.

"You wouldn't believe this," he said. "Son, my party decided to invite you to be our keynote speaker on the same day!"

We then arranged reciprocal days, and he would reserve day two of his convention for me to speak.

Every time I passed through Barbados on an early transit flight, Errol was at the airport for an early chat. He rose early and loved to be at the airport to see what was happening. His love of the sky and the sea pervaded his spirit, and my presence, I suppose, refreshed his love of sailing and made him look forward to another voyage. When Errol died, Cameron Tudor asked me to do the eulogy at Errol's funeral in Barbados. We met, we embraced and did not speak. I wept. My propensity for crying spontaneously is embarrassing to me.

A politician will always be shocked when he encounters thanks. Never do I pass through the airport in Barbados that a redcap does not abandon the hundreds of tourists to offer me help.

"You're the only politician that made me cry. You're the only one that made the whole of Barbados cry," one redcap told me. He began to recite, "Sunset and evening star and one clear call for me ..."

When Owen Arthur became Prime Minister of Barbados, he greeted me with the poem from Tennyson that was my farewell to my wonderful friend Errol. I was not surprised to learn that Errol had specified in his will that his ashes be thrown out from the sky into the blue Caribbean Sea.

I will have more to comment on Errol and his successors later. Suffice it to say here that to a large extent, Bequia got its airport through my bonding with Errol. We were kindred spirits of different ages. With the European Commission and the Caribbean Community agreed on the sector allocation of our regional aid under the Third Lomé Convention, my task at home was to ensure that plans were effectively executed to draw down the funds for Bequia Airport, while preparatory studies were undertaken in the Ministry of Education for an A-Level Community College as our second project. I had told the Caribbean Community Secretariat that I expected the other islands to draw down on education before me, but that, nevertheless, St. Vincent had to be included in the overall regional education project. Eddie Seaga, when he saw that the Bequia Airport was succeeding as a regional project, promptly lodged his bid for dormitories in Jamaica for UWI students to be deemed a regional project also.

To move forward the airport, I had to deal with the feasibility study being financed by the European Investment Bank (EIB). Following up a meeting of the CDB in Grenada, I had arranged with the EIB Director and his assistant economist, to visit the Grenadines with me to get a flavour of our tourism potential. I chartered a plane at government's expense to fly us from Grenada to Union Island for breakfast, and a CSY yacht at my expense to tour the islands. There was no way I could explain a yacht charter to the Treasury or to an incredulous electorate.

While at breakfast in Union Island the excursion flights could be seen and heard from the Anchorage dining room overlooking the shark pool. Our host, Charlotte Honnart, laid on a true French breakfast with coffee, fresh croissants, pain au chocolat, Danish, and jams for the sweet tooth.

We sailed to Palm Island 20 minutes away for a swim and lunch, courtesy of the Caldwells. By evening we were anchored off Petit St. Vincent watching the sunset over Petit Martinique and Carriacou, and dined American style in PSV. Hazen Richardson joined us at the table and revealed how he had moved from being the yacht captain to helping his boss build the resort. The message of success from the private sector of their rewards for investment in the Grenadines was coming through loud and clear.

I think our next day and night in the Tobago Cays brought the Bequia Airport even closer to realization. The translucent waters of the Tobago Cays and their truly turquoise colours, and the constantly refreshed white sand beaches surrounded by the World's End reef, are always guaranteed to send the most powerful message: "The ultimate Caribbean destination."

I was determined to put the five small islands and their reefs into a national marine park in perpetuity. Thanks to intervention by the Multilateral Investments Guarantee Agency (MIGA) and their representative Loren Weisenfeld, I was eventually able to succeed, with Ambassador Layne shuttling between the State Department and the MIGA offices in Washington. These environmental concepts heartened my visitors.

For lunch in the Cays, it was time to indulge my culinary skills. Some lobster divers I knew personally were commissioned to secure us some beautiful fresh specimens. Having approved the selection I requested the fishermen to boil them on the beach in sea water, and return. I cleaned them meticulously, marinated the lobster flesh in rose wine, lime juice and onion for half an hour. While the EIB Director was hanging his washed underwear to dry on the guard lines, I served chilled classic white burgundy. With the salad prepared, our feast was at hand. The planes were ready to land in Bequia.

That night we listened to the BBC World Service and the ship's short-wave radio. A *coup d'état* had taken place in Fiji. My guests wanted to know what I would do if there was a coup in St. Vincent. I produced the phone number of Buckingham Palace, and indicated that the coup plotters would have to secure each island while I asserted our sovereignty during my call to the Queen.

And so on to Mustique and Bequia. My guests were satisfied that the statistics on Grenadines travel were suitably presented.

My Director of Planning, Karl John, accompanied me to yet another meeting in Brussels. There we learnt more of the conditions that had to be met to secure disbursement. After some indulgence in one of the side-street restaurants off the Grand Place that evening, we took the train the next day to Luxembourg for a successful meeting with the EIB. (They helped us redraft our feasibility study which we then took to London to be addressed by the consultants at Halcrow.)

With access to European funds safely in the pipeline, the complementary projects for jetties, roads, water and housing had to be put in place from other sources, and satisfactory documentation sent forward to the European Office in Barbados for evaluation and onward transmission to Brussels.

The next hurdle was the European Commission itself and the bureaucracy of the Development Division, DG VIII. I had got to know the officials in the meetings on allocation of resources. The German Director, Dr. Wirsing, had before him the Caribbean requests in the transportation sector to be decided on.

Beyond the bureaucracy was the imposing figure of the former Italian Minister dealing with the Navy, Lorenzo Natali, now the Development Commissioner. His English was almost non-existent. I invited him to visit Bequia and the Grenadines. To ensure he had a good picture of the site, we used the coastguard, and sailed to Bequia, not in the calm waters of the lee, but over the turbulent northern end, where the uplifting currents against the wind made the journey a horror. Natali's translator turned green. He had to rely on another in his party to keep our dialogue going. Natali, much older than his young English assistant, relished the voyage. By the time we reached the Frangipani for lunch, he was in an ebullient mood.

I thanked Natali for the enthusiastic response from the Europeans as regards help in my land reform programme. However, I went on to complain about the Americans who ideologically opposed funding my land reform programme. I explained my problem as a liberal politician in the Caribbean, opposing communism while advocating private-sector advancement. The Americans wanted me to transfer my hard-earned gains over land for the workers into a company controlled by foreign investors in a winter vegetable garden. When I expounded the need for technical assistance to peasant farmers, the request was declined.

My London reading had exposed me to Ignazio Silone's *Bread and Wine*, a political novel about the Italian countryside.

"Ignazio Silone," Natali beamed. "He wrote about my constituency. I financed his early play! How do I hear about Silone in this Bequia?"

From then on I had direct access to the Commissioner. No stumbling block put forward by the bureaucracy in Brussels withstood my offensives. The VIP lounge in Bequia Airport is affectionately dedicated to Lorenzo Natali. Unfortunately, he did not live to attend our opening ceremony.

The project went forward to competitive bids in Europe. The Germans Kocks Consult GMBH became the engineering design consultants and the Dutch J. V. Interbeton/Ham secured the building contract.

Even as we had a public launching for the commencement of construction, I visited the school in Paget Farm and lectured the children on courtesy to the visiting Europeans. Even after the massive dredging began work, skeptics, including school teachers, were in denial.

The opening of the airport was a grand affair. All those who had helped, whether in office or out, were invited to the party. Bequia deserved to celebrate. Bequia and the Frangipani had laid the foundations of the New Democratic Party and the airport in Bequia would be a permanent monument to our political maturity on the international scene.

But mischief was afoot. A few hours before the ceremony, a bomb scare to the Frangipani Hotel came through on the telephone.

"Ignore it," I told the staff and the police. "This is my place, if it has to blow up, today is a great time. The mischievous in this country are not yet bright enough to make a bomb." For me the hoax was equivalent to anonymous letters in the press, written by troublemakers without the courage to attach their name to their cause.

My friend, the long-suffering regional journalist Rickey Singh castigated me on the lavish expenditure. "Prime Minister Mitchell, normally careful and meticulous with expenditure, went overboard," he declared.

"Ricky," I said. "Three points I wish to make. Firstly, the Bequia Airport is the largest single grant project in the entire Caribbean. It was executed in time, on budget, with additional funds merited on performance. I doubt if this level of project will ever again be approved by 14 governments in the Caribbean and 12 in Europe. Secondly, I belong to that soon-to-be-extinct species of Caribbean men who knows how to say thanks. Thirdly, the development of St. Vincent and the Grenadines is not complete. I will need these folks again."

Robinson came to the party, but had not even remotely expected the level of celebrations we had. "Son Mitchell puts on a hell of a show and this airport is not even as good as mine in Tobago; I didn't put on a show like this!" he said.

"That is why he is still Prime Minister and you are not," Karl Hudson-Phillips told him.

In the period of the development of Bequia Airport, I had triumphed over much personal anguish. The geography of the islands had always imposed itself upon our family's lifestyle, with sailing ferries confining communication to once a day, five days a week. With my wife cultivating the family business, the Frangipani, in one island and my administering a government in another, opportunity was created for diversion of our interests. Drifting with the rhythms of a guitarist, Pat was soon lecturing me on some theme about loving someone and setting them free as a test of sincerity. With this and my subsequent loss of government, both new baptisms of adversity, I was to learn that in affairs of the heart, as well as in politics, you need, for your sanity, the creativity of a boxer: when you are floored, never rise until you have a game plan for triumph. (The lesson was to come useful later in the Banana War.)

With the loss of the premiership, valium came to my rescue and in due course I resolved never to cry for St. Vincent or a woman again. When my fruit trees on the farmland I had purchased were razed to the ground by a malicious fire, and all the early morning attention by my young daughters, watering them in drought, had come to nought, my children were shocked that I was ready to replant three times as many seedlings.

Opposition in Parliament turned out to be conducive for managing the business and mending the strands in the loosened family. With the business growing again, and Sabrina, Gretel and Louise to educate, we resolved never again to allow any change in political fortunes to erode our investments.

But the drifting scenario was to repeat itself with my absence from home as Prime Minister, charting around the world a course for a newly independent land. One weekend at the head of the stairs at home, Pat informed me that she supposed I was aware that she had a friend. I replied simply: "These things evolve." I had managed to monitor certain indulgences. I had ensured that she had properties in her name.

She left home the very night I was hosting the top official from Brussels whose support was critical to the success of the Bequia airport project. It was the culmination of a period in which I had not only had to arrange a divorce, but also reorganize the family business, plan the expansion of the hotel, and ensure the continuing education of my children in Toronto, even while it looked as though our fortunes were sinking. And so before I delivered my feature address at the opening, I obtained the score of an old-time favourite tune out of New York, had the police band practise it and play for me: "Nobody knows the trouble I've seen." I could understand Pat's tears.

While my Caribbean colleagues approved of my Bequia airport project from its inception, I think they mostly went along with it assuming it was a pie in the sky. My eventual success galvanized them, and each set about looking for a way to take advantage of the Lomé Convention, that, until then, had played second fiddle for them to apartheid, jobs for the boys at UN agencies, and other inter-island rivalries.

Nevis was well positioned for airport development. Kennedy Simmonds had become Prime Minister, launching St. Kitts and Nevis into Independence and settling with the British, once and for all, on the virtual separation of Anguilla. Simeon Daniel, the Nevisian leader, had sought my advice in Bequia before he attended the constitutional conference in London. I advised that he insert a clause in his constitution allowing for a referendum on a separate Nevis, and also specify the proportion of seats to which Nevis would be entitled in the St. Kitts/Nevis Parliament. Constitutional niceties inspire respect. Anxious to please Nevis, St. Kitts had agreed.

With this background, I was happy to help Nevis get an improved airport. Although Simmons launched the project, I was not satisfied that he was doing the preparatory work in getting the entire economy and other local infrastructure in shape to meet prerequisites for the aid. At the Antigua Caricom meeting, my interjection to that effect was misconstrued, with many concluding that, having succeeded, I did not care about the others.

Their approach, I insisted, would mean the project would be likely to take more than five years to complete, if it happened at all. Bequia's success, beyond the Caricom support, came as a result of considerable local strategic planning, including satisfying the World Bank and the IMF on the execution of appropriate policies – my experience in which I would readily make available to their technicians.

As discreetly as I could, I was trying to bring into focus, without any hectoring, the new religion in the fiscal cathedral, far more inflexible than any real religion's, called "Conditions Precedent to Disbursement" (or "the CPD Doctrine," as I named it). Devised by the formidable

Paris Club of international donors, we had to worship or perish. I was to preach the sermon to my colleagues over and over again.

The IMF asked me to have a word with St. Kitts. I addressed Kennedy's party and the private sector, and explained how I closed the sugar industry and how they should diversify into more tourism. Nevis, in due course, got its airport.

Ralph O'Neil of the British Virgin Islands did understand my point, and I was able to shepherd the Beef Island Airport along the way from time to time. The heavy-set Chief Minister was contemptuous of the St. Kitts fuss and simply said to me, "Son, give me the formula." In a way, the BVI had it easier, in that as a dependent territory they had the British on their side, and there were two avenues to be pursued for their funding in Europe. I was already retired when the new Beef Island Airport was ready for opening and Ralph invited me to the ceremony. And then one evening, at the Frangipani barbeque, above the sound of the steel band, Ariane, a charming and fair youngster with her hair in braids accosted me: "I remember you. You are the one who helped Grandpa with the airport!"

"Which airport?" I asked.

"The Terrance B. Lettsome Airport. I am the granddaughter; I cut the ribbon at the ceremony!" she reminded me.

I bent down over her: "Give me a kiss."

As schoolboys, we recited from the Bible all about sowing seeds among thorns and on good ground, and how the thorns choked some but others bore good fruit. Similarly, the BVI under the umbrella of British security enjoy thriving tourism. Some of my people are reaping fruit there. I enjoy that. A prophecy I made to my journalist friend, Ricky Singh, however, has become a reality. With Haiti and the Dominican Republic now sharing the European pie with us, and poverty topping the agenda, there was no way that the middle-income Bequia I created could secure the biggest slice of the pie again.

Sir Arthur Lewis, first President of the Caribbean Development bank (CDB), in one of his annual statements to the Governors of the Bank, pointed the way to how successful services could be provided decades before we dreamt of becoming a service-based economy: "When you go into a store in a developed country, they say, 'Good morning, Sir, what can I do for you?'"

"In the Caribbean, they say, 'What you want?'"

With the enthusiasm of a young Minister of Agriculture, Trade and Tourism, leading the thrust for our economic development, I once took Sir Arthur to visit the plantation at Ottley Hall, owned by the government to seek his guidance on resort development. He had one look at the valley, the black sand beach, and the empty view to the horizon. "This place is hot, airless and has no view. You can't be serious, Son!" That was the end of that idea.

When news broke of Sir Arthur's Nobel Prize in 1979, Harold Kuhn of Princeton, famous for his Game Theory of Mathematics, and another of our regular guests at the Frangipani, told me that the recipient of the honour instructed the cleaning lady they shared to say he was not at home. She explained to Harold why she left early that day: "I was not going to stay and lie for that man any more."

In one meeting of the Monetary Council of our East Caribbean Central Bank, where we were contemplating putting selected scenes of the islands on the notes, I proposed that Sir Arthur be on the $100 bill. With the Queen on the opposite side of Sir Arthur, we probably became the first country with two heads on a note. We wanted the world to realize that emerging out of our noble tradition (symbolized by the Queen) we aspired to attain the higher echelons of intelligentsia (symbolized by Sir Arthur). What better way to signal dignified stability and wise maturity! For I did not imagine these islands, settling too easily for mediocrity, would produce another genius in research in economic development in the future.

I once asked Sir Arthur for his views on the cause of the collapse of the West Indies Federation.

"I'll tell you a little story which I trust you will not repeat. John Mordecai had been trying to find an answer for two and a half years. We were examining the events with Eric Williams. We asked him if he and Manley were such good friends, why didn't they get together and straighten things out, like the oil refining issue. Williams kept blurting out, 'Manley was no friend. Manley was no friend.' Williams then confided that at the London Conference he had dropped his bombshell that he would not honour the Chaguaramas Agreement. Unlike the Jamaica, Antigua and St. Lucia agreements, it had never been agreed by any local authority, so it was not valid. Then there was a caucus that night to discuss the next day's strategy.

"Williams had won the day. That night he was saying to Grantley Adams, 'You'll say this, I'll say that, and to Manley you'll say this, I'll say that.' Then came the historic blunder. Manley shouted to Williams, 'You're only a little boy, you're not going to tell me what to say.'"

I asked Sir Arthur how Mordecai avoided saying this in his book. Sir Arthur was frank and enthusiastic. "There are certain things you cannot say." He then quoted a line from the text that went something like this: "That night there were certain extreme exchanges which, possibly, seriously influenced the turn of events."

Sir Arthur and Mordecai had checked with Manley on return to Jamaica, but Manley did not recall the incident. (I am fully aware that Sir Arthur enjoined me to keep this story private, but fifty years on, with no one else privy to this important footnote in the collapse of the Federation, for which he cared so much, I felt the episode should not remain only in my diaries.)

When we elected Willie Demas, then of the Caricom Secretariat, to the Presidency of the CDB to succeed Sir Arthur Lewis who was returning to Princeton and a Nobel Prize, we were confident that Willie would deliver the language and substance attractive to the international financial institutions.

I enjoyed working with the tall, lanky Demas. He was my house-guest for a weekend in our small house beside the Frangipani, and we had long discussions on the cohesion of Carifta and the way forward. We shared a passion for political union. Many a day he would be on the phone, not about any infrastructure project but about political union. Up to this day, no other regional civil servant seems to have shared his enthusiasm on the subject. I was able to glean an interesting background to his academic life, from his Trinidadian colleague, Karl Hudson-Phillips, who is now a judge at the International Criminal Court.

When he was at Cambridge, the housekeeper complained that it was totally impossible to clean Demas' room as his thesis was scattered across the bed and floor and desk and washroom. His friends had ventured in his room to bestow some order, but could not do enough to help him receive a doctorate because in those days to write on Development Studies in an English university could earn no more than an M. Litt. His talent, though, shone through and the eminent economist, Dr. Ursula Hicks, took him to work with her on Development Studies in Oxford for three years. He then moved to London to work at the Trade Commission of the West Indies, and on its demise was taken on by Eric Williams. It was in that capacity in Trinidad that I first met him.

He was married to a charming medical doctor but seemed incapable of interrupting his workaholic routine for even a good meal. He bore with fortitude the blackmail imposed on his presidency of the CDB for loans to re-establish the St. Vincent sugar industry. The government of the day, headed by Milton Cato, threatened to leave the bank if the loans were not granted. Demas found himself torn between his passion for unity in the region and his intellectual hostility to poor economics. When I left Opposition and became Minister of Finance, despite our friendship I raged about the $45 million sugar debt accumulated in a short spell of five years, expecting a forceful rebuttal. Before all the CDB Governors who had supported the loan, all I got from Willie was "mea culpa, mea maxima culpa." He cast a long shadow over his successors. He was not one of those regional bureaucrats enjoying fat salaries awarded by politicians while secretly contemptuous of them.

I have spoken of Sir Arthur and Willie Demas. I want to return now to another figure in my Pantheon of remarkable colleagues: Karl Hudson-Phillips. The son of one of Trinidad's original black aristocrats, he was like his father, well-known for his excellence at the bar. He distinguished himself very early as an Attorney General prepared to resign from the all-powerful Williams government in the oil boom years if there was any attempt to make him compromise his conscience, signing an undated letter of resignation.

In due course he accumulated the wide and unchallenged experience required for election to the International Criminal Court (ICC), riding off into the sunset, dusting off the vestiges of politics, a final tribute to his brilliance and strength of character that, alas, was anathema to his countrymen. Trinidadians resented the discipline he attempted to impose on the society, for which, I think, they are paying a high price. I preferred his sobriquet "King of the Afrosaxons" to the calypsonian's title "Ah fraid Karl." Successive Trinidad Governments of different political persuasions, however, redeemed themselves in their sponsorship of his candidacy to the ICC, a candidacy that advanced the image of impartial jurisprudence in our region. Karl's intellectual powers never flagged and we in the Caribbean were convinced that he would help guide the fledgling institution toward pre-eminent respectability, a task essential in thwarting American chauvinism. Moreover, he made the transition from the elegance of his St. Clair residence in Port of Spain, graced with one of the city's magnificent saman trees, to the old world splendour of the Hague, with great dignity.

The judicial hierarchy of the English bar, on his elevation to the ICC, never reticent about recognizing accomplishment on their own terms, added their own accolade by investing him with the status of Bencher of the Honourable Society of Gray's Inn.

We shared a passion for language, both I suppose from an early and rigorous introduction to Shakespeare, Chaucer, Dickens and the English poets, all suffused with a touch of richness from the King James Bible. As though I needed further evidence that we were kindred spirits, I got it in full measure when he once called from London, with me fast asleep, and all I could hear was his chuckling laughter at the end of the line. He laughed and laughed and laughed and put down the phone. That was his response to the bedroom farce *Run for your Wife* which I had recommended out of the relief it brought my soul after a turbulent week in Europe on the Banana Wars.

At the end of a long day in court, or on the road, as he relished his first glass of his favourite Dewars Special Reserve, he would prayerfully intone: "Oh yes, Redeemer!" I asked him once, as we dined at Villa Helianthus, where did he get that invocation, so distinctly religious for an old sinner. "I am an Anglican," he said, "and it came from an old arthritic fisherman who looked after my cottage at the beach in Blanchisseuse. When I heard him use that plea, it reminded me of a wonderful experience, listening to Kathleen Ferrier at her last performance at the Albert Hall, singing Handel's "I Know That My Redeemer Liveth!"

Oh yes, Redeemer! Will our islands be redeemed?

Success, staying in office, at the pinnacle of political power, does not simply come through great campaigns, proper administration, management of the economy, or brilliant public relations. Success comes too from warding off the hypocrites, evading treachery and the selfish ambition of even those who pretend to be close friends. Long before I dreamt of being in politics, I had read the wonderful lines in Nehru's biography, how he developed an infinite capacity to recover from shock and he therefore expected to die of old age. Information is vital and when I learnt of treachery, I would simply bury it deep inside and build up my defences. The traitor never knew what I learnt until the battle was over, when it became appropriate to prick his conscience.

That I was able to lead St. Vincent and the Grenadines for such a long time in many ways reflects the advice of Karl Hudson-Phillips, including his understanding of the West Indian mind. Trinidad and Tobago's loss was my gain, and I trust, those whom I served. The glorious conclusion of his career at the ICC in The Hague did however not absolve him from his basic humanity and concern for his country. The political hurt in his homeland left the permanent scar of cynicism that escaped in his utterances from time to time. Acclaim abroad allowed him to choose whether or not he took on further battles in the islands, and when he did not, even his silence was eloquent.

With the sugar industry no longer burdening the public pension funds, the Treasury and the Bank, it was time to construct a home for our Ministry of Finance to demonstrate our coming of age, away from, and beyond our British handouts. I had lived too long in Europe not to know how much we needed foreign technology and the injection of new ideas. The longer I stayed in government, the more aware I became of the real enduring evil of the colonial legacy in the form of a protective cloak around laziness and incompetence in the civil service where civil servants, seemingly strident anti-colonialists, never recognize that their status is the last disease of colonialism in dire need of constitutional surgery.

The Food and Agricultural Organization (FAO) of the United Nations had served us well in the report I had commissioned on the revised sugar industry, declaring unambiguously that the derelict factory from St. Madeline, Trinidad, reimposed on St. Vincent growing varieties of cane not tested on our soils, would never be profitable. It was the first time since Independence that a UN agency was to guide our destiny. I closed the sugar industry. In so doing, I closed a chapter of our vainglorious encounter with sugar.

It was time to come of age. It was time to respect for all time the image of our city, unique in the Caribbean with its shaded brick and stone arches over cobblestone pavements. The red and yellow bricks had ballasted the wooden ships sailing from England in the famous triangular trade to Africa, the West Indies and Newfoundland. These arches were our constant reminder of our place in the history of the Empire, how those ships disgorged their brick ballast and slaves, to be replaced with indigo, cotton, sugar and molasses for England and returning later with a cargo of salted cod, thereby creating an enduring legacy in our Sunday morning breakfasts and links with the Canadian Maritime Provinces.

Eric Williams had instructed me and the world about the Mercantile Theory and the Navigation Laws. His analysis had certainly influenced my thinking, but it was disappointing that his clear understanding of how the sweat of slaves enriched England did not match his deploying the OPEC bonanza to enhance the architectural landscape of Trinidad. Imbued with a deep understanding of the relevance of sound education, he built many schools, but sadly did not insist that they match the inspiring edifice of his Alma Mater, Queen's Royal College. Trinidadian society followed, building new houses with new wealth that did not come close to former colonial elegance.

I resolved not to make Trinidad's mistake. One day at the Frangipani, a British architect came to present me with his plan for a new parliament building to be financed with some of our Independence grant. Our meeting was brief. I told him: "The day I form Government, I shall return to our original colonial Parliament building. This matchbox you are prescribing will suit a magistrate's court."

After we won the elections in 1984, an enthusiastic crowd of thousands collected me off the ferryboat when I arrived in the city to take the oath of Prime Minister. For hundreds of yards, my feet did not touch the ground. Kisses from a myriad of women blew toward me. They lifted me up. I had to reward them. I knew I had to transform their lives, their homes and the country.

Pigs had captured the heart of our city, Kingstown. Cattle, too, were flogged through the streets in the commercial district on the way to the abattoir. The pigs and dogs competed for the discarded guts from the fish market. "The poor had to make a dollar" was the justification, as it had been for the removal of sand from beaches. The pigs belonged to the poor. I, however, in all my battles with the communists, had always eschewed equality in the gutter. The centre of our city reclaimed by my Alliance Government a decade ago had remained a wasteland. I was not going to preside over a capital city that remained a pigsty.

We were the garden of the Caribbean, producing the most exotic selection of fruits and vegetables, but the farmers needed a market in the city that demonstrated the pre-eminence of their agriculture. And while the Law of the Sea Convention gave our archipelagic state vast fishing rights, we did not have an appropriate display of our red snapper, king fish, dorado and rock hinds. I was determined to build good markets. And I thought a Finance Centre would be a good place to start.

We commissioned an architectural competition. We could not keep allowing the Ministry of Works to abuse the landscape in which they were born, and think that ugly matchboxes defiling a small city was progress. To make an impact on Kingstown, I realized I had to face eventually some historic challenges. Colonialism had imposed a distinguished Parliament building. Self-rule before I came along had done nothing. The St. George's Anglican Cathedral in which I had served and cleaned brass, built in 1820 in its Georgian splendour, had dignified many symbolic occasions. In his own indomitable style, a Belgian monk had designed his St. Mary's Catholic Church with its minarets rising like pinnacles in children's sand castles.

The British firm, Tomlin Voss, represented by Trevor Thompson, won the competition handsomely. They sustained the theme of arched colonnades which lifted the building gracefully, and gave it a hollow centre that allowed cool breezes inside.

I had insisted on the winner being chosen solely on merit, and I did lose a friend in the process. Milton Mayers, a self-made man, who won neither the design nor the construction contract, was peeved that his hard work on the campaign trail and his family's generosity to my team around the dinner table on Sunday evenings did not enhance his chances in the competition. Fortunately, though, his son Moulton later returned from New York, and won the tenders for the Forestry Building and Revenue Office in Bequia. Moulton was amenable to my suggestion that the revenue building match the style of a Vietnamese structure in a current issue of *Architectural Digest*, complete with the easiest of facilities for yachtsmen clearing customs and immigration.

Richard Joachim, who had established his reputation in building European-financed projects like the hospital, various schools and villas, won the contest for construction of the Finance Building. Mustique was impressed with his job on "The Terraces" for the Lawrences, a tropical exuberance comparing well with their "La Fiorentina" beside the sea in the south of France where I had spent time as a young hitch-hiker.

The enthusiasm around our architectural standard infected the private sector for which Sprott Brothers, across the street, set the tone. The Jiandini's next door, having secured planning approval, were proud to show me their plans and were not ashamed to go back to the drawing-board when I thought they could do better.

As our Finance Centre rose from the ground, it became an object of derision for the Opposition: too tall; too big; its walls destined to crack. Its interior finish (under the influence of Italian architect and Mustique resident, Professor Paolo Piva, also of the Vienna School of Architecture) included a marble fountain, and a Cabinet Room and the Prime Minister's Office were all too lavish for my opponents.

The green marble we chose really graced the entrance. Our original design did not include these things. I was appalled to see finishes in plywood and summoned the planning officials to upgrade the counters and floors in marble. Again the critics emerged. When I opened the building, I reminded them of what they should have seen in their travels, but apparently did not see, that every self-respecting hotel where standards in the eyes of the world counted, had a marble foyer. But it was all built by local artisans and I insisted too that the mahogany doors came out of local furniture shops.

I was vindicated when Desmond Hoyte, President of Guyana, visited and commented to his security head, "We should have built something like this when we had money!" But the lifts were almost broken on the first day as schoolchildren had a lovely time riding them up and down for the first time in their lives.

I requested Calvin Nicholls, my old dutiful assistant at the Campden Park Experiment Station, to plant royal palms along the building and down Bay Street, which with each rain shower still rise majestically over the town. In a succession of budgets I allocated funds for the renewal of the cobblestone streets until, fed up with tedious criticism, I decided to terminate the project. To my surprise in Parliament the funds reappeared in the expenditure column. I summoned the planning director, Randy Cato, for an explanation. "Sir, we kept them in, as we know the cobblestones are dear to your heart!"

And then *the* fountain! We needed one. I remembered as a little boy when my father brought me to Kingstown to buy nails and visit the blacksmith named Gibson making fittings for the ship, we'd see all the donkeys and mules drinking from a trough with a trickling fountain beside the great shade trees. Our country had rivers, waterfalls and exciting streams in the countryside with crayfish slipping between the rocks, and in that symbolic view of flowing waters, I wanted a marble fountain in the city.

In the Caribbean region, we realized we needed a uniform strategy for investment and development. I had been much involved in the studies of harmonization of fiscal incentives, which had created levels of responses varying in accordance with levels of development. Indeed, a level of advantageous disharmony was formulated with the less developed territories securing the right to a more advantageous regime. In this way, we hoped the weak would become stronger.

Following this exercise, I realized our policy on tourism in St. Vincent and the Grenadines needed to be reviewed. So I set up a committee to examine the impact of existing legislation. It became obvious that our tourism plan needed upgrading, refurbishment and expansion. We secured British technical assistance in redrafting the laws and my experience as an hotelier was useful in determining what the industry needed. The criteria for 15-year concessions, and casinos with one hundred rooms, after further advice from The Bahamas, were established.

The 20-year Mustique agreement was coming to an end and the home-owners wanted a continuation. But I wanted expanded employment and a better deal for my constituents and the fishermen in Mustique. It became apparent that Colin Tennant, the original owner, had no stomach for negotiation with me 20 years after the first exercise. Moreover, he wanted out. He wanted a new indulgence and he found it under the Pitons in St. Lucia, where he had brought an elephant, the first in the Caribbean.

I had met Hans Neumann while in opposition at Seven Springs, Vermont, during the weekend symposium of intellectuals looking at the Caribbean Basin Initiative. It was there I learnt that he had a home in Mustique. He published my "What kind of Caribbean do we want?", delivered at the symposium, in his English-language newspaper in Caracas, the *Daily Journal*. Barney Frank of Massachusetts later got hold of it from a guest at the Frangipani Hotel and put it into the *US Congressional Record*.

I was able to gain some insight into possible new trends in development from John Kenneth Galbraith. In his talk on "The living industry," he postulated, long before computers became a household appliance, how increasingly persons will seek more amenable places in the countryside to be self-employed on industry-related matters while dirty, heavy industry will be transferred to developing countries. I kept this at the back of my mind as I conceptualized our own course in my corner of the world.

Colin Tennant could come to no agreement on sale of the island with a group. Hans Neumann, Venezuelan industrialist, Czech emigré Jew, concluded the purchase. The modern art in Hans' home in Caracas was lost on me, but I was amenable to the suggestion that he buy out Colin Tennant, set up a new framework of mixed ownership by the home-owners, with himself, naturally, holding a golden share. We put this into the context of negotiation of a new agreement without government imposition of punitive alien taxes.

The Mustique negotiating team reflected various backgrounds and disciplines. John Trafford had homes in Spain and Chile and was into oil. Pierre Marais, a retired General in the French Army, had a legal mind and was experienced in procurement. Robert Worcester of the Market Opinion Research Institute (MORI), was an emphatic environmentalist. Diego Arria, a former Governor of Caracas, was politically compatible with the rest. José Alvarez Stelling, a banker from Caracas, understood clearly how to create confidence in investment. Patrick Fauchier, in tune with Cartier elegance, sensed how to make a good thing better. Danny Wyler, a Dutch commodities trader, had established a comfortable relationship with Princess Margaret with regard to the maintenance of her home on Mustique. The management of Mustique's finances achieved new heights during his chairmanship.

Having gone through the seismic change from Colin Tennant, and from English pre-eminence to Venezuelan control, Mustique now faced an aftershock: Colin's anxiety to dispose of the Great House. I wrote to Colin expressing my alarm at his total abandonment of the place and his Mustique identity. He was keeping only a few acres around the swamp to the south. But he told me that he needed the money, and that was that. He presented me with a farewell gift, a beautiful 1824 water-colour of the Kingstown botanic gardens by the Reverend Lansdown Guilding BA (which made me realize how the name of our special parrot *Amazona guildingii* came about).

The recently formed company sought my assistance to research the background of the prospective purchaser of the Great House, a Russian named Sergei Kaouzov. The English element in the company was not sure if the Russian met their standards, but our due diligence gave me excellent assurances about him which I duly communicated. The sale now approved, Kaouzov brought in his team of engineers, architects and a horticultural expert, Stephen Gamble, from Oxford. The original building was pronounced rotten to the core. Built with saline beach sand (which had destroyed the beach), the steel was rusted and the walls were cracking. The Mustique planning committee had approved Kaouzov's expansion and design, but somehow did not envisage demolition of existing structures. They were up in arms with Kaouzov, and wanted to stop his project.

Having settled in my own mind that Colin Tennant no longer wanted to be in Mustique, I felt that the new owner had a constitutional right to develop the property as he wished, and that, in fact, the Indian images of the Taj Mahal that he wished to incorporate into his building were true to the original by virtue of Kaouzov's research into the hunting lodges on the sub-continent. He was bringing marble from India, stone elephants, Indonesian carvers, and the finest of silk carpets.

Later, the Kaouzovs became godparents to my daughter Gabija and introduced her to school in Villars not far from their home in Gryon. Gabija too was alarmed one Sunday when I took her to see the demolition. "I'll have to tell Marsha Kaouzov [their daughter] they're destroying her house," she said.

What remains fascinating about Mustique is the preservation of its very English image highlighted by Princess Margaret, that was in no way eroded by Venezuelan control, nor by the significant presence of French, Italian, American, Canadian, German, Swiss, and Brazilian home-owners. Hans Neuman, a refugee turned New World industrialist, was too clever and genuinely self-effacing to interfere with what worked well in the marketplace.

I was very cautious about accepting their hospitality, remembering how the Mustique folk did not even acknowledge me during my sojourn in lonely opposition. I did, however, rely on Diego Arria, who came along later, who knew the genuine souls, none more authentic than Harding and Mary Lawrence. They needed no overt displays to demonstrate the success that each had in their own way, Harding in aviation and industry, and Mary with her Wells Green marketing in New York and across the United States. Mary readily agreed to write a comment in the coffee table book I brought out on St. Vincent, reflecting the reasons for her choice of location for a home in the Grenadines. (One weekend, as their guest, I wrote one of my theses on political union. She also induced one of her other guests, Raquel Welch, to write a few lines about Mustique in the first edition of our coffee table book on the islands.)

Harding and I were to work together on the improvement of Mustique Airport and, in the end, settled for less than we thought appropriate. I have always regretted that I could only visit them for a few hours at "Villa Fiorentina" in the south of France. There was never enough time as Prime Minister to take a holiday there. I once made the mistake of giving Mary a copy of Kuzac's *Buda Pest 1900*, which I thought she would enjoy. Ever since then, she has flooded me with some two dozen new titles each Christmas, which she had already digested. Trying to match her generosity, I struggled in my travels to find another publication that she would want to discover.

When the Caribbean Heads of Government gave me the assignment to privatize the Caribbean Airlines, Harding invited Ed Acker for a dinner with me, during which we discussed a possible linkage of American carriers with BWIA. Unfortunately, no link was established despite our efforts. I never dreamt in all our interesting times together that Harding would invite me, before he passed on, to say a few words at his memorial service.

I got close to Alfred and Susan Schweitzman and took up their invitation to visit their farm in Accord, New York. They requested my return for the Bar Mitzvah for their son Simon, but I did not make it. Alfred sponsored, and I supported, the idea of producing two coffee-table books on Mustique. I was deeply saddened at the tragic loss of Simon's life in a fall from a balcony in New York. I don't think his parents ever recovered from the loss of their son.

The Mustique book was a great gift to present during my travels, selling as it did a special image of my country. I even gave one to Fidel Castro on my state visit to Cuba. He kept asking how we secured such investment.

We proceeded to negotiate a new 15-year agreement with Mustique and I was satisfied that every single villa in Mustique exceeded the criteria available throughout the country for a 15-year tax holiday for a hotel. One school of thought among the home-owners was that there should be no further development on Mustique – they wanted neither the noise of construction nor the presence of ill-kempt workers. Others felt that there should be a target for expansion up to a certain limit, something I was more amenable to. We settled on a policy of guided growth, with a new building code.

Mustique architecture was first influenced by Oliver Messel, the London stage designer, and uncle to the husband of Princess Margaret. The Royal presence was already creating enthusiasm for the island. Then the Swede Arne Hasselquist, his skills already tested with Guyana hardwoods in our other islands, took the plunge into primitive Mustique, settling his young family into the simple bamboo compound. With boundless energy, he ventured far and wide, assimilating the influences of Japan and South East Asia, transforming the cotton fields and scrubby hillsides into modern elegances.

Basically, I was delighted that new home-owners bought into the original plan I worked out with Colin Tennant: we wanted the island to be a special destination. I knew that diversifying by attracting investment from many countries would allow us to escape economic downturn in any single country. And, against the wishes of the local architects, I refused to restrict foreign architects. My mind was open to all the influences I had absorbed around the world and I wanted choice. I wanted, too, the technology transfer. I satisfied my local architects and builders with government contracts.

We had also to do something about the sordid fishing shacks and workers' houses which were incompatible with a luxury resort. Their replacement, and better housing for middle-management personnel, with guaranteed usage of the village, would be the price for further concessions. I insisted that the villas build facilities for their own staff, including gardeners, so that the permanent villagers could in time buy their homes. And so we created opportunity for our people, social harmony on the island, and a haven for troubled minds.

One afternoon I was swimming peacefully beside Basil's bar, operated by the island's supreme native icon, and promoter of the Blues Festival, Basil Charles, only to have my solitude distracted by jet skis from a mega-yacht. I told the thrill seekers that the importation and use of jet skis were banned in this country and asked them to please return them to their yachts.

"The Captain told us to use them," one of the defiant tourists said in a dismissive tone.

"You tell your captain," I said, "that the Captain of this land says, 'No!'"

Ignoring me, they went to the bar for drinks, but returned rather sheepishly. The barman had confirmed that the guy in the unattractive swimsuit was indeed "captain" of the island.

Two good decisions I had taken were to ban jet skis and allow computers duty-free access. In Cuba I saw one jet ski and told Fidel to ban them before Varadero turned into The Bahamas.

In many ways, it proved easier to market Mustique in London, Paris, New York and Milan than in St. Vincent. The people who worked in Mustique were earning enough to build homes in their villages at home and were the envy of neighbours. But some on the mainland, mostly jealous of their success, were mindlessly repeating the Opposition mantra that, with tourism, I was creating a nation of waiters. The Vincentian diaspora in England castigated me on the publicity that Mustique was receiving without any mention of their villages at home.

I posed the question, why had they all gathered to meet me?

"We came to meet our Prime Minister of course," they responded in unison.

"Exactly," I said. "You did not come to meet Son Mitchell. It is the Royal family, Mick Jagger and Jerry Hall, David Bowie and Iman, and others like them whose presence draws attention to us. Nevis gets publicity through the visits of Diana, Princess of Wales."

And all those criticizing my efforts in Mustique were only too happy to dine in style there when they became the Government, easily setting aside their nationalist and anti-foreign investment diatribes, relishing the flattery and food bestowed.

Mustique helped me secure projects for the rest of the country, too. Our first dinner for the Kuwaitis, for instance, was a disaster at a sea-coast restaurant in St. Vincent. The food was ordinary, the music was too loud. We were talking to them about funds for a new generator and could not be heard. So I instructed my Director of Planning, Randy Cato, to charter a plane to carry us to lunch at the Cotton House the next day. My friend Mario Ferrari, the designer, who was very much into Italian fashion, enhanced the visit by indulging us in a tour of his villa, "Black Stone." There was no doubting the difference in the Kuwaitis' reactions.

They really looked after me on my visits to Kuwait. With their help, our country now boasts a fine cruise-ship terminal. I secured funds, too, in the twilight of my ministry, to help extend our Arnos Vale Airport.

Mustique is a perfect example of what our real resources are: great location, right hemisphere, wonderful views, and good people. I have tried hard to get our people to understand that, but regret that I cannot boast outstanding success in this endeavour. Even now, the serenity of our country's beauty is all too readily abused with noisy amplifiers. The silence of a Mustique evening makes it an oasis of enviable calm in our Caribbean confusion, a model waiting to be transposed into the creation of wealth elsewhere. Indeed, a visionary like Prime Minister Mahathir of Malaysia, when he visited me after one of his turbulent elections, told me he would like to replicate our model in his islands.

I have always been thankful for having my own establishment in Bequia to reciprocate the wonderful hospitality of the Mustique home-owners at no cost to Government. I am not one who is disposed to flattery of status. After all, our family business had been the only one in existence on the same land in the Grenadines for the entire twentieth century, and so I could welcome newcomers into our islands without the slightest sense of inferiority.

It is time to talk of some of my valued constituents, and I'll start with Sigbert Ollivierre of Mayreau. His slender wife, Anastasia, a melodious voice in her church choir, thin as a wafer, with a beautiful chiselled countenance, had borne him some 13 children through all the poverty of the isolated island. She shed a fountain of tears when I told her I was attempting to find another constituency seat, warning me that I would never be "beloved" elsewhere as I was on this island. She was not impressed that I was engaged in the process of Party building.

After the Union Island Uprising was quashed, and the State of Emergency lifted, having lost the seat in South Central Windward, I was anxious to regain the seat I had vacated in the Grenadines. My Little boat, *Colibri*, with its limping engine, had barely made it beyond the reefs into the northern anchorage at dusk. Early on the Sunday morning, I waded through the thickets and scruff land to the early morning church service to find the entire island on their knees, facing the altar, and their priest(ess) Tante Jess Alexander, invoking the blessing. No one saw me as I entered and knelt behind them, and heard: "Lord, thou gavest St. Peter the keys of the Kingdom. Let that key for which we shall vote tomorrow bring us out of poverty and into the Promised Land."

Years later, in the Prime Minister's office one morning, I was informed that a fat, black old lady from Mayreau was in hospital asking for me. It was Tante Jess. She needed blood. She turned out to have my blood type. I gave her my blood. Tante Jess was the first woman priest with her stewardship finally recognized by Pope John Paul II. Mayreau is a special place.

My paternal grandfather had also owned lands in Paget Farm, opposite the family island, in the heart of my first constituency seat, where his workers and their children had settled, and built their homes, with title still registered in the name I shared with my grandfather. I simply told the folk to continue to occupy the land. Should they prepare a deed, I would sign.

After I had secured land for the Mayreau people from the Eustace family after a long day of useless negotiation in the presence of the fisherman, Sigbert Ollivierre, I began a painstaking subdivision of the property. It was taking time and Sigbert's son was furious with me. I exploded in like manner. But the old father was philosophical. "PM, you must forgive my boy. He does not know when you are poor of pocket you don't spend. When you are poor of speech, you listen. The young people don't know our struggle!"

Canouan prospered more than Mayreau. It was my daughter, Sabrina, who sparked the creation of Canouan's luxury resort. My first-born certainly did not inherit any of the "early to bed, early to rise" maritime genes of the Grenadines, but, like me in my youth, was ready to wander through Europe, enjoying its glories. With Canadian citizenship inherited from her mother, Sabrina, not being subject to the visa nuisances as I had been, enjoyed several international vacations from the University of Toronto financed with her savings from waitressing during the summer. But I never imagined that her exposure to the museums, cafés and the culture of Europe would yield dividends in my constituency and our nation as a whole. Once I sent her on a train from Paris to Madrid to be the guest of my Mustique friend, John Trafford, and so to bring her Spanish up to the comfort zone. When after a Cabinet meeting, I read out her letter of experiences as a young teenager from the West Indies on a train making her way in French and Spanish, my Ministers expressed the view that this kind of torture was incomprehensible and an awful reflection on me. I was supposed to be a kind man.

On her first summer vacation in 1986 away from the University of Toronto, she found herself beside a pool in Capri, at "Villa Materita," accompanied by two Canadian friends. ("Villa Materita" was owned by a Mustique friend, Pepponi Della Schiava, who had loaned me his house for the famous Guyana/Mustique meeting.) Another guest in the villa was Baron Carlo Amato, a genuine descendant of the Kingdom of the Two Sicilies, whose grandfather was the first Sicilian Senator in

Rome after Garibaldi and his thousands united the Kingdom of Italy. Baron Amato, a banker, was regaling the college students with his travels in Burma, Thailand, Malaysia, Indonesia, French Polynesia and islands off the Australian coast looking for an island to create an ultra-luxurious tropical haven. But he had not yet found anything suitable. The major setback for most of the places he had seen was distance from the major capitals of the world.

And thus, ensconced in her luxury holiday, Sabrina impressed upon the Baron the possibility that Canouan was just what he was looking for.

"Why don't you get in touch with my father and check out Canouan?" she suggested. "It has the best beaches in the Grenadines."

"Is it available?" Amato had asked her.

"You'll have to check," she told him, passing on the contact information. And thus changed the history of that island forever.

About that time, Michael Wilson, the Canadian Finance Minister I met at the Toronto Commonwealth Meeting, visited me one New Year's Eve in Bequia. The friendship had already yielded some funds to upgrade the Canouan airport, which had remained a dirt track throughout a decade of Labour Party rule. Without much engineering study, the flat runway that had been filled in over the swamp got its long overdue surface, and was certified for small aircraft use. We knocked up a terminal building out of the construction tool shed, got the French to finance lighting, and the Canouan Airport was in business, and ready to be shown off, I thought, to the world.

Sabrina, back in Canada at the University of Toronto, called to make arrangements for me to meet Carlo Amato and discuss investment. I received him at the PM's residence. He produced glossy reports on Banco Gottardo and Gesfid and enough information to keep me and the officials at the Ministry of Finance occupied. But his was not just a presentation on figures. I was impressed that he was a polished gentleman of good breeding, a mind enriched by contact with many cultures, as Sabrina had told me, and that he was interested in our islands beyond Mustique. Several meetings and dinners later, we were ready to get off the ground in Canouan.

Carlo and I inspected the island. Sgt. Thomas, the Officer in Charge of the Station, and two other policemen, drove us around in the only jeep on the island, which South Korea had given me in appreciation of my anti-communist stance. We drove up toward Carenage as far as we could, where we glimpsed the spire of the old Anglican Church reclaimed by the forest after the area had been largely abandoned following the hurricane of 1921. Canouan with all its beauty was largely an island of women and children, as the adventurous menfolk usually took to sea on foreign ships.

It was a struggle for me to find an allocation of $3,000 from the Treasury at Christmas to provide work for groups in the island to clean the dirt roads. I had been castigated for bulldozing the trees beside the salt pond, and wanting to destroy an ancient cemetery when we tried to establish the dirt-strip airport in 1974. The Catholic Bishop in Bridgetown and Kingstown came to my rescue, deconsecrating the burial grounds and conveying the old bones to hallowed ground in another cemetery, which allowed me to get on with the project. I knew that only infrastructure development would lead to the tourism that would transform the beautiful landscape into a land of hope.

The islanders thought that I was abandoning them when I split my constituency into two, so I had to assuage their fears by offering to build a hotel (or at least a home) to be among them and nurture further development. I bought some land in the island just to reassure them.

But the poverty of the area greatly pained me. It was so remote, the jungle and underbrush so thick, that the Regional Security System established in the Grenada communist aftermath accepted the location for insurgency training.

"You will not lay your hands on this land," I told Baron Amato, "unless you can guarantee an expenditure of US$20 million in 20 years."

"I can give that guarantee and more," Amato replied. "All we need beyond that is the price you will charge."

I informed him that the price would have to be fixed by the Chief Surveyor, approved by Cabinet, with further environmental studies and planning requirements tied to a covenant on performance.

My Minister Burton Williams, attending a World Health meeting in Geneva, made his way to check out Carlo Amato's backers in Lugano, the investment trust Gesfid and the Banco Gottardo. Needless to say, his report went beyond the diligence checks I had instituted. Carlo brought along the Bank President of Gesfid, Antonio Saladino, to see me and explained that, apart from being a banker, he was one of the world's bridge champions with a formidable memory capable of great strategic planning. The group had made great profit investing clients' money in US property. They were ready to invest in Canouan, even though Antonio could find no ashtrays in my office. They would, of course, want an agreement similar to the one in Mustique.

With agreement in principle, I made it to Lugano to check for myself. Banco Gottardo, in Lugano, was the quintessential Swiss centre for

Italian finance. It occupied a whole block in the city. Fascinated by the tales of the vast wealth of the world secreted in Switzerland, I was taken on a tour of the famous vaults that seemed to have no drawers or doors but mysteriously opened in response to the punched codes on the computer.

From Lugano we drove to Italy, and all the way to Rome, where I received a far better understanding of the evolution of the Christian religion in the time of the Caesars. I discovered in the catacombs to my absolute horror that I was the ultimate claustrophobic. The instruction from the short Philippine guide that we should be in touching contact with each other and be able to see her and hear her from time to time, and not wander off away from her path, that if we lost our way amidst the miles and miles of catacombs, we would not be found, certainly inspired no confidence. If it had been my destiny to follow St. Paul into these catacombs, I would have settled to be a Jew or Muslim.

"Breathe deeply," the Philippine said, so I snorted like a dying horse. When we got back to the surface in the little sanctuary, I knelt and prayed and thanked God for my deliverance from the fate of early more devout Christians.

It was more fun meeting Gina Lollobrigida, who was Carlo's old girlfriend. Among other things, they had been on safari together in Africa. She accompanied us to the Piazza di Spegna for the fashion show where Pepponi was enjoying himself as current President of the Italian Fashion Industry Association. Fall fashions in their glory: Gianfranco Ferre, Tussardi-Cavalli, Dolce-Gabana, Egon Von Furstenburg, Rafaella Curiel, who invited me to the Grand Hotel to see her showrooms, and continued to invite me back to Rome.

All the fashion designers were there with their top models. I wished I could pick up one of the girls, and jump into the fountain with her, a fantasy that, even our Islands, so tolerant of impulsiveness, would not countenance. I could just see the celebrity magazines: "Lunatic leaves Lollo for younger stuff." Not a headline to help me sell bananas in Europe.

Carlo took me and my new girlfriend Jeannette Cadet to Sardinia to meet the renowned Italian architect, Luigi Vietti, where he showed off his designs for us at Costa Smerlda. Along with Marco Aldaco of Mexico, they would conceptualize the themes of the Canouan resort. Frankly I was worried about Vietti's great age (he was 90 then), but stopped worrying when I saw that he was capable of drinking more wine than me at lunch and dinner.

Vietti visited us in the islands. I was about to build a second home expanding my estate house and did not like the plans presented. Vietti was willing to help. I told him I wanted a religious cloister of arches around a garden looking toward the ocean. He obliged. I am grateful to him. Mine became the only piece of architecture to demonstrate his genius in the islands. Canouan just toyed with his plans.

Often in this goldfish bowl atmosphere around a Prime Minister, my mind would drift back to my spartan sojourn in Europe as an unknown hitch-hiker. Now in the Murano showrooms in Venice I could choose heavy green and blue vases that I would never have been able to carry in my rucksack. In gracious Villa Collavini in the province of Udine as guests of Manlio and Anna, we could sample their fine *pinot grigio* nurtured by four generations of Collavinis, surviving world wars, and imbibe too a *grappa* that would have made Hemingway and his ladies smile.

Occasional anonymity exposed what others thought my true worth was. On the pier in Naples, guarding our luggage and courteously shepherding an old lady along, I got my desserts. "Idiota!" she shouted when I didn't move fast enough for her. Chivalry, I thought, had expired at the foot of the volcano in Naples. A similar contempt awaited me in retirement, outside the post office in Pianello where another friend left me to look after his blind dog, Camillo. The Italians all greeted Camillo. Sir James Mitchell was ignored.

But I became a friend of the Chief of Police in Rome, Mario Esposito, a little man who had dimmed the lights of the Red Brigade. He requested my autographed picture to join the Presidents on his wall. He visited us in the Grenadines.

Environmental studies by the American engineer, Bill Reynolds from Indiana, meeting after meeting at home, in the Cabinet room, in Lugano and Miami through the decade, with about $200 million spent, all combined to create the magnificent ambience in Canouan where I hosted the 21st Conference of the Heads of Government of the Caribbean Community, each head becoming a life member of the golf club, and planting a commemorative tree on the island. The trees in the resort survived. The rest, in the village, were devoured by goats.

I wondered, though, if Canouan was to be my last success. The Caribbean Development Bank had established criteria for minimum disbursement on a project. Their time-and-motion studies, which presumably included hotel bills and airfares in evaluation of projects, set the threshold beneath which a certain level of funding became too small. So a 1,000-metre road was out and so was a 50-foot jetty. It all meant that my Grenadines was out. No single project met the $1 million criteria. I proposed that several projects be lumped together to get into the $1 million bracket and that the Bank put multi-disciplinary teams in the field for evaluation. And so was born the Multiproject in the Grenadines that was duplicated in other Caribbean islands.

It all took time. My constituents were impatient, but it was part of my strategy in the first NDP term to satisfy the villages on mainland St. Vincent so that no one would claim the Finance Minister was partial to projects in his own constituency. To still their impatience, I devised a scheme. When the projects reached the early stages of procurement, I bought a piece of 4 × 8 plywood, glued to it all the advertisements which listed every project, and posted the board under the almond trees where all the taxi drivers, retired citizens, and know-alls gathered. Great educational stuff. And I explained every time I walked by what each project meant to them and who had tendered.

The road at the southern end of the island beyond the village of Paget Farm toward our proposed airport was strewn with five-foot boulders, a veritable obstacle course all the way to Moonhole. The bulldozers moved in. The rains came. The sticky clay was exposed. I went one Sunday to inspect our progress only to be confronted by three ladies, all dressed for church, with their shoes in their hands, delighted to meet me, and voicing their complaints about the awful condition of the unfinished road. In as civil a manner as I could muster, I asked them one by one how many children each had. The answers came: three, five and six (including names and current addresses in Trinidad, Canada and Tortola).

"Did you give birth to any without pain?"

"No," they chorused.

"There's no birth without pain," I reminded them.

When it all got too frantic, there was always home for me. If you need a little peace and quiet, Bequia is the place. With our new ferries, airport and hotels in place, thanks to private-sector response to our policy of getting the loss-making government enterprises out of the way, we entertained at our hotel many distinguished guests, not least of whom was Leonard Bernstein, who came often with his sister Shirley. After lunch he was tapping and drumming on our teak dining table singing a medley of old tunes from the 1920s onward. Under the painting of Captain Bligh landing his breadfruit plants by the English painter, Anna Zinkeisen, commissioned by the Royal Society, Bernstein spotted a Chopin score. He began to play. Ellen Schwartz, a friend living aboard her yacht *Prana* in the bay, was in ecstasy. She was relishing an experience that would not have come her way in New Jersey. She did not know what to say.

Almost speechless, I volunteered a comment to the maestro. "I've never heard Chopin so beautiful."

"Yes," Leonard Bernstein replied, feigning anguish, "but what would I have given, even a part of my hand, to have composed it."

Being a Prime Minister with a hotel in the Grenadines has its moments. Bernstein's playing remains in my memory. But there were other moments not so filled with grandeur, which brings me to the tale of Rudy Matthews, our Chief Engineer, who had been a school-mate in the cadet corps at the grammar school. Along with Karl John, he had advised me in Paris in the first joint commission with France. (The French were previously concentrating their assistance with the patois-speaking St. Lucia and Dominica, on either side of Martinique, until I secured for them the fugitive responsible for the terrorist attack on a Guadeloupe restaurant. The French Ambassador had called one night, while I was hosting Willie Demas lecturing on political union, to say that the terrorist was in St. Vincent, having been refused sanctuary in Suriname. My response was straightforward: they should send a plane at dawn into St. Vincent and I would deliver the gentleman before the lawyers awoke.) Unfortunately, I could not get either Karl or Rudy interested in exercise, even simply walking home after the evening's indulgence in a French restaurant. The most rigorous action these two grossly overweight fellows could think of after gorging on cheese following a main course extravaganza with serious wine, was ordering a taxi home.

One afternoon, we were celebrating the opening of a village road in Mesopotamia that we had paved to the delight of the villagers when word came that Rudy would not be joining us. He had just died. After dropping off Karl John, he had diverted to the home of a lady friend directly from the office.

We had to get his body to the hospital quickly and arrange a postmortem the next day. Rumours of how he had died were rife. A massive heart attack was established as the cause. I hung about the postmortem room for a long while. Taking the bull by the horns, I found a phone. After a series of calls, and getting a friend of a friend of a friend to suggest a thing or two, I invited two women to the Prime Minister's residence: Rudy's wife and the lady friend in question. The fury of jealousy like an erupting volcano could scatter lava everywhere. I steeled myself for an explosion. I knew I had to be exceedingly careful with every word I uttered. I expected raging emotions: jealousy, pain, ecstasy and the anguish of betrayal. And all those emotions there were. The eyes of the two ladies pivoted from mine to each other's unflinchingly. I was no trapeze artist, but I knew I could not afford to falter on the thin line I was walking. I would have to make it to the end of the rope. I did all the talking. Quite simply, though, a chapter of life for both of them had closed, and I could only put the book away. I was doing all I could for someone dear to three of us. Although I took part in other family disputes, I refused to hold a therapeutic session for an encounter between a wife and lover again.

In Barbados, Cameron Tudor, or Cammie as he was called, who had invited me to deliver the eulogy at Errol's funeral, chaired the succession meeting soon afterwards. Erskine Sandiford was the new Prime Minister – a sapling anxious to seek light under the old tree. So I kept my eyes and ears on my neighbour from Barbados following the death of an irreplaceable friend. His seat in Parliament was taken in the constituency by the up-and-coming erudite young lawyer David Thompson.

All was quiet in Barbados until Sandiford secured his own mandate in the new election. However, declining sugar prices offset only by tourism was no recipe for long-term stability. The CDB, the World Bank, and the IMF put up the warning lights, demanding an 8 per cent cut in expenditures. The Cabinet, after some anguish, approved, but the Trade Union wouldn't play ball. The World Bank continued to put on pressure. Perhaps Sandiford's greatest stand was his exchange in Washington with Shahid Hussein, the Pakistani Vice President of the World Bank.

"Is devaluation still your recipe?" Sandiford asked.

"Yes," Hussein replied.

"In that case," Sandiford replied, "we discuss cricket."

End of meeting. Caribbean applause, but little else. A succession of impositions by the Prime Minister began to rock the normally stable Barbados ship of state. He appointed Governors of the Central Bank without proper consultation. Richie Haynes, the brilliant Finance Minister and physician to Errol Barrow, who was first at the bedside of his dying leader, found that he could no longer stay in the Ministry of Finance. With his own ample resources and a well-established medical practice, he was ready to form his own party.

We met in the home of my doctor Harold Rampersaud one evening for dinner. I tried to dissuade Richie from forming a political party, telling him that he should seek the presidency of the Caribbean Development Bank which I would support and get other Prime Ministers to support. After all, we were the only region that did not put in a brilliant politician to head our institutions. All that would be necessary would be Barbados' sponsorship.

I explained to Richie that he could go off into the ivory tower of the CDB Presidency, collect his tax-free US$100,000 a year, and when the economy in Barbados went into recession, as it surely would, he would be recalled, as De Gaulle was in France, and be the Saviour of Barbados. He would then have control of the DLP. He should not think that, like me, he could break the mould of two-party politics. I explained my own history and how the major parties had got together to exclude me and left the field of opposition open to me; and how I had had an impregnable constituency and independent income.

Ritchie liked the idea and I undertook to market it with Sandiford at a meeting set up by Philip Greaves. In the end he did not follow through, but persisted with his third party.

Sandiford had a similar mishap with appointments in the Ministry of Tourism. The Minister, Wes Hall, famous fast bowler of the West Indies Test cricket team, resigned. Next to go, in sympathy, was Evelyn Greaves. And so the government, in one term, suffered the resignations of Don Blackman, Leroy Trotman, Richie Haynes, Wes Hall, Evelyn Greaves and Keith Simmons. It was, therefore, not long before a motion of no confidence in Sandiford reached the Parliament. The Government lost it. Sandiford had steered the ship through all the turbulent IMF storms, all the rough seas of public protest, only to end like a captain getting rid of the crew that, with him, had weathered the storm, then turned over the ship to a new captain in calm waters to go into a safe harbour.

The new captain, Owen Arthur, was a glib, fast-talking technocrat, whose ascendancy defined the end of charisma, replacing it with minimal error on a well-calculated course, with the ship, once more, on an even keel. Philip Greaves held one more audience with Sandiford. Philip was very popular at this time because it was he who had stood up to the unions and the Churches in various negotiations. He pleaded that a government which had lost direction would be unappealing both to the voters in an election and the private sector, whose financial support was critical. Sandiford idiotically replied that financial help wasn't necessary.

"In that case," Greaves concluded, "you will be consigning our party to the wilderness for a long time."

I was hounded by the media to comment on the drama unfolding in Barbados, but could only say that such could not happen in my home. Unlike Sandiford, I was the founder of my party, and was not about to destroy my creation. To me, a political party is no more than a treaty among friends. Single-minded selfishness at the expense of your friends will eventually only lead down an avenue of loneliness in old age.

I can still remember being seated at a banquet beside the Governor General Dame Nita Barrow with Sandiford across the table. As I have already noted, she had made a great name for herself, visiting Nelson Mandela in prison when she was the sole lady in the Commonwealth Eminent Persons group, reporting on apartheid South Africa. (Indeed, at Namibia's Independence, she was waiting with a large group of African Presidents in the VIP lounge in Windhoek. The President elect, Sam Nujoma, kept everyone waiting until he returned with the recently released Mandela who was overjoyed, most of all, to see Dame Nita, the only one among them who had visited him while he was incarcerated.)

Under the din of the voices at the banquet, I whispered to Dame Nita: "What do you think your brother Errol would think of Sandiford's stupidity?"

"Son," she replied. "It's a good thing he is buried at sea, he does not have to turn in his grave."

I was more fortunate with my neighbour in Antigua. Old man Bird was an institution and no political storm caused him any loss of sleep. Commissions of Inquiry, like cumulus clouds, descended with a vengeance on Antigua, one after the other. And after the showers had soaked and saturated the landscape, the sun shone again. Vere Cornwall (or VC as he was called) Bird was a big man physically and truly larger than life. My image of him as a Salvation Army major rekindled my own memories of the white-jacketed folks marching to the big drums and tambourines. So too he marched his labour troops through colonialism and the securing of all the land for Antiguans when the sugar market collapsed.

The Italians with their export credits had built the Royal Antigua Hotel. VC was ready to use it to host our Heads of Government conference. His invitation to me on the phone was crisp. "We're putting you up at the Royal Antigua. We can't afford it but we will enjoy it," he said.

Sometime later, he wanted some Vincentians to work in his police force. His request again was quite crisp. I was short in my own reply. "Send your commissioner to meet my commissioner and let them talk," I said. Fifty Vincentians joined his police force and a few months later I got another of those single-sentence calls.

"Prime Minister, I want 50 more," VC said.

"OK, Prime Minister, send your man," I replied.

Later, when VC took John Compton and me to lunch when we were in Antigua on a short visit, I asked him for an explanation for the increasing demand for policemen.

"The fellas you sent are marrying Antigua girls and taking other jobs, and I can't kick them out of the country," he said.

"In that case, Prime Minister," I retorted, "the next generation of Antiguans will be better-looking."

The old man, with a glint in his eye, roared with laughter, raising and pounding his legs on the floor.

His son Lester had quit the government, embarrassed by the shortest budget speech in history, which had been given by VC when his Finance Minister resigned. Lester, too, resigned and somehow imagined he could carry the Cabinet with him, only to discover that his brother, Vere Jr., had quietly positioned himself beside the old man to succeed in the dynasty.

The old man was not going to be brushed aside that easily. Antiguans were not going to forget how he ushered in the tourist paradise when the sugar plantations were collapsing. The dying Federation had prescribed a future for Antigua raising cattle, goats and sheep.

"Antigua will not be a paddock," was VC's famous rejoinder.

I asked VC what had happened between him and Lester.

"The boy walked out of the home. He could walk back," was his only comment.

We called on Lester, marooned in his Heritage Cay office, and advised that he call on his constituency to demand he return to the Government. The press learned of my intervention, and sought clarification of my interference in Antigua's affairs.

"What I discussed with friends remains between us," I said.

"You will not confirm or deny?"

"I've responded already and have nothing to add."

In due course, Lester became Antigua's Prime Minister. I visited the old man once more, in his graceful retirement. He was really pleased to see me and was happy how things had turned out.

Low-lying Antigua. Named in honour of a Catholic Church in Seville. Led to Independence by the Salvation Army. A bird sanctuary with few birds.

Jamaica was a more turbulent place than Antigua. In the heyday of anti-communism in our Caribbean, Eddie Seaga, Jamaica's Prime Minister, on the fringes of a Heads of Government meeting, brought together the lot of us, John Compton, Eugenia Charles, Kennedy Simmonds and Herbert Blaize, to form what became the Caribbean Democrat Union (CDU). His scholarly aide, Senator Hector Wynter, was appointed our Secretary General, and the attractive Jamaican MP, Joan Webley, was given the job of Assistant Secretary.

We set up an agenda of training for electoral campaigns and how to manage election day procedures. Lectures in leadership training became the norm. Seminars in all the islands were organized explaining detailed responsibilities to party groups. The Adenauer Foundation in Germany and the Republican Institute in Washington funded regional youth conferences teaching the role of international institutions like the World Bank and the IMF in a country's development.

Young people whose previous opportunities for getting together had been in scouting, guiding, and sports discovered with relish their regional role in politics, creating a new wave of friendships, touring the islands, getting to know intimately the leadership of islands other than their own.

Eddie Seaga became the natural choice to be Chairman of our CDU. We linked up with the Republican Institute and the Christian Democrat Union in Germany and became part of the International Democrat Union that later sponsored my presence as an observer of elections in Nicaragua and Hungary. In response to this alliance of centrist governments, the oppositions in the region got together under their umbrella, SCOPE, or Standing Conference of Opposition Parties in the East Caribbean.

With the established pattern of democracy in Jamaica, alternating parties in government every third election, Seaga's Jamaica Labour Party lost. He then suggested that a sitting Prime Minister take over the Chairmanship of the CDU and I was duly elected.

Our group became rather disillusioned about events within the JLP with Seaga, not a good loser in the best of times, ranting about what he deemed (in language reminiscent of Mao Tse-tung) to be the Gang of Five, the former ministers who thought it was time for him to resign. Among the dissidents were Pernell Charles, Edmund Bartlett, Karl Samuda, Douglas Vaz and Errol Henderson. Then there were also people like Bruce Golding, well respected by the private sector and all ranks of Jamaican society, and Joan Webley who was working with us in the CDU.

Seaga saw everything and everyone as a personal challenge, which, in our view, was not in his party's interest. In defeat, one needs friends and this certainly was not the time to dispense with competent colleagues. So the Prime Ministers dispatched me to speak to Eddie. He set up a breakfast meeting in his office. I was ushered into his grand scene amidst the pictures of his former glory among world leaders.

"I'm here, Eddie, with a message from colleagues in the islands," I began, then went on to explain how we sincerely hoped he could recapture the Government but that the fractious image of his party seeking to dispense with high-profile former ministers was giving the appearance of personal pique beyond the collective wisdom of a well-established party. We saw it as a recipe for continuing disaster for the party in Jamaica. To my utter amazement, I became the one in the dock, so to speak. He proceeded to give me a lecture on leadership. Here was someone leading a defeated opposition, lecturing me who had captured all seats in our Parliament, about leadership.

"Would you like some more scrambled eggs?" he asked. "There's plenty."

"No thanks," I replied. "I have had enough cholesterol to cause one heart attack."

Seaga did not seem to understand that devoid of lieutenants, the governing party's strategy would be to preserve him like a goose to be plucked at election time, let him loose again, only to be plucked again before the next electoral ravishment!

I reported my failure to the Prime Ministers, and Seaga persisted – and lost and lost again. His Opposition members consolidated. Michael Manley, the PNP leader, in none-too-good health, retired. He came to see me with our mutual friend Butch Stewart of Sandals and Air Jamaica to discuss tourism issues while I held regional responsibility on air transportation.

I asked Michael how he felt in retirement while his successor continued to win elections against Seaga. "My cup runneth over," he replied.

P.J. Patterson, a colleague since Carifta days and early Lomé negotiations in Europe, became a reliable friend, as we struggled together in the banana wars. He also stood up with a statement in support, when I was faced with American pressure over the murder trial of an American in St. Vincent. Did they really expect me to interfere with my country's judiciary?

We were struggling too to defeat the monopoly in telecommunications held by Cable and Wireless. At one lunch, hosted by the boss of that company, I moved into the attack as PJ graciously sat by, amused. When his turn came to speak, PJ likened our host's entry into the Caribbean to that of another Englishman beginning a Test cricket career facing West Indian fast bowlers and getting pounded on various parts of his body.

"Welcome to Test cricket," he said.

We broke the monopoly. AT&T, Orange and Digicel got into the ring.

In Grenada, though, there were real troubles brewing. Herbert Blaize was not much better than Seaga. From day one, I knew that the assemblage of parties I put together to fight off communism would not withstand his arrogance. His Ministers were resigning. One of the brightest, George Brizan, who had published a scholarly work on education in Grenada, had gone. My CDU colleagues sent me on a rescue mission. I met with Blaize, Ben Jones and Danny Williams, who later became Governor General, in the Prime Minister's office.

"What is the successor scenario?" I asked Blaize.

The whole world knew he was painfully stricken with prostate cancer, but I was not referring to his health.

"I am not dead yet!" was all he said.

We joined hands as I was leaving. "Bind us together, Lord, bind us together." He was reverting, as usual, to his unfailing hope the good Lord would straighten things out.

On another occasion I had tried to rationalize lobster fishing in our adjoining territorial waters.

"God made the lobsters," he said to me.

"Yes," I replied. "But God did not draw the boundary line between St. Vincent and Grenada of which the lobsters in the deep are ignorant."

I could not get him to understand that environmental protection, our joint responsibility in the Grenadines, meant that St. Vincent and Grenada should have identical closed seasons for lobster fishing. I had to threaten that if Grenadian ships were found in our waters with lobsters in the closed season, the ships would be confiscated even if the lobsters were caught in Grenadian waters. Eventually, in the interest of the lobsters, I shifted my closed season to be identical with theirs. "Bind us together, Lord, bind us."

When Blaize died, I called Ben Jones and told him he should go to the Governor General and be sworn in as Prime Minister. Blaize had not been a builder of institutions, so it was anyone's call in the power game. I did not attend his funeral. Jones became Prime Minister.

And Grenada?

All the hand-wringing around the world about the American invasion of Grenada was over. Blaize's government had crumbled, cookie fashion. His country had collected no crumbs from America's victory and Carriacou's pathetic surrender to the bow cannon of a yacht. Grenada was falling unceremoniously off the strategic map. Invaded and then ignored. President Reagan got his second term.

22

Second Term: After the Berlin Wall

Michel Camdessus, Managing Director of the Internal Monetary Fund, visited us in Kingstown, to attend a meeting with all the Caribbean Finance Ministers, most of whom were also Prime Ministers. The Berlin Wall had fallen, Cuba's communist influence had been contained, and we, the small Caribbean islands, had dropped off the strategic map. Funds took new wings into the Eastern Bloc, as the IMF dreamed of a repeat of the post-Second World War German economic miracle. The dismemberment of the Soviet Bloc provided impetus for the isolationists among us even as the competition in the market intensified. We could only plead with Michel Camdessus to ensure our market preferences were sustained, and that our aid on concessionary terms be extended while we diversified our economies.

My reliable friends in Mustique, Harding and Mary Lawrence, were always ready to respond to a special request, and were delighted to receive the IMF for an evening's celebration at the Terraces. To my utter amazement, Michel turned up for dinner in one of our campaign T-shirt's, inscribed with the accolade, "Much to please, little to fault," bestowed on our country at the previous IMF Article IV Consultation.

The next day, the IMF moved on to Moscow. The Berlin Wall was really down. Throughout Soviet rule, Moscow was ignored if not shunned by the Washington financial institutions. Now every financial institution wanted a piece of the action in Russia's emerging market economy.

The leader of a small Caribbean island should always know his place in the international pecking order. He should never let the "Mr. Prime Minister" business inflate his ego to the extent of believing he is any great concern of the high and mighty. Despite that, I never felt ill at ease among the leaders of other lands. Anxious to learn more about the world and other people's problems, I always thought the leaders' views of events, other cultures, and other civilizations were fascinating. Some, of course, were always rushing to be photographed among those they deemed of higher status than themselves. It is amusing sometimes, too, to look back on random placements and seating arrangements. The shunned usurper, General Musharraf, lunched with me at the Millennium Summit in New York, with not a single American at our table, a situation unimaginable after the collapse of the Twin Towers. But it is sad to remember conversations with those later assassinated, like Rajiv Gandhi and Yitzchak Rabin of Israel.

My draw at UN speeches seemed always to place me close to Israel. All politicians need a word of encouragement. I told Ehud Barak after we had both spoken how I had closed my restaurant at home so as to invite all guests to witness the television report on Rabin's assassination, and encouraged him to press on for peace. Great ideas like peace will never perish because, with all the excitement we can seek in life, peace of mind is the greatest goal for a human being, and you can't have peace of mind if there is no peace around you.

CHOGM Meetings were always fascinating. In my time, I attended these Commonwealth specialties in The Bahamas, Vancouver, Malaysia, Cyprus, Zimbabwe, New Zealand, Scotland and South Africa. One that stands out in my mind is the Zimbabwean CHOGM, where a white Zimbabwean environmentalist in his traditional bush jacket and shorts drove Robert Mugabe and me into the game reserve and carefully walked us through the bush to see the elephants. Our safari leader was obviously in love with the elephants. The souvenir books we had been presented with on our arrival – *The Presidential Elephants* by Alan Elliott and *The 1991 Zimbabwe CHOGM* – seemed to be an embodiment of an independent country proud of the land, its heritage, its national parks and all the people, black and white, moulding the old and new Zimbabwe.

Today, with all the misery imposed by ruthless plunder and inter-racial strife, I can hardly believe that my friend Robert wrote a preface to Elliot's book with the line: "The concept of a white African may be hard for some to grasp, but Zimbabwe is a much loved homeland for many of these people. For most white Zimbabweans, the rest of the world is a foreign place."

I feel a sense of total stupidity that when I reflect on that day with the elephants, I discerned no clue about the anger lurking in the soul of my host. When we met again in New York at the UN Millennium Summit I got for him a copy of the paper by Karl John on our work on land reform, urging that, in my small way, I knew the jungle of international funding for land reform and that there would be no greater contribution I could make in life than help in peaceful transition in Africa. We had succeeded in getting the British, the Danes, the French, the European Union, the OAS, and World Bank to help our land reform programme. Over 35 per cent of the beneficiaries were women. I would have loved to help Zimbabwe. It was not to be. The Harare Principle of Governance, presided over in plenary session by Robert Mugabe, has been ignored in Zimbabwe.

The splendid golf resort at Elephant Hills, where we enjoyed smoked crocodile, has since crumbled, I understand, with but a few good souls tending the greens. I had amused colleagues by suggesting we subscribe to a new venture in which I thought we could invest in Zimbabwe – crocodile tears. Why not? London smog was bottled! Think of the ultimate in presents in gift shops around the world!

Back home, too, I was once faced with the pain of an old white planter who was born in our country and suddenly felt alienated. Jack Punnett, a relic of our white plantocracy, had shot his drug addict son in a terrible altercation but was exonerated by a jury. His life style was predictable. On Wednesdays, he journeyed to his bank in the city and collected wages for his farm workers. On Thursdays, he put it in envelopes. On Fridays, he paid. The robbers decided to interrupt this time-honoured sequence and shot up his house and collected the payments one Thursday night.

He called and wanted to see me. I inspected the damage. He was definitely going to leave St. Vincent for good and join his daughter in Ireland, and I could have his property, he said. He thought I deserved to own an old plantation house overlooking the verdant Vermont Valley with a great view of the sunset.

His wife prepared tea. We sipped it on the verandah. As evening closed in, she nervously suggested we return into the living room out of harm's way.

"We will stay on this verandah into the night," I said. "I want the crooks to see that I am here. You should go to Ireland on holiday and get this trauma out of your system. Then come home. We are more peaceful than Ireland. You have already sold one part of your plantation for my land reform programme. The Rastas settled there are happy. You must stay and enjoy the rest of your days in your home. I will not be the one to buy you out when you are depressed. I will send some of my crack SSU troops to patrol your place until things settle down."

"Well, Son, will you at least take the billiard table?" he asked.

"No. I do not have a place to put it. Go on your holiday."

I knew that the Zimbabwe Constitution did not have a suitable clause on land acquisition, and I could not understand why Bob did not negotiate a deal with the international community.

Other memories of Zimbabwe and our meeting there linger, like the discussion on "youth" and what we could do with this explosion of information technology impacting on young minds, diverting them from all traditional values. Museveni of Uganda related one of his experiences on the subject: "When I was fighting in the bush to free my country of the baboon Idi Amin, I took a little holiday in Sweden to meet up with my family in exile there. I get to the airport. My little boy was getting taller. He shouts to me, 'Hi, Dad.' I had to pause and reflect on how Sweden was killing all our traditional values. A boy calling to his father 'Hi, Dad.'"

It was rather amazing listening to this tale. Deep in the collective consciences of CHOGM meeting was the recollection that while his rival was at an earlier conference, Idi Amin got rid of Milton Obote. There would be no deposition this time, only a complaint about an errant child.

Our easy-paced deliberations on methodologies to enhance democracy meandered like the tributaries toward a great African river under the guidance of our Chairman, the host Robert Mugabe. Democratic systems were evolving. All these fine statements were presented before a third of the world's leaders for sober appraisal. Our Harare Principles emerged, a beacon of light, to be extinguished, alas, in Harare itself!

In the isolated Zimbabwean countryside the Heads of Government had gone in various directions in the game reserve. The planes were ready to take us back to Harare. The protocol officer was having a dusty time. "I've lost one King, five Presidents and three Prime Ministers," he said. My Cabinet Secretary, Irma Young, who had agreed after much persuasion to come to Africa, could not contain herself. "These people can't be serious. An African King lost?" Irma, Afro Indian, with her African sensibility mixed with Jamaican anxiety over slavery, her Indian culture swamped by Catholicism, could not countenance the chaos.

On the way home in Harare, a jeep from the Ministry of Political Affairs slammed into our bus at the traffic light, putting many, including Lady Pindling, in hospital. Discussing the accident, Irma was quite contemptuous at breakfast. "If they can lose a King, what is a bruise?" Until then, she had been so passionate about her African roots!

My next destination was Cyprus. *Bitter Lemons* by Lawrence Durrell had provided the sum of my knowledge about Cyprus, apart from the personal contact I'd had with the President Glafcos Clerides, at various previous conferences. He had told me of his escape in the Second World War and walking home across Europe, and I even offered to listen to him and transcribe his story. As usual I relied on the local knowledge of my security detail to find me a restaurant that they frequented. Their choice was a marvellous fish restaurant, complete with live fish in a tank.

I had to find my daughter Louise who was to join me from Egypt where she was taking time off after McGill University to venture into Islamic Studies. The police found her relaxing around a pool. Typical of her (probably inherited) wanderlust, she had arrived in Cyprus before our official programme commenced.

The morning the Conference opened, for more than an hour driving to the capital, we witnessed the longest demonstration of women I have ever seen, mainly dressed in white, standing elegantly beside the road, protesting the division and occupation of their country by the Turks. A presentation of pure Greek tragedy.

As the days progressed and resolutions on the subject were debated and passed, I felt that the weight of the Commonwealth behind our friends in Cyprus would solve the issue. My naiveté in international relations did not discover in Cyprus what a victim of the Cold War that the country had become, with Turkey as a listening post for espionage against Russia. The Commonwealth, alas, could never influence American Cold War pursuits. I could not at the time understand the British indifference to the Turkish occupation when British troops were also ensconced in the island. Were they frozen into inaction by the lessons of Suez?

On the way back from the Archbishop Makarios' tomb we visited a home-based pork-curing operation, sampling the products. Cyprus had a wonderful variety of large white grapes, a cutting from which I brought home to propagate without much success. But my olive tree is still growing at Mt. Pleasant, though there are no olives.

Louise was delighted to meet Benazhir Bhutto and her husband, and particularly to be seated with them at the Queen's dinner on the *Britannia*. She left the Conference to return to Cairo and I made my way back to London. She wrote an editorial in the *Egyptian Gazette* about the conference which attracted the Cyprus Ambassador to Egypt, who visited her offices to commend her. I sent through a copy I received to Glafcos.

Several weeks later I got a call from Pat, panicking about Muslim fundamentalism in Egypt and their attack on tourists in Luxor. She deemed that Louise should leave immediately. I called only to receive a flood of tears, objecting to leaving. Through my friend Carlo Amato, the Canouan developer who had friends everywhere, we checked with the Police Chief in Cairo, who was close to Mubarak through marriage, and had been the Governor of Sinai when it was returned by the Israelis. He saw no cause for alarm. Pat set out for Egypt. On her return, leaving Louise where she was, she confided that my education was incomplete until I experienced Egypt.

After Cyprus, there was the Caricom Summit in Chaguaramas where we converted Carifta into Caricom. Michael Manley had proposed his father's Norman's birthday, July 4th to be Caricom Day as the date of our annual meetings. For me, it meant an annual conflict between being at home for Carnival and at the Heads of Government Conference somewhere else, with myself as Prime Minister doing no more than crowning the Carnival Queen and taking off for the meeting. This may seem an over-reaction. However, I have an unbounded fondness for human spectacles, and none is grander in our part of the world than a carnival. It is a festival of flesh, with energetic young women radiating happiness and the harmony in our history out of Africa, India and Europe, the sunshine and the rain glistening on their skins, bodies revelling in glorious costumes and swaying to vibrating music with total abandon. But when the spectacular becomes drowned in boisterous noise, I admit now I preferred to put some distance between my delicate ears and the cacophony, even at the price of denying my ageing eyes another feast.

After the Caricom Summit I went to Lugano for further discussions on the Canouan development project, including getting the German firm Kocks Consult to design the expansion of the Canouan airport. Thence I travelled to Egypt on holiday to see Louise accompanied by Jeannette.

It was Egypt that showed me the architectural magnificence of ancient civilizations. Once more I realized how important it was to ensure that my time in leadership advanced the architecture of my country.

Our friend Carlo Amato had been a godfather to Mohammed El Menshawy, whose father had given guidance when we were worried about our daughter. Mohammed, or Majed as he was known, accompanied us up the Nile, and I was lectured among all the other tourists on the extraordinary indulgences of the Pharaohs. Louise proved a wonderful guide, bargaining in Arabic with the taxi drivers, but refusing to show me the hole she rented. We visited the offices of the *Egyptian Gazette* where she was enjoying being a part-time journalist. She was toying with the idea of returning to university to study journalism or law. Quite firmly I insisted that she would not be studying journalism with my money. Journalism was a struggle in the Caribbean. The alternative was law, but she had not yet made up her mind.

One day weeks later, she called in tears. Her Editor had proposed she do an interview with the Prime Minister of Pakistan and she had spent weeks preparing for the interview, with Benazir on her visit to Egypt. One morning the proof of the interview reached her desk, ready for press. However, she discovered that the interview was already prepared for publication, having been done by the Editor himself. She charged into his office and demanded an explanation. "How could he dare waste her time to prepare for the interview and not tell her he was doing it himself?" she complained to me. The truth turned out to be very simple. The article was being published as an interview, but the Pakistani Embassy requested the questions and returned the replies.

And so Louise went on to a career that took her to Manchester, the Inner Temple, and Oxford, appearing at the Privy Council with Karl Hudson-Phillips, and into the law offices of Tim Scranton in South Carolina and the International Finance Authority at home, thanks to the editor of the *Egyptian Gazette*, suitably named Mohammed Ali.

Guyana always fascinated me. The word "Demerara" floated into my consciousness in my youth, and I can still remember the rice my father brought home from Guyana in his laden ships, enough to feed all of Bequia for a month. And in my London period, I had dined a few times in Holland Park with Wilson Harris and his English wife Margaret after he had published his wonderful book on Guyana, *Palace of the Peacock,* and we discussed the country in detail. I knew my Bequia could vanish in the Essequibo jungle of Guyana, but the diminishing quality of life in that country in the midst of such vast resources was, to me, yet another indication that the quality of life in a nation depended on leadership and policies and had nothing to do with natural wealth. Jamaica, for instance, had fallen victim to Michael Manley's socialism: "All those of you who don't like my policies," he shouted, "there are five flights a day to Miami."

Desmond Hoyte was ready to change policies toward privatization, even though I understood he had to be sensitive to the lingering influence of Forbes' wife Viola in any abandonment of the socialist rhetoric of the past. His economic adviser, the buxom Darlene Harris, was the point-lady dealing with the London-based consultations with S.G. Warburg for his privatization experiment.

In our previous Colombian trip my colleagues and I had had a useful insight into the linkage between flour and rice in the milling industry. Ken Boyea, the CEO of our East Caribbean Group of Companies, with

my help as Government shareholder, secured the authority to proceed
with the feasibility study of getting into rice milling by expanding the
flour mill, ideally located with its own jetty.

Next, I tackled Desmond Hoyte, seeking a few thousand acres for
the production of rice. Guyana needed the investment and we could
do it. Desmond advised us to contact Warburg to get the financing not
only to purchase one thousand acres of paddy fields, but also so we
could lay our hands on two under-producing factories.

Ken Boyea went down and checked out the scene around the
beautiful flat landscape along the magnificent Essequibo River. There
was also a defunct earthen airstrip which meant we could commute
with one Aero Commander into Georgetown and fly direct to our mill.
ECGC put in a bid for US$4 million, complete with a 20-page dossier
on management, up-front payment to the farmers, provision of rental
equipment for all field operations and routines for the maintenance of
equipment. Dr. Ptolmy Reid, a grand old man in Burnham's Peoples
National Movement, and retired Agriculture Minister, was dispatched
to St. Vincent to examine our operation and determine our competence.
We passed the due-diligence exercises of both Dr. Reid and Warburg.
Our four million dollars was less than an American-telexed offer of six
million, but we had convinced them we could succeed whereas the
Americans could not. We had also set aside 10 per cent of the shares
for the Government as a sop to old socialists.

I then tackled the Organisation of Eastern Caribbean States in a
meeting I chaired in Kingstown to get their support for my regional
project. All went well except for an admonishment from Eugenia
Charles, still sensitive to the Indians deprived of control of their country.
"The Indians are the farmers. The Africans are the civil servants in the
city. You will have to deal with the Indians in the countryside, otherwise
doom awaits you." Eugenia never minced words. She was our Iron
Lady.

We researched the Guyana social and economic structure to get a
feel for the place. We discovered that some 30,000 acres with rice
farmers on them had released their cattle in the fields out of frustration
with delayed payments by the dominant millers – sometimes waiting a
year to be paid. The millers complained that the peasants were cheats,
adding earth to rice to supplement their weights.

After our two mills were completely refurbished, I had to inspire
confidence in the farmers and the community. Hoyte had invested a
lot in me and I had to deliver. I called a press conference and lectured.
Working in the paddy fields of Trinidad in my youth came in handy. I

40. With Prime Minster Errol Barrow at a conference in Barbados, 1984

41. Monitoring the Nicaraguan elections with Violetta Chamorro (left) and Steve Norris (far right)

42. With regional colleagues at Mustique Meeting to resolve the Guyana electoral dispute with Kennedy Simmonds (St. Kitts), Dame Eugenia Charles (Dominica), Desmond Hoyte (Guyana), 25th January, 1986

43. Cambodia refugee camp in Thailand, 1989

44. Announcing the Land Reform Programme, May 5th, 1985

45. With European delegate and EIB Officials touring the Grenadines

46. Presenting the Bequia-built model of the HMS *Britannia* to Her Majesty Queen Elizabeth, built by Lawson Sargeant

48. Her Majesty Queen Elizabeth meeting my nanny Amelia Duncan, at Frangipani Hotel Tea Party, Bequia, 1985

47. Receiving Her Majesty Queen Elizabeth in Port Elizabeth, Bequia, wearing the sash of Venezuela's Order of Simon Bolivar

49. Christmas Party at the Prime Minister's residence with daughter Gretel, David Bowie and Mick Jagger

50. With Deputy Foreign Minister of Kuwait, Prince Al Sabah, and Sabrina, Japan

51. At the convention of Kenneth Kaunda's political party, in Mulungushi, Zambia with Oliver Tambo and Joachim Chissano of Mozambique, 1988

52. With Yasser Arafat at same

54. With Rajiv Gandhi and ANR Robinson at CHOGM Conference, Vancouver

53. With Kenneth Kaunda and Shridath Ramphal at CHOGM Conference

56. Celebrating inaugural flight of Carib Express with Sir Geoffrey Cave, Kyffin Simpson and Manager Roy Barnes

55. Ceremonial Opening of Parliament with Commissioner of Police, Randolph Toussaint

57. With Bozo Dabinovic, SVG Maritime Commissioner

58. Christmas card photo, family 1997. From left: Sabrina with Ondine, self, Gabija, Louise, Gretel

59. Picnicking with Princess Margaret and Pat on Morpion

60. PM with Mustique school children

61. Flying a kite with Gretel

62. With Jeannette and Baron Carlo Amato, National Day, San Marino

63. Gabija at Helianthus, 2006

64. Knighthood at Buckingham Palace, KCMG, May 1995, Gretel, self, Sabrina, Louise

gave them the statistics, where their industry was, and where we wanted to take it. We would rent the farmers their equipment and deduct it from sales, paying 50 per cent on purchase and the other 50 per cent on determination of quality. All the farmers on the 30,000 acres were ready to sell to us and the other private millers had to pay on time. The rice industry boomed.

St. Vincent became a player in the rice negotiations in the region. We had to take on the vested interest in Jamaica that was sneaking in subsidized rice from the US. Our mills were producing more than all of the Guyanan ones put together. It was a good time for all of us, and I even spent a few wonderful nights in a house on stilts in the manager's compound, eating sumptuously of the *roti*, crab, and curried goat.

In due course we built two separate dining rooms for the workers at the factory; one for the Afro-Guyanese, one for the Indians, each with an appropriate menu. Productivity was excellent. The mood of the community was cheerful. The testing for quality was beyond reproach. Some minor illegal practices (such as cheating on weights of paddy) arose, but these were quickly stamped out. The Caribbean media commended our efforts and declared our business style and financial planning to be a model for the region.

Desmond hosted Sir Philip and Lady Veira, the major shareholders in our company at home and in Guyana. Sir Philip, who rose from humble beginnings selling chives he had grown at home to a shopkeeper renting premises from my grandfather's sister, had become a premier industrialist in our region. Sir Philip had supported every political party in St. Vincent at different stages and was the first businessman to build a pavilion on the cricket field.

When the PNC lost the Government in Guyana, I called Cheddi Jagan from my hotel room in London to congratulate him, and he said he wanted me to come to Guyana right away to witness his inauguration. That surprised all those who had linked me with Hoyte after Mustique. My relationship with the Jagans had begun long before politics, when, as a deck third-class passenger on the Italian liner, I met Cheddi strolling the deck from his luxurious cabin. And, purchasing lumber from Guyana to construct the Frangipani, I had established a friendship with the greenheart dealer, Sam Ghany, who would invite me on various occasions for good Indian food at home where Cheddi was often the other guest.

Cheddi Jagan, the cheated outsider, always floated around the Heads of Government Conferences complaining about fraudulent elections. I never told him that although we had given Hoyte the benefit of the doubt on his election to the presidency, we had decided to monitor every election after that. After my Nicaraguan experience observing the election when the Sandinistas lost, I had written a letter to Desmond Hoyte, alerting him to this new phenomenon of election observation, and that the process would go well beyond what we had initiated. I never published this letter, but Desmond sent up an election official for a briefing and I supplied a dossier on monitoring procedure.

Cheddi requested an audience with me at the Jamaica Caricom Meeting. We met for breakfast. I remember Cheddi being choosy about the menu, while I happily indulged in my good salt fish and ackee. He informed me that he was not going to contest the upcoming election. He did not trust us in Caricom and did not trust the Commonwealth Secretariat, which he thought was under the lingering influence of Sir Shridath Ramphal, Burnham's former Attorney General. And he was not accepting any imposition by his African successor, Chief Anyaoku.

India, Africa, Slavery, Indenture, all were crashing in my ears. Tito and his non-aligned movement suddenly made no sense. My Caribbean had done nothing to halt the rigging of elections in Guyana, and the Indians felt we had cheated them. But then, the Caribbean was also silent when the Constitution of St. Vincent was rewritten to cheat me.

I explained to Cheddi what we had done in Malaysia to set up the mechanism for Commonwealth Observer Missions. I told him that since Nicaragua's election the world of election observation had changed and that he should go to London and meet the High Commissions of the Indian and White Commonwealth if he did not trust the Africans. Mrs. Thatcher, Bob Hawke, Brian Mulroney and Dr. Mahathir would see that he was not cheated. He must contest the elections, I said. I would see to it that Caricom sent a clean team. Cheddi seemed to soften and said he was going to check also with President Carter.

I reported to Desmond that we had had a good meeting and that I hoped Jagan would contest. Desmond listened to me in good faith. I didn't think he felt he was cheating Jagan.

There was a delay of the poll when the Carter Center declared that the lists were not in order. When London confirmed that Jagan had indeed won, Ken Boyea called to tell me he was very concerned that our high-profile relationship with Hoyte would jeopardize our Guyana investment. I told him about my call to Cheddi from London and his invitation to celebrate with him. I sent Parnel Campbell, my Attorney General, to say that I would come when he was ready to do business.

Ken Boyea and I chartered an SVG Air plane in time for the swearing-in of the PPP Civic Ministers. Cheddi was delighted to see me. Five of his Ministers had to share reading glasses to read the Oath of Office. They had barely survived the struggle.

After the swearing in ceremony, we went into the President's office. Cheddi's address book had only one number that was of some use, Fidel Castro's. All of his other friends were out of office, or had just simply passed on. I gave the secretary, whom I had known from the Hoyte days, the numbers for my contacts in Washington, DC.

We asked the World Bank/IMF if they wished Cheddi to make a policy statement now before they came or would they prefer to have it issued after they had discussions in Georgetown. They decided to call back. Rather quickly, the answer came that a mission would come to Georgetown and President Jagan could then make his policy statement after they had met with him.

So the new PPP/Civic Government was on the way.

The leader of the Civic group, Sam Hinds who became Prime Minister, flew up to tour our rice mill and meet the farmers. Our only request was that the empty silos in the area be made available to us to enhance our storage. Years passed with no action. It was difficult to sustain our interest. Cheddi's initial policy statement won early approval. Never had a new government assumed office with so much good will only to let it dissipate. A year afterwards, I met the aid officials from Washington and they lamented the inaction. A lot of money was allocated for projects only to be stuck in bureaucratic delays, and the talent in Guyana continued to emigrate.

Still, when both Jagan and Michael Manley died about the same time, Caricom had to decide how we would share representation. Who would stand at the grave of the socialist Manley, and who would stand beside the communist Cheddi Jagan? I opted for Cheddi, along with Basdeo Panday of Trinidad and Tobago. When I heard later that President Clinton had visited Cheddi at Walter Reid hospital, I knew that the Americans were atoning for their CIA sins in the past, and that Cheddi must obviously have been on the way out. An American President would not visit a communist who may recover.

We were all gathered, the diplomats and dignitaries, outside Georgetown at the monument of the national slave hero, Cuffy, waiting to proceed miles into the countryside for Cheddi's riverside cremation. Poor Cuffy had tall grass all around him. The national hero's statue had been erected on that site after his great inaugural ceremonies were abandoned.

One witty diplomat near me said that Cuffy's statue had once complained to a tourist who had come to take his picture, "Please go to President Burnham and tell him I want a horse. I am the only hero in South America who is not properly mounted. I want my horse." The tourist returned with an irate Burnham. Cuffy remonstrated with the tourist: "I told you I wanted a horse, not an ass."

Two hours later we were stuck in the traffic. The ferries couldn't take all the cars across the bridge. I was chatting with the Foreign Minister Clement Rohee who was assigned to accompany the foreign dignitaries when word came through the radio that the funeral was postponed. Cheddi's wife Janet had quite rightly decided that the supporters in every village must pay their respects. I informed Rohee of the postponement: "The show is off," I added. The Canadian High Commissioner invited us to share in the bounty at the back of his jeep. I was ready for a drink and sandwich. I knew that on the way back there would be no crowds and I would be able to take the stress off my prostate on the roadside.

I visited Desmond and we had dinner with some of his friends and drank the champagne I brought. He lost the election gracefully and we remained friends. Guyana moved to a new era, but Desmond retained his humanity. We in Caricom had worked too to secure Guyana's turn to provide the President of the UN General Assembly and eventually the tireless Foreign Minister Rasleigh Jackson was designated.

Cheddi's new government focused immediately on all the external jobs where Caricom had placed Guyanese: the International Court of Justice, the ACP Secretariat in Brussels, the UN General Assembly Presidency. Rasleigh Jackson had served in the Foreign Ministry through all Cabinet shuffles under Burnham and Hoyte. He had appointed Rudy Insanally as Permanent Representative at the UN, only to discover that Caricom, at Cheddi's urging, was now to place Insanally into the Presidency. Rasleigh was deprived of winding down his illustrious career riding off into the sunset. The next time I saw him he was a consultant with an NGO and had also lost his wife in tragic circumstances.

Jagan was facing the legacy, of which he was a part, of the decade-old fruitless conflict between socialism and communism, and racial conflict between the Afro-Guyanese and the Indo-Guyanese, a climate that forced the people from a land of plenty to migrate even to the islands that could all fit into Guyana's jungles.

23

Entries from My Diaries, 1988 to 1990

Entry dated September 24, 1988

Hurricane Helene has avoided us today. The Caribbean had been traumatized by Gilbert's 140 mph devastating Jamaica a couple weeks ago. So this morning, Saturday is beautiful and quiet.

I hope to sort out my miseries this weekend and finalize my divorce settlement with Pat.

Last weekend I hosted President Luchinchi of Venezuela, his Foreign Minister German Carillo and Education Minister Dr. Laura Gurfinckel on a State Visit in response to my invitation to him when I was in Caracas.

We had had very long discussions in Caracas and the length of our dialogue had made the news even before we were finished. We met several times for discussions here, more than in Caracas – in this residence, on the helicopter to and from Mustique, and at the dinner he hosted at the French Restaurant.

Our subjects ranged from Caribbean unity and its relevance to security, to the economics of surplus and deficits, and the drug war. He brought silence to the table and all conversations ceased when he declared, "The drug lords of Colombia have a US$12 billion reserve to deploy in expanding their empire and they will move anything out of their way by all the means they can procure."

I told him how I could not get my colleagues to understand how much more significant we would become if we became a single archipelagic state controlling the access to the Panama Canal. He saw the point. He made reference to the Japanese wanting to build a second canal in Central America.

My target in the discussions was to consolidate relations with Venezuela for all time. I had started in the period 1970–74 with Calvani, but the energy crisis had benefited Venezuela without any benefit passed on to us. Now I wanted my Spanish Institute funded beside the French Institute I planned in an A-level college being built by the Europeans. Fluency in language here will lead to the flow of goods, people and services. Our links with Venezuela and Martinique would be permanent. I suggested we could structure the Spanish Institute with Venezuelan procurement and exchange student scholarships between us.

Such could be the tribute to my father who perished in 1940 with the Venezuelan crew in the Bermuda Triangle aboard our schooner.

Entries entitled "Looking back on my mission to Zambia"

Kenneth Kaunda

A gracious gentleman. A pity that he should do so well in liberating his people and not lead them with the sensible policies for their economic development. I am reminded of Lee Kwan Yew's statement to the Commonwealth Heads, making reference to China's Cultural Revolution, "How many millions more must die before a country determines the right direction for progress?"

He ate with his hands with great delicacy. His basin was brought to the table to wash his hands. He got up at the end to clean up; a great sense of humour and assured authority.

Chissano

Friendly. I was surprised by his rather naïve statements about suing the foreign elements that helped to destroy his country. I wondered too if *perestroika* had reached him. But he was an easy man to talk to, and you only realized his Presidential status when his aides gathered. I would like to visit him.

Museveni

We always got along well and seemed to be often placed beside each other at the table. "The biggest problem in Africa is backwardness," he intoned. A straightforward fellow, with scholarly pretensions for he is familiar with and possesses a sense of history.

Arap Moi

An aristocrat, no nonsense.

Mobutu

A super-aristocrat. He is familiar with his own power and struts like a peacock. He sounds the cymbals of liberation against South Africa like anyone else, talks of co-operation with Zambia, but I understand the Zambians have great difficulty taking the short-cut across Zaire [today, Democratic Republic of Congo] to other parts of Zambia in the hollow.

Dos Santos

The most reclusive of the lot in that region. He ate often by himself. On the last day I pushed in to chat with him through his young interpreter. I explained to him how the IMF was not an American-dominated institution, even though they had a heavy hand in policy. That policy was accepted by the members of the Fund. The staff were mixed from several countries, including Africans, and that my World Bank man was from Ghana.

I suggested his interpreter take a picture of both of us with my camera. He insisted that approval had to be secured from the Zambian Protocol! I did not bother.

He was not close to the Cuban delegation as one would have thought. The man who was negotiating for Cuba was there and I seldom saw them together. This Cuban had to struggle to get an audience with Kaunda.

Mengistu

You couldn't tell the difference between him and his aides. They were all there and in the same blue costumes. Only his camera crew had a slightly different blue hue. If you spoke to him about his problems, the drought in Ethiopia and starvation, he said little but claimed that everything was all right. He was praised by Kaunda as a revolutionary:

"One world," was the cry.

"One revolution," the answer.

Sam Nujoma

Smiles. Recognizes that he is not yet a Head of State, but biding his time. A friendly fellow. You could talk to him.

Oliver Tambo

A pleasant fellow. He does not come across as a revolutionary leader or intellectual. He speaks slowly, measures what he says, does not say anything profound, but certainly does not talk nonsense or sound inflammatory. He questions what you say – as for example when I told him of the article I had just read in a US magazine on Winnie Mandela discrediting herself with some American would-be PR Ambassador; he wanted to know more. I was worried about the way he held his cutlery and wondered how he would fare at a state banquet in Pretoria. He eats slowly. It will be a treat to see how he handles the South African economy if given the chance.

Musokotawene
The Prime Minister. A real gentleman. I think he would lead Zambia in new economic directions – just a feeling, not based on what he said. His interests tell me this. If he ever took over from Kaunda, I would love to invite him to see how in a poor country we developed tourism.

Our people here have responded positively to the African visit. My copper bracelets to friends suffering from arthritis in St. Vincent and Bequia were a success. So were the necklaces of malachite. A fisherman was glad to have a stone from Africa in the bow of his seine boat to ward off evil spirits and bring good luck.

Entry (undated) entitled "Notes on Air Canada En Route Vancouver to Toronto"

Award of distinction
Universities in rich countries today, with their exorbitant fees for foreign students, not like in the past when you could enter the intellectual kingdom without a work permit, working even as a sleeping-car porter, will seldom again claim a foreign Prime Minister as one of their favourite sons.

My old University of British Columbia barely made it, producing a Prime Minister when John Turner slipped in for a few months in Canada. And, I suppose, they were pleased to identify me for the Alumni Award of Distinction for 1988, 33 years after I had graduated, then too with distinction.

So it was a sort of triumphant return to Vancouver, this time with my daughter Louise, and an entourage including my High Commissioner in Canada, Dr. Bernard Yankey, and our Attorney General, Parnel Campbell.

It seemed as though my previous return to majestic Vancouver, still glorious with its imposing mountains, with a high-profile speech at the opening of the Heads of Government Conference, had reminded the

UBC authorities of my existence. My lingering regret, though, of that conference, was that my daughter Sabrina and I had not taken up the invitation to India from Rajiv and Sonia Gandhi, as Rajiv had since been assassinated.

This visit to Vancouver had been put together as a whirlwind tour, beginning in Miami at the Caribbean Latin American conference, and ending in Ottawa as the guest of Brian Mulroney.

Miami

The Miami gathering regretfully seemed to be becoming an annual circus, with its co-ordinator, Peter Johnson, vainly struggling to steer investors our way under the Caribbean Basin Initiative. At least we met the odd Senator and Congressman to whom we could hope to explain our problems with Washington. The big treat was the formal banquet, on the top floor of a bank overlooking Miami, where a Prime Minister or President had to do the honours with an after-dinner speech. Nelson Rockefeller was ahead of me. Ray Robinson, John Compton, and Maria Peters of Curaçao were to speak after me.

I had to find something topical. President George Bush Sr. had just been elected. I had watched the election results from the Manor Court Hotel in New Orleans where I was taking a break. The president elect's campaigning theme on taxes – his famous "Read My Lips" – gave me my cue. With three words, I told my hosts, while all America was wondering what kind of President they would be getting after the Great Communicator Ronald Reagan, their new President had converted the United States into a nation of lip-readers. My advice to all Americans, therefore, was that they look out for a ventriloquist. Not just ovation for me, this time, but total uproar.

I left Miami for the long haul to Vancouver, but not before a breakfast session in my hotel with Dr. Wirsing of the EEC, his delegate Eberhard Stan, and Dick Gunn, my High Commissioner who got along well with Wirsing. Dick had been a great asset in following through on the Bequia Airport. I had allocated special funds to him to service St. Vincent and the Grenadines with this project in particular in Brussels. We confirmed that the project was on stream. I reported on the fine job being done by the German engineers Kocks, that we had held discussions with the DCA and settled on an approach slope of 5.3 per cent rather than 4 per cent. We discussed also the education project (an A-level college) and spent most of the time on the tourism project for the OECS. I told them I would give the highest priority to tourism education rather than promotion.

Vancouver

In Vancouver, I was met by John Diggins, President of the UBC Alumni, and Deborah Alps, who was to be my gracious host. We went to the Sylvia, an old-style hotel where I had stayed with the children when I took them years ago to see the pastures that nurtured me in my youth. I realized, though, that I would not be able to prepare my mind for the ceremonies the next evening if I stayed in that place. So I called Deborah early the next morning to get me out. We moved to the three-bedroom suite of the Hotel Vancouver, courtesy External Affairs.

Receiving the Award of Distinction from the University where I laboured was the highest point in my life. It was as great a moment as when I took the oath at the Privy Council in the presence of the Queen, but that was one for Prime Ministers, and my predecessor had gone through that road. This was mine and mine alone.

I recounted the hard days of my youth. I thanked the University for all the experiences I had put myself through after my grandfather's funds were exhausted, the gardening, the dish-washing, picking up pins in the bowling alley, delivering post – and heavy telephone books at Christmas – and the three mornings a week in the winter, before lectures, delivering mail on campus.

My theme, however, was that the opportunity which I secured in 1954-5 was not available to people from my part of the world today with fees doubled for a foreign student. I spoke with affection of how Professor Laird taught me the meaning of earth to earth, ashes to ashes in funeral rites, as he pointed out the fundamental laws of our universe embodied in the principle of change. I also recounted how my tutor, Professor Brink, after being delayed one morning by a meeting with lawyers, pointed out to us the essential difference between lawyers and scientists. The lawyers are confined to interpreting definitions, while the mind of the scientist works in the framework of cause and effect, a reality that stayed with me throughout my political life.

Dinner with the President of the Westbrook Society was a great honour. I was very pleased that my daughter Louise was there. The next day she was taken on a tour of the campus and the site of my old coffee shop haunt. She loved it, and the Chinese cafeteria in between.

Vancouver was warm, bright and endearing.

Ottawa

Ottawa was to turn out to be the crème de la crème. Brian Mulroney, the Canadian Prime Minister, and his Yugoslav wife Mila, had been great friends ever since I welcomed them to the west coast of Canada at the Vancouver Summit. He invited me to make an official visit to Ottawa, and put me up in the official lodge, Rideau Gate, for a few days. A little snow on the ground before Christmas in the tree-lined driveway was a great pleasure to someone like myself who had not seen snow since he was a youngster.

We lunched upstairs at the Lester Pearson Building and had a fine get-together. I was accompanied by my High Commissioner Bernard Yankey, a Dominican. Brian was warm, pleased with his election victory and cracking jokes. "A pleasure it is to host the leader of the NDP to lunch." I briefed him on the imminent defeat of Seaga, the chaos in Grenada, and the delays on our unification.

Brian's letter to me offering to help with our Caribbean unity project is now only a historical footnote, a noble endeavour, although he did tell John Robinson of the Canadian International Development Agency (CIDA): "Now I've just come out of an election and I won, I want Son to win. We've got to keep his voice strong in the Caribbean. Fix him up."

After that, I met with Robinson to go through the details of CIDA's planning of the Diamond Industrial Estate and ensure the increased funding.

Entry (undated) entitled "After Ottawa"

I was to find out later that, in Barbados, when the Canadian High Commission discovered I was to meet Mulroney the next day, they had a rather uneasy time preparing a rushed brief. Out of that visit to Ottawa I got the financing for the vegetable market in Bequia, so useful to the yacht visitors. This was to be our second useful Canadian gift for Bequia. The earlier, when I was Trade Minister, came from Russ McKinney – the financial allocation to build our first jetty where planks had to be placed on the beach to allow trucks to drive on to a schooner.

In Canada I also saw the Saudi Ambassador who was to put me on track for relations with the Kingdom. I set in train the recognition procedures through his Washington office.

I then had to go home to deal with problems on the home front, which turned out to be an amicable divorce. I hosted the annual Christmas party. My children had come home on holidays from school in Toronto. Friends from Mustique turned up too, Mick Jagger and David Bowie among them. Everyone had a good time, but I was in a contemplative, not a party mood. I was beginning to understand that, for all the love the public showed me, no one really cared about the mental anguish or personal health of their leader unless it affected their rewards.

When I learnt that the Queen had summoned John Major to inform him that Charles and Diana would soon separate, I rose early the next morning at 4 a.m., and called the Palace. I got in touch with Sir William Heseltine and told him that this Minister of her realm wished to convey his moral support to Her Majesty. He assured me he would do just that later that day during his audience. And in the style of a military commander, he concluded, "You carry on, Prime Minister."

Entry dated February 2, 1989

Caracas

So much water has passed under the bridge that I have been paralyzed in keeping these notes. Today I'm in Caracas for the inauguration of Carlos Andres Peres. The last time we had met was at the inauguration of Barco of Colombia. I have hardly had the spirit to record the visit of Michael Wilson, the Canadian Finance Minister, as my personal guest for the New Year's Eve celebrations of 1988 at the Frangipani. My divorce went through. My brother has been diagnosed over the last week as suffering from cancer of the colon. My children came with their boyfriends for Xmas. Nasty press comments stating that if my children disappeared at sea I would instruct the coastguard to search more thoroughly than I did for those missing required an apology on their part, and failing to receive same, I sued the Vincentian newspaper. A sort of apology followed the court proceedings.

One thing is certain. The status of Prime Minister does not match that of a President. While there is no international distinction between countries based on their size, you really get the short end of the stick if you are only a Prime Minister.

The pressure of things at home hangs over me as we move to another election. Ends to be tidied up in the Parliament, in my constituency, and other constituencies. While down here I will speak to Desmond Hoyte and Ray Robinson about their letters of support on the Bequia Airport. Also the continuing problem of Sandiford.

Desmond has just come here from Cuba. I am at a loss to understand his timing. His standby credits are about to come through on his IMF deal and he goes to Cuba – a bad move in my view. Bad timing. He said at the reception last night he wanted to visit me for a weekend chat on some ideas he was turning over. Ray, too, regretted our not being in touch. The same thing he said when we last met in Miami. The popular man on show last night was Daniel Ortega. The girls wanted to be photographed with him. The crowds were eager to see him. Vice President Danny Quale is in town; I'm looking forward to seeing how close he and Ortega get to each other. I was at the table next to Ortega last night. In the lift on the way to the dining-room, I exchanged greetings with Barco of Colombia. We recognized each other's faces. But one cannot assert oneself as a leader in this part of the world without a working knowledge of Spanish. I mean this as a Caribbean person. I have to press on developing our capability in both the Spanish and French Institute. Our relations with Europe are critical. I must see to it that my daughter Louise keeps up her Spanish and French.

Tim Eggar of the United Kingdom who had visited me with his wife in Bequia was the first I ran into in the hotel yesterday. He said he had moved out of the scramble to his Ambassador's residence. I don't suppose we will ever have a residence here.

Entry dated 3 a.m., February 3, 1989

Hopeless. Only one word could describe the performance of our protocol officer and my security yesterday. They did not brief me, or my delegation.

On my arrival, one of the things that my protocol said was that I did not have to attend the official greetings of Heads of Delegations to the President Perez at Circulo Militar. So when I came home from lunch with Quale, I went to bed for a rest under the influence of my allergy pill (to combat air conditioning). Then I was awakened at 2.00 p.m. to go downstairs immediately.

I arrived at the palace grounds only to find empty seats for my delegation who had been told not to come. We waited about an hour between functions before going to the military display which I really wanted my Commissioner of Police, Randolph Toussaint to see and again no arrangements had been made to get him to the function. The car for my delegation was taken up by military personnel.

When we returned to the hotel, I went to the room of my COP – he was relaxing and waiting for the protocol officer. It was clear the Venezuelans lack the organization to look after foreign delegations properly. They put on a good show, but they do not pay sufficient respect to visiting dignitaries. All this could not happen in the Far East. Yesterday, after the inauguration of the President, I saw a military man brush ex-President Jimmy Carter's face with his cap. The people in the auditorium do not wait for dignitaries to leave. They crowd them. They push.

So we met Danny Quayle. He is as green as grass. He seems to know little about his responsibility for the US and less about the world. The Embassy had made arrangements for a lunch with Caribbean delegations. He asked Hoyte what Castro was up to. Hoyte assured him that Castro was taking his troops out of Angola, quoting Castro's opinion, "I'm not getting into that trap." I asked Hoyte if he thought Castro was responding to the changing scene around the world and whether things could get out of control in Cuba. He said Cuba was thinking of tourism development to secure foreign exchange in order to expand social services. Hoyte said also that he had gone to Cuba to ensure Castro did not meddle in Guyana's politics.

Quayle is like the nice neighbour on the block, but a small-timer. He does not come across with intellectual strength. Vice Presidents are supposed to be Presidential material.

Castro and Quayle were the fans of the press and the crowds here. People wanted to see them. Castro sat a few seats down the left from me and Quayle two seats to the right.

This show is a splash. The Latins gather around the splash. The splash is Carlos Andres Perez and they will disappear I suppose with the ripples and turn up at the next splash. We in the Caribbean need our own direction if we are to be identifiable in this world.

There is a move afoot, started yesterday in my discussions with Ray, to take the Caricom Heads Meeting away from Grenada. We see disaster there with Blaize. But I'm not going to push anything until my election is out of the way.

The behaviour of my protocol officer from the Venezuela Foreign Ministry has spoiled my enjoyment of this inauguration. They push me to leave the main room, only to have me standing around for at least half an hour waiting on the car. If I have anything to do with inaugurations again, unless I have some special contact to make I will send a junior Minister and some policemen. I really thought I was going to advance relations between our countries with Perez in charge. I am pissed off. I have an idea of how to mediate the boundary dispute between Guyana and Venezuela; I doubt now if this is on the cards. The mood around Caracas is that Carlos Andres Perez's social programme will increase Venezuela's debt.

Last night there was a great concert and the hero was an extraordinary 12-year-old lead violinist. Perhaps the most useful outcome of my visit was my chance to talk to Ray and Desmond about the Bequia airport.

Entry dated February 4, 1989

Caracas

Yesterday was a good day. The meeting at La Casona with Carlos Andres Perez, Baena Soares, the OAS Secretary-General, and other Heads was great. We discussed the threat to democracy posed by the military in Argentina, the coup in Paraguay, world debt and the call for a summit, the problems in Haiti. I put on the agenda the celebration of the quinquennial arrival in the West Indies of Columbus in 1992.

Last night a party's party at the Blancos in the stupendous hill over Caracas. Perez was there.

Entry dated February 5,1989

Back home in St. Vincent

It was good that last day in Caracas. Perez had a listing of private meetings on his agenda. The Prime Ministers were informed individually that we'd meet to go in together as there was nothing different between what he'd say to either of us or we to him. I said I'd let Carlos Andres Perez decide. I wanted to keep my option on the Guyana dispute open.

We went on a tour of La Casona. Never have I seen such extraordinarily large hanging plants, and they made a grand show along the covered porches. They hung with clips showing that they were obviously moved from time to time. Ornate curved furniture, and in various rooms the gifts, one each in a different room received by a former President from a foreign government. I was impressed with the elaborate gift from Saudi Arabia, a palm made in silver and platinum with nuts in gold – a delicate piece. Not easy to cart about.

We waited for the Group of 8 meeting with Perez to conclude. When it did, I reported on it. It called for a Summit with Bush, the EEC and Japan to deal with the debt situation that has reached crisis proportions. He circulated a communicado in Spanish, agreed by the G8, to Alfonsin supporting democracy in Argentina. It took the Caribbean by surprise and gradually they began to respond, I'd say limply, by going along with it.

I asked two questions: (1) To whom was the text addressed other than the President of Argentina and what are we getting at? Perez replied that he had been on the phone early that morning to Alfonsin and he had got from him that he'd appreciate such a release which could influence the military. (2) If the military did take over, would the Governments that signed such a declaration not recognize them? Venezuela would not, but it would be up to governments individually, was his answer.

Perez then spoke of the need for a Marshall Plan for the development of the Caribbean and Latin America. He was really launching himself as an instrumental Third World leader – a man of fertile imagination anxious to spread himself across the globe. How effectively he'd do this in the light of his debts, his economic mess at home, will be interesting to see.

That gave me my cue. I took the opportunity of the presence of Soares to reflect on 1992, the year of the Single Europe Act, a year that threatens Caribbean trade with Europe and one that could devastate our economies if not handled correctly, and the 1992 that is, ironically, the quinquennial of Christopher Columbus bringing European civilization into the New World. I called for the inauguration of a special plan to be called the Columbus and not Colombo plan, to be financed by Europe to produce specific development projects in our region to commemorate the arrival of Columbus.

When I had suggested this at home, the press revealed a hostility to the idea of European discovery, to which I replied that Latin America and the Caribbean will be celebrating 1992 for Columbus whether we like it or not because the Europeans will be celebrating it. Without the arrival of Columbus and the Europeans, our lands may have remained only with Caribs, and there would be no people of African and Indian descent in the West Indies. Let's forget the overworked word "discovery." We should, I thought, capitalize on the European celebration of the quincentenary to get the Europeans to focus on our needs.

My argument was well received in Caracas. Perez called on Brazil's Soares to get the message across to the European capitals that the impact of the single market in 1992 could threaten many of us in the Caribbean. It was particularly important that Phillipe Gonzales, Prime Minister of Spain, knew of our concern as he was President of the EEC.

We talked of Haiti. I referred to our mission to Haiti before the last election. Namphy had given us a good lunch but he did not accept our advice. I pointed out that with 40 people wanting to run for President, Haiti needed legal advice and a new constitution. I recommended the style of France, two elections, and a run-off for the front-runners. They needed to structure elections so that the government has a more than 50 per cent mandate.

I was the only one from the Caribbean speaking out. I was the closest one to Perez, but I wanted the others to speak up. I had urged Ray to do so, but he spoke only vaguely about democracy, so I had to carry the battle for the Caribbean needs once more.

Castro and Ortega were at the lunch as were all the men and wives of everybody who was anybody in Caracas. Ortega was to sit with me, but he went to the Presidential table. So the seat beside me was vacant. And a great thing too. A beautiful woman out of my past descended like an angel, and her wings kept fluttering during the lunch as she rose to kiss so many who sought her and whom she sought. It turned out to be Beatrice Rangel who had been my wife's guide on our first visit to Caracas in my Premiership when I got the Order of the Liberator. She was now Deputy Minister in the President's Office. She had two graduate degrees from Harvard in Economics, had been anchor for two TV stations, was married and divorced, and at present without a boyfriend. When I told her that I too was divorced, she said it would not last long. She's coming to Mustique at Easter and promised to visit me. How I am going to handle this and Jeannette is still to be seen.

At the lunch, we also spoke about the coup in Paraguay. No one was upset at the departure of Stroessner. Beatrice tells me that the reason for the coup in Paraguay was that Stroessner had wanted to restructure the distribution of bribery. There were three sources of bribery – banking, trade, and drugs. One part went to people in the administration, one to the generals, one to the colonels, in that order. Stroessner wanted to centralize and redistribute all from himself.

Beatrice told me that when she sent the dispatch to Perez on the coup in Paraguay he did not take it seriously. He thought she was making another joke! I wondered vaguely if she's one of his women.

But at the last-night party at the Blanco's, I was to discover that Perez's love was his girlfriend Cecilia with whom he had lived for 20 years and had two children. Cecilia was at the party with her mother, and was graciously accepted by the other guests as the real First Lady. (I had met Perez's wife at lunch, where she informed me that she was interested in wheelchairs for retarded people.)

Ortega and I exchanged greetings. I had my aide translate. I told him that I had chaired the Caribbean Heads of Government session that dealt with acceptance of the Asia Peace Plan for his region. He wanted to know when I was coming to Nicaragua. Later in the hotel when we met again, after a luncheon, he asked again about my coming to Nicaragua. I told him I had an election. He asked how many parties we had. I said four. Mine was a centrist party, there were two communist parties and the last was right-wing.

After leaving Caracas we went to Maiquetia for the official send-off. There we met with the Foreign Minister. I told him that I'd be available after my elections to deal with the Guyana dispute if Venezuela was interested. He saw new opportunities for improved relations now that Burnham was gone. He felt that my concerns as stated in the meeting on Haiti were the more urgent to address at this point.

One thing that emerged in Caracas was the Caribbean view that we not go to Grenada because of the resignations from Blaize's government. Ray Robinson was firm. He felt we should send a mission and say so. Sandiford was anxious to take on the Heads of Government meeting, but did not want to be seen to be asking. Poor St. Vincent and the Grenadines without a big hotel could not cope. I was not going to push as I had just got from Blaize my endorsement for Bequia Airport. I repeated my request to Ray and Desmond for renewed support for Bequia Airport. Desmond explained that the request must have come when he was in Cuba, but I could rely on him as usual.

Entry (undated) entitled "The General Elections, 1989"

I called elections after my loyal Commissioner of Police, Toussaint, told me security was in place. My mind and my body had to be ready. So I got back to Lower Bay five days a week and swam the whole length of it. I exercised every morning and treated my body like a racing car being prepared for a Grand Prix. One Sunday, I climbed Soufrère, our tallest mountain, without a drop of water to drink until I reached the summit. Looking into the Crater Lake, I announced to the police security who reached the summit after me that I was ready for the election. The word was not leaked as they thought it a joke. I dissolved Parliament the next day.

Campaigning now was not like my old biscuits and cheese days in the yellow Volks. Police were driving me around in two cars, and solicitous friends were delivering baskets of well-prepared food. Not for me, however. The other candidates and the police escorts could eat. I thrived on dried apricots and water, having learnt from doctors in New York how little the body under stress needed.

I dined only at the end of the day and after all the meetings at night. A few times the security at Shrewsbury House enjoyed my basic pasta, the food of the poor in Italy: pasta, olive oil, garlic, salt and pepper.

Sabrina, her boyfriend Andrew Tile, and Gretel came home to be with me and I loved having them throughout the final push of the campaign. Rallies of over 10000 in this population of 110000 were commonplace and our biggest was 25000. Every time I asked the crowds "Will you give the Opposition any seats?" "No Son, No Son, No." The presence of my daughters beside me in the campaign eased the anguish that led to the divorce. The result was a resounding 15 to 0.

Entry (undated) entitled "Visit of Kenneth Kaunda"

The tallest of them all in Africa came on an official visit. It was right on the heels of the election. I can't describe the affection between us – and the warmth of our feelings. The people, too, spontaneously loved him and waved their flowers and tree branches as he went by. My own Bequia was great. The butlers from Mustique served him royally at Government House.

On the last morning we spoke of the Secretary General. KK felt that we should ask Ramphal to continue. He could not believe the quality of housing, the relative prosperity of our people, and especially the peace in St. Vincent and the Grenadines. As we strolled around the grounds of the Governor's House, he told me that 22 people had been killed in his border towns the night before by bandits. He spoke of the chaos in Zaire; how Mobutu had one crack battalion that protected him, and which he paid well, but the rest of the army lived by plunder. They often seized cars in Zambia. Mobutu was annoyed with the Belgians for publishing that he had $4 billion in foreign banks.

At the end, he presented me with a beautiful carved wooden chest. It is in my home, and will one day to be in a museum I hope to establish in Bequia.

Entry entitled "Official Visit to the UK"

I met with Mrs. Thatcher at 10 Downing Street on July, 26, 1989. At last I felt I'd gotten over the hump. I had gone through quite a bit, but had been burnt out more by the personal stresses of my divorce than winning a second term with all seats for my NDP. I did not even have the strength to keep full notes on the important visit of Kenneth Kaunda to St. Vincent and Bequia. I thought I would sketch a few impressions as I recalled them in due course. It was more important that I caught up with immediate events on this, my first official visit to Britain.

Margaret Thatcher invited me to Britain. In the hierarchy of protocol, Official Visits are one step below State Visits with flags along the Mall. But I was happy with the single enormous St. Vincent flag I had redesigned fluttering over the Hyde Park Hotel in Kensington.

Mrs. Thatcher had just mutilated her Cabinet. I had written congratulating her on pushing the tunnel into France (thanks to the private sector, she had replied) and here I was trying to get the privatized British Airways into bed with the new Caribbean airline, Carib Express, in the hope that this new airline would remove the burden our existing airliners imposed on the taxpayers. I had gathered that my invitation was based on "he's one of the sensible ones."

It was lovely in Suite 428 at the Hyde Park Hotel. I could keep the bedroom cool and the living-room warm. It has been a glorious summer in London. The Hyde Park was the most luxurious hotel I have ever stayed in. The Otani in Tokyo was more modern and fascinating with its dashboard behind the bed, but only in England would one have a room with a cupboard of porcelain statues, an antique golden statue of a reclining Indian lady with a tambourine over a marble fireplace.

The previous night I was the first guest of honour of the new Foreign Secretary, John Major, the star that had risen most pre-eminently in the Cabinet reshuffle that dominated events during my stay. My earlier programme had listed a reception hosted by Sir Geoffrey Howe, but he had just been dismissed.

John Major was a youngish man with a trim figure without the middle-aged paunch of tired politicians who had enjoyed too many banquet spreads. Bowen Wells, who I had known for a long time since his Guyana years, and who sat on my right at the dinner in elegant Carlton Gardens, noted that John Major was tired. I realized I should try getting my message across as quickly as possible, making it as easy as possible for him. The poor man could hardly keep his eyes open. When I told him how I wished him the best of luck in his new job, he said all I should wish him is six hours' sleep a day. He had not slept the night before and only three hours the night previously. He did, of course, state that Mrs. Thatcher had given us her assurance on bananas and so there was no need for me to say more than that the IMF analysis has shown that we would have to devalue 100 per cent if the banana market collapsed.

Bowen, who had come to prominence in the Tory party with his defeat of Shirley Williams took an interest in our bananas and was always ready to advance our cause. When he suggested that I put my case on bananas before the Foreign Secretary, I told him Major had already indicated that the policies and assurances given by Mrs. Thatcher would be seen through.

When the dessert arrived and we were set for coffee and port, I studied the Foreign Secretary, and realized he was burnt out. The poor man was really making an effort to stay up. No more business that evening, just light conversation When I asked him how his friends had taken his recent promotion, he replied wryly, "I don't have any, any more."

His after-dinner toast was lucid, friendly and appreciated. He would help us protect our economies, etc. My toast was one of congratulations, wishing him the best in his new career but warning that the honeymoon of a Foreign Secretary is short. I pleaded that Britain should not forget old friends in their re-discovery of Eastern Europe.

I saw Mrs. Thatcher the next morning on August 16th. She remembered me well from the Commonwealth Conferences and was very gracious. She seemed utterly relaxed that Wednesday morning, showing not the slightest sign of wear and tear from her most controversial reshuffle. She ushered me around showing me the best photographs in Downing Street, beside the clock on the mantelpiece, and then up the stairs to the elegant room where we chatted. My High Commissioner was with me, dutifully silent and respectful. I thanked her for the assurances she had given on bananas and mentioned the threat posed to our currency should our banana economy collapse. She congratulated me on the election. I told her that I regretted I couldn't report any progress on my Caribbean political union project, and that my neighbour Grenada was having leadership problems. I asked her about Eastern Europe and her impressions of the speed of its recovery. She told me that the farmers complained that they had to penetrate the bureaucracy to get tools, fertilizers and chemicals. She felt a great deal of reorganization was necessary before they would become productive.

One other thing about which we agreed was the need for Cabinet reshuffles. She applauded my view that it was important to bring younger people into the cabinet to build up the knowledge and experience in the party that would ensure continuity.

I asked her if she thought we should respect the opinion of some quarters in the US that we should consider legalizing drugs as a way to deal with the drug money. I said we in the Caribbean could not implement such an idea unless the British and the Americans led the way. She was at her most emphatic best: "Absolutely not. Dealing in drugs is dealing in death. If drugs become more available more people will die. Absolutely not."

On the upcoming CHOGM in Kuala Lumpur, we discussed the election of the new Commonwealth Secretary General, with the choice being between Malcolm Fraser of Australia and Chief Anyouku of Nigeria. We agreed the best man should get the job, that we should avoid block voting. I suggested that we would need a committee of five to check the opinions in various areas and leave it to a Trusted Committee of Prime Ministers to determine and inform the group without voting. She did not respond specifically on this. I told her that Caribbean opinion was split.

At the door, on my departure from No. 10, as she said goodbye, she said to the press, "The Prime minister has done a great job organizing his country. And we're very proud of him." She reminded them that during the Falklands War, British ships and their crews had rested in Bequia at Admiralty Bay. They found no respite all the way from the battle along the South American coast. We had been pleased to receive them.

The next day, they took me to the Isle of Wight. I met up with Princess Anne, the Princes Royal, at the reception at the Royal Yacht Squadron at Cowes. I raised the flag to start the race on the committee launch.

Entry (undated) entitled "Unofficial Visit to the UK"

Going through London *en route* to business in Italy and a side-trip holiday on the Nile, High Commissioner Dick Gunn informed me that my lady Jeannette and I were invited to join Prime Minister Major, as he had by then become, at the Trooping of the Colour, the next day. Sandiford, the Barbadian Prime Minister, was going to be there also. And so I sat beside the Prime Minister enjoying the pomp and spectacle of the day with my friend Jeannette ensconced beside John King, the Defence Minister, who she regaled with her Mustique tales.

As the parade concluded, we went through the back door to Downing Street, for drinks. I presented my card to the ancient functionary as we got up the steps. "The Prime Minister of St. Vincent and the Grenadines...and his lady!" (pronounced "loidy!")

The protocol was perfect.

Entry entitled "Bangkok, Singapore, Malaysia CHOGM (October 12, 1989)"

After winning the elections, I kept the Finance Minister portfolio but shed Foreign Affairs, which I gave to my colleague from North Leeward, Alpian Allen, a school teacher and Methodist preacher. Soon afterwards, we were off to Malaysia for my third CHOGM, via London. Our High Commissioner, Dick Gunn and his wife Flora, were accompanying us. Alpian, the preacher, had a suitcase (a "grip" in our parlance) that looked like a family heirloom, battered in the buses of our native country side by sacks of tannias and potatoes.

Our hotel in London, The Tower, was fortunately within walking distance from our Kensington High Commission. After breakfast, I announced to Alpian: "The House of Fraser for you!"

I had his neck measured. His collar always sagged and his ties usually fluttered below his waist. His attire might have impressed the parents in a rural school, but in cricketing language, his dress were short of a length to be that of a Foreign Minister. A dinner jacket, too, was in order. And in the basement of the House of Fraser, we selected a modest bit of luggage for £125. Ties, shirts, suits, belts and socks were dumped into the suitcase. I pointed him to Marks & Spencer where like me he could purchase the cotton essentials.

Back at the hotel I warned that the Irish maids may not know what to do with his grip, so it might be wise to leave it with family in London.

"Prime Minister, I am in your care. I am saying goodbye to this old suitcase and big collars. I don't care what the Irish maids do with it," he said.

Entry entitled "Friday in Bangkok; October 13, 1989"

One of the greatest things about political survival in the Caribbean is that the fledging diplomats you met in their youth, you meet later as a big wheel in high drama. So it was for Larry Smith who held the fort at the Canadian Embassy in Bangkok and was familiar with the King and Thai Royal Family, and in touch with Sihanouk and the Khmer Rouge, Hung Seng and so on.

"A *cordon sanitaire* should be put around Cambodia and leave the Cambodians to sort out their own affairs," said Larry at dinner last night at his official residence.

I also gleaned from conversations at the dinner table that the old man Sianouk was a waste of time, in the pocket of the Chinese who had supported the Khymers and hated the Vietnamese. Nadia Thomas, who was another old Caribbean hand in the US Embassy, said that the US had supported the Khymers – not exactly the view known in the international media. So how could the US and the Chinese be backing the same horse, I wanted to know. Larry thought "personally," that Hung Seng could win a popular election in Cambodia with a comfortable 80 per cent.

The following day was real fun. I bought a 12-piece native nickel bronze dining set, and the small spoons were similar to those Jeannette and I had used on a yacht in Italy the previous summer as guests of Pierro Busnelli, the furniture magnate who owned a Mustique home.

Entry (undated) entitled "Thailand/Cambodia"

I had the greatest time touring Bangkok. I was a real tourist, even more so than in Italy. The river cruise was especially fine.

I was amazed that the silk ties in the Bangkok shops were rather poor in design. The Italians who imported silk obviously do a better job of design than those who produce it. I bought two suits – charcoal grey and silver grey – for US$600 dollars, a little expensive, but I did not want to take the chance of going back to a tailor without recommendations I had found the day before who offered suits at lower prices.

My greatest excitement was purchasing my collection of orchid plants. The man and young people he employed were very knowledgeable. I was impressed by the way they selected my requirements and cut the coconut husks bare for packing.

Then we visited the Royal Thai Handicraft Centre where they carved the teak with some 300 young people chiselling away. I would have loved to import a whole collection of teak doors and tables for the Frangipani. I prevailed on my Foreign Minister, who was also Minister of Tourism, to join me in Pat Pong to experience Thailand's flair for tourism. I taunted him on the way home.

"Temptation, Prime Minister," he lectured, "is not a sin."

Entry entitled "Singapore," October 16

Red silk with an elegant Chinese pattern, a high neck and long sleeves, shoulders embroidered in gold, two long slits down the skirt – never was apparel on a woman more elegant than on the waitresses at a banquet hosted by Lee Kwan Yew the following night. Other girls supporting them were in black skirts and white tops.

At the tea hosted by the Singaporean President, Brian Mulroney and his wife Mila, after exchanging pleasantries, asked about the vote for Commonwealth Secretary General. I told them that I viewed the Commonwealth as a club of Prime Ministers, and if one of the boys wants a job, we give it to the club member first. I had already written to Bob Hawke confirming my position even before the Nigerian offered himself and started lobbying.

At dinner I sat close to the President of Tanzania who brought up the Secretary General vote and wanted to know our position. I told him the Caribbean was divided. One thing I insisted was that we would not want the compromise position of keeping Ramphal on the job for a fourth term as the Caribbean would not want to establish a reputation like Africa at UNESCO. We cannot allow individuals to destroy the image of our regions, I told him.

Entry entitled "Malaysia CHOGM (Electing the Secretary General)," Tuesday, October 17

I had an early appointment with Bob Hawke in his hotel. A swarm of officials and some 20 reporters with television cameras were around him. They were ready for my arrival and recorded our hand shake. We had arranged the meeting at the President's tea the previous day.

He began by thanking me for coming and regretted not getting an early confirmation of my position on the vote. He said he had tried four times to contact me.

I had sent a signal to him from home after the Kaunda visit to St. Vincent and the Grenadines, trying to let him know that Kenneth Kaunda was not enthusiastic about the Nigerian for Secretary General, that he would settle for Ramphal continuing. I told him that we were not behind Ramphal and that Dominica, St. Lucia and I were still honouring our commitment to Australia. I promised to get a fax from Eugenia confirming that.

Bob outlined his position: We had two well-qualified candidates. We should pick one or the other. We should do so by secret ballot. He was satisfied it appeared that a secret ballot would serve Australia best and that we should vote at the beginning of the conference.

I told him I'd speak to Kenneth Kaunda and sound him out.

He did not want Australia to be perceived as running the show. It emerged that he saw that it would be good if someone from the Caribbean launched discussions of the agenda for voting. I agreed that the secret ballot should be used, that we would move on it early, and keep in touch.

He then asked about Barbados. He was disappointed that after all the hassle he had put up with pressure from the Argentineans on the Falkland Islands issue by holding fast to a Commonwealth position behind Britain, that Barbados was not supporting him.

I said that I would speak to Sandiford, but that I was not hopeful.

We talked about the three-year election period in Australia, my own success and having five years ahead of me. He said they tried everything in Australia to change the three-year term, but to get agreement for a referendum was impossible.

In Singapore, I watched, listened and learnt. I begged for a copy of their environmental sign: "$1,000 penalty for littering." We saw the litter wardens, their communication systems, their vigilance, and their smart uniforms. A waterfront port that had little vegetation chose an orchid, the most beautiful flower in the world as their national flower. We in St. Vincent chose the Soufrière tree that never flowers and no one knows about.

I had to leave Singapore in a hurry because a call came through from Kuala Lumpur that I was to have lunch with the Queen. The Singapore officials got my delegation on to Singapore Airlines where I sampled their excellent service on the short flight with a local barbecued dish of meat and peanuts and champagne in crystal.

Entry entitled "Kuala Lumpur," October 18

The hotel in Kuala Lumpur had Indian décor, a crazy combination of colours, and was not restful at all – greenish, freckled carpet, brown and off-white walls, ugly pictures, brass stands for lights, and patterns of cauliflower on the seats.

I was rushed after 15 minutes in the hotel to the restored residence of the British High Commissioner where Her Majesty was staying.

Only three of us were there for the lunch: Brian Mulroney, the Prime Minister of Papua New Guinea, and I. Papua New Guinea was at her left and I was between the secretaries Robert Fellows and Sir William Heseltine. I couldn't understand why this combination of the three of us was selected, except that both Brian and I had just changed our Governors General. How Papua New Guinea fitted into this I didn't know.

Brian brought up the subject of his GG appointment and seemed anxious to explain why he had picked Ray Hnatyshyn. I told the story about Ray being upset that I could not get a bitter lemon when he gave me a ride on a Canadian Air force plane to Ottawa after Barrow's funeral, and how the Canadian High Commissioner arrived in my office one day with a case of Canada Dry bitter lemon. I said I thought Hnatyshyn was too young for the job, and Heseltine agreed. Governor Generals should be a bit ancient.

I spoke of a speech given by my new GG, Sir David Jack, and how well it was received by a national audience. I mentioned his humility and humble upbringing in a remote country village.

I told Her Majesty and everyone at the lunch about my visit to the Thai/Cambodian border. They listened with interest. The Queen questioned me on many points. She said a delegation from Papua New Guinea had been to the camp in 1984, and added that, from what I was saying, things were as they had always been, with no improvement.

After lunch, when it was time for my private audience with Her Majesty, I asked how Princess Anne was doing. The Queen remembered when I mentioned Princess Anne that I had started the yacht race at the Admiral's Cup in Cowes and that was where I had met the Princess. Her Majesty said she had not seen her daughter and that it would be good to get her sailing.

So I did not go out on this first night in Kuala Lumpur. I drafted my opening statement on the agenda item dealing with the Secretary General's election. (I am not feeling too well. I have been urinating quite often. I have a slight pain on my left side in the stomach, as though the bladder or kidney is under strain, so I got up to write these notes to see if I can keep up with the rigours of another CHOGM.)

It was really fine in Singapore. Already I can see that Singapore is ahead of KL [Kuala Lumpur]. The Chinese simply have more class. Their hotels are finer in décor. The Ministers whom I met were confident about their country.

I did not have long with Lee Kwan Yew, only enough time to tell him how well he looked, thank him for inviting me to see Singapore, and say how much I was enjoying what I was seeing.

But at the President's tea and also at the Prime Minister's dinner, I sought more opinions on Cambodia. They all wanted the Khymer Rouge accommodated, as there was no sensible alternative in any transitional government. That message I gave to the Queen's lunch also. Brian did not say much on Cambodia except to ask how I managed to get to the camps. I suspected that he, like me before my Thai visit, is not familiar with the Cambodian problem.

It is damned hard to keep up with Israel, Palestine, El Salvador, East Germany and South Africa. We of the Caribbean lost our window of opportunity in Grenada due to that arse Blaize.

Entry entitled "Langkawi, Malaysia," Saturday, October 21

I was really burnt out when I reached Kuala Lumpur from Singapore and went to sleep in the afternoon. I did not go to the first reception given by the Secretary General to meet the Press. That is an occasion for the Big Wheels. We the small islanders have nothing press-worthy.

The opening ceremony was an elaborate and grand occasion, even more exciting than Vancouver with beautiful girls in lavish golden costumes welcoming us with flower petals thrown on the carpets, the treatment for each of us in alphabetic order. I wore my Thai silk, silver grey. Each leader was led into the great hall by a gorgeous young Malaysian girl.

Dr. Mahathir was in fine form. The other opening speeches were not extraordinary. The discussions on world affairs in the plenary session were introduced by Lee Kuan Yew. He was generous in revealing his secrets on how he manoeuvred between East and West. He welcomed the Russian fleets in Singapore to clean their bottoms and reprovision with supplies, but not before he ensured the US Sixth Fleet was outside the harbour. The Chinese in their Cultural Revolution killed six million; there weren't that many Singaporeans. He continued in a similar vein about how Africa was killing millions too with imbecile policies. How much anguish would the world's populations have to suffer before leaders find the strategy for the way forward? Mrs. Thatcher, in her speech, railed against communism and delivered her privatization lecture.

Prime Minister Mahathir eased the proceedings along and lectured the environmentalists about the regeneration of his newly planted forests. He did not intend to keep his people as museum pieces with early mortality to satisfy conservationists.

These Commonwealth meetings, as I said before, in the closed session of the Retreat, provide an opportunity for leaders of small nations to meet with leaders of the G7 and G5, and other distinguished people like Lee Kwan Yew at close quarters, to learn from them of the trends in world opinion, and to fashion our policies so that we remain in the mainstream of political thinking. Secondly they provide an opportunity to send our concerns to the members of the G7 through their members present in the Commonwealth.

I have had close chats with Mrs. Thatcher; we sat beside each other in the bus on the way to the tree-planting ceremony at CHOGM Park; each head of state planted a tree. When Bob Hawke, Sonny Ramphal and I were waiting for the plane in Kuala Lumpur to take us to Langkawi, we were swapping jokes. Bob told us about his visit to Margaret Thatcher to lobby for Fraser. She told him the most awful stories about Fraser in the Lusaka Conference. Apparently he had upstaged her with an early morning conference in order to catch the headlines on Zimbabwe.

"I've never forgotten 1979," she said turning to her Private Secretary. "I had gone to sleep at 1.30 and at 2.30 I got a call that Malcolm

Fraser at that hour in the morning was calling a press conference. I was re-called again at 5.00 to say he was having the conference." Ramphal says he still has some notes from Mrs. Thatcher on the subject. Bob was exceedingly funny and roaring with laughter. But that told me a lot. Mrs. Thatcher must have voted African as she really never forgave Fraser.

My proposal on the secret ballot selecting the new Secretary General was adopted. The Nigerian Chief Anyouka won the first round and was unanimously endorsed in a formal second round!

Before Kaunda left last night, he asked me to support Zimbabwe for the next conference instead of Malta so that we could put maximum pressure on South Africa. I told him I agreed, and he could rely on me.

When I congratulated Benazir Bhutto on her presentation in Kuala Lumpur, she said how much she enjoyed my own interventions. She was forever taking notes in green ink and it reminded me of my own copious note-taking at my first set of meetings as Finance Minister in Toronto when I wanted to learn the game.

I chatted with Brian Mulroney about appointing my friend, his Ambassador in Geneva, de Montigny Marchand, as Deputy Minister in Foreign Affairs. We were walking together toward our rooms located close together in Hotel Pelangi at Langkawi. He said he had settled his appointments the week before. I told him de Montigny was a good civil servant, a friend whose judgment I trusted, and that I was sure he'd serve his government well. I think Mulroney appreciated my point of view.

I called de Montigny when I got home to St. Vincent and the Grenadines. He was intrigued with my intervention and clearly understood the statement by Joe Clark on his performance. Marie Andre, his spouse, however, did not want to leave Milan and her job as Counsellor there. Joe Clark was quite straightforward. He had, on his own, been lobbying me to direct the session on the Fraser/Anyaoku election, when it was suggested that I propose we ballot early in the conference. He was pleased that I had followed through. Everyone accepted the outcome. We were sure the Nigerian, being experienced in the Secretariat, would accept the outcome gracefully.

The personal memories of the Malaysia CHOGM can't be conveyed in a few lines or an interview. In the Far East, away from the television sets, we took to the stage in our Malaysian shirts to entertain colleagues and their spouses. I remember my rendition of "I am the Great Pretender" fascinated the Head of the Kenyan delegation, the Foreign Minister Robert Ouko, whose ditty also won great applause.

"You're pretending to be a pretender!" he joked.

It was, and still is, saddening to know that on his first weekend home after that meeting, Ouko was found burnt alive in his car in Kenya.

Entry entitled "Venezuela," November 23, 1989

I'm here in a house at a conference in Venezuela at La Viñeta near the military headquarters. It's not the first time: I'd been here for a reception during the inauguration of Perez.

In Tobago, I had had private meetings with Perez en route about landing rights for our charter planes, and wanted to know if Venezuela would give us aid. We spoke on a variety of topics developing trade between us, the changing face of Europe and how that change might lead to a situation where Caribbean problems might be ignored. I speculated that the drive toward unity in Europe might encourage unity in our islands and lead to co-operation with our Spanish-speaking island neighbours. The collapse of the communist regimes in Europe might also lead to world powers concentrating on our conflicts like El Salvador, where the civil war was now being waged in the capital.

I brought up the subject of Guyana and said that I would be happy to offer my services to help in the border dispute between the two of them.

Entry entitled "La Viñeta, Caracas," November 24th

My visit has been going exceedingly well. You are treated really royally at La Viñeta, the official residence for visiting dignitaries. Breakfast downstairs in an elegant dining room with two butlers, fresh pineapple juice which I enjoyed, and a spread of other stuff – cheese, ham, arepa, pancakes – all of which I did not touch.

At the Ministry of Energy I put forward a complicated proposal on debt equity, using Venezuelan debt notes to purchase goods in Venezuela to be bought by the government and sold, the profit being shared between Venezuela and St. Vincent and the Grenadines. To make a long story short, it would reduce debts to them and allow them to provide aid. The Venezuelans were very courteous, thought the idea fascinating, and were anxious to co-operate.

At the Ministry of Communications, I told them that the agreement with their Rent Avion had not worked. We want them to designate another airline and we want access for Mustique Airways and SVG Air. They were ready to amend and sign right away. I told them we needed the details of their new carriers and we would want to specify our planes. So we decided to fix this for a meeting in St. Vincent and the Grenadines.

For the Foreign Ministry meeting, we moved to Mira Flores where there were full military honours and the playing of our anthem. There I was received by Cardonna and the protocol department. I hope my Thai charcoal silk suit was adequate for the occasion. I had a few minutes with the Foreign Minister before the press descended. I must say the Venezuelan press has the most beautiful women of any press corps I've seen, and they are of all complexions – white, brown, beige, black – all elegantly dressed and young. I did not respond to questions on oil.

With Perez, I went over the Guyana/Venezuela dispute. He is anxious to settle the matter. He recognizes that the dispute is one that he had with Britain, a colonial power, and not a newly independent country. He was not pushing for the entire claim, but would be happy with the river access to the sea. He was prepared to develop co-operation in hydroelectricity and other projects in Guyana. He confirmed that the Secretary General had chosen McIntyre to *work* with both parties, not really to arbitrate. I questioned carefully these terms of reference. He did not want the dispute to go all the way to the Court in The Hague (I pointed out that a Guyanese sat there). He said that a Guyanese citizen would not be able to take part in that issue, but he was keen to have a Venezuelan in the Court. We should support that.

He felt that COPEI's objection to McIntyre was a bad political point, for if Venezuela could not accept a Caribbean, then the Caribbean could not accept a Venezuelan. I must confess I could not see his logic there, except that he felt protected by his terms of reference. I did not want a fudge. We needed an international arbitrator.

Perez questioned my progress on unification. He told me he had also told Bush he should support this "Mitchell" initiative. I told him that the issue had lost momentum, but after the elections early next year, it would be time to bring the issue forward again. He felt it was the most important development in the Caribbean in a long time. I gave him a copy of my book, *Caribbean Crusade*, and left a box of 48 more for distribution through universities and schools.

I brought up the subject of Eastern Europe and the speed of change there. Lech Walesa was in town and Perez told me that Walesa said that he met with Kohl two days before the Berlin Wall came down, and had asked him, "What are you going to do when the wall comes down?" He had replied, "It will not come down in my lifetime."

Perez and I agreed that we would have to stimulate change to consolidate our area. He asked, "What would you like to carry home from this trip?"

I had never yet been asked so directly a question from another Head of Government. Once more, as I had done with the former President, I pressed the suggestion that Venezuela build a Spanish Institute as part of my A-level college, the European-sponsored project, and the agreement on communications. He asked what he needed to do to advance this issue on training in Spanish. I said I needed someone from his Education Ministry and an architect to work with our Ministry on assessing the requirements and design the project. This vital area is important to close the knowledge gap in our country and bring us into the Latin American mainstream.

Perez is warm. We can talk all day. Hans Neumann was at the lunch. He bridges the gap between Venezuela's private sector and his investment in Mustique. Perez then organized a visit for me to go to the Central Bank to have them look at the complicated oil-swap proposal I had made. So much ground has been covered in so short a time. Again it is obvious that unless our islands come together in a political union we will be losing a lot of opportunities.

I expect they will give me a guard of honour out again as they did on arrival. One of the most interesting creatures met on this trip was a lady security escort. She's about my complexion, has a lovely figure and is elegantly dressed down to her high heels. You had to scrutinize her carefully to see that she had a holster under her left arm for her pistol.

Going through the visitor's book I note the splendid company I have followed into this house and bed: Ceauşescu, Pierre and Margaret Trudeau (She said she wanted to stay here forever), Josip Broz Tito, Don Juan Carlos and a litany of Latin Presidents like Figueriedo of Brazil, Rohter Prada of Peru, Blanco of the Dominican Republic, Miguel de la Madrid of Mexico. Just ahead of me was Sanguinetti of Uruguay.

Entry entitled "Guatemala/Nicaruaguan Election," February 21, 1990

My family had for generations worked too hard at sea and on land for me to swallow communism and its antagonism to wealth. I preached my message the length and breadth of St. Vincent and the Grenadines. Access to opportunity, especially in education, was the escape route from poverty. And to progress, we will all have to absorb the ethic of hard work, and eschew the leftist ideology emerging from university lecture halls in Jamaica and Barbados under the camouflage of social democracy.

It bears repeating that Jamaica's Edward Seaga gathered together leaders of governments to form the Caribbean Democrat Union: Eugenia Charles, John Compton, Kennedy Simmonds and Vance Amory from Nevis, and Herbert Blaize of Grenada. We joined the International Democrat Union in London, and linked up with the Christian Democrats in Germany, the Conservatives in the United Kingdom, the Gaullists in France, and the Republicans in the United States. We received some funding from the Adenauer Foundation to stage youth conferences in the region where young people were lectured about international finance and party organization.

Then came the Nicaraguan elections. The Sandinistas were going to the polls. The world and his wife wanted to observe Nicaragua's cataclysm. The International Democratic Union Secretariat in London invited me to be a co-leader, along with a presidential candidate in Guatemala, José Serrano, to head a team from all over the world to observe the elections. Politicians past and present, and diplomats from England, France, Australia, the US and Latin America, would make up our group.

I'm now in a Lear jet to brief Perez of Venezuela about our mission to Nicaragua to monitor the elections. Accompanied by Stuart Nanton, Ewart Delves, David Maule – in their capacities as Parliamentary Secretary, Security, and Information Officer.

When Perez learnt that I was heading up an observer mission into Nicaragua and that I also wanted some guidance from him, he promptly signalled that he would send a plane for me to come down to Caracas for consultations, and from there to get me onwards to Manauga. I wanted him, also, to indicate to Ortega that I was coming in good faith.

So we left St. Vincent and the Grenadines at 7.05 a.m., seen off by Miriam Veil, the Venezuelan Ambassador. We got into Caracas in one hour, were met by the Deputy Foreign Minister and proceeded right away to meet with Perez at Mira Flores. He greeted me exuberantly. He wore a brilliant tie that made me feel very staid. His Under Secretary and my old friend, Beatrice Rangel, greeted me warmly too.

I told Perez that I had come to hear his views on the elections in Nicaragua and that there should be an understanding of how the Caribbean should proceed in its foreign relations in concert with informed opinion in Latin America. We got down to business immediately. Our meeting was early because he had to go into the interior to deal with critical responses to the inflation that was dominating the Venezuelan news. He made his points as follows:-

1. The situation in Eastern Europe with support being withdrawn has left the Sandinistas stranded. They were hoping that with Gorbachev moving away intellectually, East Germany would have continued to prop them up. So financial support has gone.

2. Baker and Shevadnadze had come to an agreement that the Russians would not support Cuba and Nicaragua any more or the Central American leftists if the US withdrew also.

3. Ortega et al. understood the changing situation. They know also that after the election they need someone to turn to.

4. Ortega knows that if the election is not fair, he will have a difficult time internationally establishing credentials.

5. Ortega knows that if the foreign observers do not find the election fair he will be in trouble at the UN.

6. The Opposition is disunited, some 14 parties, and even some of these are only movements. Mrs. Chamorro was weak, not a political person, and physically sick. Perez said she was suffering from bone disease and he had sent a plane to take her to Houston for treatment and to bring her back. Her vice-presidential candidate was a better politician but he agreed to let her be in charge. If she won, Perez said there would be chaos. He felt that Ortega would be preferable, but that he would have to understand that he was presiding over a transition.

7. Venezuela was supplying Nicaragua with oil.

8. Venezuela, since Perez was in, was helping the Electoral Commission, and sent supplies to the Commission, including gasoline for all parties.

Our meeting lasted some 40 minutes. I asked Perez if Bush, having scored politically in the US on Panama was ready for adjustment in Nicaragua. He told me that he had sent a stern letter to Bush on Panama and that Bush was worried. It took him four days to reply. At the recent inauguration in Costa Rica, Quayle had sought an audience to explain how hurt Bush was. I told him that Quayle was to meet with us in a few weeks time.

Venezuela was sending its own observer team that included ex-President Caldera and Beatrice Rangel. Beatrice and I agreed to meet in Manauga before and after the elections. I wanted to give her my own conclusions to bring back to Venezuela, but as it turned out, we went our separate ways.

Perez was worried that there were no telephone lines directly operating to him from Nicaragua on Election Day. He wanted to follow the events immediately. We touched on other matters. I told him that I had tried with General Henri Namphy in Haiti, but that he had not responded to my suggestions on impartiality by the Electoral Commission. Perez was worried and as before in our other discussions wanted to know what he could do to help. He suggested after the elections in Nicaragua, he send a plane for me so we could draw up an action plan on Haiti. I said I'd let him know in time.

He drew me out on the Eastern Caribbean unification, said he talked to Bush and Mulroney about it and how helpful they should be prepared to be. I told him Mulroney had already pledged support. I had a letter to that effect. Bush, I felt, wanted to find a new route in Latin America.

We parted on very friendly terms. I gave a short conference at the Mira Flores entrance. We went to lunch with an elderly Ambassador who had spent most of his term in Switzerland. We went to Maiquetia and had a lovely fish meal.

We took another plane, a Cessna Citation II, and passed through the Air Force base in Maracaibo. One hour there and now *en route* to Guatemala where I am making these notes. The Venezuelan military plane was not expected in the Guatemalan skies and it took a while for us to be cleared into their air space.

Entry entitled "Guatemala," February 23rd

Yesterday in the Hotel Cumino Real we spent the day going through the IDU documentation on electoral process and the information on Nicaragua. Our host here, Jorge Serrano Elias, a presidential candidate who came fourth with 12 per cent of the vote last time, was an affable intellectual with business interests in Guatemala. Our team had assembled.

Serrano had been fussing about my co-leadership, but Keith Schuette, an American co-ordinator in our group, explained that I was a Prime Minister and while he was respected as a Latin American leader, Prime Ministers, no matter how small the country, did not ever serve under other ministers. Joint chairmanship was essential.

We began to discuss Nicaragua. The economy was in shambles. The currency was useless. Everything cost tens of thousands. The *cordoba*, that had been worth six to one US dollar when Samoza fell, had hit

65,000 to one US dollar. The government couldn't print new money quickly enough to keep up with the galloping devaluation and was rubber-stamping new values on old notes. My Security Officer Delves declared he always wanted to be a millionaire and changed 20 US dollars to collect a massive wad which he put on a chair to sit on. (He was later charged at home for a criminal financial offence, but he could boast that he once sat on a million!)

At every press conference, Serrano wanted to assert his leadership, and I let him go ahead. He had brought his sons to televise his every utterance and gesture for later Guatemala consumption.

We had dinner the night before at Ambrosia's not far away. Steve Norris, the British MP, spoke fluent Spanish, is generally very articulate and a good Thatcherite. The Australian John Valder, from the Liberals, is quite rotund, pleasant, but a lightweight. Later in the day our Japanese colleague, Oshiro Shinjun, turned up fresh from elections in Okinawa, pleased with his Liberal Party's success. In the press conference he was to point out that the changes in East Europe had put the socialists back, even in Japan.

The Press wanted to know why we were here and interested in Latin American elections. I pointed out that Nicaraguans had sought our support in the Caribbean in various resolutions, that we were concerned with the peace process, and that our part of the world (Caribbean/ Latin America) should not be left in conflict when disputes in other areas of the world were being settled.

I found the discussions exhilarating. Representatives from Mexico explained how the Nicaraguans had come to Mexico to learn about fraud. Steve and Jorge who had been to Panama recounted incidents of fraud, of the military voting by driving the same truck with the same voters from one polling station to the other, and how votes in these stations exceeded 100 per cent. I had to steer the skeptics into understanding that if voting ink was to be used, the ink use should be monitored. Norris was worried about the voter's list. I told him we will have to question people whether they were excluded or not. We will not be able to provide evidence when we were not there during registration. I think the entire delegation is well primed to do the job.

We did not get around Guatemala City, but yesterday morning after breakfast I could see the majesty of the conical volcano.

Entry entitled "Nicaragua," Friday, 11.14 a.m.

My troubles continued as we entered the Nicaraguan terminal building with its glorious revolutionary murals. Perez had told the Sandinistas

I was coming and the full protocol awaited me and my bodyguard
Delves. A private home was ready for me and my party. But our hosts,
the UNO (Opposition) Party, also had special accommodation for me.
I had to choose. Do I go with the IDU team, or do I accept Sandinista
protocol?

I decided on the Sandinistas. I would meet with our team for the
reception later. Arrived at the Protocol house which belonged to a
destitute banker. The house was in a Sandinista enclave, a pale reflection
of obvious earlier glory. But I insisted that I stay as the Government's
guest and the others go with the Party. There was a security guard who
let us in. We were brought here in an old American car, not the kind of
thing you expect from protocol. The lady driver had studied 14 years
ago in Texas and wanted the Sandinistas to win the election. At the
airport I recognized my friend Hugo who lobbied for Nicaragua at our
Caricom meetings. He took me through the procedures. I was able to
pave the way for the delegation. I was first to get my accreditation. It
turned out that UNO knew the host with whom I was staying. He was
one of them.

Entry dated Friday, 6.55 p.m.

At home here we met our hosts. This morning the old lady was shy and
evasive. She did not speak much English, but tonight when I asked
for coke, she brought four for us and when I went to the kitchen and
toasted their health, they came out and I invited them to sit. It turns out
that the old man was a banker for 43 years, and studied in England at
LSE as she did. She was from Toledo in Spain. They have one daughter,
an engineer, who studied in Louisiana and also settled there. They are
satisfied that the economic management by the Sandinistas was poor.
They bitterly assailed the inflation, how the currency moved from six
cordobas to US$1 to 65,000 to one. That they got up to 100,000 and
started over again and now it is up there again.

"You can buy nothing for 1 million of our currency here."

They are very subdued. The Opposition party did not want us to go
to the Sandinista protocol houses because the Sandinistas confiscated
them. But this house was not. It was the only one in the neighbourhood
that was not. The street had sleeping policemen. There were pill boxes
of military guards around.

Our hosts continued their tale; they had lost their coffee plantation.
They had nearly lost their lives. Twelve soldiers in masks confronted
them on the plantation one day. They nearly killed them asking them

for the money which they had to pay their workers. Their daughter for six years did not come home. She had refused to go with them to the plantation.

He had his picture of the Queen and the Duke of Edinburgh. On our last night he showed me his silver-plated carriage and some miniature horsemen – his souvenir of the Coronation in 1953. He had met his wife, as a student. She had stayed through the Revolution. Nicaragua, her second home, was where she had spent most of her life and she would not leave it!

Our hosts do not expect the 700,000 Nicaraguans in exile to return. I told them of our 3 per cent of exports of goods and services, that I do not borrow externally over 4 per cent, but internally at a higher rate. Good management, they said. I asked our hosts where I should go to observe the election, hinting I wanted to go to an interesting place. They insisted I stay in Managua where the greatest population, 33 per cent of the voters resided.

This house was built some 20 years ago. It is well furnished with a collection of ornaments, ornate picture-frames carved and painted in gold, beautiful mirrors with a few blurs, the bedroom with a small chandelier, velvet curtains that long needed changing. It has all the hallmarks of a once better economy. I learnt that the only reason why their house was not confiscated was because the wife was Spanish, and the Sandinistas could not afford to alienate Spain.

Entry dated Saturday, 7 a.m.

Last night at the Japanese reception I met more people with significant interest in this Nicaraguan election. The Embassy residence had a splendid garden with ample space for an outdoor reception. Semi-formal in Nicaragua is shirt and jacket. The hallway was green marble, as was the fountain, and the pool had goldfish.

The campaign manager for the UNO was confident that all was going well. There were a few hiccups, as in León, where not enough ballots were sent. He did not complain as you would expect a campaign manager to do to an observer if he expected to lose. The wife of an important businessman, related by marriage to the candidate, was also confident of winning.

The Italian observer from the UN was satisfied that all the correct procedures were in place to have a fair election. His boss, Richardson, had released the fourth UN report at 6 p.m. that evening saying all was well, but that the Opposition did not have fair media time before the election.

I asked Mrs. Chamorro to explain how the people are talking so freely. She said that since the election all fear had gone out of the people. (Yesterday afternoon at the Conservative Headquarters when the Russian helicopters flew over, one person remarked they are doing this to show who is boss.)

I met quite a few Japanese people at the Embassy. They were pleased to hear of our relations with Japan. One journalist wanted to interview me after the election

I had my full complement of military escorts, which turned out to be useful in the entire exercise. We had three days of solid meetings with every organization in Nicaragua. Archbishop Orlando Y Bravo stood up for the church. Their Electoral Commission explained the procedures. We met with all the branch parties in UNO, the trade unions, the Chambers of Commerce and Industry, and last of all, on the Friday afternoon, the Sandinista High Command, minus Daniel Ortega who was campaigning in the countryside.

Entry entitled "Managua," Saturday, February 24th

A peaceful night. Not a sound of gunshot. None since we are here. I called home and gave them a report.

Entry dated Saturday, February 25th –"Election Day in Managua"

Up early at 4.30 a.m. At 5.30 we leave with our driver to see him vote in Managua and thence to León and Chinandega.

Yesterday, we saw first the Archbishop Ovando Y Bravo, a short stocky man in his black robe and huge crucifix, firm confident, mature. He gave the impression that the Church was playing it impartially. He repeated that the Supreme Electoral Council, in the words of Mrs. Chamorro, was doing a good job. The Church would make its pronouncement on March 1st. He stressed the Church's message on the secrecy of the poll, that the voter in addressing his conscience should ask himself what would Christ do in your place!

Mrs. Chamorro, as Perez had said, was a sick woman suffering from bone disease. A woman of obvious great courage, good looking, fine features, tall, somewhat bronzed, her right leg in a fancy cast raised on a special rest and put into position only with great pain. We sat at the same lunch table in Perez's inauguration, but both of us had taken little heed of each other at the time. Her leg was not in the strap at that time. She was confident of victory, satisfied that the secret poll would do the job for her.

The American Ambassador in our company produced a beautiful poster of her looking like a female Christ in a white robe with all the people behind her with no recognizable features. He said, "We produced thousands of these for you, but we weren't allowed to bring them in, so I brought this one in for you." She replied, "Never mind, we got them."

I told her, to great cheers, that no matter what the election results, she was doing a great job for the people of Nicaragua and Nicaragua itself.

Entry (undated) entitled "Sandinista Interview with Commandante Arce"

We met him at the FSLN Party Headquarters, a furnished place, well appointed but not like the elegant home of Mrs. Chamorro (complete with bust of her assassinated husband and plaque that was forbidden to be placed in the streets of Managua). More people at FSLN than at UNO. I gave the commandant my card. So did the Guatemalan Serrano.

The Commandant was bright, young, not more than 35, with a quick mind. He shook everybody's hand before sitting down. The room was crowded. My friend Hugo, a Sandinista, stood behind. The barrage of questions, and the fidgeting of Arce with my card and that from the Guatemalan, convey a feeling that the Sandinistas were besieged. Indeed the army of observers had intimidated the Sandinistas.

Arce had his facts, and he answered every question properly. When our Austrian team member, Heribert Stein Bauer, asked him to explain why the UNO had no posters up in the same way as FSLN, when they both had access to money, he said, the UNO spent their money on buying 100 cars, Some of it they wanted in cash, so they had to give 50 per cent of the money to the Supreme Electoral Council. FSLN used their money as gifts – and brandishing a FSLN cigarette lighter he made his point about the publicity material. The Austrian then asked if he thought the UNO were stupid, and Arce said they were. When asked about unity in Central America, he replied that we should ask our friends from Costa Rica. And the Costa Rican, Miguel Caraguiaz, dodged the question by replying Costa Rica was a democracy, and had to get approval from the Congress.

As I listened to Arce, I felt some sympathy for the Sandinistas despite my strong anti-communism and my desire that the UNO win. I always want to support the weak, downtrodden and abused. Arce was young and alert, looking very fit in his jeans and lightly embroidered shirt. In concluding I told him how in my experience I had won and lost, and I took time to explain what the responsibilities of both were. In both cases, a leader had to keep his supporters calm. Losing for a leader is hard, but you must remember when all looks gloomy, that above all, life goes on. He replied confidently and in good humour. If you lost, you have time to rest, he said. That was the last word we heard from the Sandinistas as the campaign closed. It was after 7 p.m. in the evening.

We prepared to move early on that Sunday election, beginning in the capital Managua. My assignment was to the capital, León, and Chinandega. It was a straight fight between FSLN and UNO – Frente Sandinista Liberacion National and United National Organization. The polling station sported the blue-and-white Nicaraguan flag. The election officials, with their CSE armbands, were well trained. There was no intimidation. The soldiers in uniform in the various polling stations waited in line like everyone else. Voting was quick and orderly. Our IDU observer insignia made us visible and we ran into hosts of other observers, compared impressions and moved on. Altogether my team inspected 56 polling stations.

The poverty in the countryside was frightening. Filthy drains in the villages. Swarms of flies around the local white cheese sold in the markets. Small homes with sparse furniture. I bought four tangerines for 15,000 cordobas. Lunch was a massive pawpaw while observing the peace in the square outside a church. The seeds came home with me.

A lady came up and complained that the vote in a station was not secret. We had been there. We went back to check and found that her claim could not be substantiated. In fact, the officials were laughing at an old man who refused to respect the "Tu voto es secreto" signs posted everywhere. He would not fold his ballot paper. He wanted them all to see what his vote was.

I did a personal pre-exit poll with my diary (a handout from the Sandinistas). The voters' frowns at a glimpse of Ortega's picture told me the Sandanistas had lost.

We settled down in the square in León with a good view of the comings and goings from the Sandinista building with its FSLN flag flying. All was tranquil. We moved to another park bench across the way from the church, and faced the big arched door behind which the votes were being counted. A light was thrown on the front of the cathedral. About 8:30 pm we noted an attractive young lady coming to check results. Nothing yet. She disappeared in a red van.

We left León after 9 p.m. for Managua. Serrano was at our headquarters, his sons waiting to take his picture. I suggested we go to Violetta Chamorro's house. We entered easily. She was seated with her cane in her lap, elegantly dressed and awaiting the results. I told her she had won. I explained the hostility toward Ortega's picture on my diary's cover. Her supporters in the house were getting nervous. Ten-thirty had passed and the electoral office had not yet declared anything, contrary to the appointed schedule. My American friends were ready to call foul and send the signals to Washington that a Panama-style invasion was necessary. I was pleased that my lecture to the Sandinistas on losing was being taken. They needed time to surrender, military fashion, with orders through the chain of command. I reported on the military jeeps coming to the León headquarters for instructions.

Half an hour later the OAS Secretary General, the Brazilian, Buena Soares, came with the same message, that the High Command needed time to transmit the message.

Violetta's victory came about midnight. We gathered to prepare our final IDU press conference. I sought authority to congratulate the Sandanistas on the orderly surrender of power. I was alone. It was too early for others in our prestigious organization to use the word "congratulation."

Half an hour later, President Bush was congratulating Ortega and Violetta on the extraordinary transition and victory. Schuette recognized the work I had done, and the accuracy of my predictions.

"First you live in the Sandinista territory. Second you lecture them on losing. And then you congratulate alone," he said, adding, "We need you in Europe to oversee the collapse of communism."

That's how, later, I found myself beside Walter Mondale in Budapest, overseeing another contentious election.

Entry entitled "Managua," February 27, 3 a.m.

I went to bed after some light sandwiches at 5 p.m. yesterday. So I am up early, we leave this wonderful country and its marvellous people for Guatemala and Miami this morning at 7 a.m., but have to be at the airport by 5.30.

It is all over. At the Conservative Party headquarters I witnessed the grand finale of Commandant Ortega on television. He spoke bravely.

Some of the IDU delegation, like Schuette of the National Republican Institute, scoffed. He was later to boast that this was his fourth dictator he had brought down: Marcos, Noriega and I can't remember who the other was.

Ortega's acceptance of defeat was gracious. I knew what he was going through. I tasted the bitter pill in 1974. I felt for him when he said, "We were born poor, and we will remain poor." The tragedy for the Sandinistas is that they meant well for the poor people, the workers and the peasants, but as I said to my daughter Louise before the Romanians fell, human beings cannot swim forever against the tide. The FSLN had won many skirmishes, but they had lost the war. They had taken on an uneven struggle. When the Wall came down, Russia had gone, and the East Germans were powerless. The US embargo had brought misery. FSLN had confiscated the lands and the property, the skilled people left, and production collapsed. Just giving the people land and herding them into co-operatives led to no production. The bananas and other fruit I saw in the countryside were thin; hungry cattle were roaming all over the place.

One woman in a group of three in Chinandega told us, "We vote UNO. We want change." Asked if they will celebrate tonight, she said, "We have nothing with which to celebrate."

Another outside the pharmacy told us to come back tonight or tomorrow and celebrate the victory over FSLN. "We are tired of tears, we lost our brothers and husbands, some come back crippled and we are still poor. Sacrifice for poverty."

I made my summary in my diary: The Sandinistas lost because of
1. Poverty
2. Conscription for war

The vehicle for their defeat was
1. The secret vote
2. The swarms of observers.

There were all kinds of estimates of the numbers of official observers from the OAS, UN, Carter Center, IDU, Socialist International, plus a group from Oregon. The Oregon team outside the Cathedral in León told me their story. They met a young horseman returning home from the polling station in the countryside. He had ridden 27 kilometres to the polling station and was doing the same thing on the way back. He had on a Daniel cap. He told them he was voting UNO. But you have on a Sandinista cap, they pointed out. "Yes it is a nice cap and it is free," he told them.

Quite often at home, I deployed my stratagem to gain access to the living-rooms in a village. The ruse was simple. Turn up unannounced at the entrance to the home and plead thirst. It never failed. The lady of the house would produce her most ornate glass with a crocheted doily. I knew she would boast about my presence in the home to friends. Inside the living-rooms, I could discern the family allegiance.

I enjoyed my job as an observer, but frankly I did not enjoy working with much of this IDU team. The right-wing Latins wanted to think for us, and wanted to put opinions into the releases that many of us did not share, opinions that would have undermined the international acceptability of the electoral process. I put my foot down. They were so right-wing that they felt *I* was a fellow traveller with the Sandinistas! When they wanted to say that there was a "crippling" lack of access to the radio, I asked what would justify the word "crippling" if the UNO won.

When the count was slow in coming in and the Guatemalan and myself went to the home of Mrs. Chamorro, they were ready to make statements that this was Panama all over again. Another defeated left-wing government unable to bow to the will of the majority. I told them angrily, "Give them time, for God's sake. Do you think that Ortega will buck international opinion?"

And yet the next day I had to fight them to include a statement of congratulation to Ortega on his acceptance of defeat. And even though we agreed, the Guatemalan who spoke to the press before me ignored it and I said it. I had convinced Ambassador William Mittendorf (a member of our team who had borrowed $30 from me because he had no cash and no one wanted his cheques) that there are other regimes in the world to fall and we needed to set a precedent with Ortega's graciousness.

But I had the feeling that some of them were disappointed that the Sandinistas did accept defeat. If things went wrong they would get the publicity in mounting a challenge. Some would like another Panama invasion. My security guard had kept repeating that things were far more peaceful here in Nicaragua than in Jamaica for their elections.

It was a beautiful sight seeing Ortega holding his thumbs up showing his right thumb high with the voters ink and his left hand with the five fingers apart, the campaign sign "cinco" for the FSLN. And they brought their press conference to a close in song. Ortega and Arce did not sing.

"El Frente Sandanista." But the workers and the peasants did not prevail until the end. Great ideas for the advancement of the poor will not endure with bad management and a currency that has to stamp over 100 cordobas to make it into 100,000 cordobas. The poor will not love you no matter how much you love them if you increase their suffering.

At Dona Violetta's home I kissed her like many others. I told her that I had inspected 56 polling stations including León and Chinandega. She thanked me warmly. I told her that her words on the campaign were right; the mothers were tired of tears and nothing to give their children. While we were there Carter, Richardson and Soares came to see Dona Violetta. At that time, only 55 per cent of the results were known, showing UNO with a 5 per cent lead.

I shook Jimmy Carter's hand. One of his security men remembered me from Miami.

There was no security for Mrs. Chamorro all the time we were there. The Sandinista Army did not know that it is their job to protect the new President. But otherwise they did a fine job. There was absolutely no intimidation, no guns and military presence in this election. Not a single soldier about the polling booths.

On the night after the election, we went to FSLN headquarters. There we saw the band singing and clapping, dancers with castanets, journalists longing to be a Hemingway reporting the closing stages of the Spanish Civil War, long-haired Che Guevera types from all corners of the globe. But the revelry faded. The guitarists slipped away.

(The amateur video must have helped Serrano's cause. He made it to the Presidency in Guatemala. He toyed with the military and the Constitution, over-reaching himself all the way into speedy exile.)

Entry (undated) entitled "Guatemala Airport"

Here you see immediately more signs of wealth than in Managua. Small private planes, not the round military bunkhouses and large army helicopters as at Sandino Airport.

One thing was very notable in Managua yesterday. No scenes of jubilation or celebration. The people were obviously still scared of the military. I wondered how many were like that lady who said she would have nothing with which to celebrate!

Looking back on it all, that fellow who came out of the León polling station where we stayed for 3¾ hours, 6 to 9.45, when he came out finally and chatted with the brisk young girl who had earlier taken his message without opening it to the administration building – theirs were the first faces of defeat. They must have been discussing the results.

Ortega and the FSLN must have known they lost from 10 p.m. When Carter et al. came to Dona Violetta's house it was after 1 a.m.

Now at the end of the runway I saw some military helicopters of a different design, two blades – one in front and one behind. In Managua they had only one big blade overhead. Here also are these blue planes, brightly painted, small, looking very much like reconnaissance aircraft. Time to leave.

Entry entitled "Bequia," March 12, 1990

Dan Quayle seemed more in control of himself and his job than when the Prime Ministers of the Eastern Caribbean met him in Barbados. Ted Kennedy, whom I had last met when he came to Bequia for the wedding of his niece at Moon Hole, was looking fit, his jacket button meeting about his waist comfortably. I promptly reminded Ted we had last met when he was on the way to the wedding – that the schooner *Water Pearl* on which he sailed had sunk on the way to the Pacific. That ship was the last wooden schooner to be built in Bequia and on my family's land. She was built by Chris Bowman for Bob Dylan. So we were all at ease for the meeting.

Quayle was relaxed, saying, "Why don't we move these chairs and sit more in a circle so that we can hear and see each other." His preliminary was straightforward: he wanted to hear from us how things are going, what were are our expectations, and that while they were pushing ahead in Eastern Europe (my word, "pushing"), they did not want us to think that they were ignoring our area, the Americas. Ted Kennedy then added that both US political parties maintained their interest in the Caribbean.

Quayle asked me to begin as I was on his right. I began (as I had promised John Clarke) about the continuation of the Presidential Awards Scheme that allows our young people to study in the US. Then I expounded on the need for a Skills Training Project, which Kennedy liked because it was similar to his programme in the US.

Kennedy Simmonds of St. Kitts/Nevis, said it was not too late to convert his loan from the US on a south-eastern road into a grant.

Lester Bird of Antigua and Barbuda felt our aid should be earmarked rather than discretionary on which Quayle disagreed, pointing out the advantages. The BHN (Basic Human Needs Project) got support.

John Compton spoke on the BHN in general; Eugenia was pushing for her international airport. ("After that you can forget about us for three years," she said.) That would get Dominica all the way to the economic take-off point.

I spoke again of Nicaragua, reiterating points I had made about starting afresh in nation-building. When I went to the airport, John Clarke told me that Aronson, the Assistant Secretary for Inter-American Affairs, was impressed with my Nicaraguan experience and wanted to know if I could help with Haiti, as Avril was quitting that weekend and the Supreme Court would be taking over for 45 days. and decide when the elections should take place.

We went back to the VIP Lounge and discussed details. They wanted to know if besides helping in Haiti, I would speak to Manley about the problem. I told them I would speak to Perez as he had already offered to help. I even suggested we invite Nicaragua to give technical assistance to Haiti. That night I got in touch with the Venezuelan Foreign Office. The next morning, Sunday, I got a call from Foreign Minister Figuerido who spoke English. He confirmed that Venezuela would be ready to help, but agreed that 45 days was too short if they did not have a proper voters' list in Haiti. He told me to tell the Americans that they were anxious to have the Contras lay down their arms as specified in the peace agreement, and that the lingering Contra effect was creating problems for Ortega with his own men in the transition.

I called John Clarke and told him so. I told him further that Perez had assured me that following the Shevadnadze–Baker meeting, Ortega realized that his Russian support was crumbling and that Venezuela expected Ortega to be pragmatic. I urged that they trust Ortega and encourage him to deliver. John Clarke said he'd contact Aronson who had not yet left Chile, and at my request a Perez–Quayle meeting would take place in Chile to discuss Nicaragua and Haiti.

All weekend long I could not find Manley. I have more contacts with Seaga than with him. Eventually on Tuesday I got on to his Permanent Secretary. Manley did not call. They agreed that I was right to reject the idea of an election in Haiti in 45 days. The end of the year would be better, I felt, giving time to the parties to campaign and for authorities, local and technical from outside, to organize things.

Entry entitled "Sam Lords Castle for meeting with Brian Mulroney," March 18, 1990

What a miserable time. My entire life in the last two days had ground to a halt. Since the death of my father when I was eight years old, nothing was so traumatic – the shock of a wife's infidelity in the 1970s when I was Premier, the madness endured and survived, the tortures that led to my divorce – as the reaction of my children, particularly Gretel, to the news I sent them that Jeannette was pregnant. Gretel is on the verge of insanity: I never imagined Gretel was so attached to me. Of all the children she had been more in my presence with Jeannette than any of the others.

I really wish I could quit politics now. I am on the verge of concluding the Canouan investment with the Italian Swiss, the new Grenadines jetty at Harbour Club and the cruise-ship pier to be negotiated, the Union Island marina, the Union Island Airport extension, the extension of Bequia roads, $10 million more roads in St. Vincent. I can go on and on. The new vegetable market. All taking form even as I am to go to Hungary for the 25th. Now at the zenith of my career – the end of the road.

If my children quit school, nothing, absolutely nothing, will stop me resigning from politics. My men will be stranded. The country will suffer. But I will quit. I mean it. Why the hell should I put up with the vilification with which I am treated in the press at home, to have worked so hard, praying since my father's death that I should see my children through university about to collapse? No. Let it all collapse.

The Prime Ministers want me to take on the subject of aid, while they deal with farm workers in Canada and the Trinidad refugees. I am a handmaiden of the people's wishes, but the destruction I have wrought on my children by not caring for them, not giving them priority in my communication, makes all this politics of development irrelevant. I need now only to retire to Mt. Pleasant or Isle à Quatre and say to hell with it.

I had to leave the meeting, abandon my presentation on Haiti and meet Pat at the airport – my divorced wife. She like me can't stand the jealousy of the children – Louise, not so upset as Gretel, with Sabrina a little more tolerant. What a shame for me!

I will never be the same again. I'm going to hold on a little longer, but I am definitely now going to be set on the quitting road. No nonsense now about how I'll buck up. To hell with it. My brother is dying. The person closest to me is leaving me. My children have signalled their departure. I who am supposed to be so useful to people now find myself in THE WAY of my loved ones.

Let me leave them with what I have slaved to produce for them and others. If I am ever assassinated, I want everybody to know that such a person does me a favour of relieving me of having to put up with the disappointment of my life. It is not going to be a pleasure to live to any old age and witness the new streaks of hatred in my family, having to put up with charges by my children that I have abandoned them, when all I have done is find someone to care for me when I was considered inadequate by their mother. Life is cruel. I who have given my life, my intellect, my time unreservedly for others and in the service of my children now find myself rejected, accused of sinning, and accused of abandonment, judged without a trial. I forgive them. I would want them to forgive me for whatever sins they imagine I have committed. For myself I don't see what I have done wrong. But all the more reason why I should bring my labours to an end, retire from public life, and close all the chapters of anguish in my soul.

I recovered, I thought, from insane jealousy, but my daughter Gretel has inherited it. I pray that this experience is one that she'll recover from, and that it will give her strength to deal with love betrayed in the future. I know what I have gone through. But what a way to bring a new child into this world. My real hope for the child is in Jeannette herself who has already brought up two without a father. So this child's life begins, as mine closes.

I see no daylight in this dark estrangement. I thought I'd gone through the worst with the stranger at the gates, the defilement of the sanctity of my home, the home I now must abandon. I feel indeed that the love my children had for me has left their hearts. I am, as I have always been for much of my life, alone. I struggled alone. I wandered over the face of this earth looking for my destiny. I have carried a country, extended my poor islands into Africa, Latin America and around, but I myself belong nowhere except with Jeannette. She cares. When will her turn come to abandon me also?

I will go to Canada to deal with the trauma with my children. I will listen. I will speak. Like any exam in the past, I do not expect to win 100 per cent. I will try, for the children's sake, but not for mine. The damage has already been done to my soul. No matter what they say, I know that I have hurt them deeply, and now my spirit is broken.

What energies I have left I'll use to push my land reform. Help a few more people to own so that they will remember what I have done. Let me vanish from this scene in peace. I have settled what I want on my tombstone in Isle à Quatre: "Son Mitchell 1931- Peace beyond all understanding." I will be offended if there's another name or word added. I got a ride on the plane to Ottawa with Brian Mulroney. We celebrated his birthday. He had waived the debts for all of us in the Caribbean at the meeting. Barbados did especially well with their airport loan written off.

On the plane, as we toasted Brian, his wife Mila said to me, "Son, you are one of the leaders I am comfortable with."

Entry entitled "Hungary," March 25, 1990 – Budapest (Room 415/17 – Duna Intercontinental)

I felt quite comfortable with the Old World architecture in Budapest after one had gone past the peepholes at the Immigration Authorities. Old Budapest and its romantic Danube between Buda and Pest had a grandeur no less than the banks of the Seine in Paris. My room looks over the Danube, its amber reflections of the lights along the river and the beautiful arc of lights on the bridge.

We all on the IDU team gathered at the ornate Parliament and introduced ourselves. Former Vice President Mondale, unlike Guatemala's Serrano, graciously accepted my presence as co-leader of the observer mission. He knew of a certain teahouse in the central square where we could have great ice cream, and suggested that we go there; our group included former Senator Tom Eagleton, Senator Mathias of Maryland, Brian Atwood, Keith Schuette and myself. The mouth-watering pastry excelled.

We divided up the country among the forty-odd members of our delegation, and both of us stayed in Buda and Pest. Some 22 political parties were contesting. We scheduled meetings with every party.

Each leader had a passionate view of an alternative to Communism, and even the communists too felt they were capable of inspiration. Our own group encompassed personalities from all over Europe, Eastern Europe, the Baltic States, Czechoslovakia, Yugoslavia, Poland, plus Canada and America. I was the only one from the Caribbean.

The air was full of tales of anguish from both our Hungarian hosts and the East European observers: tales of imprisonment, entire communities risking lives attempting to slip through the barbed-wire border boundaries. The Czechs told me all about their sorrows in the Prague Spring. We were flooded with well-designed election propaganda.

The next morning our interviews began. We called on Joseph Antal, President of the Hungarian Democratic Forum. He apologized for the small size of his office and went on to elaborate.

"In 1956 this building was a barracks and in it there were soldiers who decided to fight the Soviets. On this square the Stalinist coat of arms was cut out of the Hungarian flag. This is where it hung and was adopted."

He went on to explain that only a few weeks ago he had regained his office, but he had to procure security agents to remove the bugging devices the Russians had left behind. He felt he had a good chance in the elections the next day. In small villages there could be cheating. In the big cities, orthodox communists had already given up, but in the state farms and public corporations they still had a stranglehold. He was an optimist, he said, but there was not a simple solution to everything. There were many old complexes and feelings of confrontation, but in Central Europe we can't be Balkanized, he said. With the withdrawal of the Soviets, the presence of Western Europe will be a stabilizing force. He talked about the underground linkages with intellectuals in other countries, for example, Czechoslovakia: he and Hável have even been on joint TV shows.

Walter Mondale asked if he thought the election would be fair and Antal replied in the affirmative, but for the coercion in garrison towns. I referred to the Nicaraguan experience and the trust to be placed in secrecy of the vote.

HDF had rejected any coalition with any socialist party, but they would want Opposition parties to field a single candidate for President even if it meant a different party in the Congress or Parliament as in the US or France. They were not going to co-operate with Pozgay as he was in the wrong party. Antal revealed also that he urged supporters not to insult Russian soldiers. In 1956 he had personally worked on the proposal for Soviet troop withdrawal, but now was not the time to make things difficult for Gorbachev at home when the army could depose him.

One particular poster galled me – negative advertising to the uproarious limit. It was a picture of the back of the head of a Russian occupier, warts and all on the back of his neck, with the inscription "Comrade, it's over." Surely I thought this was offensive to the Russians. He replied that it was on sale in the black market in Moscow, urging the KGB to go home.

In the afternoon we met with Janos Kis. I got an explanation for the birds in his campaign poster. The doves are symbols of peace, but the red bird is being chased out. His plea was that television should be neutral with a board elected by a two-thirds majority in Parliament. He talked about the conflicts that were surfacing with democracy: sexism, racism, and anti-gypsy sentiment. Blatant discrimination could make it difficult to get mutual reconciliation.

The Socialist Independent Party's President, a lady, well dressed, took an immediate dislike to Eagleton when he asked her if she saw herself as Thatcher. The old regime was privatizing, but winding up with everything for themselves, she claimed. She had to restrain herself from showing contempt for ridiculous questions.

We met with Imre Pozsgay, the man who let the East Germans pass across the border. Mondale asked him if he was aware what such action would lead to, and did he speak to Gorbachev about it? Pozsgay realized he was taking an extraordinary gamble, and he was there to oversee the first border crossing, told the Hungarian guards to look the other way as the first three hundred went through. He felt it was important not to consult Gorbachev. He was under pressure from Honecker and Ceauşescu, but Russia had her hands full and couldn't worry about him. He agreed with our Israeli Professor Shlomo that the Russian Empire could collapse by the year 2000, that Lithuania, Estonia, Latvia and Georgia would all go. The Far Eastern republics would then go on their own, but were unlikely to join with Pakistan. There was still 400,000 Russian soldiers in East Germany who could use East Europe as their supply source, but they were still taking orders from Moscow.

I asked if he considered the trends in East Europe irreversible, bearing in mind the chaos in the USSR. Russia, he repeated, had its hands full and could not lead the region easily again. Only a change in military perspective would change that.

He expressed concern about COMECON rushing into using convertible currency rather than rubles, and how it would create inflation which the people would not understand.

In response to the question what the West could do to help, he singled out debt relief, and help to build the spirit of entrepreneurship. He planned to run for the presidency when it came up, and said that there was a future for the Left in Hungary like Willy Brandt, Craxi and Gonsalez, but recognized that such was not a popular choice in the present circumstances.

As we were about to take our leave, we expressed the view that he should take comfort in the historic initiative he was taking, influencing events in Hungary and East Europe, and that he should realize too he was influencing events even in the Caribbean and my region. We wished him well in the future.

We had sessions too with smaller parties. The Small Holders Party, the Agrarian Alliance, the Young Socialists. Democracy at last, every ten persons could form a political party.

From Jewish delicatessens around Europe, I had acquired a taste for Polish and Hungarian sausage and when I said so; my driver took me to the "best place." They did not take my US dollars, so I changed my cash with a Turkish dealer in the street outside the shop, returned and got my sausage half price.

Entry (undated) entitled "Observing the Elections"

In Hungary, bullet holes were on buildings everywhere. My restaurateur instincts imagined how one polling station, even with its scars, would make a great location.

The saddest sight, though, was human. An old man came into one polling station. He got his papers. He went to each of the political agents.

"Who do I vote for?" he asked of the first.

"The choice is yours, sir," was the answer.

He went down the line, asking the same question and getting a similar reply.

At the end of the 22nd questions and answers, he burst into tears. "I never dreamt I would live to choose."

I did not see the Berlin Wall come down. The chairperson of the Bequia Tourism Committee, Judy Simmons, daughter of a Canadian missionary and married to one of my extended cousins, brought me back a piece of the wall from the ITB Berlin Show. The real crash of communism for me took place in that polling station in Hungary with that old man in tears.

The American media of course hounded Mondale. He graciously invited me to support his opinions on the fairness of the process. I did.

The interpreter with my team on election day spoke English fluently. He was a professor and learnt his English with a good upper-class accent. He voted for the Small Holders Party because his family had lost their land when the Russians came. His two aunts were put in the servants' quarters, but in spite of changed circumstances, the servants still addressed them as "Countess," even though they became poorer than the servants as they were too old to work. Their family land was lost to Romania. They got some money for it and bought a few hundred hectares, 65 kilometres south-west of Budapest, but this too was lost.

We heard reports of 20,000 persons applying for visas in the South African Embassy in Vienna, that the population was dwindling too with more deaths than births, that Hungary had the highest divorce and suicide rate, that the "mafia" already controlled the sale of vegetables, and there were programmes of the various parties to confront these ills, and that all parties were making the same promises. Democracy had arrived.

The results were slow coming in, some 21 computers responding to 11,000 polling stations. The Head of the Electoral Commission was calm. "Our democracy is moving faster than our infrastructure," he ventured. Our earliest tally with 27 per cent of the votes in showed the MDF with 24.68 per cent, Fidesz 19.58 per cent, Small Holders 12.86 per cent, Young Socialists 10.36 all the way down to the Patriotic Election coalition with 2.13.

Our final get-together of the team was at the Ket Medue Restaurant, beginning with Russian caviar, white chardonnay, mushrooms grilled with seasoned dumplings, Hungarian meat dishes with ham and tomatoes, and piquant gravy. It was Maryland Day and Senator Matthias rendered a Maryland tune. Our Israeli friend told some Jewish jokes, which erroneously I thought were only told by others about Jews. He was for the peace process, and thought that the release of Mandela was a historic change that would impact elsewhere. I told my joke about Emperor Bokassa and the denial of his military escort that he'd had nothing to eat.

I was seated beside the wife of a banker whose name was Gabija. She was from one of the Baltic States, Lithuania. My last daughter was about to be born in a hospital in Dallas, Texas, and we still did not have a name. I had Gabija spell her name for me, and she kindly wrote it down on a napkin, which I took all the way to Dallas.

Our team met in a conference room for a final debriefing. The theme centred around the lessons we had learned in Hungary that may be useful in monitoring the other elections coming up in Eastern European counties where the communist domino was falling. First the representatives from Czechoslovakia spoke, then those from Poland. The representatives from those countries seemed cheerful and in agreement. Then it was the turn of the Yugoslavs. Hardly had one voice begun to speak than interruptions occurred. And each one contradicted the other.

Our mission in Hungary was accomplished. We were in a farewell mood. One by one the room emptied. The Yugoslavs continued to argue explosively. The collapse of communism was not their business. It foretold violence in the Balkans.

I had to rush home. My brother Reginald was near death from cancer. I spoke to him on the phone. He was anxious for my return. I had to prepare, too, to host the Caribbean Foreign Ministers at home.

Entry (undated) entitled "Home Again"

As I listen to the world news on short-wave radio on how Yugoslavia is imploding while I enjoy another clear and peaceful sunset in the

Grenadines, I wonder what ever happened to the Yugoslav folk that were with us arguing among themselves in that room in Budapest. Were they among the aggressors or the aggrieved? I kept abreast too of the situation with our unique involvement through the ship, registered under the St. Vincent flag, MV *Droit de Parole*, off the Dalmatian coast transmitting messages of hope to those trying to locate missing members of their family. The ship's flag one day turned up in my office.

Entry (undated) entitled "A friendship"

One particular friendship that started in Hungary has endured. Pavel Bratinka, a nuclear physicist who had spent much time in jail, was sure that Czechoslovakia would go through peaceful transition. Their election was the next one scheduled in Eastern Europe, and he made it into the Parliament. When the country split, he remained, even though he was born a Slovak, in the Czech Republic. The Americans sponsored him on a lecture tour. I got the Republicans to pay his way to Barbados and I chartered a plane to bring him to St. Vincent and the Grenadines for a lecture to our unbelievers. On the beach in Mustique with a banana in his hand, in an island bought out by a Czech Jew, he was ecstatic: "All my time in jail, I dreamed of another time and another place. This is it."

I visited him in Prague where he took time off from his vacation to entertain us. He was negotiating Czech entry into the European Union and I was negotiating to keep my bananas on the European table. He arranged for me to find Bohemian crystal and got them on Czech Airways.

Years later, I had the pleasure of sharing my Czech crystal with a young couple I met on my beach in Bequia. The fellow was swimming; the well-proportioned girl was collecting shells. We were alone on the beach.

"Where are you from?" I asked.

"We're from the Czech Republic and we're studying in London," the girl replied.

"You are invited to dinner. No Czech has yet drunk from my Czech crystal," I said. "They need a proper christening."

I apologized for interrupting their privacy. They had taken a cheap flight to Barbados and decided to move on to a small island, a small hotel, and a beach to themselves. They did not expect to find a Prime Minister, alone on a beach, who had once chatted with their Vaclav Hável. We listened to the Czech Philharmonic and the commemorative disc for the World Bank/IMF meetings, which were harassed by the anti-globalizers breaking into the Mercedes showrooms. They were perhaps the first Czechs in the Grenadines. I explored their country and I was happy to have them explore mine.

Entry entitled "Miami," July 15, 1990

So glad to hear that Nicholas Ridley in the UK had to resign. The SOB is the one who decided that St. Vincent and the Grenadines should get Independence during the Soufrière evacuation, when we could not discuss the Constitution. Now I'm Prime Minister and he has made an ass of himself by cursing the dominance of the Germans and bemoaning his lack of support from the French poodles in confronting them. I'm so glad the old imperialist who shed us unceremoniously should go in disgrace!

I'm here from my LIAT meeting in Trinidad where I put forward my BA proposals *en route* to Dallas holiday and the birth of my daughter.

Sabrina spoke kindly to me for the first time since the Toronto freeze-out; she asked about Jeannette.

Entry entitled "The Trinidad Coup," July 27–31, 1990

I was really winding down in Dallas in Haymeadow Circle, a comfortable unpretentious area of North Dallas beside Richardson district where I had my prostate examined by the Urology Associates, including a sonogram (that extended into a lecture to a young lady I'd never seen before on how the equipment worked – rather another new experience to have some tool up your rear for the first time). Thankfully, negative results.

I had been running about the running track every morning with some other old folks who put me to shame doing their hour, so my condition was fair. I had been comfortably relaxing too, awaiting the birth of our daughter Gabija.

And to the end of all this on Friday night, my High Commissioner Dick Gunn called from London to tell me there was a coup in Trinidad. The Government was held up by a Muslimeen group in the Parliament and the leader of the "rebel" group had announced the take-over from the TV station.

Without a quiver I knew I had to be back in the islands, and fast. We have a saying in our villages, "When your neighbour's house is on fire, throw water on your own." Jeannette said she understood why I had to go, and indeed suggested it. (She did not mind if I went back to the region, as long as it was not to Trinidad.)

Diana Williams, married into Jeannette's family, and about to assume responsibility for our tourism promotion on the West Coast, expressed confidence that Jeannette and the baby would be all right. I should go.

Once more the choice between family and public service!

I decided to terminate my isolation in Dallas. I called Eugenia. She confirmed that the news of the coup was true. I called Philip Greaves. He also confirmed. I gave them my phone number and told them to call and let me know if a decision was required by me. Dick had stated that the Army was behind the "rebel" leader, but that the coastguard and police were supportive of the Government.

The item took over the top stories in CNN around the world. Headline News. You saw Abu Bakr, the Muslim leader of the commune outside Port of Spain on TV talking about corruption and poverty of the people, and the voice of the Deputy Prime Minister Dookeran saying the armed forces were loyal, but they needed help from outside. Pictures of fires were seen of the burning buildings. Numbers of dead varied: 30 to 300. Looting. Damage $200 million and so on.

I tried to get Compton. No response. All lines to Trinidad on Saturday and Sunday were blocked. My Commissioner of Police, Toussaint, confirmed the chaos, said there was a request for our coastguard to be available and go into action. I authorized.

On Saturday night Philip called late to say there was a truce. Ray had agreed to resign. The rebels would go to Libya. The Piarco Airport was closed. Election to be called in 90 days. Dookeran to be acting Prime Minister. I know Dookeran. I did not think he would stand the pressure. A gentle economist, but not a fighter.

The British were ready to help. I felt the real help could come from the SAS in the UK who have the best experience in hostage crisis-negotiation, psychology, fire-power, co-ordinating technology. Sahadeo Basdeo, the Trinidad Foreign Minister whom I had entertained in Bequia and Mustique after the Foreign Ministers Meeting in St. Vincent and the Grenadines was in Jamaica and he was going on to Barbados. Dick and I discussed the SAS option. I told him to alert the Foreign Office and prepare for a request. I would advise Trinidad to make the request. Panday could talk to the British High Commissioner in Barbados and I would follow up on the line to London.

Dick gave me a number to get to Robin Gorham at the Foreign Office over the weekend at home. But Philip thought the truce was on and we left it at that. In the meantime Barbados had agreed to be the staging post for regional action in Trinidad.

When I left Dallas, the information I had was that the matter was settled. On the plane from Miami I told a reporter from the *Dallas Morning News* that I had told my coastguard to stand down, but that I thought the resignation of Robinson would not hold, because if he was free, the confidence of his parliamentary colleagues would restore him to being Prime Minister.

I arrived in Jamaica. There was no mechanism in place for an immediate Caribbean response. While I knew Caribbean leaders like to upstage one another I expected to be called into session to discuss Trinidad that night. Nobody called.

This morning I went into attack at breakfast with the St. Vincent and the Grenadines delegation. This so-called truce was not getting anywhere. I called my Commissioner of Police and he confirmed that our coastguard had carried 20 men to the RSS in Barbados.

I called Sandiford. He was his usual low-key self. He said the right things in terms of what he was doing in Barbados as the staging post, but he did not communicate any urgency. He also said that Patterson the Acting Prime Minister would be convening a meeting at 11.30 when we would get together to discuss Trinidad after a break in the Finance Ministers Meeting.

Desmond Hoyte turned out to be across the room from me in the Pegasus Hotel. I had a meeting with him and Rashleigh Jackson. I deplored the lack of co-ordination by us, that separate statements deploring the hostage-taking in Trinidad was not enough. We needed to formulate a strategy to save Ray's life and the lives of his colleagues. Time was of the essence. At the end of it, Desmond said, "Son, you are different from the others, you know. They take it easy." I told him we have to have a clear strategy for action. Would we support Trinidad if they requested our and foreign assistance? He agreed that we must support Trinidad on anything they agreed.

I attended the Finance Ministers Meeting. I made two short presentations. The Secretariat was doing most of the talking. Pindling was quiet. Sandiford spoke more than others. Guyana pointed out that they were getting less than they were putting in to the Canadian Multilateral Insurance fund, negotiated in Brussels together. All of us had grayed a little. He was pleased to greet all of us.

Foreign Minister Basdeo outlined the situation in Trinidad. Their forces were in charge. The Parliament and the TV station were still under the control of the extremists. Only two people killed – two suicide bombers who drove the truck into the Police Station with the bombs.

The presentation he made seemed to satisfy the others. I moved in relentlessly. He told them of the perception in the US, on the CNN world news, of the picture of chaos in Trinidad, lack of control, when only ancient pictures of Ray are in the media, and the active image and voice of the rebel leader is facing the world. Our image in the rest of the Caribbean was in tatters – we looked inefficient. We have to convey the image of action that we are in control in the area. We need a media blitz.

Basdeo said he was in contact with Trinidad and they were asking him to hold on outside the country. His first response was a query about the life of the Prime Minister and colleagues. Information came to hand, not from Trinidad, that the radio and TV station were burnt. We speculated that if this was so, Bakr was dead, and reprisals would mean that Ray was dead also. I said that we should send someone out of the room to confirm.

I told them that I approached the situation like a rescue at sea. A single moment, a single decision could save lives. They talked about waiting until the Mexican President Salinas and international press arrived. I had to knock this on the head and say that Trinidad *was* news headlines, not the development proposals coming from debt-ridden Mexico.

Anyway we agreed that Basdeo should update us from Trinidad. Our statement to the press would be that we have our forces on standby in Barbados, and we are ready to assist if requested, and that the Government was in control but for the hostage situation.

Later at the dinner for the President and after the press conference Basdeo was loud in his praises for the way I took over from the Chairman and rammed home our perspective. I had inspired him to hang tough, Ken Gordon later confirmed.

Oliver Scott of the BBC called. I was delighted, I said, to speak on my favourite world programme. He could hardly recover from my praise. I spoke of our perception, explained the hostage situation with Muslim fundamentalists, our democratic position – that the armed forces were loyal, the people were not in support of the coup, and that we might have a long-drawn-out hostage situation.

I learnt from Basdeo on the phone when I called him after the meeting to offer my help at the press conference that the US had provided the critical technical assistance in regaining the TV station and breaking the line of control between Abu Bahr at the TV and his supporters holding Robinson in the Parliament.

I met with the President of Mexico upstairs in the hotel. We established relations between St. Vincent and the Grenadines and Mexico. He spoke English fluently. I expressed my concern about their trade agreement with the US It was definitely on. He hoped we could be involved and that it would benefit all of us. I emphasized that we in our region must co-operate more, as the Europeans were. My meeting did not last very long as I wanted to rush to help Basdeo with his press conference. But both could not be done. When I arrived at the Conference Centre, the Foreign Minister was finished. Ken Gordon told me Basdeo performed well. He was strong. He said there was a settlement but that the terms would not be announced in advance of their being implemented. Gillian Nanton, the economist on my delegation, called to say that that she heard Robinson on the air saying that very thing. He had instructed his Head of the Army to institute the settlement.

I told Basdeo and Ken Gordon that when the dust settled, they should bulldoze the Muslimeen commune, go on the offensive against the human rights activists. At the banquet I went further and told Basdeo they must dissolve the House, call elections, and let the people decide. I will write Ray to this effect.

Later, Basdeo was summoned by his High Commissioner in Jamaica privately. When he returned he told me that the RSS in Barbados wanted rations and ammo from the US or they will return to base, and that Trinidad had to make the request. Accordingly he made the request to the US Ambassador in Jamaica. He could not tell me exactly what kind of ammo and he was not clear himself. But he thought that the RSS should remain on standby for at least three days until the situation in Trinidad was clarified. I supported his request, but told him I regretted that we had to ask for rations. The ammo had to come from the US. The rations we should have provided ourselves.

Next morning, he said Trinidad would need food as soon as things are settled. I told him that he should let me know and we would buy provisions to send down from St. Vincent and the Grenadines. We'd be glad to help Trinidad, our traditional buyer.

The news from CNN is that Robinson had been freed but that 40 people are still held hostage in the Parliament. I know Ray is not too well, like me suffering from a prostate condition. And the wounds of a bullet in both feet would be devastating. The news item said he is in good spirits. I called home to alert them to prepare for a food request. Dairy products also. They say Ray left the Parliament by ambulance for hospital.

Entry dated August 1, 1990

I suggested to Caricom in the first session when we were dealing with the agenda that Trinidad be on it at every session, morning and evening, as we start and then at the end of the day. The afternoon session began with Trinidad. Basdeo reported the exact time of the Prime Minister being freed, that the troops needed ammo and other supplies from the US – that he had discussed the situation with me and that he had agreed to ask the US for supplies. The Conference felt – PJ – that it would give a bad signal if troops were disbanded while 40 hostages were still being held.

I expressed my joy at the release of Ray, but stated concerns about his health and whether, given his state of mind and body, he could think clearly under stress. I reported that I had alerted our people to get food ready for Trinidad, and in the strongest language denounced any presence by either Jesse Jackson or Jimmy Carter. On Jackson, I said he did not know how to represent his own people at home, and having Carter would drag us into domestic US conflict between the Republican Administration and the Democrats. I drew on my experience in Nicaragua for this, when I had had abundant evidence that the Republicans on my side did not trust Carter. And in the situation when the US was supporting our troops, co-coordinating their activity, and technically jamming the TV station, I felt that we should not be encouraging any Jesse Jackson meddling. The US press would descend on us and be reporting on what the American meddlers were doing and not on what the Trinidadian actors had to say.

Lester Bird supported me strongly. I had made my point subject to what George Price would have to say, but he remained silent. I knew that George was close to Carter. Ramphal reported on his experience in Trinidad, his strong lecture to the head of the Army, his discussions with Pat Robinson, her pleas for help. She felt that one of us should be an interlocuter down there helping Robinson.

Then the lobbying began. Ramphal, Compton and PJ felt I could go to Trinidad and "take" Basdeo with me. They felt I had the close confidence of Ray, the strategic sensitivity and strength to deal with the situation. I baulked. By this time I was feeling more tired than I had during the day. I discussed it with my Permanent Secretary Irma Young. She was not inclined to agree. At bottom, she thought I should go, and as leader of a team.

I was inclined to respect Jeannette's opinion not to go to Trinidad. At that time she was pregnant, about to deliver. It made sense not to put myself and family into a position that would force me to step up our security for the balance of my life against disgruntled terrorists and their ilk. I thought of myself in Opposition in the old days when no one (including Caribbean leaders) cared about me personally. In the same way they were so laid back about Ray, they would be indifferent to my welfare in the event of trouble in the future.

As I got home to the hotel, Desmond came to my room and requested that I go. They had spoken to him. He said he was not flattering me, but that I was the best suited to the job. He thought Basdeo couldn't handle the job by himself.

I called my team together – Irma, Gillian, and Minister Marcus De Freitas. They all felt I should not go. Marcus, who was here on LIAT business, thought I should only go in response to a demand from the Caribbean leadership. I called my Commissioner of Police, Toussaint. He said I should not go, that the situation required military not political action.

Gillian called. She revealed the disgusting scenario of Ray's release, looking grey and ashen, in a wheelchair pushed by his captors with one of them putting his briefcase in his lap and others lifting him into an ambulance. Utterly humiliating! She thought I should call Ray's wife before deciding to go.

I really decided not to go because I felt the situation had gone in a direction different from what I would have done in the first place. I would have called in the British SAS. But these independent black countries would rather die rather than call on the knowledge and technology available to do the job. Always we want to "learn by experience"; we want always to invent the wheel for ourselves.

John Compton called to say Robinson went to Military headquarters for debriefing, then on to hospital where he is suffering from gangrene. He now agrees I should not go to Trinidad.

I can see the dire consequences if Ray dies. Tobago will demand secession. All the other hostages will be killed. All the terrorists will be killed and the religious wars I had forecast in my earlier address to the Foreign Ministers' Conference on May 7th , entitled "Chasing Rainbows over Distant Horizons," will come to pass in parts of the Caribbean.

George Brizan told me that they had suggested to Basdeo on Friday night that he call in the SAS. I sighed. For a week I had had a number to call on the weekend and at night to request just that sort of action.

Kennedy Simmonds, who is a doctor, and not a man of many words, when I told him of the gangrene, said, "It is serious."

Entry dated August 2, 1990

I called Ray last night about 8 p.m. for at least 20 minutes at the St. Clair Medical Centre. I spoke first to Pat. Her voice was relaxed. I was absolutely delighted to hear him and so was he to hear from me. He was calm, collected, in fine spirits, and not sounding as though he was in pain. He confirmed that he had been tied up, that it had been an extraordinary ordeal. I told him that I had the clippings and a tape of CNN so that he could see how the world saw him. I went on to let him know how I had pressed the item on the Caricom agenda for the beginning and end of each day. He had not heard that President Bush had expressed support for the constitutional government of Trinidad and Tobago, nor about Perez de Cuellar, Mulroney, Perez of Venezuela, all expressing offers of help. This news he was pleased to hear from me. He said we should keep in close contact as we used to do before, and not as in the last couple of years. When I said I'd be coming down to see him after the summit, he said he was looking forward to seeing me.

Entry dated August 4, 1990

Basdeo admitted to the Caucus that they had had help from the Americans. All that they had predicted about the inevitable psychological pattern of collapse of the hostage-takers had come to pass. Eugenia on the way home told me she knew they had 44 Americans all the time helping them, but Trinidad was hiding this. Patterson was anxious to ensure that Air Jamaica, and no other carrier, brought his men home.

At one stage this week, Basdeo suggested that some authorities thought we should withdraw our troops (some 300), let them get refreshed, and if they were needed later, we could mobilize them again. We told him that once they went home, that was that. Our last on this was that they wanted 150 to help with restoring normalcy. Hoyte said if any were needed he'd want to be involved.

Entry dated August 6, 1990

I leave for Trinidad today with a letter of sympathy for Ray. I hope I can go there and get home to St. Vincent tonight. I had left the Conference in the closing stages when they played a tape recording to them he had sent up.

Yesterday we had a CDU meeting: Seaga will stay on as Chairman for another year. He seems to accept as his Executive Secretary Joan

Webley, who has been useful to us in the East Caribbean. He is a cold fish. You never warm to him. When I told him I'm off to Trinidad to see Ray, you'd think he would send greetings. No way.

Before that I met with Jagan of Guyana for breakfast. He told me how they planned to boycott the polls if there was no ballot counting at the place of poll. I told him that he should concentrate his energy on pressing the Commonwealth to do a good job of observing the election. I said he should go to London to speak with the High Commissioners of all the countries whose co-operation he wanted. If he boycotted polls, he would play into the Government's hand. If the elections were rigged and the Commonwealth did not say so, the integrity of the Commonwealth would be in question. He had to get his foot in the door, and let his whole body pass. He told me also of his plan for plural economy, how he could get tractors from Brazil and get his agriculture going again, etc. I told him that the Paris Club controlled everything that Brazil's debt-ridden economy did. It would be the IMF who would dictate if he could get help. I added that he should drop that anti-IMF language he used – "They were the borrower of last resort," etc.

He mentioned Venezuela's help. I took the opportunity to point out the substance of my letter to Hoyte, in which I emphasized the importance of trying to conclude a deal with Perez, a second-term President with a Congress of the same party in control, that with the Europeans settling the boundaries in Poland and Belize on the way, Guyana should not be left long with a problem. I offered my assistance. He seemed happy with my guidance. I called on Desmond Hoyte and told him of the discussion and also that Jagan wanted a ride back to Guyana with them.

Entry dated August 10, 1900

So the Saturday morning I left for Port of Spain, as requested by the Heads of Government, to carry our letter to Robinson, to cheer him up, and to advise him. I wanted to tell him above all, call the election (general) as soon as he was fit. Don't wait on the human rights activists or the IMF to call the tune.

When I got into the VIP lounge, only a BWIA agent was there, to greet me. The Trinidad protocol people were not in existence. I thought I was stranded. An obvious diplomat, white, with an unrecognizable foreign accent was in the lounge. He was from a UN agency and was there to meet a member of his organization (a Guyanese) coming from Thailand to identify the body of his son who was shot in the chaos, and whose mother was a fourth wife of Abu Bakr. The diplomat and the woman were separated. Apparently she was in hospital wounded in the shoot-out.

Shortly two soldiers in jungle garb and obviously armed rushed in. "Prime Minister," one said, "we've come to get you. Come with us."

At the door another two soldiers joined us. Above the airport, two helicopters were buzzing. On the ground, troops were patrolling the perimeter. I was escorted to a plane. We rushed to the Savannah.

One of my escorts told me his name and of his Vincentian parentage, and serving in the coastguard. He said the Government had taken too long to declare the state of emergency – not until 10.30 on Saturday morning – and that there was still trouble. The Army had intercepted 22 more rebels earlier today coming from South Trinidad with more guns, he added.

At the Savannah we went through the same procedure. A TV camera was there to see me escorted by three soldiers. I was rushed into a car. Basdeo was there to receive me and we went to the Prime Minister's residence. We awaited the arrival of Ray. It was about 2 p.m.

Ray came in an ambulance. The soldiers in the accompanying vehicles were heavily armed. Two nurses were in attendance, and one gave meticulous instructions to the troops on how to move him into the wheelchair. His feet had to be handled with great care. He was dressed in long pants; you could not see his wounds.

I felt like crying. Would I be ever assassinated? I wondered. There, but for the grace of God, go I. Fleeting images of those like Zia Ul-Haq, Olaf Palme and a wounded Reagan, and my friend, the Foreign Minister of Kenya, with whom I sang in Langkawi, rushed through my mind.

Ray stayed in the wheelchair downstairs chatting with Panday, myself and his buddy from Tobago, who like me was seeing him for the first time since the rebellion. His wife Pat and daughter were in attendance. Two senior Army men came in and introduced themselves. It struck me that Ray did not know who they were and that he was very distant from the Army. He congratulated them on the job and so did I, telling them how proud we in the Caribbean were of them.

I mentally prepared a full report of my impressions of Ray and Trinidad and Tobago for the media at home. He told me how they made him take down his pants and tied him up with a tourniquet around his left foot just below the knee and to his hands high up behind his back in a way that every movement on his own brought pain. He was tied to Selwyn Richardson and Richardson to another Minister. The scar from the tourniquet had cut the circulation in his left foot and the bruise was clearly visible. The bullet had gone through his right foot just below the knee. The doctor had told me that it did not hit any bone, artery, vein or tendon but had damaged a nerve, creating "foot fall." But Ray showed that he was beginning to get a little movement in the blade of the foot below the instep.

I asked him how he got shot. He said that after the police started bombarding the Red House, the Muslimeen realized that both they and their hostages could suffer the same fate. They were not ready to die. He had told the head of their group, "You all have made a great mistake," when Abu Bakr announced that he was forming a government. "You have now brought in the Third Force. If you all had kept this a Trinidadian thing, you might have been all right, but the Libyan connection will be your undoing. I have been in politics for 35 years and I know you will not succeed." So they brought Ray a microphone to speak to the police to stop the shooting. Where he was lying on the ground, he shouted, "Bandits, murderers, come for them with the full power."

At that point they rammed a rag in his mouth with the muzzle of a gun and he vomited

Then they shot him in the leg. Richardson said, "You all can kill me too." And they did.

I asked him if later on they allowed him to go to the toilet? What did he eat? What did he drink?

"I had a glass of water a day. Twice I had a cup of tea. It was a battle of wills and a psychological war. I decided not to give in. I urinated on myself. We did not go to the toilet. I never messed but I urinated."

I told him when his Tobagonian friend left that he must call the election as soon as he was better. "The structural adjustment you've made won't show results for eight years. If you can't win now, you never will."

He slapped my hand and smiled wistfully, "You are an intuitive politician."

We had a light snack, four of us together, served by his wife Pat. I chatted with her and the daughter about the nightmare. She said she decided to take one thing at a time and not try to predict the future.

I gave him the CNN video, the *Miami Herald* and *New York Times* for him to read how the world saw the issue.

Ray's aide said that when they started communicating between the Red House and the Command Centre at the Hilton, the rebels heard an American voice on the phone and dropped the phone.

"The Third Force," someone said.

The game was up. They realized Ray had been correct when he predicted their fate, and they gave up.

Entry dated August 9th

Back home in Bequia, I learned the whole story about the rebels' capitulation that Ray had not had the strength (or the knowledge) to tell me at the residence. Captain Rual King of the *Lireco* confided to me that on Monday after the coup he was heading for Barbados, 30 miles SW, from Trinidad, when about 2 p.m. a US battleship stopped them. They had seen her coming a great distance away.

"This is a US warship. Cut your engine. Captain and all crew go and stand in the stern. Where are you coming from?"

"Trinidad."

"We're boarding you. Put your ladder down."

Ten of them came on board, heavily armed, with transmitting equipment. They made a search. The Commander told them, "One of our shells can cut you in two. Thanks for your co-operation. Be on your way, but not until we're back aboard and give you the signal."

So the US had sealed the north of Trinidad and Venezuela the south. Oil and gas reserves triumphant. You little fellas behave yourself! (The *Lireco*, later scrapped, is now a dive site off our island.)

Entry dated August 12th

Last week when I spoke with Karl Hudson-Phillips, he was very disillusioned. Ray was thinking of setting up his fantasy – a Caribbean Court to try the rebels. So I called Ray in Tobago, listened, and courteously told him that the people of Trinidad and Tobago could try to hang them themselves, and that his idea would create legal hurdles – retroactive law-making, relevance, proportionality and validity. "Put it on ice for the time being." Karl and I agreed the Court – if it ever came about – should have a black prosecutor and an Indian judge to satisfy Trinidad and Tobago's ethnic population distribution. Ray is a dreamer. Karl tells me they've already selected ("they" being a young Attorney General) a white group to lead the trial.

It's good to know what is going on at the start so that one can set one's agenda and response.

My last daughter, Gabija, was born in Humana hospital, Medical City, Dallas, on the 5th August. I could not leave home. Jeannette

registered the birth details: Christian name (from Hungary), Gabija;
nationality, American (Texan).

Entry entitled "Taipei, state visit to Taiwan," August 21st

Here with Louise at the Grand Palace at midnight. Motorcycle escorts.
Met by the Prime Minister at the airport and sat next to him. He was
concerned about Iraq and inflation, and effects on his economy. He
told me that he had overcome that kind of challenge before and could
do it again.

The timetable presented does not give me much room for discussion
of my agenda. I will have to talk fast. Our team meets for breakfast this
morning to plan strategy.

This bed is the firmest I've slept on. It is hardly softer than a carpet
on a floor. A firm bed but soft pillows: a Chinese version of comfort.

Entry dated August 22nd

A few years ago I would have easily dropped our recognition of
Taiwan and gone for China. But today my priority is to get the airport
in Union Island redesigned and built, get the roads in Bequia and
Canouan finished, and a few roads on the mainland to complete our
programmes.

I have not simply gone in this direction on a narrow-minded or
selfish provincial basis. My Nicaraguan, Hungarian and East European
experience has led me to conceive that one day, and in my lifetime,
China's communism will give way. It will not be able to withstand the
dynamism of the Pacific led by Japan, anchored by Lee Kuan Yew,
Mahathir and the South Koreans. I asked myself, would a billion
Chinese forever withstand the road to progress?

My people's needs in St. Vincent and the Grenadines dictate my
foreign policy. The Chinese limit their aid to C1.8 million, send in their
workers to do the job, and I doubt if their generosity will continue.
St. Vincent and the Grenadines can't be a yo-yo going up and down.
We have to establish a dependable source of income and aid, and I
see our cause being advanced better by the Taiwanese at the present
time. It could well limit our options in the international stage, but
I can't see the windows of opportunity for any Vincentian through
mainline China. The British had not built up a viable infrastructure
as the French did (and were still doing) in Martinique. I wanted our

infrastructure built so that we can get to self-sustaining growth. If we advance our unification in the Windwards, I can see Taiwan agreeing to debt relief on the US$8 million dollars they're due.

Besides, over the years, I have come to appreciate Frederick Chien, the Taiwanese Foreign Minister, and developed a relationship with him. Better the devil you know...

Entry dated August 13th

I have slept well, but I rise tired, with a bit of a headache and numbness. Is all this just personal stress because of my children's unacceptance of my new baby getting the better of me!

At dawn, 5.15 a.m., I look down from the corner room high up at 906 at the Grand Hotel to the gardens and hear the exercise leader shouting the movements toward a radiating line of people in the gardens. I had a dignified meeting yesterday with President Lee. We had two things in common: (1) professional training in scientific agriculture, and (2) witnesssing Vietnam War protest demonstrations at Cornell University. His aides were amazed at the length of our discourse.

Taipei stinks. The atmosphere is bleak. Pollution here worse than Los Angeles where we overnighted. Six million motorcycles, three million cars, and industrialization. The river does not move. The streets need repair. The houses need to be painted. You don't see beggars, but you don't see wealth on the streets. No high fashion here, none of the modern running shoes on the feet of the people. Certainly the wealth does not appear to be distributed. I have to learn more about this place.

Premier Pei-Tsun Hace is stocky, affable and constantly smiling. He does not look like the warrior general that his aides revere. He speaks English moderately. He met me at the airport at 10.35 Monday night, and saw me to the hotel step.

At the Agricultural Council, I advanced my plan for my country to produce grapes and orchids. St. Vincent and the Grenadines was no threat to them, i.e. the Taiwan market is for Japan. I told them I wanted production for the local market, and for the up-market Caribbean resorts.

Fitz Richardson, from our Development Corporation, who is here with me, reminded me of Colombia, where they were not interested in helping us with orchid production because we challenged their markets. The Council of Agriculture apologized for their old, dilapadated buildings. Through the windows you could see the new, state-of-the-art research centre behind being built. I was really amazed they were in such inferior surroundings.

Entry dated August 24th

South to Kaoshung, to the shipbuilding and steel centres, then on to an enormous furniture factory.

My officials who went off to the meeting to discuss the loan informed me in more detail that at the outset the Taiwanese informed them that their Council had agreed to fund two projects for up to US$8 million: Union Island Airport, road and drainage. So it looks as though Bequia, Canouan, Mespotamia, and South Rivers are off. I did not like this, and instructed that we list the road projects elsewhere. We would also have to specify the Union Island terminal building. It will mean that Union Island will have to be expanded. Beyond Union Island we should have flexibility in other islands.

Anyway this evening I will see the Foreign Minister who speaks English well. He told me the story of the artist who painted the extraordinary misty mountain picture on the wall where we dined with the Prime Minister after they had decorated me with the Order of the Shining Star. The Taiwanese artist he described as a "bon vivant," who went through four wives. He lived in Brazil and when that country recognized Red China, he got rid of his mansion there in São Paulo and moved to the United States, and when they recognized Red China he moved back home. A young girl said to her classmate, I'd like to study under your father, so she took her father to meet her, and he said you're beautiful, be my wife. She married, ordered his life, and restricted his painting to periods of enthusiastic energy. His last painting was given to the Foreign Minister who tried to buy him paints and brushes – just before his death.

When we returned from the south and the extraordinary visit to the room of external and endless lights in the Buddhist temple, another vision of beauty turned up in my room, the most exquisite mother-of-pearl inlaid teak table you've ever seen. The Taiwanese had already given me a piano that I could not use and it ended up in the police barracks. Three years of piano instruction had yielded only whacks on my fingers! I told them I would have preferred a round table (fascinated with the Knights of the Round Table) as they had given Eugenia, and this was it. Louise says she wants it as a wedding present. I promised her that it's hers if she spends three years in the Buddhist temple at Fokwangshan. Oh what an enchanting spectacle the room of endless eternal lights.

A general at the theatre explained to me the theme of Chinese opera – loyalty. Loyalty to your family, your country, the factory, the Army – to your situation. A great explanation of the way to their success.

The exercise classes below going again at 5.50 a.m.

We dined last night at the Hover Theatre Restaurant – an institution modelled on the Lido in my opinion. The girls were not as beautiful as in Paris, but the singing was extraordinary. And romantic! I commented to our table how our culture's music, calypso, seems to ignore romance; our lyrics are all malice and politics. What a pity!

I spent a few moments at the dinner thinking about my dead brother. I miss him so much. In a way I feel lost without him. He worked so hard and did not live to enjoy the fruit of his labours. I feel like crying every time I think of him. I want to be so loyal to his memory.

Time for some exercise.

Entry dated August 27, 1990

My last day begins. As usual I'm up by 3 a.m. and sorting things out. Wrote a series of cards to Union Island so that supporters can have a record of my work on financing the airport improvements and the road to Ashton.

If I had to rate the memorable events of this trip I'd list them as follows:
1. Visit to the Buddhist Temple;
2. The science-based industrial park where I saw and used the suitcase model of the portable communication system with its own dish and telephone that allows you to phone anywhere in the world, either using a battery or electrically operated. Louise called Sabrina in Toronto and reception was excellent;
3. Meeting with Foreign Minister, Dr. Frederick Chien.

At the dinner hosted by Premier Hau, he sat on my right and explained the painting I described earlier. At his own banquet at the Foreign Ministry he was excellent. It was 6 p.m. Friday evening, and he had just finished work. How do you have some 800 employees in a Foreign Ministry and have so little foreign recognition!? He gave me the story of his life and it seemed typical of the Taiwanese people, going from rags to riches in a lifetime, from rural agriculture to massive industrialization. He landed here from China as a little boy in clogs, worked his way through school and his fellowship in Yale, not like the youngsters that go to the US and come home for vacations.

He had told me at the earlier dinner how he used to control information – instructing the newspaper editor what to put where in the paper, the size of print, the size of the article. He felt a little guilty about it now, but I told him that he should not be guilty. He had to mobilize public opinion at a critical time and he had to fight the Communists' fire with fire. They love to use undemocratic methods to undermine democracy and destabilize an economy.

No one could have explained the economy better. He revealed how they organized their five-year plans, how the results showed how they executed these plans, in terms of growth. He said, "Let me make my confession. We set out to make our people richer. Our per capita income moved from the bottom to near the top. On this small island land is scarce. The people save – they put their money in the stock market. Housing is a problem, they want bigger highways, and they want to send their children to the best school. They laugh at me with the salary I make as Minister at NT$100,000 a month when they make that on the market in three hours. They complain about the environment. So you go from the problems of under-development to over-development and solving the problems of over-development is harder.

Very cleverly he led to the subject of aid. He talked about the CDB and how he's preferred to allocate one block to the Caribbean, because if he gave one more than the other they'd complain. I noticed Eugenia, Compton, and Simmonds never screamed about what they got. He gave me the impression that my US$8 million was more than the others received. So I could not press for more. His officials had earlier settled with me that I could choose my priorities on the roads. So I was happy with that. It left no room now for argument about amounts. My Union Island project was the best prepared; already we had the design from the German consultants in Bequia in hand.

I told the Foreign Minister how I enjoyed the visit to the science-based industrial park, to use the suitcase model of the international telephone transmitter. He said that they had ordered six for his Ministry and that they cost US$35,000 each. I told him they had got many orders from the Middle East. King Saud has one in his car. The White House has six – I learnt that when I said I thought President Bush needed the boat model to use on his fishing trips. Chien was pleased when I told him I'm recommending one for President Perez in Venezuela. They have a poor phone system and I'm sure Perez would love to have one for himself, and so would other Ministries.

I am satisfied that we advanced our relations with the Taiwanese people. Perhaps their ambition to go back to the mainland makes sense. After all, look at the Germans. What would a single government, single free-enterprise system be like? Who knows! I speculated. I wanted to know how to bring out unification between St. Vincent and the Grenadines and its neighbours.

Chien is invited to open the Union Island Airport. He agreed enthusiastically.

The procedure here as you moved from place to place was a steady ritual, always perfect timing:

1. St. Vincent and the Grenadines and Republic of China flag at door.
2. Person to meet you standing between the flags.
3. Go to briefing room.
4. Tea already poured and hot.
5. Briefing.
6. Presentation of gifts.
7. Tour.
8. Farewell.

Of all the gifts the most treasured will be the vase from the Foreign Minister, and the Peruvian marble vase at the Trade Expo site in Taipei. Since my former wife claimed the vases after the divorce, I've been making sure my house does not look empty. The last vase I brought in was from Hungary and carried by hand all the way home.

The twelve-seat teak and inlaid-mother-of-pearl table – the gift from President Lee – is something else. I was ready to reciprocate with generous hospitality for the good of my people. Europe had induced my sense of history. The East deepened that sense.

Entry entitled " En route from Hong Kong to Los Angeles," August 31st

I met with Sir David Forde, Chief Secretary and Acting Governor of Hong Kong in his office high up in the financial centre not far from the Bank of China. It was important for me to go to Hong Kong to get a feel of the place, and put my foreign relations with Taipei in context.

Sir David's view was that Hong Kong's arrangement with China was a prelude to Taiwan's. If Hong Kong went well, then China feels that Taipei would be ready to do a similar deal, namely "one country, two systems." It is fascinating to note that both see China's unification as their goal, the Taiwanese in terms of their return to the mainland, and the Chinese in terms of their absorbing Taiwan.

The Chinese are getting 45 per cent of their foreign exchange and 75 per cent of their investment through Hong Kong. The free trade zone across the border with low wages and the Hong Kong access to the world is paying off. Apparently the way China is financing their investment in Hong Kong is as follows: borrow on the Hong Kong market and let it pay for itself. This was how they did the Bank of China Building that is 75 per cent rented.

The desire for free markets in Hong Kong, Taiwan and East Europe will influence the future.

I told Sir David that while I am a democrat I have to acknowledge that the democratic path is not a speedy way to leap out of under-development and cited Singapore, Korea and Chile. If one could go through the platonic benevolent dictatorship, set the economy right and then liberalism, one can catch up. He agreed: "Hong Kong's path too, of course – we did not make it through traditional democracy."

I really felt that if China's leadership uses its authority to liberalize the economy and become an economic power, they would swamp Taiwan. Imagine China with a per capita income like Taiwan. Of course if China and Taiwan get together, we the small fish would be left in the shallow pool. We have to hurry to get our infrastructure in place, and develop the education to maintain it and expand opportunities for our people.

It was really a sad sight back in Taipei seeing the line-up of Ambassadors at the military airport for my 19-gun farewell. South Africa, Korea, Paraguay, the Vatican, Panama. (It sounds as though Swaziland will install diplomatic relations as the King had visited here after Kuala Lumpur with one of his young wives – the one whom I met. Will we in the Caribbean be Taiwan's last diplomatic bastion?)

Summing up! In our first parliament, 1984–89, a succession of my Ministers made the pilgrimage to Taiwan. I did not go. I concentrated on getting my own house in order, generating a surplus on the current account, closing the loss-making sugar industry, privatizing all enterprises that were marketable and getting government out of the way of the private sector.

By the second parliament, I was ready for serious infrastructure development. With the funding of the Bequia Airport well advanced, I wanted to ensure that the Southern Grenadines were not left behind. Our pristine Tobago Cays, the five islands circled by reefs in the clear Atlantic, were becoming a Mecca for yachts sailing from the East around South Africa, and from Europe and America. We were riding the crest of our newly discovered popularity. So I was ready for Taiwan.

The Taiwanese *chargé d'affaires* in St. Vincent was the energetic Allan Jiang and his petite, charming wife Grace. My planning official, Randy Cato, had the documentation prepared for the reconstruction of the Union Island airport, roads between Clifton and Ashton, and some roads in Bequia and St. Vincent. I intended to get rid of the Taiwanese technical assistance in rice-growing and shrimp production, against both of which my agronomy rebelled, our soils being far too porous to yield much of either. My interest would be in orchids and grapes for possible export, and to keep our growing number of satisfied tourists happy.

For Taiwan, my team comprised Randy Cato, Chief of Planning, Harold Rampersaud, Chief Medical Officer and my personal physician, Fitz Richardson of the Development Corporation, and my daughter Louise. Taiwan knew that Beijing had made contact with me in New York, but my presence with my daughter in Taipei was a signal that I was ready to do business with Taiwan. Louise attempted to go out jogging only to be stopped, until her escorts got suitably attired to accompany her. She thought the security was for the Prime Minister only.

Our St. Vincent flag was fluttering on the ships in Kaoshung Harbour.

I asked enough questions and got adequate answers about activities in various locations throughout Taiwan to assure me that their sovereignty had enough substance and was sufficiently grounded to deserve my country's support against the international currents.

(Union Island was delighted that literally a new horizon would emerge in their air transport. Pilots would no longer have to be ready to dive down over the hill and ensure that they did not have to jump out of the sea at the other end).

The environmentalists emerged. The isolated rock being incorporated in the airport extension across the sea and joined to the mainland had apparently catered to the evolution of a distinct species of lizard that must have thrived on salt. No one could show me the lizard or a picture of one. The island had no vegetation.

In turn, the Canouan and Mustique airports were developed on my watch. Taiwan's technical assistance with orchid-growing added a new dimension to our floral landscape.

So I was invested with the Order of the Shining Star. Years onward, satisfied, I suppose, with my reciprocity in international advancement of their cause, they upgraded me to the Order of Propitious Clouds! (I assumed that "propitious" meant the same thing in Chinese and in English.)

Entry entitled "Tokyo," November 12, 1990

Here with Sabrina for the enthronement of the Emperor. The JAL flight from JFK was turbulent over a rainy New York City, but settled down later. I enjoyed the excellent French red wine which relaxed my soul. When we arrived in Narita we were taken to a smaller plane where we joined the Nicaraguan representative, Orlando Trejos Sommambia. Later the Colombian Foreign Minister came in followed by President Guillermo Edara of Panama and his slender tall wife.

The protocol people checked our dress and seemed to approve what we were wearing for the enthronement. He said at breakfast that when Sabrina's picture arrived it was felt that she would rival Princess Diana at the ceremony. With expressions of some panic, they changed our departure from the room from 12.05 to 12.03. One could not help but note the changes of minutes given by the protocol officer, and how the elevator time-monitor signified our precise movement.

The Japanese originally objected to my daughter' presence at my side. The invitation was for wives only. "In which case, I shall not be going," I told the Embassy. The Ambassador got back to me. President Corazon Aquino had no husband and wanted to bring her daughter also, so did other Presidents. It would be in order to bring my daughter.

I was a little worried about my dress for the ceremony, as it did not conform to either the No. 1 specification of "white tie," or the No. 4 of "morning coat." I settled for my grey flannel and my grey tie that I bought in England for the Garden Party at the Palace. I wore my large version of the badge of the Liberator. There was a whole range of medals everywhere and it is obvious that when people are told "Decorations may be worn," they are anxious to expose all they possess. Sabrina was in a fashionable flowered silk skirt and black top, and in the evening with a black full-length skirt, white top and bright pink centrepiece that brought her outfit alive.

The Enthronement was a slow procession from different directions to the Throne. An announcement outlined the procedure and the rest was silence. Dignitaries from all over the world were present. Great space, stark furnishings without embellishments but there's not an inch of it you would want to change. This place, razed to the ground in war, and this massive turnout of Kings, Princes, Presidents, Prime Ministers and Ministers, all paying homage to the Japanese miracle.

My placement put me beside Mrs. Lee Kuan Yew and her husband Harry. I thanked him for the radio/disc player he gave me while in Singapore, my bedside companion. He asked if it worked. He had not seen the article which said that the US real threat would be if he headed China. Mrs. Lee loved the compliment. I promised to research it and send it.

Mr. and Mrs. Perez de Cuellar were two down from us. Present, too, were the Sultan of Brunei and Iremia his brother, Vice President and Ms. Quayle, Kenneth Kaunda, Prince Charles, President Tabai of Kiribati, Maumoon Gayoon of the Maldives (whom I introduced to Prince Charles as head of the country to disappear in 50 years under global warming and sea-level rise).

Then there were the new acquaintances, the jovial General Yakabu Gowan of Nigeria who chatted freely about the oil crisis – he did not seem to be doing badly but was still complaining about Third World Debt; Ion Iliescu of Romania – a merry soul, very witty – speaks good English and charmed by Sabrina; and Prime Minister Michel Rocard of France.

I introduced myself to one who turned out to be the personal representative of the Emir of Bahrain who introduced me to Sheik Nasser al Sabah of Kuwait, the Minister of State in the Foreign Ministry. I told him when he was moaning about how his help to Iraq was wasted that he would have had better results giving me a school. He promised to call on me.

The Minister of State in the Foreign Ministry turned up with his protocol officer, his cousin, at my hotel room 1460 on the Wednesday morning. We covered the ground about the Gulf. He repeated his thanks for my help at the UN.

His message was that Kuwait wanted war. He told of the Arab meeting with Assad who said to every leader present, one after another, "Can you get Saddam Hussein out?"

"No," was the unanimous reply.

"OK, then none of you can object to the foreigners getting him out."

I told the Sheik that I really did not want to go swimming in deep international waters where my country would sink, but I was planning my three-year cycle of salary increases and the Gulf was making inflation unpredictable. I have OPEC loans and it becomes harder to make my contribution to capital projects if my revenue base is eroded. The Sheik promised, "When our country is liberated, you will be the first from your area to get loans from the Kuwait Fund. We'll want you to visit us. We'll send people to you." I invited him to be my guest.

But that was not the end of it. My meeting with Sheik Nasser went on. My speech in the UN, he blurted out, was played on radio and TV for the Kuwaiti people and Arab countries for three days, but they did not have my picture. He described Hussein as an even madder Hitler. Iraq, he insisted, had lost the war with Iran four times and Kuwait and Saudi Arabia are the ones that came to his rescue. He believes that Saddam's missiles will misfire, that he has killed six of his generals, his army will collapse in 10 minutes, and is crazy enough to think the West is bluffing. China had warned him today that they will vote in the UN on Article 51 to force Iraq out and Saddam said to them they should abstain, and China repeated, "No, we'll vote against you" – and he still thinks China is bluffing!

I was lucky to have made the Sheik a new contact. But my greatest fortune of all was my seat at the Enthronement Banquet. St. Vincent and the Grenadines must be doing something right to be placed on the right of Mrs. Tosiki Kaifu and opposite Perez de Cuellar at Table 2. (The Kings and Presidents were on table No. 1.)

In my conversation with Prime Minister Kaifu and his wife I mentioned that SVG had issued stamps commemorating both the death of Emperor Showa and the Japanese gift of our Kingstown fish market. Before the court banquet at the Imperial Palace, during the presentation to the Emperor, I requested we be permitted to issue stamps on his Enthronement. He accepted and said it would be an honour. I told the Prime Minister that the Emperor had agreed, but that I will formalize my request on my return home. In fine Japanese style I gave him my card and secured his autograph on our menu.

I took Sabrina around with me and introduced her to everyone. She expressed concern about how St. Vincent and the Grenadines would fare when I'm no longer there to push our cause on the international scene.

Our warmest Caribbean greetings were from my old pal Philip Greaves and also from Desmond Hoyte, who is looking forward to my coming to Guyana on December 1st.

The Emperor graciously thanked us for coming. The most important souvenir will be my photos with him to show to my Japanese visitors.

Entry dated November 9, 1990

Yesterday afternoon at the garden party in the Akasaka Imperial Garden, as Sabrina and I were mingling, a tall gentleman introduced himself, "Belgium." After a second, I caught myself: Kings do not explain who they are! "Your Majesty! I am delighted." I reminisced with King Badouin and Queen Fabiola about my hitch-hiking days in Belgium, and how I had lost my passport and money. The King asked if I had prayed. I said I prayed, but I also cursed myself. Later, I met President Kurt Waldheim, told him of my young days in Austria and how I helped to save a drowning girl in the Danube. I wished him continued good luck politically.

Met almost all the Royal Family of Japan. One Prince who smokes a great deal told me how he had complained about his head-gear for the occasion, and had that altered, but he did not check the shoes, and they were too tight! Sabrina knew about one of the princesses and her recent marriage. They had met at University.

Last night at the banquet. At one table Lee Kuan Yew and Mrs. Perez de Cuellar on my left, and Sabrina between Lee and Perez de Cuellar. Not far away was an MP from Yemen who explained to me how South and North Yemen after several wars had brought about unification in a two-year transition period. I've invited him to lecture in St. Vincent and the Grenadines. He was Prime Minister in the North and now has a different rank in the Union. Everybody got a job, he said

The second night at the Prime Minister's dinner at the New Otani Hotel, we were seated again at the Prime Minister's table with Perez de Cuellar and Lee Kuan Yew. I asked Mrs. Lee Kuan Yew about her husband's retirement, due soon. She said he was not retiring. They exercised a great deal to stay fit, she said in response to my comment about how well he looked.

Lee Kuan Yew told some wonderful stories. We were discussing Israel and the intransigence of the Israelis. He said, however, that at Singapore's Independence only the Israelis would help him and trained his Air Force and Army. He had spoken to Nasser and told him he did not want to offend the Arabs, but he needed help. Many years after, he invited back all the advisers and trainers from Israel. They marvelled at the country's stability and transformation both of the Air Force and Army and asked him to explain how he did it, while they themselves in Israel had turmoil.

"I chose to make peace, you chose war," I told them.

On Japanese leadership, he said he learnt a great deal from a man who worked with him landscaping his garden.

"It takes one year to grow rice.

It takes ten years to grow a tree.

It takes a hundred years to grow a man."

At one point I asked Kaifu what his main problem was in Japan. He pointed to the Secretary General and said the United Nations. Japan wanted to be a permanent member of the Security Council.

CNN is full of the trial of Noriega.

Our Honorary Consul, Akiro Watanabe, made arrangements for me to call on former Prime Minister Suzuki. He has an office in an office block in town. The Foreign Ministry protocol officer accompanying us, Fumi, was not impressed with Suzuki who in his opinion only talks fish; he said Suzuki had bored Mrs. Thatcher frigid on the subject. I could only thank him for the project we have in St. Vincent and the Grenadines, but did not see a way to get his help with aid I wanted for new directions, although he was in favour of 600 million yen to be allocated for fishing boats.

Entry dated December 7, 1990

So I introduced President Violetta Chamorro to the Miami Conference at the Thursday banquet. A packed hall, certainly over one thousand at the feast.

A message turned up at my room looking over the bay (where a small island was reclaimed to the left of the Barnett Bank, and three hotels going up that can hold more than all the visitors in St. Vincent and the Grenadines) – saying that she wanted to see me at 10.30 before the noon engagement. Of course she was surrounded by security.

She was dressed in a beautiful maroon/pink outfit. She was walking without crutches, but informed me that she was on her way to Houston for medical checks after leaving us. I met with her, her secretary and another gentleman. She was surrounded by men; only one woman was with her.

Three of us went into a dining-room of the suite. I reminisced about Nicaragua and opened up the conversation, how she was so right about her forecasts, about my telling the Sandinistas how to lose in a democratic election – never allow yourself to think that the world was at an end and cheer up your supporters.

I presented my speech. She loved it. There were a couple of functional economic analyses, a difference from the IMF figures, she sent for her Economic Minister and he corrected it. She said my lovely words brought her a feeling of tears. We chatted for over an hour.

I asked if she had dismantled all the Sandinista symbols, and had she put up her plaque for her husband in the street. She said she had decided not to. I agreed. If the people of Nicaragua wanted a plaque, I said, let them copy yours. But I cautioned that she should keep some, like the liberation statue, even in a museum for tourist purposes. She said that Fonseca was no longer at the airport. Gradually she was removing the Sandinista labels and images.

PART V

Onwards to Retirement
(1994 to 2004)

24

Third Term: Keep the Home Fires Burning

With an amicable divorce now behind me, I was able to win all constituencies in the next Parliament, expand the Frangipani with loyal staff and move on with my life. I had purchased the neighbouring family property from my American aunt, Dr. Lee, who had tried to renege on the deal, but settled after a court order. Pat and I built the Gingerbread Restaurant. I had to deploy my maritime skills to hoist the tall masts supporting the Spinella-designed roof. The restaurant, and later the hotel, became quite successful under Pat's management. We hosted some great banquets there, one for the airport opening and some years later, for my friend President Jammeh of The Gambia, who left a musical souvenir behind.

Our Cabinet, for 16 years, met at 2 p.m. on Wednesdays. Within an hour and a half we were finished. Cabinet was a decision-making body, not a deliberating chat house. With the formal meeting over, the civil servants left, and we could hold discussions on unresolved issues. The civil servants comprised the Cabinet Secretary, Irma Young the Assistant Secretary who kept the minutes, Jo Anne Veira, and the Director General of Finance Maurice Edwards, who guided on cost implications when specified. Our Cabinet papers contained the opinions of the Ministry of Finance, the Attorney General's Chambers, and the recommendations of the sponsoring Ministry. At subsequent meetings I reported to the full Cabinet on issues settled.

I had learnt from my position as Minister in other Cabinets, and in the Colonial Executive Council, that meetings beginning at 9 a.m. lasted all day. A day's ministerial work was lost in usually useless discussion massaging egos. And our government lasted 17 years while those that spent all day in Cabinet were not surviving. Cohesion in Cabinet is not a result of lengthy discussions.

An opening prayer was instituted in our last term of office when we were reduced to a single majority. The "Yes, Minister" syndrome

355

which seeped into the consciousness of the office holder I am afraid all too readily became a tinted glass case hiding the occupant from harsh reality. Occasionally I would warn of the crucifixion of Christ after the betrayal. The masses that sang hallelujah in the morning chanted "crucify him" in the evening.

All too readily those without inward strength would unknowingly be trapped into revealing the secrets of the inner circle, and abandon the oath of secrecy to which they had subscribed, all because an imagined slight had to be put right.

With Canadian technical assistance we had completed an overhaul of the public service, evaluating the relative responsibility, work load, and incentives needed for the balance among institutions: the police, the nurses, the teachers and the general administration. Every individual through their organization or Ministry had the opportunity to advance their cause. Salaries all shifted upward between 20 per cent and 110 per cent. It was the biggest structural change since the across-the-board $75 I instituted as Premier in response to the 1973 energy crisis and which favoured those at the bottom of the pile and later created a confrontation between the teachers and the Government in a subsequent administration.

On my own initiative I expanded the ranks of officers and the size of the police force, creating greater opportunities for promotion. But the greatest discrepancy was the legacy in the colonial framework sustained in the Independence constitution. How was a young developing country going to be competitive with a public service entitled to 30 working days holiday a year!? All subsequent studies on efficiency ground to a halt on this stumbling block along with the structural tenure of public officials enshrined in a colonial-inspired Independence constitution. After I retired I published a summary of my views on the type of Constitution these islands require.

My Ministers kept together. Once every three months they would spend a day at my residence from nine in the morning until they individually wanted to leave. The menu was baked red snapper, glazed chicken, and curried meat of some kind, a host of salads, sorbet and ice cream with lavish services of good red and white wine, and the harder stuff to those so inclined. Unresolved issues were put to bed. My Minister of Agriculture, Allan Cruickshank, an Adventist, did not maintain his objection to wine when he had to spend weeks in Rome at FAO meetings.

As Minister of Finance I was determined to advance the restructuring of our economy, keeping growth positive while increasing expenditure on education and health. We advanced the women's cause with a Ministry of Women's Affairs. A third of the beneficiaries of our land reform programme were women. The Prime Minister's office had only two men, the messenger and me. And the ladies were promoted head of several Ministries.

Nora Peacock, the editor of the Vincentian newspaper, fell over herself praising our amendment to the Constitution to give Vincentian women the right to confer citizenship by marriage to foreign men, equal to the status already enjoyed by women marrying Vincentian men.

In a mini-state, easy access to a Prime Minister, unfortunately, brings home serious consequences. The flood gates opened on marriages, especially among the Syrians and Lebanese immigrants, consolidating their hold on commercial activity. I found myself having to explain that it was the democratic right of our ladies to enjoy a better life through a good marriage.

The absolute irony of this constitutional change was visited on my office one dreary day when an unkempt, ungainly creature waded in. She demanded that I sign the citizenship for her husband, who it turned out to be one owing bills all over Bequia and not averse to using the term "nigger." He claimed to be a Count, a direct descendent of the illustrious dynasty of the House of Habsburg, with a fortune alas controlled by trustees, rather "niggardly" in their dispensation to him. In the pursuit of extended residence, our authorities had sought his bank references and a rumour quickly spread that it was my personal ambition to steal his money. If he were in the line of Hapsburgs, I was sure he was also the end of the line.

"So you are in love with this German?"

"Yes."

"Where is he?"

"I get a phone call."

"Are you getting any money?"

"Yes."

"Is he taking you to Germany?" (Silence.)

"Listen lady, tell this man to get a lawyer. Take me to court for constitutional infringement."

I did not bother to inform her that Germany does not recognize dual citizenship.

We inaugurated a Family Court, complete with the rights of privacy for abused virgins, abandoned mothers and jilted husbands. But perhaps a more salient improvement in our way of life came through the abolition of death duties and inheritance taxes. At least, the dead could rest in peace, knowing that their children and not the lazy state exploited their savings.

Winning all the seats in Parliament had imposed serious responsibility. I set out guidelines for our Parliament, that we should enact no law that we could not accept were we out of power, that we must be fair and distribute the wealth among the villages, and consolidate the impact of the land reform among the poor. We should always remember that however strong we were, ours was still the "in and out" club, and that the membership of the "out" club could always with indecent haste join the "in" club – and vice versa.

My cynicism after a decade in Opposition never left me. I was in Opposition twice, and now in Government for the second time. I warned colleagues about the middle class and the foreign investors. The alacrity of their genuflection before any newly empowered elite exceeds the enthusiasm of a prostitute strutting before another client in the evening. President Reagan had sponsored, too, a Justice Improvement Project. We used the funds to air-condition the Supreme Court and improve a couple of Magistrates' Courts. We recruited John Havers, a retired jurist in the UK, as a commissioner to improve and consolidate our laws. With no Opposition, drafting new laws and consolidating the old was a breeze in the Parliament. Our country became the first in the Caribbean to have a brand new set of laws. Our Attorney General, Parnel Campbell, with a careful eye to history, ensured his contribution would be recognized in his writing of the foreword. We invited the Bar Association and other organizations to comment on the laws. There was no response. I was delighted that I could challenge my opponents in the ensuing election to indicate which laws they would revoke on coming to office. No response.

We brought harmony. We sought political union for the islands. My proposals for a mixture of the Westminster system and proportional representation got nowhere. Caribbean unity is on the lips of every Head at the opening of every conference in the Caribbean standing before his flag. Reports of decades of conferences, grandiose speeches fascinated with the theme of unity fills the libraries of our academic institutions, and is used over and over again for graduate theses and critical essays from one student to another. Always a theme, only a dream, never substance in my time. Fascination, like beauty, without pursuit, yields no embrace.

Only The Bahamas, from Pindling to Ingraham and on to Christie, consistently know where they were, where they are and where they will be on political union, that is "out." With no agricultural produce to export, no industry to manufacture, a tourism market linked to the US and Canada and Europe, that's where their business was and will be. They'd co-operate with us. Fine, and no more.

I returned from England once with a brass plaque: "Grand Caribbean Unity Movement," a piece of inspiration that was so irrelevant, I could find no place even in my own country to hang it. I ventured only once with the flag for a unified country I designed and had made up in England, and after the curses and screams confined it to a cupboard.

Nevertheless, I tried to bring the islands together. In my first May Day speech in 1968 to my constituents in Paget Farm, I alerted them to the fact that voting for me would always be a mandate to bring the islands together. My speech in the Virgin Islands as Prime Minister established my credentials among the Prime Ministers and Chief Ministers, the media and all who wanted to hear. We set up a constituent assembly in the Windwards. We moved from island to island: Grenada, Dominica, St. Lucia and St. Vincent. We listened. We spoke. I was determined that the blame of failure to unite should not be upon the shoulders of our generation of leaders.

When I heard Billy Herbert, adviser to the St. Kitts Prime Minister, declare that the "boys up north" (the Leeward Islands governments) wanted to keep their flag in the United Nations; when I saw the St. Lucians, with a dominant Roman Catholic majority, appoint a Methodist to be a spokesman for the Church; and when I heard the Dominicans insist there would be no unity until Dominica had an international airport, I knew that for all my unforgiven sins, I was closer to Heaven than a Union of Caribbean States.

And so "functional co-operation" became the buzz words. We, the leaders were a Cabinet, and each Head of Government would have special responsibility for something, and there were plenty of somethings to go around. And when we met in preparatory conclaves, as we would do to prepare for the Summit of the Americas, each leader would get his two minutes, or perhaps four.

And thus Trinidad got energy, Jamaica got external negotiation, Barbados the single market and economy, Grenada, hassle-free travel and later science and technology, St. Lucia, good governance, and yours truly moved into airline privatization and later bananas.

Vincentians were frustrated with the monopoly airline LIAT and its indifferent service that meant you were unlikely to arrive home with your luggage. The government shareholders invited me to put forward a restructuring proposal, and I did. My reason and instinct told me to produce competition, private-sector ownership and management driven by market forces. Free from all corruption, and without loss-making regularly bailed out by taxpayers, I believed we could produce profit and efficiency. When we put forward, the Heads of Government assigned me overall airline responsibility in the region.

I quickly understood that the mandate excluded Air Jamaica, as they clearly indicated they were already contemplating and negotiating partnerships with international carriers. The successful Jamaican entrepreneur Butch Stewart of Sandals was coming to their rescue.

From meeting to meeting, I produced reports. I held discussions with every Head of Government, every Minister of Communications, Chief Executive Officers, pilots, flight attendants, and travel agents. The Caribbean Development Bank came on board, anxious to have its debts honoured by the LIAT. The CDB commissioned Bank Paribas to advise me.

But soon, rumours started around the region that British Airways, privatized by the Thatcher government and leading the industry in profitability, was wining and dining me. Before I presented another report, this time in The Bahamas Summit, I sought the indulgence of the Chairman, Hubert Ingraham, to deal with the rumours.

I explained that I recently had been suffering from a urinary tract infection all the way to my kidneys. Jamaican consultants gave me temporary relief that allowed me to make it on our mission to Haiti to intercede with Namphy and the latest impositions at dictatorship imposed in that poor land. A French doctor in Martinique and the laboratories there diagnosed the cause of my urinary troubles, prescribed antibiotics, and instructed me to avoid spices and liquor. I wanted to know, and asked him, if this included wine.

"A French doctor," he said, "would not exclude wine forever, but perhaps for two months."

"Mr. Chairman," I concluded, "I want to tell this conference, including all the bureaucrats that are travelling the world, that I own two restaurants. I can serve two hundred and fifty people in an evening. This whole conference cannot eat or drink me out. Do you think I can be bribed by a glass of wine provided by British Airways? Now for my report."

A linkage to Europe was not going to upset our American tourism, I explained. The airline world was getting into alliances and I did not think we should be left out. Linking British Airways with LIAT and BWIA could be an answer. But this was destined to get nowhere.

So we attempted to link up with British Airways, investing in a new regional airline, Carib Express, based in Barbados. Our leading entrepreneurs in commerce, industry, aviation, insurance and construction invested in it with enthusiasm, inspired by the presence of British Airways. The Barbadians dominated: Jeffrey Cave, Kyffin Simpson, Bernie Weatherhead, and the firms Goddards, Bryden, Barbados Shipping and Trading. From St. Vincent there were Mikey DeFreitas, Sam Goodluck, Richard Joachim and Jonathan Palmer. Grenada's presence included Lyden Ramdhanny and Dominica's industrialist Philip Nassief. Much of the planning was co-ordinated by Steve Hobson, an Englishman resident in Barbados, and David Holmes looking after BA's interest. Such were the pioneers in private-sector involvement in airlines in the East Caribbean.

But the airline could get no route to and beyond Antigua. Venezuela's new government took ages to approve the Barbados/Caracas route. BWIA launched predatory pricing between Barbados and Trinidad to fill the empty seats after the tourists had got off in Barbados. And the BAC 111 we were using, with its four engines, was uneconomical on short routes. After a few months, British Airways decided to withdraw from our joint venture in Carib Express.

I chaired the final meeting in St. Vincent that threw out my proposal on privatizing the regional airlines, effectively taking the subject off the agenda. All the debts of LIAT to the CDB were cleared, leaving the old regime in place to start accumulating debts again and not paying landing fees.

Cheddi Jagan, the newly elected President of Guyana, flushed with victory and supremacy at long last for his long-suffering Indian majority, was in absolute glee. We should countenance no private-sector control of communication, he declared. All the right-wing policies since the CIA overthrow of Mossadeq in Iran, Arbenz in Guatemala and Allende in Chile did not improve the lot of mankind. He lectured on and on with a theme we were to receive time and again. Socialism was still relevant.

"Rip again!" Prime Minister Compton would whisper on every occasion, to me. "Rip Van Winkle has surfaced again!"

The Antigua delegate was as happy as a cat that had driven off all the mice from the cheese, ready to eat it all alone: LIAT would remain under Antigua control. Patrick Manning as Prime Minister of Trinidad and Tobago, the owners of BWIA, was also rejoicing. After all, Trinidad had enough natural gas to subsidize incompetence and indifference.

I would have to be honest and tell my Vincentian people how the Caribbean ganged up on me to keep St. Vincent poorly served in air communication. But I would forever remain unrepentant toward private-sector control of aviation, albeit with government facilitation!

I would explore other options. My country was not to be held hostage. I would still seek a way for us to escape from being at the mercy of a monopoly. Our skies would not forever be manipulated by governments. I wanted open skies.

Daylight dawned for us years later when American Eagle decided to fly between St. Vincent and Puerto Rico. Our Vincentians in New York rejoiced. All the objections to route rights rejected by Antigua for Carib Express going from St. Vincent through Antigua and on to Puerto Rico became totally irrelevant. Antigua had vehemently objected to routes for a Caribbean-based airline with Caribbean investors, but would not dare to reject demands from an American carrier.

American Eagle requested that we extend Arnos Vale Airport. I saw the way to do this in due course. One morning I had a visit from Allen Stanford, owner of the new airline, Caribbean Star. He requested rights into and out of St. Vincent. I agreed instantly. He established himself in Antigua, created jobs there, and sailed through the bureaucracy in the islands which had plagued Carib Express. He knew too how to limit the influence of our British Civil Aviation regulations and to blend the American Federal Aviation rules to create new opportunities for his carriers, Caribbean Star and Caribbean Sun.

Even with a renewed lease of life, LIAT continued to lose money, relying on the taxpayers. I was asked about the possibilities of a new merger between LIAT and BWIA, a re-invention of the wheel. All I could say was that drowning men had difficulty saving one another. Ian Archer, a Barbadian expert in aviation matters, had the last word, "LIAT," he said, "is living proof of life after death."

But it was not only the Caribbean which occupied me. So when the opportunity arose to help The Gambia return to democracy, I seized it. It was a really exciting feeling, my going to the land where the slaves were sold to the Europeans. I was not a subscriber to the back-to-Africa syndrome, nor was I in the league of the culture vultures seeking an identity. The wanderings of Mungo Park in The Gambia three centuries ago had given me an historic point of reference. We set out with our arms lacerated with shots and our immune systems prepared against malaria, yellow fever and all that my doctor thought necessary.

On the way to The Gambia, I attended a meeting of the European Democrat Union in my capacity as Chairman of the Caribbean Democrat Union. Our organization had been ably guided by Hector Wynter of the Jamaica Labour Party, and was managed by Joan Webley, of whom I have already spoken, who devoted much attention to the East Caribbean after the murder of her husband in Jamaica.

The retired Prime Minister of Sweden, Carl Bildt, became Chairman of the EDU. It was fascinating to hear of the billions being laundered in West Germany, and the structural problems of the economies plagued by growing unemployment. I dined in good company, including Michael Hesletine and Giscard d'Estang, and the personal contact put new perspective into my understanding of the people forging the way forward in Britain and Europe, while our own integration at home was lumbering along.

The main thing for me was to outline my agenda dealing with the military government in The Gambia and secure some international support for my mission beyond the Commonwealth. Karl Hudson-Phillips had agreed to come along as a constitutional adviser. I took along one of my top police officers, William Harry, on the advice of Commissioner Toussaint and my Cabinet Secretary, Irma Young. They deemed it proper that I should meet a military government with someone in uniform beside me.

Thousands of people were in the airport to greet us at the ungodly hour of the night we arrived. It was a noisy reception. Foreign Minister Jagne who had initiated my activity on The Gambia's behalf in New Zealand was at the foot of the steps to introduce me to Captain Yahya Jammeh, Leader of the Provisional Military Government. They had broken their isolation following the coup that threw out President Jawara when they did not allow him back ashore from the British ship where he was being entertained.

We were put up in a home beside the river that had been an official residence in the previous administration.

In due course we met all the military men. My message was simple. I was there to follow up the help the Commonwealth wanted to provide, and to ensure they avoided expulsion like Nigeria.

A whole programme of visits was arranged, accompanied by Captain Jammeh and his men. I was invited to open a market and a newly paved street. Neither were of any great distinction, and I concluded that if they represented progress, the country could not have been well served in the past. The people were ecstatic about both projects. One woman I spotted in the crowd in a beautiful yellow dress and with a glorious shawl about her head seemed to be a Vincentian beauty. Indeed I found the faces in The Gambia almost identical to people at home, far more so than the faces in Zimbabwe or Zambia.

Every day I savoured the popularity of Captain Jammeh and his *coup d'état*. In the meantime Karl was digesting the draft constitution produced by Commonwealth technical assistance. Neither of us was pleased with some sections and Karl advised appropriately. At the final banquet in my honour, before all the assembled dignitaries of the land, I urged the military men to publish the Constitution and secure the support of The Gambia's intellectuals. The draft as it stood should not be imposed by the Military Council.

I encouraged Captain Jammeh to form a political party and contest elections while his political honeymoon lasted. I convinced him that I had enough political experience to be able to read crowds and their reaction to him. All he had to do was to ensure that the Constitution allowed the country to progress beyond the military coup. He should place one of his team as Head of the Army. He could retire and contest the presidency.

The Captain was in good humour. He accepted my suggestions. He and the people thanked me for bringing them out of diplomatic isolation. I invited him to visit us after the election. He presented me with a magnificent carving of a woman with a fish wrapped around her, saying that he had noted how I had observed the Gambian ladies in the crowd and he wanted to give me one to carry home.

I broke ranks with previous dignitaries visiting James Island, where the slaves were imprisoned before shipment to the West Indies. All distinguished visitors' names were to be carved in the bark of a magnificent Baobob tree in front of the prison. The cameras were all ready. I objected and said that there were so many carvings on the tree that it may perish and I would not be another one to destroy anything on James Island. The Gambia had long carved its imprint on our history. I only wanted to etch a line on their history, but certainly not in the bark of a tree.

On return, I informed Secretary General Anyaoku that The Gambia was not ready for election. They needed a few more months. I informed the European Democrat Union also. It takes courage to tell the international community a military government should be left in place a little longer.

Captain Jammeh won the election. He made it in full glory in his blue robes to the CHOGM in Edinburgh. The Gambia was back on the democratic path. Foreign Minister Jagne became Permanent Representative at the United Nations. But I shall never forget how on the elegant grounds of the presidential residence he introduced me to his business-like wife, only to be confused when I thought I was greeting her at the dinner the next night.

"You have changed your hairstyle from yesterday," I blurted out.

"No, I am the second wife!"

The return visit was rushed upon us with little notice. My Governor General, Sir Charles Antrobus, and his wife Gloria hosted the President at Government House. My second visiting African Head of State addressed Vincentians, this time at the Independence ceremonies at the Arnos Vale Playing Field.

My help in restoring The Gambia to normalcy became more significant as chaos turned to carnage in Sierra Leone. I got a call from a diplomat friend in New York, asking if I would be prepared to broker a settlement in Sierra Leone. I replied that a location outside Sierra Leone and with representatives of the warring parties would be a necessary start. An old friend from ICTA student days, Jake Davies, who had been for some time High Commissioner for Sierra Leone at the Court of St. James wrote me a distracted letter about the hopelessness in Freetown. I could not get a further response from him. I wonder if I had paid earlier attention to Sierra Leone rather than The Gambia whether it would have made a difference.

. Back home, my attention focused on Mustique. The US Federal Aviation Authority in its unfettered right to protect Americans in the sky and on the earth, slapped Category 2 on our airport in Mustique, deeming it unsafe. I understood they had dared to impose the same extraterritorial sanction on Ben Gurion Airport in Israel, an imposition that lasted only half-an-hour. The hotelier in me, and a family inheritance of managing ships, had driven me both to understand the ultimate doom of publicly owned airlines and the absolute imperative of getting our airports and their regulatory authorities right to preserve our tourist industry.

I could never forget the admonition by Lee Kwan Yew that Singapore Airlines through first-class service sought to inspire Australian businessmen to fly with Singapore rather than Quantas. After my failure in selling the message of airline privatization, I concentrated on getting my airports free of Category 2 irritants. Union Island had come up to the mark with Taiwanese help, Canouan with that of the CDB. Bequia had settled down. St. Vincent required further consultancy. Mustique was next on the agenda. The local pilots, like taxi drivers knowing the pitfalls on bad roads, never had any difficulty, but a few strangers did, coming over the hills and veering into the swamp. The

Directors accepted my view that the airport needed drastic attention. Harding Lawrence, the former Braniff President, still a passionate lover of airplanes after all his millions of air miles, suggested I chair the committee to examine plans for the airport. I accepted on condition that he be on the committee. We contracted with Gordon Hamilton of Sypher Mueller, out of Ottawa, and in tune with IATA, to pilot us through the maze. In the new dispensation we had to say goodbye to the brilliance of Mustique Airport's long-suffering air-traffic controller, George Fields, who with the anemometer inoperative, could confidently signal the pilot on wind speed and direction from his intimacy with a flagging windsock.

Sypher Mueller came up with two angles. One, a new direction across part of the swamp and easterly between the hills to Rutland, the other to shave some of the exit hill to the left, and transpose the landing threshold. The latter course meant further extension.

Mustique is a land of passion. Harding and I were inclined to take the decision for safety, but the traditionalists, including the new purchasers of homes, would not agree to an extension to accomodate executive jets or interference with their mosquito-ridden swamp. Nothing could deflect their hostility. Felix Dennis (who had bought out David Bowie) led the charge with his "No JFK" on T-shirts. His prestige in the island had taken root with the library he built. Not since Andrew Carnegie built libraries of some architectural merit early in the twentieth century in the Caribbean, has another philanthropist in our midst pointed us towards a better life within the covers of books. But Felix, in his rekindling of excitement in English poetry went further, securing his own place on the bookshelf. He had gone far beyond his early beginnings in publishing when, as in the case of *Lady Chatterley's Lover*, he was charged (and dismissed) for "conspiring to debauch and deprave the morals of the young of the Realm." In Harding's home, where he lavishly entertained the gathering of illustrious Mustique shareholders, our first suggestion for change was set aside. I nevertheless urged the Director of our Civil Aviation Authority, Herald Wilson, to work closely with Sypher Mueller and come up with a final design and regulations that we could all live with. After all, with 65 per cent of the traffic being Vincentians, including my own precious daughter Gabija, safety could not be trifled with.

*

Let me share with you a few final memories and reflections on Mustique.

I love the idea of throwing flowers at sunset from the shore into the blue Caribbean Sea, drinking a toast in champagne for a soul that will never join you again. A glorious sunset, for all the joy it evokes, still tells another day is gone, forecasting that another period will be over.

No one in Mustique expressed greater enthusiasm over the way the island should develop than Gilbert Le Coze. When I was contemplating my retirement from politics, he was furious because he did not want to conceive of the Grenadines without my guiding hand. No argument I could muster on the importance of continuity that would ensue after my resignation ever impressed him. Along with his sister Magui, and their chef Eric Rippert, they always had a table for me at their restaurant, Le Bernadin, in New York. Indeed, they once even hosted the lawyers who had worked for me on an agreement with the US on the procedures for intercepting ships with St. Vincent flags in international waters.

Sadly we had to throw flowers in the sea for Gilbert. He passed out in the gym in New York. Flowers in the sea at sunset is the Mustique goodbye.

The Mustique Board in its September meetings varied from London, New York, Toronto, Paris or wherever a board member chose to be host. My last was in New York and coincided with the UN Millennium Summit. Eric Shaw, the company lawyer since its inception, was our host. Paul Channon, now Lord Kelvedon since he resigned from the Thatcher Cabinet, was our chairman, and he presented me a silver model of Mustique at the dinner in the Waldorf Astoria. Paul had paid the price for being in Mustique at the wrong time. A Minister of Transport could not be out of England on holiday while a plane crashed in Lockerbie.

My role in Mustique throughout the decades was simply to promote the climate for investment while I protected the public interest.

My friend Jeannette Cadet had risen to prominence in Mustique following her management of the OECS pavilion in Vancouver and management of the villa rentals, astutely also surviving on the tight-rope between demanding homeowners and excitable visitors. She and the Hon. Brian Alexander managed the villas and catered to the fantasies of the celebrities, helping to mould Mustique into a destination to satisfy the meticulous. Brian Alexander had inherited from his noble father, a Field Marshall, a strategy toward life that allowed him to plan an advance on a new territory, and know when to keep the guns silent and consolidate. To his eternal credit, ages before the emergence of glamour in Mustique he kept the dream of the island alive in the days when there was no money even to cut the grass. He survived the retinue of company chairmen, becoming the self-effacing boss of Mustique, quietly aware of the turbulence simmering beneath the surface choosing well his opportunity to become a homeowner with his superb beach villa. I arranged for him to be invested with the CMG (Companion of the Order of St. Michael and St. George) by the Queen for his contribution to tourism in the islands. He had inherited the "honourable" title, so I had pleasure in ensuring he received an insignia he earned.

And with the German engineer Peter Ernst meticulously supervising technical operations, the island functioned. As the first set of designers and builders departed, Tony Milsom from England, with his years of tropical experience in Barbados, moved into prominence, easily blending an elegant ambience into the Grenadines scenery as sought by the new elite. Local contractors, nurtured under Swedish and Italian influence, also emerged. Quality smoothly flourished.

In the vacuum in medical services which Dr. Gun-Monro declined, as did other Vincentians refusing to abandon lucrative practice in the capital, there was opportunity for the adventurous. Michael Bunbury agreed to settle in Mustique, bring up his hearty young family, endure the myriad complaints of workers and the demanding emergencies of the visitors, while his wife Lottie designed her unique silk sarongs to be made in China. His care of Princess Margaret during her sad decline earned recognition by the Queen.

The competitive modern world is made up of thrivers and survivors. So too Mustique. The thrivers can comfortably sell their assets derived from their encounter with Mustique and retire into indolence in other corners of the globe, be it up-country America, England or South Africa. Meantime the long-suffering survivors, faithfully plodding on amidst restrictions, are lucky to be debt free in a modern home in St. Vincent before old age, with its attendant infirmity, descends.

But the beautiful serenity of Mustique was ruffled one evening. Tatiana Copeland, getting ready to build her Moroccan motif on a hilltop in the south, had thrown a sumptuous birthday party in *Rosa dei Venti*. It was one of those "everyone on the island" evenings. A glamorous ambience with the distant lights of other Grenadine islands embellishing the skyline: fine wines and champagne, exotic canapés, delicate presentations, and the world discussed. The next morning we all learnt that Susie Mostberger, a regular visitor, and who had sat with her plate on the arm of my chair, was dead. I rushed to the scene. I knew I had to do my utmost and this meant a rush back to the office. I called the French Ambassador in St. Lucia, notifying about what had happened to her citizen on holiday from Strasbourg. I requested her

65. With Prince Hans-Adam II of Liechtenstein, Bryan Jeeves and Burns Bonadie

66. Playing golf at St. Andrew's, Scotland with Lester Bird, CHOGM Conference

67. With Athneal Ollivierre (right) and his whaling successor "Baylum" Ollivierre

68. With President Mandela in New Zealand, CHOGM Conference

69. With President Jerry Rawlings of Ghana

70. With President Museveni of Uganda at CHOGM Conference

71. Dressed up in the market in The Gambia

72. Prime Minister Mahathir of Malaysia meeting the ladies from church in Paget Farm, Bequia

73. Meeting President Chen Sui Bian of Taiwan on his inauguration

74. Meeting President of the World Bank Jim Wolfensohn in Prague

75. Meeting Fidel Castro on official visit
    to Cuba

76. United Nations address

77. With Prime Minister Margaret
    Thatcher at 10 Downing Street

78. Receiving the Alumni Award of
    Distinction from University of British
    Columbia with daughter Louise, 1988

79. Meeting President George Bush Sr. at the White House

80. With President Jacques Chirac of France at Sommet France Cariforum, Guadeloupe, March 2000

81. With President Bill Clinton and wife Hillary at Summit of the Americas

82. With Canadian Prime Minster Brian Mulroney

83. With President Ronald Reagan, Caspar Weinberger and George Brizan (Grenada Minister)

84. With Edward Seaga of Jamaica

85. With Lee Kuan Yew, Singapore

86. With Antal József, observing the Hungarian elections,
Budapest, 1990

87. With Walter Mondale co-leading
election team in Nicarague

88. Enthronement of the Emperor of
Japan with daughter Sabrina, 1990

89. With President Mbeki and his wife and Chief Anyaoku and his wife at Durban
CHOGM Conference

90. Cyprus CHOGM with Robert Mugabe, Cheddi Jagan (Guyana), Goh Chok Chung in
friendlier days

91. With Perez de Cuellar at the United Nations

92. Caribbean Heads of Government, 1991; Front: John Compton (St. Lucia), Sir Lynden
Pindling (Bahamas), John Osborne (Montserrat), Kennedy Simmonds (St. Kitts/
Nevis), Eugenia Charles (Dominica), ANR Robinson (Trinidad & Tobago)
back: Lavitty Stoutt (BVI), Desmond Hoyte (Guyana), Rodney Williams (Antigua),
Roderick Rainford (Secretary General), Michael Manley (Jamaica), Erskine Sandiford
(Barbados), Nicholas Braithwaite (Grenada), self, George Price (Belize)

pathologist and security presence and chartered a plane to bring them immediately, as she said she could not find a plane. It was a difficult time for us, anxious to preserve the idyll of the island, when motive for murder could not be confined to our shores. We even amended the law to recognize French laboratories in our system. Despite all the efforts of the French authorities and our own, questions still remain.. The French media ploughed on.

It was a better experience in the Great House, celebrating the Millennium with the families of Lawrence Stroll and Tommy Hilfiger. There was champagne sealed in wax and sunk in the Baltic for most of the century and secured through auction, Cheval Blanc 1900, all out of reach of a banana dollar Prime Minister. I could only reminisce about the sailor on my father's ship, early in the century who reported on foreign ladies with perfume costing a dollar a drop. I was also quite embarrassed when Lawrence invited me on another occasion to dine with Denzel Washington, and neither of us had heard of each other.

The artistic coming of age of Mustique arrived with Felix Dennis' sculpture. After all Rome had for 400 years preserved the inspiring Raphael Fountain of Tortoises, Fontana delle Tartarughe. Why should Mustique not commemorate the glory of romance in perpetuity, with a sculpture of two buxom tortoises copulating forever?

In Paris, after I had already retired, showing the sights to our daughter Gabija, Jeannette called up Bethy Lucas who promptly invited us to tea in her home not far from the French Ministry of Agriculture. Then we were to meet her partner Jean Luc La Gardiere at Le Duc Restaurant off Boulevard Raspail, and occupy Mitterand's favourite table. Surprisingly Diego Aria and his new wife Maria were in town. So we had a Mustique evening. Great wine. Great seafood. Jean Luc was relaxed. That day he had concluded the purchase of Vivendi's French interests, placing him on the pinnacle of French publishing. Billions again. We discussed the tensions at the UN over Iraq, the protests in Venezuela, aviation industry competition between Europe and the US, between Airbus and Boeing. Jean Luc was sure that France and the US would be together, that there would be a *grande rapprochement* before any battle in Iraq. Diego, with his experience as Chairman of the Security Council in the Gulf War, could give us real insights. Jeannette found it really offensive when I took out my camera to record the evening. I could not imagine that it would be our last evening with Jean Luc. His obituaries reached me back in Bequia. He was not going to attend another of my birthday parties for Gabija at Macaroni Beach, as he had said he would love to do again.

*

The sequel to my meeting with the Kuwaiti sheik at the Japanese Emperor's Enthronement took place in Washington. I had brought along my Minister of Works, Jerry Scott, to the meetings of the World Bank and IMF where I hoped he'd glean a little fiscal expertise and discipline. I had kept in touch with the Kuwaiti Foreign Ministry exchanging Christmas cards, apparently appreciated even in a Muslim country. After the Environmental Summit in Brazil, Kennedy Simmonds of St. Kitts and my Foreign Minister Alpian Allen informed me that the Amir of Kuwait had announced that the restored Kuwait was ready to give some assistance to us.

At the following WB/IMF meetings in Washington I sought out the Director General of the Kuwaiti Fund for Arab Economic Development, Bader al Humadhi, a tall, distinguished Arab with a penchant for worry beads. From the day we met we became friends, and I was anxious to draw down a new source of funds with alacrity.

Realizing that an oil-producing country would find it appropriate to fund an electrical diesel generator, I promptly switched the package already prepared for European Investment Bank funding to the Kuwaitis and had it before Bader before he left Washington. He was anxious to get to see and know our islands, so we fixed a tentative date for his visit.

When he arrived, we ate at a restaurant under new (mis)management. It was a disaster. I informed our guests that lunch would be in Mustique the next day, and had Randy Cato charter a plane, and book lunch at the poolside of the Cotton House. My friend Mario Ferrari received us for coffee in his "Blackstone Villa" and we were all set to secure Kuwaiti loans before anyone else in the Caribbean.

We made our first visit to Kuwait. We toured the looted Museum. We visited the home of Loay Al Karafi which had been totally wrecked and later restored, the golden faucets gleaming, the new crystal chandeliers replacing those that had been stolen and shipped to Iraq. We were excited by the distinctive national Arab styles in the building that housed the Arab Fund. Our first loan was for diesel generators.

Then came the magnificent cruise-ship berth, jointly financed by the Kuwaiti Fund and the European Investment Bank. I had to return to Kuwait to settle the structure of the joint financing and procurement procedures, an experiment not to be repeated. I took along the young economist Isaac Solomon for the exposure. We all learnt that it would be better to compartmentalize funding on different components of projects in the future. And by the time I left office the Kuwaitis were ready to join with Taiwan and France in the extension and improvement of our airport at Arnos Vale. I had to visit Kuwait again.

Next came Europe and bananas – Europe, the US, Latin America and Chiquita. What a war! And how do you get the farmers at home to understand the Banana War? To secure our banana trading status with a Europe preparing for the Single Market and the convergence of the EEC into the EU post-1993 constituted a monumental task. France and Spain were friends, but we had to go all the way into every European capital to secure a qualified majority vote in favour of our banana exports. And when I explained it all to the farmers in their annual convocation, pleading with them to be aware of the new quality standards required by our major markets, all I got was, "Roads, we want roads."

I should explain the intricacies of the Banana War and how our small farmers became ensnared by American vested interests in the Latin American plantations (the so-called banana republics), thus prying open our small share of the European market. The Banana War threatened our livelihood, becoming a drama played out around the world with diplomacy in mathematics yielding a nought for us.

The WTO came into being with its level-playing-field language, while our field workers on hilly slopes were earning US$20.00 per day, targeted to match $.20 cents per day on the vast plains of the Latin American Chiquita Plantations. I kept thinking what is it going to be like when America has to level the playing field with China?

In the 1950s, fresh out of university, I was a soil scientist in the Windward Islands, researching nematode infection and potassium deficiency in the banana fields. By the close of the twentieth century, I found myself as lead negotiator in the Banana War between the United States and Europe. I had recommended to the banana authorities in the islands, even while I was working in London in the early 1960s, that they should appoint a representative in the UK to guard their interest. Deemed a rolling stone, I was not considered to be a suitable person to implement my own suggestion.

In keeping with the old mercantile theory of the British Empire, as a colony we kept in place our two-tier tariff, one for British Commonwealth goods, and another for the rest of the world. Britain, too, effectively protected our exports of bananas to the United Kingdom. With the decline of sugar production, even as we were moving from colonial status to statehood, the precursor to independence, Britain was ensuring that we moved from grant-in-aid administration to self-sustaining growth, alas dependent on a protected banana market.

Suddenly, we were overproducing, and the first conflict emerged in a battle for market share between our English marketing company, Geest, who were handling Windwards bananas, and the other company, Elders and Fyffes, working with Jamaican producers. We sought British arbitration. The British Board of Trade indicated to us that we should settle the matter outside of Britain, as settlement in Britain would contravene the rules on monopoly. We duly negotiated a settlement in Puerto Rico, with the Windwards and Geest at 40 per cent of the market, and Jamaica and Fyffes at 40 per cent, leaving 20 per cent for the smaller agents. Britain recognized the agreement, and kept things going for us until independence, when we had to face the next hurdle, the implications of British entry into the European Economic Community, which then meant we had to get European agreement to save our place in the British market, especially as Europe moved towards the single market in 1993.

We had friends in Europe. Spain ensured the voters in the Canaries sustained parliamentary majorities. Portugal had similar interests in the Azores. France wanted to ensure that the 45,000 persons engaged in banana and sugar production in Martinique and Guadeloupe did not become a further drain on French social security. All these were deemed Community bananas, and we all fitted into the definition in various protocols in the European Commission as "traditional" suppliers. Germany, shrunken since Versailles in 1919, and without colonial appendages in Africa and the Pacific, was only interested in cheap bananas.

Then the Berlin Wall fell. Communism collapsed both in Europe and in the Caribbean, except for Cuba. We in the English-speaking islands fell off the geopolitical map, amidst the detritus of the Berlin Wall. The Grenada spotlight on the world stage had long been dimmed. America was ready for the pre-eminence of American companies.

Africa, the Caribbean and the Pacific remained united in the ACP grouping we had forged in 1973, and by the time the Lomé Convention was signed with Europe in 1975, productive arrangements were enshrined for traditional suppliers – Belize, Cameroon, Cape Verde, Dominica, Grenada, Ivory Coast, Jamaica, Madagascar, St. Lucia, St. Vincent, Somalia and Surinam. In 1990, the fourth ACP--EC Lomé Convention stipulated that "in respect of its banana exports to the Community markets, no ACP state shall be placed, as regards access to its present markets, in a less favourable position than in the past or at present."

The Dutch did not hesitate to tell me they had been free traders for centuries. I should target tourism. With the success of their company Interbetton building the airport, they would give US$75,000 to examine a cruise-ship terminal facility. Their consultants produced three options. The first was to extend the Grenadines jetty where all the chickens, goats, cattle, cement, furniture and trade, as well as passengers, moved between the islands. The second was to extend the port into shallower water and against the wind. The third, under the hill where I swam as a youth and knew to be suitable, was considered too expensive. Nevertheless, I convinced them that there was no suitable alternative to the last. Always in dealing with foreign consultants you have to know clearly what is inadmissible.

But in Europe we made the other point. While tourism was the medium- and long-term strategy, we needed the weekly circulation of the banana dollar to keep social stability in the islands to preserve and increase that tourism. France needed to keep 45,000 persons employed in subsidized agriculture in Martinique and Guadeloupe to prevent unrest.

George Bush succeeded President Reagan. He appointed Carla Hills, a formidable lady, to lead the American attack in establishing the rules of the World Trade Organization. He received all of us from the OECS in his office and gave us a wonderful audience. At the end of it his gracious wife joined us and I stole her away from the group.

My colleagues were impressed. "Son, what the hell you kept chatting so long with Mrs. Bush about!"

"Dogs," I said. "You fellas don't read your literature. The Embassy circulated copies of the book written by her dog Millie. I told her that every American President had a dog, but no other would ever write a biography."

The President arranged an instant audience with Carla Hills. Eugenia Charles led our group to Carla's office. My Ambassador Kingsley Layne and Jamaica's Richard Bernal who were carrying much of the intellectual arguments on our trade and subsidy accompanied us.

Eugenia was ready to fume. Appropriately dressed in fiery red she was ready to take on the redoubtable Carla Hills, seated beneath a photograph of her receiving a crowbar from President Bush, the tool with which she was ready to crack all skulls before her. Eugenia, an independent heiress and the darling of the Washington Republicans ever since her sortie on television beside President Reagan requesting troops to liberate Grenada from communism, was ready to blast.

"If you destroy my bananas I will kill you!"

Never in the history of diplomatic negotiations had a meeting begun and ended so precipitously. You needed an ice plough to clear the freeze. Back to officials and committees. The graceful meeting with the President was dead and buried.

Dominica had really benefited from US aid under Eugenia's leadership. When I saw a drunk with a T-shirt labelled "We're fed up with Eugenia," I could only reflect on Eugenia's banana salvo to Carla Hills: What Price Glory? And when I witnessed one of her successors, the Labour Prime Minister Rosie Douglas, pleading with President Chirac to make Dominica a part of France, a request justified on the basis of the great number of Dominicans in Guadeloupe's jails, what a contrast to the brave and bold Eugenia blasting Carla Hills.

The next challenge was the looming 1993 Single European Act, unifying the banana regime. A further complication was the convergence of the GATT into the WTO. Without the benefit of costly embassies in Europe, we all had to mount missions to European capitals to plead our cause, while the Latin American countries in league with American multinationals mounted challenges to our diplomatic initiatives. More than any other Prime Minister in the Caribbean, I was quite familiar with the European scene as a result of my rambunctious hitch-hiking days. Eugenia Charles, John Compton and I split up Europe, with me in the south and they in the north, occasionally overlapping. I did not bother to return to the Netherlands after I was told that the Dutch were free traders since the fourteenth century. I was more comfortable in Italy and Spain.

Waging the Banana War became more complicated each day. The indifference of our farmers to the 1993 marketing regime in Europe was certainly not the response in the trade-liberalizing world. The Latin Americans with their expensive and well-appointed embassies in Europe could not understand how we overcame their lobbying against us. Our message was simple. The combination of our democracy, our hilly country, and no economies of scale in small islands made us uncompetitive. We were not fighting for more than 3 per cent of the world trade in bananas. The hurricane-relief package from Europe was only a survival package; we needed the benefits of trade to sustain us.

Regulation 404 of 1993 awarded a quota of 2.2 million tonnes for Latin American bananas, and each of us in the ACP got an autonomous quota. In an attempt to further unify the market and to provide an inducement to traders and operators to handle the more costly ACP and European bananas, a system of "B" licences gave them a share of import licences for "dollar bananas."

We managed to get this all in place with the European Union with a qualified majority vote, Germany, Belgium, the Netherlands and Denmark objecting. However, we sent a prime-ministerial delegation to meet the Danes, who held the chairmanship of the Council of Ministers, and so we influenced a critical vote in our favour.

Excitement raged in the regional media with the news that the new President of the United States, William Jefferson Clinton, would meet the leaders of the Caribbean big Four: Jamaica, Trinidad, Guyana and Barbados. We were excluded. What did I have to say? My answer was crystal clear, namely, how dare I tell an American President how to do his business? Then came the second release, that Vice President Gore would see the rest of us. We consulted. We decided that Dame Eugenia Charles of Washington/Reagan media fame would represent us with a troop of Ministers. One Prime Minister only. The rest declined the invitation.

The upcoming convention of my New Democratic Party in a country village had the usual American Embassy representative. I told him, "I like America. I have great American friends and we love their tourists. Washington needs to know a lot more about us. There are not two classes of Prime Ministers in the Caribbean, those who meet with Presidents and those who meet with Vice Presidents." And I let him know that my beautiful islands would survive, and I was not hungry, thanks to smart grandparents!

Bananas then became the focal point of our foreign relations. When Clinton's Secretary of State, Warren Christopher, kept calling me one weekend at the Frangipani, lobbying to install ex-president Cesar Gaviria of Colombia as Secretary General of the OAS, and secure him sanctuary away from the drug lords, he seemed aghast to learn that Colombia's banana policy had already earned my support, rather than the American *imperium.*

When Bill Clinton won the presidency, I won a five dollars' wager with the British Representative by betting that Perot would pass 15 per cent of the vote. Ken Boyea, the manager of our flour mill, had a sister, Betty, who was close to Clinton in Arkansas, and we made it to Little Rock before Christmas, meeting some of his confidants. I warned that Haiti would be a flashpoint and that I thought I could help. But Little Rock was thinking about how to divide the new Washington spoils, not about foreign policy toward a black island. The mayor of Little Rock gave me a key to the city.

The Venezuelan Embassy in Haiti had become the refuge for President Jean Bertrand Aristide, the charismatic Catholic priest driven from office by the military. Our patois-speaking colleagues in Dominica and St. Lucia were superbly qualified to monitor the elections there on our behalf. The poor were sure that salvation and manna from heaven would descend with the ascent of Aristide. The day before the election our monitoring team, led by John Compton, decided to go to the market and purchase some art, only to escape back to their vehicle in fear of the irate vendors unable to sell their wares. "Tomorrow Aristide will be President!" they predicted to Compton.

The deposed Aristide came up with Carlos Andres Perez from Venezuela to meet with us. A military plane deposited us in Cane Field, a runway in Dominica, just before sundown. And so we were ready to do our part to restore democracy in Haiti. I had met with Aristide a few times in Washington and New York. His spirits were high, even though the negative gossip about his lifestyle was drifting through the diplomatic corridors.

Meanwhile, I left Washington for some Miami shopping. The United States Ambassador at home, Jeannette Hyde, a charming, elegant North Carolina lady, had left a number for me to call.

"The President wishes to meet with you and all Caribbean leaders at the White House tomorrow," she informed me.

"I just left Washington."

"Sorry. We did not get you in time."

"How do I get back to Washington? It is Saturday night."

"We will make the arrangements."

At five o'clock there was the knock on my door. My Secret Service escort was ready. And so I was dutifully deposited in the White House and committed myself with my colleagues and the Czech Ambassador to join in the liberation of Haiti with my dozen soldiers in our Special Forces. The Clinton Administration was preparing for its first foreign policy success, keeping the black Haitian boat people out of Miami. No one had taken up my offer made long before in Little Rock, Arkansas.

Jeannette Hyde's diplomacy had some early tests. Her mission had issued a statement to the effect that all political parties in St. Vincent were supported by the drug trade. A prominent lawyer in the opposition was well known to be the defender of the dealers in the courts, but I was not aware of any drug money in my campaign. I wrote a blistering letter to the Embassy refuting their "unsubstantiated allegations" which like mud, if enough were thrown, would to some extent stick.

I invited her and her husband to tour our islands. She came, accompanied by her DEA specialist. We were entertained in Mustique. She got a feel for the confidence we inspired from those celebrity home-owners absolutely distant from the drug trade. The brilliantly lit Mustique, the last set of lights bordering the Atlantic all the way to Africa, we understood to be the navigation point for the nefarious. The South American clique were flying our way in the night, and we needed the responses from the satellites to do our part. I explained the problems caused by our geography.

I showed the Ambassador my island, Isle à Quatre, all 400 acres of it in the family for a century. We visited our hotels, and she took a room at the Frangipani. The hotel was full and I put up the DEA agent in my home, inviting him to swab every corner. I threw a party for all the American home-owners in Bequia, suggesting that she summon them to the Embassy and discover all the gossip behind my back, as they knew everything that was going on in the islands. After dinner, the Ambassador, the DEA agent and I talked into the night.

"If there is something you know that I don't please tell me. I am what you call in your country old money. We have a lot of property, but I don't want to enjoy life out of the anguish of others."

We signed up to marijuana-eradication programmes in the hills and to interceptions at sea from Venezuela and Colombia.

The next call from Ambassador Jeanette Hyde found me at a Finance Meeting in Malta.

"President Clinton wishes to proceed with the international force into Haiti, and we would like to get your men."

"But what's all this I am hearing about President Carter and General Powell settling the problem."

"Prime Minister, we still need your people. Jamaica seems to have changed its mind, and they are getting Caricom to wait on a report from their Admiral."

I never knew Jamaica had a Navy, let alone an Admiral, and President Carter, what was this modern-day St. Jude, patron saint of lost causes, up to? I knew from Nicaragua what the Republicans thought about him.

"Ambassador Hyde, I am not the Grand Old Duke of York. You can rely on me."

"What do you mean, Duke of York?"

My southern aristocrat had apparently not been brought up in English poetry. American foreign policy could rely on my obstinacy. I quoted:

"The Grand Old Duke of York,
He had ten thousand men,
He marched them up to the top of the hill and he
marched them down again.

And when they were up they were up, and when they were down
   they were down
And when they were only half way up
They were neither up nor down."

My men, I assured the Ambassador, would be ready for deployment. Get them to Haiti. I was not going to let American foreign policy, in the words of another nursery rhyme, to be like the cheese, standing alone. After all I may not have the opportunity to come to the rescue of America again – Uncle Sam needed me!

And so my dozen troops landed with the Americans in Haiti. Aristide was restored to power. My troops witnessed real poverty and would never again feel that our St. Vincent was poor. After a few weeks, the Jamaican Admiral deemed Haiti to be safe for his men to land. Caricom followed suit.

In due course I dispatched my Deputy Commissioner of Police, William Harry, to inspect our men in Haiti. I wanted the leadership of my police force to savour the sadness, the hunger, the deprivation and absolute misery induced by unrelenting misrule. Let him witness the squalid life in the gutters and open sewers on our doorstep. It might toughen him up, ensuring our standards did not slide. Haiti had known success early in its history. The slave leaders had outsmarted France and Napoleon, and won their independence. But corruption set in and through the centuries, it had led to poverty and despair among its people. Haiti needed to start all over again. A war-ruined West Germany started again, but it was, even with its division into two countries, a *big* country. A big country supported by its conquerer, the United States. But how does a *small* country start again? Especially if it is not supported by the greatest superpower the world has ever known. It is not easy for a small country that falls foul of America. I can attest to that. But our few troops were there – a condom over US policy.

President Clinton was getting ready for the greatest occasion of all times in our hemisphere, the Summit of the Americas, to be held in Miami. The Presidential Envoy, former Congressman William Gray, had toured the region, and among other things I told him was that force had to be used to remove the military junta in Haiti. Jean Bertrand Aristide, the exiled President in Washington, seemed to be a bit of an embarrassment. During the IMF/World Bank meetings, I had hosted a meeting of Caricom leaders at a breakfast session at the Wyndham Bristol Hotel, co-ordinated by my Ambassador Kingsley Layne. We told the media that Caricom recognized Aristide, a gesture for which the lonely exiled leader was grateful.

All of us in the Caribbean leadership were excited about the Summit of the Americas. With experience of the Commonwealth Heads of Government Meetings where informal get-togethers were the routine, we expected some of this with the various Presidents and Prime Ministers. But lo and behold, the final preparations among delegates at Airlie House in Virginia, drafting the Declaration and Plan of Action, totally excluded reference to our vital banana industry. The Americans and the Latins were pleased that this was so.

We were fortunately at the same time holding a meeting of the OECS Authority in Dominica. I received word from Ambassador Layne about the banana exclusion. Promptly we decided that the East Caribbean states would not be attending any Summit if bananas were not to be discussed. Layne held his *tête-à-tête* with Thomas "Mack" McKarty III, the Presidential Envoy, who secured the subject's inclusion by the direct intervention of President Clinton himself.

Our special banana meeting took place at the Baltimore Hotel on Friday 9 December, 1994. Ambassador Mickey Kantor, United States Trade Representative, promised US co-operation and understanding in addressing the critical issues of the smaller economies. My Foreign Minister Alpian Allen and Ambassador Layne felt satisfied that our Airlie intervention was bearing fruit.

After the Miami Conference, the US reverted to the old position. My best recollection of the conference was a friendly chat during the evening boat cruise with Mrs. Clinton. I did not and could not anticipate then that one of her earliest pronouncements as a New York Senator would be in support of the banana industry in the Caribbean. She joined the ranks of other distinguished ladies who had stood up for our cause, such as Mrs. Thatcher, and Mrs. Glenys Kinnock in the European Parliament.

Philip Hughes, who had been the American Ambassador in the Bush Administration, breakfasted with me at Montrose overlooking Kingstown, lobbying for the American position on bananas.

"You needn't worry about me, Your Excellency," I told him. "Should you bring about the collapse of the banana industry and create the vacuum for the drug dealers, you'll be dealing with another Prime Minister. I'll be gone."

During the Clinton presidency, Philip returned to see me, this time in his true colours. He was advocating we link up with Chiquita.

I love America, particularly a place like Vermont where they outlaw advertisements on the highways and where nature is allowed to be supreme. Trained as a scientist, I respect the brilliance of American research. But it seems as though no virtue other than American virtue exists. I was in Geneva on my way home, in the Hotel du Rhone, in 2001 when the television screens exploded with the Twin Towers collapse. Though already retired by then, I called on my New Democratic Party to hold a candlelight vigil at Democrat House to signify our empathy with America. The Embassy expressed thanks.

Henceforth it looks as though we should take our guidance from Mark Twain, supporting friends even when we know they are wrong. But it would be great if we were invited to subscribe to the error!

The Appellate Body of the WTO ruled against our banana regime in 1997, and the EC introduced a new system, which was challenged by Ecuador. The panel ruled in Ecuador's favour, and this further defeat allowed the WTO to impose trade sanctions amounting to US$191 million against the EU. Naboa of Ecuador and the American companies Chiquita, Dole and Del Monte, were unrelenting. Chiquita even tried to buy into our interests. We refused. We set up a regional negotiating machinery under Sir Alister McIntyre and Sonny Ramphal as technical experts reporting to Prime Minister Patterson of Jamaica and to Caricom, while Ambassador Edwin Laurent (East Caribbean) kept his finger on the pulse in Brussels and Ambassadors Kingsley Layne (St. Vincent and the Grenadines) and Richard Bernal (Jamaica) studied Washington manoeuvres.

We deployed Washington lobbyists. I enrolled friends from the International Democrat Union to use their influence. The Black Caucus had their say. Randall Robinson dumped bananas at the entrance of the office of the US Trade Representative. Alas, the Chiquita dream in the Lincoln bedroom was to become the nightmare of our farmers in the hills. The *Cincinnati Enquirer*, in a headline dated Sunday May 3rd, 1998, entitled "Contributions buy influence", spoke of the US helping Chiquita fight tarriffs in Europe, Island economies on the line, and contributions buying influence". The article stated that CEO of Chiquita, Carl Lindner had spent two nights in the White House and had influence on both sides of the aisle in Congress, making large financial contributions to both parties. We were losing the battle. The turbulent twentieth century was not destined to close with any inspiration for our trade in the New World Order. Islands at sea, again.

There were also skirmishes at home. It was difficult to explain the negotiations in distant Europe and America to country farmers. In their eyes, there was always a market for bananas. They never questioned "whose" bananas. When I lectured them on new quality standards, I felt I was fighting the politician's persistent battle against visions of "what ought to be." At every general meeting, when I outlined the difficulties we faced abroad, all I could get was a cry of "roads, roads, we want roads." I did not have the courage to reply that some roads lead to a dead end. I knew I had to pursue our cause in spite of their ingratitude.

The United States, in response to the WTO decision, imposed import duties of 100 per cent on luxury goods from Europe, including cheeses from France, Italy and Greece, Italian leather goods and cashmere garments, and German equipment. (The Scottish cashmere fraternity quite rightly screamed.) The European Ministers with whom we negotiated were constantly changing. We had to explain again and again to new Ministers. American policy did not change between Republicans and Democrats.

The banana regime had moved into a system where only operators, or registered companies that had imported bananas during the specific reference period, were eligible for import licences. My proposal to establish our presence with the joint purchase of Geest Industries with the Irish firm, Fyffes, allowed our industry to survive.

Throughout the exercise we were at pains to explain to the world that we, with our hilly topography and our thousands of small farmers, could not compete in production costs with the vast flat plains of Latin America. Their fiscal policies had devalued their currencies. Our democracies could not compete with dictatorship. Did Europe want our quality of life to descend into the miseries of hunger and exploitation found in the "banana republics"? Did they want our social structure to collapse and carry down the tourism alternative we were trying to create? We needed time to diversify. We sought protection as we diversified. The banana dollar circulating each week in our islands helped to create a property-owning democracy propelled by my land-reform programme, in stark contrast to what was happening in Latin America.

There was a time when our trade in fruit and vegetables within the Caribbean dominated the economy. Banana income at independence in 1979 was EC$15.8 million. With the dynamism of our land reform programme and in response to the European regime, our banana income peaked at EC$102 million in 1992. We were able to generate a surplus on recurrent account and meet the counterpart contribution to external concessionary financing on development projects. Expenditure on education and health tripled, our per capita income doubled. Cement imports escalated and pleasing homes sprang up amidst the lush greenery of the banana fields. With the inputs of electricity, telephones, jetties, roads and airports, the private sector in the Grenadines (formerly defined as dependencies of St. Vincent) began to flourish. Tourism boomed. The beauty and serenity of the islands reached out to the discerning. Then, while banana protection in Europe shrank, tourism exceeded bananas. By 1997, banana income had declined to EC$37 million and tourism was up to EC$190 million. We were into another round of restructuring our economy, this time into services.

Whenever we lost revenue with declining production, caused too by drought and hurricane, Europe produced a stabilization fund, kept in the bank in Brussels and released in medicinal proportions. Europe's sanction against genetically modified beef also got mixed up in the Banana War. America and Europe came to terms in 2001. Our protection was agreed to the end of 2005. With luck and a little panache, you can only defer the inevitable.

I left office before I could get a monument built in memory of the Banana Farmer. Our only monument is to soldiers killed in the First World War.

I knew that our neighbours, including the American territory St. Croix, had had a dusty time with the murder of Americans. We too had the unfortunate legacy of the unexplained murder of the Commodore of the New York Yacht Club, on a lonely coast on a dark night. Terrible, if a single American is killed. I never expected such wrath if an American killed a Vincentian. The horror this time was not murder, but justice on trial.

I can still recall with great vividness the morning in bright sunshine three days after Joseph's disappearance, and the discovery of his beached water taxi in Hamilton, his native village. On that sunny morning, the floating body of Jolly Joseph, swollen and bullet-scarred, was fished out of the water by the crew of the small freighter, *Kingfisher*, and landed on the jetty. The corpse's unceremonious arrival attracted me to the scene, along with hundreds of Joseph's irate, shouting friends, who had been searching all this time for his body. I dispersed the crowd, assuring them that justice would be done. "Please go home quietly," I urged.

The police took the body to the mortuary. A postmortem was performed, pictures taken, forensic analysis begun. Two Americans, James and Penelope Fletcher, husband and estranged wife, the last to be in the company of Jolly Joseph alive, were taken in for questioning and charged for murder. Their preliminary trial took place in the new Paget Farm Magistrate's Court (rebuilt with funds provided ironically under the American Justice Improvement Project) and looking splendid.

Paula David, a Jamaican with secure tenure appointed as Magistrate by the Judicial and Legal Services Commission of the entire East Caribbean (not by St. Vincent under my jurisdiction), with storm clouds of hostility gathering around her by the American media, committed James and Penelope Fletcher to stand trial in the Supreme Court, there being sufficient evidence for the case to go forward.

An interview was requested of me by a team commissioned by American television. They came to Shrewsbury House one Sunday evening, arranged where I could be seated, fixed my tie, and asked me to explain our judicial system, how Magistrates and Judges were appointed, how the institutions functioned. I took pains to explain the various appeal procedures and that the final judgment was totally beyond Caribbean control in the Judicial Committee of the Privy Council in London.

It was murder in paradise. Not a single word, not a single frame of my interview was included in the scathing attack by Ted Koppel of CBS on St. Vincent and our legal system. The American people had to be protected. Fletcher came from a wealthy family in Virginia.

The American Consul from Barbados took up residence. He had all the access he wanted to his jailed citizens. A special dietician was assigned to ensure balanced nutrition for the American inmates (the lady put on weight). Dr. Johnny Cheltenham of Barbados and Dr. Ralph Gonsalves, a prominent local criminal lawyer well-established in the defence of drug dealers in the region, represented the Fletchers.

Our Superintendent of Prisons, Bernard Marksman, came to my office. He revealed that Mrs. Fletcher had requested a visit from a Catholic priest. The priest had come to see her, and a confessional was arranged. She confessed to the priest that she had killed Jolly Joseph and she sought forgiveness. A female warden overheard the confession. I instructed the Prison Superintendent to get a written record from the warden, but said that it would not be released. I would be saying nothing. Nor should he.

In response to the CBS onslaught, it was decided that I should go on American television, CNN and Fox News, accompanied by a trusted friend, the South Carolina lawyer and Professor in the Colombia Law School, Tim Scrantom, who practised law in the United States, Britain and St. Vincent. He would be eminently suited to carry the message of fairness to the American people. We were briefed by another friend, Dick Reed.

And so to a studio in Miami, and Greta van Susteren and her programme "Burden of Proof." In the room where Tim and I were, audio only was arranged. We could hear her and the other person on the interview, a friend of the Fletchers. The cameras were on us, the ear-pieces connected. The interview began. In the intervening time it takes to hear the question being transmitted, and before I could hear the question and give an answer, there was another blast. She was neither interested in my reply nor in any fact about our judicial system. Finally, I could take her abuse no more. I blasted out: "Listen, woman..." I did not, however, reveal the confession. I preferred to take the abuse than undermine my judicial system; even though I knew taped evidence in prison was used in the United States courts.

The Fox interview was more civilized. Unfortunately it was not seen in the West Indies. Vincentians in New York and the world over were horrified. At the Jamaica Conference, the Heads of Government issued a statement in support of the integrity of our judicial process.

Then came the Barbados meeting with President Clinton. Our agenda dealt with free trade in the Americas. I was briefed by Caricom officials on my two-minute address to the President. It was clear, though, the American media was not interested in our trade discussions. It was not a story to be followed. They were only interested in the Monica Lewinsky scandal and the President's involvement.

As we were leaving the meeting President Clinton, who had caused me to rush my troops to Haiti, enquired about the Fletchers' trial. Almost as a reflex gesture, he tried to bring down an American curtain on the drama of the disgraceful behaviour of an American, Penny Fletcher.

"I can't interfere, Mr. President, but I can assure you the trial will be fair."

"I have to ask. I hope you don't mind."

"Not at all, sir."

It was totally inappropriate, I thought, that I should bring to his attention the disreputable behaviour of his citizen. I assumed as a lawyer who studied in England that he would know how the Privy Council functioned in the Commonwealth.

But the American media which supported the President had their own version. "The Prime Minister was spoken to." I was back in primary school learning the past participle and being lectured to like a rebellious schoolboy. And Madeline Albright was poised, too, to have her say, cancelling the appointment with me after her President had already intervened by questioning our justice.

Roger Durham, a retired American who was knowledgeable about weapons and was living in Bequia while researching the surrender of St. Vincent in the eighteenth-century Carib Wars, testified about the time and type of gun that was fired, as he heard it, on the night of the fatal shooting. The sound was the same as a previous incident in which Penny Fletcher had shot up her dinghy on the beach during her birthday celebrations. Other Americans who knew Jolly Joseph from his protective guidance to their children over the years, Ray and Molly Snead, owners of the classic French House in Bequia, were not ashamed to reveal the facts as they knew them about the character of Jolly Joseph. Businessmen Nolly Simmons and Nik Kuhne testified that they had heard the accused boast that she "would kill a nigger before she left the Caribbean." Peg Murta and Mary Cororan of Connecticut, regular visitors over 20 years to Bequia and thoroughly familiar with the scene, wrote in rage to CBS and Ted Koppel.

The American Embassy kept on top of the case with its frequent presence in Bequia and St. Vincent. The witnesses to Penny Fletcher's shooting-up of her dinghy were warned by Sandra Ingram, a US Foreign Service Officer, that visas would not be available to them to travel to the United States. Their testimony was thrown out by the Judge.

The morning that the trial was about to conclude, and before the Judge instructed the jury, I received a call from Audrey Ballantyne, manager of the Camelot Inn where the Fletcher family were staying for the duration of trial, informing me that the Fletchers were in a jubilant mood, and were checking out. They were sure their son and his wife would be released.

So said, so done. The Judge did not permit the jury to deliberate. The Fletcher father left the Court and read out his written statement about his satisfaction with the trial. But I knew that the trial was over before it started.

The Internet, however, revealed more. Bruce Zagaris, a lawyer with extensive knowledge into lobbying, published a 21-page dossier called "Lost in Paradise: Lobbying strategies for Public International Law Issues." It pointed out how Washington supported Americans charged abroad. Before I left office, I decided in the final political campaign in Hamilton, the village of Jolly Joseph, to unburden my conscience and inform the family and the village that I had known before the trial was completed that Penny Fletcher had confessed to a Catholic priest that she shot Jolly Joseph.

The next week, a Catholic priest sought audience with me in the Prime Ministers' Office. It was the Irish priest, Father Jim. He had listened to my meeting in the village.

"I would never have taken the confession in the prison if I knew it was overheard," he said.

"So you are the priest who heard the confession."

"Yes. But the Catholic Church does not hear confessions if they are overheard by someone else." Father Jim too had to unburden his conscience.

I met our Acting Chief Justice, now Sir Denis Byron, when we were both passing through Puerto Rico. We were unfortunately having difficulties getting all the Prime Ministers to agree on his confirmation. I wanted him to be appointed unanimously, as our constitutions stipulated, and was refusing to compromise with changing the rules to appointment by consensus.

Denis commiserated. Like retired Judge "Sleepy Smith" whose analysis in the Barbados press upheld the dignity of our process, he realized that it was not Jolly Joseph, but me as Prime Minister, our systems and government that went on trial. And we were both aware of the form of the external pressures exerted.

Penny Fletcher, I gathered, was divorced on the Fletchers' return to the United States. We in the Caribbean have got to demonstrate to the world that we are not all stupid. We also have pride. Only the hungry have to be obsequious. Small states, though, are not always recognized as nations. Seeking to extend the destiny of a small state was always an encounter with reality, beautifully illuminated by the fishermen. "Big fish eat small fish, small fish eat mud." Fortunately there are no territorial boundaries to the mind.

The trial of the Fletchers was not the only occasion when we had to face up to America in order to preserve our integrity and way of life. Throughout the Cold War, with socialism in the Caribbean often tolerant to communism, I dared to be a liberal politician, building up my hotel business, and standing whenever justified with the United States. The floods of literature from East Germany, Czechoslovakia, Hungary, Russia and North Korea did not influence me. I was the first to call publicly for intervention in Grenada when the tiger they were riding consumed them, as I had anticipated.

Nothing dramatized the difference between Opposition and Government like the attention emanating from internal security. A call would come from the British or Americans informing me that so-and-so would be visiting. I would receive a written briefing, unsigned, undated, without letterhead, updating me on the communist activity in the region.

With the fall of the Berlin Wall, this meticulous attention to security soon became history. Attention shifted from communism to the drug trade. Solicitous concerns, palliative meanderings, all vanished and in their place came instructions and confrontations, none worse than in the Banana War. The US Government's succumbing to pressure from American banana interests would have been unthinkable during the Cold War. Our democratic credentials then had value.

A ship named *Lucky Star* sailing in the Pacific Ocean under Vincentian registry was assumed to be transporting drugs worth billions in street value. The US wished to board and seize the ship. I needed advice. I needed to know the framework of international law and our responsibility. A ship-owner and Mustique home-owner, Sergei Kauzov, who was rebuilding the Great House, offered the services of his legal experts in the United States, and they met with American officials. We were offered the proceeds from the sale of the ship when brought into Hawaii. The question bothering me was how to avoid such a problem in the future within the context of international law – my problem, not an American one. I decided that a new rule would be imposed on the registration of all ships seeking to carry our flag, that carriage of illegal substances would result in immediate termination of the registration.

That I should seek to put legal structures in place did not temper the international blistering we received in the media. No funds came our way from the sale of the ship, as the cost of the coastguard operation exceeded the ship's value! No publicity was given to the two Americans found among the crew on board the *Lucky Star*.

In due course along came the Ship Rider Agreement authorizing the US coastguard to operate in our waters in drug interdiction with a couple of our personnel aboard. I would have preferred an agreement under the umbrella of our Regional Security Treaty, that had paved the way for the Grenada intervention. One by one the Caribbean governments signed on. So did I. I felt this transferred responsibility as to where the capacity to deal with the Colombians lies, and rescued our good name on the cocaine trade. At least, so I thought. I had to be stern with one of our journalists. "The stuff does not enter the Caribbean through the Internet. The US has the right to do their thing in our waters."

Then came the Mutual Legal Assistance in Criminal Matters. I signed, but sent a letter stating my reservation in respect of civil taxation information. I made it clear that the country under my jurisdiction would not be a haven for crooks and such information as I could find on request was always transmitted.

25

Third Term: Europe, the Middle East and the Americas

In November 1997 I should have been revisiting the Cooper Clinic in Dallas for a medical check, but found myself at the other end of the world in New Zealand for another Commonwealth Heads of Government Conference.

I had become quite fond of Kenneth Cooper and looked forward to my visits. He personally had my appointments arranged to fit his own schedule so that we could have a chat about the world in his gracious office. The strange types I ran into turned out to be the World Cup referees being checked for the first time by American technology. Ken Cooper was a friend of Pelé, and unusually for an American, was an avid soccer fan. His clinic failed half a dozen of the referees, and they must have been glad to know the truth about their health. So instead I was in New Zealand with my daughter Sabrina and Minister Jerry Scott.

I have written at some length in Chapter 1 of the expulsion of Nigeria and the near-expulsion of Sierre Leone and The Gambia. But there were some other important aspects of the CHOGM to mention.

This was Nelson Mandela's first CHOGM. Nigeria had supported his battle for which he was eternally grateful. But he could not turn his eye away from injustices, be it friend or foe, and so he supported the ousting of Nigeria. At the final plenary in Auckland, I commented to him that I thought he showed deep pain in being party to the expulsion. In the profusion of our goodbyes, President Mandela thanked me for my observation on his feelings for Nigeria. I took the opportunity to lobby for my proposal for Honorary Consul for St. Vincent and the Grenadines in South Africa, a trusted and personal friend named Donald Gordon. However, Donald did not pursue the appointment as he was too involved with business connections. When we subsequently held the CHOGM in Durban he met me on departure from Johannesberg.

389

Before I left the New Zealand CHOGM I fell quite ill with a 'flu bug. By January back home my heart was acting up. And I knew why. Before dawn one morning I learnt from our Chairman, Geoffrey Cave in Barbados that British Airways was pulling out of our joint venture which immediately brought about the collapse of our meticulously established carrier Carib Express. Within minutes news from Italy came through that Valdettaro, the contractor in our project to build a yachting marina had also become bankrupt. In one fell swoop, my vision of diversifying the economy with development of marine resources to service yachts from around the world, and another to link our air communication into Europe, seemed to collapse. The confident expansion that was flowing from the IMF's blessing of our performance "much to praise, little to fault" seemed threatened.

Equally threatening was my heart condition. I continued to have heart palpitations, and so sought my doctor's advice. I was resting after the avalanche of bad news when he arrived at 7.30 a.m. He kept checking and re-checking my pulse rate, and decided that Freddie Ballantyne should see me immediately. I set up an appointment for noon. By lunchtime I realized I should have gone to the Cooper Clinic instead of the New Zealand CHOGM. My friend Diana Williams checked the Cooper Clinic and they directed me to the Heart Place. It was only years later before another hospital visit in Trinidad that I learnt from my doctor that my heart had raced up to 200 beats a minute. I should have died.

To my enemies' great disappointment I lived on to the Edinburgh CHOGM

Accompanying me was Stephanie Browne, who had succeeded Mary Hutchinson when the Grenadines was split into two constituencies. She was having a difficult time with the demands of constituents even though the economy was thriving. Canouan, a place for which I struggled to find $3,000 to create employment for Christmas, was in the early throes of the millions being spent on the resort. The Union Island Marina, promised for decades, saw construction initiated, and more restaurants were coming to life in Mayreau than Carriacou, the island in Grenada that led the Grenadines before I took over. So in keeping with the principle of exposing my Ministers on the international stage and building up experience in our party, Stephanie went with me to Edinburgh. My daughter Louise, then studying in Manchester, joined us over the weekend.

New Labour and Tony Blair had captured Britain. Accordingly we were entertained with a video extolling the latest technology in Britain, a ceremony I had to attend with the clothes in which I had travelled because Security had lost my luggage!

Prince Charles and the Queen Mother were conspicuously present at the reception. I requested the Queen Mother to send us an invitation to her hundredth birthday party, really as a gesture of encouragement. But she did make it, and our Governor General Sir Charles attended. I was glad to see Prince Charles circulating among the Heads of Government of the Commonwealth. There was so much speculation as to whether he deserved this extra honour as Head of our Commonwealth should the Queen die or abdicate. When what became Queen Elizabeth's Annus Horribilis was expressed in her Christmas Day Speech, I had made one of my early morning calls to Europe, to the Palace, and sent through the message to her Majesty that this Prime Minister conveyed his moral support.

I remember Robin Cook's tie, perhaps the most flamboyant I had seen at an evening reception. We chatted away and I pleaded for continuing British support in Europe for our bananas.

The well-established weekend retreat, two nights at a resort, which gave us time to make personal contact, was relegated to a day's outing and a train ride to St. Andrews. I rode in the carriage with Nelson Mandela and his lady from Mozambique, along with the Prime Minister of India Inder Kumar Gujral and his wife. I had seen the world go full circle, with Nelson Mandela at a CHOGM in Britain, and it was perhaps the most significant event in Edinburgh. Poor divided Cyprus was still languishing on the agenda, waiting to be included in the communiqué.

There was no way was I going to be in St. Andrews and not get on the golf course. I hadn't swung a club for almost 15 years, but I was confident after a few minutes' practice at swinging I would find the ball. So I set out with Lester Bird and our Scottish caddie, running in to Basdeo Panday and his wife Oma as we went. I did not play very well, but I was happy that as we approached the final hole in front of dozens of spectators, my final stroke some 100 yards away landed on the green for an easy sink.

My Foreign Minister, the trusted Allan Cruickshank, one of the popular figures from the countryside, a schoolmaster who was in my original 1984 team, accompanied me to the Durban CHOGM as he had to Zimbabwe. Your career as a Caribbean politician was not complete, we felt, unless you had touched the soil of the land for which we had laboured in every international circle to depose apartheid.

Also in the team was our High Commissioner Carlyle Dougan. I had eased him out of the constituency to make way for the economist Arnhim Eustace whom I had brought back from the CDB as Fiscal Adviser. Carlyle was a phlegmatic individual, but fortunately steered by his wife. I had made him three proposals in the overseas diplomatic corps, Washington, New York or London. Knowing that I had tried in the previous election to get him to quit politics altogether with a QC, and that he was being manoeuvred by another Minister who did not like the idea of the retired Permanent Secretary Judith Leigertwood taking the seat, I was taking no chances a second time.

"You will be here with your wife Elma for breakfast in the morning at Shrewsbury House!"

While I was circling around to the proposal I had made earlier, Elma blurted out, "We'll take London."

"You will then get your Constituency Council together and we will have a dinner at Eustace's house."

The Durban trip was therefore an added prize for Carlyle and his wife – and I had taken the first step in paving the way for a suitable successor as Prime Minister!

At our first reception hosted by Thabo Mbeki, I met up again with my cocktail-party friend from Edinburgh, Foreign Minister Robin Cook, who was making quite a name for himself with his British troops in Kosovo. On the night I spent in London on the way to Durban, I had seen the programme on TV of the difficulties of getting young men into the British Army, so I tackled Robin. "We supply you with policemen in the Virgins, in the Turks and Caicos, Bermuda and Cayman. Would you like some men for your Army?"

"Certainly. If I can get them as tall and intelligent as you."

"You will get them taller and more intelligent."

"It's a deal. Have your High Commissioner follow up in London."

And so Vincentians made it to the war in Iraq, some in the Special Services, fighting behind enemy lines. The British sent a 45-member team, including medical personnel, to test the 750 who had volunteered. We got the Deputy British High Commissioner, Brian Robertson, to get on the radio and TV to encourage enlistment recruitment by pointing out that there were hundreds of jobs available in the Army (and later the Navy), that training was provided which was not all about guns but included engineering and information technology. We made the arrangements with the Bank to advance the passage money for the 170 that made the grade. Years after, as the House of Commons was voting on the Iraq war Resolution, I witnessed the pain with which Robin

Cook parted company with the Labour Government and I thought how ironical it was that, the man who paved the way for Vincentian opportunity in the British Armed Forces would not be visiting our boys in the field.

In South Africa, I played golf at the resort in George the Sunday morning with Canadian Prime Minister Chrétien and Singapore Prime Minister Goh Chok Chung. They were both better than me, and tolerated my company gracefully. But we came upon a great pond in one of the fairways, with the green on the other end.

"Lake Ontario now," I said, to them both.

Chrétien sank two balls in the water. Goh and I got comfortably to the other end. A little witchcraft, I suppose.

I kept my eye out for the South African wines served at the Queen's banquet. Meerlust Rubicon was especially fine. I wished Mrs. Thatcher were around to share it.

Months later, an urgent message was awaiting me at the hotel reception desk from our Geneva Maritime Commissioner, Najla Dabinovic. Normally I was quite indifferent to emergency calls for I had learnt, like Somerset Maugham, that whenever you get an urgent call, it is urgent for the caller and not for you. When I took such calls at home I would ask "Who's dying now?", only to discover it was a request for an appointment.

This time it was serious stuff. A St. Vincent-registered ship had been chartered to carry all the Canadian weapons, ammunition, tanks and ordnance back from Kosovo to Canada, because Canada had no ships to deliver the hardware. The owners of the ship were refusing to go into port and deliver the armoury, bargaining for some extra consideration, while the Canadian Government was being harassed in the media. Could St. Vincent and the Grenadines intervene?

I told Najla that she should inform the owners that I would be instructing the Canadians to escort the ship into port with their Navy and that any dispute on the contract should be resolved in the courts. I instructed the Acting Prime Minister, Jerry Scott, to inform the Canadian High Commissioner in Barbados accordingly.

My golfing companion, the Prime Minister of Canada, met me later in the United Nations during the Millennium Summit. Closing his hands before his chest, he greeted me warmly.

"Do I kneel and say thanks?"

"Not at all. Canada deserves more from us."

I did not add that I hoped he was not still dunking golf balls.

While all the Caribbean politicians at the Durban CHOGM were making the pilgrimage to Soweto, anxious to tell those at home that they had paid tribute to the fallen in the struggle, I was heading for Kuwait to secure further funds for the extension of our Arnos Vale Airport into a jetport, adequate for regional jets, and something that with careful scheduling could link us via Antigua with London, and certainly make the Puerto Rico hub into the US a serious proposition.

I took with me Allan Cruickshank and Rocky McIntosh (whom I was expecting to be my successor in my constituency). We went via Dubai where we had to wait for a few hours between the South African Airways flight and the Emirates into Kuwait. Dougan had gone back to London anxious to follow up on the military recruitment of our young folk.

I sat with the hand luggage while Allan and Rocky went shopping. They were shocked to see gold bracelets sold by weight and not design. Then it was my turn and I returned with a fully dressed Arab with only his eyes identifiable. He was the top economist Dr Nabeel Raheem of the Kuwaiti Fund. My colleagues were duly impressed that I could identify a friend when, to them, all the Arabs looked alike. As we took off, we supplied the economist with the airport proposals and the studies on three alternate sites. In 15 minutes he came to me and said, "You are going for the sensible option."

Our progress on the project had followed years of studies by various consultants and it was only after when those under the auspices of the CDB became involved that a feasible design under US$50 million for the Arnos Vale extension emerged. It was the first time I saw daylight for serious investment on the mainland for tourism. Without an airport capable of accommodating the new generation of regional jets and frequent daily flights we would not secure investment in hotels, which was essential for diversification from the threatened banana industry. Already we had moved the road inland on the leeward coast. The site was suitable for a large golf-style hotel, casinos and a jetty for yachts. I was sure this could break the unemployment on the leeward side of the island and reduce the marijuana-growing option in the hills.

The Kuwaiti Fund had previously signalled that they would be interested in the project if we had secured funds in excess of the half-way mark. Recovering from my prostate operation by Dr. Lall Sawh at Dr. Rupert Indar's Southern Medical Clinic in Trinidad, I witnessed the devastation of the earthquake in Taiwan. I dictated a letter to the secretary and sent it off, expressing my condolences to the Government and people of Taiwan.

After discussions with the Taiwanese Chargé d'Affaires, Tom Chou, while I was still incapacitated at home, I summoned the Finance Minister, Arnhim Eustace, and suggested we send US$50 thousand to Taiwan as a gesture of moral support for the earthquake victims. Arnhim agreed. We had more than that on hand from Taiwan, so it was no pain to our Treasury.

In two weeks, we got a further US$6 million dollars, half grant, half loan, from Taiwan toward our airport project. So the Taiwan contribution was up to US$26 million. The first US$20 million had come with the unceremonious eviction of Taiwan from diplomatic recognition by the Kenny Anthony Labour Government in St. Lucia, replacing them with Beijing. St. Kitts/Nevis, Dominica, Grenada and ourselves were the beneficiaries. I decided to put all into the airport project, but not as recurrent expenditure for civil servant salaries, as the other governments were doing from time to time.

Bader Al-Humaidhi, the Director General of the Kuwait Fund, a friend now of long standing since our first meeting in Washington after the Iraqis were ejected, met us at the airport and installed me in the Amiri Suite of the Sheraton, a facility far beyond my needs, three reception rooms, three lavish bedrooms, living-and dining-room bedecked with fresh fruit, sweets of all descriptions, fine china and silver and two butlers. It was a good thing the Fund was paying our bills, for my credit card would not have withstood the shock, spending more than my monthly salary as Prime Minister on a single jaunt.

The Fund did not waste time. US$8 million could be put into the airport. We added up the numbers: US$26 million from Taiwan, US$8 million from Kuwait, and the French had promised to upgrade the terminal building and lighting should we confine ourselves to Arnos Vale, for an additional US$5 million. With US$39 million and the CDB not yet on board, I was sure that we could find our counterpart funds.

In earlier visits we had paid our respects to the Amir, thought to be rather frail, in his palace. He was grateful for my stance in support of the Gulf War. The Crown Prince, more a ball of fire, entertained us during a long chat with him, and I invited him to visit us. My daughter Gretel, who during one summer vacation had done an internship with the Egyptian architect El Gohary on the design of a resort, found the experience a boost to her confidence. One of the young economists whom I had brought for exposure, Isaac Solomon, eventually moved into our Central Bank.

This visit I called on the Speaker of the Kuwait Parliament, and he was at pains to explain the slowness of reforms in their electoral process. I argued for the inclusion of women as a force for stability, compared with the men with their foraging instinct that induces greed. But I got nowhere. Kuwait wasn't ready for the liberation of women.

Bader warned me, however, that in light of the dispute with the EIB on the funding of the cruise-ship berth, the Kuwaitis would fund only a separate component of the project. The Taiwanese were not concerned with procurement, so I was satisfied that the Kuwaiti construction company, having completed the cruise-ship-berth part of the overall project, would be well placed to bid on the construction. French companies would deal with the terminal building and lights. Following the preliminary work done by consultants Marshall McClelland Monighan (MMM), the final designs were allocated to another Canadian firm, Sypher Mueller, who had done a fine job making Mustique Airport safer and getting it certified as such.

Then the news broke that Hurricane Lenny, the first storm originating west of us, had made a swipe into the Caribbean, destroying the Kuwaiti-funded work in St. Kitts/Nevis. Hours later it was confirmed that our cruise-ship berth was also being hammered, much to the delight of the Opposition, who swore that God was ready to destroy our wickedness – a sentiment that did not inhibit their lavish use of the facility in due course. Civilization for us had not advanced beyond the situation in early Roman times when the overflowing of the banks of the Tiber was attributed to the Christians deserving of persecution for luring citizens away from their pagan gods!

That cruise-ship berth, with the help of the architect Maxim James who had returned home from Canada, had significantly advanced my dream for the enhanced docking facilities I envisioned for our city. But we had had our share of problems with the Florida Cruise Ship Lines' objection to paying user fees. I saw no reason for our taxpayers to take on any extra burden. Indeed the cruise-ship operators, unified in their pressure on the Caribbean which was their premier destination, already forced the governments, led by Kennedy Simmonds in St. Kitts, and Sandiford in Barbados, to settled for the bottom end of the fees. Yet I proceeded with construction, and reworked my figures to justify expenditure. The taxi drivers were happy. They are the main beneficiaries of the cruise industry, and we set the policy for the large ships to visit St. Vincent, the smaller ones Bequia, and none in Mustique or Petit St. Vincent. My sloganizing that the cruise passengers, in terms of the local economy, did not go beyond three Ps – a Pepsi, a postcard and a pee – still lingers even though I agree that the cruise ship does give wonderful service to its clientele, if not to the ports they visit. Those destinations are seldom more than a backdrop to romance aboard the liners.

Only one thing was certain at the Millennium Summit of the United Nations. None of us parading on the world's stage would be there for another 1,000 years. The luck of the draw had delivered me a paper slip with the number of a table. Bureaucracy and democratic protocol had relegated the newly ensconced President of Pakistan, General Pervez Musharraf, to be luncheon companion of Lester Bird and myself in the UN dining room.

I am one of those who cannot ooze into acceptance of a new leader especially when he is there through a *coup d'état* without comparing him with his predecessors. In Musharraf's case I kept thinking of Zia and his pointed waxen moustache and his execution of Benazir Bhutto's father which paved the way for the triumphant return of Benazir with her silken shalwars gracing the halls of the Commonwealth. To my enquiry about the major issue facing Musharraf, he launched into a description of his preoccupation with revenue collection. The Twin Tower attack in New York, while I was shopping for gifts in Geneva, had elevated the Pakistan general into respectability. No longer would he be skewered off to a table with Lester and myself. I was the first at the airport in Geneva the next morning expecting total chaos in airline travel, a view which, when expressed to the personnel checking me in, was greeted with amazement.

My three-minute speech at the UN 50th Anniversary had focused on the relationship between religion, in particular the Muslim faith, and terrorism. It had fallen on deaf ears.

In my last term, as well as in my earlier ones, I was concerned with agriculture. *Via colendi non facilis est*. The motto of my old Imperial College of Tropical Agriculture ("the way of the farmer is not easy") was at the forefront of my thoughts throughout my professional life, as an agronomist, Minister of Agriculture, and Prime Minister negotiating for the Caribbean on bananas in the diplomatic jungles of the world. We not only had to convince the Europeans, the Latin Americans and the Americans, we had to bargain with the producers of coffee, cocoa and rice to enlist them in our cause for subsidies, and the inequities of world trade. The producers of food could well have initiated the communist slogan with a "Farmers of the world unite; you have nothing to lose but your farms."

We were able to negotiate hurricane compensation, and use licences to import fruit at a profit when our fields were destroyed. All this disappeared under WTO rules impacting on Europe.

Life kept pointing me back to a lesson heard in college: "Experience we can't teach. When a flood washes out your crop and you replant, you can earn another hundred dollars. When disease wipes you out...when pests destroy everything...when a hurricane flattens everything...when you are still going after all these tribulations, you will deserve more than a thousand dollars. It is called experience."

As Prime Minister, though, I learned there were other plagues faced by farmers: praedial larceny and the WTO. I have lived through pestilence and natural disasters. I have seen them all. I tried to get my country ready for them by putting the infrastructure in place before the donors abandoned us, encouraging savings to respond to storms, personal, natural and institutionalized.

When Warren Christopher, Clinton's Secretary of State, was constantly calling me in my office and even at the Frangipani, requesting my support for Caesar Gavira, the retired President of Colombia to be Secretary General of the Organization of American States, confidently I assured him of my vote because Colombia was supporting our position on bananas in Europe, whereas Costa Rica was lukewarm. Not an argument to inspire America, but with the same result: he got the job. But he needed to get to Washington beyond the reach of the drug lords to be sworn in. I was the only Head of State present at Gaviria's inauguration at the OAS.

My moral argument for the protection of our bananas got all the confirmation required on our visit to Honduras to commemorate the tercentenary of the expulsion of the Caribs from St. Vincent to Roatán, the island off the coast of Honduras. My delegation included Minister Monty Roberts, Parliamentary Representative of the Carib Country, the farmer, Shim Baptiste, the social worker Pat Fraser, and Ambassador Layne from our Washington Office. From my third-storey room in the hotel at La Ceiba, I looked out each day on four women at the back of a restaurant, peeling green bananas from seven in the morning until sunset. I understood that boiled green bananas were the main fare for those who could afford it in the restaurant.

The slums, the shacks of rusted sheets over the earthen floors, beside the vast manicured Chiquita plantations, provided ample testimony of the quality of life competing with our middle-income farmers in the Windward Islands. My modern-day Caribs on my delegation could boast of our land reform programme to our hosts organizing the celebrations and who sought from us a contribution to relieve their own condition. The President joined us for the unveiling of a monument to commemorate the Garifuna presence, and I could see the teeth marks of the bulldozer that had hastily enhanced the dirt road for my visit. Their fishing boats were not even up to the standard in the Grenadines before I introduced outboard engines.

So when American advocates for free trade objected to our European dispensation, I could retort that levelling the playing field meant that our farmers would revert to a quality of life enjoyed by those who laboured the Chiquita plantations. When has the American farmer played on a level field?.

Glenys Kinnock in the European Parliament visited us and carried our message back to Europe forcefully. I met her again with her husband Neil at a dinner hosted by our excellent Ambassador in Brussels, Edwin Laurent, and his charming French wife Thérèse. Edwin understood the banana issue thoroughly and knew the opinion and position of every important player in the European Parliament, the European Commission, the trade lobbies, and the technicians in the embassies. He was well respected, and I enjoyed working with him. He accompanied me in France, Luxembourg and Italy.

At the dinner, Mike Moore, Director General of the WTO, a former New Zealand Prime Minister for a short while, could not do less than listen to our entreaties. How could the US seriously propose the argument that our dispensation would harm the potential production of bananas in Hawaii for a European market! And I went on later to demand, on television with CNBC, that the US invest the penalties it earned from the WTO ruling on Europe's favourable treatment of our bananas to build an airport to enhance tourism in St. Vincent. I still think that would be fair compensation.

My accompanying delegate, Burns Bonadie, could talk trade unionism with Neil Kinnock, as Burns had been Secretary General of the Caribbean Congress of Labour, and had contact with mutual friends. I felt comfortable in Neil Kinnock's presence, relishing his humour. That a Labour leader should be enjoying respected office in Europe after retirement, with the blessing of a Conservative government, reaffirmed the maturity in western civilization. Nothing like this was happening in our Caribbean. The norm for displaced leaders was harassment to the grave, crowned with an obsequious state funeral, with tears from those whose silence promoted the persecution of the dead man.

At the same time we were in Brussels, the British were hosting a meeting with their dependent territories who were seeking to leverage some funds out of the European Union under the special dispensation in Part IV of the Aid Treaty. Montserrat's Chief Minister Brandt had brought along Ken Boyea, in his capacity as private-sector investor from ECGC in the rice mill obliterated by the volcano. Ken had successfully launched his political career inside our opposition Labour Party by winning the argument against the leadership over using an

American public relations firm led by the beautiful Jennifer Lazzlo out of Washington to run their campaign. In the process he had beaten our former Attorney General, in spite of the latter's new-found image in Baptist regalia.

I invited Ken to join my delegation in the various meetings and also to the dinner at our Ambassador's residence. We were looking for a location for an embassy and he approved the location in Louise Street that Laurent had found. He was roundly criticized by his party for deviating from their policy of making our country ungovernable. Ken enjoyed the meetings in Brussels and I was happy to expose him to our negotiations there.

Burns and I moved on to Liechtenstein to assess the work of the St. Vincent Trust Service, our premier offshore finance operative, under the direction of Bryan Jeeves and his son, Alex. Most of our international companies doing business in SVG were registered under Bryan's umbrella. He had cultivated a good relationship with Bozo Dabinovic and his daughter Najla in our shipping flag registry. Bryan had already established his elegant office in Kingstown and he was investing for some office space in Liechtenstein.

A call on the Reigning Prince was arranged. I was informed that our car was allowed further into the Palace grounds than Margaret Thatcher's. Prince Adam was delighted to meet a kindred soul who had also been much maligned for involvement with a totally legal offshore sector. As I sipped his *krug*, he advised that I should not bow to pressure from America.

"Your Majesty," I intoned. "You are a Prince. I am elected."

I had nothing but awe for the flow of trillions of offshore finance over which the Reigning Prince so calmly presided. While I could see the benefit in co-operation among offshore jurisdictions, I was not going to presume to equate my fledging steps in that sector with His Royal Highness's pre-eminence in it. You don't take a bicycle into Formula One, but you can hope one day for a new car.

That night in Vaduz, Bryan gave a dinner in my honour at the Restaurant Real, complete with the local Riesling Sylvanner and a Wilfersdorf Castle Merlot. He was well established as British Honorary Consul and I knew he moved in the right circles and dining clubs in London. The personalities present that night I was sure were managing more millions than our entire SVG budget and I wondered if the fruits of our modest ambition to keep our quality of life beyond bananas would ever materialize. Economies of scale were beyond us. The question was: could we service the wealth others produced?

Ambassador Laurent, the St. Lucian who represented his country and mine in Brussels, was quite fascinated with St. Lucia's UN standing in Paris and thought I could make similar arrangements. At a fine restaurant in Paris one evening, Wafic Said, an accomplished entrepreneur, met with us. His passion for education I immediately savoured. He was willing to be our Honorary Ambassador at UNESCO, deploying the resources of his well-appointed Paris office. My Minister of Education and Foreign Affairs readily complied. Subsequently, I was delighted to receive him and his charming wife Rosemary, along with friends at my Bequia home, Villa Helianthus, and follow the developments in England as his Said Business School at Oxford University became a reality.

My last banana mission with Ambassador Laurent to the French Ministry of Agriculture brought home to me that we must diversify out of agriculture by using our natural resources of the sea once again. When you get an invitation to meet with a Minister at eight in the evening, you have to be a social bore not to know that his working day was finished, and he is slipping you in before his dinner elsewhere.

"I know your country, Prime Minister," Jean Glavarry said. "I have just come back from two weeks' sailing in the Grenadines. Your sailing waters are wonderful. France will support you on bananas, but we're also supporting the development of a first-class marina in your country. It will have more future than bananas."

The same message had come years before in the Italian Foreign Ministry in Rome.

In the US Dan Rostenkowski, the formidable Congressman from Chicago from whom I was looking for a quota on garments asked, "What you want a quota for when God has given you these beautiful sailing waters in the Grenadines?"

So easy to hear the message! To pass it on at home, however, was more akin to the fate of the messenger bearing ill tidings in the ancient Gallic wars!

I have written earlier in detail of how Jean Bertrand Aristide had taken refuge in the Venezuelan Embassy in Port au Prince and had been spirited out of there to Venezuela. President Carlos Andres Perez urged that Latin America and the Caribbean should be making a co-ordinated response to Haiti and try to have Aristide restored. A Venezuelan military plane with the President had picked me up in St. Vincent, we had collected John Compton, gone on to Dominica to meet with Eugenia, and had a meeting with Aristide. I certainly would not like to make another trip in that military plane into the awful little

airport just before sunset again. We took our lives in our hands hoping
to restore democracy in Haiti.

Now years on, chaos again reigned. A new President of Haiti, Dr.
René Preval, invited Caricom to send a mission to Haiti to be apprised
of the forthcoming elections. That was July 1999. Caricom chose
me and Janet Boswick, the Bahamian Foreign Minister, along with
Orlando Marville of the Secretariat, to fulfil the mission. I decided to
bring along Foreign Minister Cruickshank. I was very much aware of
the futility of the earlier exercise with Seaga trying to steer General
Namphi into electoral propriety.

Very sensibly, Janet was accompanied by Carlton Wright, an
Immigration Secretary in the Bahamas. I brought on board Kingsley
Layne, Ambassador to the US and the OAS, to be secretary of the
mission. Clem John, Electoral Officer from Dominica, along with my
Press team, added to our numbers.

My experiences in Nicaragua and Hungary had prepared me for
the kind of action needed in Haiti: to get a sounding of all ranges of
political and administrative opinion, and to determine the status of
democracy and the electoral process in the country.

René Preval, not much different in size to the Napoleonic Aristide,
made every effort to ensure we had access where we wanted and that
all personalities in the political spectrum had access to us. He met
us at the airport. We held a joint press conference, opening up the
avenues of dialogue. We were treated to a sumptuous banquet in the
Palace on the Sunday evening. I was glad to see he was drinking his
champagne, unlike my encounter with his predecessor, Baby Doc. I
told of how Baby Doc passed the stuff over his shoulder to the military
attaché. Haiti had really made progress with its President being able to
drink in company in the Palace.

The Hotel Montana was our base and many delegations met us
during the three days of interviews with every political party, the private
sector, and the Chamber of Commerce. We were totally shocked by the
plethora of political parties. Indeed some who called on us represented
others that did not turn up. The Fammi Lavalas, the party of Aristide,
was the most dominant in the country and universally disliked by the
others. Ambassador Colin Granderson, Executive Director of the UN/
OAS International Civilian Mission in Haiti and Ambassador Denneth
Modeste, guided us through the political terrain. There were the
Organization of People in Struggle (OPL), Espace de Concertation
(ESPACE) – five major political parties, the Patriotic Movement for
National Rescue (MPSN); seven minor parties, the Rally of Progressive

National Democrats, led by former President Manigat (overthrown soon afterwards), the Movement for the Restoration of Democracy in Haiti (MIDH) led by Marc Bazin, the Democratic Initiative (ID), and the Patriotic Initiative Committee (CIP). The private sector comprised the Centre for Free Enterprise and Democracy (CLED), the Association of Haitian Industrialist (ADIH), and the Chamber of Industry and Commerce.

We were so overwhelmed by sectional interests that I could not help asking one group how many political parties there were in Haiti if you counted in the splinter parties. About one hundred, I was told. When I responded that they had more in Haiti than the whole of Caricom, I was instructed that they had a greater population than us. I could only mutter under my breath to Ambassador Layne that they had more parties than India.

Haiti was not short of opinions on the make-up of a future government's structure. I thought they could do with a de Gaulle-type government, in which you had a long-term President and a Prime Minister. A Canadian team was contracted to complete the registration of voters for the November election of Senators, but there was no way that we could see the deadline of three months achieved what with the hopeless transportation, lack of electricity and other facilities in rural areas. We advised accordingly.

Janet and I had to ensure that the Haitians understood that accession to Caricom did not mean freedom of movement within the islands, even among the members. Their support for their government's bid to join Caricom was coloured by this hope. In general they wished us to be a bridge to an international community that I knew was already suffering from Haiti fatigue. The international funds committed had not been forthcoming. I explained the slow process of procurement in a democracy to ensure firstly that donors facilitated their own services and secondly to allow the bidding process rather than deals between a dictator and his friends.

We called on Aristide and his wife in his home, a fine residence replete with marvellous Haitian paintings. It was in a new residential area. I was fascinated to see that the first thing built for any home was a 10-foot tall perimeter concrete fence. The former President denied that he was holding up the electoral registration, but he objected to the use of income-tax identification for electoral purposes, since the poor majority did not pay taxes. The discussions were amicable. The old friendship survived. He was waiting in the wings to have another go at the presidency.

One afternoon, I allowed Cruickshank and our TV and radio personnel to go on a tour of Port au Prince. By ten o'clock they had not returned. I was ordering dinner to be put in their rooms when they turned up.

"We cannot eat," Allan blurted out. "The poverty and misery I saw has driven all thoughts of food out of me. I have to go to sleep without eating."

Jimmy Prince, Kendol Morgan and Chester Connell agreed. The criticism at home that we were in Haiti's bracket of poverty was demolished and the pictures they were permitted to take would expose that lie for what it was.

The sense of despair in Haiti is deep. The system of government is not trusted. It does not seem to work. Haiti has gone from dictatorship to nominal democracy. Without constitutional reform to bring a better political structure, the country, already a failed state, will hardly escape its misery. Their new constitution does not work. Religion and superstition seem both to orient and to disorient the people. I wished I could teach them the unforgiving doctrine of development I had learnt: stability and education must precede a fairer distribution of wealth — the new religion.

Legend has it that the slave liberator, Henri Christophe, inspired by Brimstone Hill Fort built by the English in his birthplace, St. Kitts, and desperate to sustain his rebellion against Napoleon, was determined to build his own fortress in 1807. Because of the refusal of some of his men to pull 365 cannons up a 3,000-foot hill, he split his crews of 100 men assigned to each cannon into two crews of 50, then marched one crew of 50 to their death over the cliff as an incentive to the other remaining 50 to complete the task. The building of this Citadelle La Ferriere took some 13 years to complete.

Napoleon never came, however. Christophe committed suicide in 1820.

Such was the birth of the first black republic. The building of that fortress to this day remains the greatest triumph of Haitian leadership. Some say the spirits of those who plunged to death over the cliff have put a curse on Haiti from which it never recovered, a theory that satisfies not only the voodoo-worshipping Haitians but *obeah* believers in the rest of the West Indies. Even if it was only a part of legend, the reputed curse was certainly a good excuse for failure.

England was the first country to abandon giving Vincentians scholarships to study there. Canada followed. I discussed the subject with Brian Mulroney, and he explained that education was a matter for each Canadian province's discretion. Cuba came to the rescue, with hundreds allowed from every Caribbean country to study there on scholarships.

I had helped Ambassador Cabesas, the long-serving Cuban diplomat in our region, to patch up relations with post-revolutionary Grenada, getting Grenada to drop objections to Cuba being a member of the Caribbean Tourist Association, a collector of statistics. It became Cuba's first step into regional organizations.

Some scholarships were processed in the Caricom Secretariat. I secured a place for Juanna Osborne, a young Bequia girl, to study dentistry. She had begun an apprenticeship cleaning teeth in our hospital with visiting goodwill American specialists. On my official visit to Cuba, she was among the group I brought along to meet Fidel.

As mentioned earlier, my first gift to Fidel was a copy of my father's pilot receipt form of a voyage from the US to Cuba with a cargo of timber when his ship, *Gloria Colita*, perished. I told Fidel that my father had sailed from Bequia to Cuba in the early 1930s and my mother who accompanied him was still alive. She sent greetings. She fondly remembered that it was in Cuba where she went to the first hairdresser in her life. Fidel invited me to bring her next time.

My second gift to President Castro on my official visit to Cuba was the elaborate coffee-table book on Mustique. Castro brought up all subjects under the sun, but on each occasion we met he wanted to know how I secured this magnitude of investment in a small island.

"Tax concessions and building regulations," I explained, giving him details on the freedom to choose architects internationally and how I encouraged diversification of sources of finance in England, France, Italy, Germany, Austria, and Switzerland, plus North America, Brazil and Venezuela. I entertained him with stories of my hitch-hiking days in Europe, including having to leave a restaurant in Hamburg because of my resemblance to him.

My students complained about the compulsory course in Marxism in the first year. I took this on board, but expected I should present a diplomatic alternative. So I had my Foreign Minister Alpian Allen press for alternate studies in the rich mine of Cuban history.

When I saw the simple accommodation and the unkempt grounds of the university campus, we savoured first hand the implications of the American boycott. There were no lawn-mowers.

The Ministry of Tourism presented us with their plans. They were obviously tackling the demands from the tour operators, small-rooms providers and mass transit. I enquired into housing adjacent for workers, and was told they would be transported to and from work. Their tourism model, apart from historic old Havana, was a totally different mode from our own. Cuba was going for volume.

The Cubans provided a house on the 20-kilometre beach of Vayadero, the widest and longest beach with shallow water, in the Caribbean. We had excellent service from military personnel who passed on my interest in cheese, only to find massive slabs as my going-away trophy.

My visit to their biological research laboratories produced an invitation to address a seminar on a return visit when they discovered I could discourse on microbiology. They were working away on an AIDS vaccine and worried about plagiarism of their earlier research in other areas.

Unashamedly I have to admit that, securing scholarships for the young people apart, my great reward in Cuba was a night at Tropicana nightclub, the nightly festival of beautiful Cuban girls that survived from dictatorship through communism and that I prayed would survive to all eternity, constantly refreshed with the beauties issuing from their multi-racial society.

For my daughter Louise, whose accompaniment on the mission was a prize for success in her law studies at Manchester, her joy was to be kissed by the legend Fidel himself and bumping into, in a piano bar in Havana, the novelist Gabriel Garcia Marquez, whose books she had read and re-read.

Our students, coming back home for Christmas, sought audience with me at Democrat House to lodge all their complaints about conditions in Cuba.

"You are complaining to the wrong person. To get my education in Canada, I cleaned shoes and spittoons on the trains in Canada. I worked 20 hours a day in the summer. I had only sardines and raisin bread and chocolate milk for Christmas. I could not get home for Christmas for three years. I could not phone home. If you can't put up with Cuba, if you can't stoop to conquer, let your parents find $30,000 a year to send you elsewhere." I did not for a moment assume that Castro's successor would be imbued with the same generosity to the student world. I don't suppose they liked my reply – or ever voted for me. I agreed to give them a monthly allowance.

With the passage of time, our neighbours Grenada, enjoying the scholarships to Cuba also, under the new leadership of my friend Keith Mitchell, invited Fidel Castro to Grenada. To ensure that Keith was not singled out for criticism, I took a group of friends, including the businessman Lambert Baptiste from Union Island, to show solidarity with the triumphant return of Cuba to Grenada.

When I heard and saw the Grenadian students on the waving gallery of the terminal, built by the Cubans, singing the Cuban national anthem, I was pleased to have lived to witness Grenada's acknowledgement of the help that was launching their tourism programme. Not a word of gratitude was expressed at the airport opening ceremony under the previous regime, still under the sway of America, and not a word of thanks could be given to Cuba.

At the UN Millennium Summit in New York, the Japanese Prime Minister Yoshiri Mori held a luncheon reception for the Caribbean. Fidel Castro embraced me again. Our similarity in colour, height and beard was often remarked upon.

"Thanks to you I am still alive," he said. "They do not know which of us to shoot!"

My heart operation had put much wind in the sails of the Opposition. Even a few investors whom I had welcomed to enjoy the fruit of my policies were carping, "He ought to go!" I addressed the convention of my party for several hours and no one would go to lunch until I categorically stated that I would stay and thrash them one more time.

I was satisfied that my health was still good enough. Five doctors, led by the head of the cardiology unit in Miami's Jackson Memorial hospital, Dr. De Marchena, told me I was cured, a rare accolade from doctors. My friend Carlo of Canouan had accompanied me to the hospital. I had called Sir Charles, our Governor General, who was no stranger to heart operations himself, and told him what I was up to, and that should I not make it, he could choose someone to take over. My Minister of Tourism, Alpian Allen, was in Ft. Lauderdale, and apparently spent the night in prayer on his knees.

One of the nurses preparing me for surgery confided that her name was Petrona, interpreted by my Roman friend to be the feminine in Latin for Peter. So I challenged her not to open the pearly gates for me.

"No one," she said, "who goes into theatre in great spirits does not come out in fine form."

"In which case, you shall join me for dinner." An appointment that was in due course honoured.

We won our fourth election with a majority of one (described in the next chapter). I had expected that with the sharp businessman Ken Boyea on the other side, Labour was going to have fiery American marketing in their campaign, and indeed their hired team had experience in the Clinton camp and with Basdeo Panday in Trinidad. So I took on the

English psychological analyst Nigel Oakes. My Ministers Campbell, Jones and Wyllie could not bring themselves to conceive that a foreign public relations firm could poll and analyse our scenario while the others who pleaded for help succeeded.

New leadership was emerging in the region round me. Lester Bird took over the Bird fortress in Antigua, P. J. Patterson took over from Michael Manley. Eugenia Charles had retired, so too had John Compton. Neither Eugenia's nor John's appointed successors proved capable of being elected. In Guyana, Sam Hinds understood that his was only an interim job after the passing of Cheddi Jagan. It had to be another Jagan in power. So his wife Janet it was.

So while my new opposition was espousing how they would make the country ungovernable, they soon realized they were not up to the task of dealing with regional historic animosities. Keith Mitchell, coming to the end of his term as Chairman of Caricom, had tired of intransigence between the People's Political Party and the People's National Congress in Guyana and was happy to pass the baton on to the newly elected Kenny Anthony in St. Lucia. Janet Jagan and Desmond Hoyte were at war. Fresh with my victory and being very old friends of both Desmond and Janet, Keith suggested to Kenny that I bridge the gap. I was able to persuade Janet to agree to meet with Desmond in St. Lucia, but away from the conference venue. She was not going to give Desmond the propaganda tool of a presence at the Summit. Kenny sent on the fax I drafted as an invitation to Desmond.

In St. Lucia I became a virtual messenger shuttling between the conference and Desmond's hotel with various drafts. I quietly made my point to Desmond and his assistant who had personally been victimized by the Jagans and forced to abandon his studies in London.

"I do not want your children and a second generation of Afro-Guyanese to be sacrificed. Go for constitutional change. Get a piece of the action. Only through a federal system with Guyana divided into provinces, like the regions you have now, will Afro-Guyanese see power again. If you have a great Governor of Georgetown province, like a Guiliani in New York, all the people could well call for his presidency, irrespective of colour."

We got the retired Attorney General of Barbados, Maurice King, to liaise between the two warring factions and report to me along the way. Fortunately, I had kept up delivering champagne to Desmond ever since he lost office. He trusted my friendship. But alas, my friendship with Desmond (and Janet) bore no fruit. The PNC insisted on a carefully observed electoral process and were beaten into second by the PPP.

Kenny Anthony was allocated Caricom responsibility for governance. I was put in charge of banana negotiations in Europe, the United States and Latin America. After a dinner in Canouan, Kenny sought my advice on how to deal with the Nevis referendum on succession from the St. Kitts/Nevis federation.

I suggested he should state the Caricom view and stay away from Nevis until the referendum was completed. He thanked me publicly in a statement made in Tobago. So it became my brief to talk to the parties after the inconclusive referendum I knew would occur. Denzil Douglas, the new Prime Minister of St. Kitts/Nevis, even though he knew I was in sympathy with the Opposition at home, had appreciated that I had refused to send Special Service Unit (SSU) troops from St. Vincent after the voting. I was quite comfortable about meeting with all the contending parties after the Nevis referendum.

The secession of Anguilla from the St. Kitts/Nevis Federation had not been constitutionally settled until Kennedy Simmonds' Peoples' Action Movement (PAM) came to power. The embarrassed British Government had been pressurized by Bradshaw's deputy, Paul Southwell, into agreeing to build an international airport in St. Kitts in return for their co-operation on resolving the matter. But the Bradshaw Government did not honour their commitment to Britain. The airport was well advanced and still the Anguilla question remained an international embarrassment. I was in Opposition after my spell as Premier when I got a phone call from Simeon Daniel of Nevis for some advice in advance of the upcoming constitutional conference in London.

I told him the British would want them to tidy up the situation with Anguilla. If you do that, they'll be sympathetic to your concerns, I suggested that Nevis should be permanently entitled to one-third of the seats in the St. Kitts/Nevis Parliament, and secondly that a clause on self-determination as a last resort should be included.

When I met Vance Amory, the Premier of Nevis, and his Cabinet, I was a little saddened. The Cabinet table was a sheet of plywood, the chairs and the furniture distinctly amateurish. Colonialism had left them with little. Lord Nelson (whose historic presence is part of Nevis folklore), I am sure, had a better oak table aboard his ships. Their economic bastion was the Four Seasons Hotel, the choice of Princess Diana who launched Nevis' tourism. Their sporting facilities were well below the quality of even Bequia's. They were boiling with resentment over this treatment by St. Kitts, but St. Kitts owned the ferry between the islands and had used the threat of taking away the ferry to get "no" votes in the referendum.

I advised that the ferry service be privatized as I had done at home. Privatization produced several ferries at competitive prices. They took me to see the airport which I had had a hand in creating with European funds, like the one in Bequia. Simeon Daniel seemed to have been out of favour in Nevis. He joined me for a drink at the Four Seasons.

I met an old girlfriend from St. Lucia days, Lucille Walwyn, for an amicable breakfast. She was a stunner in her youth and still had a lyrical voice. Her husband had been an Attorney General, but had passed on. She was very upset by the rift between Nevis and St. Kitts and prayed I could point them both in the sensible direction. The draft new constitution by Sir Fred Phillips was a fudge. No reasonable person could think it practicable.

I had a dinner at Ocean Terrace Inn with all the contending parties, except the Government. So the St. Kitts Opposition, and all sides in Nevis, were present. I reminded Kennedy of the glorious days when I secured the presence of the St. Kitts' steel band at the Vancouver Expo, funded by Maple Leaf Mills and Canadian Pacific Airways, in order to market our flour in the islands and strengthen our joint venture with the Canadians.

What could I report to Caricom on this mission? I came, I saw, I *had not* conquered. The referendum had passed by 50 per cent but not the two-thirds needed. Nevis had made its point. I hoped St. Kitts was listening. The only real way forward, as I told Kennedy and PAM, was through constitutional change, by holding direct elections for a President and Vice President, one to be from each island. The islands needed a bond deeper than a ferry service.

Being born in a neglected offshore island was the obvious genesis of my interest in secession. The question was thrown at me: how do you reconcile your Grenadines Declaration on self-determination with your passion for Caribbean unity? While detractors were preoccupied with their criticism of me, I was busy promoting land reform on the mainland and endearing myself to farmers. When the volcano erupted, I was the only one to surrender my salary to the evacuation fund even though later many of my colleagues thought I deserved no proper pension.

My next involvement in the thorny problem of the right to secede was in the second Quebec Referendum in 1995. I was guest of the Vincentian Organization in Montreal, one of my favourites in our diaspora and headed by my old school friends George Richardson and Alfie Roberts. They had invited the Minister of Multicultural Affairs, Sheila Finestone, in Canada to honour the occasion. She promptly informed me that she would not stay for any length of time as she had to get on with the campaign for the vote on Monday. She thus provided me with my text. I reminded the Vincentians and all the West Indians in the audience that they did not leave their islands to migrate to Canada in order to participate in the destruction of Canada. They needed a Canadian passport. Should Quebec secede, Quebec would need to negotiate with the rest of the world on visas, as it would not be automatic that the Quebeçois would have the same travelling rights as Canadians. They would all need to become fluent in French, an easy exercise for the children, but a hard one for those who had long abandoned language studies.

"You have to get on the phone tomorrow all day calling every West Indian you know and get them to vote for a united Canada."

The illustrious General de Gaulle, whom I really admired, had illuminated the idea in one sentence – of a Quebec Libre, but he had also debunked our islands as specks of dust – "poussiers." Here was my opportunity to show that in the right location a speck of dust can reflect light.

The Canadian Minister stayed through my speech. She was delighted. My speech, she confided, was as important as any she could give that night to Canadians.

I was back home by the time the referendum results were announced. I was pleased by the statement of the losers that but for the immigrant vote they would have won the success on referendums. The Royal Canadian Mountain Police who had accompanied me must have filed a report. Who knows? Perhaps I saved the day for Canada. At least I repaid Canada for my education, and better still, my Canadian/West Indian family.

At home again, I kept an ear to the ground. My chief source of information was a woman named Vermena, sweeper under the Almond tree, Bequia's "Parliament," deemed to be illiterate, who picked up all the gossip and kept me briefed on the bane of all politicians, the home-grown hypocrites. I had learnt the importance of this kind of source from Eric Gairy once when I visited him on business in Grenada, and he explained the purpose of the earlier visitor whom he had bank-rolled to cook chicken on a St. George's street. "She's more valuable informing me on the mood in St. George's than the foolish Special Branch policemen concerned only with promotion." The Greek engineer who came to work on the Bequia Airport felt at home when he saw the scene of taxi drivers and layabouts under the Almond Tree. It reminded him of the information exchange under the olive trees. "Bequia is a Greek island," he cried.

The islands that in my youth knew nothing of telephones, jetties, airports or public transport, have become digital, accessible by plane, and easy to get around. They are even subjected to opinion polls. But for all the modern-day analysis of the voice of the people, opinion polls do not identify hypocrites. We need our Vermenas. This way you can have the hypocrite comfortably ignorant of your insight into his mind when you embrace each other.

Balancing the budget from year to year, generating a surplus on recurrent revenue to splice into the external funding of infrastructure, spreading out the scholarships abroad for the young people, we could feel comfortable with our steadily improving quality of life.

But time was running out on our lifeline, the banana industry. Europe was not going to hold out indefinitely against the US, pressured relentlessly by Chiquita and Dole. We had to diversify. Further quality tourism investment was the obvious answer.

Aldo Rolla, a middle-aged Italian engineer, came to see me with a proposal to build a super-yacht marina to complement what we were already doing in yachting, for which he could find financing in Europe. Word about the excellent sailing in the Grenadines had spread through the yacht clubs in France, Italy and Germany, and all over Europe, and maintenance and repair facilities were sadly lacking. Insurance costs would decline and a high-quality yacht would spend more time in the Caribbean if all the services were provided. He had already explored our coastline and found a site at Ottley Hall.

My training in agronomy had, I like to think, positively influenced the results in our agricultural economy. St. Vincent and the Grenadines, under the new Law of the Sea Convention, became defined as an archipelagic state and in the process assumed the largest domain in the East Caribbean. Developing our maritime resources, linking it with the long tradition of the sea in the Grenadines, seemed a logical step. We were after all on the same route the explorers had sailed centuries earlier, the winds and currents bringing ships from Europe and South Africa directly to the Grenadines. A marina in St. Vincent had inherent strategic geographical value.

Pierro Busnelli, a Mustique homeowner, had begun making his fortune by selling furniture on the back of a bicycle in Milan. He invited me to see his factories, design technology, and the annual furniture and light exhibition in Milan. I had visions of furniture manufactured at home for export to Europe under the Lomé Convention we had negotiated. But I was quickly disabused. His research unit had half-a-dozen physicists and mathematicians re-inventing three-dimensional chairs. You needed a good design that would be replicated in millions by B & B Italia for export all over the world – and you needed a showroom in Manhattan.

Professor Paolo Piva of the Vienna School of Architecture guided me through the exhibition. The gold-plated B & B Italia stall cost US$750,000, all to be dismantled in a week, and there were thousands of stalls in an exhibition area as large as the commercial centre of our Kingstown. I could take no more. My absorptive capacity was exhausted. The next day I tried to take in the marble tables and lighting designs. All too grand. We would have to do what we could with our local market and low prices.

From the exhibition grounds I flew by helicopter to Rolla's La Grazie repair shipyard near Genoa. Indeed the geography was similar to our Ottley Hall. I inspected the work being done on the luxury cruiser for the Middle Eastern sheik, supervised by a former British naval captain. A luxury yacht was being built and the hull of Tito's *Istranka* had been gutted for restoration. The yard had been functional since 1915. All that was left for me to determine was Rolla's competence and the financial arrangements with the bankers in Rome and Dusseldorf.

Piva wanted me to see his work beyond modern factory and furniture design. So we went to Oropa where an altar he designed was being constructed for a weekend mass by the Pope. Jeannette and I stayed in the monastery. Not a bad ambience for a romantic evening for two original sinners.

Oropa's investment of hundreds of thousands in the temporary edifice to be torn down paid ample dividends with the Papal visit. I wished I could ship the whole thing home – such wastage. Italian design and ingenuity was overwhelming me. How could we get all this expertise at home? Our economists were merely thinking about value-added concepts. In Italy it was a reality everywhere, in silk scarves and ties, in the veneer on tables, in the carvings of marble. All these successors of Michelangelo exuding charm in every direction. How was my Third World going to leap into this league?

In Venice, we stayed in another Mustique friend's palazzo (no hole in the floor toilets this time). I missed my old companion in Venice, Philip Greaves, now Deputy Prime Minister in Barbados. I would have to tell him I was touring the glass factories in Murano. And it was not snow on the mountains of Carrara: it was all white marble, great shaved chasms of it, and common as the volcanic andesite at home.

It is not often that history grants an opportunity to a leader to remould the centre of his capital city. Small, if it is going to be beautiful, must capture the ultimate in aesthetics. The Japanese were fashioning my fish market. The Canadians had taken on the meat market. I wanted a vegetable market and to take my small vendors off the street and out of the sun and rain, no matter how exotic were the photos of them taken by tourists, I did not want the visitors in the twenty-first century finding our tomatoes and fruit sold on a dirty street. After I had seen the markets in Barcelona and Paris and Santiago, I was determined to lead the Caribbean in the design of markets. My second visit to Taiwan produced the money. How better for Taiwan to demonstrate its influence in the world than the greatest contemporary market in the Caribbean. And so Piva designed it.

Italian direct foreign investment of millions in Canouan. Italian investment in a massive marina. Italian furniture in the Prime Minister's Office. And now an Italian-designed market. Surely the Italian mafia was taking over the country, the Opposition screamed. That Italy was supporting us in the Banana War with the US only to be hammered with punitive tariffs on its silk fashion, cheeses and proscuito made no difference to the gripers. Gratitude!

There was further criticism of the market design. It was too large. The sacred location of our war memorial should not be disturbed and every session of Parliament had some objection raised about its removal, even though the British Legion in London and its representative at home, Donald Browne, supported its transfer to the Botanic Gardens established by Captain Bligh when he brought us the breadfruit plants to feed the slaves.

The Italian designer Mario Ferrari was importing marble and other fittings from Italy for Mustique homes. We had the monument copied, elevated and suitably inscribed on white Carrara marble. The opposition to the transfer now dutifully lay wreaths each year, at Remembrance ceremonies, unmindful of the transformation we wrought in our city, inspired by my visits to Italy.

On one of my missions to lobby Italy on the Banana War, the Foreign Minister excused himself. Forty thousand Albanians, now the Iron Curtain had lifted, were on all manner of craft besieging the Italian coast. His deputies and the officials were wondering why I was not paying more attention to the Ottley Hall marina and economic diversification. Rolla had done a great lobbying job. He had told me that he had lobbied every political persuasion in Rome. He took me to see bankers in Rome. The Italian Government was ready to deploy their export credit facility, SACE, behind the project, which would use 85 per cent Italian goods and services. With these assurances my Cabinet was ready to proceed.

I took two parliamentarians to Dusseldorf with me to meet with West LB, Stephanie Browne and the engineer Glen Stewart, along with the civil servant, Maurice Edwards, Director General of Finance. The West LB Chairman and executives could not have been more charming. Our credit rating was excellent and they were ready to finance, not only Ottley Hall, but other projects as well. Their people had done a thorough analysis, including diving to examine the sea bed. Any investment had to be environmentally sound to attract European finance.

In the festive mood of the German beer parlours, eating away at our pork knuckles and potatoes, they went on to talk about unlimited investment in hotels, with package tours of thousands at US$50 a day. Beer fortunately does not flow upward to my brain, and I was not the slightest interested in US$50 single-bed employees on holiday. Our tourism was for employers.

Our honeymoon with West LB did not last very long. The project was not completed. Loans to us were called in. Suspect correspondence between the bank and the contractors surfaced. Italy's exports would increase through SACE, but German banks would be the beneficiaries. I felt that even Mussolini got a better deal out of the Germans than St. Vincent. I shipped all the documentation to the World Bank. No one was going to ensnare me in any funny business.

A friend came to the rescue. Carlo Amato, the pioneer in luxurious development in Canouan, retained his enthusiasm always for high-level diplomacy and was excited at the prospect of our deepening relations both with Rome and the Vatican. His friend Raffaele Ranucci, of old Italian stock, who was very involved with the football club AS Roma, an hotelier, and had multiple investments, would be a great Honorary Consul. His mahogany-lined office savoured the elegance of a super-yacht complete with the model of Hitler's ship, *Skagerrak*. He had bought the original ship and restored it, but it was too delicate for an Atlantic crossing. At a dinner at the home of his mother, Signora Gabriella Ranucci, we were pleased to meet the leaders in industry and politics, including Pier Fernando Cassini who was a Minister in the Italian government, with a political career very much in ascendancy. They were all sympathetic about my debt with West LB and SACE. A meeting was arranged the next day with Umberto Dini, the Foreign Minister. It was another day of political crisis in Italy.

I went into the room alone, Carlo Amato staying in the waiting room. Minister Dini was accompanied by one official. Several SACE people, I gathered, had gone to jail. None of the people with whom I dealt were still around. I thanked the Foreign Minister for Italy's support of our bananas. We knew our banana exports would have a hard time competing with the cheap exports from Latin America and its starvation wages. We had to keep our democracy alive. We had to diversify. I trusted the signature of Italy. I was naïve with the German banks.

"How did we get into this mess?" Dini asked his official.

"Sir, it is worse in Russia."

The Foreign Minister began to summarize. I began to write on the napkin under the orange juice. He got me a sheet with the letter-head of his Ministry.

"You made mistakes. We made mistakes. Let us split the difference, and share the burden fifty-fifty."

I could ask for no more, certainly not at this meeting. We would need to demonstrate good faith before seeking further relief.

Arnhim Eustace, now my Minister of Finance, was in Washington at the World Bank. He was negotiating to employ the services of the Antiguan adviser who had secured a postponement of their debt, but abandoned the idea on my news of debt relief. He and our legal expert Karl Hudson-Phillips would convert my napkin notes into the million-dollar write-off. But Ranucci could not take up our offer of Honorary Consul. He visited me in Bequia on a yacht one Christmas. He had too many appointments with the Italian Government including overseeing Italy's Olympic Committee.

26

Last Election and Fourth Term: Concluding the Agenda

Like the great cities of Europe, each island in the Caribbean has its individual intrinsic flavour. We all contend to find the phrases to propel our own island into the marketplace. Lovely beaches. Beautiful sunsets. Clear pure water. Wonderful sailing. Exciting fishing. St. Vincent has all of these. But with geology giving us a hilly topography, St. Vincent's scattered family-owned hotels could not in the beginning of our tourism efforts receive large conferences. Therefore, we were all excited for the first time to host the Heads of Government Conference, an opportunity created by the Lugano investors under the guidance of Luigi Vietti of Costa Smeralda fame, and Marco Aldaco, Mexican designer of presidential homes. They created the Tamarind Beach Hotel and the splendid Carenage Beach and Golf Resort in Canouan. Vietti by this time had sadly died, but his disciple Antonio Ferrari carried on his work. We who had never been capable of returning decades of hospitality in other islands were suddenly plunged into the limelight with a premier resort, showing how far we had diversified from a banana economy.

Canouan was launched as a wonderful destination and a place to return. I secured tickets for the leaders of our diaspora in America to savour the success of their island home, alongside some leaders of opinion on the mainland. My new Cabinet Secretary, JoAnne Veira, co-ordinated the administrative troops, and my youthful personal secretary Angela Mercury, with that rare capacity to do three things at once, hovered around me ready to smooth any troubled diplomatic waters at their inception, without even being seen.

The Guyanese President Bharrat Jagdeo fired off a blast against Caricom's acquiescence to the curtailment of his five-year electoral mandate. Had we in compromising about the length of his term compromised democracy itself? We thought not.

417

At the Canouan Heads of Government Meeting, Guyana and Suriname were squaring for a fight. The Surinamese Navy, its flotilla of three ships, attacked the Canadian offshore rig drilling for oil in Guyanese waters, which were claimed by Suriname. The wars in the search for El Dorado's liquid gold were not over. As host and Chairman, it became my solemn duty to keep amity afloat and postpone enmity. Both heavily indebted countries with no proven oil reserves were not going to let a neighbour even attempt to explore for it.

We played with words, settled on a communiqué for the press and left the ocean floor to hide its secrets, perhaps for generations, while poverty in both lands advanced. I did not have the courage to tell the leaders of Suriname and Guyana what I was really thinking, that a federation between them was the answer. My old penchant for political union again!

Other offshore battles raged in the conference. Barbados's Owen Arthur, never mincing his words on subjects he felt passionately about, charged that statements made in certain publications by Antigua's Ron (now Sir Ron) Saunders on taxation agreements made by Barbados besmirched the region. He however succeeded at the WTO against the US attempts to stop credit card gaming.

But I kept the wine as well as the words flowing. My *vin nobile* selections supplied by the resort's sommelier superbly compensated for our previous inadequacies as a Caricom host.

I was ready to take on the Commonwealth Finance Ministers meetings, and our newly elected Secretary General, Don McKinnon, was on hand in Canouan to satisfy himself that we were up to the tasks. All dignitaries were made life-members of the Golf Club, a generous gesture from the lead developer Antonio Saladino and his partner Carlo Amato who joined us in the formal banquet. Following the example in Langkawi, where at the CHOGM all leaders planted trees, we arranged for tree-planting by Caricom leaders in the village and the resort.

Sadly, Canouan, elevated by the Caricom Conference beyond the Caribbean onto the world stage and ready for the next step of receiving Finance Ministers from the Commonwealth, committed economic suicide. St. Vincent and the Grenadines with more beautiful white sand beaches than any in the Caribbean its size, became jealous of the single beach expanded beside the resort. Opposition mischief took over. Local home-owners with suddenly improved status lost their tenants. The banks were upon them. I was getting a lot of evidence that common sense is not common. In politics you begin helping human need, and you end up facing human greed. The island was moving ahead of its people.

In April 1998, I had gone to Chile with friends and quickly discovered the early-morning frost of the southern hemisphere. My experience of lunch, looking down on the stalls with an abundance of fruit, vegetable and chilled sea food in the century-old wrought-iron market designed by the Frenchman with the Eiffel tower to his credit, inspired me, along with the markets in Barcelona and Paris, to have our city market designed as a showpiece of the diligence of our farmers and market ladies who needed to be brought off the pavements into the shade.

It was marvellous to tour the vineyards, sampling the wines that bore comparison with those in the Napa Valley, France, Spain and Italy, and dine in the seaside restaurants in Valparaiso, with the sounds of the gulls and the aroma of the seaweeds on the shoreline. The Chilean success story of the economic turn around under Augusto Pinochet was an added fascination. I bought the General's memoirs.

So I was ready for the Summit of the Americas in Chile, and to revisit my friend Eduardo Aninat, the Finance Minister, in whose company we had had great discussion on the survival of small economies within the free trade of the Americas with Robert Rubin, the American Treasury Secretary who hosted us one evening at the restaurant in New Orleans. I understood quite clearly the impediments to liberalizing our economies so that we could be competitive in attracting further direct foreign investment.

The Caribbean delegations had got together in The Bahamas where we held a session with the Canadian Prime Minister, Jean Chrétien, to establish our agenda for the conference. He kindly was offering us a ride on his plane to Chile. We were going to be allocated three minutes each for our speech. The subjects were discussed and a Caribbean spokesperson selected for each topic. I was in no rush. I was ready to deal with anything. The last item on the agenda was telecommunications, which I gladly accepted. Today the subject would have been at the head of the list with several jockeying to deal with it.

President Eduardo Frei was holding preparatory meetings with various delegations. Keith Mitchell led off for the Caribbean group. When my turn came I told the Chilean leader that he should not judge our market for his wines by the size of our populations, as this did not encompass the discerning visitors. Moreover, we were ready to receive Chileans in their winter season which was our season of low prices. He replied that he had already visited the Caribbean.

I was the last leader to be given the microphone. The Chairman regulated all speeches with buttons before him, green, amber and red, signalling the time left for each speaker. Very few speeches concluded in the amber light. I began by saying that unlike previous speakers I never liked lingering in the red light district, a reference that made the entire conference roar with laughter. I got a beautiful round of applause. My hand was pointedly shaken by every Latin leader as I went by. I also made the point that at the next Summit of the Americas, I trusted that the presence of Cuba would go beyond the circulation of Cuban cigars at banquets.

When the session in Santiago adjourned, I met up with Bill Clinton in the washroom. He loved my speech on the internationalization of mischief on the Internet, and was chuckling again about my "red light" reference. When the conference finally was finally concluding with the choice of Canada to be the next venue, Jean Chrétien promised, "I will hire my friend Son Mitchell as the gendarme."

Lunch was at the prestigious restaurant, Entre Rios, in elegant surroundings beside a stream. Host governments know good places. Beverly Arthur, Jamaican wife of Barbados Prime Minister Owen Arthur, drew my attention to the fabulous wine cellar from which, in an adjoining room, glorious vintages were on sale. She took me on tour. Her husband was not impressed. Knowing that we were flying home all the way to Barbados courtesy of the Canadian Prime Minister, I was inspired to dent my credit card a few hundred dollars for a random selection of a few cases. Settling on four bottles for Beverly, on the morning of our departure I had Chilean security deliver them to her room. Barbados had been cultivating sugar cane on the same soil for 300 years with rum shops on the perimeter of the fields providing the background for daily social encounter, and it was I suppose, presumptious of me to expect anyone nurtured in this culture to make the sacrilegious leap in a single generation from the stale aura of the rum shop to savouring fine wines.

The party convention in our new headquarters did not take lunch, late in the afternoon, until I had assured them I would lead them into the election once more. Keith Mitchell, to whom we had loaned our equipment and who had taken over the leadership of Grenada, was our guest of honour.

We won with a single-seat majority. I was therefore confronted with the final political structure in my experience of the Westminster system, from Coalition through Opposition and gaining all seats, to winning the majority of seats with a minority of the popular vote. Our New Democratic Party suffered one violent death in the 1994 campaign. A supporter in a motorcade, Elizabeth Keane, travelling in an open truck, was hit by a brick on her skull. She left a baby, Kizzy, to be cared for by her grandmother, and remaining for all time in our memory.

With the demise of the banana industry in sight, I had to press on with tourism and the next essential for economic survival was the expansion of our airport to take regional jets.

I saw no daylight until the CDB-sponsored study showed we could extend Arnos Vale with less than US$50 million. This was a figure I could find. The French had long ago pledged US$5 million for terminal and apron improvement. The Taiwanese, after St. Lucia had unceremoniously kicked them out in order to establish their international respectability, had committed US$20 million in loans and grants. I have written earlier of how on my sick-bed at the Southern Medical Clinic, recovering from prostate surgery, to my horror I witnessed the devastation of Taipei by the earthquake, sent a letter of sympathy and a $50,000 cheque to aid with the relief programme, and received $6 million in return.

I knew that I had passed the halfway mark on the Arnos Vale airport project, enough to overcome the early reservation of the Kuwaitis. So after the Durban CHOGM, Kuwait was ready to receive us.

Our next pilgrimage was to Taiwan itself. In the meantime, a new President had emerged, the Kuomintang vote being split, with our old friend, now a dissident, James Song, coming second in the election. Keith Mitchell and I were the sponsors of the Kuomintang among the Europeans, when as members of the IDU we were hosted in Madrid by the then Opposition leader, José Maria-Aznar.

The new President of Taiwan, Chen Shui-bian, was delighted to receive us, being very appreciative of the slender number of Government Heads present for his inauguration. He was a pro-independence advocate for Taiwan, and warmed to a country that was happy to risk identification with his cause. My political hunch, however misguided, was that one day China might split apart. While the country did not have the historic enmity of Yugoslavia, overcome by the strength of a Tito, I could not imaging a billion people with language and economic disparities being fused for all time without the communist imperative. I hope my fantasy of a fractured China may never dawn, but I was actually sensitive to the reality that should we all declare, in the classic style of *The Three Musketeers,* all for one China, we will be all together ignored. In any event, we had to be careful. The small state, like the small child (as America was teaching us) can be easily spanked and confined in a corner. Whenever I met with the Beijing representative I pleaded that they be patient with me. "You Chinese know how to spend one hundred years carving a single piece or ivory." (I was referring to a piece I saw in the Taipei museum.) But all along I was painfully aware

that the strings of the Lilliputians would not deter Gulliver indefinitely.
You have to be smart to postpone the inevitable. All I wanted was my
jet airstrip.

I was at pains to communicate that St. Vincent and the Grenadines
was in for the long haul as far as my party was concerned, and that we
would be friends if even we were the last at their side. He confirmed
that the funds committed by his predecessor for airport development
would be sustained. I expressed the view that even as we had the
distinguished presence of the Deputy Foreign Minister at the opening
of our Union Island Airport, there would be no greater pleasure for me
than to receive him at the inauguration of our airport extension, the vital
link in our economic development under pressure from liberalization
of world trade.

The saga did not end there. Two of my Ministers, John Horne and
Jerry Scott, were hostile to this extension. They were firmly switched
on to the building of a new international airport on other locations.
The MMM consultants from Canada, in the fashion of preliminary
consultants fattening a report, had investigated other sites, one with
a cross-wind, and both running into hundreds of millions of dollars
without any reference to the cost of removing the island's main highway
or the social disruption of destroying a sizeable number of the best
homes in the country. Moreover my first-year studies in the geology
of the Caribbean had provided sufficient warning about the andesite
and obsidian of volcanic substrata that made nonsense of the under-
estimates represented by the consultants' costing.

The dissenting Ministers were both of the view that the monies
could be found. Minister Horne, always the upright gentleman, with a
niche in the hierarchy of the Anglican Church and privately branded
"Minister of All Affairs," exceeded us all in his passion for native
culture. He failed to understand why our tourism representatives could
not get American tourists to come to our 4th July Carnival and be away
from their own Independence Day barbeques at home. A great man on
causes, the essential *fidei defensor* (defender of the faith) as inscribed
on our old coins, had come into his own creating the insignias of
honour for our country.

His committee with nationalistic exuberance was ready to recommend
that all British honours be disbanded and replaced, a historic injustice
in which I was certainly not prepared to lead, as it would have meant
renouncing my beloved acclaim as Knight Commander of "Our Most
Distinguished Order of St. Michael and St. George." And what was I
then to do with insignias from Portugal, Venezuela, Taiwan, and the

Knights of Malta? Even my Chevalier d'Honneur De La Chaine des Rotisseurs, an honour which I shared with President Reagan, would be chucked into the sea. I was not ready to shed my honours, and knew that even the reconstructed "anti-colonialists" would not discard their recognition by the Queen.

Jerry Scott simply felt that certain old friends in New York had the contacts to deliver millions. He had successfully introduced our traffic lights. And so we retired to Union Island in the Big Sand Retreat organized by our former parliamentarian Stephanie Browne. The verdict was that the two Ministers be given two months to produce the documentation of their proposals to the Ministry of Finance.

I tried to get everyone to understand that the Arnos Vale option had evolved through procedures at the Caribbean Development Bank and that the donor community would be in a position to evaluate any choice we made. The French would not commit to building a new terminal in a new location. The Bank would not lend without some semblance of propriety. The Taiwanese would not want their contribution to be indistinguishable in a *pot pourri* design. The Kuwaitis would be studying procurement.

The fudge at the Retreat delighted the Opposition.

As the prospect of the extension of the airport receded, so did my enthusiasm for governing wane. A small country had to run fast just to stand still. To go upward, it had to race. To lose its airport with the new emphasis on regional jets in the aircraft industry would jeopardize serious hotel and golf-course development on the mainland of St. Vincent. I also could see clearly that daily frequent flights to and from Puerto Rico, Miami and Caracas would open us to the world and take our country and its economy safely to another level with minimum disruption to our social order.

I arranged consultancies in our conference room in our lavish administrative centre. The private sector supported the Arnos Vale option. The local pilots and airline managers clearly understood their interests and explained to me one night at Shrewsbury House that there was no sensible alternative to the Arnos Vale extension. The representative of American Eagle repeated the plea they had made on the inaugural flight for a little more length. It had taken years of entreaty to get American Eagle into St. Vincent. Proudly our Dallas tourism agent Diana Williams and I inaugurated the placement of the SVG flag in the American Airlines atrium at the Dallas headquarters. Butch Stewart, darling of Caribbean hospitality entrepreneurs with his Sandals Resorts and Beaches, and Air Jamaica, added his voice in support of the extension of our existing runway. His thanks were to be accused of interference in our domestic politics.

Those who knew too much were accused of wanting too little, while those with little to offer sought too much. The Opposition, very much in tune with the longings of the diaspora in Brooklyn and High Wycombe, claimed to be in touch with a friendly government that would build the international airport if only they were elected. Within 200 miles we were surrounded by international airports in Martinique, St. Lucia, Barbados and Grenada, but this was irrelevant.

A slender parliamentary majority provides a platform for blackmail by the public service. Strong governments ride out storms. But it was time for infinite demands on the public purse. A 12 per cent salary increase in the public sector was a joke. They wanted 30 per cent. Spurred by the teachers union, the nurses and doctors got in the queue. A Catholic priest and nun led demonstrations of school children demanding more allocation of funds to private schools, for they were suffering from the withdrawal of foreign subsidies for the same reason that we in Government were experiencing the withdrawal of concessionary finance since we had attained the status of middle-income country. In my time as Prime Minister we had doubled our per capita income.

In the previous Parliament I had sought to secure a gratuity for senators, a plea not inconsistent with the normal severance pay laws in the country. The Opposition felt that salaries and conditions should be guided by independent and well-respected persons. The suggestion was accepted. The Governor of the Central Bank, Dwight Venner, who had undertaken such an exercise in the Virgin Islands, agreed to chair. He agreed also to work with the Chairman of our Chamber of Industry and Commerce, Martin Barnard, Henry Gaymes, a former Director General of Finance, and the retired Judge, Barry Renwick. Barry's pithy epithet, bestowed on me on a previous occasion, was to prove a prophecy: "No kindness goes unpunished."

My Government's acceptance of the Venner report on terms and conditions of service of parliamentarians, even though we had agreed with the 12 per cent increase throughout the public service, aroused bitter complaint. Disenchanted offshore interests, unable to manipulate a Ministry of Finance trying to come to terms with the scrutiny of the Financial Action Task Force, found an opportunity to finance mischief. But their beneficiaries were in due course forced to abandon them when the courts in Florida called.

The police proved useless in dealing with the Opposition blocking the roads into the city. While I had tripled opportunities with expansion of the officer ranks in the force and expanded too the total numbers and improved their accommodation, I learnt that the police would never be satisfied. As soon as an officer secured promotion he was ready for the next rank the next day. Disloyalty triumphed. I knew that as soon as the strategic plans to deal with demonstration were formulated, techniques of frustration were implemented.

There was no way I was going to end my political career calling on the support of the Regional Security System. I understood quite clearly that the salient truth of democracy is that the majority has the right to be wrong. Our country could not spend 60 per cent of its revenue on salaries. Parliamentarians deserved equity. The poor and youth also had a right to a place in Parliament, not just the professionals and those with inherited comfort.

I who had helped to resolve conflict in the region was ready to have colleagues work with me to resolve our issues. Basdeo Panday and Denzil Douglas came in to meet with the patched-together Organization for Defence of Democracy (ODD) and the Cabinet. The visiting Prime Ministers were given short shrift, and had suffered acute indignities in diversion from the main road, crawling through the barbed-wire security fence around the airport to get to the meeting at Sunset Shores.

At the meeting of the OECS in Grenada I put the matter on the agenda. Our Authority of all the Prime Ministers and Chief Ministers agreed to meet with the ODD. Accordingly, they arrived. Hardly had the meeting got under way in the evening, when I invited the Leader of the Opposition, Ralph Gonsalves to join me outside the room. I wanted the ODD isolated and ignored. That was accomplished when I walked out of the room.

I was ready to make a compromise as the Guyana government had done, shortening the life of their parliament for the preservation of peace. My spirit was already shaken by disappointment with the public servants, for whom I had done so much, the disloyalty of the police, and my Ministers not seeing the wisdom of developing our opportunities with jet transport to Miami before the banana industry collapsed.

On the beach Gonsalves and I agreed to have elections the next year at the end of March. We would also incorporate the recommendations of the former Barbadian Attorney General Maurice King on the status of the Pension and Gratuity Bill before Parliament. The only voice that furiously rejected the curtailment of the life of a Parliament was Lester Bird of Antigua. Keith Mitchell did not like the speed of the resolution, but accepted that I did not fear the electoral process. Rosie Douglas of

Dominica enjoyed himself. He was not to attend, however, many more meetings beyond his excursions to Libya.

Alone in the hotel room in Grenada I said my usual prayer. My thoughts were simple: I do not fear elections. I fear ignorance. Ignorance fomented by intrigue, and blown up, like the soap bubble of a child can glisten in the sunshine but only for a while. I do not despair.

I did not despair even as an eight-year-old when news of my father's disappearance at sea made me weep. Even then I was ready to be a Captain conquering foreign seas, far away from home. My ship now was the New Democratic Party, soundly built in the hearts and minds of those whose quality of life was our creation. The mirror that is democracy allows us to see, in time, the reflection of our stupidity. I was sure my party would survive the storms. I had found the best intellects in the country to lead the party forward. I knew that beyond the elections the storms of liberalization that lay ahead. I had made Government look easy.

After the Grand Beach Accord, the only thing left on the Opposition's agenda was to threaten again to disrupt the country if we proceeded with the extension of the Arnos Vale Airport. After I surrendered the leadership of the party, stepping aside as Senior Minister, the new Prime Minister Arnhim Eustace declined to sign the final design contract won by Sypher Mueller in competitive tender. He also cancelled the technical visits of the Kuwaiti Fund.

My Director of Planning, Laura Anthony-Browne called on me in anguish. She felt that brochures were taking precedence over engineering analysis. (In retrospect, she was pleased to have videoed the ceremony of my departure as Prime Minister. She knew it was history, she said.) I had assumed that my successor would be wise enough to value our legacy and deploy our experience toward new triumphs. Instead I could see my vision of a jetport in St. Vincent vanishing, our direct linkage to Caracas and Miami receding like a mirage in a desolate landscape, and the ship of state drifting inexorably, only to founder in the turbulence of the Taiwan Strait. When you can no longer climb the mountain, enjoy the valley. It was time to go home and smell the Frangipani flowers.

"Much to praise, little to fault." No failed state on my watch. The Opposition exposed our dissension on airport development. A new music was in the air. The Barbadian entertainers staged the old calypso on the invasion of Union Island, some twenty years before: *Boots, boots.* The young people danced and so came the swing. All eyes were focused on Libya. The new government delegation was hardly out of Tripoli when the Twin Towers in New York collapsed. I could drink a Riesling in Alsace.

I prepared to retire. I had won election in the Grenadines constituency nine times, in 1966, 1967, 1972, 1974, 1980, 1984, 1989, 1994, 1998. I began with 56 per cent of the votes and ended with 88 per cent, with 92 per cent on one occasion. No one had served in Parliament in our country longer than I did. No one had led a party to four consecutive victories.

The path to success, not always glorious, like flotsam washed up on an Atlantic shore was strewn with the detritus of human mischief, often regretfully condoned, allowing for example, a supporter in Mayreau, to claim expenses for the jack ass he borrowed from Carriacou to carry sand uphill, on the US funded Basic Human Needs Project, village road building. On the other hand, I objected to writing in a will for a returning seaman, in his pique, leaving a glass of water for his errant wife. On another occasion, late one evening, after a political meeting in the countryside, I responded to a young man begging for 25 cents, "What can you get for 25 cents at this hour of the night?"

"A girl," he said.

Pleasure out of poverty and pain for me. Footprints in our history.

The Grenadines, at the time of adult suffrage in 1951, had one seat out of eight. The totals were changed to nine and thirteen, and when the Parliament extended the number to fifteen, it was time for the Grenadines to have two seats. My loyalties were torn between the northern and southern islands, but I had a superb candidate, Mary Hutchinson, already a Senator, whose husband, a respected businessman, had been jailed by the Labour Government during the Union Island uprising.

She beat me into second place in percentage of votes, securing a cool 92 per cent. I had had to tell the people in the Southern Grenadines that I would buy land and build a home or even a hotel to be a presence among them. I did not proceed, after investments with which I could not compete gained a foothold.

I was not happy with the ugly shacks along Britannia Bay where the fishermen squatted, nor were the indigenous people of the island satisfied with their landless condition. Cardinal Simon, a returner from England, who boasted that his culinary skills had been tasted by Her Majesty, had his own ideas. I helped him form the Mustique Indigenous People's Association to hold its own with the Mustique Company, and I had the institution incorporated in Parliament. I became Patron of his organization, while being a member of the Mustique directorate. Together we secured the rights of persons born in Mustique and those living in the village. The edict of Colin Tennant that there be no funerals in Mustique, so that the island's image is one of perpetual joy and happiness, was set aside and a cemetery was established. Before this, all the dead had to be buried elsewhere.

But with the passage of time, home-owners too in Mustique were passing away. Like my friend Harding Lawrence, who requested I deliver a eulogy at his memorial service in the Bamboo Church. In quick succession, I was called on to do the honours for Princess Margaret, along with Colin Tennant. I substituted for the Duke of Kent whose sudden departure was occasioned by the death of the Queen Mother. I thought it singularly significant that the descendant of a pirate should be paying homage to the Royal Family.

Passionately I had pursued building up the infrastructure of the country, saving a little at home, creating a modest surplus, and blending our resources with funds sought and secured beyond our borders. The construction industry boomed. Heavy equipment could now be imported duty free. Scholarships for young people flourished. The land reform programme produced a property-owning democracy. A middle class emerged even in the countryside. Potable water was available everywhere save the dry Grenadines. Electricity reached the remotest end of our Carib country.

Progress with infrastructure was more easily accomplished than human development. At the switching-on ceremony, putting lights into the Carib country for people ignored since the end of the Carib wars in the eighteenth century, a young teacher asked if I would be paying her light bill. I had no answer for her taunt. Her question made me recognize that in spite of my land reform, many hoped to reap without sowing. She could easily be bribed.

Sometimes, though, I enjoyed my success all alone. After switching on the lights in Union Island, I spent a night at Petit St. Vincent, the southernmost island of my domain, courtesy Hazen Richardson, the current owner. He gave me an isolated cottage in the north-west. I enjoyed the lights of Union Island miles away, across the water. I went to sleep in the hammock enjoying what I had done for those loving old ladies in Ashton.

The governor of our Central Bank, Dwight Venner, once enquired of me, how I had succeeded in finding so much financing out of Europe.

"Simple", I told him. "Call Europe at 3 o'clock in the morning, and be the first on their agenda. Don't wait until you get into office at nine o'clock, and Europe is at lunch."

He digested my advice, for when news broke about the pending bankruptcy of BARINGS, who were in charge of over US$50 million of our reserves, he was first on the line to the Bank of England. I guess I saved us millions.

My turn for the calypso came with "Nancy," where I was compared with the legendary spider that ensnared the entire animal kingdom. Now, I was not gifted in music. Everyone seems to have accepted my rendition of "Oh God, our help in ages past" when I opened my political meetings assisted by the old ladies. Beyond that, any vocal rendition was greeted with immediate derision. But I could listen to music and discern a good tune. At the end of one budget debate, early in the Carnival season, I complained, "Believe you me; I will never ban a calypso as my predecessors did. I don't mind a calypso being made up on me, but for God's sake, give me a good tune."

The calypso flopped. "Nancy" became only a shout at my passing car. I accepted the nickname and used it to taunt all and sundry when my strategies triumphed

I became increasingly concerned with balancing healthy attitudes with material progress, and the legislative formula was to no avail in this regard. Noise pollution with imported radios and churches proclaiming their God-given right to place amplifiers outside the churches, disturbing entire communities, always imposed in me a sense of regret for introducing electricity into the villages.

Our police, brought up in this noisy culture, did not enforce the law. I felt a sense of impotence as Minister responsible for the police when at midnight I could give no comfort to the entreaties of an old lady or to the folk in hospital. Our culture was becoming noise. Three notes pounding away became music. The centres of entertainment could not afford to be air-conditioned. The whole Caribbean was losing its serenity. A cynical travel writer, witnessing the environmental purity in Mustique declared it was a rather "unCaribbean" island with the absence of chaos. With failure in the system, the law, and the police, I had no refuge but to disconnect my phone so that I could sleep and recover my sanity.

I once endured an indoor Carnival celebration in Canouan, seated in the front row between two massive boom boxes. For two weeks after it I thought I was deaf. My hearing eventually recovered a bit, but whenever I do not hear the telephone ring I recall my prime ministerial ears being deafened. The island that I loved, to which I brought millions in investment, stole from me, for all time, the beautiful melody of a child's voice.

It was painful too to experience individual selfishness. A lady on the ferry complained about the water on her property coming down the hill toward her house. Did she know I was returning from a nasal operation in the hospital? Yes, but she had not seen me for a few weeks, and the rain was ruining her land.

Many a time a small-island politician wishes he could get away from the immediacy of the constituency. My 35 years at 15 hours a day meant that compared with the clock-watchers in the Civil Service I worked for 70 years. But perhaps the most intriguing demand imposed was a midnight call when I had finally reached my own bed after flying from Taiwan.

"Prime Minister! There is a donkey in my yard knocking down my paw paw tree with the paw paw I sell to the tourists. When are we going to get the law to shoot donkeys?"

I duly legislated for such a law.

How the scene has changed. Eugenia Charles, John Compton and I shared out Europe. Centuries ago, a Pope had shared out the New World, giving Brazil to Portugal, and the rest of South America to Spain. Our sharing, though, was not ambitious conquest but simply allocating responsibility for lobbying in Europe to maintain our small share of the banana market in England, threatened by invasion from the "banana republics" and the persuasive clout of the American multinationals.

Europe too was moving beyond the European Economic Community into the European Union. We could not afford embassies in every capital. Prime Ministers received courtesies abroad but we all had our mini-states to run.

So we alternated our visits to Europe, restricting ourselves to our allocated countries. We all did London, Brussels and Paris. Eugenia and John concentrated on the North while my territory was Spain, Portugal, Italy and Ireland. Our message was that we were democracies, and democratic competition influenced our high cost of production on mountainous terrain while the American interests benefited from the penury they imposed on the Latin American plantations.

We were moderately successful, with the humorists at home playing upon the acronym of the OECS: Only Eugenia, Compton and Son.

Sensitive to the limited time Europe had given us in the protection of our banana market, aware too of the concessionary financing that had come our way by dint of prudent fiscal management at home while our anti-communist stance inspired confidence, I became acutely aware of the transition in those historic times. I told my colleagues that, while I had faith in our beautiful countries and their resources, like the empires that had risen and fallen, we should recognize that a country was never aware of its golden age until it was over.

I wanted to see my friend John Compton placed so that his illustrious career could be capped with another glory. He had been the longest-serving Minister of Finance in the region, with a voice respected in World Bank circles. Our joint family background of the sea and shipbuilding had led him into the University of Wales, and the London School of Economics, where he did Economics and Law. He too, would make a good President for the CDB, the institution he co-founded.

Compton retired and ushered Vaughn Lewis, the Secretary General of the OECS, into the leadership of his UWP. In discussions, we resolved the issue of a seat in Parliament for Vaughn. George Mallet, the long-serving Trade Minister, would vacate and become Governor General. Everything fell into place and the voters obliged.

Vaughn seemed set to expand the glory of the Lewis family name, following Sir Arthur's Nobel Prize and Sir Allen's tenure as a Chief Justice. The British were ready to flatter. On becoming Prime Minister, Vaughn was invited to deliver a lecture at his old stamping ground at the University of Manchester.

I began my lobby for the vacant post of CDB President. P.J. Patterson of Jamaica was willing to withdraw his nominee Rodrick Rainford if the retired Prime Minister of St. Lucia was put forward. But the new Prime Minister of St. Lucia did not nominate Compton for the post.

I urged too that Vaughn name the Vigie Airport in honour of George Mallet who had done more as a Tourism Minister than anyone else in St. Lucia and who had vacated the seat, making Vaughn's leadership possible. "It will cause a fuss," was Vaughn's response. Two weeks after he lost the general election, the incoming government named the airport after the resurrected George Charles.

As the old order changed, once more I had to welcome a work with a new dispensation among my neighbours.

Eugenia Charles was the first to go. She called a convention of her Freedom Party and her Attorney-General, Brian Alleyne, was elected, much to her dislike. She refused to let him act as Prime Minister in her absence, but still found herself on the rostrum supporting him during the general election. The party lost. Brian took a job as a judge in our Supreme Court. Keith Mitchell agreed to have him in Grenada, and soon he was burnishing his non-political credentials.

Edison James took over the leadership of Dominica. I sent Arnhim Eustace, my Fiscal Adviser and Chairman of the Banana Company, WIBDECO, to brief him for two days on the banana market. He joined me on a banana mission to Europe. I had to distance myself from his plea for funding recurrent expenditure on school books, but in Paris I introduced him to good red wine, as his dislike of the stuff had come from the obviously poor, probably smuggled stuff from Guadeloupe which he had imbibed. We became good friends.

The departure of John and Eugenia, my trusted buddies in the OECS, meant the end of the early morning phone-calls, plotting our banana strategy for Europe, the US and Latin America, fortifying each other, our currency and our islands. Between us we had logged 100 years of parliamentary experience.

Democracy, and the never-to-be-worn-out political slogan, "time for change," was selling around the region. Communism and socialism, the self-righteous blessing emanating from the intellectuals, was buried without a eulogy or apology.

My other neighbour Barbados underwent singular trauma, losing two Prime Ministers by heart attack, Tom Adams and also Errol Barrow. Erskine Sandiford succeeded Errol. He made the fatal error of assuming he had the mantle similar to a founding father in a political party. He was no Errol Barrow, Battle of Britain spitfire pilot, a charismatic figure who put the partnership between business and the trade unions together.

So all around me I was outliving changes. In my time, Trinidad had gone from Williams to George Chambers, A.N.R. Robinson, Patrick Manning and Basdeo Panday. Guyana had gone from Burnham, to Cheddi Jagan, Janet Jagan, and Bharrat Jagdeo. Jamaica from Shearer to Seaga, Manley and Patterson. Gairy in Grenada had been followed by Maurice Bishop, Coard, Nicholas Brathwaite, Blaize, Ben Jones, Brathwaite again, George Brizan, and Keith Mitchell. Antigua went from V.C. Bird to Lester Bird. I'd seen St. Kitts/Nevis through from Bradshaw to Southwell, to Kennedy Simmonds and Denzil Douglas. St. Lucia went from John Compton to Vaughn Lewis to Kenny Anthony, that charismatic enigma, my friend the Oxford-educated George Odlum, always on the periphery. And Dominica ended up with the unreconstructed socialist, Rosie Douglas, putting his faith in help from Gadaffi.

In the wider Commonwealth there was a sea-change of faces. All that was left of the league I joined were Mahathir of Malaysia, Museveni of Uganda, Gayoon of the Maldives, and Mugabe of Zimbabwe. Even Mandela had come and gone, followed by Mbeki.

It was time for me to go. In the language of cricket I wanted to declare my innings closed. Not bowled, caught, or run out. I had enough runs on the tins. Michael Manley had come to see me with Butch Stewart to discuss tourism and airline privatization after he had given way to P.J. Patterson, outliving his own socialist credentials.

"How do you feel to have your successor win an election without you?" I asked.

"My cup is full and running over." He replied. It was the last time I saw him.

Mine had been the role of eulogies, for Barrow and Gairy, and kneeling at the state funerals for Bradshaw, Jagan and Pindling.

My first three daughters were out of university. My health seemed to be holding. Political endurance kept me wondering how many more new faces I would welcome. It did not stop me from thinking about moving on, just as the shock of the disappearance of my father in the Bermuda Triangle, the image of the masts of his ship still standing with torn sails and the decks awash in the ocean, did not eliminate my lust for distant lands.

My nanny Amelia had wanted me to be a priest. I couldn't imagine myself stuck in a parish with old ladies. Love of science took me into agriculture and contact with the English hierarchy in the Imperial College in Trinidad that was luring me, like them, into the management of the resources of the tropics. Then beautiful distant Vancouver. On to a spell as an agronomist in the islands. Wandering again in Europe until the collapse of the West Indies Federation found me one Sunday morning searching for earrings on a beach in Italy after a night of grappa. I would reunite the Caribbean. Big dream. But at the end of it all I wanted above all to retire from politics undefeated. No enemy will ever boast of my defeat.

I had enough runs on the scoreboard. Let others try to surpass my score. With 35 years' service I was the longest-serving parliamentarian in St. Vincent, and at the time, the longest-serving Prime Minister in the Caribbean. I had also done a lot of firsts. First to be Premier as an Independent. First to break the mould of two-party politics with a third party. First to win four consecutive general elections. The only leader left that had seen his country from colonialism to Independence. From the twentieth century into the twenty-first.

I had founded a political party. I knew that its ultimate proof of success would be for it to succeed without me, and that I should establish a series of traditions within my party. And our country needed to have in its history, for the first time, a leader who retired undefeated. Before me, they had all perished, and were defeated. Up to the moment of retirement, I controlled 85 per cent of the votes in my Grenadines constituency, easily bestowing this legacy on my successor. My party had lost three Secretaries-General, Owen Walker, Stuart Nanton and Kelvin Gibson. All three had died.

In order to retire I had to find two successors, one to lead the party, a tricky task, and one to take over the constituency, an easy gift. All that was necessary in Bequia was to summon the faithful. Hundreds. A few of the curious slipped in. The venue that Sunday afternoon was the dining-room of our neighbouring Gingerbread Restaurant, anchored beside the beach with enough engineering expertise to challenge a tsunami, and delicately finished in an intricate fretwork, an imaginative fantasy by the architect Mario Spinella, evoking a graceful whale courting a frangipani flower, two icons of land and sea, seeped in the culture of Bequia, and a suitable setting for the changing of the guard. My ex-wife Pat, now a business partner, and Managing Director of Gingerbread, had the place prepared.

Four candidates emerged, my dutiful Parliamentary Secretary Rocky McIntosh; Jeannie Ollivierre, retired from my Women's Affairs department; Cosmos Cozier, now retired, hoping to return from New Jersey to recapture the glory when he stood in for me while I experimented in another constituency; and Loraine Friday, a lawyer with a Canadian doctorate – his candidacy espoused by the charming boutique manager, Cynthia Marks, reading out his credentials in his absence. He made it.

The crowd was boisterous. I tried to bring some order. We tried out writing the names on paper. Confusion. But the trend was clear. They wanted someone whom they imagined would replace my fighting spirit and said so noisily. Loraine Friday was finally agreed on.

My New Democratic Party did not want me to retire. My health was sending other messages. I did not want to perish on the job. Earlier encounters with accidents, at sea, and once being almost electrocuted, had hinted at mortality. Two nasal operations, one in Dallas, and the second at home, carried out by St. Clair Thomas (who became a candidate, Senator, and my Minister of Health) had toned down my expectations. (Our hospital had ensconced me in the maternity wing for security reasons, a great place for a Prime Minister to be reminded by screams of his responsibility for the next generation.)

The Heart Place, the Tom Landry Center in Dallas, prescribed medication. So did our visiting specialist, Grady Hendrix, who lectures in our offshore medical school, after another set of tests in South Carolina. Then at the University of Miami, Dr. Eduardo de Marchena arranged with his specialist Dr. Alberto Interian to straighten me out. It would be the next day or in three weeks. I was ready for the operation the next morning, called my Governor General, and told him he should prepare to find another Prime Minister.

As I recounted earlier, the next day Eduardo and his team doing the rounds at Jackson Memorial Hospital informed me that I was "cured," a term that I pointed out had never come my way from the medical profession. I was ready for some good wine.

Our party convention, bolstered by the presence of Keith Mitchell from Grenada, would not be satisfied until I declared that I should run one more time and thrash the opposition. But it was going to be my last election. After a lunch at the residence, I invited my colleagues to contemplate my succession.

"Gentlemen, are you ready to choose my successor? Which of you are ready to come forward?"

The long-serving Jerry Scott put forward his name. The newcomer, the economist I had brought in – Arnhim Eustace, my Finance Minister – timidly indicated his willingness. In popularity inside the Party, Jerry would win, but our constitution confined choice to the parliamentarians, and I was sure, the capacity for economic management would prevail.

My mother had gone to high school with Arnhim's mother, and she was at hand next door in Edinboro when he was born. He was one of the economists on my team, the other being Ambassador Kingsley Layne, when I assigned the task of import substitution in the energy crisis of October 1973. A series of appointments at home and at the CDB propelled him forward. I had brought him home to help me implement my plan to restructure the banana industry in the Windward Islands. With the guidance of Samuel Montague in London, we had successfully negotiated the joint-venture purchase of Geest industries with Fyffes of Ireland as our partner, with funding from the Allied Irish Bank. I had found him a seat in parliament, by luring his predecessor Carlyle Dougan into being High Commissioner in London, a transition encouraged by his wife Elma. On the conclusion of one of my budget addresses in Parliament, Arnhim's wife Jennifer congratulated me on my presentation. I told her that one day I expected her husband to deliver a budget before I left the scene.

We summoned a convention in Victoria Park, the place I had brought the first African President, Kenneth Kaunda, to address St. Vincent and the Grenadines. The additional royal palms I had had planted dignified the location. In this park where I once hit a single six outside the grounds in a cricket game, and failed to win even a third prize in athletics, before a cast of thousands, my successor was selected. I took the parliamentarians aside in a private room. We agreed that the Minister Glenford Stewart collect and count the ballots. We returned to the throne. I said my favourite prayer and announced my successor.

So we had a new President of the party, Arnhim Eustace. I would demit office as Prime Minister at a time of my choosing.

At Independence Day, after my final overview, returning to the arms of my four daughters, I demitted office, holding on as Senior Minister until elections. I advised my successor to launch his new career, staking out his concern for the poor. Their monthly allocation called poor relief was to be raised from 60 to 100 dollars a month.

I could feel the tears in the pavilion. The aftermath of my loss of the premiership in 1974 had taught me to anticipate the wave of ensuring ingratitude and one abiding reality: the friends you meet on the way up are the friends you meet on the way down. Retirement, I knew, would be a variation of that theme. Many times, I would think back on the fortuitous, but difficult decisions of my mother, which made me a Vincentian. Had not my father's ship the *Fauna* been wrecked, with the family having to return to Bequia to build another schooner, I would have been born in Curaçao, as a Dutchman. Had she not left me behind with my grandmother when she took her other children to St. Lucia, I would have been a patois-speaking St. Lucian.

But that disappearance of my father, and my mother leaving me behind in Bequia, taught me at an early age to say goodbye. Retiring from power was just another goodbye. For all my 16 years, the Prime Minister's residence was a lonely house, not a home. My children and friends were only occasional visitors. It was a work-station. My last daughter Gabija, in the naïve perception of youth, asked her older sister Sabrina, "Why does Daddy not come home every night like other fathers?"

"You'll have to learn to put up with it, as we did," Sabrina replied.

But sacrifice has its compensations. I can reflect on many tributes, the best being the simplest. In the early days before the jetties were built in the islands and container ships unloaded delicatessen specialties, adulation took quite primitive form. I remember visiting Canouan, before Rosewood and Raffles introduced refined cuisine, when a fisherman greeted me with beaming enthusiasm: "Son Mitchell, when I see you I feel so good. It's like I eat goat."

In these modern times I would like to assume I would be elevated to proscuito.

In retirement I attended the funeral of the old salt, Officer De Roche, who had on occasion sailed me in his fishing boat between the islands. His son Louis, a trader between Miami and Haiti, regaled me on how I had brought Canouan out of the Dark Ages. Before my time, an old lady, Tante Lizzy, had received her first US dollars and pasted them on her partition. Her son Job had sent money home "to pretty up the house." I had seen out the last four decades of the twentieth century. My team had brought home the information revolution. Computers were duty free. Young girls, the daughters of peasants, were sporting mobile phones as a fashion statement. We had broken monopolies in the region.

Glenford Stewart, our Minister of Communications and Works, himself a Consulting Engineer, and his partners from the other islands, Calixe George in St. Lucia, Cedric Liburd in St. Kitts, along with our technical expert Donny DeFreitas were in turn properly advised by the World Bank experts, with assistance from the International Telecommunications Union and the US Federal Communications Commission. They exposed the imbalances and carried the battle to Cable and Wireless.

As a young Trade Minister, I had negotiated that company's entry into our islands providing us with reliable service, and I had now survived to spawn the challenge to their exploitive monopoly. As I said earlier, at a lunch in Jamaica I could taunt their Caribbean Director that I was satisfied they had made more money out of us than we had received from Britain as independence grant and loan, a remark that P.J. Patterson equated with the unkindness of our fast bowlers. Digicel, A T & T, and Orange descended upon us.

My government too had broken the television monopoly and licensed the cable company Karib Cable owned by Kelly and Jankie Glass. And we unleashed the licences for FM radio stations, swinging the pendulum of abuse and praise in the holy name of democracy.

We were becoming the victim of the revolution of rising expectations. The careful restructuring I had done of public-sector grades and salaries was long forgotten, the pending collapse of protection for our banana industry ignored. And I was not prepared to summon the help of the Regional Security Forces to compensate for the disloyalty in our own ranks. The upper echelons of the police force were saturated with ingratitude. When you have conquered many mountains, lifting generations of your citizens to new heights, delivering sumptuous reward to them beyond their dreams, and joy out of your own anguish, and when at the end of it they all become puppy dogs nibbling at your ankles, it is time to take off the socks, throw them away, time to move on.

A Prime Minister receives many gifts. It seems that biblical prophesy has to be fulfilled in this regard: "He that hath, to him shall be given." So it was with a series of wrist watches, many of which I passed on to needy supporters. I kept the gold Rolex given to me by Bozo Dabinovic, but it spent its life in my safe. I was not going to wear a Rolex to a meeting with the donor community, nor I was going to wear it as lead negotiator on bananas.

Safely out of politics I took out the Rolex. I joined my good friend Carlo taking his 1948 Bentley from Miami to Portland and on the ferry to Yarmouth. Vintage Bentley and Rolex go together. In glorious anonymity we took the corner table in the dining-room of the ferry boat, *The Scotia Prince*, and summoned the wine waiter.

"Sir James, delighted to have you at my table." It was one of the Webbs from the village of Edinboro at home. He had heard my farewell speech "Nothing" in Democrat Square, voted for my party and returned to his ship the next day. "Without you in charge, Sir James, I will not be going home for a long time," he intoned. Like the beautiful people we had lured into the landscape of Mustique, surprised to discover friends of friends, I had finally become a small-worlder.

27

Reflections

Religion and politics

One relic of my religious youth as an acolyte in the white alb with a silken cord tying up the waist, which served me in trying times, was the evening prayer. It served me several times when I was alone in the Opposition fighting the regime that described itself as the "strongest government in the world." It served me in the pain after double knee replacement in Copenhagen. And in my final days as Chairman of Caricom in Montego Bay, when we were all set to receive Prime Minister Chrétien for a Canada–Caribbean Summit, and he called to say that be would only grace us by shaking hands, because on the plane to join us he had received the tragic news of the death of Pierre Trudeau, the prayer provided my only speech. The Canadian delegation joined us around the banquet table; I called for a minute's silence and then prayed:

"Oh, Lord, support us all the day long of this troublous life, until the evening comes, the shades lengthen, the busy world is hushed, the fever of life is over, and our work is done; then Lord, in Thy mercy, grant us a safe lodging, a holy rest, and peace at the last."

It was and still is a very comforting prayer.

Protocol required that I represent the community at the funeral of Trudeau as I had done for Lynden Pindling in The Bahamas, but I was exhausted from travel. John Compton, retired, and of the group (including Barrow) who sailed with us when we entertained Pierre Trudeau in Isle à Quatre on his honeymoon, represented us instead.

But it was amazing how much strength I received as I would say this prayer. I governed myself and others, but always keenly sensitive to my own mortality. In the glory of office I always knew its transience, its fleeting happiness. When we captured all the seats in 1989, and a cartoon of a painting of Vincent Beache, the defeated leader depicted on a beach of garbage, much to the amusement of thousands at Victoria

Park, I called for the return to the stage of the painting for my personal observation, saying to the crowd, "Let me enjoy this, for one day you'll be laughing at me too."

My religious training had taught me some serious lessons in politics that I used to advise my new Cabinet at our first meeting: "We are all worshipped now. Remember the fate of Christ. I expect one of you disciples will betray me. And remember too, those who say 'Hosanna' in the morning will say 'Crucify him' in the evening." Ultimately, history engenders cynicism in politics. Democracy reflects the other lesson of the crucifixion, that the thief Barabas will be chosen rather than Christ. With such philosophy ingrained, a leader can be bold and stride forward while ahead.

Above all I warned that one particular tenet must always be with us while we have all the power: "We must do nothing with this power that we could not face without it as ordinary citizens." This has been my repeated plea. I had concluded, too, a philosophy of life: moderation in all things, including moderation.

But it was not all sadness while I was alone in Opposition. I found ways and means to laugh, and have the whole country laughing, and my laughter on the radio once a year at budget time was heard in Barbados and St. Lucia. A mechanical blurry sound like an engine was deliberately put on radio to accompany my speech and make it inaudible. But my prayer fortified me. When we lost in all seats but mine in December 1974, all my friends in my home in Bequia were speechless. They did not touch a drink on the table. But my spirit never broke.

One Sunday morning, I had a visit at my home in Bequia from the Chairman of the Banana Association, Martin Barnard, briefing me on the draft Bill before Parliament to confer authority on the Cabinet to control the Association's directorate. I gave him my answer. "The Grenadines have no bananas, but that would not stop me from representing the farmers in St. Vincent who are my friends. I would not however be objecting to more power over the industry being given the Government, as one day I hope to be the Government."

All that I had gone through in childhood, the loneliness away from my mother, the discipline in university, coupled with the financial independence, however limited, allowed me to withstand the trials of Opposition. My yellow Volkswagen had become the symbol of resistance in the remotest village as she faithfully scaled the ridges and troughs of the rough roads all the way to the deprived Carib country.

The St. James Bible which had been presented to me at my confirmation, a gift from the Archbishop of York to my English priest

Father Mallet, at his ordination earlier in the century, accompanied me to Trinidad, Canada, Europe and into the Prime Minister's residence. The Kingdom of Heaven, for me, lodged within. As a young man in Kingstown I would visit four churches on a Sunday night, catching up on friends, mainly the girls, be they Catholic, Anglican, Methodist or Gospel Hall. My stepfather had some books on the Rosicrucian faith that he allowed me to read. In Trinidad at college, I was invited to a lady's home for discussions on theosophy and the writings of Annie Besant. One evening at her home in Woodbrook, we got together with Adrian Coli Rienzi, a trade unionist but passionately into theosophy also.

In London I drifted into existentialism, Sartre, Camus, Kierkegaard. Once, an Australian girl had taken me to a play, *Waiting for Godot*, in a funny little theatre, and the images of the play transposed themselves into my grande finale in the last campaign speech on "Nothing." (In response to the charge from opponents that I had accomplished nothing, I listed the institutions built and had the thousands in the audience shouting "Nothing.")

All this exposure saved me from being a "born-again Christian" for I had long been on the religious road, and the churches that probably thought I would be embarrassed to preach on their invitation to a Prime Minister found that I was not a lost soul. A plethora of little churches got going. We helped them with lumber and galvanize roofing, and paved the strips to their entrances. All to advance the religious cause. But freeing up the airwaves to include Spiritual Baptists and Adventists did not go down well with the established churches, the Catholic and Anglicans. The Canon in charge of the Anglican Cathedral let it be known that he would not be on our radio again!

My deep-seated understanding of religion with its attendant adoration of fanaticism inspired my lecture in 1990 to our Foreign Ministers in the region that with the collapse of communism and apartheid and the Cold War put aside, the cause of conflict in the twenty-first century would be religion, the battle between Islam and Judaism in the Middle East, and the internecine hatred between the Catholics and Protestants in Ireland. But who would listen to a small voice in the wilderness of the United Nations at the 50th anniversary singling out the terrorism inspired by Islam to be the main unfinished business of the world body!

Even as the celebration of a phase of life as Prime Minister prevailed, I never allowed myself to forget the stark loneliness of Opposition and vacant days when I would place the map of our country before me and pick random villages, one by one, to be visited with only a friend or two beside me. So too, many nights before the Prime Minister in me went to sleep, my mind would drift to those villages again, one by one, and contemplate what I could do for them, the only difference between the dreary old days and the present season of flattery being that my car no longer broke down in the darkness of night.

Portugal had invited me to their Expo, a splendid reminiscence of their early conquest of the oceans, and exposure of the technology of modern oceanography. I had developed good relations with Professor Joao de Deus Pinheiro, Development Commissioner of the European Union whence we were extracting funds for irrigation projects. Portugal had been on our side in the Banana War with the US. I also promoted their cause, all the way to a seat on the Security Council of the UN. So I was to be invested with the Order of Infante Dom Henrique, Grand Cross. I took along our Honorary Consul for Portugal, Richard Joachim and his wife Nancy, and his brother Jack. Jeannette and Gabija were with me. High up on my list of special restaurants in various corners of the globe to which I would willingly return is the Tromba Rija in Mazzazes, where the Deputy Foreign Minister, Luis Amado entertained us to the ultimate in Portuguese cuisine, complete with the local wine. The Tromba Rija is two storeys deep with an open court, the customers above looking down on the extraordinary range of specialties. The meal was a three-hour affair and through all this array of dishes, beautifully prepared, my eight-year-old Gabija, having discovered the enormous difference between fresh Portuguese tuna and our tinned import, concentrated on the sardines.

In solitary moments too, my memory often floats back to the evening in the cathedral of San Francisco in Quito, where at the end of a session of the Economic Commission for Latin America in the 1970s, entertained by the diminutive dictator (who had lectured us on democracy in the morning), a single spotlight beamed on the long fingers of a beautiful Argentinean harpist before the altar, in an ambience of the reflected golden décor emerging out of the darkness, as we listened to the single notes issuing from her, filling the cathedral and inspiring my raptures of appreciation.

Into this century, and more recently, when requested to finance musical instruction for my teenage daughter, I wondered if by chance it would be the harp? With stern realism I got the answer. "What, Daddy! You think I am an angel?"

Sins, faux pas and misdemeanours
My life from youth had gone through a strange gamut of experiences: acolyte in the Anglican Church, sailor, navigator, agronomist, hotelier,

husband, father and lover. All had produced in me a kaleidoscope of images which surfaced in response to random demands for speeches at odd moments. So I would sometimes refer to schoolboy thinking in the language of cricket or the religious stuff I imbibed under the tutelage of a matriarchal grandmother, or my inherited language of the sea that pervaded the rhetoric of the fishermen and sailors in my constituency. To the untutored in these indulgences, I was easily deemed a lunatic.

When a Minister got himself into trouble, becoming an electoral liability, I defined my strategy as "easing the jib sheet, letting the sail flutter a while, and getting the ship back on course." There were times too when the ship needed to jettison some cargo to save itself. Or, on another occasion, I would comment in the heat of a political storm that any member of the crew could hold the wheel when the sea was calm, but rough seas meant all hands on deck with the captain at the wheel.

When my strategy was in question, I told of a fisherman who explained to me how he never set out to fish with a thin line or a small hook. "I like a thick line and a heavy hook. When a fish big or small takes my bait and begins to fight me, I say 'beg the curve, not me.'" (The fish could only get away if the hook straightened, so "beg the curve".)

No points were scored when the Church and moralists raged against my response to teenage pregnancy at a youth rally, advising: "Bat, but don't score." What I should have said is, "If you have to bat, please don't score." But I don't know if the rephrasing would have made a difference to the Church.

Holding up three fingers toward me, a passenger in transit around the baggage carousel in Miami accosted me, and said, "Congratulations on the three!" Wondering which three accomplishments could produce such effusive praise, I sought clarification from the stranger. "Three executions in one day," he said. 'That's balls. I like it."

Then I realised what he meant by his gesture and words. Our committee on the prerogative of mercy, which included a priest and a physician, had firmly recommended the executions, and I signed the warrants and had the condemned prisoners promptly executed. I would have been crucified by the press had I, as was often the case, commuted these sentences. For one of them in particular, there could be no mercy. He stole the victim's car and drove it around the countryside, exhibiting the head he had severed.

Then came the time when the courts in Grenada sentenced the murderers of Maurice Bishop and his colleagues. Knowing the timidity of Prime Minister Braithwaite, I ventured to help. "It is not often that St. Vincent can provide technical assistance, but should you require

it, we can help you with the gallows," I said. I also informed him that
I had sent a policeman once to Dominica with our noose in response
to their request. Braithwaite let his lady Minister excuse herself as she
commuted the sentences.

My citizenry found it totally indigestible that I should describe those
in our society who wished to reap without sowing as possessing the
mentality of a breadfruit tree. The wonderful tree that Captain Bligh
had suffered to bring us required absolutely no attention, no fertilizing,
no pruning, no spraying. It is a tree to be reaped without any care.
"Breadfruit mentality! Mitchell is a wicked man." And so, my "breadfruit
mentality" comment became my curse, not a plea to turn away from
our sins, and to sow before you wanted to reap. But I made no apology!
Still, I wished I could have commissioned a statue of Captain Bligh in
our ancient Botanic Gardens, as a centre-piece for our school children
and tourists. Our city, too, needed a modern statue, dedicated to the
banana worker. I could envision him with the banana tree, cutlass and
a bunch of bananas in his hand. He did more for this country than the
public servant city-slicker clock-watchers. He sweated!

Attending the graduation ceremony in a school is thought by some
to be the ultimate in a leader's dedication to the youth, or in Caribbean
parlance, "the youths." My early training in the English language
imposed an abhorrence of the plural in abstract nouns, so I had great
difficulty with the term "youths." But the real issue that bothered me
was the elaborate expense to which parents were put when forced
to comply, buying elaborate outfits for their children for a so called
"graduation" long before the final exam results were known.

A headmistress explained that if she waited on the publication of the
results, very few children could turn up. So the graduation ceremony
was no more than a party, protecting the incompetence of the teachers,
a fraud that left me uncomfortable. In this mood I was forced to endure
the spectacle. In the results so far, however, there was one salient fact:
the girls won prizes in a three-to-one ratio over the boys. I congratulated
the girls to loud applause. Our society had advanced I told them,
since my youth when male performance exceeded that of the females.
"The trouble with the success of you girls will nevertheless bring you
misfortune later in life," I declared. "Where will you find intelligent
men to marry? What is going to become of our country?" Another of my
misdemeanours, another awkward truth.

After several entreaties, I had permitted myself to break my deliberate
reclusion upon retirement, giving an interview to a young aspiring
journalist whose Barbadian editor impressed upon him the value of

getting his byline on an article with reflections by the longest-serving Prime Minister. So I launched into the subject of diversification of the economy being primarily a problem in the mind of our people, overcoming inertia, and abandoning local prejudices. My bananas-and-tourism diatribe exceeded his ambitions of the day, and beyond him and toward me, arousing the slumbering hostility of the tedious sociologists who had happily assumed my sun to be safely set below the horizon, only to find it still radiating and well outside the reach of their malevolent slander. I told the young man, "We delude ourselves to think that agriculture is local, and tourism is foreign. Both bananas and tourism aim at the same market: white people." The media did not like it but found the courage to make it the quote of the week!

At some stage, every Finance Minister in the developing world has to explain himself to the international finance institutions. They call it Article IV consultations. My healthy trade in bananas, anthurium lilies, plantains, eddoes and mangoes with Barbados had ground to a halt when it was discovered that St. Vincent's produce was infected with the mealy bug, *Maconilli coccus*, which had probably come from Trinidad. Barbados prohibited our exports of fruit and flowers, an imposition that was causing a loss of thousands of dollars a week to our farmers, and kept my friend Captain Snagg and his cargo ship, *Admiral Bay* tied up for months.

"What are you going to do about this balance of payments issue with Barbados?" the IMF official demanded. I explained that we were installing fumigating equipment at our port, and in the countryside, we had released the ladybird beetle, *Crytolaemus montrouzieri* and the wasp *Angyus kamali* for biological control. "And if that doesn't work?" he continued. "For my sins," I replied, "I am, beside being a Minister of Finance, a trained pathologist and entomologist; I shall infect Barbados!" There were no further enquiries about my management of the economy. For the record, it should be stated that the biological control worked in ridding St. Vincent's produce of the mealy bug, and it was not necessary to level the playing field by deploying my alternative action plan.

I certainly had no reason to be unkind to Barbados. Their protocol ladies with unfailing regularity shepherded me to and from the international carriers, having me unwind in their VIP lounge. When I found Billy Miller, now Dame, the Minister of Foreign Affairs, whose uncluttered intellect made her a lady to be trifled with at your peril, pouring over plans to remodel the lounges that had become quite jaded and frowzy since Independence, I thought I would make a decorative gift of a boat. Consternation descended on the Foreign Ministry. Where would the boat be placed? How could an oddity inconsistent with the culture of Barbados be accommodated? Surely it would be better consumed in the cane fires. My boat was to their surprise no more than a finely crafted Bequia model sailing boat. Sighs of relief. It found its quiet corner in a glass case in the lounge greeting all the dignitaries.

My other gesture of help to Barbados fell by the wayside. Prime Minister Arthur was not impressed with my aside at a finance meeting when I offered to help with the controversy surrounding the post-colonial pique over the removal of the statue of Nelson in Bridgetown. I had become an expert on new placement of statues, having successfully triumphed over my barrage of criticism over the war memorial at home. I could accommodate the valiant admiral in my village of Hamilton beside Admiralty Bay. Surely the amorous Lord Nelson would love to look over a flotilla of yachts and be poised on the land dedicated to his Lady Hamilton. Certainly a more romantic idyll than the fumes of traffic in Bridgetown.

Good and bad government
I'd certainly recommend every leader to make the pilgrimage to Sienna in Italy and spend a minute in the company of fourteenth-century Ambrogio Lorenzetti's depiction of it in his fresco, to see the joy or anguish that flows from our decisions.

Observing Lesotho's elections, May 2002

I had called on Don McKinnon, our new Commonwealth Secretary General, when I was in London once more on banana business, to present him with Karl John's treatise on our joint efforts in land reform at home. A little technical competence, and respect from leadership in Africa, combined with Caribbean credentials, we both thought would be appropriate experience to help Zimbabwe out of its perilous land policies. But nothing could be done under the Mugabe regime. At that time, there was the thorny problem of whale-fishing quotas to be dealt with.

For 300 years the British had done nothing to enhance our fishing industry. It had taken us two decades to draw down the Independence gift and loans. The Japanese were delivering assistance to our fishing industry within the financial year committed, and had given us over US$15 million in a decade. My constituency was the only whaling constituency in the New World, a tradition learnt from New England and continued in the ancient Moby Dick style with hand-held harpoons. I had sponsored the reduction of our quota from the International Whaling Commission from three to two whales a year, and I knew that one day the courage of the new generation of whalers would be lost. Our whaling will come to a graceful end. I said to the British Trade Minister, "Foxhunters should not claim moral superiority over whalers." Before Japanese assistance our fishermen were obliged to store their fish overnight in the city morgue. I respected the fun of foxhunting in the English countryside; they should respect too our tradition of whaling.

My delegation of Carlyle Dougan, and Cenio Lewis from the High Commission in London put on a brave front at my arrival. They would have to face the British after I had gone home.

"The British should know me well enough," I said, "not to expose green Ministers. When you are negotiating, you go to the brink and see who first falls off. And balls outside the wicket have to be dispatched beyond the boundary. How dare they think I'm one to exterminate a species on this earth?"

So in retirement I found myself again in Don McKinnon's office being briefed on leadership of the Commonwealth Observer mission for Lesotho elections, a process I had helped to set in train in the Malaysia CHOGM. Quite a combination of personalities and origins comprise a Commonwealth Observers team, and mine included citizens of Australia, Ghana, Nigeria, Namibia, Sri Lanka, Mauritius, Uganda and the United Kingdom, as well as former ministers, senators, diplomats and current secretariat bureaucrats.

We arrived in Maseru at different times, our advance team being Joram Rukambe of Namibia who had already been monitoring the registration of voters and getting to know the lie of the land. The affable secretary Nishana Jayawickrama, whose name not even Sri Lankan cricket had prepared me for, had established our secretariat in the Lesotho Sun Hotel, beside the South African media centre.

My introduction to the Australian member of our group Dr. David MacGibbon, got off to a good start, with my relieving the agony of his lost luggage with my gift of toiletries from the British Airways travel pouch together with replacement essentials from Marks and Spencer I'd picked up in London, a courtesy repaid with a lecture on Australian wines. We had a wonderful day in the rain and the mud at the back of the villages in Mohale's Hoek searching for polling stations when I had to commandeer the wheel from the driver and bring to bear my experience of driving tractors on farms. MacGibbon had held firm, months earlier in the Zimbabwe elections, demanding that the nonsense be exposed. Lesotho was now easy stuff for him. He had been a Senator and Select Committee Chair in Australia.

Terry Waite had spent his most glorious days as secretary in Britain's anti-apartheid movement, and was now teaching Physics, the flame of struggle, alas, still glowing in his veins. Ready for sacrifice, we deployed him and the Ugandan from Marlborough House, Martin Kasirye, a diplomat in the making who presumed to lecture me on dealing with the media, into the remote corners of Qacha's Nek, where horses and donkeys were the preferred transport.

Professor Akinjide Osunkotum, Presidential Adviser in Nigeria along with Chief Anyaoku, had been Ambassador in Bonn, and in an earlier incarnation had lectured in the Caribbean. He had fond memories of his Caribbean stint, including cruising on my friend Moses Matalon's yacht. He was absolutely confident that had he not been married already, a West Indian woman would have gone back to Africa with him. As kindred spirits, we noted an African young lady of much distinction crossing our paths in the Lesotho Sun Hotel; he assured me that she could not be Basotho. My presumptuous check revealed his acute sense of Africa; she was Namibian. His assistant in the heartland of the mountain kingdom was the dedicated Kishner Falkner, inured in the culture of India blended with old England.

We settled down to serious business, interviewing every political party, every organization including the Church, the media, the electoral commission, the Interim Political Authority and the Ambassadors, satisfying ourselves that the preparations for elections were in order. I was impressed with the high profile of the Irish Embassy. The previous elections had led to disorder, quelled by troops from South Africa and Botswana, even though my predecessor as Observer, Sir Lynden Pindling, had been satisfied with the credibility of the election. With Lesotho's turbulent history, including assassination and exiling of kings, we recognized the seriousness of our responsibility in monitoring the election this time around. A new constitution calling for a mixture of constituency seats and proportional representation had been formulated with Commonwealth guidance.

Having satisfied myself that Lesotho was a constitutional monarchy, I called on King Letsi III in his Palace. His father had been the king "lost" by the Protocol in Zimbabwe on our famous Sunday outing, and had later died in a motor accident. The streets around the Palace told the simple story of poverty.

Every day the newspapers, the *Mirror* and the *Mopheme Survivor*, in their top right-hand corner advertised "the latest option to protect women against STIs and HIV/AIDS: Use it and live," an ad. sponsored by Japan Trust Fund. The glossy object spurred total revulsion by our female companions on the observer mission, who also felt that my comments that their deployment was better than death were quite unnecessary.

The Police Commissioner and his officers were pleased with my visit, hoping that all the observer missions would make their job light. Not far from their offices, huge signs advised policemen to travel with their condoms. Funeral parlours were prominent in several villages, telling the truth about the 37 per cent infection rate of HIV/AIDS, much of which they claimed came back home from the mines in South Africa. Dozens of bodies abandoned in the mortuaries were buried in mass graves by prisoners.

The mountain kingdom of Lesotho is a beautiful but sad country. Along the fairly well-kept highways herds of cattle roamed with a blanketed herdsman, woman or child. The cornfields were dry, the stalks were thin, and beyond the grazing here and there no real agriculture to speak of. In one Catholic compound beside the church I found one citrus tree. All the citrus fruit came in piles on trucks, like everything else, from South Africa. The Chiefs told you where to build your home, a shack with one door and window. I felt powerless. We could do our best for them, but I felt they would be poor for a long time, and they had no slavery to blame. One youthful trade union leader had formed his own party specifically to raise wages in the Parliament. I stepped outside my terms of reference, revealing my experience that legislating on minimum wages and equal pay for women led to closure of factories and production in other countries.

Each day as we returned from the field, we filed reports to Marlborough House. We reciprocated the hospitality of the Southern African Development Community, inviting them to our reception. After the normal exchange of greetings I invited the President of the Lesotho media to say a few words. Still stung by the invasion after the previous elections, he blasted SADC. He did not trust them too after their reports on Zimbabwe elections. I had a diplomatic mess on my hands. I called on SADC to reply. I told the Lesotho media that I am guided by the Commonwealth regional principle. In the Caribbean we did not expect Africa to settle our disputes, and I would expect the same tradition to develop in southern Africa.

Don McKinnon had intimated to me that I should be careful not to be seen as trampling on what was deemed Southern Africa's prerogative. They would not be keen to have us observing elections beside them, but we had an international responsibility. That night I called Don and explained that it was all the other way round. The Basotho people wanted the Commonwealth presence. South African television interviewed me regularly after they got over the shock that I, and not someone from Australia or Nigeria, was leading the team.

Late one night I checked on Ama Kwaw-Swanzy, to see what our Ghanaian assistant was filing to London. I added a note to the Secretary General, that the Chairman, yours truly, wanted authority to hire some donkeys to assist in the transporting of ballot boxes in the mountain paths. My assistant, the chain-smoking Diane Stafford, head of the legal department in the Secretariat, confronted me with the e-mail reply: "Sir James, what have you been up to?"

"Absolutely nothing, I slept all night."

"Well the SG says you are not allowed to hire asses!"

General Lekhanya's sophisticated posters dominated the lamp-posts in Maseru. You could hardly find posters of the Government's Lesotho Congress for Democracy (LCD) or their breakaway faction, the Lesotho People's Congress (LPC). The other 15 parties were not visible at all. The race as we assessed all presentations seemed to be between Prime Minister Mosisil's LCD, Lekhanya's Basotho National Party and Kelebone Maope's LPC.

We were delighted to be able to facilitate the SADC team, whose group in Thama-Tsaeka had run out of petrol. In our inspection tour, Marie-Claude Arouff-Parfait and Joram Rukambe were to meet us half way beyond the Mohale Dam construction site and the Blue Mountain Pass. Marie-Claude, the former Mauritius Minister, had pleaded for a blanket, bemoaning the Parisienne wardrobe she had left behind, so we had to shop for her in Maseru to keep her alive. I added some good South African wine, and chocolates from the hotel boutique that she would certainly decline in her normal figure-watching routine. But the cold recesses of bare rooms in the mountain kingdom were no health spa. Our drivers showed us the ridge where the assassinated ministers were dumped.

Maintaining the Commonwealth Observer tradition, now in excess of some 50 missions, the Chairman and official team leader concentrate on the capital and stay in contact with the office. So Diane Stafford, with whom I had toured several districts, was on the go with me before the polling stations opened. We checked with political agents that they were satisfied with the process. All was going well until we found a half-mile-long queue in Mabole constituency where there was some concern about the integrity of the ballot boxes, a problem not resolved until noon, forcing the IEC to extend voting until the next day. It meant that some were voting while results elsewhere were declared on radio.

And so into the night for checking the voting. We selected a tent. Meticulously each ballot was shown to all agents after being checked for total numbers. With two colours of voting cards, one for the constituency and one for proportional representation, this meant a long drawn-out process. I abandoned Diana and returned to the car for warmth. When I returned it was obvious that the cold had me in agony. One political agent loaned me her blanket, which Diane was not too embarrassed to share. The wonderful warmth in the day had not prepared me for the freezing night temperature. My system folded. I could not swallow when I returned to the hotel. My first experience of hypothermia. All in the interest of advancing democracy in Africa. We filed a report on fairness.

The BNP called a press conference, after the LCD's massive win of constituency seats, to quibble on procedures. I had dealt with that kind of mischief before, all the way to the Privy Council. General Lekhanya was being steered by his South African consultant. I demanded to know if any political agent had registered a complaint during the voting. There being none, I advised silence. Nearly all the constituency seats went to the LCD, but proportional representation placed several other parties in the parliament, including the lone trade unionist. The new constitution seemed to have worked.

For our final evening at the Lesotho Sun we commandeered the high table in the dining room. The Mauritian *maître d'*, anxious to please Marie-Claude, dished up a feast, producing his Mauritian best. He was determined to redeem himself after I strongly recommended some nights before that the osso-bucco be taken off the menu.

We were all making our ways back home to other parts of Africa, Europe, Australia and the Caribbean. I was going to hear my daughter in a school choir, in a different world, at Villars in the Swiss mountains. My driver said goodbye at the airport. He was the son of a former Minister in Lesotho, and was now making a living driving a South African jeep. Along with our tokens of appreciation I gave him one of my ties as a souvenir which he promised to hang in his house. "Sir James," he said, "remember we are starving here."

28

Finale

Bequia, Becouya, island of my birth, my home, the land that nurtured this wandering soul, the quintessential island, the Rock. To the Caribs, it was an island of clouds; nobody there, I suppose. But the early English had fun with it, naming its hills and valleys: Friendship, Hope, Spring, Industry, Paradise, Mt. Pleasant, Sugar Hill, and Cinnamon Garden. Where else on earth has a fragrant spice and the labours of life been blended with dreams of eternity?

The French, too, either in grief or mirth knew what they were up to in their Carte des Antilles: Mustique, Isle des Moustiques, for millions of years the habitat of mosquitoes, and in my time, through three steady decades of my nurturing, the elite sanctuary for the discerning; the Pillories – a ritual to the best of my knowledge never invoked; Isle à Quatre, Quatre Isle, the last pristine idyll – an island haven of turquoise lagoons and peaks with magnificent views that must have looked out on the naval skirmishes between the French and English; Morpion – crab louse; and Punaise – bed bug; deserving tributes to the plight of wrecked ships and adventurers drowned in uncharted waters. (I too once in an open boat at nightfall ran aground there and was missing for several hours.) One imaginative entrepreneur sought my indulgence to cede him Morpion and confer on him the title, Marquis of Morpion. I loved the thought, but I did not know how to begin! Heraldry was not my métier.

Then St. Vincent, named by Columbus and jealously engraved in its people's affection, with pledges of loyalty in the anthem: a title defined by the Italian in honour of the Saint, a slice of history finally frowned on by our emancipated heretics. And the other islands, Canouan, Mayreau, Union Island, Palm, Petit Nevis, and Petit St. Vincent. Never least among them, the Tobago Cays, glorious gems in blue sparkling waters, refreshed from the beginning of time by the Atlantic, a marine park now after my 30 years of persistence.

These then, are my islands. Images of land and water that nurtured my affection for mountains and lakes in distant continents, embuing me with a love of nature, a love of life and a fascination with the way other souls responded to their piece of Mother Earth.

From hitch-hiker to Prime Minister, my wanderings over the face of the earth taught me that the world has many idyllic locations with a wonderful quality of life. I always loved the sound of church bells ringing as they had done for centuries across the rolling landscape in France and Italy where battlefields had become vineyards.

I helped many careers rise upwards. My heaven was still in the soil. In my islands I may have presided over their loss of innocence but I did not surrender their charm. Retirement afforded me time to relax in the country home of my publisher in Vermont. Jill Bobrow, with the help of her business partner, Dana Jinkins, was able to put together my last collection of speeches, *Season of Light*. In one of their yachting publications, *Captain's Log* distributed with *Boat International*, I found an article casting doubts on the integrity of our flag registry, meticulously managed as it was in our Geneva office, ensuring compliance with international standards. I replied, getting out the message to the mega-yacht fraternity, that SVG had, among other things, secured the first judgment on behalf of ship-owners at the Court of Law of the Sea Convention in Hamburg. In retirement, I was still ready to defend our cause.

Returning home and settled each morning in the company of the chirping mocking-birds, flashing hummingbirds and the busy banana twits among the gliricidia and apple-blossom cassia flowers outside my study, I began to write these memoirs, finishing 1,200 pages from memory. Then I collected the old diaries out of the bank vault, matched them up with the appointment books and spliced, cancelled, rewrote and rewrote.

Operations on knee replacements in Denmark, both at once, arranged by Danish friends who had been my Bequia guests, and another operation in Trinidad on bladder route cleansing (like recovering log jams in a stream) ground my enthusiasm for writing to a halt. To get out of it, I wrote about writer's cramp.

In the midst of this anguished exercise, my daughter Sabrina informed me that her co-author friend, John Bowman (they made a joint effort on the coffee-table book, *Discover St. Vincent & the Grenadines*, with pictures by Jean Marc Le Cerf, published by Fabre-Domingue, with a foreword written by me) was pleased to know that I was writing an autobiography and wanted to know if I needed an editor. Instantly I accepted. John's poem "Why," inspired by the untimely death of Jolly Joseph, the water taxi driver, and the exoneration of the Americans, had left me with an indelible imprint of his brilliance. The might of America, deployed to grind our sovereignty into insignificance, did not extinguish the light of his spirit or mine. John disappeared from Bequia for years and resurfaced in Caracas, working for Dow Jones as a journalist, writing for among others, the *Wall Street Journal* and the *Economist*. He took time off from the anti-Chavez demonstrations and referendum manoeuvres to be with me at Villa Helianthus, enjoying guava jelly that reminded him of his native Sri Lanka. He spent a week digesting my story. Then he wanted to see some published biographies. I loaded him up. In three days and long nights he absorbed them like a desert drinking a deluge of rain and concluded, "we have the genre." I discovered later that his real name was Jehan Senaratna, John being a pen-name.

We worked together each morning after breakfast. I responded to his queries, his unravelling of my ramblings. "Your thoughts soar like a bird. You burrow like an earthworm. We have to bring the strands together." He had to return briefly to the Chavez chaos, and to London to visit his sister Sharmini, while I had to visit Gabija for parent's weekend in Villars. He said goodbye to Dow Jones, the *Economist* and his journalist's life to return to Bequia to finish my book and to write his own novel. After Caracas, we picked up the thread. Three weeks and we would be finished the preliminary stage. I read for him one morning a passage from Edward Gibbon's *Decline and Fall of the Roman Empire* describing how the Germans in the age of Tacitus were unlettered and how great was the distance between the man of learning and the illiterate peasant, no better than an ox. "Without some species of writing, no people have ever preserved the faithful annals of their history."

"Yes," Jehan replied, "let's get on with it!"

We were about to finish the morning's work. I knew I had got it right when, reading and reshaping my thoughts, his feet under the table would begin to do a little dance like the baton of a conductor vibrating in ecstasy with a phrase being perfectly rendered. We were chiselling away at a sculpture. We were happy with the shape it was taking, our minds in splendid harmony. He loved the labyrinth I had created out of my life.

Suddenly, on that fateful day in December, he rolled over. I caught him falling away from his laptop. With my maintenance crew we rushed him to an oxygen tank in the hospital. The heart attack, his second in ten years, like an unseen assassin had lurked around the corner. Two of us were paddling a boat across a flowing stream. Now, its brow was broken, my friend fallen overboard. I was left alone to paddle to the shore. The friend beside me had drowned. There was no water in the sinking ship. The only water sinking the ship was my tears. His ashes now, with his wonderful spirit, have returned to the family site in Sri Lanka. The mystery in his life unfolded, with an American daughter isolated from him. We held a ceremony for him at my home and threw the petals of the flowers from his friends at Associated Press in Venezuela in my Monet garden pond amidst the lilies, and the flirtatious dragonflies dipping their tails in its mirrored surface.

My father had vanished when I was not yet nine. I was alone in Opposition. Loneliness has been my destiny. I had to go on. Sabrina, my daughter, who had been shepherding the text with Jehan, took the reins and brought the work to conclusion. So much more to tell, so much to reveal.

Fortunately, the attention I had paid to improving the family inheritance was enough to yield some comfort in my retirement. Enthusiastic hugs continued to reveal the thanks from those whose life I suppose was enhanced by my toil. But the curious still wanted to know how I judged myself, what was the greatest thing done and the worst sin. It was as though Pilate should reconsider the Crucifixion of Christ or Da Vinci embellish the mystic smile on his Mona Lisa.

My time was once more, my own. I am still in love with rainbows. Where others see ocean, I see currents. From my home, when I look up in the quiet evening sky and see the magnificent frigate birds, the ocean abandoned, devoutly yet carelessly circling together high up over the land as they must have done for millions of years, with barely a flicker of the wing, I know their portent of the rain showers I need. I can contemplate in my ancient youth how I sought their discarded feathers on the Atlantic shore to make a quill pen for school.

In silence I hear symphonies. On a dark peaceful night, alone, it is inspiring to see from my deck, the lights of a candlefly and a satellite, both vanishing. Can either tell me what ever happened to the baby I refused and returned to the arms of the mother in the Cambodian refugee camp?

Forty years on, I could revisit the scenes of my early odyssey, where once I dared not stop, dishevelled and unkempt, rucksack on my back filled with all my soiled earthly possessions, and find myself in a new fantasy, breakfasting beside the Wörthersee, relishing the fall colours outside the windows of Hotel Schloss Seefels. Kind friends, the Oblaks who had been our guests in the islands could take us also to Igor's restaurant to enjoy white truffles in Croatia, where in those early days my fare and that for all the poor peasants like me, trundling along the dusty roads in Tito's unified realm, was sausage.

Hosted in like manner by the O'Hanlons in Ireland, I would stray from company and hike alone. I relished the anonymity of the wasteland of Connemara. So, too, on the other side of the chilly Atlantic, I could spiritually inhale the long twilight, the sunsets glowing across the wide horizon; sitting on the rocks beside the still waters, my feet patting the polyps of the seaweeds, while lying backwards, gazing at streaking jets, contemplating the lives of those above plying between the continents in a voyage that I once made, and no longer missed. And then it would be time to walk down the gravelly path, glimpse the deer, thank creation for the gorgeous plumage of the pheasants, and pick up the mezzaluna and roll it through the onions and garlic, helping to prepare dinner with friends at Carlo's Shangri La, graciously secluded in Nova Scotia.

And so always, back home, rounding the corner into Admiralty Bay, a feeling special only to lovers of "the rock," our diamond, our Bequia. My home faces the East. Early morning, as it must have been for my ancestors living in these hills, it is still wonderful to rise, breathe slowly the fresh air coming across the ocean and discover beyond the islands, the dawn.

Index